EUROPE BY

Katharine Wood-de Winne was ̄ ̄ ̄ ̄ ̄ ̄ ̄ ̄ ̄ ̄
was educated there, reading Communications, then English language and literature at university. Interspersed with working as a freelance journalist, she travelled extensively by train in Europe and North Africa, and in 1981 she started research for this guide. She now works as a full-time travel journalist, having to date clocked up 55 countries, and is involved in numerous books which cover everything from first-class round the world air travel to backpacking holidays.

The success of this book has led to her publishing a further 15 guidebooks, and she also regularly contributes to travel programmes for radio and TV, and writes articles for magazines and newspapers including the *Daily Telegraph*, the *Sunday Post*, BBC's *World* magazine and the *Sunday Telegraph*. In 1990 she was awarded a fellowship of the Royal Geographical Society. European train travel is still her greatest love, however, and she takes to the rails regularly to update this book. In between travelling she lives in Perth, Scotland, with her husband and two young sons, Andrew and Euan, who frequently accompany her on her worldwide travels.

George McDonald was born in Dumfries, Galloway, and was educated at Fettes College and Edinburgh University. He developed a taste for train travel after a journey on the world's highest railway in Peru and a trip through the Soviet Union. Since 1981 he has been constantly on the move fact-checking for this guide, and considers it unusual to be in one place for more than three weeks at a time. Home, when he's there, is Guernsey in the Channel Islands. He now works on various other projects, including his own publishing concern.

KATIE WOOD AND GEORGE McDONALD

EUROPE BY TRAIN
THE COMPLETE GUIDE TO INTER RAILING

Chief Editor: Katie Wood

Head Researchers:
Tim Cook, Timothy Page and Alison Pickard

Fontana
An Imprint of HarperCollins*Publishers*

This revised edition first published in 1991 by
Fontana Paperbacks

Copyright © Katie Wood and George McDonald
1983, 1984, 1985, 1986, 1987, 1988, 1989, 1990
Copyright © Katie Wood 1991

The maps, drawn by Illustra of Maidenhead, are based on
Thomas Cook's Rail Map of Europe.

Set in Linotron Times
Made and printed in Great Britain by
William Collins Sons & Co. Ltd, Glasgow

CONTENTS

EUROPE - Major Rail Lines

FOREWORD

What makes this book different from other guidebooks on Europe is that it's train orientated and economy minded. Research for this guide stems from travel all over Europe. Thorough investigation and very tight budgets have been the basis of this work. This is the only guide of its kind giving train and station information, as well as accommodation and the sights. It was written because I, like thousands of others, needed a book like this and it didn't exist. Now it's here I hope you'll be able to learn from my mistakes and benefit from my experiences. The book tells you of the finds made when going round Europe in recent years and explains the different ways of using the various rail passes which offer an exceptional opportunity to see the sights, meet new people and broaden your horizons – all for an amazingly low price.

• **Prices and exchange rates:** Because these fluctuate, we can only give a rough guide. As a reference this book uses £1 = $1.70, but this rate and all the prices mentioned are subject to change. The costs in the former communist countries will be particularly vulnerable to inflation, as these countries move towards a market economy.

• **Any potential researchers or budding journalists out there?** Many of you write unsolicited to me, asking if I need researchers to help update this, and my other fifteen guides. I do, but there are very stringent rules that apply. If, after reading this, you still feel you would suit, please send on a full CV, photo, list of where you've travelled, sample of any published writing or any travel writing, and send it to me care of Fontana.

Criteria

1. You must have travelled very extensively in the countries and on the forms of transport written about in the book (eg on Inter Rails for *Europe by Train*; on round the world air passes or long haul flights for *The Round the World Air Guide*; on alternative 'green' holidays for *The Good Tourist In . . . series*).

2. You must be very interested in travel. And I mean manically interested, not just keen on going to foreign parts. Are you the type who never misses a travel programme; who immediately turns to

the travel sections of newspapers and magazines; who yearns for foreign travel more than anything else? Do you know, or are you prepared to learn, a lot about the travel industry?

3. Do you write well? Are you at least up to 'A' level English, preferably degree level, and are you competent with your language? These formal qualifications need not matter if you have a natural talent, but without training, few do, so be honest about this. You will have to be concise, yet interesting; you may have had to write it at 1 a.m., but it mustn't show. Can you read a booklet and translate it into a couple of sentences? This is what guidebook writing is all about. Could you pick out the most salient points?

4. Can you work to deadlines? Publishing schedules wait for no man. If a guide isn't on the shelves by the holiday season, forget it. I work to very strict deadlines, and I am a hard task mistress! Could you deliver in time? You will be contractually bound to do so.

If you can do all of this, and want to travel, write to me now.

Katie Wood
c/o Fontana Paperbacks
HarperCollins Publishers
77–85 Fulham Palace Road
London W6 8JB

INTRODUCTION

For my part, I travel not to go anywhere, but to go. I travel for travel's sake. The great affair is to move; to feel the needs and hitches of our life more nearly; to come down off this feather-bed of civilization, and find the globe granite underfoot and strewn with cutting flints.

ROBERT LOUIS STEVENSON, *Travels with a Donkey in the Cevennes*

Anything is possible on a train, a great meal, a binge, a visit from card players, an intrigue, a good night's sleep, and strange monologues framed like Russian short stories.

PAUL THEROUX, *The Great Railway Bazaar*

Taking it for granted that the vast majority of eurorailers are looking for the most competitive prices in accommodation and food, the aim of this guide is to help you to get the very most out of a meagre budget. While this is the main motivation behind this book, you are meant to be enjoying yourself, and if you try to rough it too much or for too long you'll grow disillusioned with the seamy side of Europe that goes along with rough living. If you know where to look, cheap hotels or hostels or campsites can be found, as can good supermarkets and eating places – thus leaving you as much time as possible to see the sights on a full stomach secure in the knowledge that you've somewhere to stay the night. Far too many travellers spend the best part of their holiday walking round the wrong part of town on an empty stomach and with a heavy rucksack.

Preplanning should not be regarded as a constriction on your flexibility. There's nothing to stop you changing your plans while you're away but, with a little well-structured forethought, you can ensure you see everything you'd ideally like to, and don't waste precious time waiting in the long tourist and train-information queues. It's also a good idea to do a bit of background reading to keep the myriad of sights in perspective. I recommend you get Kenneth Clarke's *Civilisation* from your local library, but most cultural histories will serve the same purpose.

In Part One you'll find information on different aspects of eurorailing which will be of interest to everyone, regardless of your routes. Following this there are individual chapters on the countries of Europe in alphabetical order; these follow the pattern you're best advised to take from the minute you step off the train at your chosen destination. I'll guide you to the accommodation service, the campsites, hostels and hotels, the tourist information office, the eating places, and then the sights themselves.

Europe in late 89/90 was an exciting place. The number of eurorailers who headed for the ex-Eastern Bloc countries was staggering. In response to this demand, it is with great joy that I bring you the 1991 edition. I have added new parts of Europe to this book: researchers have scoured Turkey, Bulgaria, Czechoslovakia, Hungary, Poland, Romania and what was East Germany. The result is an edition packed with new places to see, and things to do. As someone who fell in love with much of Eastern Europe even back in the bad old days, a decade ago, it thrills me that eurorailers can now enjoy this part of the world without the restrictions of a Communist dictatorship. Travel there is not easy yet; it's still a challenge to get round and there are still far too many queues as there's not enough of an infrastructure to make a traveller's lot easy, but *go* despite this.

Good eurorailing.

Katie Wood
Chief Editor *Europe by Train*
January 1991

FACTSHEETS

Last year I brought out a series of factsheets in response to the great demand for itineraries tailored to suit your individual preferences when travelling. They were an enormous success. There were times in the summer when I dreaded the mailbags arriving! Many of you wrote to say nice things about them and to tell me how useful they had been when planning your trip, and when away, so that makes it all worthwhile.

For 1991 I have nine factsheets. Again they are split into the sections of The Sun Worshipper (where to find the best beaches); The Sightseer (where the most interesting sights are and what to look for); The Socialite (where best to people-watch; catch nightlife, and annual fiestas and events); The Nature Lover & Recluse (where to escape the crowds and head into the hills or most scenic countryside), and the Grand Tour (a taster itinerary, encompassing all the aspects above). Every type of traveller is therefore covered and will be directed towards the parts of Europe best suited to their needs.

Basic Accommodation suggestions are given for places not in *Europe by Train*, the guide, and sights, and rail links are covered. Many places never before featured in the guidebook are in the factsheets.

Make your selection of factsheets from the choice below:

1. Europe – a brief run down on all 26 countries. This is ideal for planning your route. It also reads like an appendix to *Europe by Train*. This was the most popular 1990 factsheet, though the 1991 one has been substantially enlarged, updated and re-structured.
2. Italy
3. France
4. Germany
5. Greece
6. Netherlands
7. Spain
8. Eastern Europe – covering all Eastern European countries*
9. Scandinavia – covering four Scandinavian countries*

* New for 1991. All 1990 countries thoroughly updated.

Cost

In 1990, one reason why I dreaded the success rate these factsheets were having was because each time I sent one out, I actually became poorer! The cost of manufacturing these factsheets was nowhere near met by the £1.75 per sheet I was charging in 1990. The Italy sheet alone is 18 pages of A4 photocopies (and you know the price of professional photocopying). Plus most of you, unfortunately, sent minuscule envelopes and 15p stamps to return them in! The result was I had to buy A4 envelopes and pay the postage differential of an average 50p per person! Others didn't even send an SAE, and then I had the joys of bouncing cheques (after the sheets had gone!) to contend with on top of that.

This year, therefore, I am having to lay down the following provisos:

1. Send your A4 SAE, but ensure there is a first class stamp *per factsheet* on the envelope. Don't ask for seven factsheets and put on a 22p stamp please! NB. If writing from abroad for factsheets, send an International Money Order for the amount in sterling, plus £1 for postage.

2. Ensure your cheque really is inside the envelope before posting (you wouldn't believe how many I had to return because of this!), and that it's made out to K. Wood for the correct amount.

Europe costs £4.50
Eastern Europe costs £4.50
Scandinavia costs £3.00
Italy, France, Germany, Spain, Netherlands and *Greece* all cost £2.50 each.

Send your cheque, SAE and a note of the countries you want to:

Katie Wood
c/o Fontana Paperbacks
HarperCollins
77–85 Fulham Palace Road
London W6 8JB

Please clearly mark your envelopes EUROPE BY TRAIN FACTSHEETS. Allow five weeks for delivery.

Part One: EURORAILING

The advantages of train travel

Besides the fact that eurorailing is a real bargain, there are many advantages to travelling by train which make your European travels more pleasurable. The train is without doubt the safest, most convenient and interesting means of transport to really uncover some hidden corners of Europe that hitch-hiking can never show you. You can cover a lot of ground in a very short time – you leave from, and arrive at, stations which are invariably in city centres; and you don't lay yourself open to the vagaries of the weather – trains are very rarely cancelled due to fog or rain. You also cut out the inevitable traffic jams you would land in if you van round the roads of Europe in the high season. The advantages of eurorailing over hitching are numerous, but the main one is clear: you can rely on getting to your destination and can thus cram far more into your trip. All in all, there are virtually no tourist centres in Europe that cannot be conveniently reached by rail, and even if there were, there's always buses or bikes at the nearest station.

Believe it or not, the train (assuming you take a high-speed express and not a local shunt-about) can actually travel faster than a plane on a distance of under 400 miles, allowing for the time it takes to commute to and from airports. If you're on a long journey, the train allows you to walk about and stretch your legs, and to go for a meal or a snack when you please. You'll also find trains a wonderful meeting-place to chat to people, both the locals and other euro-railers. It's almost impossible to make a trip on one of the popular routes in a summer month and not end up swapping stories with groups of fellow travellers. On overnight journeys, the intimacy of the train compartment makes it *quite* impossible!

Almost all European trains are diesel- or electric-driven, and most are government-owned (the main exceptions being some lines in Switzerland). A long-distance international train may use rolling stock from several countries along its route, so it pays to discover quickly what each country's carriages look like, and head for the good ones (i.e. the Swiss, German or any of the Scandinavian ones) when the train rolls in.

Every year the main roads of Europe become more and more congested and road improvements move at a slow pace, compared to the investments continually being made on the European rail networks. In northern Europe, second-class seats today are comparable with the first-class ones of twenty years ago. Speeds of 125 m.p.h. and more are common now in France, Britain and Germany; as networks expand, new and simplified routes emerge, allowing you greater choice as to the particular part of the country you'd like to travel through in order to get to your final destination.

Anyone who has travelled by train in North America will notice the difference straight away. European trains are faster, more plentiful and more punctual, serving many more destinations. Historically the European networks have not been maintained on a profit-making basis – few networks actually 'make' any money. They are essentially a public service, and the Inter Rail/Eurail pass is a good measure of this. For example, for the £175 the Inter Rail ticket costs, you end up with an average saving of £200–400 off the fares you'd normally have to pay, and even these are subsidized at source so, economically speaking, you can't really go wrong.

From the environmentalist's point of view, trains are good news when you bear in mind they consume up to seventeen times less energy than aircraft, and five times less than cars, to transport the same volume. Per square foot, a train can carry more people than cars can – and without the same pollution problems.

One of the main beauties of eurorailing – and one of the main pleasures you'll look back on – is the immense feeling of freedom you enjoy. It's entirely up to you where you spend your time, when you move on to somewhere else, and how you choose to get there. It's quite a heady feeling, never really knowing where you'll be this time tomorrow. To preserve this, it's advisable not to book too many hotels, hostels or trains ahead of time – if you bother to book any. However, to counteract the negative side-effects of total flexibility, it's a good idea to arrive in the major cities as early in the morning as possible in order to get yourself a bed for the night. The best option is to send for Katie Wood's *Cheap Sleep Guide* (p.16), or get to the tourist accommodation office (often on the station premises) before noon if you possibly can, otherwise you might end up having to spend precious sightseeing time searching for a room. Nearly every town has affordable places to stay within a few blocks of the station so don't worry, you will not have to walk far.

Eurorailing: the options

Basically there are three schemes you can choose from: a BIJ (Billet International de Jeunesse) ticket or rover ticket covering a set route, an individual country pass or an Inter Rail/Eurail, depending on where you live. BIJ operates under the auspices of the continental railways and offers reduced fares to the under 26s. Eurotrain is now the largest company in this scheme, with Wasteels as a newcomer to the market. They offer fares to over 2,000 destinations in Europe, Turkey and North Africa, with discounts of up to 40 per cent. As they allow you to break your journey anywhere you want on the route you've chosen, you have the flexibility to use your ticket as a sightseeing pass, so it's important to pick the route which takes in the places you most want to see. There are seven or eight routings to some cities, so it's possible to go one way and return another; for example, if your final destination is to be Rome, you could go out via Paris, the south of France and Genoa, and on the return stop off in Florence, Innsbruck, Munich and Belgium. The extra cost in taking two singles is only £5–10 ($8.50–17), and it lets you see a lot more of Europe.

The price of 'add-on' fares (to get you to London from your home town) is another factor to consider. (Eurotrain tickets can be issued for travel from any British Rail station you nominate.) Before committing yourself, always check that British Rail aren't offering an even cheaper fare to London – but bear in mind that these concessions are usually only for restricted services, whereas Eurotrain's ticket is good for all trains to London. Another tip: don't overlook the coach services to London offered by National Express, especially if you're travelling down from Scotland.

At the end of the day, it all depends on where you want to go and how much distance you intend to cover: an Inter Rail/Eurail would undoubtedly work out better value if you want to do the grand tour of Europe, from Copenhagen to Casablanca. Eurotrain sell Inter Rails through their offices anyway; their staff, who are generally very helpful, will advise you which scheme would work out cheapest. Before you rush out to buy any pass, do your research to find out if it will save you money. Add up the total second-class fares for the major routes you plan to cover (or get a travel agent to do it for you). If the sum comes near the price of the pass, the convenience of the pass is nearly always worth the extra.

• **Group travel:** Six or more constitute a group, as far as Eurotrain are concerned. This allows you all to travel at still further reductions. Further information from Eurotrain (071–823 5517). They offer a free place to a leader in a group of fifteen or more. Phone for a brochure.

INTER RAIL

• **Quick history:** The Inter Rail scheme was thought up by the UIC (the Union of International Railways) in 1972. It was devised to commemorate fifty years of international transport law; its price is decided upon each year at a conference of all participating countries. Around half a million Inter Rails are sold each year.

• **What is Inter Rail?** It is a ticket anyone living in Europe under the age of 26 can buy; it allows you to travel an unlimited distance for one calendar month on the rail networks of the countries listed below, and in the country of purchase at discounts of up to 50 per cent (34 per cent in Britain). If you want to travel for more than a month, buy two or more tickets at a time, getting the dates to run consecutively. The price fluctuates each year, but for 1991 it is £175 ($332).

There is now only one form of Inter Rail ticket available. With it you can travel free in the following countries: Austria, Belgium, Bulgaria, Czechoslovakia, Denmark, Finland, France, Germany, Greece, Hungary, Italy, Luxembourg, Morocco, the Netherlands, Norway, Poland, Portugal, Republic of Ireland, Romania, Spain, Sweden, Switzerland, Turkey, the United Kingdom and Yugoslavia. It also includes the Brindisi–Patras ferry crossing. As you can see, this allows the Inter Railer to visit the vast majority of European countries, either taking in as much as possible on a whistle-stop tour or concentrating on areas with particular appeal to the individual.

• **Who qualifies?** Anyone under the age of 26 on the first day the pass becomes valid – and it's up to you to decide when it will start and finish. You must hold a passport of a country participating in the scheme or be able to prove residence for over six months.

• **Rebates:** When you return home, take your Inter Rail pass back to the station where you bought it and you'll get a rebate; it varies from year to year, but it's around £4 ($6.80). The train authorities use the information (where you travelled on your Inter Rail, etc.) for market research.

• **Reductions:** An Inter Rail pass bought in the UK entitles you to discounts of up to 50 per cent on British and Northern Ireland trains and on the ferry services to the continental ports, including Hoverspeed hovercraft. Reductions on some of the private European railways are also granted, and these include most of the Swiss mountain railways. For real train buffs, the Inter Rail gets you a reduction on admission into the various transport museums of Europe.

1. *Europabus* have an agreement with the Inter Rail scheme by which they give a 25–30 per cent reduction on many of their runs. These tend to be slow but scenic and the best ones are mainly in France, the south of Italy, Sicily and Switzerland as they often cover areas not on the main rail network and go through small, out-of-the-way places. If you want further information, pick up a Europabus route-planner – but don't forget: they get busy in summer, so reserve ahead. See Appendix I for a complete list.

2. *Ferries:* 30 per cent concessions are available on Sealink and P&O and 50 per cent on B&I ships; you can also obtain reduced rates on many continental services. The Irish Continental Line from Rosslare to Cherbourg or Le Havre offer 50 per cent reductions. See also the individual countries later in this book. See Appendix II for a complete list.

If you need help with travel arrangements you should get in touch with the local station or tourist information.

NB In the UK, Inter Rails can only be bought from British Rail stations or through authorized BR agents. Do not attempt to get one on the black market as the railway authorities do very rigorous checks now, and you'll just end up being packed off home early, not to mention the local repercussions against you.

EURAIL

• **Quick history:** Basically, Eurail came into existence because Europe had a new and expensive network of intercity trains that needed riders. Its purpose was to entice potential passengers from the other side of the Atlantic, by offering two months of unlimited second-class travel on any or all of the member rail systems. The first pass was issued in 1959 when 5,000 tickets were sold. Later developments were one- and three-month passes, 15-day passes, first-class passes and such fringe benefits as free access to many ferry and steamer connections and free or discounted bus transportation. In addition, the 21-day pass was developed in 1966 to complement air excursion fares.

The popular Eurail Youthpass was introduced for anyone under the age of 26, to capture the market of students who were making use of cheaper transatlantic air fares. The value and enjoyment of eurorailing soon became apparent as Europe developed its own Youthpass system (Inter Rail), followed closely by the individual country passes.

• **What is the Eurail Youthpass?** It is an unlimited-mileage pass available to anyone who can prove they are under 26 years old on the first day of travel. The price of one month's Youthpass is $425, and for two months, around $555. The ticket may be purchased and used only if you reside outside Europe or North Africa.

Eurail Pass and Eurail Youthpass are personal and non-transferable. They are forfeited if presented by anyone other than the person for whom they were issued, or if they bear any evidence of alteration or mutilation. Presentation of a passport to European train personnel is compulsory. Therefore, if the issuing agent has made a mess-up with the spelling of your name, don't use it, but return it to the issuing office and get another. Your pass is valid until midnight of the last day of validity so be sure to take a train scheduled to arrive at your destination before midnight.

A Eurail Youthpass is valid in second class exclusively. This entitles you to unlimited travel on the national railways (except on special chartered trains) and many private rail lines, steamers and ferry crossings of the following countries: Austria, Belgium, Denmark, Finland, France, Germany, Greece, Hungary, Ireland (Republic of), Italy, Luxembourg, Netherlands, Norway, Portugal, Spain, Sweden and Switzerland. It also entitles you to free or reduced travel on buses run by the railway companies and some ferries. (For a full list of concessions granted to ticket holders, see Eurail Bonuses in the individual country sections.)

Reservation fees, meals, refreshments, sleeping accommodation and port taxes when using some steamers and ferries are not included in the price of the ticket and will have to be paid extra. It is sometimes obligatory to have a seat reservation (on Spanish express trains, for instance), so check first with station information. Also, a surcharge is required for travelling on some trains (IC, Eurocity/ TGV, Rapidos).

A new pass has been introduced for 1991 – the *Eurail Youth Flexipass Saver*. A second-class ticket, it allows 15 days' travel within three consecutive months. Three people under 26 years old must be travelling together, and the pass can only be bought in India for use in Europe.

From 1 June to 30 September, Adriatica di Navigazione and Hellenic Mediterranean Lines operating between Brindisi and Patras require $15.00 high season surcharge. During July and August advanced reservation ($7.00), is recommended.

Having a Eurail Youthpass does not guarantee a seat on a train nor space on ships unless a reservation has been secured in advance.

• **Refunds:** A Eurail Youthpass is not refundable if lost or stolen. It can only be replaced after having been validated, and provided the validation slip can be presented at time of replacement to a Eurail Aid Office. Any refund, if granted, is subject to a deduction of about 15 per cent from the price of the ticket.

• **What is the Eurail Pass?** It's the adult equivalent of the Youthpass, and has no age restrictions placed on it. It's a first-class go-as-you-please pass with prices of $390 for 15 days, $476 for 21 days, $582 for one month, $810 for two months and $1006 for three months. These are available from the same outlets as the Youthpass.

• **Eurail Saver Pass** (USA and Canada only): A 15-day Eurail Pass for two or more people travelling first-class off-season (1 October to 31 March) or a minimum of three people during the high season is now available at a cost of $298 per person. This new pass represents a saving of around 25 per cent compared to the regular 15-day Eurail Pass and provide the same services, including free or reduced bus, ferry and steamer passage.

• **Eurail Flexipass:** This is a first-class Eurail Pass which allows a limited number of chosen days of travel inside a given time period. The prices are $230 for 5 days of travel in a 15-day period, $398 for 9 of 21 days.

• **Where to buy your Eurail:** Eurail Passes must be bought outside Europe. Nearly every travel agent in North America and Canada will be able to supply you with a pass. For more information contact CIEE (Council on International Educational Exchange), 205 East 42nd Street, New York, NY 10017 (Tel. 212-661 1450), or CUTS (Canadian Universities Travel Service), 44 George Street, Toronto, Ontario M5S 2E4 (Tel. 416-979 2406).

• **Before you begin:** The pass must be used within six months of purchase, and must be validated before use by a railway official who will enter the first and last dates the pass can be used. It is important to get this done when buying the pass as validating it on board a train costs $6.23 extra. Rip out the counterfoil card from the pass as soon as you get it, and carry it separately and in a safe place. If you lose the pass you'll need this counterfoil as proof before a replacement can be issued, and if a railway official checks your Eurail during the trip this is considered your confirmation of ownership.

Eurail Aid Offices are there to help you if you have any problems. They also stock timetables and maps free of charge and can be found at the following stations:

AUSTRIA
ÖBB
Wien Westbahnhof
A–1150 **Vienna**

ÖBB
Salzburg Huptbahnhof
A–5010 **Salzburg**

ÖBB
Innsbruck Hauptbahnhof
A–6010 **Innsbruck**

BELGIUM
Société Nationale des
Chemins de fer
Belges
Salon d'Accueil
Service International
Gare de Bruxelles-Midi
Brussels 1070

DENMARK
DSB Travel Agency
Central Station
Banegärdspladsen
DK–1570 **Copenhagen**

FINLAND
Valtionrautatiet
Rautatieasema
VR Lipputoimisto
SF–00100 **Helsinki 10**

FRANCE
Société Nationale des
Chemins de fer
Français
Service International
Gare de Paris-St Lazare
F–75008 **Paris**

Société Nationale des
Chemins de fer
Français
Bureau Information-
Réservation
Gare de Paris-Nord
F–75010 **Paris**

Société Nationale des
Chemins de fer
Français
Bureau SNCF d'Orly
Aéroport
Cedex A 222
F–94396 **Orly-Airport**

Société Nationale des
Chemins de fer
Français
Bureau SNCF de Roissy
Aéroport Charles de Gaulle
BP 20215
F–95712 **Roissy Aéroport
Charles de Gaulle**

Société Nationale des
Chemins de fer
Français
Guichet 'Billets
Internationaux'
Gare de Marseille
St Charles
F–13232 **Marseille**

Société Nationale des
Chemins de fer
Français
Gare de Nice-Ville
F–06000 **Nice**

GERMANY
Deutsche Bundesbahn
Fahrkartenausgabe
Hauptbahnhof
D–6 **Frankfurt/Main**

Deutsche Bundesbahn
Fahrkartenausgabe
Hauptbahnhof
D–69 **Heidelberg**

Deutsche Bundesbahn
Fahrkartenausgabe
Hauptbahnhof
D–8 **Munich**

Deutsche Bundesbahn
Fahrkartenausgabe
Hauptbahnhof
D–5 **Cologne**

Deutsche Bundesbahn
Fahrkartenausgabe
Hauptbahnhof
D–7 **Stuttgart**

Deutsche Bundesbahn
Fahrkartenausgabe
Hauptbahnhof
D–2 **Hamburg**

GREAT BRITAIN
French National
Railways
179 Piccadilly
London W1V 0BA

GREECE
Chemins de fer
Hélléniques
Bureau des Voyages et
du Tourisme No.2
1, rue Karolou
Athens 107

Chemins de fer
Hélléniques
Gare Centrale des
Voyageurs
Thessaloniki

HUNGARY
Magyar Államvasutak
Déli Pályaudvar
Budapest

Magyar Államvasutak
Keleti Pályaudvar
Budapest

Magyar Államvasutak
Nyvgati Pályaudvar
Budapest

IRELAND (Republic of)
Coras Iompair Eireann
International Rail
Ticket Sales Office
35 Lower Abbey Street
Dublin 1

ITALY
Ferrovie Italiane dello
Stato
Stazione Santa Maria
Novella
Officio informazioni
Florence

Ferrovie Italiane dello
Stato
Stazione Centrale
Milan

Ferrovie Italiane dello
Stato
Stazione Santa Lucia
Venice

Ferrovie Italiane dello
Stato
Stazione Termini
Rome

Ferrovie Italiane dello
Stato
Stazione Centrale
Naples

Ferrovie Italiane dello
Stato
Stazione Centrale
Bari

Ferrovie Italiane dello
Stato
Stazione Centrale
Palermo

28   Europe by Train

LUXEMBOURG
Société Nationale des
Chemins de fer
Luxembourgeois
Bureau des
renseignements
Gare de Luxembourg
Luxembourg (GD)

NETHERLANDS
N.V. Nederlandse
Spoorwegen
Marketing
Reizigersvervoer
Bureau 13
Kamer 935
Katreinetoren (in the
Hall of Utrecht
Central Station)
Utrecht

NORWAY
NSB Billettekspedisjonen/
Utland
Oslo Sentralstasjon 0154
Oslo 1

PORTUGAL
Companhia dos cominhos
de ferro Portugueses
Departmento commercial
Estação de Santa Apolonia
Lisbon

SPAIN
Red Nacional de los
Ferrocarriles Españoles
Alcala 44
Madrid

Red Nacional de los
Ferrocarriles Españoles
Madrid–Barajas
International
Airport
Madrid

Red Nacional de los
Ferrocarriles Españoles
Estación central de
Barcelona Sants
Barcelona

Red Nacional de los
Ferrocarriles Calle
Zaragoza 29
Sevilla

Red Nacional de los
Ferrocarriles Españoles
Plaza Alfonso el
Magnanimo 2
Valencia

SWEDEN
Swedish State Railways
Ticket Office
Stockholm Central Station
S–105-50 **Stockholm**

SWITZERLAND
Schweizerische
Bundesbahnen
Auskunftsbüro
Hauptbahnhof
CH–4051 **Basel**

Schweizerische
Bundesbahnen
Auskunftsbüro
Hauptbahnhof
CH–3000 **Bern**

Chemins de fer fédéraux
Suisses
Bureau de Renseignements
CFF
Gare de Genève
CH–1211 **Geneva**

Chemins de fer
fédéraux Suisses
Geneva Airport
Geneva

Schweizerische
Bundesbahnen
Auskunftsbüro
Bahnhof
CH–6000 **Lucerne**

Schweizerische
Bundesbahnen
Auskunftsbüro
Hauptbahnhof
CH–8021 **Zürich**

Schweizerische
Bundesbahnen
Auskunftsbüro
Zürich Flughafen
CH–8058 **Zürich**

• **How to get the most out of your pass:** There are three basic ways you can use your Inter Rail/Eurail Youthpass.

1. Cover as many countries as possible on a grand-scale European tour, sampling each country (however sketchily), and deciding which ones you're most keen to return to on a later pass.

2. Head for a specific area or destination (the Greek islands, say, or the south of France or the art towns of Italy). Use the ticket to get you there by planning a route which takes in some of the European highspots, and come back by a different route. Often this can combine the best of both worlds since, if you stop off at three or four places en route and tire yourself out, you can relax, safe in the knowledge that you've still got two weeks' sunbathing on your Greek island before you have to set off, seeing more sights on your way home.

3. Concentrate on one specific country or area and tour it in depth by rail, stopping at every place that catches your eye.

Having carried out and enjoyed trips on all three principles, all we can say is that each is great fun in its own way – the choice is yours.

• **The BritRail Pass:** To travel in Great Britain, which is not covered in the Eurail scheme, it is best to buy a BritRail Pass or BritRail Youthpass. These passes are valid for unlimited travel anywhere by rail in England, Scotland and Wales, excluding the London underground system; they do, however, include 50 per cent reductions on steamship cruises on Lake Windermere, in the north of England. Below is a table of current prices valid until the end of December 1991 in American dollars.

	Gold	Silver	Senior 60+		Youth 16–25
Consecutive days	1st	Standard	1st	Standard	Standard
8	$319	$209	$289	$189	$169
15	$479	$319	$429	$289	$255
22	$599	$399	$539	$359	$319
1 month	$689	$465	$619	$419	$375

Age 5–15 half price.

Since 1989 a second BritRail pass has become available. This new, more flexible pass allows you to travel for either 4 days in a given 8-day period, or 8 days in a 15-day period. The table below quotes current prices up to the end of 1991.

	Gold	Silver	Senior 60+		Youth 16–25
	1st	Standard	1st	Standard	Standard
Any 4 days in 8	$269	$179	$239	$159	$145
Any 8 days in 15	379	255	339	229	199
Any 15 days in 1 month	549	369	495	329	—
Any 15 days in 2 months	—	—	—	—	295

Age 5–15 half price.

BritRail Passes can be purchased from over 22,000 travel agents throughout North America or by writing direct to BritRail Travel International, 10th floor, 1500 Broadway, New York, NY 10036. Don't forget that BritRail Passes cannot be purchased in Britain after you arrive. For visitors to London, the new 'London Extra' is of interest: 3-, 4- or 7-day passes for travel in and around London and the Home Counties cost $75, $90 and $135 for 2nd class; $95, $120 and $170 for 1st class. The London Visitor Travelcard (within London city) costs $18, $23 and $40 for 3, 4 and 7 days.

EUROTRAIN

Eurotrain is the leading UK operator in continental rail travel for students and young people. Generous discounts on normal rail fares are available to anyone under 26 to 2,000 destinations in Europe. Tickets are valid for up to 2 months (Turkey and Morocco returns for six months) and you can start your journey from any UK station.

Eurotrain fares allow great flexibility and freedom. You may choose your outward and return routes and stop off where and when you wish, and the ferry crossings are included. If you really want to see as much of Europe as possible then a Eurotrain Explorer ticket is the one for you. There are eighteen super value explorers to choose from, each combining the major cities of Europe by the most interesting routing available. The Capital Explorer is particularly popular and allows you to experience the very best of four great capital cities –

London, Paris, Brussels and Amsterdam. This summer it will cost around £75.

Explorer fares are valid for two months and you travel out by one route and return by another. You may stop off anywhere on your 'specified' route and stay for as long as you wish in the places you like best. They are introducing a scheme to allow passengers to book the first two nights' accommodation in Amsterdam, Brussels, Dublin, or Paris. For full details contact: Eurotrain, 52 Grosvenor Gardens, London SW1W 0AG (Tel. 071–730 3402). A booth at Victoria Station operates 8 a.m.–8 p.m. daily.

There were two new Explorers for summer 1990 – the Eastern Explorer and the Gaelic Explorer. The Eastern Explorer for £172.50 takes in Berlin, Prague, Budapest, covering nine countries in all. Also new in 1990 were two Explorer passes – the Polish pass selling from £10.00 and the Hungarian pass selling from £18.50 (inc. seat reservations). They are not only valid for under 26s but are also valid for students with ISIC cards (any age), teachers/academics and accompanying spouses/children. Both valid for one week, offering unlimited travel throughout the country.

WASTEELS

Wasteels are a similar organization to Eurotrain, operating under the name of Route 26. As the name suggests the tickets are valid for anyone under 26, and are available to the same destinations as the other companies. Wasteels also offer Mini-Tour tickets and have around 200 local offices throughout Europe. They also offer travel bargains from the UK to Italy for Italian nationals. They may be contacted at 121 Wilton Road, London SW1 (Tel. 071–834 7066).

OVER 26s

Those over 26 needn't despair of having to resort to boring package deals from now on; they can still eurorail by travelling according to one of the following two suggestions: take a youth hostel touring holiday or a rail touring card within an individual country. The youth hostel packages are extremely good value, based on rail travel and hostel accommodation, and operate in fifteen different countries, including Iceland, Israel, Japan, Australia and New Zealand. For further details write to YHA Travel, 14 Southampton Street, London WC2E 7HY (Tel. 071–240 5236/3150). Also, there are the regular Eurail Passes, individual country passes, and hopefully soon Inter Rail for the over 26s.

A new club has been formed for Inter Railers over 26 years. Based in Sweden, the Club +26's main purpose is to act as a network of contacts in different countries for Inter Railers, and to help those no longer eligible for the traditional Inter Rail card find out about the individual country passes available to them. Note an Inter Rail Card for those over 26 years is available in Scandinavia. Monthly meetings take place in Stockholm, but postal membership (£5 p.a.) is possible too. Write to Club +26, Nybrogatan 51, 11440 Stockholm, Sweden.

OLD AGE DISCOUNTS

The Senior Railcard (£16) gives those over 60 at least one-third off fares on British Rail. Those with this card (or the equivalent from the following countries) can get discounts on rail and ferry travel of 30–50 per cent with the Rail Europe Senior Card (£5 from BR) on first- and second-class travel in Austria, Belgium, Denmark, Finland, France, Germany, Greece, Hungary, Ireland, Italy, Luxembourg, Netherlands, Norway, Portugal, Spain, Sweden, Switzerland (most lines), United Kingdom and Yugoslavia. Information on further discounts can be had from branches of Thomas Cook or in the US from the National Council of Senior Citizens, 925 15th St NW, Washington DC, 20005 (Tel. 202–347 8800).

PASSES FOR INDIVIDUAL COUNTRIES

Nearly all Western European countries offer their own touring passes which allow you the freedom of their individual rail networks. The disadvantage of these is that it's often more expensive to get to the country where the pass becomes valid than to buy a BIJ ticket or an Inter Rail, which gets you out of Britain as well. Another point: even though you often get the use of ferries and coaches as well as trains, *you are still limited to just the one country*. It can be advantageous, though, if you're only interested in touring one country in depth, and don't want the route restrictions of a BIJ ticket. Many countries have passes with more flexible timescales, with tickets valid from four days to a month. There are no age restrictions on these go-as-you-please schemes so anyone, over or under 26, can still take advantage of them.

The Benelux countries, France and Switzerland offer a realistic alternative to continual touring: they make your ticket valid for travel on any of four, five or eight days of a holiday lasting 15–17 days, so you can spend a few days in each centre without worrying that you're missing out on the benefits of your rail pass.

The different deals range from 'very good value' to 'not worth your while', depending on currency fluctuations. Before committing yourself, decide how extensive and attractive the rail network of the country is (a quick glance at the European Rail network map – free with the BR International Timetable – will give you a good idea how much track there actually is to cover) and how much it'll cost you to get out there. A cheap flight to Greece, followed by one of their 'tourist cards' for the railways, can be an economical and effective way to see the country; conversely, by the time you've got yourself over to Austria and bought a touring card, you'll have spent well over the price of an Inter Rail. The 1991 Thomas Cook *Railpass Guide* gives full details of each country's individual rail passes.

SNCF, the French railways, introduced a 'youth railcard' called the Carte Jeune in 1983 which offers a 50 per cent reduction on any off-peak rail journeys made in France between 1 June and 30 September. This ticket entitles you to half-price travel, and includes travel on TGVs – the fastest trains in the world. There's also a free couchette thrown in on any overnight journey on a French domestic route, so if you're confining your travel to France this could well work out as your best alternative. Also in 1984, SNCF introduced the Carré Jeune which offers a 50 per cent reduction on off-peak and 20 per cent reduction on standard journeys on four single trips (or two returns) made within a period of one year. Both tickets cost around £14 and are valid on both first and second class.

Apply in person with your passport and passport photo to SNCF, 179 Piccadilly, London W1V 0BA (Tel. 071–409 1224), or any other SNCF address.

The enormous changes in the East have made it one of the most fascinating places to visit. Danish State Railways have introduced the East Rail Pass (available in the UK through British Rail's Victoria Station (Tel. 071–834 2345), and open to any nationality), which gives unlimited travel for 15 days in Czechoslovakia, Hungary, East Germany, and Poland, as well as Denmark, for £115. This is also valid on Danish ferries, as well as Danish trains. To start the journey, travel from Gedser in Southern Denmark by ferry to Warnemunde on the East German coast (£4 rebate when pass returned).

Eurotrain now offer the East European Explorer (£172.50), which journeys to Berlin, Prague and Budapest, as well as the Netherlands, Austria, Switzerland, France, Luxembourg and Belgium. Inter Rail is valid in Czechoslovakia, Hungary, Romania, Yugoslavia and Eurail is valid in Hungary. Individual 'Explorer' country passes are also available from Eurotrain for Hungary and Poland. These are open to all ISIC holders (i.e. students of any age), teachers and academics; and those under 26 years. The Polish pass costs £13 for first-class and £10 for second; and the Hungarian pass costs £26.50 for first-class; £18.50 for second (1990 prices).

These are one-week passes, and are available in multiples of one week. The Polish pass includes all seat reservations and express train supplements.

We've listed full details of *all* the available European touring passes in their respective chapter. Many can be bought in Britain from the European Rail Travel Centre, P.O. Box 303, Victoria Station, London SW1V 1JY (Tel. 071–834 2345 for information; 071–828 0892 for credit card bookings) or any BR Travel Centre. For further information, write to the individual country's tourist authority (their addresses appear on pages 55–58).

SPOIL YOURSELF

If you have the opportunity, there are some trains which are a delight to travel on. They connect the major European cities and are called:

LEONARDO DA VINCI	Milan–Innsbruck–Munich–Cologne–Dortmund
LIGURE	Marseille–Milan
ETOILE DU NORD	Paris–Brussels–Amsterdam
CATALAN-TALGO	Barcelona–Geneva
ARBALETE	Zürich–Paris
MERKUR	Copenhagen–Frankfurt
FRANZ HALS	Amsterdam–Munich

All are accessible with a first-class Eurail Pass (Eurocity etc.). The Intercity trains carry both first- and second-class passengers and are available to Inter Rail, Eurail Pass and Eurail Youthpass holders, as are TGVs, the world's fastest, linking Paris to Lyon in two hours at 168 m.p.h. TGV trains also link Paris to the south of France, the Alps and Switzerland.

If you've suddenly come into money (like a lot) treat yourself to a trip on either the Venice Simplon – Orient Express or the Queen of Scots. Both trains, run by different companies, use original restored coaches from the Pullman era of the 1920s. The most famous is the Orient Express which leaves London twice a week for Venice. You don't actually use the same train for the whole journey; the coaches for the British sector stay in Britain and when not on Orient Express duty are used for day excursions from London and private hires. On the continent, you use a different set of coaches which travel the original route of this train for the rich, famous and thriller writer through Paris, Basel, Zürich, Innsbruck, the Brenner Pass and Verona before arriving at Venice. London–Venice one way in mid-summer will cost around £700–750. London–Venice with two nights in a first-class hotel in Venice and return air fare is something more than £1,200. For further information pick up a brochure at your travel agent.

The Queen of Scots stays entirely in Scotland and leaves from Edinburgh's Waverley Station. You can have a three-day tour of the south-western Highlands (which includes a steam-hauled section on the West Highland Line) or the northern Highlands including Inverness and the far north – or go the whole hog and do the full six-day trip. The sheer opulence of both trains almost defies description, the coaches have been beautifully restored and the food, wine and service are simply superb. As a guide to the quality of service, the Queen of Scots carries a team of 12 staff to look after a maximum of 28 passengers. Both trains come into the category of 'if you have to ask the price you can't afford it' and they may even be outside the price range of first-class Adult Eurail travellers (£1,200 for the three-day tour, £2,800 for the whole trip).

Station information

The average major European city station will have most of the following facilities:

1. *Ticket desk:* At most large stations, tickets for domestic and international travel are purchased at different windows, so make sure you're in the right line.

2. *Train information office:* Marked with a blue letter *i*. Here you can find out the times and availability of trains from multi-lingual clerks. If the office is packed, see if large timetables are posted up on boards in the station. There are normally separate posters for arrivals (white background) and for departures (yellow background). Fast trains on both are given in red instead of black print, running chronologically from 0 hr to 24 hrs. Next to the time is the name or number of the train, together with its routeing, from point of origin to final destination, with the most important stops in between. Finally, the track and platform numbers, at which the train departs or arrives. Major stations provide this information on computer-ized boards. Train composition boards are always useful as they indicate where on the platform each coach stops. That way, you don't waste any time running to get your seat when the train rolls up.

3. *Left-luggage:* In the big stations, you'll find there'll be a manned depot (usually open until midnight – then it closes down till 5 or 6 a.m.) and automatic lockers. If you're catching a train before the manned depot opens again, get a locker, obviously. Note: Check that your rucksack will fit into the locker first. There are several sizes of lockers, and if you've a large pack you'll be very lucky if you can cram it in the smaller ones.

4. *Lost property office:* Usually open 9 a.m.–5 p.m., from Mondays to Fridays only. If it's desperate (say, you've lost your ticket, rucksack, passport or money), go to the station master.

5. *Station master's office:* In theory he's in charge of the trains not the passengers, but as he's the 'king pin' in the station he's your best bet if it's a real emergency.

6. You can always count on there being *telephones* and *post boxes*. Some stations have an international telephone service on the spot, and in some you can even find a full post office operating.

7. Assorted *shops* and *news-stands*.

8. Often a *first-aid post:* In Germany and France there are travellers' aid organizations: 'Bahnhofsmissions' and 'Bureau accueil'. They'll help if you're ill, lost or generally in distress. If you're ill and there's no first-aid help, again go to the station master.

9. *Toilets:* Vary dramatically in degrees of cleanliness and are not always free.

10. *Waiting rooms:* Again, these range from quite OK to diabolic. Nevertheless, they are useful, obviously, to Eurorailers. Many close at night, so you shouldn't count on them for spending the night in.

11. *Baths/showers:* Most large stations have these facilities where you can buy or rent towels, soap, shampoo, etc. They cost on average £1.50 ($2.55) a bath, £1 ($1.70) a shower.

12. *Foreign-exchange desk:* Unless you're really in need of the local currency, these tend to be a bad idea as their exchange rates are rarely competitive and there are usually long queues.

13. *Tourist information desk:* Extremely useful for eurorailers. Apart from handing out free maps and guides, they invariably run an accommodation service for a small charge, about 50p–£1.50 ($0.85–2.55). Watch out here as there can be long queues.

Obviously, the larger the station, the more facilities you can expect. If there are any outstanding facts relevant to a particular station, for instance, a cheap and good snack bar downstairs in Stockholm station, we mention that under 'Stockholm'.

PICTOGRAMS

Nearly every station is clearly marked with universal pictograms which overcome the language barrier very efficiently. Most of these are extremely straightforward and don't need explanation. There are some, however, which might cause confusion to first-timers:

Meeting Point

Lost and Found

Luggage and baggage store pictograms can even catch the old hands waiting in the wrong line, for example the self-service luggage-cart sign is:

Self-Service
Luggage-Cart

while that for a porter is:

Call for Porter

In some stations you will have enough trouble fighting the porters off without going out looking for them.

Confusion can also occur between the Luggage Registration Office (for sending luggage through to your next destination):

Luggage Registration
Office

and the left luggage or baggage check room:

Baggage
Check Room

Coin-operated lockers are different again:

Locker

Lockers are
also indicated by: CONSIGNE DES BAGAGES
GEPÄCKAUFBEWAHRUNG
CONSIGNA DE EQUIPAJES
DEPOSITO BAGAGLIO

You'll get a ticket which you have to present when you pick your
luggage up again.

RESERVATIONS

Unless you don't mind slouching in the corridor for hours on end, a
seat reservation can make a lot of sense on a busy route in summer.
On many services reservations are compulsory.

If you choose not to reserve, at least try to check how busy the train's going to be. For the equivalent of 50p–£1 ($0.85–1.70) a reserved seat is worth it. If you suspect that your departure train's going to be mobbed, check up and reserve before leaving the station on your arrival. In many Western countries, reservations can be made up to two months in advance. Some countries have obligatory reservations, whilst in others you have to make your reservations at least two hours before departure (all this is noted in the chapters on individual countries). When making a reservation try going along at a time when the office should be quiet (generally 9–11 a.m., and 3–5 p.m., Monday to Friday). You'd be amazed how many people roll up at lunchtime and at weekends when all the locals are out in force trying to make their own reservations. In Sweden, if you board a train in which reserved seats are compulsory without having reserved a seat for yourself beforehand, you will be charged an extra fare in addition to the reservation fee on board the train. Trains requiring compulsory seat reservations are indicated in timetables.

If you find yourself on a train without having reserved a seat, quickly shoot down the corridors looking for free seats on the reservation notice located outside each compartment or on the actual seats themselves. If the train seems to be completely booked up, try asking the guard whether there are any other carriages being added on, or any cancellations.

When you're making a reservation, tell the clerk exactly what you want – unless you specify, say, a non-smoker, it will be presumed that you want a smoker! In southern Europe especially, you're rarely asked what you want, so make your wishes clearly known when booking. Bear in mind the following:

1. *Class:* Make sure you don't end up unintentionally in first class.

2. *Non-smoker/smoker.*

3. *Which side of the train* you want to sit. On some journeys this can be quite significant; for example, a seat on the south side of the train on a Riviera journey ensures you a good view, but you'd miss most of it by sitting on the north side.

4. *Facing/back* to the engine: Some people have a preference for looking either in the direction of travel or away from it.

5. *Aisle/window seat:* Often the window seat has a pull-out table which is useful for eating or writing, whereas the aisle seat allows more leg room.

SOME TIPS

Always check the name of the station if you're dealing with a city with more than one (see below). Don't assume that, as you're travelling north, you'll necessarily be leaving from the city's northernmost station – it doesn't always follow. The following towns and cities have more than one main station (the towns marked with an asterisk are those where the station used by trains connecting with ferry services is separate from the main station):

ANTWERP	*DOVER	LONDON	ROTTERDAM
ATHENS	DUBLIN	LYON	SAN SEBASTIÁN
BARCELONA	ESSEN	MADRID	SEVILLE
BASEL	EXETER	*MALMÖ	STOCKHOLM
BELFAST	*FOLKESTONE	MANCHESTER	*TILBURY
BELGRADE	GENEVA	MARSEILLE	TOURS
BERLIN	GLASGOW	MILAN	TURIN
BILBAO	HAMBURG	MUNICH	VENICE
*BOULOGNE	*HARWICH	NAPLES	VIENNA
BRUSSELS	*HELSINGBORG	*NEWHAVEN	WARSAW
BUCHAREST	HENDAYE	OPORTO	ZÜRICH
BUDAPEST	IRÜN	PARIS	
*CALAIS	ISTANBUL	*PORTSMOUTH	
*CASABLANCA	LIÈGE	PRAGUE	
COMO	LISBON	ROME	

Refer to the city centre maps on the reverse of the European Rail map to see which cities have more than one main line station.

Bear in mind the distances between stations in these cities are usually quite substantial (in London, between Paddington and Liverpool Street is about five miles; in Paris, between Gare de Lyon and Gare St Lazare is about four and a half). The moral is: don't count on split-second connections between stations.

Train information

NIGHT TRAVEL

Travelling at night has distinct advantages for the eurorailer who doesn't mind missing the scenery of a particular area or the fact that night trains invariably take longer to get to their destinations. The advantage of night travel is that in effect you add an extra day to your stay by arriving in the morning, ready to start your tour. How exactly you spend the night, and the consequent amount of sleep you manage to get in, depends largely on which of the sleeping arrangements you opt for, and how good a sleeper you are.

Basically there are four ways of travelling at night: sit up in the normal seats; get a seat which pulls down (as on the German and Italian trains) and allows you to lie down; buy a couchette; buy a sleeper. Taking each in turn, you can:

1. *Sit up all night* in a seat. It's free, but not guaranteed to find you fresh enough for a full day's sightseeing the next day. A neck air cushion is a good idea.

2. *Pull-down seats.* These are great when you can find them, as they're free yet still allow you to stretch out, thus increasing the chances of sleep. Once all six seats are pulled down, they join together to form a massive 'bed'. How much room you end up with depends on how full the compartment was originally; if there are only two or three of you in the compartment, you're home and dry for a free sleep. Reserve one if you can.

3. *Couchettes.* This is a seat by daytime, which at night is converted into a proper full berth. In second class, there are six to a compartment (four in first class). There is no sex segregation but this is not normally a problem even for single girls as the couchettes are nearly always full. For your £8 ($13.60) (average cost, but see under list of individual countries) you get a sheet, blanket and pillow, and there's a bed-light. You can use the washroom next to the toilets for washing. Each couchette has a luggage rack, but it's always wise to take your valuables to bed with you. Standards of couchettes vary enormously as they're run by the individual national rail networks, so that in Germany

they're very good, while in Spain and Italy they're pretty awful. Reservations for couchettes are more or less essential in the summer. You are required to book at least five hours before the train leaves the station.

4. *Cabines*. In 1986 French Railways launched Cabine 8, a compartment (in new air-conditioned coaches) with 8 semi-reclined bunks enabling you to stretch out in your own sleeping bag. They are completely free, but as they were an overwhelming success you might find it worthwhile reserving ahead. Sleepers are operated either by the Wagons-Lits Company (an international concern) or by a subsidiary of the railway. Many of these are developing into combined groups, collectively calling themselves 'Trans Euro Nuit/Nacht/Notte'. The Scandinavian and East European countries operate their own sleepers, as does British Rail. The average two- or three-berth sleeper is £16 ($27.20) a person, but price often depends on the distance you're covering.

5. *Sleepers*. Sleeping cars are a great step up in comfort from couchettes, but they're also a lot more expensive. As in Britain, European sleepers come in two classes and offer: a proper bed with all the trimmings, a sink with soap, towels and warm water, an electrical outlet and occasionally your own WC. The Thomas Cook European Sleeping Cars Book (£1.60) details the different types of cars in use.

A bit of general advice on travelling at night. Very often, your train gets into the station an hour before departure; if you've had a hard day, this is good to know as you can get yourself bedded down earlier. If you take the train right through to its final destination, you can often lie on for another half-hour or so in the morning, once it arrives, before getting ousted.

If you're reserving a couchette or sleeper, try for the top berths as they're roomier, there's more air and they afford you a slightly greater degree of privacy. Watch out when the train enters for the yellow stripe along the outside of the carriage, just below roof level. This indicates first-class coaches only.

If you're going by sleeper or couchette on an international trip (or even for some internal ones in Italy, for some strange reason), the attendant will take your passport and ticket from you so that, in theory anyway, you won't need to be woken up at the border in the middle of the night.

Once you're all in, lock the door and hope you've not landed yourself – as I have so often in the past – with a collection of snorers!

The best trains for a good night's sleep are those that don't cross international borders (difficult to avoid) or stop every couple of hours at stations en route, otherwise you'll have customs officials coming in for a nose-around at 3 a.m., or train announcements blaring out all night long (you can bet it'll be your carriage that stops right beneath the loudspeaker). Our advice to eurorail insomniacs is to have a heavy meal before the journey, take some ear plugs, and don't hold back on the local vino.

A few years ago, however, many travellers on Italian and Spanish trains accepted the 'hospitality' of their fellow travellers in the form of doped orange juice and other drinks, and woke up many hours later to find they had been robbed. These incidents, which were widely publicized, unfortunately gave others the same idea, and in Scotland several travellers on the East Coast between Edinburgh and Dundee fell victim to the same trick. The culprit was later arrested and sent to prison.

Most night trains don't have a bar or eating facilities on board so if you're the type of person who enjoys a midnight feast or gets thirsty in the night, you had better bring your own supplies along or you'll wake up with an empty stomach and a throat like a vacuum cleaner.

• **Main night trains:** Below is a list of just some of the many good night trains in Western Europe. Remember you can save money by sleeping on these night trains and cover more ground during your vacation.

Amsterdam–Copenhagen	Madrid–Algeciras
Amsterdam–Munich	Madrid–Lisbon
Barcelona–Geneva	Madrid–Santander
Barcelona–Madrid	Milan–Paris
Barcelona–Nice	Nice–Geneva
Barcelona–Paris	Ostend–Munich
Barcelona–Pamplona	Paris–Amsterdam
Basel–Hamburg	Paris–Copenhagen
Belgrade–Thessaloniki	Paris–Munich
Brussels–Genoa	Paris–Nice
Brussels–Munich	Rome–Nice
Copenhagen–Hamburg	Vienna–Cologne
Hamburg–Munich	Vienna–Frankfurt
Heidelberg–Lugano	Vienna–Lindau
London–Edinburgh	Vienna–Venice
Malmö–Stockholm	

Don't forget that it's often preferable to sleep in a good compartment than in a crowded youth hostel. Try pretending you're sound asleep when the train pulls in to stations and you'll raise the chances of being left undisturbed.

EATING

Few eurorailers can afford to indulge in buffet or restaurant meals on the trains because they're never cheap. The majority of the dining services offered on European trains are run by the Wagons-Lits Company. However, the quality of the food and service varies from country to country, as it really depends on the staff and hygiene of the host country. Don't be fooled by the mobile mini-bars that wheel temptingly past you – they're a rip-off pricewise, and on top of that the food and drink is of very poor quality. As a general rule all Eurocity and most InterCity and long-distance express trains have a separate dining car with set-price meals from £5–15 ($8.50–25.50) or a bar/buffet car serving drinks, sandwiches and light snacks. It's a very satisfying experience having a leisurely meal along one of the scenic routes even if you can only afford it once.

Remember: You can't drink the water from the train washrooms anywhere in Europe. Buy your drink before you get aboard. The best bet is to stock up with food from the supermarkets before you leave and treat yourself to a good picnic on the train. 1987 saw the introduction of Eurocity, an international branding of high-speed and quality trains with first and second classes. Eurocity have absorbed International InterCity trains, and most former TEE trains, with the exception of those in France.

TRAIN SPLITTING

As the trains of Europe undertake some pretty complicated routes and use one another's rolling stock, trains on long international journeys often split into various sections at certain points, so obviously it's important to check that you get on the relevant part of the train. The best policy is to ask and make sure you're on the right segment before you settle down. If your coach is going to be shunted about on to another train, find out at which station it's due to happen and at what time. It's all made quite easy by the signs posted on the doors and windows at intervals along the train:

CALAIS

PARIS   ————————   MILANO
(Nord)   (Centrale)
                 VENEZIA

This shows that the coach starts at Calais, stops at Paris (Nord) and Milan (Centrale) and terminates in Venice. There will also be a '1' or '2' to tell you the class of the carriage. Whatever happens, don't get out of a train which is due to split up, and then get back into another section of it with the intention of walking along to your seat – you could find you're no longer connected to that bit of the train! Just in case you do get separated from your fellow travellers, carry your own money, ticket and passport at all times. This advice is also relevant in case one of you gets mugged – that way you won't lose everything at once. In some stations, mainly termini, you'll find the train reversing and going back in the direction you've just come. This is often the case in Switzerland. Don't worry about it. It's just a standard shunting procedure. This usually takes place on the last stop before, or first after, an international frontier, and is used to reduce or add on extra carriages. If you're in any doubt about your train splitting, ask the ticket inspector as soon as you are on board.

• **Supplements:** An Inter Rail or BIJ ticket alone is not sufficient to travel on some of the express trains of Europe, or on many of the Eurocity services. If you want to use these trains, you'll have to pay a supplement, and this is calculated on the distance you're travelling and the type of express you've chosen (unless you have a regular Eurail).

Some countries (notably the Scandinavian ones) don't charge supplements as such, but make seat reservations compulsory on expresses. (Full details of all the supplements and surcharges are to be found below under the individual country chapters.)

It's often worth inquiring how much the additional first-class supplement is, particularly if you're feeling under the weather and the train's packed out. (As a survivor of the Spanish Olive Oil Epidemic of '81 trying to get home, I can vouch for it!)

TIMETABLES

One of the best timetables is Thomas Cook's European Timetable. This is published on the first day of each month. The June to September issues have a full summer schedule, and there are summer service forecasts from February to May. The full winter schedule appears in the October to May issues, with forecasts in August and September. In this book you'll find most of the trains that run in Europe and most ferry services. Although it seems expensive at around £6.40 a copy, the timetable is worth its weight in gold and can save you hours of queueing (particularly at Italian stations). It also has a number of tables from the Thomas Cook Airports Guide Europe. Back editions can be ordered for half price from Thomas Cook Publishing Office, 10/12 Eningsby Road, Bretton, Peterborough PE3 8SB. If you do this, watch you buy one which has the appropriate summer or winter schedules. It is available from all Thomas Cook travel agents or by post at £7.35 from Thomas Cook Ltd, PO Box 36, Peterborough PE3 6SB (£7.80 in Europe and £10 outside Europe). Also worth thinking about is the Thomas Cook Rail Map of Europe which costs £3.95 or £4.40 (£4.90 in Europe and £5.40 outside Europe) by post, published biennially, and the new Railpass Guide, published every year at Easter at £1.95 (£2.40 by post, £3.05 in Europe and £3.75 outside). NB A voucher appears in the 1991 Inter Rail brochure in the UK entitling the purchaser to £1.45 off the combined cost of the European Timetable and European Rail map when purchased together at a Thomas Cook Travel Shop, providing you have bought an Inter Rail card.

The best value is the free UIC international timetable on ABC lines, though copies are like gold in most travel agents. Also good to have is the Eurail timetable free from any Eurail issuing office.

If you want the more detailed national timetable and railmap for a particular country (often hard to find), contact the SBB Timetable Shop, Office 224, Hauptbahnhof, CH–9001 St Gallen, Switzerland, which runs a mail order service.

Bear in mind the change from winter to summer schedules: all European rail networks start their summer schedules on the last Sunday in May and the winter schedules on the last Sunday in September, except in Britain. Check also the time zone the country's in, and keep an eye out for local and national holidays.

• **Public holidays affecting trains:** At public holiday times, you'll find services are amended, and those trains that are operating will be busier than usual and with more reservations. Check with stations for details and turn up earlier for the train. We list all the relevant holidays under the individual country chapters. In many countries the day, or at least the half-day, preceding an official public holiday is also regarded as a holiday. Note also that in the Eastern Bloc countries religious holidays are often locally observed but not nationally recognized. We give below a calendar of moving holidays for 1991:

Shrove Monday	11 February
Shrove Tuesday	12 February
Maundy Thursday	28 March
Good Friday	29 March
Holy Saturday	30 March
Easter Sunday	31 March
Easter Monday	1 April
Ascension Day	9 May
Whit Monday	20 May

Muslim holidays:

Ramadan begins	17 March
Id-ul-Fitr	16 April
Id-ul-Adha	23 June
New Year (1412)	13 July

• **Hazards:** On those long hot runs in southern Europe, where temperatures are high and trains aren't air-conditioned, the temptation is to stick your head out of the window to cool off. Be warned: you may cool off more than you anticipated. When you feel that unexpected drop of rain upon your face, you may fear the worst . . . someone's been to the loo further up. Moreover, don't be reassured by the notices announcing that it's illegal to throw rubbish out of the window. Expect anything, and be on your guard, especially for cans and bottles. Most importantly of all, always be on your guard for open or unsecured doors; even the safety-conscious DB (Deutsche Bundesbahn) estimate that nearly 200 people have been wiped out in the last five years by falling from their trains. Always carry your valuables with you when you go to the loo, and be extra careful on night trains as this is when most theft occurs. Often a small padlock securing your bag to a fixed point is enough to deter a thief.

TRAINS IN EASTERN EUROPE

To avoid unbelievable anxiety and frustration while travelling in Eastern Europe, it's useful to remember the following:

1. Tickets are often only valid for the specific date and class of the train stated on your ticket. To change your date is more trouble than it's worth, so always be sure of the exact date and time you wish to leave before buying your ticket or making a reservation.

2. Queueing is a fact of life, so try to buy tickets and make reservations at odd hours: one of the best times is late at night, since queues begin long before offices open in the morning. Whenever possible, try to buy your ticket/make your reservation from Western Europe (say, Vienna) at the appropriate student office.

3. For all international journeys, tickets and reservations must be made through the official government travel agents (listed below under each country). Otherwise use the train stations where queues are slightly shorter.

4. Make sure you're in the right queue. There's often one queue for journeys over 100 kilometres, another for reservations, etc. These are not immediately obvious as often there are no signs and it's quite possible to stand for up to an hour in the wrong line.

5. When you reach the front of the queue try and get everything possible done in one go, so you don't have to queue again later: buy your ticket, make your reservation, ask what platform the train leaves from, etc. Write it all down, in case the assistant doesn't speak English.

6. Try to view the whole exercise as an initiative test, and always be prepared for any eventuality. It's not uncommon to discover that all second-class seats are fully booked so, unless you fancy another hour's wait at the end of the queue, it's best to have considered alternative trains or routes, or whether you're prepared to pay the extra. Compared to the West, you'll find that train fares are much cheaper, and it's worth the extra cost to go first class for the added comfort, space and – sometimes – cleanliness.

Increasingly, the Eastern European stations are being re-modelled on Western lines, but until the mid 90s anyway, don't expect comparable standards. The station facilities are basic, so don't expect luxuries like showers or permanently staffed Tourist Information booths.

TRAIN AND BIKE TRAVEL

Those wishing to combine a cycling and train holiday will find the situation very different in the various countries. In some it is easy to arrange transport of your bike with you, in others almost impossible. In some countries it is also possible to hire a bike. For advice and details contact the Cyclists' Touring Club, Cotterell House, 69 Meadrow, Goldalming, Surrey GU7 3HS. They publish Country Information Sheets, and have many other services, including insurance.

Before you go

FLYING THE ATLANTIC

The basic rule is the more you pay then the greater your flexibility will be, or conversely the less you pay, the more restrictions you will have to face. As always, forward planning can not only save you money, but also buy you time in Europe. It is a good idea to spend time in countries not covered in the Eurail scheme (Great Britain or the Eastern Bloc, for example), either before your Eurail Pass becomes valid or when it has expired. Don't waste precious days of your pass in countries where you can't use it. Consequently, it's important to choose the right city as your gateway to Europe.

Flying to London with Virgin Atlantic or Pan Am is one of the most popular starts and it's easy to see why, with return fares at only around £200 ($340) low season and £375 ($640) high season. To make a reservation, write or telephone Virgin Atlantic, 43 Perry Street, New York, NY 10014 (Tel. 212 242 1330) or Ashdown House, High Street, Crawley, West Sussex RH10 1DQ (Tel. 0293 38222); Pan Am, 100 East 42nd Street, New York, NY (Tel. 212 687 2600) or 193 Piccadilly, London W1V 0AD (Tel. 071–409 3377).

Reservations can normally be cancelled or changed up to three days before departure for a £40 ($68) charge, or even after that for an increased charge. Virgin Atlantic work out slightly more expensive but offer bonuses included in your ticket cost, such as in-flight snacks, a hot meal with wine, and a low-cost hotel scheme. During the peak season, June to September, both airlines are well booked up and unless you reserve well beforehand you may be forced to travel standby. If this happens, you stand a better chance midweek than at weekends. Also check out the Icelandair route from New York to Frankfurt via Reykjavick, which might be worth considering if you intend to start your trip in continental Europe.

There is no shortage of airlines or types of tickets to get you over to Europe, but if money is the prime consideration set yourself the task of getting a really good, reliable travel agent. After briefing him on how much cash you have to spend and where you want to go, leave it to him to come up with a few ideas for you to think about. Do your own homework, too, and plan early as most reduced air fares are payable thirty days in advance. Scan *The New York Times* (especially Sunday's) and talk to as many other eurorailers as you can to pick up tips. Midweek days are usually the quietest for flying, so flexibility is an advantage, particularly if you're flying with Pan Am or Virgin Atlantic.

If you can't afford the luxury of being flexible, go for a charter flight which gives you a seat reservation but can involve you in backtracking to get back, for the return journey, to the airport you arrived at. If you've a bit more cash, an APEX (Advanced Booking Excursion Fare) allows you greater freedom as you can return from a different airport. Make sure you will land at an airport that has its own railway station: Amsterdam, Brussels, Frankfurt, Geneva, London LGW, Paris CDG, Zürich, etc.

● **APEX:** APEX flights represent one of the most flexible options on the reduced fares market, as they are not so restrictive as charters. With an APEX ticket it's possible to arrive at and depart from different cities (countries) and even on different airlines in some cases. If you decide to fly with a particular airline, ask if they operate a Super-APEX package which can mean an even cheaper deal.

● **Standby:** If you want to keep your options open until the last minute without committing yourself, a standby ticket is your best bet. Not all airlines offer standby, and your choice of both

American and European gateways is limited. However, if you are flexible the rewards are high for apart from being the cheapest ticket around, it doesn't commit you to any particular time or place when returning to the US.

There are only a limited number of standby seats on each flight, so it's important to be well organized to improve your chances, particularly in peak season. A few days before you plan on leaving, phone up the airline's reservation desk and check out the seat availability on your optimum flight. Don't mention that you are planning to fly standby, as many officials are cagey about giving information away. Seats are always given out on a first come, first served basis, so be there in good time, and be prepared for a wait, even overnight if necessary. Most sales desks open at around 7 a.m. and it's not unusual for a queue to form before then. As soon as you've bought your ticket don't hang around, go straight to the check-in desk and get your name down on that list.

• **Budget fares:** Pricewise a budget fare is similar to a standby, yet it offers a confirmed seat reserved in advance. The only problem is that you must tell the airline which week you would like to fly out and return (if desired), and they will get back to you at least a week before your flight with the details. In this way, the airline gets to choose the exact day, at a time which is convenient to them, not you. In our opinion, it's only worth considering if you cannot find a suitable APEX flight, and don't want to take the risk of flying standby; even then, it only makes sense if you've got plenty of time on your hands before your rail pass begins.

• **Charter flights:** Charters are back and more competitive than ever. While most charter operators who have survived the last ten years in the hectic US marketplace can be considered reliable, you should still exercise care in booking a charter. Read the charter operator-participant contract to be fully aware of the rules governing a charter flight. Try CIEE's Council Charter (Tel. 800 223 7402) or Travac (Tel. 800 872 8800). Council Charter's brochure *Charter Europe* includes year-round low-cost flights to several European cities. Get a free copy from your nearest Council Travel Office or write to Council Charter, Charter Europe, 205 East 42nd Street, New York, NY 10017. Finally, try and keep an eye out for good deals in the Sunday papers.

• **Other options:** There are cheap scheduled flights from New York/California offered by Virgin Atlantic, World, Transamerica Capitol and Icelandic. Check with Council Charter for your best option, for apart from being the 'grand-daddy' of charter flight operators for students and young people, they also know what else is on offer.

TYPE OF AIR FARE	MIN/MAX STAY REQUIREMENT	ADVANCE PURCHASE REQUIREMENT	CANCELLATION PENALTIES	STOPOVER POSSIBILITIES
STANDBY	None	None	None	None
BUDGET	None	21 days	$50+	None
APEX	Varies from 7–180 days	Varies 21 days round trip only	10% of fare	Sometimes Check with airline
SUPER-APEX	Varies 7–180 days	Varies 21 days round trip only	10% of fare	None

• **Travel agents:** No special licence is required by travel agents in the US so anyone can set themselves up in business regardless of experience. At present, there are about 100,000 to choose from, so be selective. Only a small percentage are members of the American Society of Travel Agents (ASTA) which requires at least three years in business prior to membership. For a list of ASTA members in your area write to the American Society of Travel Agents, PR Dept, 711 Fifth Avenue, New York, NY 10022. They also produce free brochures giving general advice about travel overseas. Alternatively look out for the ASTA globe which is the symbol of membership.

Another good sign is the Institute of Travel Agents certificate which means that the agent must have worked in the industry for at least five years and have passed the relevant exams. For listings of CTAs in your area write to the Institute of Certified Travel Agents, 148 Linden Street, Wellesley, MA 02181 (Tel. 617 237 0280).

Always go to a travel agent after you've done your own research first to see if they can come up with a better deal than you were able to. Most travel agent services are free, so if it's necessary to make a transatlantic phone call let them make it. Never forget, the cheaper your ticket is, the less their commission will be, so the temptation will be for a travel agent to recommend APEX as opposed to standby unless they see you've done your homework beforehand.

PREPLANNING

This can give great pleasure and add to the fun of the trip, as well as ensuring you get the very most out of your time abroad. After looking at the map of Europe, plan out a rough itinerary in your head and check its feasibility in your timetable (use last summer's one rather than a winter schedule); then write it down and roughly allocate days to it.

When planning a rail itinerary for a complete tour of Europe, there are three main considerations to take into account: the interesting destinations you'd like to go to; how many days you want to spend there; and the most scenic and enjoyable route to get there.

● **Time allocation:** Most cities require a minimum of two or three nights, though obviously you could mix a few 'one-nighters' into your schedule to make your time last out. Time allocation is a more serious consideration for those attempting a 'whistle-stop' tour, whereas those touring only a few countries can be more lax about it.

● **Time differences:** Bear in mind the different time-zones of the countries you'll be travelling in and allow for this when you're making connections. Remember: all these are based on GMT (Greenwich Mean Time).

COUNTRY	SUMMER	WINTER	COUNTRY	SUMMER	WINTER
AUSTRIA	+2(A)	+1	MOROCCO	+2(A)	+1
BELGIUM	+2(A)	+1	NETHERLANDS	+2(A)	+1
BULGARIA	+3(A)	+2	NORWAY	+2(A)	+1
CZECHO-			POLAND	+2(A)	+1
SLOVAKIA	+2(A)	+1	PORTUGAL	+1(A)	GMT
DENMARK	+2(A)	+1	ROMANIA	+3(A)	+2
FINLAND	+3(A)	+2	SPAIN	+2(A)	+1
FRANCE	+2(A)	+1	SWEDEN	+2(A)	+1
GERMANY	+2(A)	+1	SWITZER-		
GREECE	+3(A)	+2	LAND	+2(A)	+1
HUNGARY	+2(A)	+1	TURKEY	+3(A)	+2
IRELAND	+1(B)	GMT	UNITED		
ITALY	+2(A)	+1	KINGDOM	+1(B)	GMT
LUXEMBOURG	+2(A)	+1	YUGOSLAVIA	+2(A)	+1

(A) = Summertime runs from end of March–end of September.
(B) = Summertime runs from end of March–end of October.

• **When to go:** Most eurorailers find themselves on the road (or rail) between June and September – for obvious reasons. Travelling in the high season gives you the advantages of encountering more people, getting better weather and being sure all the museums, hotels and places of interest are going to be open.

However, the counter-argument is obvious: prices are higher, the character of a place tends to get lost beneath the throngs of tourists, accommodation is difficult to find, people involved in the tourist industry have less time for you, and in general there are more hassles on the trains.

For the lucky few able to choose when to go, we'd personally recommend spring to early summer – but whenever you go, you'll find it a fascinating experience.

• **Destination and routes:** Most eurorailers have a few special places in mind before they set off, maybe an urge to see Paris, Rome and Athens, and by using a timetable and the information given later in this guide you'll be able to work out the quickest and best routes between these places. Often there are two or three alternative routes to major cities, and there's bound to be one that appeals to you more than another. The *Europe by Train* factsheets aim to provide helpful information for those wishing to find the very best route for their particular needs (see p.16).

• **Advance tourist information:** If you know all the countries you're going to be visiting before you set off, write to their main Tourist Office in your own country and they'll gladly send you back free booklets and maps to whet your appetite for their country and give an idea as to what you'd like to see and what you can afford to miss out.

Addresses in the UK:
AUSTRIA, 30 St George Street, London W1 (071–629 0461)
BELGIUM, Premier House, 2 Gayton Road, Harrow, Middlesex HA1 (081–861 3300)
BULGARIA, 18 Princes Street, London W1 (071–499 6988/9)
CZECHOSLOVAKIA, Čedok, 17–18 Old Bond Street, London W1 (071–629 6058)
DENMARK, 169–173 Regent Street, London W1 (071–734 2637/8)
FINLAND, 66 Haymarket, London SW1 (071–839 4048)
FRANCE, 178 Piccadilly, London W1 (071–499 6911/071–491 7622)

EAST GERMANY, Berolina Travel Ltd, 22A Conduit Street, London W1 (071–629 1664)

WEST GERMANY, 65 Curzon Street, London W1 (071–495 3990)

GREECE, 195–197 Regent Street, London W1 (071–734 5997)

HUNGARY, Danube Travel Ltd, 6 Conduit Street, London W1 (071–493 0263)

IRELAND, 150 New Bond Street, London W1 (071–493 3201)

ITALY, 1 Princes Street, London W1 (071–408 1254)

LUXEMBOURG, 36/37 Piccadilly, London W1 (071–434 2800)

MALTA, 207 College House, Wrights Lane, London W8 (071–938 2668)

MONACO, 50 Upper Brook Street, London W1 (071–629 4712)

MOROCCO, 174 Regent Street, London W1 (071–437 0073)

NETHERLANDS, 25–28 Buckingham Gate, London SW1 (071–630 0451)

NORWAY, Charles House, 5–11 Lower Regent Street, London SW1 (071–839 6255)

POLAND, Polorbis, 82 Mortimer Street, London W1 (071–580 8028)

PORTUGAL, 1–5 New Bond Street, London W1 (071–493 3873)

ROMANIA, 29 Thurloe Place, London SW7 (071–584 8090)

SPAIN, 57–58 St James Street, London SW1 (071–499 0901/071–834 6667)

SWEDEN, 3 Cork Street, London W1 (071–437 5816)

SWITZERLAND, 1 New Coventry Street, London W1 (071–734 1921)

TURKEY, 170–173 Piccadilly, London W1 (071–734 8681)

UNITED KINGDOM, 12 Regent Street, London SW1 (071–730 3400)

YUGOSLAVIA, 143 Regent Street, London W1 (071–734 5243)

Addresses in the USA:

AUSTRIA, 500 Fifth Avenue, 20th Floor, New York, NY 10110 (212 944 6880)

3440 Wilshire Boulevard, Los Angeles, Ca. 90010 (213 380 3309)

BELGIUM, 745 Fifth Avenue, New York, NY 10151 (212 758 8130)

BULGARIA, 161 East 86th Street, New York, NY 10028 (212 722 1110)

CZECHOSLOVAKIA, 10 East 40th Street, Suite 1902, New York, NY 10016 (212 689 9720)

DENMARK, 655 Third Avenue, 18th Floor, New York, NY 10017 (212 949 2333)

FINLAND, 655 Third Avenue, 18th Floor, New York, NY 10017 (212 949 2333)

FRANCE, 610 Fifth Avenue, New York, NY 10020 (212 757 1125)
645 North Michigan Avenue, Chicago, Ill. 60611 (312 337 6301)
9401 Wilshire Boulevard, Beverly Hills, Ca. 90212 (213 271 6665)
GERMANY, 747 Third Avenue, New York, NY 10017 (212 308 3300)
444 South Flower Street, Los Angeles, Ca. 90017 (213 688 7332)
GREECE, Olympic Tower, Fifth Floor, 645 Fifth Avenue, New York, NY 10022 (212 421 5777)
611 West Sixth Street, Suite 1998, Los Angeles, Ca. 90017 (213 626 6696)
HUNGARY, 630 Fifth Avenue, New York, NY 10111 (212 582 7412)
IRELAND, 757 Third Avenue, New York, NY 10017 (212 418 0800)
ITALY, 630 Fifth Avenue, New York, NY 10111 (212 245 4822)
500 North Michigan Avenue, Chicago, Ill. 60611 (312 644 0990)
360 Post Street, San Francisco, Ca. 94108 (415 392 6206)
LUXEMBOURG, 801 Second Avenue, New York, NY 10017 (212 370 9850)
MOROCCO, 20 East 46th Street, New York, NY 10017 (212 557 2520)
NETHERLANDS, 355 Lexington Avenue, New York, NY 10017 (212 370 7367)
605 Market Street, Room 401, San Francisco, Ca. 94105 (415 543 6772)
NORWAY, 655 Third Avenue, 18th Floor, New York, NY 10017 (212 949 2333)
POLAND, 500 Fifth Avenue, Rockefeller Center, Suite 520, New York, NY 10110 (212 391 0844)
PORTUGAL, 548 Fifth Avenue, New York, NY 10036 (212 354 4403)
ROMANIA, 573 Third Avenue, New York, NY 10016 (212 697 6971)
SPAIN, 665 Fifth Avenue, New York, NY 10022 (212 759 8822)
845 North Michigan Avenue, Chicago, Ill. 60611 (312 944 0215)
1 Hallidie Plaza, San Francisco, Ca. 94102 (415 346 8100)
SWEDEN, 655 Third Avenue, 18th Floor, New York, NY 10017 (212 949 2333)
SWITZERLAND, 608 Fifth Avenue, New York, NY 10020 (212 757 5944)
250 Stockton Street, San Francisco, Ca. 94108 (415 362 2260)
TURKEY, 821 United Nations Plaza, New York, NY 10017 (212 687 2194)

UNITED KINGDOM, 40 West 57th Street, New York, NY 10019 (212 581 4700)

612 South Flower Street, Los Angeles, Ca. 90017 (213 623 8196)

John Hancock Center, Suite 3320, 875 North Michigan Avenue, Chicago, Ill. 60611 (312 787 0490)

Plaza of the Americas, North Tower Suite 750, Dallas, Texas 75201 (213 623 8196)

YUGOSLAVIA, 630 Fifth Avenue, Suite 280, New York, NY 10111 (212 757 2801)

Remember though, Tourist Offices are in the business of selling their country, so take some of their claims like having the 'most beautiful city in Europe' with a pinch of salt. However, as their brochures are nearly all free and usually very well produced, you've nothing to lose. Make sure you ask for country and city maps; often the tourist authority will send you free the same ones you might otherwise have to buy, once in the country.

• **UK red tape:** A valid passport, with the relevant visas for Poland, Czechoslovakia, Bulgaria and Romania if you're going there, will get you in without problems. (Visas for Eastern Europe are in a great state of flux, and the best advice for the early 90s is to check with the London Embassy of the country concerned.) Likewise a British visitor's card is fine for many countries in Western Europe but no good for Eastern Europe. It costs £7.50 and is valid for twelve months. Apply at a post office in person with two recent passport-type photos and either your National Health Service card or your birth certificate.

For a full ten-year passport, get an application form at a main post office, complete it and send it on to your nearest passport office. This costs £15. Allow a month at least if you're posting off the form and at least three weeks if you take it in person.

• **US red tape:** A valid US passport will get you into the following countries for up to three months without the need for a visa: Austria, Belgium, France, Germany, Greece, Ireland, Italy, Luxembourg, Morocco, Netherlands, Spain and Switzerland. Portugal allows you 60 days without a visa, and of course, all Eastern European countries, excluding Czechoslovakia, require a visa. Apply to the nearest consulate/embassy of the country concerned (see under US visas).

As far as the Scandinavian countries are concerned (Denmark, Finland, Norway and Sweden), the three-month period without visa is for holidaymakers and can be spent in all or any of the four Scandinavian countries. But a US tourist who has spent three months in, say, Sweden, cannot go on to spend a further period in, say, Denmark. A residence permit would be required in that case.

If you're applying for the first time or your current passport was issued before your eighteenth birthday or if it's more than eight years old, you'll have to go along in person to any US Post Office or Passport Agency, otherwise you can send off a DSP 82 form by mail. Along with your application you should include two recent passport-type photos, signed on the back, plus around $40. If you have to go along in person, you'll need your US birth certificate and around $48 ($32 if you're under eighteen). Passports are valid for ten years if you're over eighteen, five if you're under. If you've any problems, contact the Passport Office, Department of State, Washington, DC 20520, and ask them for their free booklet 'Your Trip Abroad'. Canadian passports are valid for five years only and can be obtained by mail from the Passport Office, Department of External Affairs, 125 Sussex Drive, Ottawa, Ontario K1A OG3 for CDN $25. Allow six to eight weeks' processing time from March to September, and four to six weeks from October to February.

VISAS

Don't be put off from visiting a country because of the visa situation. The procedure is extremely straightforward and is invariably easier than most people imagine, especially with the increasing liberalization in Eastern Europe.

A visa in advance is required for all East European countries *except* Yugoslavia and Hungary, and where possible it's best arranged in advance, by writing to the relevant embassy for their application form (see below). When you send off your application, don't forget to include two passport-type photos signed on the back, plus the relevant fee, which now seems to be standardized at £20. Don't forget that you still need a visa for Bulgaria, Czechoslovakia, Poland and Romania even though travel is valid using an Inter Rail.

Allow up to four weeks for the processing of your application form, although it is usually turned round in a week or ten days. Get yourself organized early and do as much as possible by post as far in advance as possible (not too far in advance, as visas are only valid for certain periods). If you've left it until the last minute don't worry as you can normally pick up visas from the relevant embassy in London, Paris or Vienna. Bear in mind, though, that many embassy visa sections are only open for a few hours each day and that queues are inevitable. You may also find some countries insist you leave your passport overnight so don't count on obtaining more than one visa per day. Always take cash, as they often won't take cheques.

It goes without saying that you must be very careful not to lose your passport or visa; if this should happen, contact your embassy immediately (addresses are given under the individual countries). It is also important to have a recent passport photo.

• **UK visas:** For ROMANIA you can only get a visa in advance if you have prepaid accommodation, so it's best to buy your visa at the frontier, where you should have no problems. If you feel more comfortable with things arranged in advance, contact 4 Palace Green, London W8 (Tel. 071–937 9666). £20.

For HUNGARY, you can buy a visa on the border for £17, or by post in advance. At the time of going to press, it looks like even this will be abolished. Check first. On receipt of your first letter they'll send you an application form which you'll have to send back, along with two passport photos and the fee, £14, to the Consular Section of the Embassy of the Hungarian People's Republic, 35B Eaton Place, London SW1 (Tel. 071–235 2664/4462). Allow at least a month for the whole procedure, and don't leave it to luck by hoping to buy a visa at the frontier, as you'll only be disappointed.

POLAND'S consulate, visa section, is at 47 Portland Place, London W1 (Tel. 071–580 4324). Apply in advance. £20.

CZECHOSLOVAKIA'S rules state that you need to buy a visa in advance. Write to their embassy at 28 Kensington Palace Gardens, London W8 (Tel. 071–727 3966) for an application form, then send this back with two photos, the fee, £20 or £12 if under 20 (in cash or a postal order) and a self-addressed registered envelope to Čedok, 17–18 Old Bond Street, London W1 (Tel. 071–629 6058).

BULGARIA requires a visa if you're travelling independently or if you're staying at private accommodation. Send for forms to the consular section of the embassy at 188 Queen's Gate, London SW7

(Tel. 071–584 9400). £20. You must change the equivalent of $15 per day.

Contact the Visa Shop, 44 Chandos Place, London WC2 4HS (Tel. 071–379 0419) for the latest visa information in today's fast-changing world.

UK passport holders now need a visa for TURKEY. This can be obtained upon arrival anywhere in Turkey for £5.

• **US visas:** For CZECHOSLOVAKIA it is no longer necessary to get a visa in advance.

A visa must be obtained in advance for BULGARIA. For the relevant forms, write to the Bulgarian Embassy, 1621 22nd Street NW, Washington, DC 20008. You must change $15 per day.

A visa for POLAND must be obtained in advance. For the relevant forms, write to Polish People's Republic, 2224 Wyoming Avenue NW, Washington, DC 20008.

A 30-day visa for ROMANIA will cost you around $15 at the border, and can be extended for up to 90 days for an extra $10. For further information contact the Romanian Tourist Office at 573 Third Avenue, New York, NY 10016.

Visas for HUNGARY must be obtained in advance when travelling by train. For an application form, write to the Consulate General of the Hungarian People's Republic, 8 East 75th Street, New York, NY 10021, or the Hungarian Embassy, 3910 Shoemaker Street NW, Washington, DC 20008. If you left it too late, it's possible to get one in 48 hours if you go along in person to the Hungarian Embassy in Vienna at Bankgasse 4.

When you cross the border into YUGOSLAVIA, a customs officer will take your passport and return it sometime later with a free 90-day visa. At smaller crossings, you may be asked to get off the train and follow him to the customs office while he does the paper work.

Because visa requirements can change quickly these days, it's worth contacting the Visa Centre Inc., 507 Fifth Avenue, Suite 904, New York, NY 10017 (Tel. 212–986 0924).

BUDGETING

Exactly how much money you have to spend will affect your

'lifestyle' on InterRail in many ways. I'm making the general assumption that the average eurorailer is perennially short of cash and won't ever be keen to spend more than he has to on basics such as accommodation and food. There's no shortage of information for those wishing to spend more – other 'budget' guides to Europe you can buy will list hotels for £30 ($51) a night, or restaurants for £20–25 ($34–43) meals. I'm not interested in that. After all, who needs advice on how to *spend* money in Europe? Also, you experience more of the real country when living like the locals on a budget.

It's a straight fact that £25 ($42) a day in Norway will just about get you a hostel bed and a cafeteria meal; the same £25 in Spain will give you a hotel bed and a restaurant meal, so take into consideration the countries you want to go to, and budget accordingly. The most expensive countries are: Norway, Sweden, Finland, Denmark, Switzerland and Austria; the intermediate ones are: West Germany, United Kingdom, Ireland, Netherlands, Belgium, Luxembourg, France, Italy and Yugoslavia; and the cheap ones are: Spain, Greece, Portugal, Turkey, Eastern Europe and Morocco. The southern part of Europe remains much cheaper than the northern, but to take full advantage of this cheapness you have to be prepared to accept the local standards of hygiene, cuisine, etc. Eastern Europe is cheap for food, drink and entertainment, but hotel accommodation is expensive, so hostel or camp. (Yugoslavia is a tricky one as the food in the local markets is very cheap but the accommodation prices are ridiculously high.) The basic fact of the matter is: camping and hostelling are cheap all over Europe, and if you are prepared to do this and buy your food in the local shops and markets to make your own picnics, you can eurorail for very little money.

On average, for your bed and daily food, you'll need at least £25 ($47) a day for the expensive countries, £15 ($25) a day for the intermediate ones, and £12 ($21) a day for the cheap ones. Remember: if you're travelling on your own and you insist on a single bedroom in a cheap hotel, it can double your costs, so double up with fellow travellers where at all possible.

• **International Student Identity Card:** This saves you money all over Europe – often as much as 75 per cent on museums and art galleries, etc., or even free entry. It also entitles you to 10–15 per cent discount on rail travel (useful if you want to go into a country not covered in the Inter Rail scheme, e.g. Bulgaria), and up to 50 per cent reduction on some air fares. You need a certificate from your college or university, a photograph and £5. Remember to take the book of discount vouchers with you. The ID card when purchased in the USA even provides you with automatic accident/sickness insurance anywhere you travel (outside the US) for the entire validity period of the ID card. Apply to your local Student Travel Office or to one of these addresses:

UK: International Students' Travel Centre, BJC, c/o NUS Marketing, Old Co-operative House, 8 Ashton Street, Glossop, Derbyshire SK13 8JP or Campus Travel, 52 Grosvenor Gardens, London SW1N 0AG (Tel. 071–730 3402).

USA: CIEE, New York Student Center, Sloane House YMCA, 356 West 34th Street, New York, NY 10001 (Tel. 212–564 0142).

CANADA: Travel Cuts, 44 George Street, Toronto, Ontario M5S 2E4 (Tel. 416–979 2406).

AUSTRALIA: Australian Student Travel/STA, 220 Faraday Street, Carlton, Victoria 3053 (Tel. 03 3476911).

SOUTH AFRICA: SASTS, Anreith Corner, Hans Strydom Avenue, Cape Town. Post address: PO Box 1381, Cape Town 8000 (Tel. 21 6438).

NEW ZEALAND: Student Travel Bureau, Students' Union, University of Auckland, Princes Street, Auckland (Tel. 375 265).

Ask for a copy of the ID discount guide for 1991.

For the Eastern European countries you should officially have the IUS (International Union of Students) card which is the ISIC's counterpart. This is now incorporated in with new ISIC cards.

● **International Youth Card (YIEE):** This is offered by the Federation of International Youth Travel Organizations (FIYTO) and is meant for young people who are not eligible for the ISIC card but wish to take advantage of travel concessions open to them; it is not necessary to possess both of these cards. The card is available at any student travel office. To get it you need proof that you are under 26, one passport-sized photograph and £4. The card comes with a FIYTO booklet of discounts.

• **Discount Cards:** One way to save money in Europe is to take advantage of an expanding network of discount card schemes for those under 26. In Scotland, there's the *Young Scot* card, in Belgium the *Cultureel Jonger en Passport*, in France the *Cartes Jeunes*, in Portugal the *Cartao Jovem* and so on. The cards cost about £5, can be bought from a variety of outlets, and offer literally thousands of discounts on meals, clothes, souvenirs and other goods. The cards can all be used interchangeably – so you can buy a Scottish card and use it to get discounts in France, for example.

• **Student travel offices:** There are about 60 STOs in the UK. The good thing about them is that they nearly all sell BIJ and Inter Rail tickets, and the staff will work out the cheapest alternative for you. They also sell ISICs and are usually found in university or college complexes. Note: They offer their services to anyone under 26, not just students.

• **The Council on International Educational Exchange (CIEE):** The CIEE is a non-profit, membership organization based in the US, and is one of the foremost organizations concerned with student travel.

They are there to help budget travellers with low-cost travel (air, train, etc.) as well as accommodation problems. In fact, they cover every aspect of your trip from your Student ID card to your airline ticket and reservations. Get hold of their 1991 Student Travel Catalogue which is a mine of information by writing to CIEE, 205 East 42nd Street, New York, NY 10017 (Tel. 212-661 1450). They also have offices in other US and European cities (see Appendix II). The catalogue provides information on Student ID cards, travel, study and work abroad. Use the Council's expertise as much as possible to get the lowest possible air farès, eurorail passes and other travel packages.

• A useful tip is to go to your local library and explore the world of travel grants to see what's available. It's amazing what funds are around, and it pays off to do your research well in advance.

Getting yourself together

WHAT TO TAKE WITH YOU

Obviously this very much depends on where you're going and at what time of the year: if you're going to Scandinavia in the spring, an extra jumper will certainly come in very useful. However, there are various points to remember, irrespective of where you are going or the time of the year. Unless you're visiting family or friends in Europe and expect to be met at every station, we strongly advise that you use a framed rucksack (preferably with an internal frame). Its advantages are manifold: it gives one the feeling of membership of a eurorail club and this stimulates conversation and communication which otherwise might not take place. Also – and more importantly – both your hands will be left free to use, allowing you to produce your maps, passport, etc., at the right moment. Shops specializing in outdoor equipment are an invaluable source of information and help. They will, in most cases, give free objective advice on what you really need for your trip and which brand names to look out for to suit your budget. If you're starting from scratch it'll take about £100 to get together all the basic gear required to camp your way round Europe, but once bought this will see you through future trips and you'd easily spend that much on grotty accommodation in just one Inter Rail trip. An inexpensive way to get hold of some second-hand luggage is to try the Railways Lost Property shop in London, at 359 Oxford Street (upstairs). They sometimes have camping gear too. Other names to look out for in the UK are the Youth Hostel Association shops, Field & Trek Equipment (catalogue from 3 Waters Way, Brentwood, Essex CM15 9TB for £1.25), and in the US write to L. L. Bean Inc. at Freeport, ME 04033, USA for a catalogue. It's better, though, for a novice to go to a shop and check out the equipment first hand, and Blacks are best for this.

Daysacks, in which you can take all that's needed for a day's sightseeing – maps, cameras, snacks, guidebook, etc. are handy, and if you're going to northern Europe it's a good investment to go for a good duck and down bag. Although the initial cost is steep you get back the value over the years and if you can afford it it's well worth the extra cash.

Don't cut back on tents and bags unless you're only planning on using your equipment for one or two seasons. Spend as much as you can afford and take advice from the shop staff.

• **Packing:** Every summer, Europe is full of backpackers wishing they hadn't taken so much, so don't take more than you're prepared to carry with comfort. Before you set out, put out on the bed everything you want to take with you – then halve it. Before you finally make up your mind, try wearing your rucksack with everything you intend to take in it on a good walk. Remember, don't be overgenerous as you'll be returning with more than you left with in the way of presents and souvenirs, so leave room for them. All this is common sense really; however, we all need reminding from time to time, as it can make the difference between a relaxing and an exhausting holiday.

• **Essentials:** The rucksack: without doubt this will be your most important single piece of equipment, so it is essential to ensure that it is both comfortable and light. Beware of back-breakers and spine-grinders. The three most important features you should look out for are: that it sits just above your hips and, if possible, has a support belt for round your waist; that the shoulder-straps are well padded and that the tension can be adjusted; and (most important of all) that your pack is 'high' rather than 'wide', when packed to capacity. I wish we had a pound for every eurorailer we've seen creating havoc along the all-too-narrow train-corridors. If they're not pulling the door shut on someone's leg they're laying out the natives with swinging cameras and boots hanging from the rear.

A small daypack is also invaluable, especially when sightseeing, as it will hold your maps, guidebook, waterproof, camera, films, food, etc., all conveniently together. However American it may make you feel, it's well worth it as it solves a lot of problems and saves you walking around all the time with a large rucksack. It's a good idea to put your name and address in the inside of your pack, just in case – something which most eurorailers overlook.

• **Valuables:** Keep an independent note of your ticket and passport numbers. If you do lose your passport, notify the police then get a copy of the report the police make out and go along with it to your country's nearest consulate or embassy. A photocopy of your birth certificate is another very useful thing to have with you, as are a couple of passport photos, which can come in handy for impromptu visas, replacement ISICs or passports.

One idea, very popular with the Scandinavians, is to buy a pouch that you hang round your neck with all your tickets in it. Keep cash separate – in a safe inside pocket, perhaps. Another good idea is a moneybelt. You can pick up one of these in Greece or Spain quite cheaply – assuming you can get that far without getting ripped off.

• **Sleeping bag:** Unless you plan to spend all your time staying with friends or hostelling you'll need a good bag. Hostels charge for bedding and won't allow you to use your bag (in Northern Europe) which is *very* frustrating – but the rule. Make sure when you are buying that it conforms to the YHA standard. Note: at some hostels you may find it compulsory to hire sheets, even if you do have your own. Also at some stage in your travels it's likely you'll be a deck passenger on an overnight ferry somewhere. When you're shopping around for a sleeping bag, price is likely to be your main criterion, as it's not difficult to spend more on your sleeping bag than on your ticket. If you have no bag already, and can't borrow one from a friend, go along to your local camping shop and get the best you can afford. As with the other two basics, rucksack and shoes, the better the quality, the more money you can expect to spend. Do not make cutbacks in this direction: there are few things worse than a cold sleepless night before a hard day's sightseeing. Buying a cheap sleeping bag is a classic false economy. Shop assistants in camping shops are usually very helpful and only too ready to help you out as best they can.

If you're taking a bag and plan to do a lot of camping or sleeping out on southern beaches, then a foam mattress is also advisable. Try and get one that is long enough but not too wide (remember those train corridors). Lie down on it in the shop to check it out. Print your name on it as you'll find mattresses disappear with remarkable frequency.

• **Comfortable walking shoes** (already broken in) are essential as you can expect to spend as much time walking as you will on trains. Don't go over the top and wear boots that would look better on Everest rather than strolling round the Vatican. If you're heading south, a pair of sandals is a necessity to give your feet a chance to breathe. If you don't have any, don't worry: they're cheap in southern Europe.

• **Camping gear:** If you're heading for northern Europe and plan to camp a lot, get a strongish tent with a fly-sheet; however, if you'll be mainly in the south, pick a light one, preferably of nylon. A small Calor gas stove can save you a lot of money, especially in places like Norway where buying a cup of tea or coffee can cost £1 ($1.70) or so. Gas refills are widely available so don't bother carrying spares. Unless you're camping non-stop for about a month, don't carry food supplies and a lot of camping equipment with you, but do take cutlery. Shopping from the local supermarkets makes much more sense. Remember to take a torch for those late-night pitches.

• **Clothes:** Obviously it depends on where you're going and the time of year. Use your common sense, but don't take anything you don't absolutely need and remember: though you may look terrific in your white jeans when they're newly washed and ironed at home, you'll look terrible after you've sat up all night in them on an Italian train.

Take dark comfortable clothes that won't show the battering you're giving them. Laundries are often expensive, so take a little washing powder or liquid detergent and wash your own clothes. 'Washaway' tablets from Boots are particularly handy.

LAST-MINUTE REMINDERS

1. Girls: take a scarf or shawl to cover your head and shoulders as often you'll be refused entry to churches and cathedrals if your arms and shoulders are bare. Shorts are also prohibited in many churches, so go prepared.
2. A travelling alarm clock is a handy thing, especially if you have early trains to catch.
3. Don't forget toilet paper, soap, a universal plug and a small towel. You can never find a place to buy these, just when you need them most.
4. Plastic bags are handy for containing liquids, etc.
5. A Swiss Army penknife, with as many functions as possible (including a corkscrew), comes in handy.
6. A small padlock is often needed when hostelling (for the lockers) and for locking your bag to a fixed point if sleeping on a train.
7. A pre-filled water-bottle will save you cash on long thirsty journeys as prices of drinks on trains are high.

8. A good book: take your reading supply from home as English-language books cost a lot abroad.
9. Invaluable are a notepad and a pen. Get shopkeepers to write down prices before saying yes, if you don't have the lingo. This way, you'll know when you're being ripped off.
10. Postcards of your home town are a good ice-breaker and let foreigners see where you're from. It can even boost home town tourism!
11. A calculator for working out exchange rates. The cheapest one you can find will do (under £2).
12. A Walkman comes in handy if you get temporarily fed up of your travelling companions and want a bit of solitude. A pair of ear plugs can come in handy for the same reason, although you are more likely to find these useful in shutting out the escaping noise from *their* Walkman earphones!
13. Don't forget to take some camping cutlery (the type that clip together) and a sharp knife for cutting bread.
14. Insect repellant is a very good idea if you are visiting countries like Scotland or Scandinavia.
15. If you're taking the Algeciras–Tangier ferry, carry a photocopy of your Inter Rail card as you need this for the crossing and to get it done at the other end is one big headache!
16. A length of string or cord can be useful as a washing line in youth hostels.

MONEY

There's a 'Catch 22' situation with money in Europe. Undoubtedly, with violence and crime the way it is at present in Europe, especially the south, it's a big risk to carry around all your cash in ready notes on you, even in a moneybelt. To be weighed against this is the fact that by taking traveller's cheques you lay yourself open to continual queueing, especially in the summer, not to mention the hassles trying to find a bank or travel agent to cash them. If you decide to play safe and take most of your money in traveller's cheques, then get them from one of the big banks or, even better, from Thomas Cook or American Express. Don't find yourself walking around every bank in town trying to cash an obscure brand of traveller's cheque.

When buying your traveller's cheques, always buy small denominations as this is more economical on a tight budget. Anyone from the USA or a major European country should buy cheques in their own currency – unless you're planning to spend 99 per cent of your time in one country. If you offer a £20 cheque and ask for £14 in French francs and £6 in Italian lire, most banks will charge you first to change into francs, then again into lire. It's better to get traveller's cheques in denominations of £10 ($17). In general, it's a good idea to take some bank notes of the countries you know you'll end up in, especially if there's a chance you will arrive late at night or at weekends. As a rule, I take £25 ($43) cash in four or five different currencies, just to be on the safe side, in case there's no opportunity to change money on arrival and you have to pay for your room in advance. Again, it's best to order the currency you think you'll need from your bank at least two weeks in advance. It's always worth while taking along a few US dollar notes as a standby as you will find them accepted almost everywhere, particularly in Eastern European countries where goods and services for foreigners are often priced in US dollars. This applies particularly to Yugoslavia and Czechoslovakia.

Credit cards can be useful – if you're good at resisting temptation! Providing you keep them for emergencies only, credit cards may be able to get you out of a hole and are likely to be the only source of funds if you lose your traveller's cheques and are waiting for replacements. It goes without saying that you should be very careful indeed and keep them separate, so that if you are robbed you don't lose them as well. They are not as widely accepted abroad as in the UK & US, but can help if you need to pay for something but don't want to use cash or change traveller's cheques. This can be important in Eastern bloc countries where you can't take the local currency out and lose on conversion deals at the border. Watch out for exchange rules. The maximum cash advance in Yugoslavia on Access on any one day is £80, but you may find this is also the minimum you can change. When using cards you are at the mercy of fluctuating exchange rates. This can work to your benefit in a country with high inflation where the local currency is falling against your home currency – but it works both ways and an item which was a bargain when purchased could end up being more expensive when the bill is presented to your card company some time later. Remember, if you use a credit card to buy your traveller's cheques from a bank before leaving, this is treated as a cash advance and you pay interest right away. If you have a Thomas Cook Credit Card and buy your cheques from them, you have up to 55 days to settle the bill before paying interest. This also applies to currency and tickets.

Remember: take a moneybelt. Sending money on is expensive, so take a realistic amount. Also remember: apart from banks, large stations have exchange facilities, as do some hotels and travel agents, though the rate is often lower.

● **Money in Eastern Europe:** 'Hard' currency from the West helps strengthen the local stuff; as a result, some countries insist on a minimum exchange requirement. This is nearly always more than is strictly necessary, and in some cases you'll have difficulty trying to get rid of it. To discourage black-market dealings, you'll have to declare all your hard currency and any goods that the authorities think you might want to flog off while you're there. This declaration is normally carried out on the train at the border.

If you're thinking of playing the black market you will have to 'forget' to declare some of your hard currency because if, on departure, you cannot account for the missing money or produce the required receipts, you will be in trouble. This still applies – even after 1990.

● **Black market:** The freeing up of exchange is starting to finish off the black-market (as in Poland). The authorities in parts of Eastern Europe still come down with a heavy hand on those caught in the act (in some cases this means imprisonment). Hard currency is very much in demand, and many private citizens are prepared to pay far more than the official rate to get it. Some people are still prepared to pay high prices for jeans, pocket calculators, etc., though this is becoming less common. In general, never have any dealings with anyone who approaches you in the street; at best, you're likely to get poor rates and, at worst, they could be plain-clothes police or an informer. A final word: tipping is not general practice here, so hang on to your cash.

● **Banking:** You can cash a personal cheque of up to £100 in any European bank displaying the EC symbol if you've got a Eurocheque Encashment Card and appropriate cheque book with you. Check the cheque book you've got, as the style changed in January 1989, and the old style is no longer usable. Eurocheques are normally written in the local currency (US dollars in Eastern Europe) and no commission should be paid when cashing them (it's deducted from your account). Remember that the 24-hour exchange bureaux in general charge a higher commission, so don't always be tempted to cash your cheques at the first place you see in the station. They often have less favourable rates of exchange. In some countries, such as Germany, the post office changes money without taking as large a commission as the banks. In countries where there's a high service charge for cashing traveller's cheques, you're better off cashing your own personal cheques at Eurocheque banks using your banker's card, as only a small charge is made for this. Banks in all countries open in the morning from Monday to Friday, but beware of the siestas in the Mediterranean countries (see the individual countries, for banking hours).

INSURANCE

Whether or not to get insurance cover depends very much on where you're going, and for how long. If you've a lot of expensive new camping gear and photographic equipment then undoubtedly it's worth it. Shop around for the best deal; call in at your local student travel centre and see what they have to offer. It could be you're already insured through your home policy (your parents' or your own), so check up first. Eurotrain offer a travel insurance scheme. It's worth bearing in mind that train travel is very safe indeed, and it's highly unlikely that you'll end up in hospital because of an accident, but your health and your valuables are a different matter. Still, after food poisoning in Morocco and with a doctor being called out at 2 a.m., the bill for one of us was less than the insurance premium would have been, so think twice if you're really broke.

• **American and Canadian travellers:** If your personal policies don't provide adequate cover abroad, check with your travel agent or CIEE office to see what options are available.

• **Medical:** If you're only travelling in EEC countries and you're British, go along to your local DHSS office and get form E 111. This service is often neglected by eurorailers which is surprising as it provides medical cover in EEC countries to the same level that a national of that country enjoys. In theory it takes a few days to obtain, but can often be granted on the day. You may, however, have to pay part or all of your treatment and drugs. Keep receipts and claim back the cost from the DHSS when you return home. Doctors in Europe can be very expensive, and often a chemist can give just as good advice – free! To find a 24-hour chemist, either ask at a police station or go to the nearest chemist's shop and look in the window, as there's often a notice saying where one is open.

Watch out, girls: in Eastern Europe it's often impossible to get hold of tampons or sanitary towels, so take a supply along with you. (Also, if you'll need contraceptives, take them from home.)

If you've got to carry drugs or injection needles for medical reasons, take a doctor's note about them as you could otherwise be in for a hard time in Eastern Europe and Turkey.

Unless you've got an iron stomach, it's best to work on the theory that prevention is better than cure: take along some multivitamin pills to keep body and soul together during those long hauls, avoid the tap water in southern Europe, peel all fruit and make sure that meat is always well cooked. You'll be doing enough running for trains . . .

Whether or not you can drink the tap water depends a lot on where you are and how strong a stomach you have. It's really down to common sense. You should be OK in a city or large town, particularly in Scandinavia and near European countries, but in the more remote, hotter or less developed places be cautious and stick to bottled or boiled water. If you have an easily upset stomach play safe and stick to bottled water or water you have treated yourself with tablets, available from good chemists and camping stores.

In the event of your having problems with sangria, paella and the like, it's a good idea to keep some Alka-Seltzer and anti-diarrhoea tablets to hand. A mild laxative won't go amiss, in case all that foreign food and drink affects you the other way. The further south you go, the more mosquitoes and other undesirables you're likely to encounter, so if you're a big scratcher take along some soothing cream and a small pack of plasters and, should all else fail, some pain-killers.

A few weeks before you go, if possible, visit your GP to see if you need inoculations for cholera and typhoid if you are intending to go to places like Turkey or Morocco, or where sanitation is dubious. Check also if you need boosters for tetanus and polio. Also ask about anti-malaria tablets, which need to be taken after your return as well as during the trip, if you need them at all. Make sure you get an International Certificate to prove you've been protected against these diseases or you may find you're not allowed to visit places where there are outbreaks of diseases such as cholera. A certificate costs about £3. You can also get advice and all the protection you need from the British Airways Medical Centre, 75 Regent Street, London (Tel. 071–439 9584), just up from Piccadilly Circus. It is open office hours but tends to get busy around lunch time in summer, so expect delays of up to an hour. Free information is also available from the Robens Institute in Guildford, Surrey (Tel. 0483 68637/68673).

When you're there

ACCOMMODATION

As accommodation is the largest potential headache for eurorailers and we're limited for space, I'm restricting my suggestions to the main tourist centres. If you plan travelling off the beaten track or arriving late in peak season, I strongly recommend you buy the *Europe by Train (Cheap Sleep Guide)* (see p.16). For the price of two Tourist Board placings, it will save you a lot of time and trouble and money in the end.

My suggestions tend to be biased towards hostels, and to places located near stations. Basically there are four types of accommodation open to you: cheap hotels; youth or student hostels; camping and private accommodation. There is, theoretically, a fifth option for those with an open pass – and it will certainly ensure you get round Europe at a phenomenal rate – it is to sleep on the trains themselves, not just in the couchettes or sleepers which vary in price from £5 to £25 ($8.50–43) for a night's sleep, but for free in the seats. As we've discussed 'night travel' already and I do not really recommend you spending your eurorail doing this, we'll concentrate now on the other four.

• **Cheap hotels/pensions:** If you're travelling with your girlfriend/boyfriend and don't fancy camping and can't get into private accommodation, this is your only real alternative if you want to spend the night together. The advantages are obvious: relative comfort and convenience. If you're in a city and you haven't long to be there, it's best to try for one located near the centre, to save you bus journeys and hassles. The disadvantages are: it's more expensive than hostelling or camping, and if you're in a really cheap hotel, you often find a sort of 'skid row' atmosphere. The hotels I list under each country are the best compromise I could find between clean, pleasant surroundings and a fair price.

If there are two or more of you room-hunting, it's a good idea for one to wait in the tourist office queue with all the luggage, while the other goes looking for a room in one of the hotels you invariably find close to the stations. The rooms in these places are generally cheap and, of course, very convenient. Alternatively, if you all want to go off to hunt together, leave your heavy packs in left luggage. You won't regret the £1 ($1.70) you spend for the extra comfort and speed you'll get out of it.

Once you've found a suitable place and have been told the prices, ask the receptionist again if she has nothing cheaper. Often this works and you get a cheaper room tucked away near the top. The luxury of taking a room with a private bath or shower is bought at a high price, so you do best to use the communal one. Always ask how much a bath or shower costs. If you're travelling in a group it can be cheaper to have a room with a bath than to pay for four showers. In the vast majority of cheap hotels it's not included in the price, and it can come as a nasty shock when you get the bill.

Unfortunately the wonderful British institution of B&B does not exist in Europe. Breakfast is often extra and rarely does it merit the name or the cost. Anyway, it's far cheaper and more entertaining to find a coffee bar or café where the locals go.

Pensions (guest houses) are often far more attractive and friendly than hotels. A double bed is usually cheaper than two singles. Remember to check all the following before deciding on a room in a hotel: the price of the room, including all taxes; whether breakfast is included; whether a bath/shower is included; whether there is nothing cheaper; whether the hotelier would mind if three or four people used a double room; and finally when you must check out the next day, to avoid paying for another night's accommodation.

● **Hostels:** Hostels run by the International Youth Hostel Federation are good value and an ideal place to meet up with other travellers. They're the next cheapest alternative to camping, ranging from £2 to £9 ($3.40–15.30) a night. You need to be a member of your own country's YHA or that of the country you're in, though often you can buy temporary membership on the spot. If you're already a member of the YHA, attach a photo of yourself to your YHA card to allow you to hostel in Europe.

Youth hostels offer simple basic accommodation for men and women in separate dormitory-style bedrooms, washing and toilet facilities, and a common room. Many hostels have their own communal kitchen, though you need your own utensils. In this way you can buy food at supermarket prices and cater for yourself for next to no cost at all. Economical meals are laid on at many hostels (we list these below, under each country) and hostellers are expected to help with some domestic chores. Even if you bring your own sleeping bag, many hostels insist you hire their sheets – a pain, but nothing you can do about it. The general rule is that you can't stay more than three nights at any one hostel. Try phoning ahead, but they may tell you they are full, even when they aren't.

If you've never hostelled before, it's a good idea to go round one or two at home so you get to know what it's like. If you're expecting room service or breakfast in bed, forget hostelling. (Actually, if you're strictly the breakfast-in-bed type, forget eurorailing!) Average cost is £6.50 ($11) a night and average meal £2–3.50 ($3.40–6).

• **Booking ahead:** During July and August it's a good idea to book your hostel bed ahead in the major tourist cities. If you're going to be doing a lot of hostelling in Europe, a useful system is International Multi-Lingual Booking Cards: they cost about 5p each and allow one, two or more people to reserve beds and meals. You post the cards on to the hostel concerned with an International Reply Coupon (on sale at post offices). Beds reserved through this scheme are held until 6 p.m. You should be able to buy these at your local hostel or from your country's Youth Hostel Association head office.

Hostels vary a tremendous amount; generally though, the further south you go, the less strict the rules tend to be, and also the more basic the accommodation becomes. Some hostels still insist on midnight curfews and lock you out between 10 a.m. and 4 p.m., while others are far more liberal. If in doubt, it's always a good move to phone ahead from the station and check out if there's space and what rules, if any, apply. Many hostels are open only in the summer.

Beware of the increasing number of unofficial hostels which are springing up, especially in southern Europe. Many call themselves 'Student Youth Hostels' and, though they impose no curfews or sex segregation, the facilities they offer are often very poor and the charges are more than those of official youth hostels.

If you intend staying in youth hostels a lot, it's a good idea to get a full list of all YHA hostels in Europe to complement *Europe by Train*.

If you need more hostelling information, the London office of the YHA is: 14 Southampton Street, London WC2E 7HY (Tel. 071–836 1036). Head office is: Trevelyan House, 8 St Stephen's Hill, St Albans AL1 2DY (Tel. 0727 55215).

● **Student hostels:** Student hostels are similar to youth hostels, but instead of a YHA card you need an International Student ID card. Many student hostels are unused student dorms and are only open during university vacations.

● **YMCA/YWCA Inter Rail Points:** The European Alliance of YMCAs operates a series of twenty-three Inter Rail Points in eleven different countries to provide budget-priced accommodation. They also organize optional events such as sightseeing trips, hill walking, barbecues etc., as well as helping with advice if required. Most of the YMCAs involved in this programme offer hostel facilities throughout the year and reduce their rates during the eurorailing period from June to September. Unlike the YHA you do not have to be members of the YMCA to use their facilities. Many are near the station and provide showers and cooking facilities. For further details, write with an SAE to: YMCA Special Programmes, Crown House, 550 Mauldeth Road West, Manchester M21 2RX (Tel. 061–881 5321).

● **Camping:** If you're keen on the 'great outdoors', then camping in conjunction with a eurorail is ideal for you. There's no shortage of scenic sites, and even the major cities of Europe have campgrounds on their outskirts. But as a general rule we advise against it for big cities. The advantages of camping are obvious: it's cheap, if you're on a campsite you have all necessary facilities to hand, and it adds a dash of 'pioneering spirit' to your holiday. Prices on official campsites range from £1.50 to £5 ($2.50–6.80) a tent, and £2 to £7 ($3.40–11.90) per person.

The International Camping Carnet is useful if you're doing a lot of camping, as many European campgrounds insist on it, particularly those in the state forests of France and Denmark. You can buy the Carnet at most sites.

The disadvantages of official camping that spring to mind are: other people, cars, radios, tents all around, queueing for showers, etc. Unofficial camping, however, removes all these problems and can be a memorable experience. Remember to check with the farmer or landowner before pitching tent for the night, and observe strict hygiene.

It's quite feasible to camp throughout your entire eurorail. A tent, gas stove, utensils, sleeping bag and foam mattress will solve all your accommodation problems at once. Don't skimp too much on equipment, however; a good tent is far and away the most important thing.

• **Private accommodation:** This is an interesting and, in many ways, preferable alternative to hotels. Pricewise, it's slightly cheaper than hotels, but more expensive than hostels or camping. Individuals arrange through local tourist authorities for tourists to come and stay at their houses for any period of time from a night to the whole summer. It's an excellent way to meet the locals and get a home-from-home atmosphere. It also provides the perfect opportunity to ask all the questions you want about the country, but otherwise could not. Understanding the locals gives you a much better insight into the country, and, for my money, this is the best form of accommodation. Ask at the tourist office and they will arrange the details for you. The only problem is that you may find all the places full in the high season as in many cities there are more prospective guests than recipient hosts.

• **Accommodation – Eastern Europe:** Nearly all hotels are owned and run by the state tourist company of the country. They cater mainly for large parties who tend to book *en masse* months ahead, making it difficult, but not impossible, to find a room. They also tend to work out expensive, as they charge higher prices for Western tourists. Go for private accommodation where you can. It's cheaper, gives you a better idea of Eastern European life, and can either be arranged through the state tourist authority or negotiated in the street. You often find women meeting the trains to offer their rooms out; don't be afraid, it's perfectly legal and acceptable. Camping is another option, but always check first how far out of town the sites are, and how good the bus services are. During the summer, students with ID cards can sleep in university dormitories: book these through the national student organizations.

The East European tourist authorities will find a room for you for a commission, and will give you a list of campsites. Be prepared for long queues in summer and for their commissions to be higher than their Western equivalents. East European authorities work under the assumption that all young people travel in large groups, not in ones and twos. As a result, you will often be told that hostels are only run for groups; however, don't give in, but insist. Since 1990 and all the changes in the East, the situation has, if anything, worsened. Exorbitant prices are being asked for up-market hotels as tourists flock in to the cities of the East.

EATING

Whenever possible it's a good thing to sample the local cuisine, for quite apart from being an extremely enjoyable way of learning about another culture, it's often a lot cheaper and more appetizing than eating the type of food one's accustomed to at home. If all the restaurants are expensive, don't despair; you'll find that nearly every supermarket has a section devoted to regional specialities where with a little bit of imagination you can prepare yourself a veritable feast. Like everything else, a little background knowledge can add greatly to one's enjoyment. Try collecting articles on regional food from travel magazines, cook books, Sunday supplements and the like; or, even better, check out your local library. Time-Life books do a good series called *Foods of the World* and it's well worth reading the European section on the countries you plan to visit.

Here are the basic rules, accumulated over years of good and bad eating out:

1. Avoid expensive, pretentious-looking restaurants and cafés which display no prices.

2. Read the menu first, then add up the cost of your choices and all the taxes and service charges before ordering.

3. Go for 'menus of the day' or tourist menus with fixed prices wherever you can.

4. Serve yourself whenever you can.

5. Don't buy food or drink from vendors on the trains or from stalls in the stations. Buy in advance at supermarkets.

6. If you've an addiction to something like coffee in the morning, take your supplies with you in the form of a camping stove, a small pan and some instant coffee.

7. When it comes to cheeses, wines, meats, biscuits, etc., buy the local stuff. Imports are always more expensive and, anyway, it's good to sample the local produce.

8. Use fast-food chains if nothing else is available for cheap, reliable snacks. They're often far better and cheaper than local snack bars, especially in southern Europe where hygiene is often suspect.

9. Be adventurous, try something new. Ask for house wine: it's always cheaper than listed wine and there's a good chance it's the popular wine of the region.

10. Eat breakfast out when it's optional at your hotel as it's nearly always cheaper at a local café.

11. Make lunch your main meal of the day. Prepare yourself a big picnic whenever possible. Even when you eat at restaurants, it's at least 15 per cent cheaper than in the evening. Avoid tourist areas, where prices are nearly always higher. In large towns search out the university areas, where prices are generally more reasonable.

12. Look out in the stations for drinking water taps and fill your bottles for free when you get the chance.

CITY TRANSPORT SYSTEMS

If you're going to stay in one place for more than a day or two, find out about the cheap travel passes on offer. Some cities offer day passes, others weekly ones and, if your accommodation is out of town, they can save you quite a bit. Before rushing off to buy one, however, check on a map for the location of the main sights you're interested in, as in many towns these are all within easy walking distance of one another and you won't need a bus pass. If you're not in a rush, using the buses as opposed to the underground lets you see a bit more of the city – which is worth bearing in mind. Tickets for the buses and underground can often be bought at tobacco kiosks. Thomas Cook's *Railpass Guide* is particularly good on local transport.

TELEPHONE AND TELEGRAM

You will usually find both these facilities at the general post office. Some countries also offer special telephone kiosks for international calls. Find out the international dialling code (44 for Britain; 1 for the USA) before you start.

Always try to dial direct as it's much cheaper. Direct dialling codes to and from the UK and US can be found in the basic information for each country. Never telephone via the switchboard at hotels or hostels as they invariably add on a whack – sometimes as much as the call itself – for themselves. Throughout Europe it's pretty standard that calls out of business hours (7 p.m.–8 a.m.) are charged at a cheaper rate. In nearly every country, either dialling instructions in English or pictograms are to be found inside telephone boxes.

Telegrams are expensive, and in almost every case you'll find it cheaper making a quick phone call; but if that's impossible, write out your message and hand it to the clerk to avoid spelling mistakes.

MAIL

Airmail letters from major West European cities to the USA and Britain arrive within a week or so. Letters from southern or Eastern Europe take anything from two weeks to a month, so if you're on a eurorail lasting a month, it's hardly worthwhile writing. Postcards tend to be even worse. Use surface mail (by ship) for posting home any books or clothes you don't fancy carrying around. It's usually very cheap – but very slow too.

Trying to collect mail in Europe is more often than not a nerve-racking business. If you've no fixed address, the best method to use (and it's free or costs very little) is poste restante. This means your mail is sent to you c/o the main post office of any city or town. Depending on the vagaries of the country's domestic postal system, your mail should be at the poste restante office filed under your surname. Produce your passport or equivalent proof of identity and pick it up. If the clerk says there's nothing for you, get him to check under your first name too.

In Eastern Europe, get the sender to put a '1' after the city's name to ensure it goes to the main post office. American Express card holders or traveller's cheque holders can get mail sent on to AMEX offices to await collection.

SHOPPING

Unlike many other guidebooks, we don't include details on shopping. We are taking it for granted that most people won't have spare cash to blow in the shops, and if you do, you'll have enough common sense to head for the centre and find the main shopping areas for yourselves. In general, the studenty part of a city is cheaper, and for food the large supermarkets are your best bet.

Shopping hours vary from country to country but they're all based round the 8–6 routine, though lunch hours can range from none at all to three hours. As a basic rule, the further south you go, the longer the 'siesta', and you can only count on a half day on Saturday.

TOURIST INFORMATION

At most stations you'll find a *Tourist Information Office*. When this isn't the case we give directions below on how to get there. These tourist offices are easily your best source of maps and detailed information. There seemed little point to us in reproducing their maps and rewriting the minuscule details of the sights for you here. Our main aim in this book has been to direct you to the main things of interest, give you the basics, and let you fill in the rest from what you're given at tourist offices. Finally, so far as opening times are concerned, we've generally only listed irregular ones; take the rest as following the local norm.

Good eurorailing!

FREE BOOKS FOR MOST HELPFUL LETTERS

Please feel free to write in your comments and suggestions to me. If you've come across anywhere you think deserves more detailed treatment or come across a real 'find' you want to share with future eurorailers, give me as much detail as possible, like the full address, telephone number and how to get to it. Obviously in a book containing the amount of information that this does, facts and figures get out of date easily, and though I try to update as thoroughly as possible I would appreciate your help. While I enjoy reading about your experiences, please keep your letters brief and concise (2 × A4 sides maximum, preferably typed including relevant page references from this book). The writers of the six best letters of 1991 will receive a free copy of the updated 1992 guide. All correspondence should be addressed to: Katie Wood, *Europe by Train*, Fontana Paperbacks, 8 Grafton Street, London W1X 3LA.

SOME INTERNATIONAL TIMETABLE SYMBOLS

Ⓡ	Reservations compulsory	⟩ Trains running on certain days only
	2nd class	
◣	Couchette	◆ Trains subject to special regulations stated in the information notes of the relevant timetable
🛏	Sleeping Car	
✗	Restaurant Car	
⊗	Buffet/Cafeteria	
♈	Drinks service and snacks	🏛 Frontier border station; customs and passport checks
✗	Except Sundays and public holidays	🚌 Connection by bus
†	Sundays and public holidays only	⛴ Connection by boat

BE A GOOD TOURIST

As this edition of *Europe by Train* goes to press a new work is being prepared; it's something very close to my heart; something I believe in very strongly, and not since the launch of *Europe by Train* have I felt that there was such a great need for a book like this. It should be of interest to many of *Europe by Train*'s intrepid types, and the theory behind the book is of relevance to all of us who travel, in any way, at any time. Called *The Good Tourist – A Guide to Green Travel Worldwide* – the book addresses the issues of the impact of tourism on the environment and society. This may sound a bit heavy, but the reading of it is not. It's about what you are on the point of doing – travelling to a foreign country; any country. What you do; where you go; how you go; where you sleep; what you eat – it all has a great impact on that country. You can make this a positive or negative experience. For too many countries, for too many years now, the impact has been increasingly negative, and it's up to every one of us to take account of our actions.

Traditionally, travel has been seen as a good thing. Tourism generates valuable income for a country (indeed, more money is made though tourism and its related services than any other industry in the world!), and broadening the horizons and experiencing other cultures can only do good, can't it? Well, it can be good for the guest, but what of the host in this relationship? How much income goes back into the pockets of the waiters and taxi drivers in third world countries such as Thailand and Gambia from all the mass tourism in their country? How much land is given over to developments for wealthy tourists? What control do any of us as individuals have on the mass developments going on the world over in the name of tourism?

We are destroying the very things we set out to see. Europe is a classic case, and travelling through it by train is a good way to discover the truth about the tourist industry. Venice is sinking under the weight of tourists' feet; the Acropolis is being eroded by pollution and over-visiting; the once-beautiful beaches of the Spanish costas and the Med are polluted and ugly; the Alps are crumbling under the pressure of skiing.

Fortunately, the current wave of 'green thinking' is also percolating into tourism and travel. But is enough being done? Where is the mass industry going? Are you, as an inter railer, leaving your conscience at home when you travel? Have you really questioned why you are making this trip? Do you truly respect the country you are visiting? What do you hope to gain from this trip? Do you make an effort to meet the locals and get to know the real culture of the place? Are you staying in appropriate accommodation; are you adding to the litter and pollution? The chances are, you, like most educated independent travellers, are among the few who try to be as 'green' as possible in your travel. The train is one of the best means of transport in terms of low pollution and energy efficiency. Staying in locals' houses, or hostels or camping makes sense, and having a caring and aware attitude, you will probably be contributing as little as possible to the deterioration of our world.

My husband (an ecologist) and I are writing a book which looks at how to be a good tourist in detail; it looks at the impact of all different types of holidays; it tells you which companies to travel with (and which not to). Now that being green is so trendy, it's good to separate the wheat from the chaff. Reading this may make your European wanderings all the more pertinent and give you more of an idea of the overall plan of things. The book aims to take a balanced approach between tourism and related development, and the need to conserve the very things that most of us as tourists want to enjoy. Knowing so many of you from your letters as I do, I feel sure it's the sort of intelligent read you'll enjoy. I welcome your comments.

The Good Tourist is published March 1991 by Mandarin Paperbacks.

Part Two: THE COUNTRIES

AUSTRIA

Entry requirements	Passport
Population	7,600,000
Capital	Vienna (pop.: 1,300,000)
Currency	Austrian Schilling
	£1 = approx. AS 20.03
Political system	Federal Republic
Religion	Roman Catholic
Language	German (English spoken)
Public holidays	1, 6 Jan.; Good Friday; Easter Monday; 1 May; Ascension Day; Whit Monday; Corpus Christi; 15 Aug.; 26 Oct.; 1 Nov.; 8, 25, 26 Dec.
International dialling codes	From UK 01043
	From USA 01143
	To UK 0044
	To USA 001

Austria would have been no place for eurorailing during its early history, certainly not for sleeping out at the station, as one power struggle followed another until the Habsburgs emerged victorious at the end of the thirteenth century. As good Catholics and Holy Roman Emperors for four centuries, they spent most of their time fighting the Turks as well as keeping everyone at home in order. As a result of this, they provided a strong monarchy, but it was no fun to be in the army as Austria continued to be involved in political struggles till the eighteenth century. By then, Vienna had become the home of Europe's finest musicians such as Mozart, Beethoven and, of course, later on, Strauss. With the First World War the monarchy came to an end and her empire folded up. She had a hard time in the Second World War as she was joined on to Germany, and suffered heavily from Allied bombing. In 1955, Austria became a neutral country and has since made a spectacular economic recovery. This is particularly so with Vienna, which has been lovingly restored and once again fulfils its ancient role as a stopover place where eurorailers can enjoy their last few days of Western comfort before heading south-east to Yugoslavia. The Alpine scenery and Tyrolean villages make Austria one of Europe's most attractive countries and a perfect destination for those seeking the great outdoors.

AUSTRIAN FEDERAL RAILWAYS
(Österreichische Bundesbahnen, ÖBB)

As you might expect, trains run on time. They are clean and comfortable, as are the stations. However, there's generally a lot of queueing in summer, so be warned. Most intercities run two hours apart.

Train types are: international expresses (Expresszüge), long-distance expresses (Schnellzüge), semi-fast services (Eilzüge), and EuroCity trains. Apart from on the EuroCity trains, you can get by without supplements. Avoid local trains unless you have plenty of time as they tend to be slow, especially if you're on a mountainous route.

● **Inter Rail bonuses:** Half price is offered on the following services:

COMPANY	FROM	TO
	(or vice versa)	
Puchberg am Schneeberg–Hochschneeberg Mountain Railway	All	
St Wolfgang Schafbergbahnhof–Schafbergspitze Mountain Railway	All	
ÖBB Wolfgangseeschiffahrt	All	
Vereinigte Schiffahrtsverwaltungen für den Bodensee und Rhein	All	
Erste Donau–Dampfschiffahrts–Gesellschaft (steamship company)	Passau	Wien (on Danube)
Steiermarkische Landesbahnen	Feldbach	Bad Gleichenberg
	Gleisdorf	Weiz
	Peggau–Deutschfeistritz	Übelbach
	Unzmarkt	Tamsweg

Free entry to Railway Museum, 212 Mariahilferstrasse, Wien.

● **Eurail bonuses:** The following services are free:
—Puchberg am Schneeberg–Hochschneeberg rack railway.
—St Wolfgang–Schafbergspitze rack railway.
—Steamers on Lake Wolfgang.
—Steamers operated by the Erste Donau–Dampfschiffahrts–Gesellschaft between Passau and Vienna.

Reduced fares:
—50 per cent reduction on steamers operated by steamship companies on Lake Constance.

TRAIN INFORMATION

Austrian Federal Railways main information for the whole country is at no. 9 Elisabethstrasse in Vienna.

Information officers are nearly all multilingual while most other rail staff speak at least a little English. You can easily tell the information officers: they wear yellow cap bands. Luggage lockers use ten-schilling pieces.

• **Reservations:** Are not necessary. If you want to make one, it can be done until two hours before your train leaves (cost: approximately AS 40).

• **Night travel:** Austria's too small for an extensive service. Sleepers and couchettes are clean and comfortable. Reserve at least five hours beforehand. Couchettes cost around AS 260. There are also compartments with pull-down seats which cost nothing.

• **Eating on trains:** For those with money, there are dining cars on all intercity trains. Mini-bars are to be found on all trains except locals. As always, we advise picnics, but if you don't have time to go to a supermarket before the train leaves, there are kiosks at most stations. Vienna's stations, in particular, have well-stocked delicatessens which are open long hours, including Sundays.

• **Scenic tips:** The main Innsbruck–Zell am See–Salzburg line is one of the most scenic in the country. If you're going from Innsbruck to Italy, take the train to Brennero for beautiful mountainous scenery. If you're heading towards Yugoslavia, try Vienna–Trieste – this goes via Klagenfurt and Udine. If you're travelling from Innsbruck to Munich or vice versa, try the route via Garmisch – again the mountain scenery is beautiful. Bregenz, situated on the Bodensee in the west of Austria, is a good point of departure to sail across to Germany. From here you can go to Konstanz over the border (ask about reductions for train pass holders). Also at Bregenz you can take the Pfanderbahn up to the top for a wonderful view of the Alps and over the Bodensee. Go to the Vorarlberg Tourist Office in Bregenz on Jahnstrasse for information on Alpine villages and excursions. You can sail the Danube from the German–Austrian border (Passau) to Vienna or from Vienna to Passau. The trip lasts a day and a half, stopping overnight at Linz. Alternatively, there's the Linz–Vienna trip or vice versa. The prettiest part of the trip is from Krems to Melk. The train runs from both Melk and Krems. Further information from DDSG, Reisedienst 2, Handelskai 265. In Passau, go to DDSG-Schiffsstation, Im Ort 14A, Dreiflunseck. Get off the boat and take a look around as often as possible, as many of the stopping-off places are well-preserved medieval or baroque towns. If you're leaving Vienna for Salzburg, stop off at the village of Mariazell. It's beautiful. Surrounded by hills, it was a religious pilgrimage site. Take the cable-car for the view. From Vienna take the train to St Pölten from the Westbahnhof, then change there to a train for Mariazell.

● **Bikes:** You can rent out a bike in nearly every important station in Austria – 'Fahrrad Am Bahnhof'. Take a quick look at the traffic situation before committing yourself. Prices are normally around AS 70–75, but with your train ticket you get half price.

● **Rover Tickets:** The Austrian General Season Ticket (Bundes-netzkarten) for any adult is around AS 1440 for nine days, AS 1960 for 16 days and around AS 3100 for a month. These prices are second class, first class costs double. It is valid only on ÖBB, but does give reductions on some shipping services. Children under six travel free on ÖBB. Between six and 14 they pay half the adult Bundesnetzkarten fare if accompanied by an adult. Also available are Regional Season Tickets (Regionalnetzkarten), giving unlimited travel for 4 to 10 days, within any one of eighteen regions. Another introduction is the 'Rabbit' card, which allows travel on four out of ten days, for AS 490 (under 26), or AS 890 (over 26).

TOURIST INFORMATION

There's a local tourist office (Verkehrsverein) in every large town which will give you the addresses of the provincial tourist boards if required.

● **ISIC bonuses:** 50 per cent reductions on most art galleries and museums. For further information, contact Türkenstrasse 4–6, Wien (Tel. 3475260).

• **Money matters:** 1 Austrian schilling (AS) = 100 groschen (gr). Banking hours are Mon.–Wed., Fri.: 8 a.m.–12.30 p.m., 1.30 p.m.–3 p.m., Thurs.: 8 a.m.–12.30 p.m., 1.30 p.m.–5.30 p.m. The main banks in Vienna stay open over lunch. It's best to cash your traveller's cheques in large denominations as commission charges are high. You can cash Eurocheques without paying commission if you are staying at the Ruthensteiner hostel near the Westbahnhof.

• **Post offices:** Open Mon.–Fri.: 8 a.m.–12 noon, 2 p.m.–6 p.m., Sat.: 8 a.m.–10 a.m. Stamps can also be bought from Tabak-Trafik shops.

• **Shops:** Generally keep to the same hours as the post offices, closing on Saturday afternoons. Food shops usually open before 8 a.m., but close for lunch from 12.30–3 p.m.

• **Museums:** Tend to close on Mondays.

SLEEPING

• **Hostels:** To stay at any Austrian youth hostel, you need an International Youth Hostel Association membership card, though guest cards are always available. In general, they're open from about 6 a.m. till 10 p.m. and charge about AS 90–170 for bed and breakfast, from AS 60 for just bed, and about AS 60–120 for a meal, adding on an extra charge where cooking facilities are available. At many hostels breakfast is compulsory; check first. Provided space is available, you can stay more than three nights at most hostels unless you're travelling in a large group. If you are, write in advance to the warden and book your space.

• **Hotels:** Hotels are nearly always clean but wildly expensive, particularly in Vienna and Salzburg. If you travel off-season, prices are 20–40 per cent cheaper; also in May, June and September they can be 15–25 per cent cheaper than in July and August. You can expect to pay at least AS 350 for a double, from AS 500 in Vienna and other cities. Bear this in mind if you're approached by an Austrian hotelier trying to fill his hotel – he may be offering you a bargain. Don't be put off by this approach as it's a buyer's market; ask the price and location and what's included. You're under no obligation.

• **Private houses** (Privat Zimmer/Zimmer Frei): Rooms are around AS 150 per person and make an interesting alternative.

• **Camping:** The International Camping Carnet is not obligatory, but it'll get you preferential treatment on most sites. Generally, the sites are very good: clean, efficient and well laid out. Austrians are keen campers themselves, so in peak season you might find it advisable to get to the site and pitch as early in the day as you can. Charges are from AS 25 per person and AS 25 per tent, with Vienna at around AS 50 per person and tent.

EATING AND NIGHTLIFE

Austrian food is wholesome stuff and great if you've a soft spot for pastries. In general, the pork (schwein) and fish dishes are better value than lamb and beef. Tafelspitz (boiled beef) is good and cheap, and this with a noodle or dumpling soup is a filling, inexpensive meal. The coffee-and-cakes scene is good news all round, except for the price. Strudel is excellent, as is Sachertorte. Having said all this, you may well end up eating from fast-food chains most of the time, owing to high restaurant prices. If so, try and eat the local dishes at least once, you won't regret it.

The nightlife is centred round coffee houses and the opera, rather than heavy-metal gigs and bars. You have to remember that discos and bars cost money in Austria and anyway they tend to be a bit smooth. The best advice is to head towards a wine tavern or beer cellar in the studenty areas where possible, as prices tend to be more realistic there. The east of the country is best for wine. However, if you're into opera, Vienna's the place. The season runs from September to June, but prices are very high.

Vienna (Wien)

Gateway between the East and West for over two thousand years, Vienna's middle-European flavour makes it unique among all capital cities. Its position as ruler of half of Europe for over six centuries has left behind a legacy of impressive buildings and an atmosphere of solid institutionalism. This is probably helped by the fact that over a third of Vienna's 1.3 million population are pensioners.

The city is divided into twenty-three districts, with the 'Ring' in the city centre as No. 1. Vienna's not actually on the Danube – the river only runs through its suburbs – but the Danube Canal is part of the city.

If you want to sail on the Danube and are heading for Hungary it is a fraction of the price in Budapest.

Use this book, and do your sums carefully in Vienna to avoid its high costs during your stay. It's a great place, but at a price.

STATION FACILITIES

Vienna has two main stations: the West and the South, with trains leaving daily from the West Station at Europaplatz to France, Switzerland and Germany. Trains for Eastern European countries, southern Austria and Italy leave from either the South Station or the smaller Wien-Mitte Station. Finally there are three minor stations for all other regional trains, Berlin and some Czech and Polish destinations. For further info, telephone (222) 1717.

Trains to Budapest leave from West Station, trains to Prague from Franz Josef.

	SÜDBAHNHOF (South Station)	WESTBAHNHOF (West Station)
Train information	6.30 a.m.–9.20 p.m.	7 a.m.–8.30 p.m.
Reservations	7 a.m.–8.45 p.m.	7 a.m.–8.30 p.m.
Tourist information	6.30 a.m.–10 p.m.	6.15 a.m.–11 p.m.
Foreign exchange	6.30 a.m.–10 p.m.	6.30 a.m.–11.15 p.m.
Bar, Buffet	6 a.m.–10 p.m.	6 a.m.–10.30 p.m.
Snack bar	6 a.m.–7 p.m.	6.30 a.m.–11 p.m.
Bath, Shower	4 a.m.–11.45 p.m.	Mon.–Sat.: 7 a.m.–10 p.m. Sun.: 8 a.m.–noon
Left-luggage lockers	Shut midnight (AS10)	Shut 12.30 a.m.–3.30 a.m.
Left-luggage store	4.30 a.m.–11.45 p.m.	Always open
Shops	6 a.m.–10 p.m.	6 a.m.–11 p.m.
Waiting room	Always open	Always open
Station shuts	Midnight–4 a.m.	12.30 a.m.–3.30 a.m.

There are post office facilities at both stations. Tram 18 connects the South and West stations. To get to the city centre from Südbahnhof take U-Bahn 1 or Tram D. From Westbahnhof take Tram 58.

TOURIST INFORMATION

The main office is at Kärntnerstrasse 38, behind the Opera (Tel. 43 16 08 13). Open 9 a.m.–7 p.m. The station offices can also help out and provide an accommodation-finding service costing AS 40. Pick up the city map, transport map and the students' magazine 'Jugend/Youth scene'. Tourist information for all of Austria is available at Margaretenstrasse 1 (Tel. 587–2000). Open Mon.–Fri. 9 a.m.–5.30 p.m.

● **Addresses:**

POST OFFICE: Fleischmarkt 19. Poste restante. Open 24 hours.

AMEX: Kärtnerstrasse 21–23, Mon.–Fri.: 9 a.m.–5.30 p.m., Sat.: 9 a.m.–noon (Tel. 515400).

UK EMBASSY: Reisnerstrasse 40 (Tel. 7131575).

US EMBASSY: Gartenbaupromenade 2 (Tel. 315511).

CANADIAN EMBASSY: Karl-Lueger-Ring 10 (Tel. 5333691).

AUSTRALIAN EMBASSY: Mattiellistrasse 2–4 (Tel. 5128580).

POLICE EMERGENCY: Tel. 133.

MEDICAL EMERGENCY: Tel. 144.

ÖKISTA (Student Travel): Turkenstrasse 4–6, Mon.–Fri.: 9.30 a.m.–5 p.m. (Tel. 3475260). They help out with any accommodation problems you may have.

CITY PHONE CODE 01.

● **Getting about:** Information on city transport is available at Karlsplatz U-Bahn Station. There are various passes on offer, but remember you can see most of Vienna on foot. Tickets for buses, trams, U-Bahn and S-Bahn (free on Inter Rail) cost AS 20 each, AS 56 for blocks of four if bought in advance at Tabak-Trafik. You can also buy three-day unlimited passes (Netzkarte 72 Stunden Wein) at Tabak-Trafik and the Karlplatz information office for AS 102. A one-week ticket for AS 116 is also available from Tabak-Trafik (at stations and main subway stops). There is a 24hr pass for AS 40 and an 8 day 'environment' pass which can be used by more than 1 person for AS 220. Pick up a map of the city and transport system at the tourist office. Tickets can also be purchased from automatic machines in stations and on some trams, so have AS 5 and AS 10 coins to hand. Night buses, costing AS 25, radiate from Schwedenplatz. Forget the city tours, taxis, and 'Fiakers' (two-horse coaches at AS 300 a go) as they'll cripple your budget.

SEEING

Pick up leaflets from tourist information offices. These will give you all the history, details, opening times, etc.

At the heart of Vienna is St Stephan's Cathedral and its square, Stephansplatz, at the intersection of Graben and Kärntnerstrasse – it's a good place to sit and watch Viennese life go by. Rather than suggest a walking tour with everyone tramping round exactly the same treadmill like guinea pigs, we list the major sights and you can devise your own route by using the map.

ST STEPHAN'S CATHEDRAL: Built in the thirteenth and fourteenth centuries, it's the most important Gothic building in Vienna. Climb the 458 steps of the south steeple (or take the lift up the north steeple, AS 40) for a good view of Vienna, or descend to the catacombs and look at the Habsburgs' innards in the 'Old Prince's Vault' (AS 25).

THE HOFBURG: The old imperial winter palace sprawling all over the heart of the city and encompassing every architectural style from the thirteenth to the twentieth century; it includes the Spanish Riding School and the Hofburgkapelle where the Vienna Boys' Choir perform – though, crazily, both close down for periods in summer. Entry to the Hofburg is AS 15 (reductions for ISIC holders).

SCHÖNBRUNN PALACE: This was the Habsburgs' summer palace. Situated at Schönbrunner Schloss-Strasse in the outskirts, south-west from Westbahnhof, U-bahn 4. There are a limited number of English tours for AS 50 (AS 25 ISIC) which are worth it.

THE BELVEDERE: Includes the Austrian gallery of modern art and a museum of medieval art.

THE KUNSTHISTORISCHES MUSEUM, Maria-Theresien Platz: One of the great art collections and the fourth largest gallery in the world. All the treasures the Habsburgs could get their imperial hands on are here. The Breughel room contains over half the artist's remaining pictures.

The above are the main sights but, if you've any time left, take in the FREUD MUSEUM. Followers of the master can visit his house at Berggasse 19 (AS 10).

Of interest to musicians will be: HAYDN MUSEUM at Haydngasse 19; MOZART ERINNERUNGSRAUM, Domgasse 5; SCHUBERT MUSEUM, Nussdorferstrasse 54; and SCHUBERT STERBEZIMMER, Kettenbrück-engasse 6; JOHANN STRAUSS MUSEUM, Praterstrasse 54. At most of these addresses, the composers' original houses are still standing.

If museums are one of your passions, consider buying a seven-day museum ticket (AS 150) for entry to all fifty of Vienna's museums as often as you like. The charges for entrance seem to be constantly changing, but municipal museums should be free for all on Friday mornings, and national museums free for all students. But don't be surprised if the rules change – especially outside the high season. Pick up the leaflet 'Museums Wien' from the tourist office. Alternatively, as a break take a walk and a picnic in the Vienna woods which border the city on its southern and western sides. Take tram 38 to its terminus at Grinzing, then bus 38 to Kahlenberg.

SLEEPING

Write in advance if at all possible as cheap beds are few and far between in the summer. This is mainly due to the fact that they don't open their student hostels till July (making late June a particularly bad time); hotels are ridiculously expensive and the cheap pensions get full quickly. Use the ISTC accommodation booklet as it lists all the best places.

There are two main accommodation-finding services in Vienna: the tourist office (at the stations), and the student organization Ökista. If you want to save the commission charge, try phoning yourself. Most hoteliers speak English, or you can try out your phrase-book German.

• **Student hostels:** Try the Internationales Studenthaus at Seiler-stätte 30 (Tel. 5128463). The location is very central, and they give 10 per cent reduction to ISIC holders. If they are full try Asylverein der Wiener Universität at Porzellangasse 30 (Tel. 347282), tram D from Sudbahnhof or Franz Josefs Bahnhof (it is possible to walk from the latter), with doubles at around AS 130 per person (higher charge for one night stays). Also try Pfeilheim on Pfeilgasse 6 (Tel. 4384762), a 15-minute walk from Westbahnhof: turn left outside station, and continue along main road, until you reach Pfeifgasse. Alternatively, take bus 13a from Südbahnhof, until it crosses Lerchefelder. Costs AS 330 for double, including breakfast.

• **Youth hostels:** Ruthensteiner, Robert Hanerlinggasse 24 (Tel. 834693 and 8308265). 77 beds with all facilities, near Westbahnhof: turn right, cross Mariahilfer Strasse, next road parallel. Costs from AS 114 for dormitory, to AS 169 for a single room. Free showers, but no lockers. If you are going east for a few days they will store extra luggage free of charge (at your risk) if space permits. No curfew. Breakfast available at AS 22.

Myrthengasse, Myrthengasse 7 (Tel. 936316 + 939429). 123 beds and all facilities. All rooms have showers. Near Centrum. Must be IYHF member. A second house round the corner has 100 beds and excellent facilities. Walkable from Westbahnhof, or U-bahn 6 to Burgasse, then tram 48A to Neuburgasse, hostel nearby.

Brigittenau, Friedrich Engels Platz 24 (Tel. 338294). 330 beds, all facilities. Near the Danube. Must be IYHF member. Tram N from Schwedenplatz (U-bahn 1 or 4) to Friedrich Engels Platz.

Hütteldorf, Schlossberggasse 8 (Tel. 8771501). 300 beds and all facilities. Must be IYHF member. Take the underground from Westbahnhof to Hütteldorf, then a ten-minute walk. AS 125 B&B, AS 70 for evening meal.

Inter Rail Point (YMCA), Kenyongasse 25 (Tel. 936304), mid-July to mid-August. Cost is around AS 110 (breakfast is compulsory). Other meals cost around AS 75. They are unhelpful about taking telephone bookings in advance.

Another novel hostel is in the bell tower of a church at Turmherberge Don Bosco, Lechnerstrasse 12 (Tel. 7131494). Take Tram 18 from Westbahnhof or Sudbahnhof to the end. Men only. Costs AS 55. No catering, and don't expect a long lie – the alarm bell is very loud and very close!

● **Hotels:** Graben, Dorotheegasse 3 (Tel. 521531), near St Stephan's Cathedral, 46 rooms. Karntnerhof, Grashofergasse 4 (5121923). Good value for money.

● **Pensions:** Pension Columbia, Kochgasse 9 (Tel. 426757), quiet with doubles from AS 580, including breakfast.

Pension Merlingen at Zeltgasse 13 (Tel. 4219413) not far from Westbahnhof, doubles around AS 350.

● **Private rooms:** Private rooms are available, owned by Hedwig Gally, near the Westbahnhof at Arnsteingasse 25/10 (Tel. 81 29073/83 04244). Prices start at AS 340 for a double, AS 440 for a double with shower. Try the rooms owned by Irmgard Launig at Kaiserstrasse 77/8, close to the Westbahnhof (Tel. 934152). Costs AS 200 including showers and cooking facilities.

Frank Heberling runs an establishment at Siccardsburggasse 42 (Tel. 604 0229), phone first. Very friendly, walkable from Sudbahnhof.

• **Camping:** All grounds are located well out of the city with an average price of AS 50 per person and the same per tent.

Wien West II, Hüttelbergstrasse 80 (Tel. 942314). Get off train at Hütteldorf, then bus 52B. Open April–Oct.

Wien West I (just up the same street) (Tel. 941449). Open mid-June–mid-Sept. But I've had terrible reports of declining standards in Wien West I and II, and I would not advise them. If desperate, try Camping Süd (Tel. 869218), open June–early Sept., close to the Atzgersdorf-Mauer S-Bahn station. Quite near this site is the Rodaun-Schwimmbad site at An der Au 2 (Tel. 884154). Take tram 58 from Westbahnhof to Hietzing, then tram 60 to the end. Hot showers are AS 5, and there is a free swimming pool. Open end March–mid-Nov. If you are desperate, sleep out at the Prater Park.

EATING AND NIGHTLIFE

There's no shortage of places to eat in Vienna – the only problem's the prices. As usual, though, if you know where to look you'll be OK. The Hungarian and Turkish restaurants are usually good value.

The Schnell Imbiss counters (quick snacks) dotted all over the city serve cheap filling snacks (AS 30–70), and of course there's always McDonalds, one of them very convenient for the Westbahnhof on Mariahilferstrasse heading towards the city, on the left-hand side.

Cafés are a Viennese institution, serving up their delicious pastries and cakes, but they're expensive, so make your café visit on a wet afternoon when you can hang around reading the papers, playing cards and generally getting your money's worth.

For picnics, use the self-service supermarkets. There's no shortage of good breads, sausages, cheeses, fruits and wines, so picnicking is easy. Vienna's largest market, the NASCHMARKT, lying from the fourth to the sixth districts, has a few food bargains and plenty more besides. Get to it by the underground to Kettenbrückengasse.

• **Suggestions:** There is nowhere really cheap in the centre of Vienna to eat, but scrutinize any 'menu of the day' you see. Places worth trying include the Aktion Schnitzelland at Schottenfeldgasse 3 and the Naschmarkt Restaurant on Schwarzenberg Platz. The best place to head for is the seventh district around the Neustiftgasse where you will find the Phonixhof and Puppenstube restaurants. You can expect a good meal and wine for around AS 140 and if these are full there are other places in the vicinity. The student restaurant Mensa is at Universitätsstrasse 7. It's open for lunch and dinner, Mon.–Fri., and there's no problem getting in as long as you look like a student. Prices from AS 30 to AS 45 for a basic meal.

Vegetarians should try Gauthaus Wrentch, Hollergasse 9 (15th district) or Bauermarkt 10 (1st district).

The Viennese are happier at the opera or the theatre than engaged in active nightlife. Young people tend to congregate in the Kaffeekonditorei rather than in pubs or discos, but Vienna still has a few surprises up its sleeve. A good night out can be had at the Prater – Vienna's large amusement park on the outskirts of the city. Entrance is free and the rides average AS 15–25, although the big wheel, built in 1895 by British engineer Walter Bassett, costs AS 25. Open from Easter to October. Take Tram 79A or 81, it's reasonably obvious where to get off, or U-bahn 1. Those interested in seeing the other sights of the film 'The Third Man', should also try one of the trips to the sewers (ask at tourist info).

Bars and nightclubs can be sleazy and expensive, so watch out. Try U4 Disco, Schönbrunnerstrasse 222; it's very popular with the young Viennese and it's easy to get to. In general, though, you're better off heading for a wine tavern or beer cellar. These represent best value by far. Try: Esterhazykeller, Haarhofl, good studenty crowd with the best prices in town; or Zwölf-Apostelkeller, Sonnenfelsgasse 3, near St Stephan's, so low down from street level, the walls are covered with straw to diminish the dampness. Go down to the lowest level – it's liveliest. Open Sundays, but closed all July. There's a good atmosphere here. And for the connoisseur, Melkerkeller, Schottengasse 3, run by Benedictine monks, has excellent wine.

For enthusiasts, Europe's largest bowling alley is in Vienna. It's the Bowling-Brunswick at Hauptallee 124 and costs around AS 25 a line. Plenty of students congregate here.

If you're keen on opera and classical music, check with tourist information, but when buying tickets don't use an agency as they charge a 20 per cent commission.

Southern Austria

If you're travelling south on to Italy or Yugoslavia, you'll pass through the southern regions of BURGENLAND, STEIERMARK and KÄRNTEN.

Burgenland is the province next to the Hungarian border and is famous for its wines. EISENSTADT is its capital and between late August and early September this turns into a pretty lively place, thanks to its Weinwoche (wine week). Steiermark is in the south-eastern area of Austria, along the Yugoslavian border which the 'Weinstrasse' (wine road) runs through. The journey between Salzburg and Villach is particularly scenic and if you fancy visiting a typical alpine town you could do worse than to choose Badgastein. Although expensive, it is worth while spending a relaxing few hours here, taking in the wonderful views down the valley from the station and seeing the powerful waterfall at close range.

Kärnten (Carinthia) has as its capital KLAGENFURT. This is an attractive region with lakes, wildlife parks and rolling hills. Klagenfurt itself has two campsites, and a youth hostel in its centre, and is a good place to base yourself to explore the surrounding Naturpark Kreuzbergl.

Central Austria

South of the Linz–Salzburg line lies a region of Austria that the tourist hordes haven't as yet discovered or spoilt. It consists mainly of mountains, lakes and tiny old villages – the sort of Austria you'd optimistically imagined. Not being commercialized, prices are low, so it's really got everything going for it.

From Vienna or Salzburg catch a train to Attnang Puchheim, then take a local train going in the direction of Stainach Irdning, passing through Gmunden, Hallstatt and Obertraun.

GMUNDEN, a town at the northernmost end of the Traunsee by the largest lake of the region, is particularly lovely. Tourist information is at Am Graben 2. Traunsteinstrasse is one of the best streets in which to look for accommodation.

HALLSTATT is the third stop after Bad Goisern. It is a particularly beautiful village with lakes, cliffs and a waterfall as the backdrop to your views. The small youth hostel on Salzburgstrasse (Tel. 06134 279) is open from May to September (only limited facilities), and there's camping at Campingplatz Höll (Tel. 06134 329). Tourist information is in the Prehistorisches Museum just off Seestrasse; they'll advise on accommodation. The oldest salt mines in the world (they claim) are here and can be visited, AS 85. This area is rich in walks and sails; you can rent a small boat for around AS 95 an hour. There's a ferry into the town from the station after each train arrives.

OBERTRAUN, the next stop along, has some interesting ice caves, but the admission cost is quite high. Their youth hostel is at Winkl 26 (Tel. 06134 360) and opens at 5 p.m.; it is more pleasant than the hostel in Hallstatt, As 100 for B&B.

Salzburg

Extremely expensive, touristy, but beautiful. The prince-archbishops who ruled over the town built many fine churches, palaces, mansions and gardens until it became known as the 'Rome of the North'. The town is famous for its festival (from late July to end of August), which attracts all the big international names in music and fills every hotel, hostel and campsite with the thousands who flock to this event.

Luckily, Salzburg is a university town, so this slightly eases some of the financial problems eurorailers may encounter. There are some student hostels and restaurants which are less than half the price of their commercial counterparts, but basically Salzburg is a town which caters for the middle-aged and middle-class.

Salzburg is 3½ hours from Vienna, 2 hours from Munich in West Germany, 2½ hours from Innsbruck and 5 hours from Zürich; there are daily trains to Cologne, Hamburg and Copenhagen. The tourist information office at the station gives out free maps and for AS 10 will help you find a room. It is to the left side of the building facing you as you come out of passport control.

STATION FACILITIES

Train information	Daily 8 a.m.–7 p.m.
	(Tel. 71541)
Reservations	Daily 8 a.m.–7 p.m. in train info office
Tourist information	Daily 8 a.m.–8 p.m. (Tel. 71712)
Foreign exchange	Daily 7 a.m.–9 p.m.
Bar, Buffet	Mon.–Fri.: 6.30 a.m.–9 p.m.
Restaurant	Mon.–Fri.: 6 a.m.–11.45 p.m.
Left-luggage lockers	Always open
Waiting room	Always open
Food shops (or head towards	
centre for supermarkets)	Mon.–Sat.: 8 a.m.–7 p.m.

TOURIST INFORMATION AND ADDRESSES

The city's tourist information offices are next to American Express, at Mozartplatz 5 (Tel. 80723462 or 847568) (open all year 9 a.m.–6 p.m.) and at the station. There's also an office at Auerspergstrasse 7 (Tel. 80720) which operates an accommodation-finding service. Also pick up a copy of 'Salzburg für die Jugend' – very useful. There is an information centre for young travellers, 'Jugend-Service-Stelle' at Hubert-Sattler-Gasse 7 (Tel. 80722592) open weekdays 10 a.m.–4.30 p.m. (2 p.m. Fridays). City transport information and free maps are obtained from the bus drivers. Fares are AS 10 and a 24-hour pass is AS 40, which gives free entry to the railway for the castle, although most sights are within walking distance.

POST OFFICE: Residenzplatz 9, Mon.–Fri.: 7 a.m.–7 p.m., Sat. 8 a.m.–10 a.m. or 24-hour service near main railway station.

AMEX: Mozartplatz 5 (Tel. 842501).

STUDENT TRAVEL SERVICE: Ökista, Hildmannplatz 1a (Tel. 846769), Mon.–Fri.: 9.30 a.m.–5.30 p.m. Help out with travel problems.

CITY PHONE CODE: 662.

SEEING

Gone are the days when Salzburg depended on its salt; tourists now come in their thousands to see the impressive baroque legacy of the powerful archbishops. They weren't all good, though; they did their fair share of expelling the Jews, pillaging and persecuting the local Protestants – all the usual stuff. The HOHENSALZBURG FORTRESS (their main residence) shouldn't be missed. Take the cable car up 1,780 feet and kill two birds with one stone, as the view from the top over the city is tremendous. If you're getting fed up with your travelling companion, check out the MUSEUM OF TORTURE there.

The other four main sites are the RESIDENZ (seventeenth-century archbishops' palace), SCHLOSS MIRABELL, the CATHEDRAL and MOZART'S HOUSE at Getreidegasse 9. Slightly outside Salzburg is SCHLOSS HELLBRUNN, the castle built by a bishop for his mistress, surrounded by an Alpine zoo (take the local train from Salzburg). If you've had enough of tourists, there are several escape routes: two of them a short bus or train ride away over the border in Bavaria. The first is a vist to Hitler's retreat, the 'EAGLE'S NEST', and the second is a visit to the salt mines. Organized excursions to the salt mines run several times a day from Salzburg station, although you can do both trips independently. The starting-off point for both trips is Berchtesgaden. You might find it more convenient to take the bus as it runs more frequently than the train, and since the journey is quite short the cost is reasonable at around AS 20. (Discount with Inter Rail, free on Eurail). Once you are at Berchtesgaden you need to take a bus to the mines where you can hire protective clothing for around 25 DM. Check to see if your bus passes the mine entrance on the way to Berchtesgaden. For the 'EAGLE'S NEST' you will need a local service bus to the entrance road, where you change to special buses for the trip up to the car park. Don't even think about going any further if you suffer from vertigo for the bus seems to be suspended in mid-air for most of the tortuous journey up the single-track mountain road. You then walk into the middle of the mountain before going up to the eyrie in a brass-panelled lift. Total cost about 20 DM. The view is quite spectacular, although you might be just as happy to take a cable car up to the top of the Untersberg (5,800 feet), which will give you fine views of the Alpine scenery without the same expense in time and money but even this is relatively expensive. Alternatively, take one of the regular 'Sound of Music' tours round the locations of this popular musical. Details from tourist information.

SLEEPING

Your best bet here is to go for private accommodation: ask at tourist information for their list of private rooms. Forget hotels and try one of the hostels or campsites. If you've no luck here, go to the tourist office at Auerspergstrasse and tell them the most you can afford, then wait and see what they can come up with. If all else fails, consider going out to one of the villages on the outskirts, or sleeping in the station, but be careful with your belongings.

• **Youth hostels:** The youth hostel at Josef-Preis Allee 18 (Tel. 842670) has 360 beds and all facilities, but fills up quickly so go early or book in advance. It closes from 9 a.m. to 11 a.m. and at midnight. Take bus 5 to Justizgebäude and get off shortly after crossing the river. The International Hostel at Paracelsusstrasse 9 (Tel. 79649) is only a few blocks away from the station and is a real 'find'. It is immaculately clean and well kept with a washing machine and drier on-site which can be used for a nominal amount. Although showers and breakfast are extra, you can choose from Continental, British or American. There is also a cheap restaurant/bar which has a happy hour and serves an excellent Weiner Schnitzel. Expect to pay around AS 120 for a bed. Also near the centre of town is the hostel at Aigner Strasse 34 (Tel. 23248). Buses 5 or 6 and change to 49 at Zentrum. It can get very busy and noisy, however.

• **Pensions:** Zum Junger Fuchs, Linzer Gasse 54 (Tel. 75496). Doubles about AS 350. Very good. Walk from the Staatsbrücke bridge, along Linzer Gasse.

• **Camping:** There are several campsites including Gersbergalm at Gersbergweg (Tel. 20374) and City Camping (Tel. 71169) at Bayerhamerstrasse (only a ten-minute walk from the station. Cross under the railway line, then walk behind the station). Most are open from 1 May to 30 September, and prices vary from AS 35–55 per person and tent.

EATING AND NIGHTLIFE

There are plenty of flash restaurants in Salzburg and no shortage of ways to blow your money if you have any. Try Pitterkeller, 6 Rainerstrasse, near the station. After 7 p.m. an accordion player adds oomph to your evening; the food's not bad either, and it's cheap by Salzburg prices.

For picnic food, there's a good open-air market on Thursday mornings by St Andrew's Church, and there's one every weekday on Franz-Josef Strasse. There is a cheap stand-up Imbiss place, with a larger range than most, at 10 Judengasse, where Wiener Schnitzel and chips can be had for around AS 75.

Beer Gardens: Salzburg is a bit more orientated towards beer than to wine, probably due to its proximity to the German border. The beer cellars invariably offer good value in eating, drinking and entertainment. Try Pitterkeller, Rainerstrasse 6 (meals AS 90–140), or Augustiner Bräustule, Augustinergasse 4 – there are several small stalls in this building where you can treat yourself.

If it's just a drink you're after, try Stigl Beer Cellar, Festungsgasse 10, which has a great atmosphere and views over the city to match, or Students' Centre, Gstattengasse 16, 4 p.m.–9 p.m.

Western Austria

From Lichtenstein to the Arlberg Tunnel, the Vorarlberg Alps are particularly scenic: mountains, chalets, green fields, etc. The best towns to base yourself in to explore this region are FELDKIRCH and BREGENZ.

Feldkirch is an old town with many reminders of its Gothic heyday. The tourist offices are at Schlossergasse and Herrengasse (Mon.–Fri.: 8.30 a.m.–12 noon, 2 p.m.–6 p.m., Sat.: 9 a.m.–noon). They'll suggest walking tours. There's a youth hostel (Tel. 23181) at Noflerstrasse, or use Pension Grete at Mutterstrasse 12.

Bregenz is a medieval city on the Bodensee. The information office is at Inselstrasse. There's a youth hostel at Belruptstrasse 16A (Tel. 22867) and three campsites.

Innsbruck

As capital of the Tyrol and the Austrian ski scene, Innsbruck is busy all the year round. It is beautifully situated and well worth a day or two of your time.

STATION FACILITIES

Train information	Daily 8.30 a.m.–7 p.m. (Tel. 25275)
Reservations	Daily 8 a.m.–5 p.m.
Tourist information	Daily 9 a.m.–10 p.m.
Restaurant	Daily 6.30 a.m.–midnight
Bar, Buffet	Daily 7 a.m.–8 p.m.
Left-luggage lockers	Always open
Waiting room	Always open

For food and provisions, head towards the Maria-Theresienstrasse area, two streets straight ahead from the station.

There are daily trains from Innsbruck to Cologne, Hamburg, Munich (2¼ hours), Salzburg (2¼ hours), Vienna (5½ hours), Milan, Rome, Venice and Zürich (4 hours).

There's a centre for young travellers at the station (opening times 9.00 a.m.–10.00 p.m.). It's wonderful. Seize this opportunity to be treated like a human being and use it.

TOURIST INFORMATION AND ADDRESSES

At the station, open daily 8 a.m.–9 p.m. They'll find you a room, change your cash and fill you in on what's happening. There's another office at Burggraben 3, in the city centre, open daily 8 a.m.–8 p.m. The post office is at Maximilianstrassc 2 (one block away from the Triumphal Arch). The AMEX office is at Brixner-strasse 3, and the student travel service, Okista, is at Josef-Hirnstrasse 7/2. City phone code 512.

• **Alpine information:** As you're in one of the best Alpine centres in Europe, you may feel inclined to head for the hills. Check up on conditions before setting off at Wilhelm-Greillstrasse 15 (Tel. 24107) or, if you prefer to take an organized hike, contact Verkehrsverein at Burggraben 3 (Tel. 25715).

• **Mountain hut scheme:** There are over 700 huts up in the mountains surrounding Innsbruck. They belong to various local and national Alpine associations, and doing a tour of them, or even just staying the night in one, is very rewarding, cheap and provides a good memory of Austria. All the huts have some cooking facilities and some even serve up hot food. Prices range from about AS 120 to AS 250 for a night.

Before setting out, make sure you have emergency food supplies, a waterproof and are wearing good climbing boots. The distress call in this neck of the woods is six visible or audible signals spaced evenly over one minute, followed by a minute's break, then the six signals again.

SEEING

The Nordkette mountains dominate the main shopping street – Maria-Theresienstrasse. At one end is the TRIUMPHAL ARCH and at the other the old Gothic town. The GOLDEN ROOF is the symbol of Innsbruck; it's an ornate Gothic balcony built in 1500 from 2,657 gilded copper tiles. Also see the Olympic Museum here. The HOFBURG (Imperial Palace) is the other major sight.

For an all-round perspective, take the cable car up to HAFELE-KAR. At 7,500 feet, the view is quite spectacular. Take tram 1 to the Hungerburg funicular, then the cable car, but be warned, it is expensive to go all the way. There are also two other cable car routes. The 1964 Winter Olympics were held at IGLS near Innsbruck, and if you're in the ski set you can still go and see the set-up (bus J from Innsbruck Station or tram 6). Enjoy the view but stay out of the cafés there. If you want to see a pretty Alpine village and travel on an open-sectioned train (highly recommended), go to the village of FULPMES, in good picnic country (tram 1 to Stubaitalbahnhof where the mountain train leaves).

SLEEPING

The Glockenhaus Hotel at Weihnerburgasse 3 (Tel. 85563), is situated ten minutes' walk from the town centre and twenty minutes from the station, although there is a pick-up service from the station if you arrange in advance, or bus K. The friendly owners work hard to create a happy atmosphere and lay on cooking facilities, ski rental and organize skiing, hiking, river rafting and wind surfing excursions. Prices start at AS 110 for dormitories, AS 140 for doubles and AS 170 for single rooms. The Pensione Tautemann, at

Stamser Feld 5 (Tel. 83715) charges AS 350 for a double room with shower *en suite* WC, and includes breakfast. Very comfortable. There is also a small hostel at Sillgasse 8a, although reports on the cleanliness vary. Only five minutes' walk from the station, it charges AS 100 for bed, breakfast and shower (Tel. 31311). Alternatively, there's the popular youth hostel at Reichenauerstrasse 147, which despite its distance from the town centre and 10 p.m. curfew is well worth a visit. Take bus O or R to Campingplatz or a 30-minute walk. Cost is around AS 120 (Tel. 46179). Also try the hostel at 17b Rennwegg (Tel. 25814). Open July and August only. Small rooms at AS 100 including breakfast.

The nearest campsite is Reichenau at Reichenauerstrasse (Tel. 46252), 30 minutes' walk from the station, follow river downstream, or take buses R, O or OA. It is expensive at AS 70 per person. You can also try the Westerdorf campsite, but it is further out and you need to take a chairlift there.

EATING AND NIGHTLIFE

Head towards the university area. Try Gasthaus Gruber, Innrain 160 (between university and Old Town). Also, the Mensa (off Innrain) at Herzog-Siegmund Ufer 15, 2nd floor, offers cheap meals for ISIC holders, lunchtimes only.

There's a free Tyrolean evening in front of the Golden Roof every Thursday evening at 8.30 p.m. Or try the St Nikolaus Kellerei, Innstrasse, open 8 a.m.–12 noon, 2 p.m.–8 p.m. Good wine, but no English spoken.

BELGIUM

Entry requirements	Passport
Population	10,000,000
Capital	Brussels (pop.: 1,200,000)
Currency	Belgian Franc
	£1 = approx. 60.58 BF
Political system	Constitutional Monarchy
Religion	Roman Catholic
Languages	French and Flemish (English widely spoken)
Public holidays	1 Jan.; Easter Monday; 1 May; Ascension Day;
	Whit Monday; 21 July; 15 Aug.; 1, 11 Nov.;
	25 Dec.
International dialling codes	From UK 01032
	From USA 01132
	To UK 0044
	To USA 001

To confuse the Flemish with the Walloons is like calling the Scots English; it is a mistake to be avoided in a country where the two major ethnic groups each speak their own language and are equally proud of their historical and cultural differences. The Flemish speak their own language closely akin to Dutch, live in the north and west, and still carry the hard-working characteristics of their Germanic forebears. The Walloons, on the other hand, speak French, often in the 'old French' dialect and are in every way more like their French neighbours.

During the early Middle Ages, trade and commerce created a rich town life unrivalled in northern Europe. All this was to change, however, as Belgium got caught up in the crossfire of European affairs through marriage and alliance. The French, Spanish and Austrians all fought to secure her strategic ports and the fertile lands of Flanders, until she gained independence in 1830.

The four main centres of interest are: Bruges, Brussels, Antwerp and Ghent, and although Belgium is the second most densely populated country in Europe, it's still possible to find solitude among the forests and hills of the Ardennes in the south.

BELGIAN NATIONAL RAILWAYS
(Nationale Maatschappij der Belgische Spoorwegen, NMBS)
(Société Nationale des Chemins de Fer Belges, SNCB)

Belgium's train network is one of the most reliable and extensive in Europe. The trains are frequent and go just about everywhere. To cross the country takes only 3½ hours, and trains leave for most internal destinations every hour or two. The fastest services are the Eurocity services and the semi-fast services are 'Inter-regional' (IR numbers). No supplements are charged for any trains running wholly within Belgium, but supplements are payable for travel by certain international trains, even for journeys wholly within Belgium. Eurorailers get a good deal here as normal train fares are expensive. Inter-Railers and Eurail pass holders have an extra bonus as it's possible – and often advisable – to use one city as a base and tour the rest of the country from it (it only takes 1 hour from Bruges to Brussels).

• **Inter Rail bonuses:** RTM (P&O) ferries give 30 per cent reductions from Dover to Ostend, and vice versa. SNCB gives free entrance to the Railway Museum, Gare de Bruxelles, Nord.

• **Eurail bonuses:** The following half-price reductions are granted by Europabus on transportation costs only and by local offices in Europe.
—Antwerp–Brussels–Menton
—Antwerp–Brussels–Barcelona
—Ostend–Brussels–Frankfurt (M.)
—Ostend–Lille
—Antwerp–Brussels–Le Havre–Lisieux

TRAIN INFORMATION

Information officers speak good English, other rail staff speak both Flemish and French. If you're spending any time in Belgium, ask for a copy of the official SNCB timetable ('indicateur'/'spoorboekje') from any station. It has an introduction in English and explains all you need to know about schedules and supplements. If you don't get one, don't worry as there are large posters everywhere, giving departure and arrival information. Lockers take 5 BF coins.

• **Reservations:** Are not necessary, or even possible on inland routes. International reservations cost about 100 BF and can be made up to two months in advance, if you're that highly organized. If you are, you'd probably also like to know that you can reserve seats on trains leaving for Austria, Denmark, Germany, Italy, Luxembourg, the Netherlands and Switzerland, at most large stations, as the SNCB's computer is linked up with these countries.

• **Night travel:** Belgium is too small to warrant inland services, but SNCB have couchettes and wagon-lit sleepers on international routes. (Look out for the German rolling stock with pull-down seats, to save a bit of money.)

• **Eating on trains:** There are not many services on inland trains; some have a mini-bar and a few have a buffet. Don't let that worry you, though, as Belgium's supermarkets are renowned for their food. International trains have all the usual expensive facilities, so either way prepare a picnic in advance, and don't count on station shops to supply it as there aren't any, except in major cities.

• **Bikes:** SNCB run a scheme called 'Train + Vélo' (Trein + Fiets in Flemish) which allows you to take advantage of Belgium's perfect cycling conditions. You can rent a bike for around 110 BF per day (with a rail pass) from over 30 stations and hand it back at over 100. Most roads have cycle tracks and it's flat going all the way to explore the surrounding countryside. (Don't forget to ask for a free tour map.)

• **Rover Tickets:** There are three types of ticket which can be purchased for rover travel within Belgium. The 50% reduction card allows you to buy an unlimited number of single-journey tickets at half normal price. It is valid for one month on the whole of the Belgium network. The 5-day Tourrail Card is valid for 5 days of your own choice within a 17-day period. For adults over 26 the second class card is about 1600 BF, juniors (12–25) pay around 1200 BF. First class costs 50% extra. The 16-day Tourrail Card is valid for 16 consecutive days giving unlimited travel over the Belgian network. The cost is about 4380 BF first class and 2920 BF for second class. There are no reductions on this card.

TOURIST INFORMATION

Local tourist offices are to be found in every large town. For any extra information on the provinces and the country, ask at the main office in Brussels. If you've any problems tourist information can't help out with, try the Info-Jeunes (Info-Jeugd) office. There are branches in most large towns.

• **ISIC bonuses:** 50 per cent off most museums. For further information, contact Connections, 13 rue Marche au Charbon, 1000 Brussels (also a Eurotrain office), or ACOTRA, rue de la Madeleine 51, 1000 Brussels.

• **Money matters:** 1 Belgian franc (BF) = 100 centimes.
Banking hours are Mon.–Fri.: 9 a.m.–12 p.m., 2 p.m.–4 p.m. Late opening, Friday till 4.30 p.m. AMEX are the only bank that won't charge a ridiculous commission of around 90 BF on each transaction involving traveller's cheques. Eurocheques are thus the preferred means of payment. The station exchanges take no commission, but their rate of exchange is about 10 per cent below the official one. The ferries give a good rate and their commission is considerably less.

• **Post offices:** Open Mon.–Fri.: 9 a.m.–4 p.m.

• **Shops and museums:** There are no hard-and-fast rules here, but museums tend to shut either on Mondays or Fridays, and some in the afternoons. Shops open from 9 a.m. to 6 p.m., Monday–Saturday, with lunch 12 noon–2 p.m. Bakers and newsagents open early in the morning, and you can also find a grocer open on Sunday somewhere. Many shops stay open till 8 p.m. Late night Friday.

SLEEPING

Apart from tourist information, the Info-Jeunes offices also give help with accommodation. Unmarried couples wanting to sleep together might find problems if they are under 21 as hoteliers can be imprisoned for up to three years under Belgian law for allowing this.

Hostels are your best bet – either the IYHF ones or those run by an organization called 'Amis de la Nature'. There are a few unofficial ones as well as student hostels which offer a more relaxed atmosphere. All of these are given in the Budget Holiday booklet which you can pick up at any tourist information office.

Hotels tend to be expensive (absolute minimum 500 BF single, 900 BF double) but clean, and offer an inclusive continental breakfast.

EATING AND NIGHTLIFE

The Belgians love their food and take eating very seriously, a fact which is borne out by the well-stocked supermarkets you will find even in the small towns. Always be prepared for an impromptu picnic. If you're eating out, go for your main meal at lunchtime as the fixed menu is not available at night, so making dinner a more expensive affair. Belgian cuisine is similar to French, both in quality and in price. If possible, try some local specialities: carbonnades flamandes (beef stewed in beer) and waterzooi (chicken and vegetables stewed in sauce). Don't miss the Belgian waffles served with fruit or cream, or the excellent pastry and cakes, and if you think the Swiss are the only Europeans who know how to make delicious chocolates, try the Belgian pralines (especially the fresh-cream-filled white chocolates, available from any branch of Leonidas). Apologies for making your mouth water if you're really broke, but there are always Belgian chips, which are small, thin and delicious and are served with mayonnaise. In fact, the 'friterie/frituur' is the cheapest and most prolific source of fast food in Belgium. There's always one near a station, and they serve kebabs, sausages, etc., too.

Belgium's selection of bars would satisfy the most demanding drinker. While wine is good and cheaper than at home, you'll do best to try what they're famous for: beer. In the cities, it's quite common to find pubs serving up to fifty varieties (La Houblonnière in Brussels boasts a hundred). Try one of the Trappist brews, a good nightcap, or for those willing to try anything once, kriek, a cherry-flavoured beer.

There is no shortage of theatres, cinemas or discos, and the set-up is very similar to at home. Don't waste your time looking for cheap seats or student discounts, as there aren't any.

Ostend

If you're coming from England by ferry or Jetfoil, chances are you'll land here. There's not much to see, but if you want to stop overnight, the youth hostel 'de Ploate' at Langestraat 82 (Tel. 805297) is only five minutes from the docks and station. It is however difficult to get a bed during summer, so try to book in advance.

Bruges
(Brugge – Flemish, Bruges – French)

This beautifully preserved medieval town is more like an open-air museum than a twentieth-century city. If you're going to stop off anywhere in Belgium, make sure it's Bruges, as this is definitely one of the most attractive towns in Europe. For over 200 years, Bruges was one of the most important commercial centres in Western Europe, and the Counts of Flanders spent their money making the town's guildhalls, palaces and churches as impressive as they could. All this glory came to an end when their harbour silted up and made trade impossible. Bruges is known as the 'Venice of the North', and its network of canals, bridges (Brugge means bridges) and tall Gothic buildings reminds you very much of its Italian counterpart.

STATION FACILITIES

The station is on the southern edge of the town, one mile from the city centre. If you don't feel like a walk (although it is quite pleasant through the large park) get any of the buses going to the Markt, close to where the main tourist information is situated.

Train information	Mon.–Fri.: 7 a.m.–7 p.m.
	Sat.–Sun.: 9.30 a.m.–5.30 p.m.
	(Tel. 382382, multi-lingual)
Reservations	Same hours as above
Tourist information	Room reservation only, Mon.–Sat. 2.45 p.m.–9 p.m.
	(mid April to mid Oct. only).
	Other services, Burg 11.
Foreign exchange	Mon., Wed., Thurs., Fri., Sat.,
	June–Sept.: 9 a.m.–6 p.m.
Left-luggage lockers	Closed 1 a.m.–3.30 a.m.
	No access 1.30 a.m.–4 a.m.
Buffet	6.30 a.m.–9 p.m. (Sundays from 7.00 a.m.)
Cycle hire	7.00 a.m.–9 p.m.
Station shuts	1.30 a.m.–4 a.m.

Daily trains to: Cologne, Vienna, Koblenz, Berlin, Belgrade, Munich, Salzburg, Basel, Brig, Milan, Brussels, Paris.

TOURIST INFORMATION AND ADDRESSES

The tourist office is at Burg 11 (Tel. 448686) and is open April to
September, Mon.–Fri.: 9.30 a.m.–6.30 p.m. Sat. and Sun. 10
a.m.–12.30 p.m., 2 p.m.–6.30 p.m. and October to March, Mon.–
Fri.: 9.30 a.m.–12.45 p.m., 2 p.m.–5.45 p.m. Sat. 10 a.m.–12.45
p.m., 2 p.m.–5.45 p.m. Closed Sunday. They will sell you a map (20
BF) and give you leaflets, fix up a bed for you and change your
currency. The post office is nearby at the Markt.

City phone code 50.

SEEING

The main things to see are: THE BELFRY on the Markt, built from the
thirteenth to the fifteenth century. Climb up for a good view of the
layout of the old town and listen out for the CARILLON (bell concert).
Two museums right next door to each other on the Dyver are
GRUUTHUSE and GROENINGE (closed at lunchtime, and on Tuesdays in
winter). Gruuthuse is a museum of applied arts, housed in a
particularly beautiful fifteenth-century mansion, while Groeninge is
devoted to Flemish Renaissance painting and contemporary art.
Joined on to Gruuthuse is the thirteenth-century CHURCH OF OUR
LADY, containing Michelangelo's 'Madonna and Child'. The BEGIJN-
HOF (a Belgian type of convent) is in a peaceful location off the
Wijngaardplein. You can wander around the interior and the grounds
for free or pay a few francs to visit the museum. The canal boat trips
may seem a rip-off at around 130 BF a go, but they're actually quite
good value as you get an added perspective on the town and they don't
rush. Bus fares are 30 BF for any distance, but as you can see most of
Bruges on foot, you shouldn't need to use them much. If you're
wanting to see 'Alternative Flanders', try taking one of the cheap bus
tours offered by Quasimodo's. They are very good, covering
everything from beer tasting to the WWI and two cemeteries, expertly
guided (Tel. 318657 or call at 52 Engelendalelaan).

SLEEPING

Try and stay central as all the sights in Bruges are close together;
bear in mind that the town gets its fair share of visitors in summer, so
get there early. The Youth Hostel is at Baron Ruzettelaan 143 (Tel.
352679). It's not too central, but OK, although more expensive than

some of the other hostels in town. There is an 11 p.m. curfew and you'll need an IYHF card and 295–360 BF for B&B. Closed 10 a.m.–5 p.m. and all through October to mid-February. Take bus 2 to Steenbrugge and get off shortly after the canal.

Camping St Michiels is at Tillegemstraat 55, St Michiels (Tel. 380819), 75 BF per person, 90 BF per tent. Quite a way out: take bus 7 from the station or 't Zand. Change traveller's cheques here free of commission.

The Snuffel Travellers Inn is good value, from 310 BF for B&B. It's at Ezelstraat 49 (Tel. 333133). Though not exactly luxurious, it is comfortable, central and friendly and has recently been reno-vated. There is a good choice of reasonably priced meals and the bar has a 'happy hour' each evening. Get there early as there are only 50 beds. Try Bauhaus at Langestraat 135–137, which has 105 beds (Tel. 341093). Cost from 300 BF to 900 BF for double, B&B, five minutes from market place, near the windmills. Also Bruno's Youth Hostel, Dweersstraat 26 (Tel. 340232). Rooms booked per group, smallest group is four people, cost 1500 BF inc. breakfast. 10 minute's walk from station, five minutes from market.

EATING AND NIGHTLIFE

As Bruges is not a university town, there's no specific cheap studenty area, but you can get by. The Lotus at Wapenmakers Straat do a good 'plat du jour' for lunch, and the Ganzespel at Ganzestraat 37 do a 'menu du jour' for about 220 BF. There are late-night cafés dotted around the old town; Vlissinge on Bleker-straat claims to be among the oldest in Europe.

Brussels
(Brussel – Flemish, Bruxelles – French)

Brussels is a real patchwork of old and new: a city of extreme contrasts, from the seventeenth-century GRAND' PLACE to the modern skyscrapers of the multinationals, and the new EEC headquarters. The main part of this capital which is worth seeing is enclosed in quite a small area of the old town; don't waste your time on the new 'cement heap', as predictably there's nothing unique or particularly Belgian about it. The city revolves round 'the most beautiful square in Europe' – the Grand' Place. Try to view it in daytime, and then again when it's floodlit at night.

STATION FACILITIES

Brussels has three main stations: the Gare du Nord, Gare du Midi and Gare Centrale. Though Centrale handles few international trains, it is conveniently located for the Grand' Place area, and there are interconnecting trains between the three stations every 15–20 minutes. Trains leave daily for Holland, Denmark, Germany, Switzerland, Italy and France. It takes less than 2½ hours to get to Paris or Amsterdam from Brussels.

	NORTH (Nord/Noord) STATION	SOUTH (Midi/Zuid) STATION	CENTRAL (Centrale/Centraal) STATION
Train information	6.30 a.m.–9 p.m.	6 a.m.–10.15 p.m.	6.30 a.m.–9 p.m.
Reservations	8 a.m.–8 p.m.	Mon.–Fri.: 8 a.m.–8 p.m. Sat., Sun.: 9 a.m.–7 p.m.	8 a.m.–8 p.m.
Foreign exchange	7 a.m.–11 p.m.	6 a.m.–11 p.m.	8 a.m.–8 p.m.
Bar, Buffet	Mon.–Fri.: 6 a.m.–10 p.m. Sat., Sun.: 7 a.m.–9 p.m.	6.15 a.m.–9.45 p.m.	Mon.–Sat.: 6.15 a.m.–9.45 p.m. Sun.: 7 a.m.–9.45 p.m.
Restaurant	Mon.–Fri.: 7.30 a.m.–10 p.m. Sat.–Sun. 7.30 a.m.–7.30 p.m.	6.15 a.m.–9.45 p.m.	Temporarily closed
Left-luggage lockers	Always open	Always open	Closed 1.20 a.m.–3.50 a.m.
Left-luggage store	Always open	Always open	Closed 1 a.m.–3.50 a.m.
Waiting room	Always open	Always open	6 a.m.–10.30 p.m.
Duty officer (Sous-Chef de Gare)	Always open	Always open	Always open
Station shuts	Mon.–Fri.: 1.30 a.m.–2.30 a.m. Sat.–Sun.: 1.30 a.m.–4.45 a.m.	2 a.m.–4 a.m.	1.20 a.m.–3.50 a.m.

There are some booths near the South station selling food, and friteries in the nearby rue de France. For tourist information go to Gare Centrale and walk across Place de l'Europe for three blocks. There's a post office near Gare du Midi (open 24 hours) and at Centrale. You'll find social segregation at the Midi station in the form of the Brussels Tavern, which provides a snack bar, etc. Officially, these are only for the use of Eurocity or IC passengers, but in practice you can get in if reasonably dressed. Don't be tempted to buy anything as the prices are roughly double what you can pay elsewhere in the station. For information on city transport, head down to the metro station at Gare du Midi. Finally, if you arrive late at night when the tourist office is shut, head for the Gare du Nord as there are several student hostels in this area.

TOURIST INFORMATION

The main office is at TIB on Grand' Place (Tel. 513 8940). Open 9 a.m.–6 p.m. (Sun. 9 a.m.–6 p.m. April to September 10 a.m.–2 p.m. in October and November). They'll fix you up with accommodation and give you maps and all the usual handouts. Other organizations providing help with accommodation and what to see are: ACOTRA, rue de la Madelaine 51 (Tel. 512 8607 and 512 5540). This youth organ-

ization provides a *free room-finding service*. They're open weekdays 10 a.m.–6 p.m., Thurs. to 7 p.m., Sat. to 1 p.m. INFO-JEUGD/JEUNES, in rue Marché-aux-Herbes 27 (Tel. 512 3274) is near the Grand' Place and is open Mon.–Fri.: 12 a.m.–6 p.m. National tourist information is available at rue du Marché-aux-Herbes 61 (Tel. 5123030), just behind Grand' Place.

• Addresses:
POST OFFICE: First floor of tall building at Place de la Monnaie, poste restante here.
AMEX: 2 Place Louise (Tel. 512 1740), open Mon.–Fri.: 9 a.m.–5 p.m., Sat.: 9.30 a.m.–noon.

UK EMBASSY: Britannia House, 28 rue Joseph II (Tel. 217 9000).
US EMBASSY: 27 Boulevard du Régent (Tel. 513 3830).
CANADIAN EMBASSY: 2 Ave. de Tervuren (Tel. 735 6040).
AUSTRALIAN EMBASSY: 6 rue Guimard (Tel. 231 0500).
AMBULANCE: (Tel. 100)
POLICE: (Tel. 101)
24-HOUR CHEMIST: Tel. 479 1818, 648 8000
CITY PHONE CODE: 2

• **Getting about:** Basically, there's a flat rate of around 35 BF within the city which is valid for transfers between metro, bus and tram. There's also a tourist pass which gives unlimited travel for one day, costing 140 BF. You can also buy a ten-trip pass from metro stations for 220 BF, or a five-trip pass for 155 BF. For information on city transport, there are offices under the Place Rogier, Porte de Namur and Gare Midi.

One tip – if using the metro take a map with you, there is limited information posted.

SEEING

If you have only a single day, a bus tour is the best bet. But try to avoid the traditional ones in luxury coaches, six languages and which end your tour at a lace shop where the driver gets a backhander – there's usually a much better alternative with Chatterbus. It's run by the former manager of one of the city's youth hostels and aimed at the eurorail type of customer. Chatterbus takes in all the places you want to see in Brussels – and a few of the ones the city authorities would rather you didn't. You'll get a good tour of the city and an honest assessment of the places not worth exploring further. The cost is 650 BF, or 500 BF if you are staying at one of the youth hostels. The same group also runs Brussels on Foot tours during the summer at around 250 BF each. If you're in a group they will arrange off-beat tours such as hijacking a tram, or a beer tasting night, including beer-flavoured food and they also have lists of ordinary Brussels residents who are prepared to act as guides for the price of the telephone call to book them. Book through youth hostels, or call Chatterbus directly (Tel. 673 1835). As Chatterbus is more of an informal service than a profit-making business, you may find it only runs on certain days and at certain times. But it is well worth making the effort to try to catch one of these tours.

If you've a bit more time or like to be independent, head for the GRAND' PLACE which is *the* sight of Brussels – a well-preserved collection of Gothic guildhalls and public buildings from the seventeenth century. In the mornings a flower market is held there and at night it's floodlit. Opposite the MAISON DU ROI (the city museum) is the TOWN HALL, considered Brussels' most elegant building. MANNEKEN-PIS (a small statue of a boy having a pee) is the symbol of Brussels and is situated behind the Town Hall on rue l'Etuve. There are several stories as to his origin, the main one being that he saved the city by damping down some dynamite – in a natural and effective fashion.

The MUSÉE DES BEAUX ARTS has a good collection of early Flemish masters, including Rubens (free; closed Monday). In contrast, next door is the modern art gallery: the MUSEUM OF ART AND HISTORY, one of the largest in Europe, covering absolutely everything (closed Monday). It is situated at the Parc du Cinquantenaire. The MUSICAL INSTRUMENT MUSEUM has the largest collection in the world (over 4,000).

The FLEA MARKET at Place du Jeu de Balle is at its best on Saturday and Sunday mornings. If you've any time left, try and see the PALAIS DE JUSTICE, closed weekends, ST MICHAEL'S CATHEDRAL and ERASMUS' HOUSE.

Paris has the Eiffel Tower and London Big Ben, but Brussels' big monument (apart from Manneken Pis) is the ATOMIUM, an immense model of an iron molecule, which was built to celebrate the 1958 International Exhibition at Heysel. At the foot of the Atomium is MINI-EUROPE, a collection of 75 models of well known European sights. Spot the places you have seen, but at a price, 350 BF. Open June–October. Also in the same area, known as Bruparck, there are a water theme park, a planetarium and an IMAX cinema.

A few interesting day-trips from Brussels are: LEUVEN, a medieval university town (20 minutes by train); WATERLOO, site of the battle, now with museums; and BOKRIJK, the largest open-air museum in Europe with over a hundred reconstructions of medieval buildings (April–October). Trains from any Brussels station (90 minutes). Note that it is quite a walk from the Waterloo station to the Wellington Museum – and too far to walk to the battlefield (though a bus runs in peak season).

There is a good amusement park at Bierges – a half-hour journey from Gare du Nord. Called 'Walibi', it costs around 450 BF (all-in ticket).

SLEEPING

Unless you're prepared to go a long way out of town, your choice is limited to hostelling or hotelling (the campsites are miles out). There's not much difficulty getting a bed in Brussels, even in summer, and things are getting easier. The best area to concentrate your efforts on is round the Gare du Nord. If you have any trouble ACOTRA (see under tourist info) will find a bed for you.

● **Student hostels:** Sleep Well at rue de la Blanchisserie 27 (Tel. 218 5050) is the best value in the city. It's clean, central (near Gare du Nord and next to City 2 shopping complex), cheap and has a good atmosphere. It makes an effort to be different, and in fact the piped background music is all classical. Dormitory beds are around 280 BF, singles 430 BF and doubles 780 BF. Closes 10 a.m.–5 p.m. In July and August it has a big dormitory 'Sleep In' at only 200 BF including breakfast and showers. Try to reserve ahead as it's popular. In summer, it arranges city tours by local students. Sleep Well will be moving in 1991, but intends to stay in the same part of town.

Another student hostel which offers good value is CHAB at 8 rue Traversiere (Tel. 217 0158). It has 190 beds in dorms (290 BF), 3/4 bedded rooms (370 BF), twins (440 BF), singles (540 BF) and a 'Sleep In' (240 BF), close to the Botanique metro station, or 10 minutes' walk from the Gare du Nord. Although school groups are accepted in low season, the preferred age range in summer is 18–35. Open from 7.30 a.m.–2 a.m. This hostel also has bike rental (150 BF/day) and has kitchen, laundry and locker facilities. They organize walking tours of Brussels and free (or very cheap) music and art events plus an open-air cinema at the nearby Botanique Culture Centre.

● **Youth hostels:** There's a hostel at Heilige Geeststraat 2 (Tel. 5110 436) near the Kappelle Kerk/Église de la Chapelle, head down Keiterslaan from the Central station. It's known as the Breugel and costs from 340 BF to 560 BF including breakfast. You'll need an IYHF card. Also try Maison Internationale Etudiants, Chaussée de Wavre 205 (Tel. 648 9787), metro to Porte de Namur or bus to Place de Luxembourg. Open June–Sept. Costs 290 BF to 350 BF including breakfast and shower.

The International Accommodation Centre Jacques Brel, at rue de la Sablonnière 30 (Tel. 218 0187). It has 134 beds and charges between 340 BF and 560 BF including breakfast. It is open all year round, but booking is essential in summer. Has a cafeteria, information and TV room.

• **Pensions/hotels:** There are a few at Avenue Fonsny (opposite Gare du Midi): the Merlo and Hôtel le Petit Coq are both OK and reasonably priced by Brussels standards. Hôtel Sabina at 78 rue du Nord (Tel. 218 2637) and Hôtel De L'Yser, 9–13 rue d'Edimbourg (Tel. 511 7459) are worth investigating. The Hotel Du Grand Colombier at rue du Colombier (Tel. 217 9622 or 219 5136) charges around 980 BF for a double, including breakfast. Ask at TIB for other suggestions.

• **Camping:** Try Beersel, Steenweg op Ukkel 75 (Tel. 376 2561), 9 km south of the city, or Paul Rosmant, at Warandeberg 52 (Tel. 782 1009) although the latter, while nearer town, is only open between April and the end of September. Metro to Kraainem, then bus 30 to Place St Pierre. Also Grimbergen at Veldkanstraat 64 (Tel. 269 2597), bus G from Gare du Nord to terminus, then walk.

EATING AND NIGHTLIFE

It's easy to eat cheaply and well in Brussels. Use the stalls on the main shopping streets for waffles. There are plenty of fast-food chains and no shortage of cheap restaurants with fixed-price meals. For a splash out, go along the rue des Bouchers, trying the varieties of moules marinières (360–400 BF). The department stores offer good food at reasonable prices and the shopping centre, City 2, located off Place Rogier (5 minutes from Gare du Nord), has several cafés; the one on the top floor does soup and as much salad as you can get on your plate for around 100 BF. Open 9 a.m.–8.30 p.m. The Vietnamese and African restaurants are also good value and Le Breton, 59 rue des Drapiers, offers authentic Belgian food, beer and wines in a studenty atmosphere.

Head for the Gare du Midi – the student quarter – for pubs, clubs, etc. Discos are expensive, so make do with a lively pub if you can.

Try Le Dolle Mol, 52 rue des Eperonniers, for the young crowd. To meet the locals go to La Morte Subite at rue Montagne aux Herbes Potagères or Bierodrome, Place Fernand Cocq 21. Films are good value (usually 160 BF for students), and the Styx, 72 rue de l'Arbre Bénit, shows revival films with midnight meals, which usually attract an interesting crowd.

Southern Belgium

The main line to Luxembourg passes through Namur and the Ardennes. To explore the area, it's best to base yourself at NAMUR; the regional tourist office is at rue Notre Dame 3 (Tel. 22 29 98). For information on the city, go to the pavilion next to the station or the Info-Jeunes at the belfry in the town (Tel. 714740). Namur has one of the friendliest youth hostels in Europe at Avenue Felicien Rops 8 (Tel. 22 36 88, bus 4 from the station).

Antwerp
(Antwerpen – Flemish, Anvers – French)

Belgium's second city is famous for its flourishing diamond trade, its shipping and fine art. There are two stations: Berchem and Central. International trains stop only at Berchem, except for those coming from Paris and Amsterdam. Opposite Central Station is the information pavilion (open 8.30 a.m.–8 p.m. weekdays, 9 a.m.–7 p.m. Saturdays, and 9 a.m.–5 p.m. Sundays). They'll give you maps (20 BF) and brochures on what to see, and city transport information. The main tourist office is at Grote Markt 15 (open 8.30 a.m.–6 p.m. weekdays; 9 a.m.–5 p.m. weekends). Most sights are concentrated in the old town: OUR LADY'S CATHEDRAL, PETER PAUL RUBENS HOUSE, the ROYAL MUSEUM OF FINE ART with over 2,500 paintings and an excellent exhibition of eight centuries of northern painting, the GROTE MARKT, ST CHARLES BORROMEO'S CHURCH, the PLANTIN-MORETUS MUSEUM of sixteenth-century printing, and CASTLE STEEN – a maritime museum. Three-quarters of the museums are shut on

Mondays. There are free diamond-cutting exhibitions and tours of diamond works – ask at tourist information.

The student hostel 'Boomerang' at Volkstraat 58 (Tel. 2384782) is centrally located and reasonably priced, though reports of standards vary. Take bus 23 from Central Station or tram 8 from Berchem Station. Hôtel Florida, at De Keyserlei 59, is right in front of Central Station. Don't be taken in by the 'rooms for tourists' advertised in cafés around the station – they're brothels. The New International Youth Pension at 256 Provinciestraat (Tel. 2300522) is clean, friendly and near the station, down Pelikaanstraat, 20 minutes to Provinciestraat. The campsite is at Vogelzanglaan (Tel. 2385717), bus 17 to the Crest hotel, and is cheap. The youth hostel is at Eric Sasselaan 2 (Tel. 2384782). Tram 2 or bus 27 from Central Station, to just after bridge across main road. For food, the Prinsstraat area (round the university) has several cafés doing fixed-price menus. The docks area is lively in the evenings and round the Grote Markt there are bars and restaurants – but they're expensive.

CITY PHONE CODE: 3.

Ghent
(Gent – Flemish, Gand – French)

Renowned for its art and flowers and a glut of historic buildings. Day-trippers from Antwerp should get off at Dampoort Station which is nearer the centre, but from all other destinations you go on to St Pieter's Station.

Train information	Daily 7 a.m.–9 p.m. (Tel. 225721/224444)
Reservations	Daily 7 a.m.–8 p.m.
Tourist information	In centre
Foreign exchange	Hours variable, generally 9.00 a.m.–4 p.m., closed lunchtimes and Sundays
Left-luggage lockers	Always access
Buffet	Daily 6.30 a.m.–10 p.m.
Cycle hire	7 a.m.–9 p.m.
Station shuts	Always open

Daily trains to: Cologne, Vienna, Koblenz, Berlin, Belgrade, Munich, Salzburg, Basel, Brig, Milan, Brussels, Paris.

Tram 1 will take you to the centre, Koornmarkt. Tourist informa-
tion is at Botermarkt Crypt, Town Hall (Tel. 253641 and 241555)
April to October: Mon.–Sun.: 9.30 a.m.–6.30 p.m. November to
March: Mon.–Sun.: 9.30 a.m.–4.30 p.m.

CITY PHONE CODE: 91.

All the sights are central and within easy walking distance of one
another. The main sights are: the CATHEDRAL OF ST BAVO,
containing Van Eyck's, 'The Mystic Lamb'; next door is the
BELFRY, 'S'GRAVENSTEEN' – the twelfth-century FLEMISH COUNTS'
CASTLE – and the guildhouses by the KOORNMARKT. As the youth
hostel closed down you are limited to pensions or the university
halls of residence during holidays which are at Stalhof 6 (Tel.
220911), just off Overpoortstraat (open 24 hours, all single rooms).
The university at Overpoortstraat is also your best bet for eats and
nightlife, and has the added advantage of being near the station –
take bus 9, 70, 71 or 90. There is camping at Camping Blaarmeer-
sen, Zuiderlaan 12 (Tel. 215399), bus 51, 52 or 53 to the
Europaburg, then bus 38, or a 20-minute walk from St Pieter's
Station.

BULGARIA

Entry requirements	Passport and visa
Population	9,000,000
Capital	Sofia (pop.: 1,000,000+)
Currency	Leva
	£1 = approx. 5.54 leva
Political system	Republic
Religion	Eastern Orthodox
Language	Bulgarian (Russian widely spoken; some German, French and English understood)
Public holidays	1 Jan.; 3 Mar.; 1, 2, 24 May; 9, 10 Sept.; 7 Nov.
International dialling codes	From UK 010 359
	From USA 011 359
	To UK 0044
	To USA 001

Every year, swarms of tourists from East and West alike flock to the Black Sea coast for the sun. Few venture far from their hotels, leaving much of the country's interior unspoilt. The original Bulgars were an Asiatic tribe who were eventually conquered by Slavs from the north. By the tenth century, Bulgaria had her own empire in which literature and the arts flourished. This process continued till the fourteenth century, when trade helped Bulgaria to become the leader in south-eastern Europe. In 1396, the Ottomans became worried at what was going on and moved in. For the next 500 years they hung about to keep a check on things, and only left after the Russo-Turkish war of 1877 obliged them to do so. Fortunately during this long period the Bulgarians managed to preserve their native culture by giving refuge to writers and artists in their monasteries, many of which survive. The Bulgarians backed the losing side in the First World War, and supported the Allies in the Second. Shortly after the Soviet liberation from the Germans in 1944, Bulgaria became a Socialist People's Republic, in the Russian mould. The ousting, during 1989, of the hard-line communist leader, Todor Zhivkov, led towards democratic reforms. With the emergence of political parties and the free elections of summer 1990, Bulgaria followed the trend in other eastern bloc countries, but with the reformed and renamed communists holding power.

With new freedoms, ethnic tension between the Bulgarians and the formerly repressed Turkish muslim minority occurred. Prices here are extremely low and hard currency buys the traveller a lot.

BULGARIAN STATE RAILWAYS (BDZ)

Trains tend to be overcrowded and slow in Bulgaria. Occasionally things come together and they run on time, but this is the exception rather than the rule. There are three types of trains: express (Ekspresen), fast (Brzi), and slow (Putnichki). Avoid the latter at all costs. Unfortunately, BIJ only run as far as Sofia. In theory, it should be quite easy to cross the country to the Black Sea coast and return again the same day – trains leave Sofia early every morning, arriving at Burgas in the early afternoon. In practice, there are often delays at intermediate stations. Whenever possible, buy your ticket at least a day before setting off (reservations are compulsory on all expresses), or arrive early at the station to be sure of a seat. An alternative would be to take the overnight sleeper trains. Fortunately for eurorailers, Sofia is not too far across the Yugoslavian border: take the 'Marmara' Express from Belgrade to Dimitrovgrad, then the normal fare to Sofia. Try to buy the ticket before getting the train, if possible elsewhere in other Eastern countries, as the fare charged on board is higher. Bulgaria is now part of Inter Rail.

TRAIN INFORMATION

Few of the staff speak English, so you might find German and French more helpful. Timetables are given in the Cyrillic alphabet, but there is a Latin equivalent shown against international trains. If you're stuck, try: 'Ot koi peron zaminava vlaka za . . . ?' (From which platform does the train to . . . leave?) Depend on your Thomas Cook European Timetable for most of the time.

• **Reservations:** To be sure of a seat you'll have to reserve at least one day in advance. Reservations are obligatory on international expresses and can be made through a Balkantourist or RILA office.

• **Night travel:** All couchettes and sleepers are operated by the state railways and fall well short of Western standards, and cost a fraction of the price.

• **Eating on trains:** There's either a buffet car or mini-bar on all fast trains.

• **Sofia** has one of the most modern and impressive stations you are ever likely to find with all facilities except showers. It is open from 4 a.m. to 1 a.m. and the Balkantourist money exchange office is open from 6 a.m.–10 p.m.

TOURIST INFORMATION

There are Balkantourist offices in nearly every large town. They answer all your travel and accommodation problems as well as giving out tourist information. With the recent political upheavals be prepared for street names changing.

• **ISIC bonuses:** With an IUS card (obtainable from ORBITA Youth Travel Bureau, 45a Boulevard Stambolijski, Sofia), you can get reductions for international train travel within the Eastern Bloc, and cheaper entrance charges to many museums and galleries.

• **Money matters:** 1 leva = 100 stotinki.
Banking hours are 8 a.m.–12 noon. Visitors to Bulgaria now receive a bonus when they change cash or traveller's cheques at Balkantourist exchange bureaux. In theory, you're supposed to have prepaid for two nights' accommodation, but in practice they don't worry you. A compulsory currency exchange for tourists of $15 per day, in any hard currency, is payable on entry. There is no need to use money changers now that the official rate is so good.

• **Shops:** Open 9 a.m.–8 p.m. with a siesta on Monday from 1 p.m.–2 p.m. Look out for Corecom which sell Bulgarian goods at favourable prices.

• **Museums:** Tend to shut on Mondays, but there's no fixed pattern; opening times also tend to vary.

• **Language:** Like the Russian language, Bulgarian is written with the Cyrillic alphabet.

CYRILLIC ALPHABET	ENGLISH EQUIVALENT	SOUND VALUE	CYRILLIC ALPHABET	ENGLISH EQUIVALENT	SOUND VALUE
А а	A	for Anglia	П п	P	for Park
Б б	B	for Bed	Р р	R	for Road
В в	V	for Vault	С с	S	for Soft
Г г	G	for Garage	Т т	T	for Trail
Д д	D	for Day	У у	Ou	for Cool
Е е	E	for Engine	Ф ф	F	for Fair
Ж ж	Zh	for Azure	Х х	H	for Hot
З з	Z	for Zebra	Ц ц	Ts	for Tsar
И и	I	for In	Ч ч	Ch	for Cheese
Й й	Y	for Yes	Ш ш	Sh	for Ship
К к	K	for Kirb	Щ щ	Sht	for Ashtray
Л л	L	for Lip	Ъ ъ	U	for Under
М м	M	for Morris	Ь ь	J	for Yodel
Н н	N	for Nut	Ю ю	Yu	for You
О о	O	for Austin	Я я	Ya	for Yard

It is also useful to remember that in Bulgaria a nod means 'No' (Ne), and that a horizontal shake means 'Yes' (Da).

SLEEPING

When dealing with Balkantourist offices, bear in mind that they always try to fill up their own hotels first. Ask for a room in a private home whenever possible, as they're always a lot cheaper and more interesting. If you decide to bypass the tourist office and take up a local on the offer of a room, you're supposed to register this with the police. There's no real need to do this if you've already got a couple of official stamps on the card you were given at the border, for the mention of the police will bring many a host out in a sweat. Be careful here, for if you cannot account for several nights, you could face a fine. ORBITA (the student travel service) will find you a bed for about 6–7 leva in one of their hostels any time between mid-July and mid-September. For advance bookings write to International Tourist Relations, ORBITA Youth Travel Office, 45a Boulevard Stambolijski, Sofia. Camping costs about 1.50 leva per tent and 2 leva per person on any of the hundred or so official campsites. Accommodation has to be paid for in hard currency.

EATING AND NIGHTLIFE

Eat as much as you can in Bulgaria as food is tasty and cheap. National dishes have a strong Turkish influence, with lamb and pork as the most common meats. Try haiduchki kebab (lamb cooked with onions, white wine and pepper) or one of their wonderful meat and vegetable dishes, slowly cooked in an earthenware pot, known as gyuvech. You cannot go wrong with any of the charcoal-roasted meat dishes with fresh salad. Yoghurt originated here and the Bulgarians are addicted to it, the thick sheep's milk type is particularly good, but not always available. Their ice cream is excellent, too. Vegetarian travellers should try shopska salad, vegetarian versions of gyuvech, or one of several aubergine dishes, including iman bayaldu. For drinks try any slivova, a spirit made from plums. Bulgarian wine has become well known in the West, and can be enjoyed cheaply here. Avoid the Bulgarian beer, it has little to recommend it. (Jippy tummy is not uncommon when in Bulgaria and as very few loos supply paper, bring plenty with you!)

Most Bulgarian towns have at least one theatre, several cities having open-air ones. A range of plays, operas and ballet can be seen. See the local Balkantourist office for details and tickets. They will also give information on arranged folklore events. Also look out for occasional rock concerts with local bands.

Sofia

The 5,000-year-old city of Sofia lies in the middle of the Balkan peninsula. It's got a lot going for it: it's the 'greenest city in Europe', has skiing (from December to April) less than half an hour away, and has some fascinating buildings – mosques, museums and churches which range from Byzantine to Roman, Turkish and Greek architecture.

TOURIST INFORMATION

The Balkantourist office at the station will change money but does little else. It's open 7 a.m.–10 p.m. The main office is on Dondukov Ulica 37 (open 7 a.m.–10 p.m. daily); they will find you a private room and give you a map and general information. Take tram 1 or 7 and look out for the Banya Bashi Mosque, this brings you to the centre. The Balkantourist office is a short walk away, down the side of the

Central Department Store (TSUM). For train information telephone 311111.

● **Addresses:**

CENTRAL POST OFFICE: Gurko Ulica 2, open daily 7 a.m.–8.30 p.m. Also poste restante here.

ORBITA – STUDENT TRAVEL OFFICE: Will grudgingly find you a room in a student hostel. 45a Boulevard Stambolijski (Tel. 879552), continue along Georgi Dimitrov to Pl. Lenin, then head down Stambolijski away from Balkan-Sheraton hotel. Open daily 9 a.m.–12 p.m. and 1 p.m.–5 p.m., but times unreliable.

RILA: International Railway Bureau, Gurko Ulica 5 (Tel. 870777). All tickets for international journeys, except those wanted for today's date, are to be bought here. Open daily 8 a.m.–11.30 a.m., 12 noon–4 p.m. Make sure you have your exchange forms with you.

UK EMBASSY: 65 Boulevard Tolbuhin (Tel. 885361).

US EMBASSY: 1a Boulevard Stambolijski (Tel. 884801).

24-HOUR CHEMIST: Alabin Ulica 29 (Tel. 879029).

CITY TELEPHONE CODE: 02.

● **Getting about:** The city buses and trams are fair enough. Buy your tickets in advance from the special kiosks, and also grocery stalls. The main area worth seeing, however, is easily walked around. A metro system is under construction, expect changes to bus/tram routes as this is opened.

SEEING

The two main churches of Sofia are the twentieth-century, neo-Byzantine ALEXANDER NEVSKY, and the sixth-century ST SOPHIA on Nevski Square. The former, topped with its golden domes, is dedicated to the Russians who fell liberating Bulgaria from the Ottoman Empire. The fascinating crypt is stuffed full of beautiful · icons from all over the country. Also worth seeing is the BOYANA CHURCH, at the foot of Mount Vitosha, with its restored medieval frescos. In the courtyard of the Sheraton hotel is the fourth-century ST GEORGE ROTUNDA, the oldest standing building in Sofia. During 1989 the St George and St Sophia churches were both closed for restoration, for an unspecified length of time.

The NATIONAL ARCHAEOLOGICAL MUSEUM, 2 Boulevard Stambolijski (closed Mondays) is in the former Buyuk mosque. It has lost many of its artefacts to the new NATIONAL HISTORY MUSEUM. This museum, at 2 Boulevard Vitosha, contains the national treasures, including Thracian gold and ecclesiastical art plus much more. Probably the best one to visit, open 10.30 a.m.–6.30 p.m., Friday 2 p.m.–6.30 p.m., closed Mondays. The MUSEUM OF THE REVOLUTIONARY MOVEMENT IN BULGARIA, 14 Boulevard Russki, is the official version of the takeover and a monument to party members long gone. In the light of recent events it would be an interesting insight into the past, but has the drawback of being presented entirely in Bulgarian.

At one end of Boulevard Russki is the September 9th Square, with, on the South side, the MAUSOLEUM of GEORGI DIMITROV, the first leader of the People's Republic. His embalmed remains can be viewed three afternoons a week and are protected by goose-stepping guards. On the opposite side of the square is the former royal palace, built during the Ottoman empire. This now houses the NATIONAL ETHNOLOGICAL MUSEUM, but has lost many items to the National Museum. The NATIONAL GALLERY OF PAINTING AND SCULPTURE is being relocated to Alexander Nevski Square, previously open 9 a.m.–6 p.m., closed Monday afternoons and all day Tuesday.

On Georgi Dimitrov Boulevard there is the sixteenth-century BANYA BASHI MOSQUE, behind which is the run-down mineral baths building. Both of these are undergoing renovation during 1990. Opposite the mosque is the HALI market hall, built in the National Revival style in 1910; due to 'restoration' the inside has been spoilt.

SLEEPING

Use either Balkantourist on Dondukov Ulica 37 or ORBITA for private accommodation and expect to pay 20 leva for a double through Balkantourist, and less through ORBITA. Do not be surprised if Balkantourist give you the keys of the house, and there is no one there, and be aware that your host will probably not speak English. If you're arriving late and these offices are shut, stay in the station and 'look lost'. You'll find locals coming up to you and offering a place in their house for about 10 leva a person. People do halve this price by *discreetly* paying them in hard currency (sterling, dollars, marks, francs). If the trend in Bulgaria follows that in other eastern European countries, expect the cost of accommodation to soar in 1991.

ORBITA Student Hostel, Anton Ivanov 76 (Tel. 652952). This official students' residence (you'll need ISIC) is OK and not too far out from the centre, tram 2 or 9 to road junction of Anton Ivanov and Georgi Trajkov.

Hotel Pliska at 87 Boulevard Lenin (Tel. 723721) is one of the cheapest available. Singles cost 20 leva, doubles 36 including breakfast. Also worth a try is Hotel Bulgaria at 4 Boulevard Ruski, near the Dimitrov Mausoleum (Tel. 871977) or Hotel Slavia at Ulica Sofijski Geroi 2 (Tel. 525551), tram 13 from station, about three stops down General Totleben.

If things look desperate, make your way to the university, set in a park off Boulevard Lenin (trams 1, 2, 7, 9, 14 and 18, then change to 4 or 10) and ask around for a student to let you share. Camping Vrana (Tel. 781213) is on Boulevard Lenin and offers campsites and bungalows. Bus 313, 213 or 305 from station and then bus 5 or 6. Another site is Cherniya Koss (Tel. 571129), take tram 5 from the city to the end of the route, then bus 58 or 59.

EATING AND NIGHTLIFE

Food's cheap and good, and eating out in Sofia can cost far less than picnicking in Western Europe, although the price is expected to rise rapidly. Count on 10 to 15 leva for a full and excellent meal. For Bulgarian specialities, try Koprivshtitsa, on 3 Boulevard Vitosha; for Russian food, try Krim, 2 Dobroudja St; and for German food, Berlin on 2 Boulevard V. Zaimor. There are new 'European' restaurants too, Forum and Havana – both centrally located. If you're really cutting corners, there are plenty of self-service places and an open-air market on Georgi Kirkov Ulica near the station. There are also Bulgarian-style fast food places on Vitosha.

Balkantourist fill you in on what shows and concerts are on. These tend to be more classical than popular, but the National Folk Ensemble put on some good things.

EXCURSIONS

If your long journey to Sofia has filled your lungs with smoke, hike up to the VITOSHA MOUNTAINS NATIONAL PARK, five miles from Sofia. Take tram 5 to its last stop, in the Kinyazevo district, then a short uphill walk to the cable car. Alternatively there are several bus routes up to Vitosha, ask at Balkantourist. The mountain air will do you good, and if you're feeling energetic ZLATNIY MOSTOVE, the glacial moraine, should provide the necessary challenge.

As Bulgaria is known for its monasteries another possible excursion from Sofia is to the RILA MONASTERY, around 75 miles south. Balkantourist arrange day trips; alternatively you can get yourself there, with difficulty, by bus from the Ouchna Koucha terminus, or by train to Kocherinovo station, then bus. Camping Bor is within walking distance of Rila. Ask at Balkantourist or the bus station for the services, and book accommodation in advance.

Plovdiv

Plovdiv is only two-and-a-half hours from Sofia by train and is Bulgaria's second largest city. Whilst much of this city is now industrialized, with many modern grey apartments, there is much worth seeing in the old town.

The main Balkantourist office is at 34 Moska Boulevard (Tel. 55 51 42), trolley-bus 2 from the railway station, to just over the river. Pick up a map here, but they are of little help with accommodation. Try Hotel Bulgaria, 13 Ul. Patriarch Eutimii (Tel. 22 60 64/22 55 64), upwards of 15 Leva, or Hotel Leipzig (Tel. 23 22 50), 76 Rousski Blvd, similarly priced. The nearest campsite is Trakiya (Tel. 55 13 60), 4 km west, bus 4 or 23.

For food try the cafes around the 19 Noemvri Square, restaurants in the old town, or in the cheaper hotels. If you are really cutting cost there is also a self-service canteen on Maksim Gorki, and another opposite the railway station.

The main attractions are in the old town, located on the three hills which gave rise to Plovdiv's Roman name of Trimontium. Around the maze of cobbled streets rise houses of the National Revival Period and the remains of the old fortress walls. A restored ROMAN AMPHITHEATRE is situated in this area, and is now used for theatrical performances. Also in the old town is the ETHNOGRAPHICAL MUSEUM and an Icon Exhibition. The partial remains of a Roman stadium may be seen in 19 Noemvri Square and other ROMAN REMAINS in the Tsentralen Square. Also in 19 Noemvri Square is the fifteenth-century DJOUMAYA MOSQUE. The ARCHAEOLOGICAL MUSEUM, in Saedinenie Square has many relics of ancient Plovdiv. However much of its excellent collection of Thracian gold has recently been moved to the National History Museum in Sofia, and replaced with mock-ups.

Veliko Târnovo

The capital of Bulgaria until the Ottoman invasion of 1396, this old city on the Jantra river is stunning, and well worth the trouble of getting there. Take the train from Sofia towards Varna, and change at Gorna-Orjahovitza, use table 822 of Thomas Cook's timetable. You will arrive at the station, on the southern outskirts, at the foot of the Sveta Gora hill. Use one of the many buses to the centre.

Balkantourist is at 1 Vasil Levski (Tel. 2 18 36). Try Motel-camping Sveta Gora for tents and chalets, bus 14 from Balkantourist, or bus 15 from the station. A moderate price hotel in the old town is Hotel Jantra, 1 Velohova Zavera Square (Tel. 2 03 91).

The two main areas of interest are VAROSHA and TSAREVETS. Walk around these to get the best from them, but prepare for tired legs – it is not exactly flat. From Balkantourist head into Varosha, the old Ottoman town, armed with your map. The National Revival Museum is on the site of the Ottoman town hall, or Konak, with the Revolutionary Museum nearby, in a former Turkish prison. All museums are shut on Monday. Tsarevets, almost completely enclosed in a loop of the river, is approached by a stone causeway. The continuing digs turn up more each year. Parts of the impressive ramparts are on view, as are the Palace ruins. The views from Tsarevets make the uphill struggle, literally, well worthwhile, even for those not interested in old stones. One of the views, in an adjacent loop of the river is the Trapezica Hill. Here excavations of several of the old Bulgarian rulers' churches and other buildings is in progress.

Black Sea Coast – Varna and Bourgas

The two main cities are Varna and Bourgas, each reachable by around six trains a day from Sofia. Along the whole coast accommodation is difficult, if not impossible to find during the summer, due to the increasing popularity of the area, both to eastern and western tourists. Varna has more going for it, with Roman remains and several reasonable museums. Buses can be taken from either Varna or Bourgas along the coast.

In Varna there is a Balkantourist office, open all year, opposite the railway station, at Ul Avram Gachev (Tel. 222389). A hotel that is worth trying is the Moussala, 3 Ul Moussala (Tel. 223925). The nearest campsite is Galata, bus 17 to the end, then a short walk. Bourgas has a Balkantourist office at 2 Ul Purvi Mai (Tel. 45553). The cheapest hotel is probably Primonets at 1 Liliana Dimitrova (Tel. 44117).

CZECHOSLOVAKIA

Entry requirements	Passport and advance visa (under review)*
Population	15,500,000
Capital	Prague (pop.: 1,500,000)
Currency	Koruna
	£1 = 50.1 Kčs.
Political system	Federal Republic
Religions	Catholic and Protestant
Languages	Czech and Slovak (some German and English understood)
Public holidays	1 Jan.; Easter Monday; 1, 9 May; 25, 26 Dec.
International dialling codes	From UK 01042
	From USA 01142
	To UK 0044
	To USA 001

The independent state of Czechoslovakia came into being in 1918 with the political union of Bohemia, Moravia and Slovakia, all former provinces of the Austro-Hungarian empire. Czechoslovakia prospered until 1939. Geographically, Czechoslovakia is at the very heart of Europe – not a good place to be at the best of times, but before the Second World War it was positively disastrous. Hitler was chafing at the bit, demanding that Czechoslovakia became a German-speaking land. France, Britain and Italy agreed to let him have it in 1939, and before long Poland and Hungary got in on the act and divided up the rest. After the war, Czechoslovakia was restored to its original boundaries, except for Ruthenia which the Russians decided to hang on to.

Dubcek's ill-fated attempt to combine Communist ideology with democracy in 1968 brought Soviet disapproval and occupation. Twenty-one years later the peaceful revolution, led by the Civic Forum Movement, saw the collapse of the old order. 1990 confirmed the former dissident playwright, Vaclav Havel, as president, and brought free elections and the departure of the majority of Soviet troops. The country is now undertaking the slow and painful path to a market-led economy. In the meantime expect the exchange rate to vary rapidly, and inflation to take hold.

*For UK passport holders under 21 years the visa fee is £12, the normal fee is £20.

CZECHOSLOVAK STATE RAILWAYS
(Československé státní dráhy, CSD)

The service is a hot contender for the title of slowest in Europe. Like Britain, they have their own 125 – the only trouble is it's 12.5 m.p.h. However, the system is relatively dense, and so most places can be reached by rail. Trains are frequent and tickets are sold according to the speed of the train. Don't cut corners here as it's generally recognized that even buses are faster than the expresses. Go for the fastest possible (Expresní or Rychlík). Unfortunately, these sometimes require seat reservations and supplements, and that may mean queues, either at the station or at the Čedok office. Generally avoid travel on Friday and Sunday afternoons. Substantial price rises in September 1990 will almost certainly be repeated during 1991. Since 1990 Inter Rail includes Czechoslovakia.

The delays and hassle of crossing the Czech border have now almost vanished, the trains no longer stopping for a seemingly interminable time. The number of trains crossing the border is expected to increase during 1990–91. The compulsory currency exchange of around £10 (£6 for under 23s) is not now always carried out on board, depending on the crossing. Any 'hard' currency will be accepted.

TRAIN INFORMATION

Take it for granted that the staff will be friendly but won't speak English at information offices so have the German vocabulary at the ready. If you still have no success, try: 'Z kterého nástupiště odjíždí . . . vlak do . . . ?' (From which platform does the train to . . . leave?). However there are generally plenty of timetable boards available. Express trains are marked in bold or red letters, Arrival – Příjezd, Departure – Odjezd. A lot of the left-luggage lockers are vandalized – it's not that you've got the combination wrong. The left-luggage offices normally cost between 2–5 crowns. Don't expect to be able to change money on trains or in stations.

• **Reservations:** Try to reserve well ahead of time to be sure of a seat, as trains are always busy. This is obligatory on some expresses marked with an R in a box, or míst. Use the ARES office, at some 120 stations, if possible. International reservations are made at Čedok or ARES offices. If you are going on to Hungary, it is essential to specify which of the three routes you are taking and get your ticket for the appropriate counter. The crossing points are Štúrovo, Komárom and Rajka.

• **Night travel:** Sleepers and couchettes are operated by the state railways and run on all long journeys. Avoid sleepers as they tend to be expensive.

• **Eating on trains:** There's either a restaurant car or buffet on a few selected fast trains.

• **Rover tickets:** The East Rail Pass, available from Danish State Railways (see p.33), covers Czechoslovakia.

TOURIST INFORMATION

This is mostly handled by Čedok. They suggest tours and supply local information. The student travel offices (CKM) are staffed by students and issue ISIC and IYHF cards. They are normally very good.

• **ISIC bonuses:** 25 per cent off East European train fares, discounts at some museums.

• **Money matters:** 1 koruna (Kčs) = 100 hellers (hal).
Banking hours are Mon.–Fri.: 8 a.m.–3 or 4 p.m. The £10 ($20) per day you were obliged to change should be plenty to keep you going. Spend *all* your koruna, because at present it's difficult to change them back when you leave. Instead, you are given a voucher for your next visit (regardless of whether or not you intend to return). This situation will change when the koruna is made fully convertible, during 1991. It's not worth the risk for the little extra you might get on street transactions. The chances of being conned are so great that your best bet is to avoid them altogether. Until the koruna is fully convertible, expect the black market to flourish. Some private exchange offices are now open, permitted under new laws. There is a minimum currency exchange standing at about DM15 daily.

• **Post offices:** Open from 8 a.m. to 4 p.m.

• **Shops:** Follow the usual pattern, opening at 9 a.m. and shutting at 6 p.m. on weekdays and at noon on Saturdays. Tuzex is the name of the government hard-currency chain, due to be shut down.

• **Museums:** Open Tues.–Sun.: 10 a.m.–5 p.m. Closed Mondays.

SLEEPING

Despite the revolution, the accommodation situation has not improved. If anything, it has got worse. This is due to increased demand and lack of infrastructure; however, expect the situation to improve in time. The prices below are likely to be subject to inflation during 1991. Whenever possible, try (though it's not easy) to arrange for prepaid accommodation through Čedok offices outside Czechoslovakia. If booking through Čedok in London, expect to take 14 days minimum. They also will not book anything less than 3-star half board. In Vienna, their office is at Parkring 12 (Tel. 513 2609). Hotels are graded from 2 to 5 stars. A 2-star double should cost about 300 Kčs per night. Make sure you have agreed beforehand on the cost. It is quite common to be charged more when it comes to paying the bill. In a country where the first language is Czech, the second Russian and the third German, your chances of winning an argument in English are somewhat minimal. Camping is very cheap: 25 Kčs per person. Ask Čedok for their map with lists of all campsites.

Staying at a private home also works out a lot cheaper than hotels, though if you book through Čedok you will usually have to commit to a minimum of three nights.

Apart from Čedok offices, where queues are normally large, it's also possible to find accommodation through the student travel offices (CKM) during July and August. Do not use Ave accommodation service in the station. They charge 100 per cent commission on every night's stay. Go outside the station to Čedok office.

Dormitories are converted into youth hostels (strediska), many of which have good two-bedded rooms for only 60 Kčs per person on an IYHF card, or about 75 Kčs without.

The old requirement to register with the police, and have your visa stamped every night, will apply to fewer people, as visa requirements are abolished. Check the latest situation with tourist offices, before your trip if possible.

EATING AND NIGHTLIFE

Specialities include zeleninová (a vegetable and cream soup) and any dish made from pork (vepřové). For really cheap meals, try any of the self-service stand-up restaurants (automaty). You'll never get it as good again, so eat as much as you can. A lot of the grade-one and -two restaurants have dancing, but apart from this things are very quiet by Western standards. Čedok should be able to help out on what open-air concerts, etc., there might be. The best way to find out what's happening is to ask any young Czechs. They will probably advise you to head towards a wine bar or beer hall where most young people meet. Try Budvar, Prazdroj or any other beer you're recommended, for not only is Czech beer among the best in Europe, it's also the cheapest. If stuck to pay for a meal in local currency anywhere in Eastern Europe, offer to pay in hard currency – they will be delighted!

Bratislava

The largest city and capital of Slovakia, was also the former capital of Hungary. Situated on the Danube, it can be reached by boat from Budapest and Vienna, as well as by train. Despite being an essentially modern city, it still has over 400 historically interesting buildings.

Čedok is at 13 Šturová (Tel. 52002), is not far from the Danube; the student agency, CKM, is at Hviezdoslavou námešti 16 (Tel. 331607). Try Čedok or CKM for accommodation. The CKM hotel Sputnik is at Drieňová 14 (Tel. 234340). Take tram 8 from the centre to the lake on the city outskirts. For camping take tram 12 to the Zupka crossroads, then change to bus 32 for three stops, to one of the sites at Zlaté Piesky (Tel. 65170 or 66028). Pleasant lakeside sites, which also have bungalows.

As with the rest of Czechoslovakia, try the wine bars or beer halls for food. The wine bar, Velki Frantiskani at Dibrivova is in an old cellar, offering good local food and occasional folk music. The local Slovakian wine is worth a try.

The city is dominated by the thirteenth-century BRATISLAVA CASTLE, burnt out in 1811, and rebuilt after the war. Now the home of the Slovak parliament, and the SLOVAK NATIONAL MUSEUM, featuring Slovakian history and archaeology. ST MARTINA'S CATHEDRAL, dating from the fourteenth century, is the resting place of several Hungarian kings and queens. The OLD TOWN HALL, fifteenth-century, now houses the CITY MUSEUM, with a museum of viniculture nearby. A complete contrast is the ultra-modern SNU bridge, spanning the river below the castle. A good view can be had from the restaurant at the top, but do not eat there.

Slovakia

The eastern region of Czechoslovakia occupies around a third of the country. The people have their own strong personality, quite different from the Czech's. Much of the region is unspoilt mountains and forests, and ideal for hiking, as well as visiting the many small towns. From Bratislava head up into the Lesser Carpathian Mountains, an area with many vineyards. To the north of Slovakia are the Low Tatras, with the High Tatras further east. These make up the second highest mountain range in Europe, after the Alps. Take the train from Prague to Poprad-Tatry, a mainly industrialized town, then the local trains up into the hills. Trains go to Tatranska Lomnica, where there is a camping site to base yourself at. Use Thomas Cook's Tables 813 to 815, to get around the region.

Brno

The capital of Moravia and Czechoslovakia's third city has quite a lot to offer. A royal city, founded in the thirteenth century, on the rail line between Prague and Bratislava.

The Čedok office at Divadení 3 (Tel. 23303), and CKM at Česká 11, are your best bets for accommodation suggestions. The city gets filled up with several exhibitions during the year. The nearest camping site is the Obora, 15 km from Brno (Tel. 56575), not easily reached by public transport. Private accommodation may be your best bet.

The ŠPILBERK CASTLE, founded 1277, and rebuilt in the eighteenth century, now houses the MUNICIPAL MUSEUM, undergoing restoration, and ART GALLERY. See the display of torture instruments in the museum. Dominating the city and castle is the CATHEDRAL OF ST PETER AND ST PAUL. Also worth seeing is the OLD TOWN HALL and the CAPUCHIN MONASTERY, complete with mummified monks on display. Also see the colourful outdoor CABBAGE MARKET.

Pilsen (Plzeň)

Basically, this is an ugly, uninspiring place situated in western Bohemia, but if you're a beer-fan it's pilgrimage country, for this is the birthplace of Pilsner Urquell beer. See the BURGHER'S BREWERY, the BREWING MUSEUM on Roosevelt St. The ABBEY OF THE VIRGIN MARY and ST BARTHOLOMEW'S CHURCH are the town's other saving graces.

Prague (Praha)

Prague, the fourteenth-century capital of the Holy Roman Empire, is where to go if you want to step back into medieval life and have all your preconceptions of an Eastern Bloc city shattered. As far as sights are concerned, many consider Prague to be on a par with Paris, London or Rome. We feel it is too, and a good deal of the reason lies in the fact that there are only a tenth of the tourists there to spoil it. It lies in western Bohemia and is a riot of bridges, parks, hills and a fascinating array of architectural styles. Despite the hassles of getting there, we're sure you'll think it was worth it.

STATION FACILITIES

There are three main stations in Prague: Praha–Hlavní Nádraží, Oraha Masarykovo (formerly Střed) and Holešovice. The first two are located close to the centre, with the latter to the north, across the Vltava river. Hlavní is used by domestic services and international trains to Germany, Poland, the Soviet Union and Hungary; Masarykovo is mainly for domestic services. Holešovice has international trains for Germany, the Soviet Union and Hungary.

All these stations are served by the metro system, and have the usual facilities. There are showers at the Hlavni for around 10 Kčs.

TOURIST INFORMATION

From the main station (Praha–Hlavní Nádraží) or the alternative station of Praha–Masarykovo (Střed), walk up Hybernská to the centre. The Prague Information Service is at Na Příkopě 20 (Tel. 54 4444). They'll give you maps, 'what's on' (pick up the excellent 'The Month in Prague') and general information (open Mon.–Fri.: 8 a.m.–8 p.m., Sat.: 8 a.m.–noon).

Čedok, the Czechoslovak national travel organization, has offices all over the centre of town, but foreigners only deal with two. Na Příkopě 18 (Tel. 2127111) change money (you get an extra 36 per cent at this office), arrange rail tickets (expect delays) and operate a room-finding service round the corner at Panská 5 (open Mon.–Fri.: 8 a.m.–10 p.m., Sat.: 8 a.m.–8 p.m., Sun.: 8 a.m.–5 p.m.), Tel. 227004 or 225657.

- **Addresses:**

POST OFFICE: Jindřišská 14, 24-hour service. Also poste restante here.

CKM (the student agency): Žitná ulice 12, 12105 Prague 2. Open Mon.–Fri.: 8 a.m.–10 a.m., 1 p.m.–5 p.m. (Tel. 299941).

FIRST AID: Jungmannová 14 (Tel. 247771).

POLYCLINIC FOR FOREIGNERS: Karlovo náměstí 32 (Tel. 299381).

UK EMBASSY: Thunovská Ulice 14, Malá Strana.

US EMBASSY: Tržiště 15, Malá Strana (Tel. 536641).

CANADIAN EMBASSY: Hradčany, Mickiewiczova 6 (Tel. 326941).

PRAGOTUR: U Obecního domu 2; also operate a room-finding service. Open Mon.–Fri.: 8 a.m.–8.30 p.m., Sat.: 9.15 a.m.–6 p.m., Sun.: 8.30 a.m.–3 p.m. (Tel. 231700).

INFORMATION SERVICES: Na Příkopě 20 (Tel. 544444); Panská 4 (Tel. 223411).

- **Getting about:** The new underground is efficient and cheap, and the bus and tram network covers every corner of the city. Buy tickets in advance from news-stands, hotels, machines and tobacconists and stamp them on the buses. There is a special tourist ticket valid for 24 hours and giving unlimited travel on trams, buses, metro and Petöíu fernicular for about 8 Kčs. Get it from the red ticket machines at metro stations in the city centre. The yellow machines sell single tickets for 1 Kč. Forget taxis altogether.

SEEING

Don't judge the city by its station. We nearly boarded the first train out again on our first visit, but it is in two halves – the platforms ancient, crowded and dirty, and the rest of it like a modern airport terminal. Had we done so, we'd have missed a city with as much to see and do in as Paris, although many of the sights seem to be permanently closed for renovation. Prague started off as five separate towns, and each one of them merits a visit: the New Town (Nové Město), the nineteenth-century commercial centre; the Old Town (Staré Město), medieval buildings and fascinating Jewish Quarter; the Lesser Town (Malá Strana), the baroque area of palaces and churches; Hradčany, the area round Prague Castle; and Vyšehrad, the ninth-century fortress-town opposite the castle. A good way to get your bearings is to take a boat trip on the Vltava. Leave from Vltava Quay in the New Town and rather than return by boat take metro line 3 from Palacky Bridge. (Most Palackého.)

• **Nové Město:** The main sights are WENCESLAS SQUARE, locally known as Václavské náměstí, the main boulevard, the NATIONAL MUSEUM and CHARLES SQUARE (Karlovo náměstí), the largest square in Prague with a park in its centre and the NEW TOWN HALL on its north side. Also DVOŘÁK'S MUSEUM, Ke Karlovu 20, is in this vicinity.

• **Staré Město:** The Old Town dates back to 1120 – and you can feel it. The POWDER TOWER, used to store gunpowder in the fifteenth century, gives a good view from the top, while the OLD TOWN SQUARE was at the centre of medieval Prague. Here is to be found the 1490 Astronomical Clock of the OLD TOWN HALL which performs every hour. Tour round the Town Hall, and then see the TÝN CHURCH on the east side of the square. This twin-Gothic-spired church has a baroque interior and dates from 1365.

The JEWISH QUARTER houses the oldest synagogue in Europe (1270) and the fifteenth-century JEWISH CEMETERY with its 12,000 tombstones piled on top of one another. The museum in KLAUS SYNAGOGUE tells of the extermination of Jews in the Second World War.

Bordering the New Town is the BETHLEHEM CHAPEL where the Czech hero John Hus preached, and the baroque CHARLES BRIDGE has superb views of the castle, the island of Kampa and the River Vltava.

● **Malá Strana:** The rich seventeenth- and eighteenth-century merchants spent their money on this town. The LESSER TOWN SQUARE and NERUDA ST are testament to that. ST NICHOLAS' CHURCH is the finest baroque building in Prague, and just north of it is the palace of the Habsburg general, Albrecht Wallenstein. Much of this area is undergoing restoration; scaffolding is everywhere.

● **Hradčany:** PRAGUE CASTLE today houses the Czech government, but it used to be the palace of the kings of Bohemia. Try to get on a tour round it. Also in this 'royal city' is ST VITUS' CATHEDRAL which is quite incredible, and is certainly the most detailed Gothic church in central Europe. The National Gallery is in the ŠTERNBERK PALACE in the castle square and has an excellent collection of French impressionists.

A charming walk can be taken down the GOLDEN LANE where the alchemists tried to turn their lead into gold. The STRAHOV MONASTERY, west of the castle, houses the Museum of Czech Literature and offers a good view over the whole of Prague.

● **Vyšehrad:** The VYŠEHRAD FORTRESS has in its grounds the eleventh-century Rotunda of St Martin, and in its cemetery Dvořák, Smetana, and other Czech 'greats' are buried.

If you have a couple of hours to spend, the Zoo in the north of the city at Troja (Tel. 84 14 41) is well worth a visit.

SLEEPING

This is your main headache in Prague. If it's at all possible, book ahead, particularly in the summer. During 1990 the number of tourists increased ten-fold, and made the situation worse. Čedok or Pragotur are your best bets for finding a room (see above). Prepare yourself for the inevitable long queues and insist on somewhere central and cheap. They charge a small commission, but it's well worth it. Private accommodation is cheaper, but usually three nights minimum, so always ask for this or, better still, the CKM student hostels. You will probably do best contacting the campsites yourself. Get a list from Prague Information Service. If stuck, try going back to Čedok/Pragotour in the late afternoon for cancelled reservations. For those still having to register with the police, the office at Olšanká 2 closes 4 p.m. and weekends.

• **Hostels:** CKM student hostels charge about 60 Kčs a night. Go in person as the CKM office usually only books for groups. The Junior Hotel, at Zitna 12, charges less if you have an IYHF card. But don't pin too much hope on getting in as they are geared up to groups from Eastern Bloc countries and will often tell you they are full for weeks ahead (Tel. 299941 or 292984). Čedok's hostels are booked through Panská 5. They don't make waves about unmarried couples, but cost more than CKM.

Strahov, Spartakiádní Station. Reception opens at 10 a.m. (be there at about 8.30 a.m.).

Hotel Jarov, Kověvova 196 (Tel. 824641) is not terribly central (next to the Economics Institute), but pleasant. Tram 9 or 21.

• **1-star hotels:** Every year they get thinner on the ground, and those which are left all charge about the same rate. The cost of these has risen significantly over the last year. Hotel Balkan, Svornosti 28 (Tel. 540777): a good place offering good pub grub. Národní dum, Bořivojova 53 (Tel. 275365) has multi-bed rooms. The three botels moored on the River Vltava, which runs through Prague, are quite good value, but cramped. They are the Admiral (Tel. 548685 and 547445), Albatros (Tel. 2313634) and the Racek (Tel. 759513 and 723241).

• **Camping:** There are several sites around Prague, try: Sokol Troja at Trojská 171 (Tel. 842 833), Sokol Dolní Polernice at Dolní Počěrnice Nár. hrdinu (Tel. 718 034) and Katva at V ledáren 55 (Tel. 461712). Ask for a full list and tram/bus details from Pragotur.

EATING AND NIGHTLIFE

Beer halls (pivnice) and wine cellars (vinárny) are dotted all over the city. These are safe bets for cheap food and drink, as are the stand-up snack places. Don't expect a huge menu, but what there is is usually OK. There are plenty of 'Automats' – self-service restaurants – in the Wenceslas Square area, which are good and cheap. Take advantage of the Czech beer while you can. Specially recommended are: U Prince, Old Town Square, opposite the Town Hall: good and cheap in a wonderful setting; closed Thursdays. Berjozka Bistro, Na Příkopě: a good Russian restaurant next to the Prague information service.

The Prague Spring Festival (12 May–4 June) is a big draw for music- and drama-lovers. The monthly 'What's On' can be had from PIS, Na Příkopě 20. The Laterna Magika, Národní 40, is a review of films, ballet and drama which deserves a mention, but you usually need reservations of up to a month.

The citizens of Prague love their ice cream (zmrzlina), and everybody seems to be licking furiously away. One of the best ice cream places we have found outside Italy is in Prague, on Vodičkova, in the shadow of the New Town Hall. You can join the queue outside on the pavement to buy one to enjoy in the nearby Charles Square (Karlovo náměstí) or queue up inside for a seat in this popular café.

Beer halls or wine cellars are the most likely places to meet Czech students. Try: U Malvaze, Karlova 10, big student dive, U Zelené Žáby or U Kalicha on Na Bojišti 12. An excellent restaurant which serves a good meal at a reasonable price can be found at Parizska 17. It is called U Staré Synagogy (At the Old Synagogue) and is near the Jewish Cemetery between the Intercontinental Hotel and the Old Town Square. The strongest beer can be found at U Supa at Celetná 22.

• **Excursions from Prague:** Half an hour in the train is all it takes to get to the amazing fourteenth-century castle of KARLŠTEJN – Bohemia's finest example. Take the train from Smichov Station – on the Metro. The famous spa of KARLOVY VARY (Karlsbad) also makes an interesting trip. Trains to get there are relatively cheap, and take about three hours. Čedok is at Tržiste 23. Another castle of note is KŘIVOKLÁT, medieval seat of Bohemia's kings, located above the Berountia river, a worthwhile sight in its own right. Take the train from Prague–Smíchov, change at Beroun, then on to Křivoklát.

Olomouc

Czechoslovakia boasts many beautiful historic towns, and Olomouc is one which you might consider visiting. The town is on the direct line from Praha–Hlavní, taking around three-and-a-half hours. Olomouc became an important city in Moravia as early as the eleventh century, and today is a tourist's delight.

From the station, the centre is a 15-minute walk, and on several tram routes. Tourist information, Čedok is at Horní náměstí 2 (Tel. 28831), located in the city central square, providing the usual facilities. CKM is at Denisova 4 (Tel. 29009). Try these for accommodation suggestions, or in July and August the Studencentrum, at Křížhovského 14, may help to find a room. There is no campsite in the town, but half an hour away by train, in Šternberk, there is a site. If really stuck try sleeping out at the Smetanovy sady park. There are plenty of beer halls, wine cellars and restaurants, so there should be no problems. To meet local students try Mikulovská vinárna and U Trojice wine cellars, in the city centre.

The town is a protected urban reservation. The main sight is the superb twelfth-century ST WENCESLAW CATHEDRAL, with the PRZEMYSL CASTLE, ST ANN'S CHAPEL and CHAPTER DEANERY nearby. The Renaissance TOWN HALL is also worth a look, as are some of the buildings of the University, the second oldest in Czechoslovakia. A trip on bus 11 from the railway station will bring you to the Kopeček hill, with a good view of the town, and site of the seventeenth-century VIRGIN MARY CHURCH and MONASTERY.

DENMARK

Entry requirements	Passport
Population	5,200,000
Capital	Copenhagen (pop.: 1,400,000 +)
Currency	Kroner
	£1 = approx. 11.23 kr.
Political system	Constitutional Monarchy
Religion	Lutheran
Language	Danish (English widely spoken)
Public holidays	1 Jan.; Maundy Thursday; Good Friday;
	Easter Monday; Common Prayer Day;
	Ascension Day; Whit Monday;
	Constitution Day (5 Jun); 25, 26 Dec.
International dialling codes	From UK 01045
	From USA 01145
	To UK 00944
	To USA 0091

Over a hundred of Denmark's islands are inhabited, the largest of these being Zealand where Copenhagen was founded in the twelfth century. During the Middle Ages the economy prospered, and in 1397 Sweden and Norway came under Danish rule. The union with Sweden lasted till 1523, while Norway remained united until 1814. The acceptance of Luther's Reformation was followed by a flowering of the arts and sciences and culturally the nineteenth century was Denmark's 'Golden Age'. Today Denmark enjoys a very high standard of living; from a eurorailer's point of view, the high degree of social planning and the number of public facilities available make travelling here a pleasure, whether you head for Copenhagen or one of the smaller, picturesque islands.

• **Getting there:** From Britain the cheapest way is to take the train from London to Copenhagen (26 hours). There are ferries from Harwich to Esbjerg (20 hours), Newcastle to Esbjerg (19 hours, summertime only). There's a 50 per cent reduction with an Inter Rail on the DFDS ships.

DANISH STATE RAILWAYS
(Danske Statsbaner, DSB)

In Denmark you spend as much time on water as you do on land, when entire trains clamp down on to specially adapted ferries which connect the islands with one another and with mainland Sweden and Germany. With hourly intercity trains, they've had plenty of practice and have got the whole operation down to a fine art. There's a great feeling of camaraderie once you're on board. Passengers are free to get out and wander about. This is particularly the case on the Kalundborg–Århus crossing (3 hours); a more leisurely affair than the Great Belt (Storebaelt) crossing (1 hour). The whole system runs efficiently with trains rarely running late.

The rail network is divided into four categories:

1. Lyntog–Lightning trains L. Almost as luxurious as Eurocity and used on long hauls, such as Copenhagen to Frederikshavn.

2. Intercity IC. Equally fast, serving the shorter distances between large towns.

3. Regionaltoget. Slower regional trains, connecting up the smaller towns with the main network.

4. S-tog. Copenhagen's underground, connecting up the city with the suburbs.

● **Inter Rail bonuses:**

	FROM	TO	REDUCTION %
Det forenede Dampskibs-	Esbjerg	Harwich PQ	50 (1)
selskab (DFDS)	Esbjerg	Newcastle	50 (1)
	Copenhagen	Oslo	50 (2)
Hjørring Privatbaner (HP)	Hjørring	Hirtshals	50
Flyvebadene	Copenhagen	Malmö	50

DSB – Free entrance to Railway Museum, Odense.
Inter Rails are also valid on the S-tog in Copenhagen as well as on island ferries.
(1) Reduction only allowed when travelling in couchette accommodation.
(2) Reduction only allowed when travelling in rest chair accommodation.

● **Eurail bonuses:** The following services are free:
—Ferry crossings Århus to Kalundborg, Knudshoved to Halskov, Nyborg to Korsør, Fynshavn to Bøjden.
—Ferry crossings Rødby Faerge to Puttgarden (Federal Republic of Germany).

—Ferry crossings operated by the Danish and Swedish State Railways between Helsingør and Helsingborg (Sweden).
—Ferry crossings operated by Stena Sessan Line between Frederikshavn and Gothenburg (Sweden).

Reduced fares:
—50 per cent reduction on the Danish Navigation Company, 'Øresund', on the hydrofoil between Copenhagen and Malmö.
—20 per cent reduction on the normal fares of the Steamship Company DFDS between Esbjerg–Harwich, Esbjerg–Newcastle, Esbjerg–Faroe Islands, Copenhagen–Oslo.
—30 per cent reduction on the normal fares of the Steamship Company KDS between Hirtshals and Kristiansand (Norway).
—50 per cent reduction on couchettes.

TRAIN INFORMATION

Timetables are dotted everywhere around the stations, and all the staff seem to speak fluent English. If you're spending some time in Denmark ask for the Køreplan, a timetable for all the ferries, trains and buses.

• **Reservations:** Are only compulsory when crossing the Great Belt between Sjaelland and Fyn (that is, from Korsør to Nyborg). The cost is 15 kr. on IC and 25 kr. on Lyntog trains. Reservations can also be made for Lyntog and IC trains.

• **Night travel:** Couchettes/sleepers cost *relatively* less in Scandinavia than elsewhere in Europe. A couchette costs around 30 kr. and a bed in a two-berther approximately 100 kr. Within Denmark, they operate between Copenhagen and Esbjerg as well as to Struer and Frederikshavn and cost less than on international journeys.

• **Eating on trains:** There are no dining cars, even if you could afford them, though on L and IC trains there are buffets and trolleys selling snacks, etc. The coffee is reasonably priced but the sandwiches are as big a rip-off here as they are everywhere else. If you're starving, try to survive till you get aboard the ferries as they have self-service cafeterias. The Puttgarden-Rødby service usually does a good choice at reasonable prices.

If you're on an international crossing, don't forget to check out the duty-free shops. They have good prices for cheese, wine, cigarettes and chocolates. Don't forget that in Scandinavia, and especially in Norway, normal prices are high.

• **Scenic tips:** There's good coastline scenery if you're on your way to Frederikshavn from Copenhagen or vice versa. Take the route which goes via Odense and Fredericia. If you're heading for Stockholm from Copenhagen, your best route is to train it to Helsingør (1 hour) then take the ferry to Helsingborg (free on Inter Rail).

• **Bikes:** You can rent out a bike in the summer at most of the larger stations, with the exception of Copenhagen, for about 35 kr. per day, plus deposit between 100–200 kr. Ask at stations for leaflet 'Take a Train – Rent a Bike'.

• **Rover tickets:** The best ticket to go for is the Nordturist 'Scanrail' pass, which is valid in Denmark, Norway, Sweden and Finland for 21 days. It covers all rail services and the major ferry services between the countries, with reductions on some other sailings. It costs about 1,450 kr. (£135) second class and 1,945 kr. (£181) first class. These tickets have been available to people under 26 at a discount of 25 per cent. If you are travelling with at least three paying passengers (adults and children) there are discounts of between 20–40 per cent available on the Nordic Family Ticket. Available from Norwegian State Railways Bureau, 21 Cockspur Street, London (Tel. 071–930 6666). Monthly tickets for unlimited travel on Danish domestic rail and ferry services cost 1,340 kr. In Denmark children under 4 travel free and those between 4 and 12 at half price. Danish State Railways issue the East Rail Pass. This covers travel in Czechoslovakia, Hungary, East Germany (as was), Poland, and Denmark. All Danish trains and ferries are valid. See p.33.

TOURIST INFORMATION

In Denmark the tourist offices are the best in Europe, particularly for the under 26s. They are both friendly and efficient, and if every tourist board was like them we would be out of a job.

If you tune in a radio to Radio Denmark programme 1 on 90.8 MHz at 8 a.m.–10 a.m., Mondays–Fridays, you'll hear news in English, and information about exhibitions and other events in Copenhagen for that day.

• **ISIC bonuses:** 50 per cent reductions on films, theatres and museums. For further information, contact DIS Skindergade 28, Copenhagen.

• **Money matters:** 1 kroner (kr.) = 100 øre.
Banking hours are Mon., Tues., Wed., Fri.: 9.30 a.m.–4 p.m., Thurs.: 9.30 a.m.–6 p.m. Bank commission varies from 10–18 kr. For late-night service there are facilities at Central Station and Tivoli Park in Copenhagen. Some tourist offices may exchange money out of banking hours.

• **Post office:** Opens Mon.–Fri.: 9 a.m.–5 p.m., Sat.: 9 a.m.–12 noon.

• **Telephones:** Either fully automatic or through the operator if the number starts with letters. Insert 50 øre for local calls or 1 kr. for long-distance. You don't get your money back if there is no answer, but you can continue to dial calls, and you do not get change from 25 øre coins.

• **Shops:** Hours vary from town to town; in general: Mon.–Thurs.: 9 a.m.–5.30 p.m., Friday to 7 or 8 p.m., Saturday to 1 p.m. or 2 p.m. First Saturday of each month to 5 p.m. in larger towns.

SLEEPING

Youth hostels require you to register before 9 p.m. and have IYHF membership. An average charge is 35–55 kr. per night and outside Copenhagen an 11 p.m. curfew is the norm. A free booklet listing all of Denmark's hostels and many campsites is available from the tourist office. There are over 500 campsites and the Camping Carnet is required. An average overnight stay will cost 30 kr. Town mission hostels are excellent, clean and cheap. If you can't get into a hostel and don't want to be bothered with camping stay in a private home (anything but a hotel, as these really are very expensive). Tourist information will put you in touch with a Danish family who'll put you up.

EATING AND NIGHTLIFE

Danish food is expensive, but don't despair: shop at the well-stocked supermarkets and prepare your own smørrebrød (open sandwiches). Pølser (hot dog) stands are on most street corners, and the famous Danish brews round off picnics in style. Look out for cafés with signs 'Madkurve kan Medbringes' (literally, 'bring your own food'), so just buy a coffee.

ISIC gives you 50 per cent off films, theatres, etc., and there's no shortage of pubs in Denmark. For Copenhagen, 'Use It' have a useful magazine called 'Playtime' which gives you a rundown on what's on, and if that's not enough they also have special information sheets on entertainment.

Copenhagen (København)

The largest city in Scandinavia, situated on the north-eastern shore of Zealand, Copenhagen is a well-run, exciting place with lots going for it and an almost Parisian *joie de vivre*. The Danes are known to be a socially-minded lot, and this shows particularly in their capital where they operate two free services for young travellers which are almost too good to be true. The YMCA and YWCA get together and open two centres for eurorailers in high summer where you can go for advice on what to see and where to go, and for help with problems. They're at St Kannikestraede 19 (Tel. 3113031). Open 8 a.m.–12 p.m. and 2.30 p.m.–3 a.m.; 1 July–14 August. Also at Valdemarsgade 15 (Tel. 311574). Open 8 a.m.–12 noon and 2.30 p.m.–3 a.m.; 15 July–15 August.

The second organization, called 'Use It', is much larger, is open all year, and is sponsored by the city youth organization. It offers countless free or non-profit-making services: free maps, tourist information and advice, a series of leaflets on cheap restaurants and hostels, free luggage storage, and at its centre at Rådhusstraede 13 (Tel. 33156518) (10 minutes' walk from Central Station along Frederiksberggade to Rådhusstraede) there is a restaurant, jazz club, rock/folk club and cinema where you can meet fellow travellers and young Danes. Pick up their magazine, 'Playtime'. 'Use It' will also find you a bed you can afford, or help you out if you've an emergency or crisis. They're open in summer from 10 a.m.–7 p.m. and off-season from 10 a.m.–4 p.m.

Bear in mind: the YMCA/YWCA set-up is a Christian organization and can be quite strict – even in Copenhagen – so if you're
after advice on the hottest places for evening entertainment, etc.,
go to 'Use It'.

These sort of facilities are unique in Europe, so make the most of
them whilst you're there, and don't expect anything remotely like it
in southern Europe.

STATION FACILITIES

Train information	8 a.m.–10 p.m. (Tel. 33141701)
Reservations	8 a.m.–9 p.m.
Left-luggage lockers	Shut 1.30 a.m.–4.30 a.m.
Left-luggage store	6.30 a.m.–0.15 a.m.
Duty officer 'Inspektion'	All hours
Chemist	7 a.m.–11 p.m.
Waiting room (in cafeteria)	6.30 a.m.–11.45 p.m.
Restaurant	7.30 a.m.–10.30 p.m.
Cafeteria	6.30 a.m.–11.45 p.m.
Bar, Buffet	7 a.m.–11 p.m.
Snack bar	7 a.m.–11.45 p.m.
Shopping	Supermarket by station open 8 a.m.–midnight
Foreign exchange	7 a.m.–10 p.m.
Station shuts	1.30 a.m.–4.30 a.m.

There are post office, banking and telephoning facilities.
Copenhagen–Malmö 40 minutes, to Gothenburg 4½ hours, to Hamburg 5 hours.

Copenhagen's 'Hovedbanegård' is the terminus for all main-line
trains. It's a particularly fine station with many facilities. The
platforms are below ground level. The 'S' trains (suburban elec-
trics) also use the station. Look out for drunks, however.

Note: These S-togs are free to Inter Rail or Eurail card holders.
Kiosk P (9 a.m.–midnight in summer) is the room-finding service in
the station. As their commission is 14 kr., best to go to 'Use It' who
offer this service free.

• **Inter Rail Centre:** DSB's Inter Rail Centre was opened on 1 July
1984 and is the first of its kind in the world. Anyone with an Inter
Rail, Eurail Youthpass or BIJ ticket can use its excellent facilities

from mid-June through till mid-September. (Open 7 a.m.–1 a.m.) These facilities include a common room and a dining room where everyone meets up, as well as toilets and washing facilities. Throughout the day, there are news bulletins in English, German and French, and tape-recorded tourist information in the same languages. There are also vending machines with hot and cold beverages and sandwiches, music and a large collection of folders. Use the showers at odd times of the day to avoid queues.

TOURIST INFORMATION

At the Town Hall Square, by Tivoli entrance, is Danmarks Turistråd – tourist information, H. C. Andersens Boulevard 22 (Tel. 33111325). Open May: Mon.–Fri.: 9 a.m.–5 p.m., Sat.: 9 a.m.–2 p.m., Sun. and holidays: 9 a.m.–1 p.m. June to mid-Sept.: daily 9 a.m.–6 p.m. Off season Mon.–Fri.: 9 a.m.–5 p.m., Sat.: 9 a.m.–noon. Their service is excellent and there are leaflets on everything you could possibly need to know. Be specific and ask for everything you might need, for instance camping, walking, other parts of Denmark, etc. Don't forget to pick up their free map and a copy of 'Copenhagen This Week'.

● **Addresses:**
USE IT: Rådhusstraede 13 (Tel. 33156518). They help out euro-railers with everything and will even hold your mail and find you a bed for the night. Not always over-friendly, but useful!
POST OFFICE: Tietgensgade 37 (behind Central Station). Poste restante here too. 9 a.m.–6 p.m., to 1 p.m. on Saturday.
AMEX: Amagertorv 18 (Tel. 33122301).
UK EMBASSY: Kastelsvej 36–40 (Tel. 31264600).
US EMBASSY: Dag Hammarskjölds Allé 24 (Tel. 31423144).
CANADIAN EMBASSY: Kristen Bernikowsgade 1 (Tel. 33122299).
AUSTRALIAN EMBASSY: Kristianiagade 21 (Tel. 31262244).
24-HOUR CHEMIST: Steno Apotek, Vesterbrogade 6c (Tel. 33148266).

● **Getting about:** The S-tog is free with any rail pass. If you haven't got one, the buses are a better bet at 8 kr. a ride, although they are cheaper if you buy a nine-ride pass from the driver for 50 kr. All tickets are interchangeable between buses and trains providing they are used within the hour. The best way of all, however, is to invest in a 'Copenhagen Card' which gives you unlimited travel by bus and rail in the whole of the metropolitan area and includes North Sealand. It also gives free admission to many sights, attractions and museums. If you don't have a pass which gives free or reduced ferry crossings to Sweden, the Copenhagen Card allows a 50 per cent reduction. It is valid for one, two or three days and costs about 105 kr., 170 kr. and 215 kr. respectively. Children aged 5 to 11 pay half-price.

If you're thinking of going to Malmö in Sweden, carefully compare the ferry lines on offer. Prices vary between 27 kr. and 130 kr., bonuses for Inter Rail may be available. The jet-foil saves you 45 minutes' travelling and costs 55 kr. with a 50 per cent Inter Rail bonus, otherwise the trip takes 1½ hours.

SEEING

Copenhagen is a great walking city and most of the sights can easily be negotiated on foot. There are six well-planned city walking tours which last about two hours (ask tourist information or Use It).

TIVOLI (the famous amusement park) is in the centre across from the station and has, over the years, become rather too commercial for our liking. Entrance 28 kr. Avoid eating there. Open May–mid-September, 10 a.m.–midnight. An alternative is the free entry amusement park of BAKKEN. Take the S-tog to KLAMPENBERG (free on Inter Rail and Eurail) and walk through the park. Open April end August, 12 a.m.–12 p.m. The CARLSBERG and TUBORG breweries run a good deal (a classic favourite for thirsty eurorailers): tours of the breweries with free samples afterwards, closed weekends. Carlsberg tours at 11 a.m. and 2.30 p.m. Take bus 6 or 18. Tuborg tours at 10 a.m., 12.30 p.m. and 2.30 p.m. S-tog line A to Svanemotten or Hellrup, or bus 6 or 21.

As you will be on foot, you will not miss STRØGET, a series of streets throbbing with life. The area around the university is host to a multitude of bookshops, bric-a-brac and a good selection of cafés. See also the RUNDETÅRNET, the summit of which affords a great view of the old town and is curiously reached by a continuous spiral ramp.

Another good view of the town can be obtained by climbing the unusual tower of VOR FRELSERS KIRKE on Princessegade and Torvegade. The spiral staircase is on the outside of the church's spire and gets progressively steeper and more uneven. Not recommended in high winds or rain!

'Alternative' Copenhagen can be experienced at CHRISTIANA on Princessegade. Occupied in 1971 by a group of hippies who enjoyed the free Danish attitudes to pot, drinking and nudism, it makes an interesting visit! The veggie cafe and craft stalls are worthwhile and it is safe to look round. Restaurants, bars and shops are cheaper than in the rest of the town. Avoid taking photographs of the inhabitants to avoid any unpleasantness.

Copenhagen has a multitude of museums and perhaps the best are the WORKERS MUSEUM and the NATIONAL MUSEUM which is best on Danish history and the Vikings. Also worth a look are the THORVALDSENS MUSEUM for the work of Denmark's famous sculptor. NY CARLSBERG GLYPOTEK (free entry on Wed.) for classical art and the interesting RESISTANCE MUSEUM, tracing the growth of opposition to the German occupation during the Second World War.

The Bellevue is a beach between Copenhagen and Helsingør, known locally as 'Fluepapiret' (fly-paper) for its ability to draw the bikini-clad blondes and the local likely lads.

The walk to the little mermaid, along the LANGELINIE, is the best part of the trip, as the statue's nothing special. Look out for the nearby Gefion Fountain. The comprehensive leaflet provided with the 'Copenhagen Card' gives full details on opening times, locations and other facilities.

SLEEPING

Hotels in Copenhagen are busy all year round, with prices starting at 200 kr.; you are better investigating the city hostels, private house schemes and campsites.

• **Hostels:** These are busy in summer, so don't waste time touring round them yourself. 'Use It' will help you find a bed (when their office is shut, they post up the latest bed situation outside their office). The main youth hostel (you'll need an IYHF card), Bellahøj at Herbergvejen 8 (Tel. 31289715), is very good and situated in a park in a nice suburb about 15–20 minutes from the city centre. The cost is around 55 kr. with and 75 kr. without an IYHF card. Take bus 2 from the station almost to the end of the route. Security can be a problem, so use the lockers in the basement. The Copenhagen

Hostel (IYHF) at Sjaellandsbroen 55 is very clean and modern. Book in after 1 p.m. (Tel. 32522908). Take bus 46 from the station on weekdays. At the weekend use bus 13 or train to Valby Station, changing to bus 37. Vesterbro Ungdomsgaard, Absalonsgade 8 (Tel. 31312070) is more expensive than the other hostels, due to its good location. Take bus 16 from the station, or a 10-minute walk along Vesterbrogade. Cost 75 kr. Active University, Olfert Fischersgade 40 (Tel. 31156175) is still very cheap (40 kr. per night) but very busy during the summer. Finally, there's 'Sleep In' which is now permanently based at Per Henrik Lings Allé 6 (Tel. 31265059). Very few restrictions; IYHF cards are not required; co-ed dorms; bring your own sleeping bag. The cost is 65 kr., including breakfast. Take bus 1, 6 or 14 to Idraetsparken; Per Henrik cuts through this park.

• **Private accommodation:** Use Kiosk P (in the station) to find yourself a room in a private house, and expect to pay up to 250 kr. for a single, 350 kr. a double. They also take about 14 kr. commission per person.

• **Hotels:** If you have no alternative and want to stay in an hotel try the Amager in Amagerbrogade (Tel. 31544008) or the Carlton on Halmtorvert (Tel. 31212551). You will also find places in the area behind the Central Station on Helgolandsgade and Colbjørnsensgade.

• **Camping:** There are seven sites costing around 33 kr. per person with Danish camping pass. The all-year site is at Absalon Camping, 132 Korsdalsvej (Tel. 31410600): take the S-tog, line B or H, to Brondyoster Station.

EATING AND NIGHTLIFE

This is varied, interesting and there is no shortage of places to choose from. For meals, you can't do much better than the set menus at Chinese restaurants. To keep you going there are pølser (hot dog) stalls, fast-food chains, daily specials (dagens ret) and smørrebrød. (See the 'Use It' brochure, 'Where to Eat'.) One of the most popular places for smørrebrød is Smørrebrødforretning at Gothersgade 10, open 8 a.m.–10 p.m.

Universitetspoppen (university refectory), 52 Kobmagergade, charge 40–50 kr. for huge lunchtime meals. You'll need an ISIC, but they are closed July and August. At Pasta Basta, Valkendorfsgade 22, eat as much spaghetti as you can for 42 kr.

Spisehuset, Rådhusstraede 13 (part of 'Use It'). All you can eat reasonably cheaply (noon–3 p.m.). In the evenings it's a pub (serving food).

There are hundreds of pubs, clubs and discos in Copenhagen. NYHAVN (the dock district) makes an interesting nocturnal wander – but it is not really advisable for girls to go there alone. The 'Use It' house is as good and cheap a place for a drink, etc., as any, and Frederiksberggade comes alive at night. Good jazz can normally be found on Norregade. Basically, in Copenhagen you don't need to look hard for nightlife.

Your best day trip from Copenhagen is 40 km north to Frederiksborg Castle at Hillerød (35 minutes by S-tog, leaving from the main station).

Århus

Denmark's second city is a busy industrial and commercial centre. See the old town (den gamle by) OPEN AIR MUSEUM, a reconstructed sixteenth-century village, the CITY PREHISTORIC MUSEUM with the amazing red-headed mummy of the Grauballe man, the twelfth-century CATHEDRAL and the VIKING MUSEUM.

Tourist information is in the Town Hall, one block from the station, and is open 9 a.m.–8 p.m. Shorter hours out of season, small charge to book accommodation (Tel. 86121600). It's a university town and the student centre is at 84 Niels Juelsgade. The youth hostel is Vandrerhjemmet Pavillonen (Tel. 86167298); closed 12 p.m.–4 p.m. It's good and well situated in a forest, near beaches. Take bus or tram nos. 1, 6 or 9 to the terminus, then follow signs. Hotel Århus Smandshjêm at 20 Havnegade, near the port (Tel. 86121599), has single and double rooms which are quite cheap. There is a Sleep-in, Kulturgyngen, at Mejlgade 53 (Tel. 86192255). Open 1 July–1 Sept. The campsite is 7 km out at Blommehavn, Ørneredevej 35, bus 6.

Your cheapest lunch is at the Matematiske Fakultet (University) off Langelandsgade; closed after 1 p.m. and all July. Even better is the 'Use It' Youth Centre at 15 Vester Allé. They also give free concerts and plays. Musik café at Mejlgade 53 is worth a try in the evenings.

Odense

En route from Copenhagen to Jutland, Odense is one of Denmark's oldest towns. It's the home town of Hans Christian Andersen; you can visit his house at Hans Jensens Straede 39–43 (17 kr., no reductions).

Tourist information is in the Town Hall, south of the station (Tel. 66127520). Open in summer 9 a.m.–7 p.m., Sundays 11 a.m.–7 p.m., ST CANUTE'S thirteenth-century cathedral and the OPEN AIR FOLK MUSEUM and operating farm on the outskirts of Odense are interesting. At Ladby (20 km north-east of Odense) is the coffin ship of a tenth-century Viking chief.

The youth hostel is at 121 Kragsbjergvej (Tel. 66130425). It has 230 beds, is on bus route 6 from the station, and costs 55 kr. There is a camping site at Odensevej 102 (Tel. 66114702), bus 1.

Aalborg

The 1,000-year-old centre of north Jutland. The main sights include the remains of a Viking village and mass grave (at Nørresundby, just outside Aalborg), the well-preserved OLD TOWN, the fifteenth-century MONASTERY OF THE HOLY GHOST, ALBORGHUS CASTLE, ST BOTOLPH'S CATHEDRAL and the baby brother of Tivoli, TIVOLILAND. All Americans in Aalborg on 4 July should make their way to the Rebild National Park, 30 km south of the city, for the most extensive Independence Day celebrations outside the USA.

The Fjord Parken hostel is at Skydebanevej 50 (Tel. 98116044), with a camping site, Strandparken, nearby. Bus 2 or 12 from centre or railway station, to terminus.

Legoland

One of Denmark's most famous exports is Lego, the children's plastic building brick. At BILLUND in mid-Jutland there is a mini-town of houses, railway, harbour, boats and cars – all made out of the stuff. Legoland is open from May to mid-September, with some indoor exhibitions from Easter to mid-December.

Take the train to Vejle and then bus 912 from the station to Billund (28 kr. each way). Journey takes about one hour.

Entrance fees cheapen during the day, costing 40 kr. in the afternoon. In summer, it stays open until 8 p.m.–9 p.m. In winter it closes at 5 p.m.

There is a camping site very near Legoland, at Nordmarksvej 2 (Tel. 05331521).

FINLAND (Suomi)

Entry requirements	Passport
Population	5,000,000
Capital	Helsinki (pop.: 500,000 +)
Currency	Finnish Markka
	£1 = approx. 6.96 mk.
Political system	Republic
Religions	Lutheran and Orthodox ministry
Languages	Finnish and Swedish (some English spoken)
Public holidays	1 Jan.; Epiphany; Good Friday; Easter Sunday and Monday; 1 May; Ascension Day; Whitsun weekend; Midsummer Eve and Day; All Saints Day; 6, 24, 25, 26 Dec.
International dialling codes	From UK 010358
	From USA 011358
	To UK 99044
	To USA 9901

Finland is an interesting mixture of both east and west, and once you reach there you really do feel a long way from home. In summer, darkness hardly ever comes and in winter daylight lasts only a few hours. Geographically, Finland is very beautiful: 70 per cent of her land is covered by lush pine forests and over 188,000 lakes; added to this is clear air and an environmentally conscious people.

For centuries, her neighbours, Sweden and Russia, played political chess with Finland as the pawn. (Finland was linked with Sweden for 650 years and with Russia for 100 before proclaiming independence in 1917.) As a result, you won't find the Finns too keen on either the Swedes or the Russians. Conflict with Russia in the Second World War lost her valuable territories and landed her with large war reparations to pay off. Today, prices are crippling for young travellers, but a quick trip into this interesting country is recommended.

• **Getting there:** Unless you're going by train and bus round the north of Sweden, your most direct route is to take a ferry from Stockholm to either Turku or Helsinki. It's a beautiful cruise (10–11 hours and 14–16 hours respectively). The main shipping lines are Silja and Viking. An Inter Rail gets you a 50 per cent reduction on both lines, while Eurail holders travel free with Silja and on a 50 per cent reduction with Viking. Facilities on both lines are excellent. Cabins are expensive, so get your sleeping bag down on deck somewhere, or, better still, head for the free 'sleep-in'. On the older ships these have 60 beds, but the excellent new ships on the Silja Lines Turku–Stockholm route have 200 places available on all sailings. It is worthwhile taking a day sailing as the route is very scenic and you pass many small islands on the way, with the ship constantly zig-zagging to keep in deep water. Snacks and coffee on the ship are reasonably priced as are the duty-free goods – by Scandinavian standards. There are several services each day with prices varying depending on the crossing. The Helsinki ferries leave at 6 p.m. and cost from 170 mk. The Turku ferries leave at 8.15 a.m. and 9.15 p.m., during high season and cost from 120 mk.

FINNISH STATE RAILWAYS
(Valtionrautatiet, VR)

Big, solid and reliable (like the Finns!), the majority of the rolling stock is new. There are four types of trains: IC-trains (IC-juna), special expresses (Erikoispikajuna), regular expresses (Pikajuna) and locals (Henkilöjuna). Their service extends as far north as Lapland and includes nearly 6,000 km of line.

• **Inter Rail bonuses:** 50 per cent reductions are offered on the Silja Line service from Helsinki to Lübeck–Travemünde, and on Oy Vaasa–Umeå Ab lines from Vaasa to Umeå. On the crossing over to Stockholm, there are also 50 per cent reductions.
VR – Free entrance to Railway Museum, Hyvinkää; Narrow Gauge Railway Museum, Jokioinen (Gare Minkio).

• **Eurail bonuses:** Free services:
—Ferry service of the Silja Line between Helsinki and Stockholm and between Turku–Aland Islands–Stockholm. Full fare is charged for cabin space.

TRAIN INFORMATION

At the major stations you'll find the staff speak English. Contact the 'Neuvonta' at the station if you've problems.

• **Reservations:** Obligatory on the IC-trains and special expresses; optional on other trains. Oddly, reserved seats are not marked, making it difficult to tell if a seat is free. Costs are between 15–60 mk., depending on type of train.

• **Night travel:** There are no couchettes, only sleepers which are reasonably priced. During the peak periods (Easter and July/ August) try and reserve sleepers as far ahead as possible.

• **Rover Tickets:** There are two tickets offering unlimited travel, either the Finnrail Pass which is limited to Finland, or the Nordic Tourist Ticket, which is valid for all the Scandinavian countries plus major connecting sailings. The Finnrail Pass is valid for 8, 15 or 22 days and costs 400 mk., 650 mk. and 815 mk. respectively for second-class travel, 50 per cent higher for first-class.

TOURIST INFORMATION

City offices, Matkailutoimistot, provide excellent maps and leaflets on their locality. For Finland as a whole the national tourist board, 'MEK', has its base in Helsinki. Museums tend to close on Mondays.

• **ISIC bonuses:** Student discounts on museums, art galleries and theatres.

• **Money matters:** 1 Finnish markka (mk.) = 100 penni (p).
Banking hours are: Mon.–Fri.: 9.30 a.m.–4 p.m. Banks give the best rate of exchange. All banks and exchange bureaux close over the mid-summer weekend holiday.

• **Post offices:** Open 9 a.m. to to 5 p.m., Monday to Friday. Stamps are also sold at bookshops, newsagents and stations. Post boxes are yellow.

• **Shops:** Monday to Friday 9 a.m.–5 p.m. (with some staying open to 8 p.m. summer weekdays), Saturday 9 a.m.–3 p.m.

SLEEPING

Youth hostels and campsites are graded on a star basis from one to four. There's no age limit to Finland's 160 hostels and you don't need IYHF membership, except in the most expensive category, which often have saunas. Prices range from 28–90 mk., though most cost around 40 mk. For further information about youth hostels in Finland contact Suomen Retkeilymajajärjestö, Yrjönkatu 38 B SF-, 00100 Helsinki (Tel. 694 0377). There are something like 340 campsites, varying in price from 23–66 mk. per tent. For more details on hostelling and camping, ask at tourist information for the current leaflet 'Finland Budget Accommodation'.

Private accommodation and small boarding houses are also available. Summer hotels are often made out of student dorms, and they're usually clean, modern and reasonably priced. The cheapest you'll get for a hotel room (double) with breakfast is 100–150 mk. per person.

EATING AND NIGHTLIFE

The baaris, grillis, krouvis or kahvilas are a mixture of cafés and fast-food chains. They're OK but vary dramatically in quality. The student-run cafés are your best bet. Finnish specialities include salted Baltic herring, rye bread, crayfish and fruit-filled pancakes.

Nearly all restaurants have set lunch and dinner menus but you're better advised to starve yourself all day, then go to a Voileipä-pöytä or Smörgåsbord (Scandinavian cold table) for a set price. This often includes hot dishes as well, and you work on the basis of eating as much as you like for a set price. Heavy tax on alcohol means consequently high prices e.g. a pint of beer 15–25 mk.

Finns are keen on dancing and there's plenty of that going on on Vappu Night (30 April). This is the students' spring festival which is a good excuse for Helsinki's 20,000 students to let rip and have a knees-up after the long winter. Whether you've been sleeping on deck or going by train and bus round the north, there's nothing like a real Finnish sauna to relax you. Most hotels welcome non-residents. (Rub birch-leaves with the Finns – it's cheaper to take a sauna in a group.)

Helsinki

A clean, bright, modern capital city. Your first impression will probably be of the colourful harbourside market, a daily event in front of the City Hall and President's Palace. Helsinki particularly reminds one visually of its geographical location: the solid eastern-looking buildings contrast with the modern department stores selling endless well-designed consumer goods. In some ways, you feel closer to Russia in Helsinki than you do in Budapest.

STATION FACILITIES

There are daily trains from Helsinki to Leningrad, Turku, Tampere, Kontiomäki, Oulu, Kemi and Rovaniemi (10–13 hours). Helsinki Central is one of the world's few architecturally famous stations. It's a classic example of *art nouveau*, designed by Eliel Saarinen.

Train information	Mon.–Sat.: 7 a.m.–8 p.m. Sun.: 9 a.m.–8 p.m. (Tel. 010115) (International queries Tel. 627804)
Reservations	As train information
Tourist information	Mon.–Fri.: 9 a.m.–9 p.m., Sat.: 9 a.m.–7 p.m. Sun. 10 a.m.–6 p.m.
Cafeteria	Mon.–Sat.: 6.30 a.m.–12 p.m. Sun. 8 a.m.–12 p.m.
Restaurant	Daily 9 a.m.–1 a.m.
Left-luggage lockers	Shut Mon.–Fri.: 1.30 a.m.–4.40 a.m. (Sat., Sun.: 1.40 a.m.–5 a.m.)
Left-luggage store	Open 6.30 a.m.–10.25 p.m.
Shops	Mon.–Sat.: 10 a.m.–10 p.m., Sun.: 12 noon–10 p.m. Shopping gallery in underground passage
Station shuts	Mon.–Fri. 1.30 a.m.–4.40 a.m. Sat.–Sun.: 1.40 a.m.–5 a.m.

There are left-luggage lockers on both the lower and upper floors. The small ones on the lower level are too small for packs and cost 3 mk. You may get a pack in the larger ones on the upper level, cost 10 mk.

'Hotellikeskus' is the accommodation-finding service downstairs in the station. They take 10 mk. commission per find. Summer hours: weekdays open 9 a.m.–9 p.m., Sat.: 9 a.m.–7 p.m., Sun.: 10 a.m.–6 p.m.; off-season Mon.–Fri.: 9 a.m.–6 p.m. They also have a list of all the IYHF youth hostels in Finland.

TOURIST INFORMATION

The main city tourist office is west of the market at Pohjoisesplanadi 19 (Tel. 169 3757). Open weekdays 8.30 a.m.–6 p.m., Sat. till 1 p.m., closed Sundays. They produce very comprehensive leaflets and are incredibly helpful. Pick up 'Helsinki This Week', 'Helsinki Guide', 'Helsinki Today', a tourist map and the four self-guiding walking-tour brochures. They have a free phone here which you can use to

ring up your accommodation. If you're staying for a while, ask them about the city transport passes. Another possibility is the Helsinki Card which is valid for either one day at 65 mk., two days at 90 mk. or three days at 110 mk. Not only does it allow you free travel on all public transport, but it also entitles you to free entry of various museums, and other discounts.

If it's a wet day or you're fed up with walking, tram 3T does an excellent round trip from the station. It takes about an hour and all the main sights are pointed out. (Weekdays 10 a.m.–3 p.m. and 6 p.m.–8 p.m., weekends 9 a.m.–8 p.m.)

- **Addresses:**

FINNISH TOURIST BOARD: Töölönkatu 11 (Tel. 403011) for information on all of Finland. Open Mon.–Fri.: 9 a.m.–5 p.m., Sat.: 9 a.m. to 1 p.m. during the summer.

POST OFFICE: Mannerheimintie 11, open Mon.–Fri.: 9 a.m.–5 p.m. Poste restante is here.

AMEX: Travek, Eteläranta 16, open Mon.–Fri.: 8 a.m.–12 noon, 1 p.m.–4.30 p.m.

UK EMBASSY: Uudenmaankatu 16–20 (Tel. 647 922).

US EMBASSY: Itäinen Puistotie 14a (Tel. 171 931).

CANADIAN EMBASSY: Pohjoisesplanadi 25B (Tel. 171 141).

24-HOUR CHEMIST: Yliopiston Apteekki, Mannerheimintie 5.

STUDENT TRAVEL AGENCY: Travela, Mannerheimintie 5 (Tel. 624 101). Near the train station.

HELSINKI TODAY: Tel. 058 for information and events in English, 040 for news and weather.
CITY DIALLING CODE: 90.

SEEING

The neo-classical centre of town, around the Senate Square, built after a fire which devastated Helsinki, makes a good starting point. On the Square stand the Lutheran CATHEDRAL, UNIVERSITY and GOVERNMENT PALACE, all built in the early nineteenth century. Heading down towards the sea front, the PRESIDENT'S PALACE, CITY HALL and ORTHODOX CATHEDRAL can be seen. The tourist board's walking tours take you around the sights. The NATIONAL MUSEUM, north of Mannerheimintie from the station, is worth a visit on route to the ROCK or TEMPPELIAUKIO CHURCH. From the museum head down Aurorankatu, then along Temppelgatan. Two island locations of note are the SEURASAARI OPEN-AIR MUSEUM, bus 24 to its terminus, and the SUOMENLINNA FORTRESS ISLAND, reached by ferry from near the tourist information. Finland is also rightly acclaimed for being a world leader in manufacturing design, and the Helsinki Design Centre at 19 Kasarmikatu brings together all the best the country has to offer.

SLEEPING

Hotels are expensive in Helsinki and are often fully booked in summer. The hostelling news is good and there are always Matkustajakoti (rooms for travellers) advertised around the station if you're desperate.

• **Hostels:** Try Youth Hostel Stadionin Maja, Pohjoinen Stadiontie 3B (Tel. 496071), up to 100 mk. with IYHF card. Located in the Olympic Stadium complex and reached by tram 3T or 7A from Mannerheimintie, right out of station. Also try the Academica, Hietaniemenkatu 14 (Tel. 4020206), head across Mannerheimintie from the station, and down Arkadiagatan, then Norra Jarnvgsgatan to the junction with Hietaniemenkatu. During the summer the Hotelli Sakuntatalo, Lapinrinne 1 (Tel. 694 0311) has dorm facilities, and single rooms. Near the station.

• **Camping:** The nearest campsite is Rastila (Tel. 316551), take the metro from the station to Östra centrum, then bus 90, 90a, 96 or 98, first stop after the bridge. Open May to September, around 25 mk. per person.

EATING AND NIGHTLIFE

There are plenty of stalls, takeaways and cafés, as well as the excellent markets, so eating is no problem. If you're really down on your luck, wait till the end of the markets and fight for the pickings of the stall-holders' leftovers. Stockman's department store have a good basement food hall, and if you're going for a restaurant meal you've the usual choice of Chinese, Indian, etc., or Russian.

Vanhan Kellari, Mannerheimintie 3. Good self-service, popular with students. Open till 1 a.m. Try Kasvio, Korkeavuorenkatu 3, for good vegetarian food. Open 11 a.m.–6 p.m.

Finns really come to life in the pub, of which Helsinki has no shortage. You don't have to look far for them. KY Exit, Pohjoinen Rautatiekatu is a popular disco with students. Also try Pub 99 at Mannerheimintie 58.

If you're in Helsinki on 12 June (Helsinki Day) or Midsummer's Eve, prepare yourself for a late night as they stay up all night dancing and drinking.

Turku (Åbo)

The old capital and main seaport of the nineteenth century. If arriving on the ferry from Sweden, take the train or bus to the city centre, from outside the terminus.

TOURIST INFORMATION

Käsityöläiskatu 3, open 8 a.m.–4 p.m., Mon.–Fri. Also at Silja and Viking line terminals, open daily 7.30 a.m.–12.30 p.m.; 6 p.m.–9.30 p.m. and at Aurakatu 4, open weekdays 8.30 a.m.–7.30 p.m., Sat.: 8.30 a.m.–4 p.m., Sun.: 8.30 a.m.–3 p.m.

Telephone code 21.

There are boat excursions through the archipelago to the village of Nauvo and the church of Seili: 6½ hours for about 40 mk.

The main sights are the twelfth-century CASTLE, originally a Swedish stronghold, which now houses part of the PROVINCIAL MUSEUM. Entry is free on ISIC but get off the train at the harbour station to see it and save a 25-minute walk. TURKU CATHEDRAL, the SIBELIUS MUSEUM containing his instruments and personal possessions, and the LUOSTARINMÄKI MUSEUM where craftsmen put on live demonstrations of their skills in an old style street. SUOMEN JOUTSEN, a sailing vessel open to the public, is anchored in the Aura River and worth a look.

SLEEPING

• **Hostel:** Kaupungin Retkeilymaja at Linnankatu 39 (Tel. 316578). 128 beds in dorms and small rooms. Bus 3B from station, to just before the Aurajoki river, or bus 1 from the ferry terminus and Market Square. Reception open 3 p.m. to midnight. 45 mk. and 20 mk. for sheets.

Turisti-Aula (Tel. 334484). Central and very good. One block north of city tourist office at Käsityöläiskatu 11, from 170 single, to 290 double. Finnhostel Kåren (Tel. 320421), Hämeenkatu 22, has 95 beds.

• **Camp:** Island of Ruissalo (Tel. 589249), bus 8 from Market Square. Buses are not too frequent and it is a 20-minute ride. Facilities are good with a worthwhile restaurant and beach nearby, also has sauna facilities.

EATING

Go to MARKETPLACE (8 a.m.–2 p.m.) where the food's good, as cheap as you can expect to find, and is a sight in itself.

Just up the road is the KAUPPAHALLI (covered market). It's open 8 a.m.–5 p.m. and Saturday morning, and is full of delights.

There are several pizza places and the department stores have good cafés. Restaurant Kåren, part of the hostel, does good meals at reasonable prices.

Tampere

Located on the isthmus between two lakes, Tampere is Finland's second city. Although an industrial centre, it has plenty going for it to make it worth a visit.

TOURIST INFORMATION

At Verkatehtaankatu 2. Open weekdays 8.30 a.m.–6 p.m., Saturdays 8.30 a.m.–3 p.m., Sundays noon–2 p.m., weekdays only off season.

The 'Tampere service card' is a 24-hour tourist card providing unlimited travel on city buses, free admission to 13 museums and discounts on cruises and entry to SÄRKÄNNIEMI AMUSEMENT PARK. Costs 40 mk.

Telephone code 31.

SEEING

SÄRKÄNNIEMI not only has an amusement park, but also an aquarium, dolphinarium, planetarium, children's zoo and the NÄSINNEULA OBSERVATION TOWER, which affords a good view of Tampere and its surroundings. The SARA HILDÉN modern art museum is also nearby (open 11 a.m.–6 p.m. daily).

The LENIN MUSEUM at Hallituskatu 19 (open Tuesday to Saturday, 11 a.m.–3 p.m.) is possibly unique as the only museum outside Eastern Europe dedicated to the life of V. I. Lenin.

The CATHEDRAL, built 1907, is worth a look for its altar piece and frescos, as is the ORTHODOX CHURCH at Tuomiokirkonkatu 27, which although it is the only neo-Byzantine church in the Nordic countries, has the largest bells in Finland.

SLEEPING

• **Hostels:** Uimahallin Maja at Pirkankatu 10–12 (Tel. 229460) is central for most of the sights and about 1 km from the railway station. Head down Hameenkatu and bear right at the end. The YWCA at Tuomiokirkonkatu 12A (Tel. 359000) is also fairly central and nearer the station, head down Hameenkatu and take the second right, but only open from 1 June to 25 August.

Northern Finland

If you want to sail in the midnight sun and walk in the forests of Europe's remotest northern land, prepare yourself for a minimum of twenty hours' train travel from Helsinki and buses and ferries which don't always connect up as smoothly as one would like.

The end goal is a unique experience, but to be honest it's easier to get up to the Arctic tundra through Norway or Sweden. OULU is the most attractive of the northern towns. The trip from Helsinki to Rovaniemi isn't too bad – a direct 12-hour train journey – and this takes you to a convenient starting point for your Lapland excursions. The tourist offices at Oulu and Rovaniemi will supply you with all you need to know and suggest accommodation. The Rovaniemi youth hostel, at Hallituskatu 16 (Tel. (960) 14644) is good and clean and costs 37 to 50 mk. Turn right outside the station and follow the signs.

Southern Finland

The lakes and woods of the south make this area an outdoor recreation paradise and one of Europe's last wildernesses. SAVONLINNA is a good centre to base yourself at. In this neck of the woods you really ought to camp to get the feel of Finland. The tourist office can arrange canoes and bikes for you.

Savonlinna, near the Russian border, 6 hours from Helsinki, has more charm than the other towns in the Lake Region.

Don't wait on the train for the main station at Savonlinna, get off at the stop near the centre, Savonlinna–Kauppatori, as you're nearer the tourist office there. It's at Olavinkatu 35 and is open 7.15 a.m.–10 p.m. every day in summer.

At the heart of the town is Olavinlinna, on a small island, the medieval castle with the old wooden houses of Linnankatu surrounding it. Take the English guided tour of the castle.

From 5–28 July, the Opera Festival takes place, and it fills up beds at an incredible rate and is expensive to participate in. Use the open-air markets to picnic from, and try to stay at the excellent Malakius Youth Hostel at Pihlajavedenkuja 6 (Tel. 23283), 40 mk., either a 15-minute walk along TulliportinKatu and Savonkatu, or by bus 2 from centre. Camp at Kyrönniemi (Tel. 21507) in summer for 25 mk., close to Olavinlinna.

Almost on the Russian border, and on the route to Savonlinna, is the small town of Imatra, on the Vuokri river. The youth hostel and campsite are on the sandy shore of a lake in the forest. Despite the 2½ mile walk, or bus, it is a great place to relax.

USSR – Leningrad

As there is a daily train from Helsinki to Leningrad which only takes 7 hours, you may feel the urge to visit the USSR. Unfortunately, due to the timetable an overnight stay in Leningrad is essential and likely to be relatively expensive. Full details from Intourist, 219 Marsh Wall, London E14, or 71 Deansgate, Manchester M3 2PW, or 8 Belmont Crescent, Glasgow G12 8EV.

Intourist will be able to arrange the necessary visa and accommodation. Allow at least two to three weeks. Intourist will probably only offer you expensive first-class hotel accommodation, unless you insist on cheaper.

A ticket from Helsinki to Leningrad is likely to cost around £25.

Despite the relatively high cost, you may feel this is more than worth it for a glimpse at one of the most historic cities of the USSR.

FRANCE

Entry requirements	Passport
Population	53,500,000
Capital	Paris (pop.: 10,825,000)
Currency	Franc
	£1 = approx. 9.82 F
Political system	Republic
Religion	Mainly Roman Catholic
Language	French (English spoken in cities)
Public holidays	1 Jan.; Easter Monday; 1 May; 8 May; Ascension Day; Whit Monday; 14 July; 15 Aug.; 1, 11 Nov.; 25 Dec.
International dialling codes	From UK 01033
	From USA 01133
	To UK 0044
	To USA 001

France is a country of great diversity whose long and eventful history has left behind a wealth of attractions and pleasures to experience. Because of the efficient rail network, you can make as much or as little of France as you want: it's just as possible to explore each region in depth as it is to take an overnight express straight to the Riviera, if time and tanning are of the essence.

France (Gaul) was part of the Roman Empire till the Germanic Franks moved in during the fifth century. Charlemagne was crowned by the Pope on Christmas Day 800, but after his death the French nobles tried to go it alone. More successful than most were the Dukes of Burgundy and Normandy. In 987 the Capetian dynasty began to centralize power which led to a period of prosperity and trade, and the eventual growth of Paris as the intellectual centre of Europe in the thirteenth century. England's Norman kings held vast estates in France till the Hundred Years War sent them packing. This further strengthened the French monarchy; a process which continued under the Valois and Bourbon kings, till Louis XIV said it all – 'L'état, c'est moi' ('I am the state').

Under the 'Sun King' (Louis XIV), literature and the arts flourished and all the stylish people in Europe wanted to speak French. From this high point things gradually turned sour, and heads began to roll with the revolution in 1789. The First Republic didn't last long; then out of the chaos emerged Napoleon and dictatorship. During the nineteenth century the French Empire continued to grow, with power constantly changing hands between democracy and dictatorship. The revolution of 1848 brought about the Second Republic, which was followed by a coup d'état and the dictatorship of Napoleon III (nephew of the first). The Third Republic of 1870 survived until the German occupation of France in 1940. After Liberation the Fourth was created, and de Gaulle got the Fifth off the ground in 1958.

FRENCH NATIONAL RAILWAYS
(Société Nationale des Chemins de Fer Français, SNCF)

Arguably, Europe's best railway with the most luxurious carriages travelling at the fastest speeds on the most extensive rail network. Until recently one had to pay hefty Eurocity or at peak periods a smaller TGV (train à grande vitesse) supplements in order to experience the speeds of 180 m.p.h. of which SNCF justifiably are proud. Fortunately things are changing as TEEs have decreased rapidly in number and Corail trains have taken over. On some routes the TGVs offer the only convenient services (Paris–Lyon–Marseille–Toulon and Nice), and in these cases are well worth the extra francs. In general, though, supplements are only required on about 40 per cent of the journeys. The high speed network is being expanded, not only within France but to neighbouring countries, and includes the Channel link with England. The general increase in speeds now means that Strasbourg is four hours away from London, with Berne only four-and-a-half hours, Nice under seven hours. Planned routes to the Atlantic coast will mean that in the future Bordeaux will be three hours away and Hendaye, on the Spanish border, just over five hours (cutting two hours off journey times). The non-supplement Corail trains are almost indistinguishable from the Eurocity in comfort and in many cases run at the same speed. The network serves over 5,500 destinations using four different types of trains: TGV; Eurocity; Corail; and Turbo-train.

There are two special overnight trains from Calais to the French Riviera. Depending on the season they may call at Paris Nord, but no change is required, see Thomas Cook 12, 12a and 12b. These trains have no seating accommodation so you will have to go for either a sleeper or a couchette at about £8.20. As with most other aspects of French life, the train network is centred round Paris, so if your route is via Paris, generally you're OK, but if you're crossing France from east to west, your impression of SNCF will be somewhat less glowing. Everyone under 26 gets a good deal from French Railways – up to 50 per cent reduction with a 'Carré Jeune' railcard valid for a year or with a 'Carte Jeune' valid for the summer months.

• **Carte Jeune:** The Carte Jeune offers you a 50 per cent reduction on any journey made within France except on Paris suburban lines between 1 June and 30 September, provided it starts in a 'blue' (off-peak) period (see below). Off-peak dates account for approximately 80 per cent of the total number of days during the period in question.

Valid in both first and second class, the Carte Jeune costs £16 and even includes a special bonus in the form of a free couchette for an overnight journey on any French domestic route. In 1987, over 180,000 Cartes and Carrés Jeune were sold, helping French Railways to increase their share of the under-26 market.

It is a good investment, as the initial cost is recouped after travelling around 190 miles in second class, if you take advantage of the free couchette offer.

Cartes Jeunes also exist for reduced entry to museums, and staying/eating at universities and should not be confused. Ask at tourist offices for full details.

• **Carré Jeune:** Travel anywhere on the French Railways network, except on Paris suburban lines, and you will get the following discounts on 4 single (or 2 return) journeys in first or second class made within a period of one year:
—50 per cent on journeys started during a 'blue' (off-peak) period.
—20 per cent on journeys started during a 'white' (standard) period.
See below for details.

If you do a lot of travelling you can, of course, buy two or more Carré Jeune railcards during the year – you'll save yourself a lot of money because you get the reduction on all French domestic train services including the 168 m.p.h. TGV, the fastest train in the world. Only seat reservations (compulsory on TGV) and supplements for travel on certain trains and sleeping accommodation have to be paid for in the normal way.

The Carré Jeune will cost you £16 which you recoup after around 200 miles of second-class travel started during a 'blue' period or 500 miles of travel started during a 'white' period.

● **The 'blue, white and red' tariff calendar:** The French Railways tariff calendar is colour coded as follows:

'Blue' (off-peak) period: generally from 12 noon Monday to 12 noon Friday and from 12 noon Saturday to 3 p.m. Sunday.

'White' (standard) period: generally from 12 noon Friday to 12 noon Saturday and from 3 p.m. Sunday to 12 noon Monday plus some French public holidays.

'Red' (peak) period: approximately 60 days in the year when no reduction is available.

To help you plan your trip(s), you are supplied with a copy of the tariff calendar when you buy your Carré Jeune or Carte Jeune.

● **Where to buy your railcard:** You can buy your Carré Jeune or Carte Jeune at French Railways, 179 Piccadilly, London W1, upon presentation of your passport, as proof of your age, accompanied by a passport-size photograph in the case of the Carte Jeune. Either card can be bought at any railway station in France for 160 F.

● **Family Trains:** Another novel idea from SNCF is the Family Train which runs on 11 long-distance routes, mainly from Paris, but also from Nice and Nantes. Each train has fully-equipped play areas where young children can while away the journey as their parents look on. Special menus are available for family groups and there are even power points for baby's bottle-warmer. There is no additional cost, and children under four travel free if they don't occupy a seat. If they do, quarter-price fares are charged – but this only applies to Family Trains. Provided at least four full fare paying passengers, including at least one under 12, are in a group, a whole compartment may be reserved.

• **Rover Tickets:** The French rover ticket is called France Vacances Pass and is valid for 9 days in any one month, or 4 days within 15 days, at any time of the year. The ticket does not cover Corsica, but it does give travel concessions on the Paris metro and buses. There are a number of other bonuses on the ticket such as special £14 cross-Channel fares (each way) when you travel on Hoverspeed, plus discounts on Pullman/Altea and IBIS/URBIS hotels in cities served by the TGV, and reduced entry fees to a large number of historic buildings and monuments. It also includes the supplements payable on Eurocity and some TGV trains, but not the TGV or TEE seat reservation charge. The 4-day France Vacances pass costs £75 for second class and £103 for first class. Children (4–11) pay £37.50 and £75 respectively. The 9-day France Vacances costs £127 for second class and £185 for first class. Children (4–11) pay £63.50 and £92.50 respectively. It can be purchased from any travel agent or at main BR travel centres in Britain and at Paris St Lazare, Nice and Strasbourg stations and Paris Charles de Gaulle or Orly airports.

• **Air France Rail Tickets:** A new bargain is the Air France Rail Ticket which can be used in conjunction with a France Vacances pass. It offers direct flights from 16 UK and Irish airports to Paris or any major French airport and unlimited rail travel thereafter, just as a normal France Vacances pass. A further discount is the free rail travel from Paris Charles de Gaulle airport to the city centre.

From London a 4-day ticket costs £176 for second class and £204 for first class. A 9-day ticket costs £228 and £286 respectively. From Manchester a 4-day ticket costs £193 for second class and £221 for first class, £245 and £303 respectively for a 9-day pass. From airports in Scotland and Northern Ireland the cost of a 4-day ticket is £212 for second class and £240 for first class, £264 and £322 respectively for a 9-day ticket.

Further details, together with a ticket, can be obtained from travel agents, Air France or French Railways.

• **Liberté:** New in 1990, this is a 4-day France Vacances pass with seven nights' accommodation vouchers. Basic package from £279. Optional extras include single rooms, first class rail and nine-day pass.

• **Inter Rail bonuses:**

FROM	TO	REDUCTION %
Chemins de Fer de la Provence	Nice–Digne	50
Chemins de Fer de la Corse	All	50
Société Nationale Maritime Corse-Méditerranée	All routes	30 (in 2nd class)
Services d'Autocars de Tourisme SNCF	France–Corsica	

Also free entry to French Railway Museum, 2 rue Alfred de Glehn, Mulhouse.

• **Eurail bonuses:** Free:
—Digne–Nice or vice versa on the Chemins de Fer de la Provence.
—Ferry crossing on the Irish Continental Line between Le Havre (France) and Rosslare (Ireland) 21 hours, or Cork (Ireland) 21½ hours, and between Cherbourg (France) and Rosslare (Ireland) 17 hours. If cabin accommodation is requested, an extra charge will be made. Port taxes are extra and payable in French francs. During July and August advance reservation is recommended. It is compulsory if cabin accommodation is requested. Check the sailing schedule always.

The following half-price reductions are granted by Europabus on transportation costs only and by local offices in Europe.
253 Besançon–Lausanne
254 Chamonix–Evian–Geneva
255 Geneva–Nice
256 Grenoble–Nice
257 Grenoble–Briançon
258 Thonon–Evian–Stresa
446 Best of Brittany

TRAIN INFORMATION

English is spoken by rail staff at the major stations. Agents d'accueil ('welcome officers') wear orange caps and armbands and are in the stations to help with travel queries and any problems you've encountered on your journey, i.e. if you've had your rucksack stolen. These guys tour round as opposed to sitting in the information offices. At the ticket barriers in all French stations you'll see a bright orange machine. Use this to validate your ticket only if you've bought it in France. Otherwise ignore it. But if you have a French-purchased ticket, you must validate it, or face a fine.

• **Reservations:** Obligatory on all Eurocity and TGVs as well as a few of the Rapide trains. If you are taking a Eurocity you'll find the reservation charge is included in the supplement you'll have to pay. The supplement depends on distance – between 45 F and 61 F. Other optional reservations cost about 13 F. Reservations can be made up to noon, for trains between 5 p.m. and midnight on that day, and up to 8 p.m. for trains from midnight to 5 p.m. the following day. For trains to or from Paris, give yourself 2–3 days if possible. If you are very well prepared you can reserve up to four months in advance. Eurocity are reservable up to one hour before departure. Generally, it's a good idea to reserve on international trains and on days before public holidays. On some TGV services the reservation ticket is known as 'Resa 300'. Note that on these services you must validate the reservation ticket along with the main ticket.

• **Night travel:** A sleeper or couchette in France will cost you more than anywhere else in Europe. Granted the service is good, but at a price. SNCF offer both first- and second-class couchettes with four and six berths respectively. Couchettes cost about 80 F and must be reserved in advance, not later than 8 p.m. French Railways introduced a super new concept in budget night travel, the Cabine 8. This is a second class air-conditioned coach with compartments containing eight semi-reclined bunks which are completely free of charge to use. Needless to say, it was an instant success and SNCF are considering increasing the number of routes from last year's eight. If you are considering a long-haul overnight journey in France, check to see if Cabine 8 coaches have been added to the train you intend to use. In view of their success, it is advisable to reserve your bunk, for the standard seat reservation fee. Unless you're loaded with cash, avoid the TEN (Trans Euro Nuit) sleepers. Second-class sleepers are either (T3) three beds or (T2) two beds.

• **Eating on trains:** Surprisingly, few stations have tempting deli-catessen selling fresh croissants, pâtés and cheeses, so you must come prepared if you want to picnic. There are restaurants and bars at stations which are good but pricey. If you're going to have a blow out, you'd do far better going for a meal which you can at least be sure will be good, rather than for a snack from the ridiculously priced mini-bar trolleys, from which a coffee, for example, will cost about 11 F.

• **Scenic tips:** Take a train anywhere in southern France and you won't be disappointed. Not surprisingly the Alps provide a spectacular backdrop on any run. If you just want to breeze through, consider the Paris to Turin route (10 hours) which goes via the Mont Cenis tunnel (8½ miles long). For those who aren't happy with anything but the best, change at Culoz or Aix-les-Bains, for Chamonix. If you want to head down to the coast, we recommend the run from Grenoble to Marseille (5 hours), then Marseille– Genoa (be sure to sit on the right-hand side of the train on the Riviera stretch). All this journey along the Côte d'Azur is beautiful.

On the other side of the country: the lines between Clermont-Ferrand and Béziers, and Limoges and Toulouse, provide fine upland scenery. The Perpignan to La Tour de Carol is another favourite, as is Valence to Briançon.

• **Bikes:** The scheme's called 'Train et Vélo', and bikes can be hired at any of 283 stations from 50 F a day, plus 500 F deposit. Note, it is not easy to transport bikes with you on SNCF.

• **Advance tickets:** Tickets to and for within France can be purchased at British Rail Travel Centres and at Continental Shipping and Travel Ltd (CSTL), first floor, French Railways House, 179 Piccadilly, London. CSTL also provides a timetable information service by telephone 071–491 1573. French Railways, at the same address, supplies the various passes.

TOURIST INFORMATION

There are over 5,000 tourist information offices in France. They're called Syndicats d'Initiative or Offices de Tourisme. Those designated 'Accueil de France' will help you out with your travel and accommodation problems, as well as booking a bed for you for a small fee. The French tourist literature is good and free. Always ask for a map. If you're touring a whole region in depth and require further information, look up the address and phone number of the Comité Régional de Tourisme, and contact them.

For further information on Andorra the tourist office is: 63 Westover Rd, London SW18 (Tel. 081–874 4806 – mornings only).

• **ISIC bonuses:** Up to 40 per cent reduction on long-distance coach journeys. 50 per cent off all state museums and galleries, museums and theatres.

• **Money matters:** 1 franc (F) = 100 centimes.
Banking hours are 9 a.m.–12 noon, 2 p.m.–4 p.m. weekdays. Closed Saturdays (main towns) or Mondays, and closed early on day before bank holiday. Shop around before exchanging currency, as banks vary with their commission charges. The best we could find was the Crédit Agricole. Not every bank now changes currency, so if you're arriving on a Sunday night you won't be able to get any anywhere except the main station in the larger cities, where commission charges average 10 F and credit cards and some traveller's cheques are not accepted. French traveller's cheques are much more useful than those in sterling or dollars.

• **Post offices:** Open 8 a.m.–7 p.m. weekdays, and 8 a.m.–12 noon on Saturday. The larger railway stations have post offices which keep these, or longer, hours.

• **Shops:** Tend to shut from around noon to 2 p.m., and even longer in the south. They generally stay open till 7.30 p.m. Some food shops, especially bakeries, are open Sunday mornings.

• **Museums:** Follow the same pattern as shops; you'll find many of the state-owned ones closed on Tuesdays, with municipal ones shutting Mondays.

SLEEPING

Your best bet is to use the facilities offered in the various Foyers des Jeunes Travailleurs which are in all major centres. These studenty hostels are usually more central and less strictly run than youth hostels (they don't make a fuss about unmarried couples, etc.). The Acceuil des Jeunes en France (AJF) has numerous hostels through-out France (5,000 beds in Paris alone). Another organization, Union des Centres de Rencontres Internationales de France

(UCRIF), operates several hostels throughout France, with sixteen in Paris.

France is well supplied with official youth hostels (auberges de jeunesse) which charge around 50 F per person. They do ask for IYHF cards, so membership is obligatory. You can join up in France: their head office is 6 rue Mesnil, Paris.

Hotels run on a one- to four-star system with the government fixing prices; these are posted on the back of hotel room doors. So always check you've been quoted the right price. One stars start at about 90 F and are perfectly adequate so long as you don't expect the luxury of a bath. In France a shower or bath (and often breakfast, too) will almost always cost extra. Try to reduce your costs if you're travelling in a group by getting a third bed put in the room – this'll cost an extra 30 per cent or so and is cheaper than another room.

Camping should present no problems in France as nearly every major town has at least one site. They also operate on a star system. The International Camping Carnet is advisable at most sites – you can buy it at site offices on the spot.

EATING AND NIGHTLIFE

Eating and drinking are about the only things in France not centred on Paris. Each region has its own specialities based on the local produce. There's no such thing as a hurried snack – the midday lunch break is at least a 12-to-2 affair. The French take their food very seriously and like to think themselves connoisseurs. Cafés are for sitting and watching the world go by, not for cheap eating. If you're desperate for a coffee, check the price and size of cup first, make it last and drink in the atmosphere as long as possible. It's far better, though, to get a baguette under your arm and head for the corner charcuterie and crémerie, where you can choose from a huge selection of cheeses (watch out: chèvre is goat). Fortunately, supermarkets are reasonable and still maintain a high standard. Look out for branches of Prisunic, Monoprix, Uniprix, or Codec.

The wines are cheap and the parks free. Unless you're really broke, it's well worth eating out in the evenings with the fixed-price menus always a safe bet. Try where possible to sample the local dishes, as they give an added interest to touring.

Rouen

It is a pity that many Inter-Railers en route to Paris pass through the fascinating and historic region of Normandy without stopping. Situated on the Seine, Rouen is the capital of Normandy and is perhaps best known for its links with Joan of Arc.

TOURIST INFORMATION

At 25 Place de la Cathédrale (Tel. 35 71 41 77); during summer open Mon.–Sat. 9 a.m.–7 p.m., Sun. 9.30 a.m.–12.30 p.m., 2.30 p.m.–6 p.m. They will hand out useful leaflets and help you find a cheap room.

SEEING

The OLD TOWN dates from the twelfth century and boasts a fine collection of beautiful half-timbered houses. A circular walking tour enables you to appreciate the main sites. Unmissable is the RUE DU GROS-HORLOGE, as it connects the OLD MARKET PLACE to the CATHEDRAL (and is adjacent to Tourist Information).

The OLD MARKET PLACE was where JOAN OF ARC was burnt at the stake in 1431 and now contains the STE JEANNE D'ARC national monument, a church and a small covered market, all designed by Arreche.

NOTRE DAME CATHEDRALE dates from the twelfth century and is a fine example of Gothic architecture.

Rouen has many fine churches; perhaps the most notable is ST MACLOU for its large five-panelled porch. The nearby ST MACLOU CLOISTER at 184–186 rue Martainville should also not be missed. This tranquil cloister is one of the last examples of a medieval plague cemetery and was used as a charnel-house until the eighteenth century.

SLEEPING

Cheap rooms are plentiful and many are in the heart of the old city. Tourist Information will assist.

• **Hostel:** Centre de Séjour at 17 rue Diderot (Tel. 35 72 06 45), bus 12 from the railway station. Alternatively cross over the river, turn left and walk along the river bank.

EATING AND NIGHTLIFE

All the Normandy culinary specialities can be found. The seafood, Rouen duck, calvados and cider are all recommended. Most restaurants are good value and offer fixed menus. The many small bars offer cheaper snacks or just one course and the universal burgers are also available.

A cheap meal can be had at the Maison des Jeunes, 114 ave. de Bretagne, close to the Centre de Séjour, weekday lunchtimes for about 30 F.

Bayeux

An impressive town, Bayeux deserves at least a few hours' sightseeing. It is most notable for its connections with William the Conqueror and the world famous Bayeux Tapestry, graphically telling the story of the Norman Conquest of Britain.

Tourist Information is in the centre of town on corner of rue St Martin and rue des Cuisiniers (Tel. 3192 1626), and will provide the usual assistance and information.

SEEING

QUEEN MATILDA'S TAPESTRY, also known as the BAYEUX TAPESTRY is now magnificently displayed in the Cultural Centre on rue des Nesmond. Open mid-May–mid-September 9 a.m.–7 p.m., otherwise closed over lunchtime. The BARON-GERARD MUSEUM has fine displays of old paintings, lace and tapestries. A combined ticket for four museums can be obtained.

The CATHEDRAL was originally completed in 1077 and is now an impressive mixture of Norman and Gothic architecture. Also worth a look is the MUSEUM OF THE BATTLE OF NORMANDY 1944 in boulevard Fabian Ware. Open 9 a.m.–7 p.m. in the summer, the museum recounts the Allied invasion of France June–August 1944 and is near a British military cemetery.

• **Hostels:** Should you feel inclined to stay, the youth hostel is about 1½ miles from the station at Centre d'Accueil Municipal, 21 rue des Marettes (Tel. 31 92 08 19). The Family Home Hostel on rue Général de Dais 39 (Tel. 31 92 15 22) is good value, follow the signs from the station. Reservations recommended.

Mont St Michel

Although not on a direct railway line, the extra hassles are well worth it to see the 'marvel of the western world'. Mont St Michel is a solitary village and abbey dramatically perched on a small island linked to the mainland by a causeway which occasionally floods completely at high tide. A tide table is available from the local tourist office, located in the town hall.

• **Getting there:** Mont St Michel is actually on the boundary between Normandy and Brittany. Take the train from Caen to Rennes and get off at Pontorson. Mont St Michel is about 6 miles away and reached by bus, 25 F return, bus from opposite station, about seven buses a day during summer.

   A further disadvantage is the hordes of tourists, but if you can be bothered to make the trip, you will be rewarded by an unforgettable sight and experience.

SEEING

The splendid ABBEY dominates the island and is open 9 a.m.–11.30 p.m. and 1.30 p.m.–4 p.m. (6 p.m. May–Sept., all day during high season). The guided tour lasts around ¾ hour, at about 1-hour intervals. Closed Tuesdays. The MERVEILLE or 'marvel' is the group of superb early-thirteenth-century buildings and is aptly named. The VILLAGE is a steep labyrinth surrounding the abbey and is itself encased in RAMPARTS which have good views of the bay.

SLEEPING

The nearest hostel is at Pleine Fougères about 3 miles outside Pontorson at rue de Normandie (Tel. 33 48 75 69). Poor bus service, so your best bet is to walk. Camping sites are better situated but do not be tempted to sleep rough on the causeway or beach as the tides are very unpredictable and dangerous.

Brittany

You'll curse the rail network if you want to visit this region in depth. Local trains all connect up to the main Paris–Brest line rather than other nearby towns. On the new TGV line from Paris it now only takes just over 2 hours to Nantes and around 2 hours to Rennes. For accommodation and general information on the area, visit the Centre Information Jeunesse Bretagne in the Maison du Champ de Mars at 6 Cours des Alliés, Rennes.

From RENNES it's possible to make a day trip to the impressive walled port of ST MALO, formerly a pirates' stronghold, and preserved almost intact. Pushing south, NANTES has a majestic fifteenth-century ducal palace, as well as a very good museum devoted to Breton folklore. The youth hostel in Nantes is at 2 Place de la Manu (Tel. 4020 5725), open high season only.

Also consider a trip to CONCARNEAU. Take the train to ROSPORDEN and then a railway bus (free on Eurail) to Concarneau. Check your timetable first, because the bus doesn't connect with every train.

The Loire Valley

This pastoral region contains many of France's most elegant and impressive buildings. To do justice to the area would take at least a week. Fortunately for the eurorailer, most of the châteaux and palaces lie between Angers and Blois, a distance of about 80 miles. Where to base yourself depends on your style. Perhaps the most impressive châteaux are CHAMBORD and CHENONCEAU. There are campsites everywhere, and youth hostels at Saumur, Tours, and Blois.

BLOIS is typical of the Loire: THE BISHOPS' PALACE, the CHÂTEAU, the OLD QUARTER – all set in a picturesque location among fine churches and gardens. The campsite at Blois is good. About 3 miles out of town, by bus or taxi from the station (about 0.40 F and 35 F respectively) or take the metro to Port Maillot and then the campsite bus. The last bus from Blois leaves at 6.15 p.m. For those who prefer a cheap hotel, it's best to base yourself at TOURS, where rooms are plentiful around the station. Try the Olympic opposite the station at 74 rue Bernard–Palissy (Tel. 47 05 10 17), or Hôtel Comté behind the station, at 51 rue Auguste Comté (Tel. 47 05 53 16). If you're out of luck, the tourist office is just in front of the station at Place Maréchal Leclerc (Tel. 47 05 58 08) (open Mon.–Sat.: 9 a.m.–12.30 p.m., 2 p.m.–9 p.m., Sun.: 10 a.m.–12.30 p.m., 4 p.m.–9 p.m.). For a fee of about 5 F they will fix you up with a room and give free advice on bus tours, etc., to the châteaux. If you can't afford the bus, don't worry as they rent out bikes at the station for around 50 F a day plus deposit, and most of the châteaux are easily accessible. The town itself, like Blois, has a charming OLD QUARTER and a former BISHOPS' PALACE which now hosts the MUSÉE DES BEAUX ARTS. Further down the line, SAUMUR and ANGERS both have very impressive castles perched on high, overlooking the Loire and Maine respectively. If you prefer to stay at this end of château country, the Syndicat d'Initiative, opposite the station at Angers, will find you a room for a small charge.

Wherever you end up, it's a good idea to go along to any train information desk in the area and pick up one of the local timetables giving all the smaller stops. .

Paris

Everyone has his or her own impressions and expectations of Paris – so much has been said and written about it, and it all seems a cliché, yet Paris is everything you've probably ever heard, and more. It's a fabulous city and you can't help but enjoy a few days there.

Paris has twenty 'arrondissements' (districts) with the Louvre as No. 1. The city is divided into the Left Bank (Rive Gauche) and Right Bank (Rive Droite), with the River Seine dividing them. Generally speaking, the Left Bank is the trendy, studenty and less expensive area, and the Right Bank is more classy.

STATION FACILITIES

There are five international stations in the city: Austerlitz serves southern France, Spain and Portugal; Est serves Germany, Switzerland and Austria; Lyon serves the south east of France, Italy and Switzerland. Nord serves Belgium, Holland, Scandinavia and Germany, and St Lazare serves Britain's entry ports of Dieppe and Le Havre.

		AUSTERLITZ	EST
Train information	Mon.–Sun.:	All hours (Tel. 482 50 50)	All hours (Tel. 482 50 50)
Reservations	Mon.–Sun.:	8 a.m.–8 p.m. (Tel. 465 60 60)	8 a.m.–8 p.m. (Tel. 465 60 60)
Tourist information	Mon.–Sat.:	8 a.m.–10 p.m. (Tel. 484 9170)	Mon.–Sat.: 8 a.m.–10 p.m. (Tel. 407 1773)
Foreign exchange	Mon.–Fri.:	8.45 a.m.–5 p.m.	7.30 a.m.–8 p.m.
Bar, Snacks	Daily	6 a.m.–12 midnight	7 a.m.–11 p.m.
Bath, Shower	Daily	5.30 a.m.–8.30 p.m.	6.15 a.m.–10 p.m.
Left-luggage lockers	No access:	0.30 a.m.–5.30 a.m.	1.15 a.m.–5.45 a.m.
Left-luggage store	Daily	6 a.m.–0.30 a.m.	6 a.m.–12 midnight
Shops		7 a.m.–11 p.m. Lower level and at Blvd de l'Hôpital	Mon.–Sat.: 8 a.m.–12.45 p.m. 2.30 p.m.–7.30 p.m. Sun.: 8 a.m.– 12.45 p.m. Rue du 8 Mai and Faubourg St Denis
Waiting room		All hours	All hours
Toilets		All hours	All hours
Station shuts		0.30 a.m.–5.30 a.m.	1.15 a.m.–5.45 a.m.

There are post office facilities at both these stations (8 a.m.–7 p.m., half day Saturdays). SNCF run buses for 14 F which connect most of the stations, or metro line 5 connects Paris Est and Paris Nord and Austerlitz. Paris Lyon is reached by buses 61 and 69 from Austerlitz, and bus 65 from Est. SNCF have recently introduced a train information telephone service in English. The number is 4380 50 50.

	PARIS LYON	PARIS NORD
Train information	All hours (Tel. 482 50 50)	All hours Office: 6 a.m.–11.15 p.m. (platform no. 1) (Tel. 482 50 50)
Reservations	8 a.m.–8 p.m. (Tel. 465 60 60)	7 a.m.–9 p.m. (Tel. 465 60 60)
Tourist information	Mon.–Sat.: 8. a.m.–10 p.m. (Tel. 443 3324)	Mon.–Sat.: 8 a.m.–10 p.m. Sun.: 1 p.m.–8 p.m. (Tel. 487 89215)
Foreign exchange	6.30 a.m.–10 p.m.	6.30 a.m.–10 p.m. Also opp. station, Mon.–Fri.: 9 a.m.–4.30 p.m. Sat.: 9 a.m.–1 p.m. at BNP (smaller queues and better rates)
Bar, Buffet	5.40 a.m.–11.30 p.m.	6 a.m.–11 p.m.
Restaurant	5.40 a.m.–11.30 p.m. (ground level) 11 a.m.–2 p.m. 6 p.m.–9.15 p.m. (upstairs)	11.30 a.m.–2 p.m. 6.30 p.m.–9.45 p.m.
Bath, Showers	6 a.m.–8.30 p.m.	6 a.m.–8.30 p.m.
Left-luggage lockers	No access 1 a.m.– 4 a.m.	All hours. (Use the ones upstairs beside the left-luggage store)
Left-luggage store	All hours	6 a.m.–12 midnight
Shops	Rue Hector Malot	Mon.–Sat.: 8 a.m.–12.45 p.m. 2.30 p.m.–7.30 p.m. Sun.: 8 a.m.–12.45 p.m.
Waiting room	All hours	All hours
Toilets	All hours	All hours
Station shuts	1 a.m.–4 a.m.	0.15 a.m.–5.45 a.m.

Post office facilities at both stations, Mon.–Fri.: 8 a.m.–7 p.m., Sat.: 8 a.m.–12 noon (rue Diderot for Paris Lyon). SNCF buses will get you from one station to another, or from Paris Lyon you can get to all the other stations by metro line 1 to Bastille then change to line 5. From Paris Nord, line 5 takes you to Austerlitz, Est and Lyon (change on to line 1 at Bastille). An additional route from Nord to Lyon is to take line B to Châtelet les Halles, then line A to Lyon (much faster). With six stations in Paris it's important to get the right one. Plan well ahead, and wherever possible use your timetables, as train information queues can be up to two hours long in the summer. At Gare du Nord reservations for the TGV to Lyons are now made at an automated machine with French instructions.

	ST LAZARE	MONTPARNASSE
Information	Tel. 482 50 50	Tel. 482 50 50
Reservations	Tel. 465 60 60	Tel. 465 60 60

FROM	TRAINS GO TO:
Gare de l'Est	Eastern France
	Germany
	Switzerland
	Eastern Europe
Gare de Lyon	Riviera
	South-east France
Gare d'Austerlitz	Central France
	Southern Atlantic coast
	Spain
Gare Montparnasse	Western France
	(Chartres, Loire Valley and Brittany)
Gare St Lazare	Normandy
Gare du Nord	North coast
	Belgium
	Holland
	Germany (Hamburg)
	Britain

TOURIST INFORMATION

The main office of 'Accueil de France' is at 127 Avenue des Champs
Elysées (Tel. 47 23 61 72) (metro to Etoile). Open Mon.–Sun.: 9
a.m.–8 p.m. in high season. Closes at 6 p.m. otherwise. They'll give
you information on Paris and the rest of France. They also run a
wide-ranging accommodation-finding service on a commission
basis. Also, it's well worth paying the 5 F for their 'Guide de Paris'
(in English). For recorded tourist information in English phone
47 20 88 98.

• **Accueil des Jeunes en France (AJF):** This non-profit-making
tourist office for the young is at 119 rue St Martin (Tel. 42 77 87 80),
across from the Pompidou Centre (Beaubourg) (Metro Les Halles
or Rambuteau.) Open Mon.–Sat.: 9.30 a.m.–7 p.m. They'll find

you a bed or a place in a Foyer for 80 F upwards. They also have offices at Gare du Nord, 139 boulevard Saint Micheal (metro Port Royal) and 16 rue du Pont Louis-Philippe (metro Hôtel de Ville). The policy these days seems to be to pay the full accommodation price over to AJF when booking, so remember to change money before joining the queue. To get the best rooms be in the queue by 8 a.m.

• **Union des Centres de Rencontres Internationales de France (UCRIF):** This centre for young tourists is at 4 Jean-Jacques Rousseau, near the hostel (Tel. 42 60 42 40).

• **Addresses:**

POST OFFICE AND POSTE RESTANTE: 52 rue du Louvre (Tel. 42 33 71 60), open 24 hours a day (metro Louvre).

AMEX: 11 rue Scribe, Mon.–Fri.: 9 a.m.–5 p.m., Sat.: 9 a.m.–12 noon (Tel. 42 66 09 99) (metro Opera).

CIEE: 51 rue Dauphine 6e (Tel. 43 26 79 65), Mon.–Sat.: 10 a.m.–1 p.m., 2 p.m.–6.30 p.m. They will help out in all your travel needs and fix you up with an ISIC (metro Odéon).

UK EMBASSY: 109 rue du Faubourg St Honoré (Tel. 42 66 91 42). The Emergency Consulate is nearby at 16 rue d'Anjou (Tel. 42 66 91 42) (metro Concorde).

US EMBASSY: 2 Avenue Gabriel (Tel. 42 96 12 02), Mon.–Fri.: 9 a.m.–4 p.m. (metro Concorde).

CANADIAN EMBASSY: 35 Avenue Montaigne (Tel. 47 23 01 01) (metro Franklin-Roosevelt).

AUSTRALIAN EMBASSY: 4 rue Jean Rey (Tel. 45 75 62 00) (metro Bir-Hakeim).

24-HOUR CHEMIST: Pharmacie Dhéry, 84 Avenue des Champs Elysées (Tel. 45 62 02 41) (metro George V).

SOS HELP LINE: English speakers to help you with personal problems, etc. 3 p.m.–11 p.m. (Tel. 47 23 80 80).

• **Getting about:** the metro in Paris is one of the world's best underground systems and you're bound to use it at some point to get you quickly round this incredibly large and sprawling city. The system is open from 5 a.m. to after midnight. The lines are designated by the terminal station. It's a cheap as well as efficient way of getting about. Buy tickets in 'carnets' of 10 for around 32 F, and hold on to them till the end of your journey. The same tickets

206 Europe by Train

can also be used on the buses – validate them in the machine on the bus, using two if crossing a zone – and central Paris RER trains.

Recently there has been an increasing number of reports of crime on the metro, including drug users and dealers causing problems for the authorities. Also beware of buying a ticket at anywhere other than an official booth: you are only asking to be ripped off.

Tourist passes known as Paris Visite, valid on metro and buses are available; three days at 70F and five days at 115F, for three zones, only first class. Ask at tourist information for full details, and other passes.

SEEING

• **The Champs Elysées:** The ÉTOILE is the great circle at the western end of the Champs Elysées with twelve avenues radiating out from it, literally a 'star'. In its centre is the massive ARC DE TRIOMPHE, Napoleon's thank-you to his army; note the sculpture of 'the Marseillaise' by Rude. At the other end of the long and elegant Champs Elysées is the PLACE DE LA CONCORDE, regarded as the most beautiful square in the world. This is where Louis XVI, Marie-Antoinette and some 1,300 others met their death in the French Revolution.

• **The Left Bank:** ST GERMAIN-DES-PRÉS, the oldest church in Paris, is surrounded by open-air restaurants and cafés and quiet little streets like PLACE FURSTEMBERG which make a pleasant stroll.

BOULEVARD ST MICHEL, the centre of Bohemian student life of the 1960s, still makes an interesting excursion. Sitting in one of the cafés along the 'Boul Mich' in the Latin Quarter (so called because the Sorbonne students were lectured to in Latin in the Middle Ages), you're bound to make new friends. The tallest building in Europe, TOUR MAINE–MONTPARNASSE (690 feet), gives you a great view over the city. (The lift up is supposed to be the fastest one in Europe.)

Also on the Rive Gauche is the beautiful church of LES INVALIDES with its golden dome and the mortal remains of Napoleon. A good view of NOTRE DAME CATHEDRAL can be seen from SQUARE RENÉ VIVIANI.

• **The Right Bank:** Opposite the LOUVRE is Richelieu's PALAIS ROYAL where the Comédie Française is based, and not far from here is the oldest square in Paris – PLACE DES VOSGES – the beautiful Renaissance square built by Henry IV early in the seventeenth century; VICTOR HUGO'S HOUSE at No. 6 is now a museum. The GEORGES POMPIDOU CENTRE (known as the Beaubourg) is a good place to meet trendy young Parisians and see interesting exhibitions. Closed Tuesdays, it's open till 10 p.m. at weekends.

The SACRÉ-COEUR is the white dome that dominates all of Paris, built on the hill at MONTMARTRE, the artists' quarter that flourished in the late nineteenth century when many of the Impressionist painters lived and worked there. The artists' quarter is more than the touristy PLACE DU TETRE. Stroll along rue Norvins into rue des Saules and check out the LAPIN AGILE, a meeting point for writers and artists and very atmospheric. A climb to the dome of the Sacré-Coeur gives you a thirty-mile view over Paris. Watch out for pickpockets in this area.

• **Île de la Cité and Île St-Louis:** The tiny island where Paris began in pre-Roman times is the Île de la Cité. The oldest bridge in Paris, the PONT NEUF, leads you to the statue of Henry IV and on to the PALAIS DE JUSTICE (law courts). The SAINTE CHAPELLE is the Gothic church which houses many holy relics and dates from 1248.

NOTRE DAME is only a short walk from here; this thirteenth-century cathedral is the first church of Paris, where Napoleon was crowned and all national celebrations are staged.

The other main sights are the OPÉRA BUILDING, 1875 (the opera is now located at Place de la Bastille) and, of course, the EIFFEL TOWER, which looks its best floodlit at night. A five-year renovation scheme costing millions of francs was completed recently and has made great improvements, but it is still expensive to ride to the top. There are three stages of lifts, getting progressively more expensive the higher you go. It is possible to walk up the first two stages to save on the cost, but if you use the lifts all the way there is a whopping 45 F charge. The queues can be long, even with all lifts in action, also check for the right queue. The view from SACRÉ-COEUR is just as impressive. If you are visiting it on 14 July (National Day), make sure you go at night and catch the spectacular hour-long fireworks display. If you want to tour the famous PARIS SEWERS, call in at 93 Quai d'Orsay.

There are various city tours: Parisvision buses with prerecorded commentary, and Cityrama tours, or the famous bateaux-mouches which sail down the Seine (go for the evening one when the illuminations are on). Shop about, as they vary from reasonably priced to extortionate. Still, if you've only a day or two, the three-hour Parisvision tour gives you a pretty comprehensive idea of the city.

• **Museums:** All state-owned museums in Paris are shut on Tuesdays and those owned by the city close on Mondays. An ISIC will get you into most places for half price. The Louvre is free on Sundays (and packed). There are over 100 interesting museums in the city; pick up a leaflet on them from tourist information.

The MUSEUM CARD (LA CARTE), available from metro stations and major museums, permits direct entry to 60 museums and monuments in the Paris region. Valid for one day (cost 50 F), three consecutive days (cost 100 F) or five consecutive days (cost 150 F); unlimited visits are permitted and access is immediate, avoiding the often lengthy queues. The card can be bought in advance, but your name and date must be written on it on your first visit in order to validate it.

THE LOUVRE: Porte Denon, Place du Carrousel (in the Tuileries Gardens). Treasures include the Venus de Milo, and the Mona Lisa. Open 9.45 a.m.–6.30 p.m. (though many departments close at 5 or 5.30 p.m.). Entry is 25 F, all under-26s half price, free on Sundays. Remember, you *must* leave your hand luggage at the entrance, and the museum shop shuts at 6 p.m. Queues are very long on Sundays.

As it now houses the underground entrance, it is impossible to miss the controversial 71-foot-high GLASS PYRAMID in the courtyard of the Louvre. Designed by Pei, it not only houses the reception area, including a complex of restaurants and shops, but has greatly expanded gallery and exhibition space.

The Jeu de Paume is now included in the wonderful new MUSÉE D'ORSAY, which has also absorbed the contents of a few other museums. It is situated on the Left (south) Bank, near the Tuileries. Closed Mondays. Admission 23 F, open 10.30 a.m. to 6 p.m., from 9 a.m. on Sundays. Reduced entry for 18–24 year olds and ISIC holders. You can spend all day in the Louvre or Musée d'Orsay.

POMPIDOU CENTRE: A modern multi-cultural art centre conceived by Georges Pompidou and opened in 1977, this eccentric building is home to just about every modern art-form you can think of. It also includes an excellent library with hundreds of daily newspapers, including most English and American ones. Although entrance is free, special exhibitions and the cinema usually incur a charge of between 10–15 F. Special one day pass is available at 40 F. There's usually plenty of free entertainment in the form of fire-eaters and street artists outside. Also known as the 'Beaubourg'.

For button-pushers, the CITÉ DES SCIENCES ET DE INDUSTRIE, at 30 Avenue Corintin-Cariou, will keep you occupied all day. A combination of science exhibitions, computer games, practical demonstrations and videos are all included in the 35 F admission. The Planetarium is included, but entry to the giant movie theatre is extra. Take buses 150, 152 or 250.

MUSÉE DE CLUNY: 6 Place Paul-Painlevé (corner of Boulevard St Michel and Boulevard St Germain). Open 9.45 a.m.–12.30 p.m., 2 p.m.–5 p.m. Medieval art housed in a fifteenth-century mansion next to the Roman baths of Paris.

MUSÉE DE L'HOMME: Palais de Chaillot, Place du Trocadéro. Open 10 a.m.–6 p.m. (5 p.m. in winter). Very good anthropological museum – documentary films are shown daily.

• **Parks:** There is no shortage of attractive parks and gardens in Paris, and they make good picnic venues or places to sleep if you're running out of money.

The BOIS DE BOULOGNE is the wood at the western edge of the city with seven lakes, a waterfall, various sports facilities and a campsite. The BOIS DE VINCENNES is the wood on the south-eastern edge which tends to be a better bet to sleep rough in, but is a bit rougher (not recommended for girls alone). There's a zoo, a racetrack and a couple of museums out here too. The two most central picnic parks are the JARDIN DES TUILERIES and the JARDIN DES CHAMPS ELYSÉES; the LUXEMBOURG, off Boulevard St Michel, is a very picturesque, formally laid-out garden in French style.

SLEEPING

Campsites are not at all central, and with so much to see in Paris the commuting may be a waste of valuable time. Private accommodation is hardly heard of in Paris and sleeping rough gets riskier each year, so if you're wise you'll choose between a cheap hotel, a student hostel or a Foyer. Your choice will be dictated not just by your pocket but also by how many you are. Paris really is a city for lovers – it's often virtually the same price for a single or a double bed so couples are on to a good deal, but singles are better off in a Foyer.

The average night in a hotel double room is anything upwards from 100 F, for 1 star, and a single Foyer stay will be about 80 F. Always ask hoteliers if there's nothing cheaper and get as many as possible into a room to bring the cost down. The youth hostel is at 8 Boulevard Jules Ferry, near place de la Republic. It was an hotel before becoming a hostel some years ago. It re-opened in 1986 after substantial renovation work which closed it for almost a year (Tel. 43 57 55 60). Take the metro to Republique. There are several others further out. A new 400-bed permanent hostel opened in late 1987 called Auberge de Jeunesse d'Artagnan, at 80 rue Vitruve (Tel. 43 61 08 75). The nearest metro is Porte de Bagnolet. The best districts to concentrate your attention on for cheap hotels and basic B&B-type accommodation are around the Place de la Bastille, Nation, St Paul, Gare de Lyon, Place de Clichy and Pigalle. If you have any problems try the UCRIF/AJF information office at Gard du Nord, but don't try sleeping there or you'll be ejected about 1 a.m. or mugged. Also try the UCRIF/AJF offices listed under **Tourist Information**.

● **Hotels:** Try: Sorbonne, 6 rue Victor Cousin (Tel. 43 54 58 08); Hôtel Notre Dame, 1 Quai St Michel; Hotel Avenir, 52 rue Lussac, 5e (Tel. 43 54 76 60), or Hotel Henri IV, 9 rue St. Jacques, 5e (Tel. 43 54 51 43). Also worth a try are Dacia, 41 Boulevard St Michel (Tel. 43 54 34 53), Hôtel Henri IV at 25 Place Dauphine (Tel. 43 54 44 53), and the hotel at 13 rue de Malta. The Hôtel Speria at 1 rue de la Bastille is also worth checking out.

● **Foyers and student hostels:** CIS Léo Lagrange, 107 rue Martre Clichy (Tel. 4270 0322, metro Mairie de Clichy); Maison des Clubs Unesco, 43 rue de la Glacière (Tel. 43 36 00 63, metro Glacière); Hôtel des Jeunes (AJF), 11 rue du Fauconnier, 6 rue de Fourcy (both Tel. 42 74 23 45, metro St-Paul), 12 rue des Barres (Tel. 42 72 72 09, metro Hôtel de Ville); Centres International de Paris (BVJ), 20 rue Jean-Jacques Rousseau (Tel. 42 36 88 18, metro Châtelet), and 5 rue du Pélican (Tel. 40 26 92 45, metro Louvre); Foyer International d'Accueil de Paris, 30 rue Cabanis (Tel. 45 89 89 15, metro Glacière). BVJ International at 11 rue Therese (Tel. 42 60 77 23, metro Pyramides or Opera) is excellent. Open all day but with a 2 a.m. curfew.

● **Camping:** Camping du Bois de Boulogne, allée du Bord de l'Eau (Tel. 45 24 30 00), take the metro to Port Maillot, then bus 244, then a short walk. Cost around 55 F per night, get there early in summer.

● **Stuck in Paris with no money for a bed?:** There are good overnight trains to Madrid (from Austerlitz), Salzburg (from Est); Venice (from Lyon), and Copenhagen (from Nord).

EATING AND NIGHTLIFE

Both are a great pleasure in Paris and can be afforded, in one category or another, by everyone. The French seem to have invented the picnic and you'd have to be completely blind or stupid not to be able to make yourself a delicious picnic of baguette, pâté, cheese, wine and fruits. There are several open-air markets and boulangeries (bakers) in every district while the épiceries (grocers) stay open till 7.30 p.m.

If you want a change from French food, there are plenty of alternatives provided by the numerous immigrants from France's ex-colonies. The centre of the North African (Algerian, Tunisian, Moroccan, etc.) restaurant area is between rue St Jacques and Boulevard St Michel.

There are fast-food chains and self-service cafés too in Paris, but you're better – and it's often just as cheap – to look for a French restaurant which offers a 'menu du jour', and eat real French cuisine – for once at a price you can afford. The areas round rue de la Huchette and rue Mouffetard in the Latin Quarter will prove fruitful for reasonably priced restaurants.

Often the best value set menus are in Chinese Restaurants. Try the Palais de Chine for especially good value. It's at 31 rue St Jacques, off the Boulevard St Germain.

For those wanting to eat at student restaurants on their ISIC, call at CROUS, 39, avenue Georges Bernano (metro Port Royal), Open Mon.–Fri. 9 a.m.–5 p.m. for a list of all the places you can eat for under 20 F in this scheme. CROUS is shut during June and July.

A few suggestions: Crêperie St Germain, 27 rue St André des Arts; Chartier, 7 rue du Faubourg Montmartre – about 60 F for 3 courses and a drink – very traditional restaurant; Restaurant des Beaux Arts, 11 rue Bonaparte – good cheap set menus – expect a really good set meal with wine for 50 F; Country Life vegetarian restaurant, 6 rue Daumou, Mon.–Fri. 11.30 a.m.–2.30 p.m.; Crêperie de la Houff, 9 rue Mouffetard; Au Grain Folie, 24 rue de la Vieuville, Montmartre, 7 p.m.–10 p.m., small but good vegetarian. Also try La Casa Miguel, 48 rue Saint Georges (metro St Georges), long queues but very cheap.

For current events in Paris, pick up a copy of *Pariscope* from tourist information.

If you were thinking of the stereotyped trip to the Moulin Rouge, Lido or Folies Bergère, you might as well forget the rest of your European itinerary, as a night out in one of these places will cost you about 400 F minimum. It's actually more of a spectacle walking round the Blanche and Pigalle areas, just down from Montmartre, or Montparnasse, but watch out for drug-pushers and pickpockets around here. For the serious red-light seekers, the place is rue St Denis.

Slightly more sedate a time can be had watching the fountains at the Trocadéro and admiring the view of the Eiffel Tower, or wandering down by the Seine; often there are buskers in the area round Place du Vert Galant. On a fine evening, wandering around the Place de Tertre, Montmartre, is also a great experience.

There's an active theatre and cinema scene in Paris – for details of what's on, see *Pariscope*. The area along the Seine on the Left Bank is best for affordable jazz and rock clubs. Le Caveau de la Huchette, 5 rue de la Huchette, is known to all Parisian students as their informal club, but they ask 50 F (60 F on Friday and Saturday nights) on nights when there's jazz or dancing. For clubs try Le Palace on rue de Faubourg-Montmartre. Closed Monday and Tuesday. Entrance £12 or free if you eat in the restaurant (£13 minimum). Les Bains on rue du Bourg-L'Abbé is the ultimate rowdy club in an old Turkish bathhouse. Live music is good at Gilbus, 18 rue du Faubourg (Metro Republique) and Le Furstemborg at 27 rue de Bici is good for jazz. The cafés at Montparnasse remain a typically Parisian vantage point from which to watch life go by, but watch out for the prices. In August, when many French restaurants are closed, these are often the only places open.

EXCURSIONS FROM PARIS

VERSAILLES, the elaborate palace of Louis XIV, is the main attraction near to Paris. Entrance to the palace costs 23 F. Get there early, or you'll be queueing all day instead of viewing. The gardens cost 14 F, but go there after seeing inside, as the fountains usually aren't switched on until after 3.30 p.m. Take a train from Montparnasse or Invalides out to it. The palace is open Tues.–Sun.: 9.45 a.m.–5 p.m. (free under 18, half price on ISIC, half price on Sundays). Also within striking distance is the palace of FONTAINE-BLEAU with its beautiful park-forest. Take the train from Gare de Lyon. Open 10 a.m.–12.30 p.m., 2 p.m.–6 p.m., except Tues. Fill in your Inter Rail and take it to the ticket office: you'll be given a free ticket for Fontainebleau or Versailles on the suburban railway. CHANTILLY is an attractive small château, reached by train from Gare du Nord, but it's open only on Sundays and holidays. CHARTRES, home of the world's most famous Gothic cathedral, is an hour away from Gare Montparnasse. If you really want to make a day of it, take the hour-long train ride to Epernay where Moët et Chandon, on Avenue de Champagne, play hosts for another enjoyable tour with free samples.

Alsace and Lorraine

After many years of occupation, the German influence is strongly felt in this region, especially in the cuisine: choucroute (sauerkraut with ham and sausage) and backaoffe (casserole with lamb, pork, beef and potatoes) are our favourites; swallowed down with some pression (local draught lager), they make a meal you won't forget.

Strasbourg

Apart from being the seat of the European parliament and the capital of Alsace, it is one of France's most attractive cities. The tourist office is at the station when you arrive. They will supply you with a map and information on the city, as well as provide a room-finding service. Alternatively there is another office at 10 Place Gutenberg (Tel. 88 325707). The youth hostel is quite far away so it's best to try somewhere more central like Hôtel du Cycliste, 8 rue des Bateliers (Tel. 88 362001). There are several hotels near the station but they are quite tacky.

STATION FACILITIES

	STRASBOURG GARE
Train information	Mon.–Sat.: 7.30 a.m.–8 p.m.
	Sun.: 8 a.m.–8 p.m. (Tel. 88 22 50 50)
Reservations	Mon.–Sat.: 7.30 a.m.–8 p.m.
	Sun.: 8 a.m.–5.30 p.m.
Tourist information	Mon.–Fri.: 9 a.m.–12 noon, 2 p.m.–6 p.m.
	Sat.: 9 a.m.–12 noon
	Outside in front of station
Foreign exchange	8 a.m.–8 p.m.
Left-luggage lockers	All hours
Left-luggage store	All hours
Showers	6 a.m.–10 p.m.
Cafeteria	4 a.m.–2 a.m.
Restaurant	11 a.m.–10 p.m.
Waiting room	All hours
Post office	Mon.–Fri.: 8 a.m.–7.30 p.m.
	Sat.: 8 a.m.–12 noon

Daily trains to: Luxembourg (2 hours), Brussels (4 hours), Munich, Stuttgart (2½ hours), Basel (1½ hours), Zürich (2½ hours), Milan, Lyon, Paris (4 hours). (The main tourist office is at 10 Place Gutenberg, open till 7.30 p.m. in summer.)

From the station, walk down to LITTLE FRANCE (well-preserved old houses bordering the canal) and wind your way through the covered bridges and narrow medieval streets to the Gothic CATHEDRAL. Try and arrive at noon when the astronomical clock comes into action or see the sound and light show in the evenings (7 F). If you fancy a climb up to see the Clock – and a good view – the entrance fee is 4 F. Opposite the cathedral, the CHÂTEAU DES ROHANS contains a fine museum of archaeology, ceramics and paintings. For eating, try the areas around Place du Marché aux Cochons de Lait and Place du

Corbeau. For cheap and well-prepared Alsacian specialities, go to 9 Porte de Kehl. If you like to eat in a crowd try Au Pont St Martin at 13–15 rue des Moulins (Tel. 324513) overlooking the river. In early June there is an International Music Festival.

• **Hostel:** There is a youth hostel, Rene Cassin, at 9 rue de l'Auberge de Jeunesse, Montagne Verte (Tel. 88 30 26 46) about 1 mile from the station on bus 3, 13, 23 from Marché Ste Marguerite to Auberge de Jeunesse.

The Alps

In our opinion, CHAMONIX is one of the best places to visit in the Alps by train. The mountain railway which winds its way through picture-book villages is an unforgettable experience; sit on the right-hand side for the best view. When you're there, the tourist office at Place de l'Eglise (open till 8 p.m.) will help you out on accommodation, etc. (prices are expensive), or you could try camping. Check out the price of 'Le Chamonard' for accommodation with the tourist office. Another unforgettable experience is the cable car to the Aiguille du Midi. The Youth Hostel is at Les Pélenus (Tel. 531 452). It does dinners and packed lunches, and you can also get discounts on cable cars here. It is about a fifteen-minute walk from town and only a few hundred metres from the nearest station, also called Les Pélenus.

If you have only a day and want to head for the hills, ask tourist information for the list of 'Promenades à Pied' (walking tours), state how long you want to walk and ask what their suggestions are, as the possibilities are endless. If you take your walking seriously, contact the *Club Alpin Français* on Avenue Michel Croz (Tel. 50 531603) for information on mountain refuges and conditions.

Even if you don't make it up the mountains, go and rub shoulders with the climbing set and have a beer with them in the Nationale, rue Paccard. Local Alpine food specialities include smoked sausage, various cheeses and, of course, fondue.

Two other very beautiful spots are AIX-LES-BAINS and ANNECY. Aix-Les-Bains is a pretty spa town on a lake, with good walks in the surrounding hills and around the lakeside which afford panoramas of the deep blue lake and of the town. The hostel at Promenade du Sierroz (Tel. 79 88 32 88) is very good. Take bus 2 towards Plage-Piscine and the Grand Port if you don't fancy the walk of about 1¾ miles. Annecy is another picturesque lakeside town. The old town with its narrow streets and fortress is well worth seeing. The hostel is 'La Grande Jeanne' at 16 route du Semnoz (Tel. 50 45 33 19). Take bus 1 towards 'Paradis'!

Burgundy

If wine is what takes you to Burgundy, be sure to visit the MUSÉE DU VIN in the Hôtel des Ducs de Bourgogne at BEAUNE and take the tour at MAISON PATRIARCHE, rue du Collège, where they even give you a little bottle for the train. Apart from wine, Burgundy possesses some of the finest abbeys in France, the most spectacular one being at VÉZELAY, and though this isn't on the rail, there's a bus from AVALLON which is. From Paris or Dijon, change at Laroche-Migennes.

Dijon

Capital of Burgundy and an important centre in the fourteenth and fifteenth centuries, Dijon went into a decline for about 400 years until the railway brought commerce and industry back in the 1850s. Now it is known for its edible specialities such as mustard, cassis (blackcurrant liqueur) and snails, and is a thriving commercial and industrial centre.

STATION FACILITIES

	DIJON GARE DE VILLE
Train information	Mon.–Sat.: 8 a.m.–7.30 p.m.
	Sun.: 9 a.m.–12 noon, 2 p.m.–6.30 p.m.
	(Tel. 80 41 50 50)
Reservations	As above
Tourist information	Mon.–Sat.: 9 a.m.–12 noon, 2 p.m.–8 p.m.
	In Place Darcy, three blocks away
Foreign exchange	As 'train information'
Bar, Buffet	7.30 a.m.–10 p.m.
Left-luggage lockers	No access 1 a.m.–4 a.m.
Left-luggage store	All hours
Shops	Regular hours. In Place Darcy
Station shuts	1 a.m.–4 a.m.

Daily trains to: Paris (2½ hours), Strasbourg (4 hours), Venice, Genoa, Lyon (1½ hours) and Marseille–Nice.

TOURIST INFORMATION AND ADDRESSES

Place Darcy (Tel. 80 434 212), near city centre; open daily 9 a.m.–12 noon, 2 p.m.–9 p.m. (until 7 p.m. in winter). Room-finding service.

• **Addresses:**
POST OFFICE: Place Grangier, Mon.–Fri.: 8 a.m.–7 p.m., Sat. and Sun.: 8 a.m.–12 noon.
24-HOUR CHEMIST: Tel. 80 412 828.
CENTRE INFORMATION JEUNESSE DE BOURGOGNE: 22 rue Audra (Tel. 80 30 35 56).

SEEING

The best way to see Dijon's well-preserved past is on foot; the tourist office gives out a free brochure on walking tours.

The former ducal palace, which houses an art museum, deserves a visit, as do the streets of the old town surrounding it. The archaeological museum has artefacts dating back to the ninth century BC (closed Tuesdays).

The youth hostel at 1 Boulevard Champollion (Tel. 80 713 212) is good but a long way from the station. Bus 6 from station to Place de la Republic, change to bus 5. The Foyer International d'Etudiants at Avenue Maréchal Leclerc (Tel. 80 715 101) requires an ISIC and is also quite far out of town. Hôtel du Miroir, 7 rue Bossuet (Tel. 80 305 481) has rooms for 70 F. The campsite is at Avenue Albert (Tel. 80 435 472), overlooking the lake. It's clean, and in the summer it fills up early, so phone first.

Restaurants can be an expensive luxury in Dijon, so buy from the market stalls along rue de la Liberté. One of the least expensive restaurants is Moulin à Vent at 8 Place Françoise-Fude. For a jar of the famous mustard, go to 'Maille' on rue de la Liberté.

The Riviera (Côte d'Azur)

EXCURSIONS

In the past you would have had to be crazy to try and base yourself anywhere but Nice on the Côte d'Azur, but that doesn't apply any more should you want to visit the swanky resorts such as Cannes, Monte Carlo, Juan-les-Pins and St Tropez. A day's sunbathing will cost you nothing and you'll find prices only slightly more expensive. The beautiful people of St Trop have not permitted such vulgar inventions as public trains to spoil their paradise, so you'll have to bus it from St Raphael to get there. Still, if you want an all-over tan – or to scrutinize other people's – it's the only place to be.

If you hit a cloudy day, go through to Monaco and put on your best bib and tucker and brave it out in the famous casino at Monte Carlo: the main gambling room is free, but you must be able to prove you're 21 or over. The palace is also worth seeing, but is expensive. If you're staying overnight, try and get into the Relais International de Jeunesse in Cap d'Ail (Tel. 93 781 858) just outside Monte Carlo, or the excellent Princess Stephanie Youth Centre (with mixed rooms!). Another good place to base yourself is at the Saint Michel Ment (Tel. 93 35 81 23) campsite at Menton near the Italian border. A tent for two people a night costs from 29 F, depending on season. Look out for bogus lifts from the station to the campsites as we've had reports of drivers taking money and leaving people at the site entrance knowing it to be full. For windsurfing, sailing and other water sports, make for St Raphael, as prices are cheaper here and there's more likely to be wind than further up the coast. Try Hotel de Geneve, 92 boulevard Felix Martin (Tel. 93 95 2335) for a night's rest (doubles 100 F) and the Wind Club for surfing (Tel. 93 95 4492).

A reasonably cheap place to base yourself is Biot. Look hard for the station between Nice and Cannes as it's easy to miss. Biot has a particularly good campsite opposite the station. Le Logis de la Brague is cheap and close to the beach.

Another good spot is Villeneue Loubet Plage, between Antibes and Nice. It is a small pleasant town with several campsites. A friendly and cheap campsite is Savoy (Tel. 93 20 16 06) which is right on the beach. Easy access to other resorts by train which runs frequently along the coast.

A good campsite just outside Toulon is Camping Bureguard, which is reached by bus 27 or 9.

The island of CORSICA can be reached from either Nice or Marseille. The cheapest fare is on a night ferry travelling fourth class (sleeping on deck) from Nice, Marseille or Toulon, one way. Corsica is very beautiful. Bonifacio, Ajaccio (Napoleon's hometown) and Bastia are the three most attractive centres on the island. Basically though, you'll need to be really keen to go to Corsica to make it worth while as rail fares are expensive and rail passes aren't valid here, though Inter Railers get a reduction. Eurotrain have reduced fares from Nice to Corsica, available from USIT.

Nice

This is without doubt your best base for a spell on the Riviera; it's cheaper than the more pretentious resorts along the Côte d'Azur and has more facilities suited to the eurorailer's lifestyle. It gets very busy, especially in August, and you might have to fight hard for your space on the pebbly beach, but at least there's the reassurance that you're only a few minutes by train from other small Riviera resorts with less crowded beaches like Villefranche, Beaulieu and Menton.

STATION FACILITIES

	NICE GARE DE VILLE
Train information	Daily 6 a.m.–10 p.m. (Tel. 93 875 050)
Reservations	Mon.–Sat.: 8 a.m.–7 p.m. Sun.: 8 a.m.–12 noon, 2 p.m.–7 p.m.
Tourist information	Mon.–Sat.: 8.45 a.m.–12.30 p.m., 2 p.m.–6 p.m. In summer, daily 7 a.m.–10 p.m. (Hotel reservations from 10 a.m.)
Foreign exchange	Mon.–Fri.: 7.30 a.m.–8 p.m. Sat., Sun. and holidays: 9 a.m.–7 p.m.
Café	7.30 a.m.–10 p.m.
Left-luggage lockers	No access 1.15 a.m.–5.30 a.m.
Left-luggage store	5.30 a.m.–12 midnight
Bath, Shower	8 a.m.–9 p.m.
Station shuts	1.15 a.m.–5.30 a.m.

Daily trains to: Paris, Strasbourg, Genoa, Milan, Rome, Marseille.

TOURIST INFORMATION AND ADDRESSES

The main office is to your left, coming out the station, at Avenue Thiers (Tel. 93 870 707). Youth Information CIJ, 19 rue Gioffrédo (Tel. 93 80 93 93).

● **Addresses:**
POST OFFICE: 23 Avenue Thiers. Daily 6 a.m.–10 p.m.
POSTE RESTANTE: Rue des Postes.
AMEX: 11 Promenade des Anglais, Mon.–Fri.: 9 a.m.–12 noon, 2 p.m.–6 p.m., Sat.: 9 a.m.–12 noon.
NIGHT CHEMIST: 7 rue Masséna. 7.30 p.m.–8.30 a.m.
DOCTOR AND AMBULANCE: SOS Médecins (Tel. 93 830 101).
SNCM: 3 Avenue Gustave V, for boats to Corsica.
USIT VOYAGES: 10 rue des Belgiques, 06000 Nice (Tel. 87 333 496). Also Eurotrain office.

SEEING

The old town of Nice with its street markets and Italian atmosphere has some typically Mediterranean walks through narrow winding alleys, which come as a sharp contrast to the commercial, touristy feeling on the main streets of Nice. To get a view over Nice and the

Mediterranean, climb the 300 feet up to the château. If you've only an hour or two in Nice, spend it walking the length of the Promenade des Anglais. Eating in the cafés is prohibitive but the manwatching scope is great.

Among the main things to see are: the PALAIS LASCARIS at 15 rue Droite (former residence of the Count of Ventimiglia), the RUSSIAN ORTHODOX CATHEDRAL, the old PORT of Nice where the beautiful people keep their beautiful yachts, the MATISSE MUSEUM at Avenue des Arènes with some of the artist's works and personal possessions, and the MUSÉE NATIONAL MARC CHAGALL, Avenue du Dr Ménard.

SLEEPING

During the Jazz Parade each July beds become very scarce, and at any other time beds are still hard to find, so come early and phone around. Most of the cheap hotels are located round the station. The youth hostel is 4 km away at route Forestière du Mont Alban (Tel. 93 89 23 64), bus 14. Use les Collinettes, the university accommodation, at 3 avenue de Robert Schumann (Tel. 93 97 06 64) bus 17, girls only. Price is around 50 F. The Relais International de Jeunesse (Tel. 93 81 27 63), Avenue Scuderi, is OK, but could mean a long wait to be checked in. However, hotels in the following streets are central, clean(ish) and affordable: rue d'Angleterre, Avenue Durante, rue Alsace Lorraine, rue de Belgique, Avenue Thiers. The Hotel Ideal Bristol in rue de Belgique (Tel. 93 886 072) charges 100 F for a double – which includes a fridge! Try Madame Garstandt, 55B rue Gambetta next to the station. Hotel Ann Margaret at 1 Avenue St Joseph is 10 minutes' walk from both station and beach and costs 70 F per night including use of the swimming pool. The beaches are closed from midnight to 6 a.m. so it is impossible to use them for a cheap sleep. You may be lucky and find one open, but it will be very crowded and a bit of a bearpit. There are lots of campsites at Villeneuve–Loubet, 8 km from Nice and on the line from Nice to Cannes. Although expensive, facilities are good. A map of the sites is available from the Tourist Information Centre at Nice Station. If stuck, go to the hostel in Menton.

EATING AND NIGHTLIFE

Food in Nice is among the best in France; the proximity of Italy (30 minutes away) is clear in the cuisine, so the pizzas in Nice are better than many you'll find in Italy, and there's plenty of fresh seafood from the Mediterranean. Sitting in an outside restaurant in one of the pedestrianized streets watching life go by is one of life's great pleasures, and Nice abounds with good set menus at prices from 45–80 F. Try Le Felix Fauvre, 12 avenue Felix Fauvre; Chez Davis, 11b rue Grimaldi; Chez Nino, 50 rue Trachel (100 beers). For self-service try the Café de Paris at one of 3 locations – 42 rue Pastorelli, rue Massena or in the Old Town. For those cutting corners there are some good supermarkets in the centre.

Discos and clubs are expensive, and anyway a walk down the Promenade des Anglais is just as entertaining.

Marseille

Marseille lacks the charm and finesse of the Riviera resorts but it does have character. It's France's oldest city (dating back to 600 BC) and one of the world's major ports, but it tends to cater more for businessmen than tourists.

STATION FACILITIES

	MARSEILLE ST CHARLES
Train information	5 a.m.–1 a.m. (Tel. 91 08 50 50)
Reservations	8 a.m.–7 p.m.
Tourist information	June–Aug.: Mon.–Sat.: 7.30 a.m.–9 a.m., 3 p.m.–8.30 p.m. Otherwise main office
Foreign exchange	6 a.m.–8 p.m.
Bar, Buffet	5 a.m.–12 midnight
Restaurant	11 a.m.–2 p.m., 6 p.m.–9.30 p.m.
Left-luggage lockers	No access 1.30 a.m.–4 a.m.
Left-luggage store	All hours
Shower	4 a.m.–12 midnight
Station shuts	1.30 a.m.–4 a.m.

Daily trains to: Paris, Strasbourg, Lyon (4 hours), Nice (2¼ hours), Milan, Bordeaux, Nantes.

TOURIST INFORMATION AND ADDRESSES

To be found at the station in summer, otherwise at 4 La Canebière (near the Old Port) (Tel. 91 549 111), open 8 a.m.–8 p.m. They have an accommodation-finding service. Youth Information is at rue de la Visitation (Tel. 91 499 155).

● **Addresses:**
POST OFFICE: Place de l'Hôtel-des-Postes (metro Colbert).
24-HOUR CHEMIST AND DOCTOR: Tel. 91 528 485.

SEEING

Marseille's most famous street is the Canebière (can-o-beer to generations of British and American sailors) which leads up from the Old Port to the Quai des Belges. This gets quite lively at night (the Bar du Téléphone was the scene of the biggest gangland massacre ever), but you're safer walking round here than in the slums of the North African quarter round the Porte d'Aix and rue Ste-Barbe.

The MUSÉE DES BEAUX ARTS in the Palais de Longchamp is the city's art gallery and the MUSÉE DES DOCKS ROMAINS (Roman docks), 12 place Vivaus, was the unexpected result of a 1943 German bomb.

The other 'sights' are the old town, ST VICTOR'S BASILICA and CATACOMBS, Le Corbusier's 17-storey CITÉ RADIEUSE, the CATHEDRAL and the park and CHÂTEAU BORLEY.

SLEEPING

The two youth hostels are a long way from the centre but are all right once you get there: Avenue de Bois-Luzy (Tel. 91 490 618) bus 8 from Bourse (near Canebière) and then bus 44, and Auberge de Bonneveine at 47 Avenue J. Vidal (Tel. 91 732 181), metro to RD–PT du Prado, then bus 44. Beware when looking round for a cheap hotel, especially near the docks – many of them are 'multi-purpose' establishments. For pensions, try down Allées Léon Gambetta and anywhere round the station. There's also camping at Les Vagues (Tel. 91 730 488), but it's pretty poor and resembles a car park. Also a long way out.

EATING AND NIGHTLIFE

Bouillabaisse, the famous French fish stew, comes from Marseille, and is at its best here. There's no shortage of restaurants-cafés and fixed-price menus can be found. The Tunisian and Moroccan restaurants are cheap, though not always good – but it's not wise for unaccompanied girls to head into the North African quarter at night. Chez Papa down by the port does a spectacular ice-cream sundae for less than 30 F.

Nightlife more or less finds you in Marseille. Just watch out you don't go into too low a dive as, if things get nasty, we've heard the police don't lose too much sleep over the odd mugged eurorailer.

Provence

Renowned for its cloudless skies and Roman remains, Provence's rich countryside has acted like a magnet to artists and eurorailers alike for years. The best time to go is May or September as

Aix-en-Provence and Avignon have Arts festivals in July and August, and rooms are hard to find.

If you're going to or from the south or west and have plenty of time, consider breaking your journey at VALENCE. Valence is a pretty, peaceful town with a good youth hostel/campsite near the station called Centre L'Eperviere. Costs are around 14 F a night and the centre also has a swimming pool and bar/restaurant.

Avignon

If you're coming from Lyon, consider getting off the train half an hour before Avignon at ORANGE to see one of the finest Roman theatres in the world.

After a fracas between the Vatican and Philip IV of France, Boniface VII moved to Avignon. The inner walled city is still dominated by his palace, the PALAIS DES PAPES, which is most impressive from the outside; they are restoring it and English tours are available. Be sure to visit the park above the palace for a superb view of the River Rhône.

Sleeping will be your greatest problem in Avignon, but there is an accommodation service opposite the station, which you're advised to use to save yourself hassle. If you don't mind large dormitories, try the Youth hotel at Camping Bagatelle (Tel. 90 863 039), located on the Ile de Barthelasse in the middle of the Rhone. Prices are good and there is a superb view of the palace. Also try the YMCA foyer, 7 Chemin de la Justice (Tel. 90 254 620), from 50–90 F. Finally, there's a youth hostel at 32 Boulevard Limbert (Tel. 90 852 778), from the station, walk around the city walls to the right. The tourist information office is at 41 Cours Jean-Jaurés and in front of the station. Open 9 a.m.–6 p.m., closes for 2-hour lunch on Saturdays, closed Sundays.

If you're camping, Avignon has several sites near each other on the Ile de Barthelasse, Camping municipal (Tel. 826 350), Camping Bagatelle (Tel. 863 039), Parc des Libertés (Tel. 851 773) and Camping des deux Rhônes (Tel. 854 970). Although they are all within walking distance of the station, the rather infrequent No. 10 bus from the station (5 F) will take you there.

Arles

An important centre in Roman and medieval times with an impressive amphitheatre which today has reverted to its function as a blood bath, imported Spanish bulls having replaced the gladiators. The MUSEUM OF CHRISTIAN ART is well worth a visit, as is the ROMAN THEATRE from the first century BC and the ROMAN CEMETERY.

Tourist information is on Boulevard des Lices (Tel. 90 962 935): they'll supply a ticket for 20 F (14 F on ISIC) for entry to all the museums and monuments as well as help you out with accommodation if necessary. The youth hostel is on rue Foch (Tel. 90 961 825), a block behind the tourist office. Try Hôtel Mistral, 16 rue du Docteur Fanton, or Hôtel du Trident, 9 rue de la Liberté for a cheap bed. If you want to venture into the Camargue, Arles is about the nearest you'll get by rail (they rent out bikes at the station and the going is flat).

Nîmes

Some of the best Roman remains in France are here, with the MAISON CARRÉE and the AMPHITHEATRE stealing the show. Tourist information is at 6 rue Auguste, and they run a similar system to Arles: ticket for the monuments, ISIC reduction. They'll also give you the best route to the PONT DU GARD, a 2,000-year-old Roman aqueduct which is almost intact, and the old Crusaders' port of AIGUES-MORTES, now well inland through silting up. Both are well worth visiting.

The hostel is about 2 miles out at Chemin de la Cigale (Tel. 66 23 2504). Either bus 6 or 20 – note the last buses are at 8 p.m.

Aix-en-Provence

Birthplace of Cézanne and intellectual and cultural centre of the region, Aix fancies itself somewhat and gives off an air of sophistication that is lacking elsewhere. Sit in any café and you'll feel a strange air of self-importance. The MUSEUM OF TAPESTRIES is particularly interesting. Avoid their festival, as prices and crowds increase dramatically. Tourist information is at Place du Général de Gaulle (Tel. 42 260 293). Try Hôtel du Casino, 38 rue Victor Leydet (Tel. 42 260 688), or the Auberge de Jeunesse on Avenue Marcel Pagnol (Tel. 42 201 599) – take bus number 8 to Estienne d'Orves or 12 to Vasarely from the Place de Gaulle as it's 2 km from the station.

Central/South-west France

The Auvergne, Dordogne and Languedoc regions are sparsely populated and consequently trains are few and far between; however, if you have the time and patience for the local trains, the rewards are great.

CARCASSONNE, the medieval gem of the Languedoc region, is on the main line and services are good. This is arguably Europe's best-preserved relic of the Middle Ages, and certainly the most interesting walled city in France. After centuries of building and fortifying the town, it was left to rot in the sixteenth century and it wasn't till the nineteenth that restoration began. The tourist office is on Boulevard Camille Pelleton; they find rooms and are generally helpful. Arrive early as Carcassonne is not a well-kept secret and in summer rooms get scarce.

CLERMONT-FERRAND and PÉRIGUEUX are not particularly interesting towns in themselves but they make excellent bases for touring the Auvergne and Dordogne. The tourist board at Clermont is at 69 Boulevard Gergovia, and Périgueux's is in Avenue de l'Aquitaine. They'll provide you with details on the surrounding area and how best to reach the places of interest. Accommodation should be no problem in either town: most of the cheap hotels surround the stations.

LES EYZIES DE TAYAC (the prehistoric capital of Europe) is about 40 minutes south-east of Périgueux by train and its cave paintings are within easy walking distance of the station, as is the tourist information office (Tel. 53 069 705). There are plenty of hotels to choose from in the village and there's camping on the other side of the river.

Bordeaux

Famed for the many quality wines it produces, Bordeaux is a good place to head for if your money's running out and you fancy a week or two working on the grape harvest which is picked in September. A short stay here will give you a totally different perspective on French life from your few days in Paris: whilst Paris is very Parisian, Bordeaux is terribly French.

STATION FACILITIES

	ST JEAN STATION
Train information	Daily 5.30 a.m.–9 p.m. (Tel. 56 92 50 50)
Reservations	Daily 7 a.m.–8 p.m.
Tourist information	9 a.m.–12.30 p.m., 1.30 p.m.–6 p.m. (weekdays) 9 a.m.–3 p.m. (Sunday) closed Sundays during low season
Foreign exchange	5 a.m.–8 p.m. At ticket windows
Bar, Buffet	All hours
Restaurant	Daily 7 a.m.–9.30 p.m.
Shower	5 a.m.–11 p.m.
Left-luggage lockers	No access 12 midnight–5 a.m.
Left-luggage store	All hours
Shops	Regular hours. In Cours de la Marne
Waiting room	All hours
Post office	Mon.–Fri.: 8 a.m.–7 p.m. Sat.: 8 a.m.–12 noon
Station shuts	12 midnight–5 a.m.

Daily trains to: Paris, Lyon, Nantes, Toulouse, Marseille, Nice, Biarritz, Madrid and Lisbon.

TOURIST INFORMATION AND ADDRESSES

The main tourist information office is at 12 Cours du 30 Juillet (Tel. 56 442 841), just off the Esplanade des Quinconces. The post office is at 52 rue Georges Bonnac. For a 24-hour chemist or doctor, telephone 56 909 275. The Centre Information Jeunesse Aquitaine is at 125 Cours Alsace-Lorraine (Tel. 56 485 550), and will help with accommodation.

SEEING

Explore Bordeaux on foot, starting your tour at the GRAND THÉÂTRE on the Place de la Comédie. From here you can work out the best route on the map to take you to the other sights: the ESPLANADE DE QUINCONCES, the largest square in France, the PLACE DE LA BOURSE with its eighteenth-century façades, the CATHÉ-DRALE ST ANDRÉ, the MUSÉE DES BEAUX ARTS and the smart shopping streets round RUE BOUFFARD. Also worth a visit is the interesting MUSEUM OF THE RESISTANCE, and MUSEUM OF AQUITAINE.

To get the feel of things, take a 'wine tour'; the Syndicat d'Initiative (in the tourist office) arrange these daily. The cost is around 70 F. per person, high season only.

SLEEPING

A bed is no problem in Bordeaux, even though many places close down in August. The youth hostel is close to the station at 22 Cours Barbey (Tel. 56 915 951). Head down Cours de la Marne, fifth turning on left. There's a bar, kitchen and a great atmosphere. Costs 37 F with IYHF card, 42 F with passport. Closed 9.30 a.m.–6 p.m., but rucksacks can be left at reception. There are several cheap hotels in the area: Hôtel Gambetta, 66 rue Porte-Dijeaux (Tel. 56 512 183) and Hôtel St François, 22 rue du Mirail (Tel. 56 915 641) are reasonably priced. For camping check out the site at Lorréjean, a half-hour bus ride on route 'B', leaving from the bus station at Quai Richelieu, down by the river. The site is a few minutes' walk from the terminus.

EATING AND NIGHTLIFE

Predictably enough, the local cuisine makes good use of the regional wines and there are all sorts of dishes using the delicious Bordelaise sauce. Set menus at affordable prices can be found in restaurants on rue des Augustins, Place Général Carvail, and rue du Maréchal-Joffre.

The main shopping street is rue St Catherine, where there are plenty of good supermarkets and eating places.

Ask tourist information for a 'What's On' and try sampling the regional wines at bistros.

Cerbère

If you are heading for Spain along the Mediterranean coast and decide to break your journey for the night at the border, give the station and the beach a body swerve. Instead walk back along the main road towards France for a few hundred yards and take the foot-path up the cliff. Both the scenery and sleeping potential here are much better.

GERMANY

Entry requirements	Passport
Population	78,000,000
Capital	Berlin (pop.: 2,960,000)/Bonn (pop.: 300,000)
Currency	Deutschemark
	£1 = approx. 2.93 DM
Political system	Federal Republic
Religions	Protestant and Catholic
Language	German (English spoken in major cities)
Public holidays	1 Jan.; Good Friday; Easter Monday;
	1 May; Ascension Day; Whit Monday;
	17 June; Corpus Christi; 15 Aug.; 7 Oct.;
	1, 17, 21 Nov.; 25, 26 Dec.
International dialling codes	From UK: 010 + 49 (western) or 37 (eastern) + number
	From USA: 011 + 49 (western) or 37 (eastern) + number
	To UK: 00 + 44 + number
	To USA: 00 + 1 + number

The new united Germany has emerged from a nightmare stretching back through partition to the 1930s. The immediate future may be rocky as the backward east is incorporated into the west, but the result may well be a new economic super-power. The east is now more accessible and well worth the visit to see not only the effects of the last 45 years but also to see its history, exemplified by the beautifully restored city of Dresden.

The Germans are a restless lot. Wherever you go in Europe, there they are. It's always been like this from the days of the Franks and Saxons. Most people have heard of the Holy Roman Empire, created by Otto I in 962, which survived till 1806, but few realize that the local German regimes were often much more powerful. The Hanseatic League of merchants, associated with the towns of Lübeck and Hamburg, controlled much of northern Europe's wealth in the medieval period.

Long after the rest of Europe had formed itself into single nation-states, 'Germany' was still divided, a fact not helped by the incredible number of feuding princedoms and the country's lack of natural boundaries. These divisions came to a head in the Thirty Years War of 1618–48 when the Catholic south defending the

Habsburg emperors and Protestant north, inspired by men such as Luther and the Reformation movement, fought it out between themselves. In 1871 Bismarck got everyone organized and the German nation came into being. The autocratic rule, attempts to conquer an empire, and rapid industrialization led to discontent, and topped with Kaiser Bill's blunderings, this ended up as the First World War. After the failure of the liberal Weimar Republic, Hitler started stirring things up again, and we all know what Nazism led to . . .

The end of the Second World War saw Germany occupied by the Allies. Cold-war tensions caused the division into two states. Germany has survived all these trials. The Wall is down and, despite the chaos, we have a united Germany again.

GERMAN FEDERAL RAILWAYS
(Deutsche Bundesbahn, DB)

DB offer one of the best deals in Europe. They're fast, clean and efficiently run. Unlike Britain and France where all the main lines radiate out from the capital, the Germans have an excellent series of interconnecting cross-country lines which serve all the principal cities and the smaller towns throughout the country.

The number of trains crossing the old border has been doubled to approximately 200 a day. This year, a single timetable is being produced for east and west.

There are five types of train, apart from Eurocity: fast intercity trains (IC) which require a 7 DM supplement – supplements for journeys across a frontier may vary; the new InterRegio (IR) trains are nearly as fast and connect to smaller cities and the IC network (require a 3 DM supplement); Schnellzüge (D) are similar to IRs but are older; the Eilzüge (E) serving the regional areas; Personenzüge or Nahverkehrszüge, which are slow local trains. This year the next generation of German trains are to be introduced – the 150 m.p.h. + electric intercity expresses (ICE). The German Rail Pass is becoming more popular each year at £80 for 4 days' unlimited travel, £120 for 9 days and £170 for 16 days second class (all within a 21-day period). The card frees you from paying supplements but travel on Eurocity is only available with the first-class card. If you are under 26 there is also a Youth Pass, which is valid for second-class only. It costs £45 for 4 days, £70 for 9 days and £95 for 16 days. The Rail Pass also entitles you to a reduced (50 DM second class) return ticket to West Berlin and a free coach tour of the city. Cards are available from BR-appointed travel agents, BR continental booking offices or DER, 18 Conduit Street, London W1 (Tel. 071–499 0577). In the United States write to German Railways for further information at 747 Third Avenue, 33rd Floor, New York NY 10017 (Tel. 212–308 3100). When in Germany anyone under 23 (students, 27) can buy a one-month, go-as-you-please Tramper-Monat ticket for 246 DM at any of the larger stations. You can also buy it from DER before you go for £90. You need evidence of age, such as a passport or IUS card. If you plan on spending a long time in Germany, look out for the DB Junior Rail Pass available for anyone aged between 12 and 22 (students, 27). It's valid for a year and gets you 50 per cent reduction on all rail tickets, although you still have to pay Eurocity and IC supplements. It costs 110 DM and can be purchased from BR travel centres at Liverpool Street and the International Rail Centre at Victoria Stations in London and DER Travel. DB also have Regional Rail Rovers which are available in 20 regions and are valid for unlimited second-class travel for 10 days out of 21. A single ticket costs £20, a ticket for two is £29 and a family ticket including any number of unmarried children under 26 is £35. For families travelling throughout West Germany a minigroup ticket can be purchased. The first two adults pay full fare, additional adults pay half price and children quarter price. The maximum group size is 5½ (children count as ½).

● **Inter Rail bonuses:**
NB All S-Bahn trains except those in Berlin are free on Inter Rail but not U-Bahns.

	SECTION		REDUCTION
	FROM	TO	%
Schauinslandbahn GmbH, Freiburg (Breisgau)		All	50
Vorwohle-Emmerthaler Verkehrs-betriebe GmbH, Bodenwerder		All	50
Kahlgrund-Verkehrs-GmbH, Schöllkrippen		All	50

| | SECTION | | REDUCTION |
	FROM	TO	%
Oberrheinische Eisenbahn-Gesellschaft AG, Mannheim	Rail sections only		50
Regentalbahn AG, Viechtach	All		50
Lokalbahn Lam-Kötzting, Lam			50
Tegernsee-Bahn AG, Tegernsee			50
Verkehrsbetriebe Peine-Salzgitter GmbH, Salzgitter-Hallendorf			50
Kreisbahn Aurich GmbH, Aurich			50
Eisenbahn-Gesellschaft Altona-Kaltenkirchen-Neumünster, Hamburg	Kaltenkirchen-Neumünster		50
Regionalverkehr Munsterland GmbH	All coach lines		50
Regionalverkehr Ruhr-Lippe GmbH	All coach lines		50
Verkehrsbetriebe Kreis Tecklenburg – Techlenburger Nordbahn – AG	All coach lines		50
Verkehrsgesellschaft Kreis Unna mbH	All		50
Vereinigte Schiffahrts-unternehmen für den Bodensee und Rhein	All		50
Frankfurt (M) Postal and Railway buses	All		50

DB – Free entrance to Transport Museum, Lessingstrasse 6, Nürnberg. Free use of S-Bahn.

• **Eurail bonuses:** Free:
—Ferry crossings from Puttgarden to Rødby (Denmark).
—Steamers operated by the Köln-Düsseldorfer Deutsche Rheinschiffahrt (KD) making regular runs on the Rhine between Cologne and Frankfurt (Main) and on the Moselle between Trier and Koblenz (except on ships making cruises of several days between Basel and Rotterdam and vice versa). For the use of Express-steamers, an extra charge will have to be paid by Eurail Youthpass holders, and for the use of hydrofoils by Eurail Pass as well as by Eurail Youthpass holders.

—Most of the bus lines of the integrated bus transport Post/Railway bus union.

—Europabus line 189 – Burgenstrasse (Castle Road) from Mannheim–Heidelberg–Heilbronn–Rothenburg ob der Tauber–Ansbach–Nürnberg.

—Europabus line 190 – Romantische Strasse (Romantic Road) from Wiesbaden–Frankfurt (Main)–Rothenburg ob der Tauber–Füssen/Munich.

Reduced fares:

—50 per cent reduction on hydrofoil service between Cologne and Mainz.

—50 per cent reduction to Eurail Pass and Eurail Youthpass holders on the normal fares of the ferry crossing operated by TT-Saga-Line between Lübeck–Travemünde and Malmö (Sweden).

—50 per cent reduction on regular steamer services operated by the German Federal Railways on Lake Constance.

—Eurail Pass and Eurail Youthpass are not valid on private railways in the Federal Republic of Germany. However, the following mountain railways grant reduced fares:

1. Garmisch-Partenkirchen–Grainau–Zugspitze (Schneefernerhaus).

2. Freiburg (Breisgau)–Schauinsland: 50 per cent on ordinary tickets, for Eurail Pass and Eurail Youthpass.

—25 per cent reduction for students producing a valid student ID card on the round-trip bus fare Braunschweig–Berlin or vice versa operated by Bayern Express and P. Kuhn Berlin GmbH.

—20 per cent reduction on some half-day or full-day excursions out of Munich operated by the Oberbayern GmbH.

—10 per cent on Munich city sightseeing tours operated by the Oberbayern GmbH.

• **Deutsche Reichsbahn, DR:** It is expected that the eastern and western systems will be combined, but this will inevitably take time. The former East German DR system is efficient and frequent compared to that in other east European countries, but slower than the western system. The faster trains – special diesel express (Ex), expresses (D) and seniorfast (E) trains – require some supplements. Avoid the local (Personenzug) at all costs, as they stop at nearly every station.

• **Rover tickets:** East Germany is covered by the new 15-day East Rail Pass, available from Danish State Railways (see Introduction). The East European Explorer, offered by Eurotrain, also covers East Germany (see p.34). Germanrail have introduced an extension pass offering 4 or 8 consecutive days' unlimited travel in Eastern Germany. Available to holders of the German Rail Pass or German Rail Youth Pass, it is well priced and a useful option for those extensively touring.

TRAIN INFORMATION

Information officers wear yellow capbands and generally speak good English, though you may have problems in smaller towns in eastern Germany. Left-luggage lockers take 1 DM and 50 Pfennig pieces.

• **Reservations:** Can be made up to 2 hours before departing, but not after 10 p.m. They are included in the price of the supplement for ICs (5 DM from an automatic ticket machine or 6 DM if you buy it on the train) and Eurocity (10 DM). On all other trains, it's optional and costs 3.5 DM. Rail pass holders are exempt from the IC supplement.

• **Night travel:** Some German compartments have pull-down seats which make excellent free beds. Couchettes have 6 berths and cost around £8.20. Tourist-class sleepers (4-berth) cost £10.90 and 3-berth compartments are more expensive at around £20.60, but it's often possible to get 1 between 2 out of season, as they're usually underbooked. DB has extended the special couchette service introduced in 1984 between Dortmund and Munich which it called 'Rollende Jugendherberge' (Rolling Youth Hostel). It is now called 'Twen-Nachttrampler' (Night Tramper) and the services last year ran between Aachen to Copenhagen via Hamburg, Hamburg to Munich and Dortmund to Munich. It allows you to have a couchette for only 4 DM and all you need is a sleeping bag or blankets. If you don't have either, you can buy a paper blanket on board for 6 DM from the conductor. You don't have to worry about reservations either as you can pay the 4 DM on board, although the number of places is limited and the service has proved to be very popular. Look out for extra services being laid on and check with DB before booking couchettes for an overnight journey in case your route has come into the scheme.

• **Eating on trains:** Prices are lower than British Rail, while the quality is higher. So if you've the money, it's worth considering a meal on the ICs. Other trains (except E-trains) have mini-bars which are pricey for what you get.

• **Scenic routes:** The Rhine valley, Black Forest, Romantic and Castle roads, as well as the Alps, all provide scenic routes within Germany. If you've always wanted to go cruising down the Rhine, it's best to do it between Koblenz and Rüdesheim or Mainz as this gives you magnificent views of both sides of the valley. If you're coming from the opposite direction and want to stay with rivers, then head to Giessen from Koblenz. To see the Black Forest, there are a variety of options. The Romantic and Castle roads are arguably best seen by Europabus, which are nearly always busy and require advance reservations. The Munich–Nürnberg, Heilbronn–Heidelberg train follows more or less the same route as the bus at no extra cost. For the Alps, try the line to Salzburg or Innsbruck from Munich – both are equally attractive. If you're going to Switzerland, try Freiburg–Basel or Würzburg–Zürich.

• **Bikes:** Can be hired from around 300 stations throughout Germany at half the normal rate (5 DM) to anyone with a valid ticket or rail pass. You can either do a circular tour of the region or merely cycle from A to B and return the bike to another station.

TOURIST INFORMATION

Tourist offices are usually called Verkehrsamt or Verkehrsverein. Many towns in eastern Germany have an office, simply described as an information office. Also expect most east German Reiseburos to be open. Many cities have free pamphlets specially prepared for the under 26s.

• **ISIC bonuses:** Museum discount, with varying reductions at some sports centres. For further information, contact Europa Sprach Club, Amalienstrasse 67, Munich 40. There are branches in all main cities. In Berlin also try the Jugendtourist office at Alexanderplatz 5, 1026 Berlin.

• **Money matters:** 1 Deutschemark (DM) = 100 Pfennig.
Banking hours vary, but generally are Mon.–Fri.: 9 a.m.–12 noon, 2 p.m.–4 p.m. It's also possible to change money at some post offices; they often give a better rate, because they make mistakes.

• **Post offices:** Open Mon.–Fri.: 8 a.m.–6 p.m., Sat.: 8 a.m.–1 p.m.

• **Shops:** Open Mon.–Fri.: 8.30 a.m.–6/6.30 p.m. In smaller towns they shut for lunch, 12 noon–3 p.m. NB On Sat. they only open till 2 p.m., and until 6 p.m. on the first Sat. of each month.

• **Museums:** Hours vary depending on locality. Check with tourist information.

SLEEPING

Youth hostels cost 12–21 DM a night and there are over 600 scattered throughout Germany. Tourist information have a free map and brochure showing their locations. Youth guest houses (Jugendgasthäuser) are in nearly all the large towns, but they tend to be stuffed with groups, so always phone first. There's no uniform system of classification for Germany's hostels and hotels, so you'll find they vary dramatically. The accommodation side of tourist information, however, is usually very obliging and you need never feel really stuck as in the end they'll fix you up with something in your price range. As in many other countries, the towns are ideally laid out for eurorailers and many of the cheap hotels are near the stations. In smaller places, look out for signs hanging up saying 'Zimmer frei' (room to let) or 'Gasthof' (inn), and for private accommodation turn to tourist information for lists. With over 2,000 campsites in Germany, you shouldn't find any problems. Again, tourist information have a free map and brochure showing where they are. Facilities are generally very good and prices usually fair.

This is still a problem in eastern Germany, due to the demand and lack of infrastructure. This is despite the fact that private citizens are now able to offer B&B, and formerly East Germans-only places are expected to become available. Inter hotel prices have now risen beyond the budget traveller's range – upwards from £50. This effectively leaves Jugendtourist hostels and campsites, but even here the demand will mean overcrowding. Ask at local tourist information offices and Reiseburo for suggestions, including veriband Christlicher Hospize which has hostels in Berlin, Leipzig and Weimar.

If possible it will be advantageous to book in advance, and certainly worthwhile contacting the tourist office in your own country (see introductory section of this guide). They will be able to advise on the latest position.

EATING AND NIGHTLIFE

German cuisine is as varied as French – the only difference is that the former like to eat more of it. There are countless types of beer and Würste (sausages), but it's unfair to think that's all there is, as so many do. The food halls of the large department stores (e.g. Hertie, Kaufhof) are real showpieces, and the quality and quantity of the produce means there's no excuse for not living off picnics and saving your Marks that way. Fast food's also available in the major cities, and Schnell Imbiss stalls with Würste and beer also crop up. Note that if you drink at one of the beer gardens, it is not unusual to be charged a deposit for your glass – remember to claim it back. Alcoholic drinks can be very expensive in Germany.

As far as regional specialities go, try some of the following: Grünkohl mit Pinkel (green cabbage with bacon sausage) from the north, Sauerbraten (braised beef in sour sauce) from the west, and for your picnics sample Westphalian Pumpernickel (black bread) or Vollkornbrot (bread made of whole unground grains of wheat). Many of the Würste look revolting, but don't let that put you off. Vegetarians tend not to be well catered for here.

The Germans are keen on large-scale celebrations: some of their festivals resemble Wagnerian opera sets, and no expense is spared. If you get a chance to join in, do. As far as music goes, the classics are always well represented and there's an active jazz and disco scene in all the major cities.

Berlin

There is literally no other city in Europe, or elsewhere, like Berlin. It was once as beautiful and cosmopolitan as Paris or London, but was reduced to rubble in the Second World War. Then in August 1961 the city was cut in two by the notorious Wall which split life on either side between the two political polarities. Recent events are obvious, and by summer 1991, very little of the wall will remain. With a background as dramatic as this, it's only to be expected that Berlin is a city of extremes and contradictions. This was the city at the heart of the Cold War of the mid-twentieth century, and that alone makes it significant enough for a visit – it's not so much the sights that are worth coming for, as the atmosphere, the world-famous 'Berliner luft'. The tremendous changes have made Berlin, once again, a vibrant and exciting city. Even so the two halves still have their differences.

STATION FACILITIES

The three main stations are Bahnhofzoo, Hauptbahnhof (formerly Ostbahnhof) and Lichtenberg. Bahnhofzoo and Hauptbahnhof currently serve international destinations, and Lichtenberg for domestic and eastbound trains, but check timetable carefully. Hauptbahnhof has been undergoing massive rebuilding of its platforms, so watch your feet. The former important border station, Freidrichstrasse, will lose its importance.

	BERLIN– HAUPTBAHNHOF	BERLIN– LICHTENBERG
Train information	8 a.m.–10 p.m.	6 a.m.–10 p.m.
Reservations	6 a.m.–8 p.m., weekdays 8 a.m.–6 p.m., weekends	6 a.m.–8 p.m., weekdays 8 a.m.–10 p.m., weekends
Tourist information	None, Reisburo provides other services	None, S-Bahn to Alexander Platz
International tickets	6.30 a.m.–9 p.m., weekdays 8 a.m.–6 p.m., weekends	6 a.m.–9 p.m., weekdays 8 a.m.–6 p.m., weekends
Shop	6 a.m.–10 p.m., to 8 p.m. at weekends	6 a.m.–10 p.m.
Snacks/Buffet	6 a.m.–6.30 p.m.	6 a.m.–10 p.m.
Restaurant	6 a.m.–9 p.m.	6 a.m.–10 a.m. and 11 a.m.–10 p.m.
Left-luggage lockers	Always accessible	Always accessible
Left-luggage store	As station	As station
Station shuts	12 a.m.–4 a.m.	12 a.m.–4 a.m.

Luggage lockers also available at Alexander Platz and Freidrichstrasse S-Bahn stations. Daily trains from Hauptbahnhof to the west of Germany, from Lichtenberg to Copenhagen, Dresden, Leipzig, Malmo and Prague, from Bahnhofzoo to Copenhagen, Cologne, Hamburg and Malmo.

BERLIN BAHNHOF ZOO	
Train information	6 a.m.–10 p.m.
Reservations	Mon.–Fri.: 6 a.m.–9 p.m.
	Sat. and Sun.:
	8 a.m.–4 p.m.
Tourist information	In the main hall, 8 a.m.–11 p.m. (Tel. 313 9063)
Foreign exchange	Mon.–Sat.: 8 a.m.–9 p.m., Sun.: 10 a.m.–6 p.m.
Left-luggage lockers	Available, but quite small
Restaurant	6 a.m.–12 midnight
Post office	Always open
Station shuts	12 midnight–5 a.m.

• **Getting around:** A variety of tickets covering different parts of the transport network are available so consider the options carefully. A single ticket covering the whole network for 2 hours costs 2.70 DM (Multiple Sammelkartir allow 5 journeys for 11.50 DM). A day ticket valid for 24 hours costs 9 DM. If you're staying for more than 3 days then the best value is the group ticket (28 DM) which is valid for 7 days and can be used by individuals. All multiple tickets must be obtained from the machines at S-Bahn and U-Bahn stations or from the BVG office in front of Zoo station. The U-Bahn and S-Bahn systems were split in 1961, with the building of the Wall. At Friedrichstrasse the S-Bahn has now been reconnected; expect the U-Bahn also to be reconnected during 1991.

TOURIST INFORMATION AND ADDRESSES

TOURIST OFFICE: On the Budapesterstrasse side of the Europa Centre, open daily 7.30 a.m.–10.30 p.m. (Tel. 2626031). Accommodation service for 3 DM. The free book 'Berlin For Young People' is excellent. Among other bits of interesting information, it lists 20 or so cheap pensions. Berlin–Information on Alexanderplatz (Tel. 212 4675) under the TV tower. Open Tues.– Fri., 8 a.m.–7 p.m., Mon. from 10 a.m., Sat. and Sun., 10 a.m.–6 p.m. Also on Friedrichstrasse near the station, at Berlin Zoo (Tel. 3139063), open 8 a.m.–11 p.m., and on the eastern side of the Brandenberg gate. In addition, the Budapesterstrasse side of the Europa Centre office still operates.

POST OFFICE: Bahnhof Zoo. Twenty-four hours. Also poste restante here.

AMEX: Kurfürstendamm 11 (2nd floor) (Tel. 882 7575), Mon.–Fri.: 9 a.m.–5.30 p.m., Sat.: 9 a.m.–12 noon.

CURRENCY EXCHANGE: Alexanderplatz, Bahnhof Zoo, Friedrich-strasse, Hauptbahnhof, also major hotels.

ARTU REISEBÜRO: Hardenbergstrasse 9. Student Travel office selling BIJ tickets and IUS card. Open Mon., Tue., Thur., Fri.: 10 a.m.–6 p.m. Wed.: 11 a.m.–6 p.m., Sat.: 10 a.m.–1 p.m.

UK CONSULATE: Uhlandstrasse 7 (Tel. 309 5292)/Unter den Linden 32–34 (Tel. 220 2431).

US CONSULATE: Clayallee 170 (Tel. 832 4087)/Neustädtische Kirch-strasse 4/5 (Tel. 220 2741).

CANADIAN CONSULATE: Europa Centre (12th floor) Tel. 261 1161.

AUSTRALIAN CONSULATE: Europa Centre (Tel. 261 8030).

TELEPHONE CODE: 030 (East Berlin: 2).

SEEING

The WALL is the tourist attraction of today. You can walk casually through the breaches in the wall, where so many people died not long ago. You should cross through the site of the old Checkpoint Charlie to compare the development of the two sides of the city separated for so long. The actual hut is now in a nearby museum. Near the checkpoint is the MUSEUM OF THE WALL which tells its story.

KURFÜRSTENDAMM (Ku'damm) pulsates with life late into the night and is the city's preferred promenade and thoroughfare. The famous Berlin institution CAFÉ KRANZLER is found on the junction with Joachimstaler Strasse, but eat elsewhere as it is expensive. The ruined KAISER-WILHELM GEDÄCHTNISKIRCHE is unmissable and the focal point of the Ku'damm and a popular meeting place. The church itself reflects the city's story – it has been built, bombed, rebuilt and preserved, and mirrors Berlin's present mixture of old and new. A few yards away beyond an elaborate fountain complex stands the massive EUROPA CENTRE, twenty-two floors of pubs, discos, boutiques and a cinema which shows a useful introductory film on Berlin's history. The rooftop café affords an excellent view of the city. Berlin's premier department store, KaDeWe at Tauenzienstrasse, is well worth a look, especially for its food halls.

The SIEGESSÄULE, celebrating Prussian victories in the 1860s and 1870s, can be climbed for an impressive view towards the BRANDEN-BURG GATE. TIERGARTEN is a beautiful park, next to the city zoo, which has more species than any other in the world. Next to the zoo is the world's most extensive collection of fish and reptiles in the aquarium on Budapesterstrasse. The OLYMPIC STADIUM conjures up images of Jesse Owens and Hitler and is worth the 1 DM entrance fee.

SCHLOSS CHARLOTTENBURG lies a few miles north-west of Berlin. This seventeenth-century palace houses several galleries and museums and is the best example of Prussian architecture you'll find around Berlin (closed Mondays, 6 DM admission, 3 DM for students). The EGYPTIAN MUSEUM opposite has a fine collection including the fabulous bust of Queen Nefertiti. DAHLEM MUSEUM is a complex of seven museums (closed Mondays), so you're bound to find something to interest you. The BAUHAUS MUSEUM with exhibits of the school's designs (closed Tuesdays and Wednesday mornings), and the photographic story of German nineteenth- and twentieth-century history at the REICHSTAG BUILDING are both interesting visits. For a good view over the city climb the Berlin Radio Mast (4 DM). Also see the TEUFELBERG not far away in the GRUNEWALD. At 380 feet high, it is the highest hill between Warsaw and the Netherlands. It is made of an enormous mound of rubble from the ruins of Berlin after the Second World War. It now has a ski and toboggan run, whilst the very peak is an American radar station.

SEEING

UNTER DEN LINDEN is the most impressive street of eastern Berlin and is at its very centre. From here you can see the Brandenburg Gate, refurbished during summer 1990, and the new city centre. Not far from here is MUSEUM ISLAND where the main eastern Berlin museums are located. Avoid Mondays, when most are shut. General hours 10 a.m.–5 p.m., but various exhibits only certain days. Go to tourist information for a three-day pass for these museums. MARIENKIRCHE is Berlin's oldest church dating from the thirteenth century. This, predictably, stands next to a huge, very twentieth-century television tower which offers a good view, if nothing else.

Old Berlin lives again in the NIKOLAIVIERTEL QUARTER, a veritable cat's cradle of narrow streets and alleys around the ST NICOLAS CHURCH. It is interesting for the half-timbered buildings, mullioned windows and the odd quaint corner.

For signs of the past, try a walk to the SYNAGOGUE on Oranienburgerstrasse. This was burnt on the infamous Kristall-nacht 1938, and in recent years has been undergoing restoration. The MONUMENT TO THE VICTIMS OF FASCISM AND MILITARISM on Unter den Linden and the SOVIET WAR MEMORIAL in Treptower Park, which is reached on the S-Bahn, will set you thinking. How much longer the goose-stepping changing-of-the-guard, outside the former, will last, is open to question.

On Museum Island are: the PERGAMON (stunning collections of Eastern and Roman artefacts), the BODEMUSEUM with its Egyptian works; the twentieth-century art gallery, the ALTES MUSEUM and the NATIONAL GALERIE of nineteenth-century art. Another museum, undergoing reconstruction, on Museum Island is the NEVNES MUSEUM. The work on this is disrupting the whole area. The MUSEUM FÜR DEUTSCHE GESCHICHTE in the Arsenal (Zeughaus), the oldest building on Unter den Linden, has German history from prehistory onwards. However much of the post-war section was closed after the November '89 revolution. During 1991 a new exhibition will open. The MÄRKISCHES MUSEUM traces Berlin's history.

The Spree River flows through the city and it's possible to take a boat ride on one of the white excursion boats (Weisse Flotte) from April to September. You can get off at various points; the best is the MECKLENBURGER DORF – a reconstruction of a nineteenth-century German village. Boats leave eight times a day from Treptower Park S-Bahn Station. (The commentary is usually given in German only.)

SLEEPING

Finding a bed isn't easy and this is one city where you would be really wise to book ahead; write about two to three weeks in advance, to the Tourist Board: Verkehrsamt Berlin, Europa Centre, 1000 Berlin 30, or DJH Berlin, Temelhofer Ufer 32, 1000 Berlin 61, for hostels, stating how much you can pay. You will probably have better luck in the old West Berlin, due to lack of established facilities on the eastern side. But here try desk 13 of

Reiseburo on Alexanderplatz or Jugendtourist, also here. If you aren't organized enough to plan ahead, don't worry; ask at tourist information for their map of Berlin with all the hotel and hostel listings. For hotels look at the board at Bahnhof Zoo, though they tend to be expensive.

• **Youth hostels:** Hermsdorfer Damm 48, Berlin 28 (Tel. 404 1610) is well out of the town centre, but good, 15 DM per night plus 4.90 DM for breakfast. Kluckstrasse 3, Berlin 30 (Tel. 261 1097) is central, 19.10 DM plus 4.90 DM for breakfast. It is the most central, being 10 minutes from Ku'damm by bus. Although it is 20 minutes on the S-Bahn to Nikolassee, try also at Badeweg 1, Ecke Kronprinzess-Innenweg (Tel. 803 2034). It is clean, cheap and very modern, price as above. The eastern Berlin Jugendtourist hostels, which should now be available to Westerners, are the Egon Schultz at Franz-Mett Strasse 7, U-Bahn to Tierpark (Tel. 512 9127), and the Jugendherberge Hans Krefert at Dahmestrasse 6, S-Bahn to Altglienicke (Tel. 681 4422).

• **Pensions:** The area round Fasanenstrasse, Uhlandstrasse and Meinekestrasse is your best bet. Also on Carmerstrasse, Grolmann-strasse and Knesebeckstrasse. Try Pension Savoy (Tel. 881 3700) at Meinekestrasse 4; just next door are Pension Zeinert (Tel. 881 3319) at No. 5 and Pension Witzleben (Tel. 881 6395) at No. 6. For good doubles try Pension Fisher at Nürnbergerstrasse 24A (Tel. 246 808), near the station (50–60 DM). Also ask at tourist information for B&B, now opening up on the eastern side of the city.

• **Camping:** International Youth Camp, DM 7 a night; blankets and mattresses free. Open 1700–0900 daily June–Sept. (Tel. 433 8640) Waidmannsluster Dam, Ziekowstrasse (subway station Tegel/bus 20). Maximum stay: 3 nights. Ages 14–23. Zeltplatz Kladow 1 and 11, Krampnitzer Weg 111/117, bus 35, then 35E (Tel. 365 2797). Zeltplatz Dreilinden, Albrechts Teerofen (Tel. 805 1201) bus 18. Kohlhasenbruck Neue Kreisstrasse – U-Bahn Oskar-Helene-Heim, bus 18 (Tel. 805 1737). Also try the former Intercamping Krossinsee site, tram 86 to end, then walk across bridge, and take the third turning on the right. If you're desperate, the Bahnhof Mission in the station will help out, or go out to the Grünewald and sleep there.

EATING AND NIGHTLIFE

The department stores have good cafeterias and there are fast-food chains and sausage stands. There are many good authentic Turkish restaurants on Oranienstrasse in Kreuzberg.

Berlin's a big cultural centre and there's always plenty happening in the evenings. Festival follows festival and the student community is large and active. Head off to the area round Konstanzerstrasse, Düsseldorferstrasse, Joachim-Taler Strasse and Lietzenburger-strasse. With literally thousands of pubs, clubs and discos you should find something to occupy you. Many of the bars in the former East Berlin are north of the river from Friedrichstrasse station. Try the 'Kleine Melodie', Friedrichstrasse 127, for a disco. For a taste of the 1930s Berlin atmosphere try Zum Trichler on Schiffbauerdamm, only a stone's throw from the Brecht Ensemble Theatre. A very atmospheric place to have a drink as the walls are lined with old photos of Brechtian productions, murals and clocks. There is even a small stage for cabaret performances. In the Irish Pub on Eisenacherstrasse (and also in the Europa Centre) you're guaranteed to meet a fellow Brit, most of the staff speak English, and in Leierkasten on Zossenerstrasse you'll bump into the local students. The Jungle, 53 Nuernbergstrasse, is the hottest club in Berlin. 'Tip' – the bi-weekly listing of what's on, and 'Zitty' are worth buying if you're staying a while.

If you miss a hostel curfew don't despair as many bars begin to serve breakfast at 2 a.m. and Berlin is literally open all night. The cafés here are an institution, try Schlander on Olivaer Platz.

For tickets for classical music and drama try Zentral/besucher-dienst below the Palast Hotel, Karl-Liebnechtstrasse, or desk 1 of Reiseburo on Alexanderplatz. The Haus der Jungen Talente, Klosterstrasse, has young musicians' concerts with cheap tickets.

Potsdam

In 1744, Frederick the Great chose this town as his permanent seat, and from then on Potsdam flourished to become one of the main imperial centres of Europe. As Potsdam is less than one hour from the centre of Berlin, it can be treated as a day trip, but, be warned, there is a lot to see.

The impressive SANS SOUCI PARK and surroundings contain baroque palaces and elaborate pavilions. The SANS-SOUCI SCHLOSS, the large NEUES PALAIS, SCHLOSS CHARLOTTENHOF, the ORANGERIE and gold-plated CHINESE TEAHOUSE, are all here. The Orangerie houses sixty-seven very good fake Raphaels, with nearby the SICILIAN GARDEN. Another large park, the NEUER GARTEN, on the shores of a lake, includes the SCHLOSS CEILIENHOF, scene of the three-powers agreement to divide Germany. Most palaces are open 9 a.m.–5 p.m., closing at lunchtime; some also close on Mondays. The city centre has been extensively rebuilt, but the Dutch quarter retains its charm and elegance. Just outside the town is the incredible EINSTEIN OBSERVATORY TOWER. Make the effort to see it if you can.

The Tourist Office is at Friedrich-Ebert Strasse 5 (Tel. 21100), take one of several trams to the city centre from the main station. The nearest Jugendtouristhostel is in the nearby village of Werder, with a campsite a couple of miles beyond this village. Ask at Tourist Information for bookings and details of buses. As elsewhere Inter hotel are now outside the budget traveller's means, or try Tourist Information for B&B possibilities. While in Potsdam eat out at a Schnell Imbiss and have a beer at the Schwarzer Adler on Gutenbergstrasse.

City phone code 33.

Dresden

Two hours from Berlin, Dresden is the cultural centre of the DDR and, though the city was virtually wiped off the map in a bomb attack in February 1945, what was left was carefully restored, though the city is still shabby and resembles a building site.

STATION FACILITIES

There are two main stations, Hauptbahnhof and Bahnhof–Neustadt. Many trains call at both, eastbound ones tend to use Neustadt only. The facilities at Neustadt are similar to those at Hauptbahnhof. There is a post office opposite the station.

HAUPTBAHNHOF	
Train information	6.30 a.m.–9.45 p.m.
Reservations	6.30 a.m.–8 p.m. to 6 p.m. on Sat. and Sun.
Tourist information	None at Pragerstrasse
Restaurant, buffet	7.30 a.m.–10 p.m.
Shops	Mon.–Fri., 7.30 a.m.–9 p.m.
	Sat.–Sun., 9 a.m.–4 p.m.
Left-luggage lockers	As station
Left-luggage store	As station
Station shuts	Train departures 24 hrs, but do not rely on all facilities being open

Through trains use the elevated platforms on each side, terminating ones the central platforms.
Daily departures to Berlin (Lichenberg), Leipzig, Munich, Prague, Warsaw.

TOURIST INFORMATION

Dresden information centre is at Pragerstrasse 10/11 (Tel. 4955025) (5 minutes from station). Open Mon.–Sat.: 9 a.m.–8 p.m., Sun.: 9 a.m.–2 p.m. Change money here. 'What's On' leaflet from here: 'Dresden-Information'. Bus and tram tickets have to be bought in advance, but most of the worthwhile area is walkable from Hauptbahnhof, along pedestrianized Pragerstrasse.

City phone code 51.

SEEING

The ZWINGER PALACE contains half of Dresden's impressive museums: the magnificent GEMÄLDEGALERIE ALTE MEISTER (closed Mondays); the HISTORISCHES MUSEUM of weapons (closed Wednesdays); the MATHEMATISCH PHYSIKALISCHER SALON (maths and physics); and both the ZINNSAMMLUNG and the PORZELLANSAMMLUNG display the famous Dresden porcelain and pewter (closed Fridays). During 1990 much of the Zwinger Palace was shut, and covered in scaffolding. This is part of a long-term restoration of the area.

On the other side of the street is what's left of the palace of Saxony's electors and kings, parts of this also are being restored.

The ALBERTINUM is Dresden's other museum complex. Included in the complex is the GRÜNES GEWÖLBE (Green Vault), containing a fabulous collection of the treasures of the Saxon dukes. It is very popular, so get there early. Opens 9 a.m. most days, closed Thursdays. Nearby are the remains of the bombed-out FRAUEN-KIRCHE behind Bruhlische Terrasse, which, like Coventry Cathedral, is a vivid memorial to the horror of indiscriminate bombing.

The 'old' nineteenth-century part of the town is across the Elbe, with its Markt.

SLEEPING

Youth Hostel Rudi Arndt, Hubnerstrasse 11 (Tel. 470667), a few blocks from the station, down Wincklemannstrasse is one possibility. The newer Schloss Eckberg Hostel, Bautznerstrasse 134 (Tel. 54403), is normally groups only. The third hostel is the Wilhelm Peck at Sierksstrasse 33 (Tel. 36672), take tram 5 to Nurnburger Platz, change to bus 61 or 93, get off 2 stops after Elbe bridge. Then it is only a short walk away. The campsites are far flung, and not really worth the hassle – ask at Tourist Information Centre for details. A series of sites are located to the north, in a wooded area. Take bus 81 to the terminus, then a 15-minute walk.

EATING

Places on Pirnaisches Tor are cheap, as are the restaurants in the 'Am Zwinger' complex on Thälmanstrasse.

Leipzig

The second city of East Germany is only 1½ hours from Dresden, and though it is more a commercial and industrial centre, there are still enough points of interest to make it worth a stop-off. The Hauptbahnhof here is Europe's largest, with 26 platforms. Tourist information is at Sachsenplatz 1 (Tel. 79590), open weekdays 9 a.m.–7 p.m., Sat. to 2 p.m.

City phone code 41.

STATION FACILITIES

	HAUPTBAHNHOF
Train information	6 a.m.–10 p.m.
Reservations	6 a.m.–9 p.m.
Tourist information	None at station
Foreign exchange	6.30 a.m.–9 p.m. to 1 p.m. at weekends
International tickets	6.30 a.m.–9 p.m.
Restaurant/buffet	6.30 a.m.–10 p.m.
Left-luggage lockers	Always accessible
Left-luggage store	As station
Post office	6 a.m.–10 p.m., Mon.–Fri.
	8 a.m.–12 p.m., Sat.
Station shuts	Train departures 24 hrs, but do not rely on all facilities being open.

This is Europe's largest station and many facilities are duplicated, so if one is shut, look around. Leipzig's small S-Bahn system departures are also from here.
Daily departures to Berlin (Lichenberg), Cologne, Dresden, Hannover, Munich and Warsaw.

SEEING

The main part of Leipzig that is worth seeing is within the Ringstrasse, a partly pedestrianized area, starting opposite the station. Bach spent 27 of his creative years working as the Kantor (Choirmaster) in ST THOMAS' CHURCH, and is buried here. The boys' choir, once conducted by Bach, can be heard on most Friday evenings and Sunday mornings. Dating from 1482, St Thomas' has been beautifully restored, as has the old, sixteenth-century ALTES RATHUS (town hall). This now houses the city history museum. During 1990 this was closed, with the area behind, for renovation. In the meantime occasional exhibitions are held elsewhere. The NIKOLAIKIRCHE, located nearby, is also worth a visit.

As well as having associations with Bach, Leipzig has other musical connections, with Mendelssohn, for example, who founded the Gewandhaus Orchestra, Europe's oldest, and erected a monument to Bach. The city also has strong literary connections, with large numbers of bookshops. Goethe set the scene between Faust and the devil in the AUERBACHS KEILER in Madler-passage, the decorations of which are now based on the book.

• **Excursion:** Near Leipzig is the small town of Colditz, location of the famous castle which was used as an officer's POW camp in the Second World War, the story of which was made into a TV series of the same name. Much of the castle is inaccessible to the public, but the trip here is worthwhile, and the beer brewed here is excellent. Ask at the tourist information centre for details.

SLEEPING AND EATING

As with the rest of what was East Germany, hotels formerly in the budget pocket are now well outside it. The Jugendtourist hostel is at Kathe-Kollwitz Strasse 64/66, take tram 1 or 2, to just before the Klingebruche bridge. For camping try the site at Auensee, Gustav-Esche Strasse (Tel. 52648), take tram 11 or S-Bahn to Wahren, then follow the signs.

There are plenty of reasonably priced restaurants and pubs, but expect the costs to be approaching West German levels. There is a mensa behind the International Bookshop, off Karl-Marz-Platz. Opposite the station's Wintergartenstrasse exit is a well stocked supermarket.

Weimar

Homeland of Bach, Liszt, Schiller, Goethe and Nietzsche, and the Buchenwald concentration camp, this town was also the site of the first German Republic (the Weimar Republic) which fell in the 1930s, just before Nazism rose to power.

TOURIST INFORMATION

Weimar Informationszentrum, Marktstrasse 4 (Tel. 21 73), open Mon.: 10 a.m.–5 p.m., Tues.–Fri.: 9 a.m.–5 p.m., Sat.: 8.30 a.m.–12.45 p.m., 1.30 p.m.–4.30 p.m. Take bus 1 or 6 from the station to Goetheplatz and walk along Dimitroffstrasse to the Marktplatz. They'll direct you to the Zentralkasse where you can buy a museum pass and tickets for concerts and theatrical events, as well as bus tickets.

SEEING

The LUCAS-CRANACH HAUS is the richly decorated Renaissance building in the Marketplatz. Close by is the SCHLOSSMUSEUM, with its collection of German Renaissance works, and the Gothic church, HERDERKIRCHE. The KIRMS-KRACHOW HAUS has displays on the philosopher Herder and poets Schiller and Goethe, among others. There are museums devoted to Schiller and Goethe, also within walking distance. Another famous son of Weimar, Liszt, also has a museum here.

• **Excursions:** the Rococo SCHLOSS BELVEDERE, a former Royal summer palace, can be reached by bus from Goetheplatz – ask at the information office for details, as this was closed during 1990 for restoration; check that it has reopened at the same time. The Nazi concentration camp of BUCHENWALD can also be reached by bus. Now a grim memorial to the more than 56,000 Jews, communists and others killed between 1937 and 1945.

SLEEPING AND EATING

There is no convenient campsite, the nearest is listed under Erfurt, and is some distance from there. The four nearby youth hostels were formerly for eastern block groups only, but should now be available, ask at Tourist Information Centre for details, and also about B&B possibilities in private houses.

People eat early in Weimar and you'll find places closing from 8 p.m., and all weekend, so get some supplies in. Try Alt Weimar, Steubenstrasse 27, or the Elephantkeller on the Markt. For a drink and to meet the local students, try Zum Pilsner, Freidrichstrasse 18.

Erfurt

The capital of the forested and mountainous region of Thuringia, a short journey from Weimar. The very well preserved medieval centre of the 'City of Flowers' makes the trip well worthwhile.

The Tourist Information Centre is on the road to the railway station, at Bahnhofstrasse 37 (Tel. 26267). The youth agency

Jugendtourist has an office at Fischmarket 6 (Tel. 63113). Your accommodation options here are limited; Jugendtourist has a hostel at Juri-Gagarin-Ring 154/6. The nearest campsite is on the outskirts of Sommerda, take the train north, then you face a one-mile walk.

The twin towers of the Gothic CATHEDRAL and ST SERVERUS CHURCH, on the Domberg, dominate Erfurt's skyline. The unusual bridge, Kramerbrucke, is lined with a collection of restored fourteenth-century houses, now becoming spoilt by an influx of souvenir shops. Not far away is the Anger, a restored street of Renaissance and Art Nouveau buildings.

Northern Germany

Northern Germany – the area between Schleswig and Bremen – is comparatively unspoilt by tourism. The main centres of interest are: Bremen, Hamburg, and Lübeck, and also you could take in the little towns of Hameln (of Pied Piper fame) and Celle, if you've enough time left.

Bremen

Bremen with its port, Bremerhaven, is the oldest seaport in Germany. The tourist information office is right in front of the station. Tackle Bremen on foot and take in the old medieval section round the MARKTPLATZ, the RATHAUS, the FOCKE MUSEUM and ST PETER'S eleventh-century CATHEDRAL with its cellar full of mummified bodies. The old section of the town called the SCHNOORVIERTEL is particularly attractive, with its narrow winding streets dating back to the 1400s and its half-timbered houses. Take a stroll down the WALLANLAGEN (Rampart Walk) with its windmill, and have a look in the craft shops round there.

The youth hostel is at Kalkstrasse 6 (Tel. 0421–1713 69), about 20 minutes' walk from the station, or bus 26 or tram 6 from the station. The campsite is excellent. Take tram 5 outside station. At the terminus, change to the bus for the Universität and then it's a 1km walk. Clean, friendly – with a good cheap restaurant. It's only open from March to October and costs 6 DM per person and 4–8 DM per tent.

Hamburg

Germany's second largest city, after Berlin, and largest seaport. Unlike many of Germany's cities, Hamburg does not lack character or things to see.

STATION FACILITIES

	HAUPTBAHNHOF
Train information	All hours
	(Tel. 339 911)
Reservations	7 a.m.–8 p.m.
Tourist information	7 a.m.–9 p.m.
Foreign exchange	7.30 a.m.–10 p.m.
Left-luggage lockers	No access 2 a.m.–5 a.m.
Left-luggage store	6 a.m.–11.30 p.m.
Bar, Buffet	All hours
Restaurant	6 a.m.–12 midnight (intercity)
Waiting room	All hours
Post office	All hours

Daily trains to: Copenhagen (5 hours), Hanover (1½ hours), Frankfurt (5 hours), Vienna, Munich, Basel, Zürich, Milan, Bremen, Düsseldorf (4 hours), Cologne (4½ hours), Brussels, Paris.

TOURIST INFORMATION AND ADDRESSES

There is a tourist information office just outside the station, and the head office is at nearby Hachmannplatz. They'll supply you with maps, a fortnightly programme of local events 'Where to go in Hamburg', and the 'Hamburg Guide'. Ask for 'Muzikszene', 'Tango' or 'Oxmox' for entertainment.

There's a separate information office (Hotelnachweis) also at the station and they'll find you a bed for a fee.

Rail pass holders go free on Hamburg's S-Bahn.

US CONSULATE: Alsterufer 27 (Tel. 441 061).

POST OFFICE: Münzstrasse 1, near the station. Poste restante and 24-hour telephone service is here also.

AMEX: Rathaus Markt 5 (Tel. 331 141).

STUDENT TRAVEL OFFICE: Rothenbaumchaussee 61 (Tel. 410 2081).

24-HOUR CHEMIST: Tel. 228 022.

TELEPHONE CODE: 040.

SEEING

The PORT dominates the city and is difficult to ignore. It's also quite interesting to watch what goes on and there are tours of it available. The best leave from Landungsbrucken. ST MICHAEL'S, the eighteenth-century baroque brick church, affords a good view from its tower, which reopened recently after extensive renovation. The view is still restricted by on-going work. Check with tourist information for latest position. Of the many museums in Hamburg the best are: the HAMBURG ART GALLERY; the DECORATIVE ARTS AND CRAFTS MUSEUM; the MILLERS VETERAN CAR MUSEUM; and the HAMBURG HISTORY MUSEUM. Take a day trip to the nearby open-air museums: the VIERLANDE MUSEUM (S-Bahn to Bergedorf) and the MUSEUM VILLAGE in Volksdorf (U-Bahn). All museums are closed on Mondays.

SLEEPING

There are plenty of cheap pensions north of the station along Steindamm and Bremer Reihe so you shouldn't have any problems. Consider spending 1 DM for the Hotelführer list available from the tourist office. Try Pension Nord at 22 Bremer Reihe (Tel. 244 693).

The Auf dem Stintfang Hostel overlooking the harbour is excellent. It is at Alfred-Wegener-Weg 5. (Tel. 313 488). Always use the lockers provided as security has recently been a problem. Nearby Landungsbrucken station is on both S-Bahn (free to Inter Rail) and U-Bahn. Less central is the Horner-Rennbahn hostel at Rennbahn Strasse 100 (Tel. 6511671). Take the U-Bahn to Horner-Rennbahn. Also try Pension Terminus Steindamm – 70 DM for a twin room including breakfast and shower and helpful English-speaking staff. The best of the campsites is at Kielerstrasse 374 (Tel. 540 4532), open summer.

For cheap hotels – and there are plenty – head for the commercial area or, if you don't mind the noise of squeaking bedsprings, the red-light district.

EATING AND NIGHTLIFE

The university Mensa is at Schlüterstrasse 7 and represents your best bet. Being a port, seafood and fish restaurants are plentiful and good in Hamburg. Try the ones along Landungsbrücken or the Fischerhaus at the St Pauli fish market – although look out for places in this area closing around 8 p.m. from September on. Landungsbrucken has recently become more expensive. Try also near the station.

One thing Hamburg's not short of is nightlife. The famous Reeperbahn area is one of the liveliest in Europe with clubs, bars, legalized sex shops, discos and porno movie-houses abounding. Try to avoid getting ripped off as thousands of other tourists do, and don't wander into the Palais d'Amour or Eros Centre looking for a room, as these blocks of flats offer more than a bed for the night . . . Before leaving Hamburg be sure to visit DIE FABRIK on Barnerstrasse, one of Germany's first and best-known youth centres for music and student hangouts. Also try the Front Club, 32 Heidenkamps Weg.

Lübeck

Only 40 minutes away from Hamburg is the attractive old town of Lübeck, former headquarters of the medieval trading group, the Hanseatic League. You'll see as many Scandinavians as Germans here as this is one of their favourite holiday destinations. Tourist information is in the station. Open Mon.–Sat.: 9 a.m.–1 p.m., 3 p.m.–8 p.m., Sun.: 10 a.m.–noon, at Speicher, Beckergrube 95.

Lübeck is known as the 'City of Seven Spires' because the skyline is dominated by the spires of five imposing churches, including the cathedral. Extensively bombed during the war, you can see the shattered bells at the foot of the former belfry in the MARIEN-KIRCHE where they have lain undisturbed since being blasted free of their fastenings in 1942. For a good view of the city the lift up the tower of the PETRIKIRCHE is good value at 2 DM (1 DM for students).

Lübeck is renowned for its brickwork, so take a close look at the gabled houses, particularly BUDDENBROOKHAUS – the house Thomas Mann (a Lübecker) used as the background to his novel *Buddenbrooks*. The actual city centre is quite small and it's possible to walk round all the sights there: the thirteenth-century RATHAUS with its original black glazed tiles, the Romanesque ST MARIEN DOM, the HOLSTEN GATE and the old city walls and MUSEUM. On some evenings during the summer the castle is illuminated and there is a spectacular fireworks display. Check out the details with the tourist office.

The youth hostel is at Am Gertrudenkirchhof 4 (Tel. 0451–33433), 14 DM per night. A good campsite is reached by bus 7 or 8 from the station to Dornbreite. Take bus 1, 3, 12 from the station; tourist information will find rooms for you.

Hannover

Primarily known as a centre for trade fairs, Hannover is nevertheless deserving of a visit.

. The Tourist Information office is opposite the station at Ernst August Platz 8 (Tel. 0511–1682319). Open 8.30 a.m.–6 p.m. (noon on Saturdays). After hours, use the City Air Terminal in the railway station, which is open until 8 p.m. (except Sundays). Ask for the booklet 'The Red Line of Hannover' which takes you around the main sights of the city by following a red line painted on the pavements.

Our advice for getting about is to follow the red line. Sights worthy of special mention are the ROYAL GARDEN, BERGGARDEN and GEORGE GARDEN. The gardens are linked to the city by the mile-long Herrenhausen Avenue lined by 1300 lime trees. The gardens are often the venue for Music and Theatre, and Festivals of Light are often held. Check with Tourist Information for details.

Look out for the Marksmen Festival and Old Town Festival during the summer. The Flea Market on Hohes Ufer every Saturday is an interesting diversion.

The KESTNER MUSEUM and LOWER SAXONY REGIONAL MUSEUM are also worth a look.

The hostel is Ferdinand-Wilhelm-Fricke-Weg 1 (Tel. 0511–322941), 20 minutes from the station on tram 7 or 3 to Fischerhof. It also has a youth guest house. There is also Hermann-Bahlsen-Allee 8, further out (Tel. 0511–691493), 30 minutes from the station by tram 3 or 7 to Spann-hagen Strasse.

Eurotrain has an office at Karl-Wiechert-Allee 23 (Tel. 0511–5670).

The Central Belt and the Harz Mountains

Frankfurt, Düsseldorf and Bonn are all fairly modern industrial centres which have little to offer that is worth breaking your journey for. You do far better to head for centres like Marburg, Göttingen, Hannoversch-Münden, Karlshafen, Goslar or the resorts round Münster: Attendorn, Alt-Astenburg and Berleburg. These have far more of the aspects of German life you're probably looking for.

Baden-Württemberg – the Black Forest

The south-western region of Germany from Karlsruhe to Basel is considered by many travellers its most enchanting. The pace of life is slower and the villages and towns dotted round the forests really are as attractive as the tourist brochures make them look. The main towns of this region are Heidelberg, Freiburg, Tübingen, Baden-Baden and Stuttgart. The first three are picturesque old university towns and worth a day or two; unless you've time, forget Baden-Baden as it's very expensive; Stuttgart is an interesting industrial city. A day trip from Heidelberg to Freiburg, Donau-eschingen and Offenburg is a good 'pushed for time' introduction to this area.

Heidelberg

Famous for its university and magnificent castle, most of Heidelberg's sights can be seen in a day, but are nevertheless well worth seeing. Start your tour (get a bus or taxi as it's a 40-minute walk into town) at the MARKTPLATZ and take in the HEILIG-GEIST KIRCHE and HAUS ZUM RITTER, a Renaissance mansion house, now a hotel and restaurant. The OLD UNIVERSITY has an interesting STUDENTS' JAIL which proves that graffiti weren't a twentieth-century invention. From here cross the Karl-Theodor Bridge over the River Neckar and take the PHILOSOPHER'S WALK to the 1,400-foot Heiligenberg. Apart from a good view of the town, there are reconstructed Roman ruins and the twelfth-century ST STEPHEN'S CLOISTER. Inside the amazing SCHLOSS (castle), 4 DM admission, 2 DM for students, is the GERMAN APOTHECARY MUSEUM with interesting reconstructions of laboratories of the seventeenth century. You can get up to it by funicular railway if you don't fancy the climb.

The tourist information office, just outside the station, is open Mon.–Thurs. and Sat.: 9 a.m.–7 p.m., Fri. 9 a.m.–9 p.m., Sun. 10 a.m.–6 p.m. They run an accommodation-finding service for a small fee and supply you with leaflets and maps. Ask for 'All Around Heidelberg' and 'Heidelberg This Week' which includes a picture map and a walking tour of the main sights. AMEX is at Friedrich-Ebert Anlage 16. HS Reisebüro, who do student travel deals, are at Bismarckplatz (Tel. 06221–27151). Try to get around town by bus and streetcar. You can buy 6 DM and 10 DM multi-tickets, valid for 36 hours.

Hotels tend to be expensive as Heidelberg gets its fair share of middle-class, middle-aged tourists, so they don't exactly cater for eurorailers in a big way. Still, there's a youth hostel at Tiergartenstrasse (Tel. 06221–412066), on bus routes 12, 13, 330 with connecting tram at night, and the Neckertal campsite is in Schlierbach (Tel. 06221–802506). You are not allowed to leave the campsite before 8 a.m., so don't pitch your tent there if you have an early start the next morning. Your passport is kept as security. There is a train station nearby, but services are limited to two trains at night, and one in the morning.

Use the Mensa restaurants for meals: there's one off Universitätsplatz and another in Marstallhof – or a student inn. These are dotted all round the city. The station café was reasonably priced, providing you picked carefully from the menu. A filling meal with beer can be had for around 14 DM.

Freiburg im Breisgau

An attractive city of 170,000 people which has fully recovered from its heavy wartime destruction and is restored and as picturesque as ever. Though the university is the source of most young Freiburghers' social life, the summer schools based there make sure things don't grind to a halt outside term-time.

Two blocks down Eisenbahnstrasse from the station is the tourist information at Rotteckring 14. They'll arrange accommodation for you for 3 DM, or, if you're staying more than two days, you can get into private accommodation (privatzimmer).

The Altstadt (Old Town) has at its centre the MÜNSTER – the beautiful medieval cathedral with its intricate carvings and gargoyles. Opposite the cathedral to the south is the sixteenth-century KAUFHAUS (merchants' hall), and nearby is the RATHAUS (town hall) made out of two old patrician houses. Medieval and baroque art of the Upper Rhine can be seen in the AUGUSTINER MUSEUM.

There's a youth hostel and a campsite in Kartäuserstrasse at 151 and 99 respectively (Tel. 0761–67656 and 0761–35054). Take tram 1 from the station to Römerhof. With woods and forests all around, you shouldn't be stuck for a place to pitch your tent, but if things are desperate see the Bahnhofmission at the station.

The last week of June sees the Wine Festival; Baden white wine is well worth trying, and Freiburg has many wine bars and cheap (by German standards) eating places. Concentrate on the university area and Augustinerplatz.

Tübingen

The University of Tübingen, founded in 1477, still makes use of the town's Renaissance castle (SCHLOSS HOHENTÜBINGEN) and though you only visit it at weekends from April to October, you can get a good view over the Old Town and the Neckar from its gardens. In the centre there are old gabled houses and a fifteenth-century church, STIFTSKIRCHE. In the Neckar on a man-made island is the PLATANENALLEE – an avenue of plane trees which makes a good walk. Reach it via the Eberhard Bridge.

The youth hostel is at Gartenstrasse 22/2 (Tel. 07071–23002), ten minutes from the station, and there's a campsite on the banks of the Neckar (Tel. 07071–23343). The university Mensa is on the corner of Wilhelmstrasse and Keplerstrasse and is open for lunches and dinners.

Stuttgart

Described as 'one of the most interesting cities in Europe' by one reader, Stuttgart has got to be worth visiting. Stuttgart is the capital of Swabia and despite being an industrial centre, boasts that over 50 per cent of the city is woods, vineyards and parks.

TOURIST INFORMATION

Tourist Centre 'i-Punkt', Königstrasse 1, near the station (Tel. 0711–222 8240). Open 8.30 a.m.–10 p.m. (Sundays and holidays 11 a.m. to 6 p.m., Sundays Nov.–April 1 p.m.–6 p.m.). In addition to providing details of walking tours and maps, they will also provide details of budget accommodation.

Also try JIZ (Jugend-Informationszentrum) at Hohestrasse 9 (Tel. 0711–293058), specifically for forthcoming events and where the action is.

SEEING

As the centre of Stuttgart is largely pedestrianized, it is best seen on foot.

SCHLOSSPLATZ and SCHILLERPLATZ are typical of Stuttgart and are surrounded by most of the major sights. The SCHLOSSGARTEN stretches northwards to the River Neckar and here you can enjoy landscaped woods, lakes and a zoo. Stuttgart is also a centre for mineral water and the mineral baths make an interesting diversion from the Schlossgarten. Alternatively take U14 to Mineral-bäder. LEUZE mineral baths has both an outdoor swimming pool and a heated indoor pool.

Museums especially worth a visit include the imposing extension of the STAATSGALERIE (built by a British architect and as seen on British stamps and TV commercials) on Konrad Adenauer Strasse and the MERCEDES BENZ AUTOMOBILE MUSEUM just outside the main city, open Tues.–Sun.: 9 a.m.–5 p.m. Take S-Bahn 1 to Neckarstadion or bus 56.

SLEEPING

Should be no problem as 'i-Punkt' will help.

The DJH Hostel at Haussmannstrasse 27 (entrance on the corner of Werastrasse and Kernerstrasse) is central and modern and is only ten minutes from the station. Take U-Bahn 15 to Eugensplatz (Tel. 0711–241583).

The campsite at Cannstatter Wasen (Tel. 0711–556696 or 561503) is less central, on the banks of the River Neckar.

EATING AND NIGHTLIFE

It should be easy to find a decent place to eat. Follow the locals to a nearby 'Kneipe' for a popular meeting place and refreshment. They normally fill up very quickly and become quite lively. Wine is varied and excellent, whilst local culinary specialities include 'Maultaschen' – lentils with Weiner sausages, and hand-made noodles or roast beef with sauerkraut.

Stuttgart has a lively youth scene and the many jazz clubs are popular. Ask at 'i-Punkt', JIZ or any young resident for the latest details.

Not to be missed in summer/early autumn are the variety of street fairs and 'happenings'. Equally, the WINE FESTIVAL in late August–September at Schillerplatz and Marktplatz is lively, whilst the CANSTATT VOLKSFEST in late September–October, should not be missed as it is only equalled in scale by the Munich Oktoberfest.

The Rhine Valley

The section of the 820-mile-long Rhine that flows through Germany is considered the most scenic, and the popular image of sailing down the Rhine is a pleasure cruiser passing vineyards, castles and cliffs. This is founded on truth but is somewhat idealistic as the Rhine today is still Europe's main commercial waterway and as such takes its fair share of barges and freight loads. Köln-Düsseldorfer lines run boats from Frankfurt to Cologne which give a 50 per cent discount to Inter-Railers and is free to Eurail card holders. The most attractive segment of the journey is from Rüdesheim to Koblenz, or vice versa.

OBERWESEL is a lovely place, but almost closes down on Mondays. The youth hostel is fantastic, complete with swimming pool. It's at Auf dem Schönberg (Tel. 06744 7046) and costs 17 DM including breakfast. Phone to book in after 8 a.m. Stop off here on your way from Köln to Bingen – it's about three hours down the line – and finish your journey by boat.

Cologne (Köln)

The main reason for stopping off at Cologne is undoubtedly the cathedral (KÖLNER DOM) which took from 1248 to 1880 to complete; see the fourteenth-century stained-glass windows, altarpiece and the Shrine of the Magi. In the Second World War, 90 per cent of Cologne was razed to the ground, but amazingly the cathedral escaped almost intact. Open daily 6 a.m.–7.30 p.m. For an impressive view of the city climb the 509 steps up the tower (2 DM, ISIC 1 DM).

Other things of interest are the ROMAN-GERMANIC MUSEUM exhibiting Cologne's Roman remains and the WALLRAF-RICHARTZ-MUSEUM/MUSEUM LUDWIG with its impressive collection of German works. The MUSEUM OF ARTS AND CRAFTS at An Der Rechtsschule includes vast collections of arts and crafts from the Middle Ages to the present day together with designs of the twentieth century. Open 10 a.m.–5 p.m. (until 8 p.m. on Tuesdays). Admission 3 DM.

Even if you can only afford a few hours you should have no
problems, as everything is near the station. Museums are closed on
Mondays.

STATION FACILITIES

	HAUPTBAHNHOF
Train information	Mon.–Sat.: 8 a.m.–10.30 p.m.,
	Sun.: 9 a.m.–10.30 p.m. (Tel. 0221–2211)
Reservations	Mon.–Sat.: 6.30 a.m.–9 p.m.,
	Sun.: 8 a.m.–4 p.m.
Tourist information	Mon.–Sat.: 8 a.m.–9 p.m.,
	Sun.: 9.30 a.m.–7 p.m.
	Located directly opposite cathedral
	Unter Fetterhennen, 19
Foreign exchange	7 a.m.–9 p.m.
Left-luggage lockers	Always accessible
Left-luggage store	All hours
Waiting room	In restaurant (with ticket only) and passageways
Bar, Buffet	7 a.m.–9 p.m. 'Milchstube', 'Bierfass',
	all hours except 4 a.m.–5 a.m. 'Treffpub'
Restaurant	8 a.m.–10 p.m. – 'Terrassen' and
	6 a.m.–10 p.m. – 'Gaststätte'
Shops	Regular hours in pedestrian mall
Post office	7 a.m.–10 p.m. Nord Tunnel

Daily trains to: Düsseldorf (½ hour), Hamburg (4½ hours), Copenhagen, Hannover
(3 hours), Mainz (1¾ hours), Frankfurt (2¼ hours), Würzburg (4 hours), Nürnberg
(5 hours), Stuttgart (4 hours), Vienna, Munich, Innsbruck, Zürich, Basel (5 hours),
Paris, Brussels (3 hours), Rotterdam (3½ hours), The Hague (4 hours), Amsterdam
(3 hours).

There are 2 hostels in Cologne which are very good but suffer from
the same problem – they fill up fast. The nearest to the main station
is at Siegesstrasse 5a (Tel. 0221–814711). It's a 20-minute walk
across the Rhine, but is only two minutes' walk from the Deutz
station and is well signposted. If it is full up you will be directed to a
nearby hotel where you can get bed and breakfast for 30 DM –
about double the hostel cost but quite reasonable for an hotel. You
can also try the Youth Guest House at An der Schanze 14 (Tel.
0221–767081), which is more luxurious, but further out. You cannot
book by phone, so get there as soon as possible after reception

opens at 11 a.m. Take U-Bahn lines 11 or 16 to Boltonsternstrasse and then a 5-minute walk. Price is 22.50 DM and includes breakfast, shower and linen. There are 2 camping sites at the end of the Rodenkirchen Bridge. Take tram 16 to Marienberg. Campingplatz der Stadt Köln is at Weinenweg (Tel: 0221–831966). Although facilities are limited, there is a good bar across the road. Cost is 4.5 DM per person and 3 DM per tent. Tourist information will also find rooms from about 35 DM upwards. Salzgasse in the Old Town is where to go for eats, and there are all the usual excellent department stores with food halls for buying groceries.

The Moselle Valley

Less commercial, and some say less scenic, is the Moselle region where wine making is the main regional industry, apart from tourism. Boats run between Cochem and Koblenz (KD lines with the same reductions as on the Rhine). The hostel at Koblenz is very good and overlooks the confluence of the Rhine and Moselle. It's at Koblenz-Ehrenbreitstein on the right bank, bus 7, 8, 9, 10 from the station (Tel. 0261–73737). The towns to get off at are: BERNKASTEL-KUES, TRABEN-TRARBACH and COCHEM. You can hire bikes at one of these stations and return them at another. This is the region for wine tasting – ask at the tourist information offices for tours of the local cellars.

Frankfurt am Main

Frankfurt is Germany's most important trading centre; a city of large skyscrapers with an important international airport and Germany's biggest red-light area right across from what is claimed to be Europe's largest railway station. (The Tourist Information Centre is open Mon.–Sat. 8 a.m.–9 p.m.; Sun. 9.30 a.m.–8 p.m.) There is nothing really to detain you in Frankfurt, but if you do have to stay overnight the youth hostel is pleasantly situated across the

River Main and on the edge of the city's liveliest area for entertainment and reasonable eating places, the Sachsenhausen. The hostel is at Deutschherrnufer 12 (Tel. 069–619058). Take bus 46 from the Hauptbahnhof right to the hostel. Camping at Niederrader Ufer by tram 15. Although the authorities tried to move the red light area in 1985 they didn't succeed and if you head for McDonald's or Burger King across from the station you're likely to be hassled. The fruit stalls and shops in the underground mall in front of the station are quite good for stocking up on picnic items like small portions of butter, cheese and jam.

Trier

Germany's oldest city and one-time capital of the Western Roman Empire (with Roman baths, arches and amphitheatre remains to prove it), Trier has many interesting churches and museums, as well as the house where Karl Marx was born. Tourist information is next to the Porta Nigra, the youth hostel is at Maarstrasse 156, bus 2 or 8 from the station (Tel. 0651–29292) and the campsites are at Monaisestrasse (Tel. 0651–86210) and Luxemburgerstrasse 81 (Tel. 0651–86921). For cheap eats try either of the two university Mensas at Universität Schniederhof or at the Tar Forst campus. The Greek restaurant next to the youth hostel serves good, filling and reasonably-priced meals. For cheap beer and good food, head for the Lowenbrau Brewerie, near the basilica. It is off the Garrenfeld Strasse, 100 yards after the railway bridge. The tree-shaded patio, where food and drink is served, is across the road from the main entrance. There is also a good market next to the cathedral and while you are there take a look at the impressive interior decor. For a good view of the city itself, follow the Romerstrasse up from the north bank of the Mosel to the Madonna statue.

Munich (München)

Munich is the capital of Bavaria and is regarded as the ultimate West German city. It is beautifully landscaped, tastefully decorated, carefully laid out and has a glut of things to do and see.

Ruled for over 650 years by the Wittelsbach family who brought the world-famous art collections and rich architectural heritage to the city, Munich seems to have continual festivals all the year round: Fasching with its masked carnivals from January to February; the beer inaugurations in March; the summer season of concerts and operas from May to August; the famous Oktoberfest beer festival lasting from end September to early October, followed not long after by the Christmas markets. And this doesn't even take into account the countless student-based activities going on round SCHWABING, Munich's lively Latin quarter.

STATION FACILITIES

	MÜNCHEN HAUPTBAHNHOF
Train information	6.30 a.m.–11 p.m. (Tel. 592 991)
Reservations	6 a.m.–12 midnight in 'ABR Reisebüro'
Tourist information	Mon.–Sat.: 8 a.m.–11 p.m., Sun.: 1 p.m.–9.30 p.m.
Foreign exchange	6.30 a.m.–11 p.m.
Bar, Buffet	6.30 a.m.–10 p.m.
Cafeteria	6.30 a.m.–12 midnight
Restaurant	6.30 a.m.–12 midnight
Left-luggage lockers	Always accessible
Left-luggage store	6.30 a.m.–12 midnight
Shops	6.30 a.m.–10 p.m.
Waiting room	All hours
Post office	Mon.–Fri.: 7 a.m.–9 p.m., Sat.: 8 a.m.–9 p.m.
Station shuts	1 a.m.–4.30 a.m.

Daily trains to: Paris, Brussels, Zürich, Milan, Vienna.

TOURIST INFORMATION

The Fremdenverkehrsamt (tourist office) (Tel. 239 1256/57) is at the front of the Hauptbahnhof, opposite platform 11, and is open Mon.–Sat.: 8 a.m.–11 p.m., Sun.: 1 p.m.–9.30 p.m. The staff are helpful, fluent in English and will supply you with maps, details of walking tours and pamphlets and find you a room for 3 DM. Get the monthly programme of events and the 'Young People's Guide to Munich', which is excellent.

Munich's city transport system is one of the best in Europe, and also one of the most complicated. There are buses, trams, the U-Bahn and the S-Bahn. Note: Rail pass holders get free travel on the S-Bahn. You need only one ticket even if your journey takes in the tram, bus and underground systems. For further information, pick up leaflets at the underground at Hauptbahnhof, or S-Bahn stations. Day tickets cost 7.50 DM for the inner zone and 15 DM for all zones.

Whilst it is tempting and easy to travel free on public transport, you take the risk of an on-the-spot fine of 40 DM if a squad of police operates a random check (which are frequent). Ignorance is no excuse, the police reason that anyone who can work out how to get to their destination can operate the idiot-proof ticket dispensers or obtain a pass! Offenders or those unable to pay are taken to the police station for a statement. It obviously makes sense to have a valid ticket.

● **Addresses:**

POST OFFICE: Bahnhofplatz 1 (opposite station). Open 24 hours. Also poste restante here.

UK CONSULATE: Amalienstrasse 62 (Tel. 394015).

US CONSULATE: Königinstrasse 5. (Tel. 23011).

CANADIAN CONSULATE: Maximiliansplatz 9 (Tel. 558531).

AMEX: Promenadeplatz 6, Mon.–Fri.: 9 a.m.–5.30 p.m., Sat.: 9 a.m.–noon (Tel. 21990).

MEDICAL HELP: Try university clinic at Ismaningerstrasse (Tel. 41401), or AOK Clinic, Maierstrasse (U-Bahn 3, 6 Goetheplatz).

STUDIOSUS-REISEN (Student Travel): Amalienstrasse 73 (Tel. 280768).

TELEPHONE CODE: 089.

SEEING

MARIENPLATZ – the attractive pedestrian zone – is at the centre of Munich. The neo-Gothic TOWN HALL is located here (look out for the glockenspiel show at 11 a.m., noon, 5 p.m. and 9 p.m. May–Oct., 11 a.m. Nov.–Apr.), as is the old town hall (ALTES RATHAUS). On Sunday mornings in summer, a brass band in full Bavarian uniform plays in front of the town hall. Just off Marienplatz is the twelfth-century church of ST PETER. If a white disc is out on the platform, climb its tower (2 DM, 1 DM for students) for a view extending to the Alps (a red disc means you'll just see over Munich). Also near here is the FRAUENKIRCHE; this church, with its green onion-topped twin towers, is the symbol of the city and houses various works of art, tombs and relics as well as the mausoleum of Emperor Ludwig IV. ST MICHAEL'S CHURCH and the baroque THEATINER CHURCH are also worth a look. Eight blocks west of Marienplatz is KARLSPLATZ, the main square of Munich. All the city transport starts from here and SONNENSTRASSE, the main shopping street, begins. The palace of the Bavarian rulers (the RESIDENZ) houses a spectacular array of riches. Tours leave Tues.–Sat.: 10 a.m.–4.30 p.m., Sun. till 1 p.m. North of the Residenz is the university area (Schwabing) with Leopoldstrasse at its centre. Nothing much goes on in daytime here, but it's a lively place at night. To the east of Schwabing lies the ENGLISH GARDEN, ideal for sunbathing (nude!) and picnicking.

The ALTE PINAKOTHEK is one of Europe's finest art galleries. It specializes in early German, Flemish and Italian works and it's free on Sundays (closed Mondays). The NEUE PINAKOTHEK concentrates on modern art.

The DEUTSCHES MUSEUM is located on an island in the Isar River; it is the largest technical museum in the world (with lots of buttons to push), and has exhibits such as U-boats, a Messerschmitt jet fighter, a planetarium and old locomotives. Entrance 5 DM (ISIC 2 DM). The BAVARIAN NATIONAL MUSEUM gives a good introduction to what makes Bavaria different from the rest of Germany and has the most extensive collection of arts and crafts in the world (closed Mondays but open till 5 p.m. even on Saturdays; if you turn up after 3.30 they sometimes let you off without paying the admission fee).

The BMW MUSEUM (part of the factory) is well worth a visit if you have had enough of trains for a while. You can't get guided tours of the factory itself, but the museum is superb and includes a spectacular audio-visual show. It's on U-Bahn 8 (Petvelring stop). While there, visit the park itself, scene of the 1972 Olympic Games and marvel at the impressive architecture either from ground level or from the top of the Olympia Tower. Entrance to the park costs 1 DM and an extra 4 DM for the lift up the tower, which is well worth it for the stupendous view, unless the weather is lousy. Don't eat in the restaurant at the top as the prices are exorbitant. An equally good panorama can be obtained free by walking up one of the hills in the Olympic Park.

SLEEPING

Munich is busy all year, particularly during the Oktoberfest when beds are very scarce. Still, there are plenty of places if you know where to look. Expect to pay about 25–40 DM for student accommodation, 14–27 DM at youth hostels and up to 70 DM in pensions. Try to arrange hostel accommodation ahead of time or turn up early! Ask at Tourist Information for the Accommodation Guide to Munich.

The cheapest sleep to be had is at the Youth Camp (Jugendlager Kapuzinerhölzl) at Kapuzinerhölzl (Tel. 1414300); open late June– early September, 5 p.m.–9 a.m. For 6 DM you get an air mattress, blankets and a place in the circus tent, not to mention tea in the mornings and evenings. You won't get turned away. Take U-Bahn line U1 to Rotkreuzplatz, then tram 12 to Botanischer Garten. Take your passport for ID to avoid paying a 50 DM deposit for blankets.

• **Youth hostels:** You must be under 27 or accompanying a child to use Bavarian youth hostels. Wendl-Dietrich Strasse 20 (Tel. 131156) is fairly central but large, impersonal, fills up early and is usually full of noisy adolescent school groups. It could be cleaner, and the lockers are dodgy. Costs 14.80 DM including breakfast. The one at Burgweg 4-6, Pullach (Tel. 7930643 and 7930644), is more fun, but this renovated castle is a half-hour journey and also fills up early. There are no lockers and it has an infuriating token system for showers. The staff, however, are very helpful and it costs 14 DM for shower and breakfast in a small dormitory. Take S-Bahn 7 (free on Inter Rail) to Pullach. Last train from Munich is 10.40 p.m. and curfew is at 11.30 p.m. Haus International, Elizabethstrasse 87 (Tel. 1850813) is good but more expensive with prices from 27.50 DM to 40 DM, so share in a large room to cut down costs. There is a disco in the basement and no curfew. Finally, there's Jugendgastehaus at Miesingstrasse 4 (Tel. 7236550), where couples need to produce a marriage certificate to share a room. Take tram 16, 26 to Boschetsrieder Strasse or S10, S22. Westfalia at Mozertstrasse 23 (Tel. 530377) is also worth a try. If you're stuck for a place to stay try the Augsburg Youth Hostel (Tel. 0821–33909), about 40 minutes away by S-Bahn.

Some of the cheapest pensions are located in Schillerstrasse and Landwehrstrasse. Try Pension Schiller (Tel. 592435) at Schiller-strasse 11; further down the street at No. 32 there's Pension Bergbauer (Tel. 591005). The campsite, which is well equipped, is at Zentralländstrasse 49 (Tel. 7231707), open March–Oct. Take U-Bahn 3, 6 to Thalkirchen Tierplatz, then bus 57 to Camping platz (or a 20-minute walk). Although central and convenient, it can get very crowded and noisy, with cleanliness suffering as a result. 4.50 DM per person, 4.90 DM per tent.

You could try sleeping in the Hauptbahnhof although it is draughty, busy and you will get woken up and moved on by the police around 5 a.m.

EATING AND NIGHTLIFE

Bavarian cooking is tasty, filling and not for the weight-conscious. Munich's speciality is Weisswurst – a sausage made of veal and parsley. You can buy it at any number of stalls and eat it as a quick snack with a beer to keep you going. The VIKTUALIENMARKT is an attractive sight, but it's invariably cheaper to buy your supplies from one of the superb food halls of the department stores, Kaufhof, Hertie, Deutscher Supermarkt or the cheaper Pennymarkt and Aldi. The displays and high standards in these places really open your eyes if you've been weaned on dull supermarkets at home.

The student canteens (Mensas) have cheap lunches at Arcis-strasse 17 or Leopoldstrasse 15, open 11 a.m.–2 p.m., and all over Schwabing you'll find reasonably priced eating places. If you're desperate there's also a Wendy self-service outside the station. A quarter of the world's beer comes from Bavaria, and Munich is at the heart of this with its social life revolving round the beer halls and gardens. These are good places to eat, drink and make new friends. Avoid the touristy Hofbräuhaus as you're unlikely to meet the locals there; try instead the beer gardens in the English Garden. Augustinerkeller at Arnulfstrasse 52, Donisl at Marienplatz, and Hundskugel (Munich's oldest pub) at Hoherstrasse are more representative. For cheap and delicious doughnuts and so on, try Strüdel Stube in Orlandostrasse (near the Hofbräuhaus).

For nightlife, Schwabing is the area to head for. Studiosus-Reisen, Amalienstrasse 73, have tickets for concerts, theatres, etc., with reductions. There's music and dancing at The Drugstore, Feilitzschstrasse 12, and the university have occasional 'events' such as open-air discos outside term-time which you can go along to if you can pass yourself off as a German student.

• **Excursions:** 22 km north-west of Munich is the concentration camp of DACHAU built in 1933. A visit here will put into perspective the atrocities that were committed and will leave an impression with you that all the opulence of Munich can't take away. The old administration block is now a museum, and a film in English is shown twice a day. Get there on the S-Bahn line 2 (free to Inter-Railers): line 2 (Peterhausen) to Dachau, then buses 720 or 722 to the camp (closed on Mondays). Buses are infrequent on Sundays but it is a fairly easy 20-minute walk.

NYMPHENBURG PALACE AND PARK is Munich's Versailles. Home of the Bavarian kings, situated in a 495-acre park, the palace makes a pleasant day trip. Closed Mondays, 3 DM (ISIC). Other ideas for trips are Europe's largest zoo, Hellabrunn, 6 km south of the city and the Benedictine monastery at ANDECHS (buses 951 or 956), whose beer hall serves some of the strongest home brew in Munich.

A good day trip from Munich is to the fairy-tale castle of NEUSCHWANSTEIN, which featured in the famous film *Chitty Chitty Bang Bang*, and was built by 'mad' King Ludwig II. Take the train to Fussen and bus Bf 971 (half-price on Inter Rail) the 5 km to Hohenschwangau. It is then a steep 1 km walk up to the entrance. The bus fare is 1.80 DM and the entrance to the castle (open 9 a.m.–5.30 p.m. April–Sept., 10 a.m.–4 p.m. Oct.–Mar.) is 7 DM (4 DM on ISIC) including a rather hurried guided tour. While on the subject of films you may wish to spend some time at the Bavarian Film Studios which are near Pullach. Although quite expensive at 10 DM (9 DM on ISIC) and the tour being only in German, you can walk through the U-boat used for the film *The Boat* and see other sights.

The Alps and the Romantic Road

The Romantische Strasse is the name for the undeniably scenic stretch from Füssen to the vineyards of Franconia. The towns en route are very picturesque, and this is the route to take for fairytale castles and medieval churches set among rolling green hills.

To get to those hidden little corners of Bavaria, the train is not the best way: use the Europabus 'Romantische Strasse'. They offer two alternative routes: Füssen to Würzburg, and Munich to Wiesbaden (free to Eurail card holders). Make further enquiries at the Starnberger Bahnhof part of Munich station.

Places of note en route are: NÖRDLINGEN with its perfectly preserved circular medieval fortifications and fifteenth-century St George's Church; DINKELSBÜHL, also with a St George's Church which is a Gothic masterpiece, 'Deutsches Haus' and Old Town Hall; ROTHENBURG – visit the Rathaus, St Jakob's Church and the Folterkammer (torture chamber); and WÜRZBURG.

Würzburg

In the heart of wine country, Würzburg is *the* baroque city of West Germany. The Franconian RESIDENZ is the magnificent palace of the prince-bishops and is the main sight of Würzburg. Open Tue.–Sun.: 9 a.m.–5 p.m., till 4 p.m. Oct.–Mar. (4 DM, 3 DM on ISIC). The MARIENBERG FORTRESS, another of the princes' homes, is on the other side of the River Main, which intersects the town. Near the fortress is the KÄPPELE, an ornate baroque church which allows you an excellent view from the top. The MAINFRÄNKISCHES MUSEUM houses sculptures and carvings and is located in the Marienberg Fortress.

STATION FACILITIES

	HAUPTBAHNHOF
Train information	7 a.m.–9 p.m. (Tel. 0931–50656)
Reservations	7 a.m.–9 p.m.
Tourist information	Mon.–Sat.: 8 a.m.–8 p.m. Pavilion outside station
Foreign exchange	Mon.–Fri.: 6 a.m.–9 p.m., Sat.: 9 a.m.–1 p.m. (in next building along)
Café	Mon.–Fri.: 7 a.m.–8 p.m. Sat.: 7.30 a.m.–2.30 p.m. Sun.: 11 a.m.–6 p.m.
Restaurant	6.30 a.m.–0.30 a.m.
Bath, Shower	6 a.m.–10 p.m.
Left-luggage lockers	Always accessible
Left-luggage store	Mon.–Sat.: 8 a.m.–5 p.m.
Waiting room	In restaurants
Shops	Regular hours
Post office	Mon.–Fri.: 6 a.m.–9 p.m. Sat.: 6 a.m.–8 p.m., Sun.: 9 a.m.–8 p.m. (in next building along)

Daily trains to: Nürnberg (1 hour), Vienna, Munich (2½ hours), Stuttgart (2¼ hours), Mainz (2¼ hours), Paris, Cologne (4 hours), Frankfurt (2¼ hours).

TOURIST INFORMATION

Located just in front of the station and in the centre at the Haus zum Falken, by the Marktplatz: Mon.–Fri.: 9 a.m.–6 p.m., Sat.: 9 a.m.–2 p.m. They'll find you a room for 3 DM (Tel. 0931–37398). STUDENT TRAVEL OFFICE: Jugendreiscentre, Blasuisgasse 11 (Tel. 0931–59150). Check your travel instructions carefully, as the tram system is undergoing renovation and repair work, and some routes have been re-arranged.

SLEEPING AND EATING

The youth hostel is at Burkarderstrasse 44 (Tel. 0931–42590) and costs 16–20 DM. The campsite is at Mergentheimerstrasse 13B

(Tel. 0931–72536). Tram 3 gets you there. The campsite is not signposted, but follow directions to the Würzburg Canoe Club and register in the club restaurant, whence you will be directed to your pitch.

Eat at the university Mensa in the Studentenhaus at the corner of Münzstrasse and Jahnstrasse. Open for lunch and dinner on weekdays.

GREECE

Entry requirements	Passport
Population	9,900,000
Capital	Athens (pop.: 3,100,000)
Currency	Drachma
	£1 = approx. 291 dr.
Political system	Republic
Religion	Greek Orthodox
Language	Greek (some English and French spoken)
Public holidays	1, 6 Jan.; Shrove Monday; 25 March;
	Good Friday; Easter Sunday; Easter Monday;
	1 May; 3 June; 15 Aug.; 28 Oct.; 25, 26 Dec.
International dialling codes	From UK: 010 + 30 + number
	From USA: 011 + 30 + number
	To UK: 00 + 44 + number
	To USA: 00 + 1 + number
Eurotrain office	Nikis Street 11, GR–10557 Athens
	(Tel. 01–322 1267)

Every year, Greece acts like a magnet to thousands of eurorailers from the north. So many come that the summertime population increases by about 50 per cent. The islands in particular offer the best under-30 social scene you're likely to find. Ironically, it's much easier to get to know Germans and Swedes here than Greeks, and you get to know them very well indeed if you share the same nudist beach, although it is, technically, only legal at three beaches in Greece. It's difficult to have a bad holiday in Greece, the birthplace of Western civilization, which provides a haven not only for lovers of nature, but also for those interested in history, archaeology and the arts.

Greek history begins about 2,500 BC with the Minoan civilization on Crete, a thousand years before the Mycenaeans got it together on the mainland. The classical period began during the eighth century BC and reached its peak in fifth-century BC Athens. As independent city-states the Greeks shared the same culture, but were always at each other's throats, until Alexander the Great sorted them out during the third century BC, uniting former rivals and himself conquering a world empire. By the fifth century AD, Greece had become part of the Byzantine Empire, and was eventually conquered by the Turks in the fifteenth century. The

War of Independence in 1821 started the formation of the modern Greek state, a process which ended in 1947 with the return of the Dodecanese. They still play cricket on Corfu which, along with other Ionian islands, was under British rule till 1864. After the Germans pulled out in 1944, civil war broke out and continued for five years, seriously hindering Greece's postwar recovery. Away from the beaches, things are less serene. Relations with Turkey remain as strained as ever, particularly after the Turkish invasion of Cyprus in 1974. High inflation and low per capita income compared with other EEC countries characterize the economy. Greece's recent history is almost as complex and unstable as her past. If stuck for conversation, it's a safer bet to have a crack at the Turks than to discuss the monarchy (of her six kings since independence, four have been deposed and one assassinated).

• **Getting there:** Travelling there by train is still the cheapest way of getting to Greece, the islands and the sun. Charter flights offer little in the way of flexibility. No matter how bad things might sometimes seem by train, console yourself with the knowledge that they would have been a lot worse by bus. But there are problems in going by train, not least of which is deciding on your route. Note that it is now illegal to take into Greece *any* substance containing codeine – for example the common treatment for period pains, Feminax. You're OK if you have a doctor's note, however.

• **The Belgrade–Athens run:** Nearly all eurorailers have their own version of this route. In theory, the journey through Yugoslavia seems attractive enough. In reality, the story is often very different: trains are nearly always late on departure from Belgrade – that is, if they depart at all. When and if they do, it's no exaggeration to say that they can be up to ten hours or more late on arrival at Athens. If you think that's bad enough, there's worse to come. The authorities don't provide anything like the number of coaches needed for what must be one of the busiest lines in Europe during the summer. Thieves also operate on this train, preying on eurorailers. Beware. If you're lucky, there's water for two or three hours; if not, I hope you have a good bladder. If you travel in midsummer you're likely to end up on the floor, or standing with your head out of a window to escape the smell of the loos, unless you heed this good advice:

1. If you can travel out of season, do so or at least try to avoid mid-July/August.
2. Go for the fastest train possible – it's well worth the supplement. Try and get on the through-train from Munich or Vienna, or travel overnight in a couchette/sleeper. (It's advisable here to book as far in advance as possible.) You can book ahead to Munich before you go. A sleeper will cost about £18 but a couchette only around £7.
3. Reserve a seat well ahead of time or, if that's not possible, arrive early and look for German or Austrian coaches.
4. Take along plenty to eat and *drink*. Remember: the trains aren't air-conditioned and you don't know how long a train may stop en route.
5. Don't make arrangements to meet someone at the other end or keep your schedule too tight unless you can't avoid it.
6. Go on board determined to make friends, and try and look on the whole episode as an educational experience.
7. On the way back keep trying at the reservations office. You may be told at one window there are no seats for several days and get a reservation immediately at the next.
8. If you get on a train try to pay (or bribe!) for a couchette or sleeper. Have plenty of 'hard' currency on you as Dinars are usually refused.
9. Look out for Turkish or Yugoslav guards trying to extract supplements on trains which are not exclusively reserved. Simply waving a Thomas Cook timetable can sometimes scare them off. Otherwise argue and kick up as much of a fuss as possible.

When you reach Thessaloniki, things pick up no end. When it comes to soft drinks and refreshments, it's a seller's market, a fact which the keen-eyed but smiling traders know all too well as they descend on those who had set off unprepared.

• **The Italian run:** The problems faced by travellers in Italy are normally a considerably watered-down version of those faced in Yugoslavia. Trains are crowded and the toilets dirty. Your real problems start at Brindisi, beginning with the mile walk straight down to the docks.

Now that the Brindisi–Patras ferry is included in the 1991 Inter Rail card, the hassles of which ticket to buy, from whom, is, thankfully, a thing of the past.

It can be windy on the sailing, but don't let the cooling breeze kid you into not taking precautions against the sun. Putting a rucksack on sunburnt shoulders rather takes the edge off your holiday enjoyment. If you are going to Corfu, seriously consider flying from Athens, rather than taking the boat from Brindisi. It costs less (about £35) and only takes 50 minutes.

GREEK RAILWAYS
(Organismos Sidirodromoń Ellados, OSE)

A quick look at any rail map will show you that Greece's network is hardly a match for northern Europe's. Greece is a mountainous country and therefore many towns are not connected by rail, although OSE uses a large number of connecting buses, and the few trains there are will seem slow except by East European standards. The international long-distance trains are somewhat optimistically called 'expresses', although some new trains on the Athens Thessaloniki route have cut the travel time from seven hours to six and a half. Some of these require a small supplement of about 200 dr. Local trains are slow enough to enable you to strike up lasting friendships. (By the time you arrive you'll feel as if you were born with your fellow travellers.) There are no Inter Rail bonuses in Greece, but always ask for student discounts.

The good news is that between now and 1997 a lot of money is being invested in OSE, particularly in northern Greece. Speeds, services and efficiency will improve things no end. The Patras–Athens run is earmarked for major investment, and that should come as a relief to many Inter Railers!

• **Eurail bonuses:** Free:
—Eurail Pass and Eurail Youthpass travellers can use steamers (*Appia, Egnatia, Espresso Grecia, Castalia*) operated by the Hellenic Mediterranean and Adriatica di Navigazione between Patras and Brindisi and vice versa. However, between 1 June and 30 September, they must pay a £7 ($11.90) high-season surcharge. During July and August, advance reservation, which costs about £2 ($3.40), is recommended. Special accommodations (airline-type seats or cabins) and port taxes are extra. Before boarding, all passengers must check in at the Shipping Line Office at the pier. Passengers who wish to break their voyage

at Corfu must declare their intention of 'stop over' upon delivery of the ticket.

Reduced fares:
—30 per cent reduction on the published full fares of the Adriatica Line between Piraeus–Venice or Alexandria and vice versa, on the *Espresso Egitto*. Contact the local Adriatica offices. Check your dates carefully when taking this run as it can work out substantially cheaper to travel outside the high summer season which usually starts towards the end of July. If you do find yourself with time on your hands waiting for a ferry, the companies will usually let you leave your luggage in their offices while you head for the beach.

TRAIN INFORMATION

English is spoken by information officers at all major stations. Also pick up the Tourist Board's booklet, 'General Information about Greece'.

• **Reservations:** Wherever else in Europe you may decide against reserving, it's well worth thinking about it here. Go to an OSE office rather than the station – the staff are more helpful and it's generally less hassle. The rule is to book a seat as far in advance as possible for international trains. On some expresses (ask at station) reservations are obligatory. You can reserve up to a month in advance. It pays to be organized here; hundreds aren't. It's possible to reserve on internal routes in Greece, but you have to do it by post in advance and unless you have an extremely well-organized schedule (taking account of the Belgrade-Athens run) it's not worth the hassle. NB There are no tickets placed on reserved seats so chaos often ensues!

• **Night travel:** Couchettes and sleepers are both cheap by northern European standards. If you can get one, go for it.

• **Rover tickets:** The Greek Tourist Card is available only in second class for 10, 20 or 30 days unlimited travel for between one and five people. There are no child reductions. Prices for 10 days range from £29 for one person to £81 for five people. For 20 days the prices range from £43 to £129, and for 30 days from £57 to £177.

TOURIST INFORMATION

For information about the country, accommodation and the main sights, see the National Tourist Organization of Greece (NTOG) known as EOT in Greece. For any other local information see the tourist police. Don't be put off by their name. Their role is to help you find accommodation and sort out your problems.

● **ISIC bonuses:** Up to 50 per cent off internal flights and ferries, up to 80 per cent on theatres and museums. For further information contact Student Travel Service, 1 Fillellinon St, Athens (Tel. 01–3227993 or 3247433).

● **Money matters:** No more than 100,000 dr. may be imported, or 20,000 dr. exported.
Banking hours are Mon.–Thurs.: 8 a.m.–2 p.m., Fri. 7.45 a.m.–2 p.m. Some branches are open till 2.30 p.m., but don't rely on it. Also a word of warning: if you still have some dinar left over from Yugoslavia, you can only change them at the National Bank of Greece. It's best to change all your drachma before you leave Greece. All banks give the same rate and there are no commission charges. You can also change money at the Post Office (ELTA) and the Telecommunications Organization (OTE). Trying to change money at weekends other than in large resort hotels is a non-starter, so be prepared.

● **Post offices:** Stamps can also be bought from kiosks. The price is the same everywhere; in fact it is illegal for anyone to sell stamps for more than their face value.

● **Shops:** Hours can vary wildly. Generally open Mon., Wed., Sat.: 8 a.m.–2.30 p.m., Tue., Thur., Fri.: 8 a.m.–1.30 p.m. and 5 p.m.–8.30 p.m. Supermarkets tend to close at 2 p.m. or 3 p.m. Non-food shops: Mon., Wed.: 9 a.m.–5 p.m., Tues., Thurs., Fri.: 10 a.m.–7 p.m., Sat.: 8.30 a.m.–3.30 p.m. Food shops: Mon.: 9 a.m.–2.30 p.m., Tues., Wed., Thurs., Fri.: 9 a.m.–6.30 p.m., Sat.: 9 a.m.–3.30 p.m.

● **Museums:** Usually open in winter 9 a.m.–3.30 p.m.; summer 8 a.m.–5 p.m. They tend to close on Mondays or Tuesdays. Students get a 50 per cent reduction.

SLEEPING

Greece presents the greatest variety of possibilities in all of Europe. Hotels are graded A, B, C, D and E. For a C-class hotel, expect to pay at least 2,000 dr. each. Student hostels are open to any paying customers. Many also offer sleeping on the roof during summer. The youth hostels are nothing to get excited about. As usual, to stay you need an IYHF card. It's possible to get one in Athens if you haven't already got one. Some pensions and hotels charge 10 per cent extra for short stays during high summer and charge extra for showers. Off season, the boot's on the other foot and it's worth bargaining to get the price down. All hotel prices are fixed and should be posted at the reception. Expect to pay an extra 20 per cent in high season.

The National Tourist Board issues a list with all the official campsites and facilities, giving an approximate price guide. Expect to pay at least 800 dr. Also on the outskirts of some towns there are unofficial camps with fewer facilities.

On the islands, accommodation is hopelessly inadequate. Camping is illegal on many islands but nearly everyone is forced to do it at some stage as during July and August all the hotels and private rooms are full. There is some 'legal' camping on licensed campsites. The police are stepping up action and the official policy of NTOG now is that you can't come to Greece by charter flight without having prebooked accommodation. Use your own discretion, but if you're camping illegally keep the place clean.

EATING AND NIGHTLIFE

Don't expect to eat as cheaply as you would have done a few years ago as high inflation continues to push up prices. Even old hands sometimes get a shock when they convert the bill into sterling or dollars. Always check the prices first in small shops and bakeries and make sure you know what you're paying for. If you're going to the islands it's easy to live off bread, cheese and water melon (karpouzi) during the day, and eat out at night. If you need that added luxury of a cup of coffee for breakfast to see you through the day, be sure to ask for Nescafé or you'll end up with sweet Greek or Turkish coffee instead. An alternative is café frappé (iced coffee). This is much more refreshing.

When eating out, as often as not you'll be ushered into the kitchen. Take your time, as this is the local custom of choosing. Arni is lamb; moschari, veal; chirino, pork; kotópoulo, chicken. Avoid the fish unless you've got plenty of money or are on the islands where it's fresh. Moussaka is a combination of meat with potato or eggplant, in bechamel sauce. Dolmades are minced meat and rice wrapped in vine leaves and are delicious hot or cold. Eating out is a leisurely affair and gives one the opportunity in the islands of seeing what people look like with their clothes on. If you're down on your luck, there's always a souvlaki stand (meat kebab wrapped in bread) not far away. For drinks, don't overdo it with ouzo (the local aniseed spirit), or you'll know all about it the next morning. For the evening meal, try at least one bottle of the local retsina (with resin) before returning (as most do) to the aretsinato wine. During the summer months, the Athens Festival takes place. This includes open-air performances in the Herodes Atticus Odeon – an experience you're not likely to forget. For details on this and other events, contact the Athens Festival Box Office, 4 Stadiou St. There are numerous local festivals celebrating everything from Easter to wine. The Greeks use any excuse to have one, as they love to let their hair down and dance. Once a bouzouki gets going, anything can happen. Nightclubs are dull and expensive by comparison. Films are shown in their original language, and are always cheaper in the suburbs.

Northern Greece

If you're entering Greece from Yugoslavia or Bulgaria, your first main centre will be THESSALONIKI. This is Greece's second city, founded in 315 BC. Although the station (like most in Greece) is unattractive, the people are very friendly and hospitable. Take a stroll through the OLD TURKISH QUARTER, visit the ARCHAEOLOGICAL MUSEUM and the third- and fifth-century churches of ST GEORGE and ST DEMETRIUS. Also see the Byzantine walls around the city – this can be an afternoon's walk. The castle at the top is closed for restoration.

As it is by the sea, Thessaloniki is relatively cool and the wide streets have many attractive shops not found in Athens. There is also an excellent copper market and several good beaches near the city with frequent buses and boats to them.

The youth hostel is at 44, Alex. Svolou Street (Tel. 031-225946). The YWCA at 11 Ag Sofias Street (Tel. 031-276144). Good 'C' grade hotels include the ABC, Continental, and Grande Bretagne.

For an impressive day-trip from Thessaloniki, or even to stay for a few days, head east along the coast to KAVALA. This prosperous market town has an amazing OLD QUARTER and a huge medieval AQUEDUCT leading in from the hills. Hourly ferry crossings are possible to the popular resort island of THASSOS. There are a number of good beaches nearby, but the best on mainland Greece are on SITHONIA, the westernmost prong of the HALKIDIKI peninsula, and well-connected to the rest of the region by bus.

Northern Greece is real 'spaghetti western' country. The mountains are rugged and the scenery wild and untamed. The two provinces of this area are Macedonia and Thrace.

South-east of Thessaloniki is the self-governing monastic commune of MOUNT ATHOS (no female has been allowed in for 900 years). If you want to visit, you'll have to go through your embassy and be able to give a sound reason for your visit.

To see some exceptional early Christian art and visit six Byzantine monasteries is much easier – just get yourself to METEORA, north of Kalambaka (take the bus from there).

The Peloponnese

The most southerly part of Greece's mainland is separated from the central belt by the Isthmus of Corinth. The Peloponnese has remnants of every people who have ever occupied that land: Greeks, Turks, Franks and Venetians. It is an untouristy region and on the main circular line from Patras to Athens lie Kalamata, Tripolis, Argos and Corinth. Near Argos lies the delightful town of Nafplion which is as yet unspoilt. (There's a good youth hostel in the town which does not require a YHA card.)

One of the major towns is CORINTH, though there are two Corinths: the new town, which has nothing much to recommend it, and the old town which has. The station will leave you in the new town, but buses leave every half-hour for 'Arhea Korinthos'. Here you can see columns from the sixth-century Temple of Apollo and the rostrum from which St Paul preached Christianity to the Corinthians. If you're staying overnight in New Corinth, try Hotel Akti (Tel. 0741 23337) down by the sea, or camp at 'Beach Camping', having bussed from station.

Just down the line is MYCENAE which dates back to 3,000 BC and is one of Greece's high spots for archaeologists. Many of the treasures found here are now in Athens, but you can still see the 'Gate of the Lions', royal tombs and the 'Treasure of Atreus'. The youth hostel is at Athens-Fihtia (Tel. 0751 66224). They offer beds for 550 dr., or the roof for half that.

Still going south, you'll come to EPIDAURUS whose main attraction is the well-preserved fourth-century BC amphitheatre, in which classical Greek dramas are staged during the summer.

SPARTA is a town worth visiting just to see the evening *volta* in the mountain-surrounded town centre; but MYSTRA, 7 km away (about 200 dr. bus journey), has an impressive display of Byzantine churches, palaces and a castle.

PATRAS is the main town of the Peloponnese, the ferry landing from Brindisi, southern Italy. There's not much to see but if you're killing time look round the VENETIAN CASTLE, ARCHAEOLOGICAL MUSEUM, MUNICIPAL THEATRE and the churches of PANTAKRATOR and AGIOS ANDREAS. The youth hostel is at 68 Heroon Polytechniou St. and costs 550 dr. (800 dr. during the summer).

Trains run (though not very often) to OLYMPIA, site of the first Olympic Games in Ancient Greece. See the stadium, the excellent museum, and stay in the youth hostel at 18 Prayitelous–Kondyli Street (Tel. 0624-22580), where there's often entertainment in the main street under the hostel (good fun but noisy).

Athens (Athinai)

Athens, 'the cradle of Western civilization', can offer you what is generally considered to be the high spot of a European tour: a visit to the 'high city' of the ancient Greeks, the Acropolis. It can also offer you dirty, squalid accommodation, unbearable heat, so-so food, and street after street of ugly concrete blocks. Modern Athens has nothing much to offer, but it's all worth while when you climb up to see the classical beauty of the white-stoned Parthenon, Temple of Athena and the beginnings of Western drama, the Theatre of Dionysus. If you're going island-hopping, Athens – or rather Piraeus, its port – is your starting point. Ferries leave from here for scores of islands (there are 1,500 to choose from in the Aegean and Ionian seas), and the average fare for a deck passenger on a 5-hour sail is about 2,000–3,000 dr.

STATION FACILITIES

If you're travelling to the Peloponnese or Patras (for the ferry to Italy) use the Athinai-Peloponnese station, adjacent to the Larissa station (six Patras trains daily).

	ATHINAI-LARISSA
Train information	7 a.m.–midnight (Tel. 522 2491)
Reservations	At OSE office, Karolou 1–3
Tourist information	7 a.m.–12 midnight at tourist police station
Foreign exchange	7 a.m.–7 p.m.
Left-luggage office	6 a.m.–12 midnight
Restaurant	6 a.m.–12 midnight
Post Office	Mon.–Fri.: 7 a.m.–10 p.m. Closed at weekends.

Daily trains to: Thessaloniki, Belgrade–Trieste–Venice, or Belgrade–Munich–Dortmund.

TOURIST INFORMATION

The tourist police are at the station, and there's an information desk in the National Bank of Greece on Syntagma Square (Tel. 32 22545), open Mon.–Fri.: 8 a.m.–8 p.m., Sat.: 9 a.m.–2 p.m. The main office of NTOG is at 2 Amerikis St (Tel. 32 23111). Pick up the free map and leaflets on campsites, hostels, etc. They don't operate an accommodation-finding service, but try the Hotel Chamber desk in the National Bank of Greece on Syntagma Square. The headquarters of the tourist police is at 7 Syngrou Avenue, and to call them for help dial 171. A good source for information on museums and shop hours is the *Athenian* which is published in English, although there are many others.

● **Addresses:**

POST OFFICE: 100 Eolou St, near Omonia Square. Open Mon.–Fri.
7.30 a.m.–8.30 p.m., Sat. 7.30 a.m.–2.30 p.m. Also Syntagma
Square.

OTE OFFICE (main telephone office): 15 Stadiou Street. Open 7
a.m.–11.30 p.m. Reverse charge calls take 2 hours on a Sunday.

AMEX: 2 Ermou Street, Syntagma Square, weekdays: 8.30
a.m.–5.30 p.m., Sat.: 8.30 a.m.–1.30 p.m. (Tel. 324 4975).

UK EMBASSY: 1 Ploutarchou (Tel. 7236211).

US EMBASSY: 91 Vassilissis Sofias (Tel. 7212951).

CANADIAN EMBASSY: 4 Ioannou Genadiou St (Tel. 7239511).

AUSTRALIAN EMBASSY: 26 Alexandros Avenue (Tel. 8211036).

FIRST AID: 21 Tritis Septemvriou (Tel. 150).

HOTEL CHAMBER OFFICE: 24, Stadiou Street (Tel. 3235485).

ISIC–USIT: 1 Filellinon Street, Athens (Tel. 324 1884).

EUROTRAIN: Nikis Street 11 (Tel. 3221267).

TELEPHONE CODE: 01.

● **Getting about:** Looking at the taxis' tariffs, they seem a huge
bargain, but by the time you've been ripped off – which seems to
happen to most tourists – they don't work out as such a hot idea
(each person pays what's on the clock so it doesn't help travelling in
groups). The buses and trolley-buses are OK but usually packed
(run 6 a.m.–midnight). You can take a bus out to the nearby
beaches from the bus station in the centre of town. The buses are
free before 8 a.m. in metropolitan Athens and Piraeus. The
underground has only one line (Piraeus–Kifissian) and is also free
before 8 a.m.

SEEING

Athens reached its zenith around 400 BC when Plato, Socrates and
Aristotle were strolling around the Acropolis which today is the
heart of the city. What's worth seeing in Athens – the antiquities –
are all clustered round the old town, or PLAKA district. The
ACROPOLIS should be seen as soon as it opens before the hordes
swarm up and destroy its atmosphere. The PARTHENON, the temple
dedicated to the goddess Athena, is held up as the epitome of
architectural perfection. See also the ERECHTHEION, TEMPLE OF
ATHENA NIKE and the PROPYLAEA, the gates to the sacred site. The

ACROPOLIS MUSEUM is a must. It contains some of the finds: statues, friezes, etc.

The Acropolis is open from Mon.–Fri. 8 a.m.–7 p.m., weekends 8.30 a.m.–3 p.m. and costs 800 dr. (400 dr. on ISIC). PNYX HILL offers a beautiful view of the Acropolis, and there's a *son et lumière* show here at 9 p.m. each night, which costs 400 dr. (150 dr. on ISIC).

The ancient AGORA, north of the Acropolis, was the marketplace and still has the remains of the old administrative centre. The TEMPLE OF HEPHAISTOS is considered the best preserved in Greece. This site is open from 8.30 a.m.–3 p.m. Tues.–Sun. It is well worth a visit (400 dr. admission, 200 dr. for students).

The NATIONAL ARCHAEOLOGICAL MUSEUM at 44 Patission St, has the best collection of ancient Greek artefacts in the world: gold death-masks, vessels, jewellery, statues, tombstones, frescoes, etc., dating from 1500 BC. Open Mon.: 12.30 p.m.–7 p.m., Tues.–Fri.: 8 a.m.–7 p.m., weekends: 8.30 a.m.–3 p.m. Admission 600 dr. (students 300 dr.).

SYNTAGMA (Constitution) Square, is the centre of modern Athens. This is where you'll find the hotels and cafés you can't afford. Constitution Square is flanked on one side by the Greek Parliament. From here take Amalias Avenue for the attractive NATIONAL GARDENS and HADRIAN'S ARCH. Also in this direction lie the PRESIDENTIAL PALACE and the OLYMPIC STADIUM.

The famous FLEA MARKET on Ifestou St makes a colourful walk and can produce some good bargains in equipment and leather goods. Beware of pick-pockets. Closes 2 p.m. Sundays.

SLEEPING

There are literally hundreds of places to stay in Athens that fall into the economical category, and even though it's up to you to find your own room, unless you're arriving very late on an August night you should be OK. That's not to say that these places are clean, friendly or have even the bare essentials, but they are cheap.

Head first for the Plaka as it's not only an attractive central place to stay (right underneath the Acropolis) but also one of the cheapest districts. Basically, the nearer to Syntagma Square you end up, the more you can expect to pay.

You may well find young blokes from various student hostels

(unofficial ones, some of which are fairly grotty) joining the trains just before Athens extolling the virtues of their establishments and handing out leaflets. This is a good way of earning bed and board for those who plan on spending some time in Athens. Don't be put off by them all, but don't believe all they tell you either. Invariably, the accommodation looks nothing like it appears in the leaflet. The cheaper the hostel, the cheaper the security regarding belongings and valuables.

If you aren't completely numbed by the long, gruesome journey (particularly if you're hot off the notorious Belgrade–Athens run), try cutting right back on expenses and sleep on the roofs. Many hostels offer you a place for about 600 dr., and at least it's cool. For a single, on average, expect to pay 700–1,000 dr., doubles 2,000–3,000 dr. and dormitory beds 700 dr. In 1987 it was announced that sleeping on roofs was illegal, as tourists were being ripped off by hoteliers charging too much. It remains to be seen how strictly enforced this rule will be.

Try Youth Hostel No 5, 75 Damareos St, Pangrati (Tel. 7519530). A bit out of town, but well worth the trouble of travelling to. Very clean, well organized and extremely friendly. Trolley buses ·2, 11 and 12. Single 1,200 dr. Also try Diethnes, 52 Peoniou St (Tel. 8832878) or Diana, 70 Patission St (Tel. 8223179). Directly opposite the station there's Olympos (Tel. 5223433). Highly recommended is Hostel Aphrodite, 12 Einardou St (Tel. 8810589). Cheap, friendly and 3 minutes from Larissis Station. The youth hostel at 57 Kypselis St (Tel. 8225860) is always pretty busy and not too central, but it's cheap (650 dr.). For hotels, try round Apollonos St or Hotel Eva, 31 Victor Hugo St (Tel. 5223079) near the station. The Art Gallery, 5 Erechthiou Street (Tel. 9238376) is friendly, clean and within two minutes of the Acropolis. Not cheap at around 4,800 dr. for a triple; but worth it if you can afford it. Hotel Acropole is two minutes' walk from the ferry port in Piraeas at 7 Gounari St (Tel. 417 3313). The nearest campsite is quite far out: 190 Athinon Avenue, Peristeri (Tel. 5814114); it is generally not worth the hassle of getting there, but if you must, take buses 822 or 823 from Eleftherias Square (Thission underground station). There is another campsite: Voula Camping, 2, Alkyonidon St (Tel. 895 2712). Take bus 118, 122 or 153 from Vass. Olgas Avenue.

If you're still stuck for a bed, drop into the ISYTS student centre at 11 Nikis St (Tel. 3233767 or 3221267), and they'll help you out.

EATING AND NIGHTLIFE

The advice is easy – head for the Plaka. There are lots of restaurants, bars and discos there. The best club in town is Aigli at Hrodon Atlikou. The port of Piraeus is also lively at night, particularly Zea Marina, and in the National Park people gather on summer evenings to see performing artists.

For cheap eats, fill up on shish kebabs (souvlaki) and dolmades (vine leaves stuffed with meat). There are plenty of cheap supermarkets. Avoid fruit from stalls as it's overpriced and the quality suspect. Try Xynos or Aerides in the Plaka.

• **Excursions from Athens:** 69 km away is the amazing TEMPLE OF POSEIDON on Cape Sourion. It dates back to 440 BC and is dedicated to the God of the Sea. Like the Acropolis, get there as early as possible; buses leave from Mavromateon St every half hour.

For DELPHI, take the local train to Levadia and take the bus direct from there. Alternatively, take a KTEL bus from 260, Liossion Street. This is the site of the Delphic Oracle and was the holiest place in Ancient Greece. Little is left of the Temple of Apollo but there's still a fascinating museum, a 400 BC theatre and the stadium where the Pythian Games were held. Bus costs around 920 dr.

The Islands

For many, Greece is the islands. In fact, it is so for very many. Each year quiet fishing villages are becoming tourist-saturated, and while some remote islands probably still have a decade or so to go before they're turned into mini Majorcas, many have only a year or two, and some are there already. For a remote haven, choose an island which has only a weekly sailing from Piraeus – the fewer the ferries, the less the crowds. Another way to find a 'goodie' is to ask backpackers. Three things to bear in mind:

1. Buy your ticket from one of the agencies in Piraeus, not on the boat – they charge 20 per cent surcharge. Some of the Athenian hostels offer what appear to be bargain tickets – beware of hidden port taxes and surcharges.

2. Unless you enjoy a good strong gust knocking your tent down or throwing sand up in your face, avoid the southern Aegean islands in August. They can receive the incredibly strong meltemi (northern wind) which can really muck up your sunbathing and sightseeing.

3. If you plan on going far afield, go for an overnight boat as it costs no extra to sleep on deck and saves you the price of a night's accommodation at the other end.

The Argo Saronics

These islands are within 4 hours of Athens, and consequently are among the most touristy and expensive. AEGINA is the closest to Athens. Look for bed and food around the port in Aegina town and admire the view from the TEMPLE OF ATHENA. The bay of Agia Marina has the best beaches but is packed out with Athenians at weekends.

POROS is packed out in summer, but for a reason. It has beautiful beaches and lush pinewoods. The tourist information in the town of Poros will help you find a bed – avoid hotels. See the MONASTERY OF KALAVRIA.

HYDRA, 3½ hours from Piraeus, is one of the beautiful people's islands, consequently the prices, especially along the harbour, are crippling. For a truly memorable view, climb up to the hilltop monastery of AGIA TRIADA. Hydra is all you expect a Greek island to be: narrow winding streets, donkeys (no cars allowed), beaches and blue sea and sky. The tourist police (Tel. 52205) will find you rooms, which are cheaper at the other side of the town.

SPETSES is a small wooded island of great charm with AGII ANAR- GIRI as its best beach. The harbour town of Spetses has the two cheap hotels (the Acropole and the Saronicos) and the tourist police on Botassi St.

The Cyclades

These are the most visited of the Aegean islands. There are 211 of them in all, but it's still possible to find a few of the inhabited ones that will offer you relative 'splendid isolation'. The 'dry islands' of SIFNOS, SIKINOS, SERIFOS and MILOS are relatively quiet, but their landscape is rather arid. ANDROS and TINOS are very attractive and large enough to allow the tourists to spread themselves out. MYKONOS is *the* Greek island. It's very beautiful, very very touristy, very expensive and very gay. There are nude beaches (the Paradise beach and Super Paradise – mostly gay) and countless discos, clubs and restaurants. There's also what was there before the thousands of tourists: whitewashed houses, windmills and 365 churches. There are a few reasonably priced hotels: the Phillippi (Tel. 22294), the Apollon (Tel. 23271) and the Karbonis (Tel. 22475).

There are boat trips from Mykonos to DELOS, ancient religious centre of the Greek world, where you can see the ruins of the Sanctuary of Apollo, the Terrace of Lions and the archaeological museum.

PAROS is is a beautiful and very clean island, but very touristy, and all that makes it worth the trip is its beautiful old church, Panagia Ekatontapiliani.

NAXOS is considered by many the most beautiful of the Cyclades islands, but the cheap rooms and tavernas in its capital, Naxos town, have disappeared as it has become more popular with the package tour operators. See the beautiful old Venetian quarter, the CASTRO. APOLLON and AGIA ANNA have the best beaches.

IOS used to be the place where students headed for – free and easy living with lots to do at night – but has now turned into a den of iniquity and is best avoided.

Santorini

4,000 years ago, a massive explosion left the outer rim of a volcano which became Santorini. From the harbour, get to the town of THIRA (ferries dock at Athinio now) where you can find rooms at reasonable prices. Alternatively, the youth hostel (Tel. 0286 22722) offers a very good deal. The best beaches are Kamari, Monolithos and Perissa with its black sand. There are ruins from the Minoans, Romans and Venetians. The boat trip out to the little island of Mikra Kameni, where the volcano started and smoulders still, is worth it.

The Sporades

Some of the quietest islands in Greece are the Sporades, as they're further off the beaten track than the others. You approach them by boat from Kymi, Agios Konstandinos or Volos which you reach by bus from Athens.

SKIATHOS is the most touristy, but that's because it's very beautiful. It's also lively, and one of the best Greek islands for nightlife. For a night's rest try one of the pensions on Evangelistras St in Skiathos town. KOUKOUNARIES is a superb beach surrounded by pine groves.

ALONISSOS is the smallest island. From the port of Patitiri, head for Marpounda or Kokinokastro where there's a good beach and some archaeological remains.

SKOPELOS has cheap rooms in its town and good beaches at STAFILOS and AGNONDAS. Inland lie the ruins of the medieval bishops' palace, and many churches and monasteries with icons. If you intend to stay in SKOPELOS try and get a room *up* the hill, even though it means further to walk, as the town sewage discharges into the harbour and can smell awful on a hot day.

SKYROS is the most beautiful and unspoilt island of the Sporades. Flat-topped white houses stand on the cliffs and folk crafts still flourish. The long dark sand beach is wonderful, and there are countless little coves for swimming and sub-aqua jaunts. Try one of the restaurants for a room, and change money at Stam Sarri on Agoras St.

North-east Aegean

If you don't mind going a bit further out of your way, the islands off the north-eastern Aegean have their rewards: Samos, Lesbos and Chios are the three most popular. SAMOS is heavily wooded with a rocky coastline and a good beach resort, Kokari. LESBOS is a mass of olive trees and has some incredible, traditionally designed buildings in its port of Mithymna. CHIOS has an interesting old monastery, the Nea Moni, plus all the usual Greek island charms.

The Dodecanese (South-east Aegean)

These are the most easterly islands of Greece, a few miles away from Turkey. The boat trip from Piraeus can take up to 20 hours, so unless you've a bit of time to spend – think again. You're rewarded for your efforts by superb beaches, mountains, medieval buildings and an air of historical importance which you don't find in any other group of islands.

The two main islands are RHODES and KOS, the latter of which is regarded as the birthplace of modern medicine as it was a healing centre of wide acclaim. The Knights of St John captured them in the fourteenth century, and they were occupied by the Italians during the Second World War. They were reunited with Greece in 1947.

RHODES: if you avoid the main town of Rhodes to escape from the package tourists, you're OK. In Rhodes town, see the old city, the Suleyman Mosque, and the Grand Masters' Palace. The tourist police and tourist information will help you out, and you shouldn't find accommodation too bad. The old town has the best cheap places to sleep, such as Steve Kefalas's pension on Omirou St. The ferries to Israel stop at Rhodes, but only for a couple of hours; you can wait for the next boat provided you say so when you book. The west coast of Rhodes is incredibly windy, especially in comparison with the east coast where the best beaches are. Of these, Faliraki Beach is undoubtedly the best, even though it's packed for most of the season.

LINDOS, along with Kameiros and Ialissos, has archaeological remains and is a particularly picturesque town, but the package-deal customers are here in swarms in summer.

KOS comes very high in the list of archaeological sites and is a fascinating island: great beaches, ancient Roman and Medieval monuments, mosques, a Crusader fortress, mansions and a wonderful atmosphere. In the town, try the tourist police for a room, but camping, though not legal, is idyllic. There is an official campsite, however; the tourist police will tell you how to get there. On the outskirts are the ruins of Hippocrates' medical school and sanctuary.

Crete

This is the most varied of all the islands, from the barren mountains to the beautiful old cities. Crete is divided into four regions with Agios Nikolaos, Rethymnon, Hania and Heraklion as their capitals. HERAKLION (Iraklion) is the main port of Crete with connecting ferries to Piraeus. Apart from the amazing ARCHAEOLOGICAL MUSEUM off Eleftherios Square, the city has little to recommend it. If staying, try the youth hostel (Tel. 081–222 947) or one of the places in Handakos St. From Heraklion you can visit the Minoan ruins at KNOSSOS or PHAESTOS, or the beach at PLAKIAS.

In western Crete look out for RETHYMNON with its Venetian and Turkish buildings. There is a youth hostel at 45, Topazi St (Tel. 0831–22848), and the tourist office is on E.L. Venizelou Avenue (Tel. 0831–29148). In HANIA (Chania), the elegant capital of Crete, the Venetian architecture makes you feel you're more in Italy than in Greece. Try the harbour area for rooms, or the youth hostel at 33 Drakonianou St (Tel. 0821–53565). For the high spot of your Cretan trip, walk along the 18 km SAMARIA GORGE, the largest one in Europe. Take the bus to OMALOS for this six-hour walk.

In eastern Crete AGIOS NIKOLAOS is the tourist trap. It's very picturesque but often short of rooms. Try the youth hostel (Tel. 0841–22823) or pester the tourist police till they come up with something. SITIA, east of the city, is near the fantastic palm beach of VAI, and the youth hostel (Tel. 0843–22693) can usually squeeze you in.

If you're camping, there are a number of good sites on the island. Camping Iraklion is only 6 km from Heraklion and has excellent facilities including supermarket and swimming pool. Camping Arkadia and Camping Elisabeth are beside excellent beaches and are just a few km from Rethymnon. Expect to pay about £3 per night.

The Ionian Islands

These are the islands off the north-west coast, lusher than most, with Corfu as its main tourist trap.

Corfu

If you're taking the ferry from or to Italy, chances are you'll stop off here. Take the opportunity if you've a day or two to spare, particularly if you can avoid the terrible crush months of July and August. Corfu doesn't look terribly Greek; in some ways it's more like the French Riviera. The Venetians, French and British have all occupied the island and left their colonial marks in the buildings, food and people. If you are travelling from Patras, possession of an Inter Rail + Boat does not make you second class (or even third class) but deck class, so the trick is to get on early and find a sheltered place to lay out your sleeping bag.

When you disembark, turn left to the Old Port; the road to the right of the Hotel Constantinopolis is where to start your search for a cheap bed. Try the Hotel Europa (Tel. 0661–39304), a short distance from the port. You are likely to be met at the port by a rep from this hotel – as well as reps from just about every other hotel with spare beds that day. The tourist police, 31 Arseniou St, will fix you up in a private home if they like the look of you. Tourist information is in the Governor's House (Tel. 0661 30298 or 30520) between Mantzaran and Dessila streets. The youth hostels are far out and invariably full. Camping Vatos, on the opposite side of the island to Corfu Town is cheap, friendly and has full facilities including bar, disco and a cheap restaurant. You can get free minibuses to and from the nearest beach as well as a free minibus service to the early-morning ferries. Pelekas Beach, on the west coast, is a favourite of Eurorailers. The bus costs 140 dr. We don't recommend you to hire a moped, but if you must, make sure you get a helmet and haggle for the petrol, which is always an add-on at rip-off prices. Moped hire usually costs around 1000–1500 dr. The lively Pink Palace Hotel (Tel. 53103/4) at Agios Gordios is right on the beach and can be reached by bus from the Old Port.

See Mon Repos where the Duke of Edinburgh was born. For your evening meal, the Old Port area is good and there's Greek folk dancing at the Fortress at 9 p.m.

Beware of some of the cheap food stalls as food poisoning seems to be a recurring hazard on the island.

PAXÍ and its little neighbour ANTIPAXÍ are becoming more touristy than is desirable due to their proximity to Corfu, but these small islands still have a lot of charm, and the sandy beaches of Antipaxí make ideal campsites although it is actually illegal to camp overnight on any Greek beach.

HUNGARY

Entry requirements	Passport and visa (UK citizens can buy one on the border now)
Population	10,713,000
Capital	Budapest (pop.: 2,200,000)
Currency	Forints
	£1 = approx. 116 ft.
Political system	Republic
Religions	Catholic and Protestant
Language	Hungarian (some German and English understood)
Public holidays	1 Jan.; 15 March; Easter Monday; 4 April; 1 May; 20 Aug.; 25, 26 Dec.
International dialling codes	From UK: 010 + 36 + number
	From USA: 011 + 36 + number
	To UK: 00 + 44 + number
	To USA: 00 + 1 + number
Eurotrain office	Szabadsagter 16, H–1395 Budapest 5 (Tel. 01–119 898)

During the ninth century, seven tribes of mounted Magyars began riding westwards, until they were stopped by the Holy Roman Empire in what is now Hungary. Gradually they began to settle down and became converted to Catholicism. Then during the fifteenth century, just when things were beginning to take off, the Turks turned up. A century and a half later, the Austrians took over and in 1867 after several uprisings they agreed to grant Hungary equal status under the joint monarchy of the Austro-Hungarian Empire. Things fell apart at the outbreak of the First World War, and Hungary went it alone until 1945. Two years later the Communist Party, aided by the Russians, took power. Hungary was then linked with the Soviet Union, despite the attempted counter-revolution of 1956. Travel within Hungary can be very slow, so think twice before heading off to explore every corner. Fortunately, the areas which have most to offer are the most accessible. If you only have time to visit one country in Eastern Europe, you can't go far wrong with Hungary. The people are friendly, but prices have increased dramatically since 1989–90. Tourism is the growth industry now. Hungary has been a pioneer regarding *Perestroika* and *Glasnost* and the number of western influences and the emerging capitalist economy are witness to this. Hungary has led the way in Eastern Europe these past two years, preferring to liberalize peacefully, with democratic elections ending the power of the Communist Party.

HUNGARIAN STATE RAILWAYS
(Magyar Államvasutak, MÁV)

Trains are considerably slower and dingier than they are in the West, as well as being crowded in the summer. There are often long gaps between services, too, but with patience it's possible to explore nearly all the larger towns and tourist centres on an Inter Rail or BIJ ticket. Trains marked 'Sebesvonat' make only a few stops at major centres; other fast trains are marked 'Gyorsvonat'. The ultra-slow local ones ('Személyvonat') are noisy and take an age to get anywhere. Bear in mind when making your plans that the railway network is very centralized and that it's always easier to enter or leave Hungary via Budapest. As in other countries, BIJ ticket holders can break their journeys at any point without having to get their ticket stamped. As with the rest of Eastern Europe, queueing is a way of life, and unavoidable during the summer. Whenever possible, make your seat reservations in advance, at the MÁV booking office at Népköztársaságútja 35, Budapest (Mon.–Wed., Fri.: 9 a.m.–6 p.m., Thurs.: 9 a.m.–7 p.m., Sat.: 9 a.m.–1 p.m.). It's worth keeping an eye out for any trains with new carriages, as they are a vast improvement on the old rolling stock.

• **Inter Rail bonuses:** Free entry to Metró Museum, Metró Station Deák Ferenc tér, Budapest V; Transport Museum, Városligeti-Körut 11, Budapest XIV; and Horse Carriage Museum, Parà-fürdo.

• **Rover tickets:** You can buy Rail Tourist Tickets before you go, from Danube Travel, 6 Conduit Street, London (Tel. 071–493 0263) but unless you intend to do a great deal of travelling they do not offer particularly good value. Available for 10, 20 or 30 days in first and second class they cost from around £35 in second class for 10 days to £107 in first class for 30 days. You can buy two types of rover tickets in Hungary from any MÁV office. One covers the whole country and costs 800 ft. for 7 days and 1,200 ft. for 10 days, second class only. The second ticket is for the Lake Balaton area only and costs 200 ft. 7 days and 300 ft. for 10 days. If you are buying tickets as you go along there is, in theory, a 50 per cent reduction if you pay in a convertible currency. In practice, you will find that you are allowed to buy your ticket to the border in forints, but have to pay for the rest of the journey in a convertible currency.

Eurotrain offer Explorer passes in Hungary in first and second class (see p.34 for details), and it is also covered by the East Rail Pass, available from Danish State Railways (see p.33).

TRAIN INFORMATION

Really, only German is understood. If you're getting nowhere, try and get your tongue round: 'Melyik vágányról indul a . . . vonat?' (From which platform does the train to . . . leave?)

• **Reservations:** (Helyjegy) To be sure of a seat, it's best to reserve at least two or three days in advance. This is obligatory on some international (Nemzetközi gyorsvonat) and other express trains.

• **Night travel:** Where necessary, Hungary borrows sleepers and couchettes from other East European countries. If you can't get a seat or lose yours to someone with a reservation (very common at Belgrade), try sleeping in the luggage car – this is more comfortable than being cramped in a single seat, but get there early. This appears to be tolerated by at least some guards in Turkey, Bulgaria, Yugoslavia and Hungary. It is, of course, against all regulations, and this is information, not a recommendation.

• **Eating on trains:** All long-distance trains have either a buffet car or mini-bar which can be unbelievably bureaucratic and grubby. Station buffets are particularly good value, however, and quieter.

TOURIST INFORMATION

All towns have their own local tourist information offices (Idegenforgalmi Hivatal) in addition to the newly privatized IBUSZ offices which deal with all aspects of travel and accommodation.

306   Europe by Train

• IUS/ISIC bonuses: 25–30 per cent off other East European train fares. For further information, contact Express, Semmelweiss 4, Budapest (Tel. 01 178600).

• **Money matters:** 1 forint (ft.) = 100 fillérs.
Banking hours are generally 9 a.m.–5 p.m. (2 p.m. on Fri.), though the Hungarian National Bank closes at lunchtime. There's no minimum daily exchange amount, so only change money as you need it. You can do this on the train at the border, if you are lucky, but don't count on it. You are not allowed to take Hungarian currency out of the country, but you can change back up to half the amount you brought in, although this is limited to £50 or US $100. You may be directed to the restaurant car instead to spend your excess forints. Not all currency exchanges will change money back into hard currency – you have to look around. You are allowed to take out 100 ft. (really just a souvenir for all its value) and while you will be asked on the train about this they are unlikely to check. You will also be hassled quite openly in the station foyer at Keleti about changing money. Commission charges are very low (usually 1 per cent) and it's definitely not worth the risk of exchanging on the black market.

• **Post offices:** Open Mon.–Fri.: 8 a.m.–6 p.m.; Sat.: 8 a.m.–12 p.m. Stamps can also be bought from tobacconists.

• **Shops:** Most shops are open 10 a.m.–6 p.m., with food shops opening at 7 a.m. Late-night opening on Thursdays is usually to 8 p.m. On Saturdays 9 a.m.–1 p.m. is the norm and many tobacconists and pastry shops also stay open on Sundays.

• **Museums:** Open 10 a.m. till 6 p.m. (Closed Mondays.) Admission is between 5 and 10 ft. (no fee on Saturdays).

SLEEPING

IBUSZ and the local tourist offices will fix you up in a private house for about 300 ft. per night (plus 30 per cent for the first night). These are your best bet, so ask for the IBUSZ leaflet on accommodation in private homes. They are graded into A, B and C, depending on the tourist potential of the area. In small towns, look for the sign Szoba Kiadó (or Zimmer Frei or Zimmer) and don't be afraid to accept offers of a room if you're approached on the street. If you're out of luck, the student travel service Express have several hostels and cheap student hotels. Beds in a hostel/student hotel start at about 250 ft. Doubles start from 500 ft. per room. Express also book rooms in private homes. There's no need to be a member of the IYHF, and it's possible for couples to get a room to themselves. Most hotels, especially the budget ones, are booked out months in advance and are expensive for what you get.

Camping is a realistic possibility; ask for a camping map from IBUSZ. There are over a hundred sites, graded from 1 to 3, depending on the facilities offered. For more detailed information contact the Hungarian Camping and Caravanning Club at Üllöi út 6, Budapest (Tel. 01 336536). During the summer, Hungary's population almost doubles and queues for accommodation can be frustrating. You can reserve hotel accommodation in Hungary through the IBUSZ office in Vienna, at Kärntnerstrasse 26, where it's possible to reserve accommodation ahead of time. They only deal with hotels, and will not help with other types of accommodation such as hostels or campsites. Also if you plan on staying at any of the Express hotels or hostels in Budapest and will be arriving before 6 p.m., you're given priority if you have an Express Student voucher, available from Ökista in Vienna but you have to do it at least 10 days in advance. Wherever you end up, don't forget that you must register with the police (KEOKH) within 48 hours of having your visa stamped, unless you're going through official booking services, where they do it for you. Don't be surprised if you are asked to pay for accommodation in hard currency – another reason for not changing too much.

EATING AND NIGHTLIFE

Hungarian food is excellent by any standards, and furthermore it's cheap. Try pörkölt (a pork stew with paprika), paprikás csirke galuskával (chicken with a sour cream paprika sauce) or goulash, and somlói galuska (sweet dumplings in rum and orange sauce) or rétes (strudel) to follow. The cheapest places are the self-service restaurants. Choose and collect your food, then pay the cashier. Look out for the tourist menus as they're normally exceptionally good value; if you're really broke and don't mind standing up, try any bisztró. Unlike the rest of Eastern Europe, Hungary has quite a bit of nightlife, particularly in Budapest. There are student discos and open-air concerts, as well as nightclubs.

If you're travelling on to Romania, Poland or Bulgaria, stock up on food in Hungary before you leave. All the Eastern European countries have menus which are heavily reliant on meat, which causes headaches for vegetarian visitors.

Budapest

The heart of the capital is the Danube, looking far more impressive than it does in Vienna, and spanned by a nice collection of bridges. Buda, west of the river and set among gentle hills, is a mixture of winding medieval streets, viewpoints over the city and neat suburbs; Pest is the centre of commerce and government. The two were united, along with Óbuda, in 1873, to become Budapest. There's plenty to see and do and because food and transport are still relatively cheap by Western standards it allows your lifestyle, for once, to rise above its usual humble level (though prices have increased sharply since 1990). All in all, Budapest is more lively, cosmopolitan and Westernized than any other East European city.

STATION FACILITIES

There are three main stations: Déli (south, Tel. 159096) which serves the south-west, Keleti (east, Tel. 136835) and Nyugati (west, Tel. 490115). For rail information within Hungary telephone MÁV Central Information (227860) and for abroad 224052. Operates between 6 a.m. and 8 p.m. Call the stations direct between 8 p.m. and 6 a.m. They are well equipped by Eastern European standards, and you shouldn't find anything too out of the ordinary here. If you are stuck, remember 'pályaudvar' means 'station'. Expect delays – especially left-luggage. Give yourself plenty of time, especially in the evenings.

TOURIST INFORMATION

There are IBUSZ offices in all the stations (daily 8 a.m.–1 p.m.; 2 p.m.–7 p.m. Weekends till 5 p.m.). In addition there are offices at

V, Felszabadulás tér 5 and Pétöfi tér 3. The latter is open 24 hours and also operates an accommodation service. If you are booking accommodation through this office, always do it before changing your money as they sometimes insist on payment in Western currencies, preferably West German DM or US $. Budapest Tourist, which arranges private accommodation, is at V, Roosevelt tér (open Mon.–Sat.: 8 a.m.–9 p.m., Sun.: 2 p.m.–8 p.m.). They also have offices near the two main stations: Baross tér near Keleti, and Bajcsy Zsilinszky u 55, near Nyugati. If you're sick of queues and know exactly what you want to ask, you can phone for foreign language tourist information (Tel. 172200). IBUSZ in Budapest are not all that helpful on general tourist information. You are often better off going to the Tourinform offices either at V., Süto ut. 2 (Tel. 179800) or Deak Ter, near the metro station or on the first floor of the Post Office (Tel. 179800).

● **Addresses:**
MAIN POST OFFICE and International Telephone Exchange is on the corner of Petöfi Sándor u and Martinelli tér (also poste restante), open Mon.–Fri.: 8 a.m.–6 p.m.; 8 a.m.–6 p.m. Saturday and in the morning only on Sundays and public holidays. Twenty-four-hour post offices are sited at Keleti and Nyugati stations.
UK EMBASSY: Harmincad u 6 (Tel. 182888).
US EMBASSY: Szabadság tér 12 (Tel. 126450).
CANADIAN EMBASSY: Budakeszi u, 32 (Tel. 387712).
EXPRESS: Student Travel Centre, Semmelweiss 4 (Tel. 176634 or 178600). They sell IUS/ISIC cards, book student hostels, tours etc.
EUROTRAIN: Szabadsagter 16 (Tel. 119898).
TELEPHONE CODE: 01.

● **Getting about:** Public transport is efficient but no longer cheap. Buy tickets in advance for buses (blue), metro and trams (yellow) from Trafik shops. Some tram services run all night. You'll pay 8 ft. for the metro and trams and 10 ft. for buses. Taxis are relatively cheap if there's a crowd of you – about 80 ft. per mile. There is also a one-day travel pass valid for the metro, yellow trams, trolley buses and suburban railways. It is also valid on blue buses, but the cheaper day pass does not cover blue buses, and neither is valid on the Pioneer railways. It's probably better to pay for individual journeys, given the cheapness of public transport.

SEEING

The old town of Buda has at its centre VÁRHEGY, Castle Hill, with its painted baroque houses and students' and artists' quarter. Crowning the hill is the thirteenth-century MATTHIAS CHURCH where the Hungarian kings were crowned. The ROYAL PALACE, virtually destroyed in 1944, is now rebuilt and houses two important museums: the HISTORICAL MUSEUM OF BUDAPEST and the NATIONAL GALLERY with its impressive collection of Hungarian art. The Margaret Bridge takes you to MARGARET ISLAND, lying in the middle of the Danube. The island is a recreation park and often has outdoor concerts and plays on summer evenings. For the best views over the city, cross the Elizabeth Bridge and climb Gellert Hill to the Liberation Monument. There is also a cable car (10 ft.) from the Chain Bridge at Clark Adam Ter. up the hill to the former Royal Palace. You can get a bus back if you're shattered. The floodlighting on summer evenings makes a walk by the riverside well worthwhile. You can also get excellent views by taking a trip on the cog railway which runs into the Buda hills. Take the Metro to Moszka Ter (opposite the Hotel Budapest) and then a short walk to the station. When you get off at the top, turn left and walk 150 yards to the start of the Pioneer railway, a narrow-gauge system operated almost entirely by children who do everything but drive the trains on the seven-mile route through the Buda Forest. When you come to the end of the line take tram 56 back to Moszkva Ter.

ST STEPHEN'S BASILICA is the impressive church on Pest beside the PARLIAMENT. A walk through the twenty-seven courtyards of this complex when the sun is setting over the Buda hills can be truly memorable. Two other museums of exceptional quality are the FINE ARTS and the HUNGARIAN NATIONAL. The Fine Arts is in Városliget (the City Park) which has rowing boats for hire on the lake, and amusement parks. If you want to cleanse the pores of the grime of train travel, try an authentic Turkish bath. It's only around 80 ft. and includes a massage. Try the old Ottoman baths of Király Fürdö on Föutca 84. Avoid the ISBUSZ organized excursions as they are very expensive. A coach tour around Budapest costs around £25 and is not worth the money.

SLEEPING

Budapest gets busy in summer, so don't hang about getting

organized on the bed front. Head for either the student accommodation office at Hotel Universitas (open only during June, July and August), Irinyi József u. 9, or the IBUSZ or Budapest Tourist Offices mentioned under tourist information, above. You can avoid long queues at the agency desks at the stations by heading straight into the city centre, depending on your arrival time, to a tourist agency who will also make bookings. Private accommodation is your best bet, although you can't get in until after 5 p.m. Expect to pay anything up to 400 ft. each. Head straight for the IBUSZ office at the station to fix up your accommodation, or try the Express Desk or any tourist agency as there's little to choose between them. You pay them in full when you make the booking. They will accept traveller's cheques and give you change in forints. If Hotel Universitas is full they'll give you alternatives in the same area. You can also try the Econotour Hostel at Kinizsi u. 2–6, which is the student quarter near the university, Hotel Lidó, Nánási ut 67 (Tel. 1886865) or Hotel Express, Beethoven u. 7–9 (Tel. 753082).

Camping out is illegal but easy to get away with (and even if you are caught you won't be sent off to Siberia, so don't worry). Try Camping Niche, 285 ft. a night with free showers. Take a bus or tram to Moszkva Ter then bus 158 to the campsite. (Chairlift out here affords wonderful views over Budapest and Brna forest.)

If you are stuck for accommodation you should get into the student hostel at Krusper utca 2. Although it is rather tatty, you may find it preferable to sleeping rough (if you don't get an offer at the station that's tempting). From Keleti take the Metro to Blaha Ter then tram 4 or 6 to the first stop after Peofi Bridge and it is on your right.

The two official campsites are a good last resort as they're rarely full to capacity. Hárshegy is at Hárshegyi u. 5 (Tel. 151482) and Római camping, Szentendrei u. 189 (Tel. 887167). Both cost around 100 ft. per person if you've a tent. Hárshegy also have four-bed bungalows around 500 ft. Bus 22 from Moszkva terminal (metro line 2). Check their availability through Budapest Tourist Office. To get to Római take the metro to Battyany Ter, where you change to the suburban railway, HEV. Get off at Romaifured, where it is within sight of the station. If you pay in a convertible currency there is a 10 per cent reduction. If you stay here you can also get free access to the outdoor pool next door.

EATING AND NIGHTLIFE

Hungarian cuisine is one of the best in Europe and in Budapest you can eat well in any price range. Fixed menus for lunch are common and rarely cost more than 100 ft. but you have to ask for them as they are not always displayed. Look out for places called bisztrós, büfés, self-services and grills for even lower prices. One night at least, though, have a real blow-out. Even in a tourist trap, with gypsy music, wine and all the trimmings, there should be change from 450 ft. per person.

Try: Hungária Restaurant, Lenin Krt. 9–11 Amazing fin-de-siècle decor, gypsy music and dancing. The carp from Lake Balaton are a speciality here.

Further along at Lenin Krt. 47 is the Royal Hotel, where you can enjoy classical music from a five-piece band along with an excellent meal with wine for less than 500 ft. (closes 9.30 p.m.). Another place worth trying is the Apostolok Restaurant, Uiggo u. 4–6 (Tel. 183704) which should provide you with a good four-course meal for around 200 ft. or Kis Kakukk, Pozsonyi út 12, which is also very reasonable.

The meals on the Danube are good, too. Boats leave from below the Duna Hotel at 5.30 p.m. and 8 p.m. and the cruise lasts two or three hours – plenty of time to enjoy the meal knowing it won't break the bank. Wine cellars (borok) often serve good meals and the Hungarian wines, particularly Tokaji and Egri Bikavér (Bull's Blood), are quite something. With food being so cheap you can also consider coffee and cakes or ice-cream on the terrace by the river at the Atrium or Forum Hotels for around 100 ft, although these luxury Western hotels, such as the Duna and Hyatt, impose fairly rigid dress standards and may refuse to serve you if you are casually dressed.

The other 'must' is a visit to a sixteenth-century pastry shop, known worldwide. Ruszwurm (Szentháromság 7, opposite the Matthias Church, closed Wednesdays) has its own varieties of cakes and strudels plus original furnishings and bread sculptures.

If you are really broke, you can lunch at the Fortuna Café for only 50 ft. Although this place is really a workers' canteen (which converts to a disco at night) you can fill up for next to nothing. It is in Old Buda near the Matthias Church. Walk past the Hilton and it is on the left up a small alley.

The Planetarium (near Nepliget Station on Metro line 3) puts on a different show each night of the week with lasers and special lighting effects set to Western music by performers like Deep Purple, The Who and Mike Oldfield. Admission is around 100 ft.

Check out the *Express Cocktail Ship*, one of the Danube cruisers which take you round Margaret Island. There's rock, dancing and boozing, all for around 150 ft., but times vary depending on the time of year, so make sure you get on the right boat, in front of the Duna Hotel. For student discos, try the Vár Klub, next to the Matthias Church. There's traditional folk dancing in Buda Park, and a list of events is published in 'Coming Events in Budapest'. There are also open-air concerts (rock and classical) on Margaret Island.

The Danube Bend

This has Hungary's most spectacular scenery and it's possible to see some of it on a day trip from Budapest. The Danube makes a dramatic sweep south, about fifteen miles from Budapest, and the mountain scenery and villages up here are the best you'll find in the country. Boats leave the capital from Vigadó tér dock at 7 a.m. and 7.30 a.m., 10 a.m. and 2 p.m. every day – later boats make it possible for you to stop off and sightsee before continuing your journey. (Further information on boats is available from Dunatours (Tel. 01–314533), Bajcsy Zs. u. 17, and also from Mahart, Belgrád RKP [Tel. 181704].) The journey to Esztergom, the heart of medieval Hungary, takes 5 hours so it's best to take a single and return to Budapest by bus (to Szentendre) and then suburban train.

SZENTENDRE is an old Serbian market town and artists' hangout. Lots of small museums (Margit Kovács ceramics collection is superb), churches and baroque houses. The main square (Karl Marx tér) is the venue for a summer festival, and the OPEN-AIR MUSEUM called SKANZEN locally (near Angyal St, about three miles' walk from the station) has examples of traditional buildings from all over the country. There is an infrequent bus service. The tourist office is by the Danube at Somogyi Bacsó part. 6. The campsite is on Pap Island (Tel. 26–10697).

A few miles up river, VISEGRÁD is right on a bend among the

mountains. This was a Middle Ages stronghold and has a FORTRESS and ROYAL PALACE. Its rich past makes it popular with tourists but you won't find any cheap commercialism, so eat in the restaurants without any fear of being ripped off. Tourist information is at Föutca 3/a (Tel. 26 28330).

ESZTERGOM has some of the oldest and best-preserved remains in Hungary. This was the residence of the Magyar kings from the tenth to the thirteenth centuries. Take in the CHRISTIAN MUSEUM and ROYAL PALACE remains, but most of all visit the BASILICA, the largest cathedral in the country. For around 10 ft. you can climb to the dome and walk around outside it to enjoy superb views over the surrounding country and into Czechoslovakia. Tourist information (Komturist) and Express is at Széchenyi tér (Tel. 484).

The Hungarian Plain

East of the Danube lies the dusty central plain which is real Hungarian peasant land. An in-depth exploration of this region will still produce pockets of rural life virtually unchanged for generations. Trains run through the Plain and the Budapest–Kelebia line stops off at the main settlements like Kecskemét and Szeged.

KECSKEMÉT, home town of Kodály, has only a small area of old town left, but what there is is good. Walk along BÁNK BÁN and János Hoffman streets. The TOWN HALL on Kossuth tér is another typical building. Express is at Rákóczi út 32.

SZEGED, near the Yugoslav frontier, was completely destroyed by flood in 1879, but the town today still has something to say of its rich past when it was under Turkish and, later, Austrian rule. See the DÓM TÉR where the VOTIVE CHURCH is, and Hungary's best Greek Orthodox Serbian church on the north side of the square. The local tourist information office is at Victor Hugo u. 1, but you're best to try Express at Kigyo 3.

EGER, in the north-east, is Hungary's Bordeaux. This is where the good red wine (Bull's Blood) you've been knocking back in Budapest originates. Tourist information at Bajcsy Zsilinszky u. 9 (Tel. 36 11724) will give you a map and information, and should you decide to stay they'll help out on accommodation, and Express at

Leányka u. 2 (Tel. 12–066) will arrange a place in the Student Hostel. DOBÓ ISTVÁN SQUARE is the town centre; just north of this is the CASTLE. The Kazamata Restaurant in the centre, by the neo-classical CATHEDRAL, is exceptionally good value and the wine is a knock-out. Eger is a good place to base yourself if you fancy delving into the forests and villages of inner Hungary for a while, and there are various cheap hotels and campsites.

Lake Balaton

Lake Balaton is Central Europe's largest lake, with rolling hills and vineyards interspersed with picturesque old towns. This is the region you'll pass through if you're coming in from Austria, and if you've hit a good spell of weather this is where to break your journey, as there are good beaches and everything you need for a few days' beach-bumming, Hungarian-style.

SIÓFOK, on the southern shores of the lake, with warm shallow waters and an abundance of Hungarian beach bums in the summer, is a bit like Torremolinos for us; but if it's company you're after, head there. KESZTHELY has more to offer. Apart from its beaches, there are various things to see: the first European agricultural college, GEORGICON; the HELICON LIBRARY, with many rare books and antiquities; and the BALATON MUSEUM. BALATONFÖLDVÁR is probably the most scenic of the Balaton resorts, with trees coming down close to the lakeside. It's a good centre for watersports and has quite a bit of nightlife. Express office at Jozsef A. u. 9 will fix you up with a room at the Express International Youth Centre or Hotel Juventus for $3–$6 a night, as will a number of other tourist agencies in town.

TIHANY and BALATONFÜRED are on the northern shore and are quieter and prettier. Tihany has Celtic and Roman ruins and a beautiful yellow ABBEY looking down on the peninsula. The OPEN-AIR MUSEUM gives a good idea of the Balaton folk traditions, and the thatched-roof houses set among the hills add to the charm.

Balatonfüred is a health spa which tends to attract wealthy Hungarians and Germans. See the MEDICINAL SPRINGS, busy HARBOUR and ROUND CHURCH.

Western Hungary

Between Budapest and Austria lies TRANSDANUBIA, which now can
be overflowing with bargain hunting Austrians over for the day.
GYÖR is a large industrial city two hours from Budapest by train.
The OLD TOWN has been lovingly preserved. See the CARMELITE
CHURCH and Baroque CATHEDRAL. For entertainment sample the
gypsy atmosphere of Vaskakas Tavern beneath the Castle or the
magnificent Kisfaludy Theatre at Czuczor Gergely utca. Tourist
Information is at Aradi Vertanuk u. 22 (Tel. 961–1557) across from
the Town Hall. Express at Bajcsy-Zsilinsky ut 41 (Tel. 28–833) can
arrange accommodation during the summer in the KTMF Student
Hotel. There is a camping ground at Kiskut-liget (open mid-April to
mid-October), take bus 8 from the station.

KOSZEG is a quiet town on the Austrian frontier (except when
the shoppers hit town!). It is famous for holding off the huge
Turkish siege of 1532. On JURISICH TER, the cobbled main square,
is the Gothic ST JAMES CHURCH with its wonderful frescoes.
JURISICH CASTLE, where the Turks were beaten back, is now a
historical museum (closed Mondays) and also has cheap accommodation from April to mid-October. The tourist bureau at Varkor
Square and Express next door will help you out with a place to
stay.

South West

Southern Transdanubia has a pleasant mild climate and has lovely
green hills. PÉCS is home to many fantastic churches, such as the
Romanesque CATHEDRAL, the former Turkish MOSQUE OF PASHA
GHAZI KASIM, and the enormous SYNAGOGUE. Walk down Kaptalan
u. to visit Péc's famous museums, including the Vasarely Museum
and Zsolnay Porcelain Museum. For a nice day out take bus 35
into the scenic MECSEK HILLS and climb the 194 m TV TOWER for a
stunning view. The tourist office at Széchenyi tér 9 (Tel. 13300)
will arrange accommodation for you. You can also try the inexpensive Minaret Hotel at Sallai utca 35 which is in an old monastery.

Twenty miles to the west is SZIGETVAR, yet another place famous for being besieged by the Turks in the sixteenth century. This story is told in the museum (open 10 a.m.–3 p.m., closed Mondays), in the fifteenth century FORTRESS. Also visit the ALI PASA MOSQUE which is now a church. The tourist bureau is located inside the Oroszlan Hotel on Zrinyi tér and will set up accommodation. From April to mid-November you can stay in dormitories in the Fortress itself.

IRELAND

Entry requirements	Passport (not necessary for UK nationals)
Population	3,550,000
Capital	Dublin (pop.: 1,100,000)
Currency	£1 = approx. 1.05 punt (IR£)
Political system	Parliamentary Democracy
Religion	Roman Catholic
Languages	English and Irish (Gaelic)
Public holidays	1 Jan.; 17 March; Good Friday; Easter Monday; first Monday in June; first Monday in August; last Monday in October; 25, 26 Dec.
International dialling codes	From UK: 010 + 353 + number
	From USA: 011 + 353 + number
	To UK: 00 + 44 + number
	To USA: 00 + 1 + number
Eurotrain office	34 Lower Abbey Street, Dublin 1 (Tel. 01–787 028)

Irrespective of when you plan to visit Ireland, prepare for the worst weather: the chances are you'll soak up more than its history and folklore. The Romans never conquered Ireland and as a result the Celts, themselves immigrants, were able to develop a native culture free from outside interference until the arrival of St Patrick in the fifth century. Ireland then became a centre of culture and learning at a period when the rest of Europe was suffering under the barbarian invasion following the collapse of the Roman Empire. This period of peaceful progress was interrupted by the Vikings who repeatedly raided the coast throughout the ninth and tenth centuries. After finally defeating the Norsemen, the Irish began fighting it out among themselves and thereby gave the Normans an opportunity to extend their influence beyond England. By the Tudor period, parliament was in the control of a British minority who gradually replaced the Irish Catholic landlords with Protestants from Scotland and England. The nineteenth century began with Ireland as part of the United Kingdom, but the subsequent failure of the potato harvests (1845–8) helped forward the cause of Irish nationalism, as well as leading to mass emigration. By 1914, home rule was passed and, seven years later, the Irish Free State was born, with the exception of the six counties of Northern

Ireland. Finally, in 1937, Ireland (Eire) became a fully independent country. Trains will get you to all the main centres, but the best way to get to grips with her past is to hire a bike and explore the glut of prehistoric and medieval monuments. The Irish are justifiably proud of their hospitality, and although not every Irishman is another W. B. Yeats, most have the 'gift of the gab' and are only too happy to pass the time of day with you. Ireland is one of the most expensive countries in Europe, and you will particularly notice the cost of eating and sleeping, apart from everything else.

• **Getting there:** The shipping lines which operate regular sailings from Britain to Ireland are Sealink and B & I. If you're a student, B & I offer the best deal on their daily service from Liverpool to Dublin with 25 per cent discount if you buy your ticket at USIT, 52 Grosvenor Gardens, London SW1 (Tel. 071–730 8111) just beside Victoria Station, or if you are an IYHF card holder, and 50 per cent if you buy a Travel-Save Stamp with your ISIC. If you're not a student, check all the other prices. Eurotrain offer a train/ferry ticket from London to Dublin for about £38 return on an ISIC which is the best value of all. Irish Continental Line operates Le Havre–Rosslare and Cherbourg–Rosslare, while Brittany Ferries operate Roscoff–Cork. Eurail Pass holders get to travel free on both services to Rosslare which is a considerable saving as the normal fare is around $90.

IRISH RAILWAYS
(Iarnrod Eireann, IE)

Eurail Passes are valid in the Republic, as is Inter Rail. The Irish Railways' Rambler tickets are an alternative, but they're quite pricey. The ticket is available for either 8 of 15 days or 15 of 30 days and you can get them for rail or buses only, or both. The cost is IR£55 for an 8-day bus or rail only, IR£75 for a combined 8-day ticket or IR£80 and IR£110 for the respective 15-day passes. An Irish Emerald Card allows 8 of 15 days or 15 of 30 days travel in Northern Ireland and the Republic on trains and major bus routes for IR£100 or IR£170 respectively, 2nd class. You are probably better off getting the Travel-Save Stamp at IR£6 which entitles you to half price on all IE train and BE bus single adult fares over IR£2 on trains and provincial buses, half price on all single or return fares on Northern Ireland Railways and similar discounts on B&I car ferries and ships to the Aran Islands. You can get these stamps from USIT in either London or Dublin. Trains are reasonably fast around the Dublin area and to major towns, but don't expect speeds similar to those on the continent. In many areas (especially in the west) buses are the main form of transport.

• **Inter Rail bonuses:**

Irish Continental Line		Reduction %
Rosslare/Cork	Le Havre	50
Sealink UK Ltd.		
Rosslare	Fishguard	30
Dun Laoghaire	Holyhead	50
B&I Line		
Dublin	Holyhead	50

• **Eurail bonuses:** Free:

—Ferry crossings on the Irish Continental Line between Rosslare (Ireland) and Le Havre (France) 21 hours or Cherbourg (France) 17 hours, and between Cork (Ireland) and Le Havre (France) 21½ hours. If cabin accommodation is requested an extra charge will be made. Port taxes are extra and payable in Irish pounds. During July and August advance reservation is recommended. It is compulsory if cabin accommodation is requested. Check the sailing schedule always.

—Free service on Expressway buses of Bus Eireann.

TRAIN INFORMATION

• **Reservations:** Are not necessary. If you want to make one, you must do so by 5 p.m. on the preceding day.

• **Night travel and eating on trains:** There are no night services in Ireland. Most long-distance trains have catering facilities ranging from bar service to set meals.

• **Bikes:** Are often the only way to get to the local hostel and see the neighbourhood. They cost about IR£4.50 a day from most towns.

TOURIST INFORMATION

There are seventy-six offices scattered throughout Ireland which are open Mon.–Fri.: 9 a.m.–5 p.m., Sat.: 9 a.m.–1 p.m. Each office gives information on its own region as well as for all of Ireland. They have a good selection of maps and literature.

Not all of Ireland is run as efficiently as the tourist board, so use their offices fully while you have the chance.

• **ISIC bonuses:** With the ISIC you can get a Travel-Save Stamp ticket. This entitles you to 50 per cent off all one-way journeys, also reductions to some cinemas and theatres.

• **Money matters:** 1 Irish pound (£1) = 100 pence (p.).
Banking hours are Mon.–Fri.: 10 a.m.–12.30 p.m., 1.30 p.m.–3 p.m. with an extension to 5 p.m. on Thurs. in Dublin. For the rest of the country late-opening days vary. The British pound is now nearly equal to the Irish pound and is often used interchangeably.

• **Post offices, shops and museums:** Tend to work around a 9 a.m.–5.30 p.m. routine. Museums vary the most, so always check with the nearest tourist information office.

SLEEPING

Hotels are very expensive so your best plan is to stick to bed and breakfast (B&B) and hostels. For advance information on youth hostels contact An Óige, 39 Mountjoy Square, Dublin (Tel. 01–363111). There are also around 50 independent hostels of all sizes and range of activities, who market themselves under the co-operative Independent Owners Association. Their information office is at Dooey Hostel, Glencolumcille, Co. Donegal (Tel. 073 30130). Get a copy of their directory, cost IR£1, from this address.

Ask at tourist information for their guide on Irish Homes (£2). This lists all the approved B&Bs. If you require it, they'll book you a bed by phone for a small charge. Youth hostels tend to be situated in the most scenic parts of the country but are not always near a station. Beds cost between IR£4 and IR£8, depending on the hostel. Camping costs IR£3.50–IR£4.50 a tent on official sites, and is only for those who don't mind getting wet. (Tourist information provide a booklet priced around IR£1.)

EATING AND NIGHTLIFE

Food is also quite expensive in Ireland and the only way to survive on a tight budget is to rely on the very good bakeries. Some restaurants outside Dublin shut by about 9 p.m., so eat early. For bargains you'll have to turn to Chinese and Indian food, or live off fish'n'chips. Ask at tourist information for their useful booklet 'Special Value Tourist Menu', which lists many restaurants throughout Ireland, that provide enjoyable three-course meals at fixed prices. The only time you're likely to get the chance of traditional Irish cooking is in a guesthouse or B&B where, if you're lucky, Irish stew or boiled bacon and cabbage may appear on the menu (if you consider this luck!). Some guidebooks politely call Irish food wholesome, rather than basic which is perhaps a more apt description. As eating out is so incredibly expensive, the pub will have to be the mainstay of the budget traveller. Here you will find great foods, good beer and a real chance to meet the Irish who are a lovely, warm lot. Ask about to discover which pubs have folk music and dancing, and where the best draught Guinness is.

Dublin

There's no denying Dublin has character. The contrast of the elegant eighteenth-century quarter with the damp dingy slums only a mile or two away is as much a comment on the Irish mentality as anything. This is the setting James Joyce used for *Ulysses* – his own home town. It's a rich experience, so don't try and hurry it.

STATION FACILITIES
Dublin has two main stations: Connolly, with northbound trains, and Heuston Station for trains to the south and west.

	CONNOLLY STATION
Train information	Mon.–Sat.: 7.30 a.m.–8.30 p.m.
	Use Booking Office on Sundays
	(Tel. 787777)
Reservations	Mon.–Sat.: 7.30 a.m.–8.30 p.m.
	Sun.: 7.30 a.m.–10.30 a.m., 4.30 p.m.–8.30 p.m.
Left-luggage store	Mon.–Sat.: 7.30 a.m.–9 p.m.
	Sun.: 8 a.m.–9 p.m.
Restaurant, Buffet	Mon.–Sat.: 7.30 a.m.–7.30 p.m.
Shops	Mon.–Sat.: 7.30 a.m.–7.30 p.m.

	HEUSTON
Train information	Mon.–Sat.: 7 a.m.–9 p.m.
	Sun.: 8 a.m.–9/10 p.m.
	(Tel. 771871)
Reservations	Mon.–Sat.: 7 a.m.–9 p.m.
	Sun.: 8 a.m.–9/10 p.m.
	(Tel. 771871)
Left-luggage store	Mon.–Sat.: 7.30 a.m.–9 p.m.
	Sun.: 8 a.m.–9 p.m.
Restaurant	Mon.–Sat.: 7.30 a.m.–7.30 p.m.
	Sun.: 8.30 a.m.–10.30 a.m., 5 p.m.–8 p.m.
Shops	7.30 a.m.–7 p.m.

Daily trains to: Belfast, Sligo, Rosslare (Connolly); Cork, Galway, Limerick (Heuston).

TOURIST INFORMATION

Main office: 14 Upper O'Connell St (Tel. 747733), open Mon.–Sat.: 8.30 a.m.–6 p.m. Money exchange facilities provided Mon.–Sat.: 9 a.m.–5 p.m.; there is also a branch at the ferry pier at Dun Laoghaire, and at Dublin Airport.

● **Addresses:**
GENERAL POST OFFICE: O'Connell St, open daily till 8 p.m., Sundays 10.30 a.m.–6.30 p.m.
AMEX: 116 Grafton St (Tel. 772874), open Mon.–Fri.: 9 a.m.–5 p.m., Sat.: 9 a.m.–12 noon.
ISIC–USIT (IRISH STUDENT TRAVEL AGENCY): Aston Quay, O'Connell Bridge, open Mon.–Fri.: 9 a.m.–6 p.m., Sat.: 11 a.m.–4 p.m. (Tel. 778117). Also a Eurotrain office.
UK EMBASSY: 33 Merrion Rd (Tel. 695211).
US EMBASSY: 42 Elgin Rd, Ballsbridge (Tel. 688777).

CANADIAN EMBASSY: 65–68 St Stephen's Green (Tel. 781988).
YOUTH INFORMATION CENTRE: Sackville Place (off O'Connell St) (Tel. 786844), open Mon.–Wed.: 9.30 a.m.–6 p.m., Thurs.–Sat.: 9.30 a.m.–5 p.m. Information on organizations, travel and accommodation.
EUROTRAIN: 34 Lower Abbey St (Tel. 787028).
PHONE CODE: 01.

● **Getting about:**
City buses operate from 6 a.m. to 11.30 p.m. Many of them start from O'Connell Street in the centre. You won't need them for sightseeing as it's all easily negotiated by foot ('shanks's pony' as they call it). If you're there for a while and can claim to be pursuing an educational or cultural project, make inquiries at tourist information for the 'Youth and Educational Travel Concession Ticket', looking earnest and intellectual. Tel. 787777 for information on all public transport. Buy a weekly bus pass (IR£9) or bus and train pass (IR£12) from Dublin Bus in Upper O'Connell Street.

SEEING

Start with O'Connell Street and your visit to the tourist office, then via the GENERAL POST OFFICE, where the Easter uprising of 1916 started, head for TRINITY COLLEGE, the university which has produced such men as Thomas Moore and Oscar Wilde, and see the beautiful LIBRARY which is the home of some of the world's most outstanding illuminated manuscripts. Pride of place is reserved for two volumes of the eighth-century 'Book of Kells' which you can look at free of charge between November and March or pay £1.75 on ISIC if you are visiting between April and October. At the back of the university, through the grounds, sit the Dail and Seanad, the seats of the Irish Parliament, at Leinster House on Kildare Street. You can visit only when Parliament is not in session. In the same street is the NATIONAL MUSEUM (closed Mondays), which is good for early historians and has a comprehensive exhibition on the 1916 uprising. Around the corner, on Merrion Street, is the NATIONAL GALLERY which has an excellent collection of Rembrandts along with a good modern section and several rooms devoted to portraits of modern Irish literary men such as George Bernard Shaw and Brendan Behan.

At Castle Street is, predictably, DUBLIN CASTLE, which has seen a lot of impressive history since it was built in the thirteenth century. Equally impressive is the plasterwork in the rooms of the State Apartments, which are open to the public during the week from 10 a.m.–12.15 p.m. and 2 p.m.–5 p.m. and at weekends from 2 p.m.–5 p.m. You can also, for a small fee, have your family tree traced by the staff in the heraldic museum situated within the grounds. As far as churches go, CHRIST CHURCH (started in 1038), and the twelfth-century ST PATRICK'S CATHEDRAL are the names to look for. Just up from Christ Church, on the way to the Guinness Hop Store is St Audoen's Church, High St. It's the location of the VIKING VILLAGE, a reconstruction of Dublin 1000 years ago. Entrance IR£2.20; IR£1.25 for students.

The most elegant buildings of Dublin are said to be the CUSTOM HOUSE, on the north bank of the River Liffey, and the Bank of Ireland in College Green (formerly Parliament House).

The JOYCE MUSEUM at Martello Tower (a little way out at Sandycove) looks at the life and works of the Irish author, James Joyce. Pick up the 'Ulysses' map from tourist information. For a breath of fresh air, head for ST STEPHEN'S GREEN, an oasis in the middle of the city and a popular place for office workers to enjoy packed lunches if the weather is fine. Just off the park, at Earsfort Street, is the new National Concert Hall, which features music to suit all tastes. Alternatively, you might like to visit the famous PHOENIX PARK, the largest enclosed park in Europe, which has featured everything from horse racing through rock concerts to a huge papal mass. Phoenix Park has the second highest obelisk in the world and one of the world's oldest zoos, famous for breeding lions. Don't be tempted to pitch your tent here, as the official residence of the President of Ireland is in the park and the police take a dim view of campers in the vicinity. Across the river from Phoenix Park is KILMAINHAM JAIL. The jail is restored and is now a historical museum, with conducted tours on Sundays from 3 p.m. to 5 p.m. and on Wednesdays from 10 a.m. to 12 noon and 2.30 p.m. to 4 p.m. For a few free pints of Guinness, go to their brewery at JAMES' GATE, watch the film about its production, then sup up.

SLEEPING

You can expect to pay between IR£12 and IR£18 in a hotel, so head

for the student and youth hostels. Go round to the Irish Student
Travel Service, 7 Anglesea St (Tel. 778117) if you're out of luck,
and a word of warning: if you were thinking of a free night in
Phoenix Park, bear in mind that the President of Ireland stays there,
so there are pockets of police to contend with.

International Student Accommodation and Activity Centre
(ISAAC), also known as the Dublin Tourist Hostel, 2–5 French-
man's Lane (Tel. 749321/363877), is a very central old warehouse
and the best deal in Dublin at around IR£5 a night. Also try The
Young Traveller at St Mary's Place (Tel. 305000). It's a lot cleaner,
but expect to pay IR£8 for B&B.

• **Youth hostels:** 39 Mountjoy Sq South (Tel. 363111/364749) and
Mountjoy St (Tel. 301766), are both very good and cost between
IR£6.50–IR£7.50. The YWCA at Radcliffe Hall, St John's Rd (Tel.
694521) and Lower Baggot St are also worth checking out.

• **Bed and breakfasts:** Try any along the Clontarf road, with views
out to Dublin Bay. Particularly good is Mrs McKenna at 110
Sandford Rd, Ranelagh (Tel. 971375), as she always makes you feel
very welcome. Or the Drumcondra area: Mrs Mooney, 20 St
Lawrence Road, Clontarf (Tel. 339097) gives you a warm welcome,
pleasant rooms and a wonderful full Irish breakfast to start off your
day. Also check out Mrs O'Neill, 6 Whitworth Parade, Drumcondra (Tel. 304733) and Mrs Ryan, 10 Distillery Road (Tel. 374147).
Expect to pay around IR£10–11. As these places are all in the
suburbs, it's a good idea to make a reservation through the Tourist
Office, approximate cost 75p + deposit, before heading out of the
city.

EATING AND NIGHTLIFE

There are the usual fast-food chains in the centre, and also quite a
few pubs now offering excellent-value lunches. If you're in town for
a while, it's worth buying the tourist board's booklet 'Special Value
Tourist Menu' which has a good choice of eating places in Dublin,
offering three-course meals at fixed prices.

Anywhere around the university is your best bet, with restaurants
catering for the student market. Try Newman House, 86 St
Stephen's Green; it's good, cheap and filled with students who can
act as a mine of information. Closed in August. Bewleys have cafés

in Grafton St, South George St, and Westmoreland St, all doing good meals at reasonable prices. Cheaper places to eat include Flanagans in O'Connell St (across from the Tourist Information Centre), and Pat Grace's Fried Chicken Store in Merrion Row – good value fish and chicken dishes. Shop for food in Moore Street.

This is the home of the pub. It's at the centre of Ireland's social life, and the atmosphere in a good Dublin pub takes some beating. The following pubs all have something unique, whether it be folk music, good beer or a great atmosphere. Most have all three, and are the sort of places you'll be looking for to eat, drink and make merry: O'Donoghue's, Merrion Row, is always lively as is the Baggot Inn, Baggot Street. Mulligan's Pub, Poolbeg Street; Scruffy Murphy's, off Mount Street; An Beal Boacht, Ranelagh Bridge and The Four Seasons, Capel Street. 'In Dublin' lists all current events.

The South-east

Counties Wexford, Wicklow, Kilkenny and Tipperary.

The WICKLOW MOUNTAINS lie only ten miles from Dublin, and a day or two exploring this mountainous area from the base towns of Glendalough (with its eighth-century monastery) or Wicklow can be rewarding. ENNISCORTHY is a small town in the Slaney valley and on the main line south from Dublin. It was a storm centre during the 1798 rebellion against the British. The sixteenth-century castle is now a folk museum, and if you hit it in the first week of July, expect an even-better-than-usual atmosphere, as the Strawberry festival livens things up considerably. In WEXFORD see the BULL RING and ruins of the twelfth-century SELSKAR ABBEY, and ask for information on the free guided walking tours at tourist information on Crescent Quay. WATERFORD, about an hour from Rosslare where the Fishguard ferry deposits you, is famous for its crystal, but apart from this and its impressive eighteenth-century CHRIST CHURCH CATHEDRAL there's not a lot doing, so head for KILKENNY and see the thirteenth-century cathedral of ST CANICE with its adjacent Round Tower, and the dominating, beautiful CASTLE. The tourist office at Shee Alms House, Rose Inn St (Tel. 21755), will fix you up with a bed. CASHEL, in County Tipperary, was a medieval ecclesiastical centre and CORMAC'S CHAPEL is the finest remaining example from this period of architecture. Rising majestically over the town, the famous ROCK OF CASHEL crowned with a magnificent group of ruins is one of Ireland's great historic sites.

Cork

3½ hours on the main line from Dublin, Cork is a convenient stopover for exploring the south-west. See the Gothic cathedral of ST FINNBARR and, as a contrast, the modern CHRIST THE KING CHURCH. If you're musically inclined, ST ANNE'S CHURCH offers you the opportunity to play its bells. The tourist office (Tel. 273251) on ·Grand Parade St (open 9 a.m.–7 p.m. in summer, Sundays 11 a.m.–1 p.m.) have guided walking tours two evenings each week in July and August. Head for the university area for B&B, or the youth hostel at Redclyffe, Western Rd (Tel. 432891) and while on Western Road call into the 'Western Star', frequent watering hole of Cork's many international rugby stalwarts.

From Cork it's only six miles to the famous BLARNEY STONE in Blarney Castle where legend has it you acquire 'the gift of the gab' once you've paid your IR£1.50 and kissed the stone.

The South-west

The south-west – West Cork and Kerry – has Ireland's highest mountains, lakes, forests and a rugged coastline. Seventeen miles from Cork is KINSALE, the culinary capital of Ireland. A pretty, small fishing village with a twelfth-century church and good youth hostel in Summer Cove (Tel. 021 72309).

The area around KILLARNEY is the jewel of this part of the world. Although the town itself is typically Irish, and very, very touristy, the scenery round about is incredibly beautiful and well worth the 90 minutes or so it takes to travel from Cork. If you want to avoid the jaunting cars and buggies (prices start at IR£12), stick to hiking instead. The Catholic Cathedral is probably the finest example in Ireland of the neo-gothic revival and took 68 years to complete, being finished only in 1914. It is set in a splendid complex of matching buildings and was extensively renovated in the early 1970s. Opposite is the entrance to KNOCKREER ESTATE where there is a very attractive garden. Walk round the beautiful BOURNE VINCENT MEMORIAL NATIONAL PARK and see the folk museum in MUCKROSS HOUSE there. Not far from the main road is the TORC WATERFALL, which is worth the trek through the trees. Use the tourist office in the town hall (Tel. 31633) to help you find a room, as beds can be very scarce in this, the most visited part of Ireland. The Youth Hostel is a couple of miles out of town at Aghadoe House (Tel. 094–31240).

The coastal road, the Ring of Kerry, is beautiful, winding its way between the sea and hills, but this would take you off the rail tracks, so only indulge if you need a few days off. Half an hour from Killarney is TRALEE, the capital of the 'Kingdom of Kerry', which in late August plays host to the world during the Festival of Kerry – a week of sport, music and song – culminating in the crowning of the Rose of Tralee. The town grew up around the thirteenth-century DESMOND CASTLE, but was almost totally destroyed in the seventeenth century. Despite that, it has some impressive eighteenth- and nineteenth-century buildings such as ST JOHN'S CATHOLIC CHURCH, off Castle Street, and the DOMINICAN PRIORY, at Day Place. Close by is a fine park, but dominated by the local council offices. There is no youth hostel in town so contact the tourist office (Tel. 066–21288) for help in finding a place to stay.

DINGLE is the gateway to the Gaelic Irish-speaking districts, and quiet, unspoilt countryside where one can unwind in an archeological wonderland, or if the weather is fine, on one of the sheltered beaches. Much of RYAN'S DAUGHTER was filmed in this area. Ferries run from DUNQUIN to the seven remote islands in the Atlantic called the Blaskets – don't go there if you get lonely easily.

Limerick

Ireland's third largest city is on the River Shannon, the longest navigable river in the British Isles. It is a port town with Georgian houses and elegant buildings which has had its ups and downs over the centuries. In recent years it has greatly benefitted from the tax-free area round about nearby Shannon Airport which has brought much employment and economic regeneration. Buildings to see in the city include THE GRANARY, a former grain store later adapated to a bonded warehouse and now tastefully adapted for modern use, housing, amongst shops and restaurants, the tourist office. It is in Michael Street (Tel. 061–317522). Also worth checking out are the CUSTOM HOUSE, TOWN HALL, KING JOHN'S CASTLE (built in 1210), and the nearby twelfth-century ST MARY'S CATHEDRAL. The town is famous for its beautiful handmade lace, and the Limerick Lace Collection can be seen in the CONVENT OF THE GOOD SHEPHERD in Clare St. (Open business hours on weekdays only). The youth hostel is at 1 Pery Square (Tel. 061–314672). Ennis Road seems to be the place for B&B, but always check the prices, for while some are cheap, there are several which are very expensive indeed.

Eight miles from Limerick City on the main Shannon Airport/ Ennis/Galway road stands the fully restored fifteenth-century BUNRATTY CASTLE which houses a superb collection of fourteenth- to seventeenth-century furniture and furnishings. It is open to visitors daily, and medieval banquets and entertainments are held twice nightly. The FOLK PARK in the grounds of the castle contains farmhouses and cottages, a forge and other typical features of the traditional way of life.

Galway

Galway is a seaport and university town which was ruled in the sixteenth century by Anglo-Norman tribes. It had extensive trade with Spain, particularly in the wine business, and it retains some Spanish architectural remains such as the Spanish Arch, the gateway to the old town.

TOURIST INFORMATION AND ADDRESSES

TOURIST OFFICE (Tel. 63081): One block east of the station, Victoria

Place off Eyre Sq. Also on the Promenade. Open Mon.–Sat. 9 a.m.–6.45 p.m.
POST OFFICE: Eglinton St. Open Mon.–Sat.: 9 a.m.–5.30 p.m.
USIT (STUDENT TRAVEL): University College, New Science Building, Galway (Tel. 24601). Open Mon.–Fri. 10 a.m.–1 p.m., 2 p.m.–5 p.m.

SEEING

Eyre Square, where the station is, is the city centre. It is also the main bus station. Note the SPANISH ARCH, which is a half-mile walk from Eyre Square down Shop St, which becomes High St and finally Quay St. LYNCH'S CASTLE, down Shop St, is fourteenth-century, as is the CHURCH OF ST NICHOLAS, where is it said that Columbus prayed before setting out on one of his voyages of discovery. Walk round by the banks of the River Corrib and see the salmon jump at SALMON WEIR BRIDGE in the spawning season, and in the summer evenings check out the *Seoda*, a traditional music presentation in the Irish-speaking theatre (Taibhdhearc Na Gaillimhe) on Middle St. In late July the GALWAY FAIR comes to town.

SLEEPING, EATING AND NIGHTLIFE

In the centre of town you have no alternative but to use B&Bs or independent hostels. Try Mrs Barrett (Tel. 23249). By far the best deal in town is actually a 15-minute ride away on a No. 2 bus from Eyre Square at the Galway Tourist Hostel, Gentianville, Gentian-ville Hill, Knocknacarra, Salthill (Tel. 25176). At IR£4.50 including a small continental breakfast and free showers, it is much cheaper than anywhere else. If full up, look around locally for B&Bs in the seaside suburb of Salthill.

There is a selection of eating places in the 'Special Value Tourist Menu' booklet, and there's plenty of fish'n'chip shops to keep you going. Cullen's Bar, Forster St, and Crane Bar, also Forster St, are lively at night and have traditional music. Also worth a try is the King's Head on the High Street, which serves what must be the smoothest Guinness in Ireland.

• **Excursions from Galway:** Three hours on the boat (Seamer from Galway Pier) takes you out to the remote and fascinating ARAN ISLANDS: Inishmore, Inishmaan and Inisheer. Again, avoid the jaunting cars as they're a rip-off. Do, however, go into the pubs to hear the Gaelic-speaking drivers and have a chat with them (they are bilingual). Life out here is traditional; a hard life based on fishing. This is where the famous Aran sweaters come from and where tweed trousers and skirts are made to keep out the Atlantic winds. If you are looking for peace and solitude among spectacular granite mountains, this is where you'll find it. Visit the prehistoric forts and remains during your hike round these fascinating islands. Inisheer has a particularly nice sandy beach. There are plenty of B&Bs and camping is IR£2 on official sites with water and toilets.

Connemara

Starting about twenty miles north of Galway is the famous rugged mountainous region of Connemara. The shoreline is unspoilt but jagged with several interesting traditional villages where English is rarely spoken, in favour of Gaelic. Connemara nees to be explored by bus or bike as there are no trains. If you are coming from Galway, the youth hostel at Indreabhán (also known as Inverin) is probably your best starting-off point. It is about 20 miles north of Galway (Tel. 091–93154). The nearby village of CARRAROE holds summer festivals and is worth a visit. Connemara ponies are wild, rugged creatures which can be seen in all their glory during August at the Connemara Pony Show in Clifden.

The North-west

Counties Mayo, Sligo and Donegal lack the charm, and warmer climate, of the south. They are serious counties, full of prehistoric remains and reminders of their turbulent past with the British. As the most inaccessible, they have also seen a lot of improvements in recent years and have much to recommend them. WESTPORT, in Clew Bay, is worth stopping at to see the beautiful estate of the Marquess of Sligo, two miles from the town. WESTPORT HOUSE is his Georgian mansion, open to the public April–Sept., full of beautiful things. You'll find Westport a busy place on the last Sunday in July, but all those people climbing CROAGH PATRICK aren't tourists, they're pilgrims as this is where St Patrick is said to have fasted and prayed. The tourist office (Tel. 098–25711) and the post office are in the Mall. Also try the Summerville Hostel (Tel. 098–25948) two miles west of town and the hostel on Altamount Street (Tel. 098–26644).

SLIGO, the county of W. B. Yeats, is incredibly rich in archaeological sites and atmosphere. This is the main town of north-west Ireland, with its population of only 14,000. The main sights are mountains – principally Knocknarea and Ben Bulben. Knocknarea is easy to climb and well worth the effort for the view you get from the summit, as well as the view on the summit itself: an 80 foot cairn, rumoured to be that of Maeve of Connacht, an amazon queen. The tourist office at Temple St (Tel. 071–61201) will give you help and information on sights and accommodation, and have guided walks at 11 a.m. every day during the summer. The main sight in the town of Sligo is the ruined thirteenth-century Dominican friary, SLIGO ABBEY, with its well preserved cloister and pillars. Also worth a visit is the COUNTY MUSEUM which has an extensive collection of first editions of Yeats. For B&B try across from the station on Wolfe Tone St.

COUNTY DONEGAL is not served by rail, but if you want to do a bit of hitching this region will provide you with an unspoilt, wild and beautiful terrain. Use the coastal youth hostels, and take warm clothes. There is much here for the visitor to admire: Slieve League, near Carrick, where a 200-foot mountain falls into the Atlantic at one fell swoop, and many other such dramatic landscapes.

The tweed industry is alive and well here and this is a thriving part of Ireland.

For Northern Ireland see United Kingdom.

ITALY (Italia)

Entry requirements	Passport
Population	57,300,000
Capital	Rome (pop.: 3,800,000 +)
Currency	Lira
	£1 = approx. 2130 L
Political system	Republic
Religion	Roman Catholic
Language	Italian (English spoken in some major cities)
Public holidays	1, 6 Jan.; Easter Sunday; Easter Monday; 25 Apr.; 1 May; 1 June; 15 Aug.; 1, 7 Nov.; 8, 25, 26 Dec.
International dialling codes	From UK: 010 + 39 + number
	From USA: 011 + 36 + number
	To UK: 00 + 44 + number
	To USA: 00 + 1 + number
Eurotrain office	Via Nazionale 66, I–00184 Rome (Tel. 06–46791)

Italy is like a spoilt child. You'll be annoyed, frustrated and overwhelmed, and yet your greatest inter-railing stories will probably originate in this exciting and beautiful country. Whatever your personal feelings on Italians are, you've got to admit they have style. Who else could make a full-scale drama out of a potentially normal situation like seeing a relative off in a train; or challenge a restaurant bill with the gusto of life and death?

Italy's history is dominated by three familiar themes: Empire, Church and the Renaissance, all of which have played a major role in the forming of European culture. From the eighth century BC onwards, there were Greeks in southern Italy and Sicily, and Etruscans in the north. By the third century BC, the Romans were on the move, conquering an empire which was to reign supreme over much of the barbarian world, until its downfall in the fifth century AD. As the civil power of Rome declined, it found a new role as the centre of the Christian Church. Italy became disunited and power was left in the hands of local lords, each seeking control of provincial kingdoms. Even the Pope and the Holy Roman Emperor could not agree as to who ruled what. Eventually the Pope, fed up with the whole affair after the city-states refused to submit to his authority, moved base to Avignon (1303–77). After this period of internal strife, the Kingdom of Naples and powerful city-states such as Venice and Florence, provided patronage for the arts. Among other factors which gave rise to this fifteenth-century Renaissance was the new humanism which produced men like Leonardo da Vinci and Michelangelo. Disunity and continued rivalry led to outside intervention by Spain and Austria and finally by Napoleonic France. This foreign domination created the desire for unity, initially under Garibaldi, leading to the ultimate unification of all Italy in 1870. After the First World War, Mussolini and the Fascists rose to power, which eventually brought about an alliance with Hitler during the Second World War. Since then, industrialization and emigration have characterized the economy, particularly in the south where poverty continues to be a problem. The wealthy north is a world away.

ITALIAN STATE RAILWAYS
(Ferrovie dello Stato, FS)

On paper, the Italian rail network should be one of the best in Europe. In reality, the railways can be quite inefficient but have improved greatly in the past few years. Most Italians accept that trains often run late and they manage to live with the bureaucracy and confusion of the whole system.

If you set out prepared for anything, you won't be surprised when a grandmother tries to board a busy train through your window, and ousts you into the corridor while she grabs your seat. Social friction within Italian society can only be worsened by the railways which ensure that those with money are provided with everything imaginable, while second-class passengers are treated as a sub-species. In peak season second class gets incredibly busy on the main lines, so either move early for a seat or, if it is a long trip, reserve. If there's a group of you, and things look busy, set one the task of getting in pronto without a rucksack to get some seats; then the rest can follow at leisure.

The late '80s have seen dramatic improvements on the Italian network – hourly services between Milan and Rome, with the first-class MiRo train taking only 4 hours to do the journey, and new sleepers and couchettes have improved overnight travel. The new rolling stock, though less quaint, is much more comfortable, and FS are spending some of the country's new-found wealth on improving the service, even for second-class travel.

The best of the non-supplement trains are the long-distance Espressos (if it's more than ½ hour late you can get a credit towards another ticket). They run frequently between Rome, Florence, Venice, Milan and Naples. Away from the main centres, things are not so rosy as you'll have to depend on the Direttos which stop at most stations or, even worse, the Locales which stop at every station. The Rapido is the top of the ladder for second-class travel, but for this privilege you'll have to pay a special supplement of about 30 per cent of the normal fare plus 2,500 L for a seat reservation. (Some Rapidos are first class only, so always check before boarding the train.) If you've always wanted to travel on a Eurocity, wait until you're out of Italy as you can pay up to 80 per cent of the ticket (usually 30 per cent). The station manager's office is always interesting as there's a 50/50 chance there'll be either a crucifix or a picture of Karl Marx over his desk.

The Italian Kilometric Ticket (no age restrictions) is valid for up to 20 trips, totalling up to 3,000 km, and can be used by as many as five different people. If this is the case, each trip is calculated by multiplying the distance travelled by the number of adults. This pass can be bought from every large station in Italy as well as from any Compagnia Italiana Turismo (CIT) office, and costs £116 first-class and £68 second-class if bought in London or 254,000 L and 150,000 L when bought in Italy. You can also get the tickets from Italian State Railways, 50 Conduit St, London W1 (Tel. 071–434 3844).

Note: When paying a supplement in Italy always check it covers the whole journey as often they're only sold in sections.

If you are intending to do a lot of travelling, it may be worth considering the 'Travel-at-Will' or BTLC ticket (Biglietto turistico libera circolazione) which is valid for 8, 15, 21 or 30 days in first and second class. This ticket frees you from paying supplements, even on Rapido trains, and is available only to tourists residing outside Italy. You can buy it in major Italian stations or from CIT in London before you go. It is possible to extend the validity of all but the 8-day ticket. Prices in second class are £65 for 8 days, £79 for 15, £92 for 21 and £112 for 30. Children under 12 get half price. Flexi Tickets are also available, second-class costing £48 for 4 days travel out of 9, £66 for 8 of 21 days, and £86 for 12 of 30 days. Tourists can

also buy circular tickets for journeys of over 1,000 km which start
and finish in the same town, or start and finish at any frontier. These
work out slightly cheaper than the normal fare but are likely to be of
limited appeal as you are not allowed to go through the same town
twice and every break of journey has to be endorsed. Day return
tickets for journeys over 50 km have a 15 per cent discount, as do
3-day return tickets for journeys over 250 km. Families of at least
four people travelling together qualify for a 30 per cent reduction on
the full fare for adults and 65 per cent for children under 12,
although the Kilometric ticket may work out better value. Fares are
worked out on the actual distance travelled and cost approximately
5,800 L for 100 km, 11,600 L for 200 km, 29,000 L for 500 km and
52,200 L for 1,000 km in second class and roughly 40 per cent for
first class.

● **Inter Rail bonuses:**

FROM	TO	REDUCTION %
Societá Adriatica di Navigazione and HML		
	Corfu	30
Brindisi	Igoumenitsa	30
	Patras	30

Via San Giovanni crossing to Sicily free.

● **Eurail bonuses:** Free:
—Eurail Pass and Eurail Youthpass travellers can use steamers
(*Appia, Egnatia, Espresso Grecia, Castalia*) operated by the
Adriatica di Navigazione and Hellenic Mediterranean Lines
between Brindisi and Patras and vice versa. However, between 1
June and 30 September, they must pay a 14,000 L high-season
surcharge. During July and August, advance reservation, which
costs about 2,500 L, is recommended. Special accommodations
(airline-type seats or cabins) and port taxes are extra. Before
boarding, all passengers must check in at the Shipping Line Office
at the pier. Passengers who wish to break their voyage at Corfu
must declare their intention of 'stop over' upon delivery of the
ticket. Holders of tickets for Corfu (as final port of destination)
can in no case continue their voyage to Patras.

Reduced fares:
—About 20 per cent reduction on first-class fares for holders of
 Eurail Pass and on second-class fares for holders of Eurail
 Youthpass on the Steamship Company Tirrenia between Naples
 and Palermo, Naples and Malta, Syracuse and Malta and for
 crossings to Sardinia.
—20 per cent reduction on the normal fares of the Steamship
 Company DFDS between Genoa and Tunis, Genoa–Alicante
 and Málaga.
—30 per cent reduction on the published full fares of the Adriatica
 di Navigazione between Venezia–Piraeus–Alexandria, on the
 Espresso Egitto and/or its return. Contact the local Adriatica
 offices.

The following half-price reductions are granted by Europabus on
transportation costs only and by local offices in Europe.
266 Venice–Florence
267 Florence–Rome
268 Rome–Naples–Pompeii–Sorrento–Amalfi
269 Palermo–Agrigento–Syracuse–Taormina–Palermo

TRAIN INFORMATION

The FS information officers generally speak English, but are
sometimes less helpful than they might be, as they understandably
get fed up with the long queues in the summer; so try and use your
timetable whenever possible.

• **Reservations:** Are optional on all non-supplement trains and can
be made up to six hours before departure. It's a good idea to do this
on runs between major cities, as the trains are always mobbed. It's
also possible to reserve a seat for the entire journey from London to
Italy or vice versa.

• **Night travel:** This is a good move in Italy where prices are low and
distances often long. You can get a couchette from Paris to Rome or
vice versa for about 16,800 L. Within Italy, they are either first-class
four-berth or second-class six-berth. Don't expect too much for
your money – couchettes can be old and dirty. Avoid bottom bunks
as headrests take up space, and it's even stuffier down there since
the air conditioning often doesn't work. If you prefer to go

up-market, there are also sleepers run by Wagons-Lits. If you're asked to give up your passport for the night, don't worry as this is standard practice. Many Italian trains also have pull-down seats. Make sure that your luggage will be secure while you are asleep.

• **Eating on trains:** There are mini-bars on all major trains, but if you're on a tight budget it would be quite a bit cheaper to take a picnic, as prices can be very high.

• **Scenic tips:** Without doubt, the finest way of arriving in north Italy is from Switzerland. The Bern–Brig–Milan and the Zürich–Lugano–Milan runs offer some of Europe's most spectacular Alpine scenery. If you plan on arriving from Austria, you won't be disappointed either, as the runs from Innsbruck–Bolzano to Verona and Vienna to Venice also offer some fine mountain views. One of the most popular routes is from Nice in France down to Pisa – which is no wonder, as there's a lot more than just the Mediterranean coast to feast your eyes on (the train makes its way past most of the Riviera beaches). Further down the same line, anywhere around the Bay of Naples has excellent coastal views, particularly along the narrow-gauge line to Sorrento, though this is a private railway. If you're arriving at Brindisi from Greece, there are three very different but equally scenic routes to choose from: along the southern coast to Catania in Sicily; up the Adriatic coast to Rimini; or over the mountains to Naples via Taranto. Another beautiful run, brought to our attention by an Italian reader, is Sulmona to Isernia, part of the excellent electrified line from Rome to Pescara.

• **Bikes** and scooters can sometimes be hired from local tourist offices.

TOURIST INFORMATION

Italy is divided into twenty regions. Each region's capital city has its own tourist board called Assessorato Regionale Turismo (ART). Each of these regions is divided into provinces which, in turn, have their own tourist offices, Ente Provinciale Turismo (EPT) or Azienda Promozione Turistica (APT). Apart from promoting general tourism in their areas, the EPTs also publish free maps, brochures, etc., as well as helping with accommodation problems. For everyday purposes, look for the local tourist offices, Azienda

Autonoma di Soggiorno e di Turismo (AAST). They have exactly the same function as the EPTs except they're limited to a particular town or resort. Before you set off to Italy, it's well worth writing in advance to their State Tourist Office (ENIT) at 1 Princes Street, London W1R 8AY, or Italian Government Travel Office, 630 Fifth Ave., New York, NY 10020, asking them to send you their excellent free 'Travellers' Handbook' which is updated annually and contains the latest information on everything you will need to know.

• **ISIC bonuses:** Between 20 and 50 per cent discounts on sea travel. For further information, contact STC Viaggi per la Gioventù, Via Nazionale 172, Rome.

• **Money matters:** The only unit of currency is the lira, for which there are notes for everything between 1,000 and 100,000 lire. Banking hours are Mon.–Fri.: 8.30 a.m.–1.20 p.m. and 3 p.m.–4 p.m.

Some exchange agencies (*cambio*) give a better rate: you will have to shop around. In general, a bank like Credito Italiano is better. The gettone (Italian phone token used as currency) is used as the equivalent of 200 L.

• **Post offices:** Open 8.30 a.m.–2 p.m. Mon.–Fri., till noon Sat. Letters can be sent to poste restante by adding 'Fermo Posta' to the name of the locality. On delivery at the central post office, you'll have to pay a small charge. Stamps are also sold at tobacconists'.

• **Shops:** Open from 8.30/9 a.m.–1 p.m. and from 3.30/4 p.m.–7.30/8 p.m., except in northern Italy where the lunch break is shorter and shops close earlier. Most stores take a half day on Monday, generally opening at about 3.30 p.m. Supermarkets can be difficult to find in town centres, so if you see one, use it.

For opening times of museums, check at the local AAST office. Many are shut on Sunday afternoons, Mondays and public holidays. Also, many churches shut between 12 noon and 3 p.m. NB Most churches, especially the major cathedrals, will not admit people wearing shorts or with uncovered shoulders (or girls with short skirts).

SLEEPING

There is a vast array of hostels, hotels and pensions in Italy to choose from; each one has its own fixed charges, mostly 15,000–40,000 L, as worked out by the provincial tourist boards. These charges vary according to the grade and the season (hotels 1–5). Always check behind the door to see if it includes IVA (Italian VAT), breakfast, and a shower, as these are often extra. There are fifty-two youth hostels scattered throughout Italy (open for IYHA members only), as well as numerous student hostels in all the main towns (open to everyone). Many Italian hostels do not accept phone reservations. For further information on youth hostels in Italy contact Associazione Italiana Alberghi per la Gioventù (AIG), Via Cavour 44, terzo piano, 00184 Roma (Tel. 06–462342). Hostels are not automatically your best bet as many operate an evening curfew and shut during the siesta period. We've found inexpensive hotels are more reliable in their cleanliness and flexibility. Look for the signs Pensione, Albergo, Locanda and Soggiorno. Girls have another option by staying at the local Casa Famiglia which are run by nuns and offer a bed for about 10,000–20,000 L. Wherever you stay, don't be afraid to give up your passport when you check in as this is standard practice. If you're determined to save as much as you can, camping represents another alternative. The local AAST office has information on the prices of the nearest sites but, for the amount you save, it's often a lot more convenient to stay at a cheap pension in the centre.

EATING AND NIGHTLIFE

Finding a supermarket in the town centre, or a public toilet can be a problem in Italy. You may be forced into a café with high prices and an old crone posted outside the toilet demanding 200 L. To avoid this it's best to be organized. In general, the breakfast at a hotel or pension isn't worth it, as all you're likely to get is a cup of coffee and a roll (it's normally cheaper at the local bar). If you can do without breakfast, go straightaway to the nearest supermarket or local market. In the evening rosticcerie, trattorie, tavole calde and osterie represent the best value. Cheap restaurants can be found quite easily and the standard of the cooking is incredibly high, even on a fixed-price 10,000 L menu. In fact, Italy represents one of the best deals in Europe for good cheap meals. The pizza stalls give you a cheap and tasty lunch, and in the evening, especially in Rome, you're spoilt for choice. Some places bump up the bill if you've chosen to sit outside to eat your meal, so check first. When your bill comes, check it. Watch the *pane e coperto* – the bread and cover charge. It ranges from 500 L to 2,500 L but the average is 1,500 L. Also check whether the bill includes service (*servizio compreso*). All restaurants are now required by law to give you an official receipt. The reason so many Italians stage melodramas with the waiter is that the arithmetic can sometimes be dodgy, and never in your favour. Snacks and afternoon coffees can be a bad idea: they inevitably end up costing as much as a meal, so bear this in mind when you're at the supermarket. Expect to pay 12,000–25,000 L for a full meal with wine in a trattoria, and 10,000–15,000 L for the menu turistico.

Once the evening meal is over most Italians wander round to a few cafés and bars, soaking up the local colour. As Luigi Barzini comments in *The Italians*:

> The show can be so engrossing that many people spend most of their lives just looking at it. There are usually café tables strategically placed in such a way that nothing of importance will escape the leisurely drinker of espresso or aperitivo.

The disco and nightclub scene is not startling, but there are a few flash – and expensive – places in the main cities. Musical and cultural events are thick on the ground in places like Rome, Florence and Milan. Pick up the 'What's On' from the local tourist office of whichever centre you're in, and make use of your ISIC whenever you can.

Northern Italy

The north is where the money's made, and to a large extent stays. Parts of it are therefore industrial, and prices tend to be higher, but there are too many interesting towns in this area simply to head south regardless. Its regions include PIEDMONT where Turin is; the DOLOMITE RANGE (part of the eastern Alps); LOMBARDY, dominated by Milan; EMILIA-ROMAGNA where Ferrara, Parma and Bologna are located; the ITALIAN RIVIERA where Genoa and the resort towns lie; and VENETO, the region of beautiful Renaissance towns such as Verona, Padua, and its crowning glory – VENICE.

Piedmont and Trentino – Alto Adige

TURIN is more of a stopping-off place than a tourist centre. It's on the main line to Rome, Florence, Naples and Paris and is one of Italy's main industrial centres. The old SIXTEENTH-CENTURY QUARTER, however, is attractive enough to merit a visit, as is the former ROYAL PALACE, the PALAZZO MADAMA and the very good EGYPTIAN MUSEUM and ANCIENT ART MUSEUM in the baroque Palace of the Academy of Sciences. Climb up the emblem of the city, the MOLE ANTONELLIANA, and look over the city from its 548-foot height. The tourist office is at Via Roma 222 (Tel. 011–535181and there's an information office at Porta Nuova.

The DOLOMITE REGION towns are a mixture of Roman ruins, medieval castles and baroque churches. The backdrop of the pink-coloured Dolomites and the proximity to Austria and Switzerland make this region feel like a totally different country. BOLZANO is on the main line from Munich, and is more Austrian than Italian in its language and character. This is the capital of the Alto Adige area and was part of Austria's south Tyrol till 1918. Tourist information is on Piazza Walther 22 and 8, where the GOTHIC CATHEDRAL stands. The MUSEO DELL'ALTO ADIGE has a rare collection of local wooden sculptures and paintings and the village of GRIES, across the River Isarco, makes a lovely walk. BRUNICO, half an hour from the Austrian frontier, still feels like a part of Austria. The dominating Tyrolean CASTLE OF BISHOP BRUNO was built in 1251. Walk for half an hour to the PLAN DI CORONES for an incredible Alpine view. TRENTO, half an hour from Bolzano on the line to Verona, is another Roman town on the Brenner route. Unlike Brunico, this town feels very Italian and, even though the inhabitants were Austrians till 1918, they now consider themselves true Italians. Walk down VIA BELENZANI and look at the Renaissance and Venetian palaces, the baroque church of SAN FRANCESCO SAVERIO, and the thirteenth-century bishop's house, IL CASTELLO DI BUON CONSIGLIO (the Castle of Good Counsel).

Lombardy

This region stretches from the Italian-Swiss border and Lombardy lakes to the plains of the Po River valley, taking in places such as intings and tapestries (closed Mondays), Via Man-

...M OF ANTIQUE ART is housed in the fifteenth-century
...E (closed Mondays). Among its collection is Michel-
...lanini Pietà' – his last, unfinished work. Enter from
, Piazza Castello. Behind the castle is the SEMPIONE
...BROGIO BASILICA, dating back to the fourth century,
...us treasures and a few dead saints as well as a
...ninth-century altar, and if you'd like to see the
...ng masterpiece, Leonardo's 'Last Supper', go to the
...to SANTA MARIA DELLE GRAZIE. The MUSEUM OF
...ECHNOLOGY, Via S. Vittore 21, is well worth visiting
...plete aircraft and ships as well as working models of
...ventions.

...t encounter many hassles in finding a reasonably
... Milan, even in summer – and you won't have to walk
...ere are plenty of suitable places just north or west of
...cept during an international trade fair. The tourist
...p you out if you've hit a fluke blackspot. The IYHF
... Martino Bassi, 2 (Tel. 367095). It's 30 minutes' walk
...on and not particularly cheap.
...ns in the 20,000–35,000 L range, try: Pensione
... Paganini 6 (Tel. 273890); Pensione Trentina, Via
... 2361208), and Pensione Soperga, Via Soperga 19
... are also close to the station and cheap. More
...re are a few pensions in Via Dante at 35,000 L per
...as the Pensione Dante (Tel. 866471). They charge
... double with free showers. Also try Hotel Rivoli at
... Lulli 11 (Tel. 2046815).
...years Milan has been taking over from Paris as
...most city for fashion and design. Consequently, many
...:ing models have been lured by the prospect of fame
... If you've been travelling on your own and miss
...:ing company, try the American Hotel, Via Finoc-
...2 (Tel. 666441) or Hotel Brussels, Piazza Castello 13

Como, on Lake Como, Bergamo, Mantua (Mantova) and its main
city, Milan.

COMO is an ancient silk-producing city on the southern tip of Lake
Como. Its architecture is very rich and you should head for the
PIAZZA DEL DUOMO to see the old PRETORIAN PALACE called Il
Broletto (1215). Next to this is the PALAZZO DEL COMUNE, and the
Renaissance Gothic DUOMO from 1396. The Romanesque church of
SAN FIDELE is reached by taking Via Vittorio Emanuele. Tourist
information is on Piazza Cavour, and at the station. Highly
recommended is taking a water bus up the lake which stops at all the
small villages en route – it makes a lovely excursion from Milan.
(Avoid the set tours as they are expensive and not good value.)

BERGAMO is divided into two: the lower city, built under the
Fascists in the 1920s; and the upper city, a medieval settlement
reached by funicular. Apart from the PALAZZO DELL'ACCADEMIA
CARRARA with its collection of sixteenth-century art and furniture,
forget the lower city. Once you've taken the funicular up head for
the Piazza Vecchia where the PALAZZO DELLA RAGIONE stands.
Opposite this is the PALAZZO NUOVO. The cathedral has a fifteenth-
century interior and nineteenth-century exterior. VIA ROCCA takes
you to a park which has a medieval lookout post from where the
view over the Bergamasque valleys is particularly good. Tourist
information is at 20 Viale V. Emanuele II.

MANTUA was one of *the* Renaissance courts, ruled as it was for 400
years by the Gonzaga family. Their sumptuous palace (PALAZZO
DUCALE) is on Piazza Sordello. There are over 500 rooms, including
the miniature suite specially constructed to house the court dwarfs.
It's free on ISIC, closed Mondays and open weekday mornings and
Saturday afternoons. Opposite the palace is the medieval CATHE-
DRAL which is impressive enough, but pales into insignificance
beside the beautiful Renaissance CHURCH OF SANT'ANDREA. The
PALAZZO DEL TÈ was the Gonzagas' summer home, built in the early
sixteenth century (closed Mon. and Sun. p.m.). The artist who
painted the frescoes decorating the rooms here was Giulio Romano,
and you can visit his sun house on VIA C. POMA, which is still well
preserved. Tourist information is at Piazza Mantegna 6 (Tel.
0376–350681) and Piazza Sordello 23; watch out for their 1 p.m.–3.30
p.m. siestas. For cheap beds, try La Rinascita, Via Concezione 4
(Tel. 0376–320607), or the youth hostel Ostello Sparafucile (Tel.
0376–372465), a renovated medieval castle, open Apr.–Oct.

Milan (Milano)

Most eurorailers don't get off at Milan, or if they do they stay in the station till their connection comes. While Milan is not exactly Venice in the sightseeing stakes, it's got a lot more than most people realize, and as the rich man of Italy (every third building seems to be another bank), it has the perks of a high living standard (and higher standards of cleanliness) and more things going on in the evenings than elsewhere.

STATION FACILITIES

There are three stations in Milan (Centrale, Lambrate and Garibaldi). The last two are mostly used for local traffic and are less important. I consider the Centrale station to be one of the most impressive in Europe, if only for its sheer size alone, which reflects past Italian confidence in their railway system. Since the fire in November 1983, the whole station has had a facelift making it even more spectacular. There are no shops nearby for picnic purchases, so buy in advance.

	MILANO CENTRALE
Train information	7 a.m.–11 p.m.
	(Tel. 222 441)
Reservations	7 a.m.–10 p.m. (6.30 p.m.–10 p.m.
	for couchettes and sleepers)
Tourist information	9 a.m.–12.30 p.m., 2.15 p.m.–6 p.m.
Foreign exchange	8 a.m.–7.30 p.m., Sundays 9 a.m.–2.30 p.m.
Left-luggage store	7 a.m.–10.30 p.m. (1,500 L)
Bar, Buffet	7 a.m.–12 midnight
Restaurant	11.30 a.m.–11.30 p.m.
Bath, Shower	7 a.m.–10.30 p.m.
Post office	Mon.–Fri.: 8 a.m.–2 p.m.
	Sat.: 8 a.m.–4 p.m.

Daily trains to: Amsterdam, Bern (4½ hours), Basel (5½ hours), Paris, Luxembourg, Vienna, Venice (3 hours), Frankfurt, Florence (3¼ hours), Rome (6½ hours), Bologna (2 hours), Brindisi, Naples, Nice (4¾ hours), Genoa.

TOURIST INFORMATION

The Provincial Tourist Boa[rd]
Marconi 1 (Tel. 809662), op[en]
and 1.30 p.m.–6 p.m., Sat.: 9 a[.m.]
(closed Sundays). For informa[tion]
walk to the left side of the sq[uare]
Galleria Vittorio Emanuele).
of the city which marks the me[ ]
useful free map gives location[s]
the commune. Get the free g[ ]
are sometimes not very helpfu[l]
you.
POST OFFICE: Stazione Centr[ale]
restante. Open Mon.–Fri. 8.1[5]
p.m.
AMEX: Via Brera 3, beyond th[e]
a.m.–5.30 p.m., Sat.: 9 a.m.–
UK CONSULATE: Via San Paol[o]
US CONSULATE: Piazza Carlo [ ]
CANADIAN CONSULATE: Via Vi[ ]
AUSTRALIAN CONSULATE: Via [ ]
24-HOUR CHEMIST: Tel. 871442
PHONE CODE: 02.

SEEING

The CATHEDRAL (Duomo),
Milanese wealth with 135 spi[res]
and out, is the finest piece of [ ]
It was started in 1386 and not[ ]
roof for the view. It's at Piazza
missing it. The famous ope[ra]
acoustics, has been the scene o[f]
and there's a museum there [ ]
other operatic memorabilia. It[ ]
gallery, on Piazza della Scala[ ]
LERY, a few blocks north of La[ ]
gallery. Housed in a seven[ ]
collection of Italian art and a li[ ]
POLDI-PEZZOLI MUSEUM is a

sculptures, p[ ]
zoni 12.
The MUSE[UM]
SFORZA CAST[LE]
angelo's 'Ro[ ]
Corte Ducale[ ]
PARK. SANT'A[ ]
houses religi[ ]
jewel-studde[ ]
rapidly decay[ ]
convent nex[t]
SCIENCE AND [ ]
to see the co[ ]
Leonardo's i[ ]

SLEEPING

You should[ ]
priced room [ ]
far either as [ ]
the station e[ ]
office will he[lp]
hostel is at V[ ]
from the stat[ion]
For pensi[ons]
Paganini, Vi[a]
Lippi 50 (Te[l.]
(Tel. 27822[ ]
centrally, th[e]
double, suc[h]
34,000 L for [ ]
Via Giovann[i]
In recent [ ]
Europe's for[ ]
English-spea[king]
and fortune [ ]
English-spea[king]
chiaro Apri[le]
(Tel. 809361[ ]

EATING AND NIGHTLIFE

There are trattorie and rosticcerie all over the city. The speciality of Milanese cooking is that they use butter, not olive oil as they do elsewhere in Italy. With the amount of money knocking about Milan, the Milanese tend to eat out a lot, so restaurants are more expensive here than elsewhere. For a cheap meal near the centre try Burghy, just out from San Babila underground station, or, even better, Ciao, just down the road at Corso Europa 12. There are plenty of cheap places in the Via Marghera area. If you want to go up-market without paying up-market prices, try Pane e Farina at Via Pantano 6 (Tel. 803274). For an interesting evening and a closer look at some of Milan's large transvestite community try Scimmie at Via Ascanio Sforza 49. For pubs go to the Brera area; and try Giamaica at Via Brera 32.

Emilia-Romagna

This is the region from the southern Po Valley to the Apennine Mountains north of Tuscany. Its towns are medieval and Renaissance: Parma, Ferrara, Ravenna and Bologna. It has the richest cuisine in Italy, where tortellini, tagliatelle and Bolognese sauce originated, and from Parma has come Parma ham and Parmesan cheese.

PARMA, in the centre of the huge plain south of the River Po, is known for its architectural and gastronomic delights. PIAZZA GARIBALDI is the old town centre with the TOWN HALL, CLOCK TOWER and GOVERNOR'S PALACE. The DUOMO (Cathedral) is Romanesque and on its cupola is Correggio's 'Assumption of the Virgin Mary'. The church of the MADONNA DELL STECCATA in Piazza Marconi is sixteenth-century and has been restored since its Second World War bombing. The PALAZZO DELLA PILOTTA is now the city's museum, and the NATIONAL GALLERY looks at the school established by Correggio in Parma, as well as the medieval–Renaissance Italian works. Tourist information is at Piazza Duomo 5 (Tel. 0521–33959). There's a student hostel both here and at Ferrara.

FERRARA today is an agricultural and industrial centre, but hopefully you'll visit it to see what's left of one of the Renaissance's cultural centres. It was an independent duchy ruled by the dukes of Este, and in their courts flowered some of the most gifted philosophers, artists and writers of the Renaissance movement. The CASTELLO ESTENSE (the Duke's Castle) dates back to the fourteenth century. This fortress, surrounded by a moat and complete with dungeons and a beautiful chapel, is open to the public. The town's CATHEDRAL is of the twelfth century and stands opposite the thirteenth-century PALAZZO COMUNALE. The PALAZZO SCHIFANOIA, down Via Scandiana, is where the dukes went for amusement; it's now a museum; the archaeological museum is in the Renaissance PALAZZO DI LUDOVICO IL MORO. Tourist information is at Piazzetta Municipale (Tel. 0532–3501).

RAVENNA was the sixth-century western capital of the Byzantine Empire, and the early Christian mosaics are outstanding. Ravenna is an hour down the line from Ferrara, and two hours from Bologna. The tourist office at Via Salara 8 (Tel. 0544–35404) will supply maps, information and accommodation help. SAN VITALE, the octagonal church, contains some mosaics, but across the cloister is the TOMB OF GALLA PLACIDIA with the best mosaics in Ravenna. Dante is buried in the grounds of the CHURCH OF SAN FRANCESCO. The high spot of Ravenna is a visit to the seventh-century church of SANT' APOLLINARE IN CLASSE (bus 4 from the station). The beaches are good, but often mobbed in summer. There's a youth hostel on Via Aurelio Nicolodi 12 (Tel. 0544–420405). It's good, quite cheap and reached by bus 1. For camping, head to Marina di Ravenna, and for a hostel try Albergo Minerva, Via Maroncelli 1 (Tel. 0544–34543), just to the right of the station, or Albergo Eva at Via Rocco Brancaleone 42 (Tel. 0544–39403). There's a student refectory at 8 Via Oberdan.

Bologna

The oldest university town in Europe (1076), one of the gastronomic centres of Europe, a Renaissance city of culture and learning, and today as red and communist as Moscow. This is where some eurorailers met a tragic death in August 1980 when the station was bombed. Things are back to normal now, and what's left of the station still stands on the northern edge of Bologna and carries trains running to Florence, Venice, Rome, Vienna, Sicily and other destinations.

STATION FACILITIES

	BOLOGNA CENTRALE
Train information	8 a.m.–8 p.m.
Reservations	7 a.m.–9.45 p.m.
Tourist information	Mon.–Sat.: 9 a.m.–7 p.m., Sun. 9 a.m.–1 p.m. (Tel. 246541)
Foreign exchange	8 a.m.–10 p.m.
Left-luggage store	All hours
Cafeteria	Thurs.–Mon.: 11 a.m.–3 p.m., 7 p.m.–10 p.m.
Restaurant	11 a.m.–12 midnight (upstairs) 7 a.m.–12 midnight (downstairs)

TOURIST INFORMATION AND ADDRESSES

Apart from the one at the station, there are offices at Via Leopardi 1, Via Marconi 45, and Piazza XX Settembre. The main tourist office is at Palazzo Comunale (Tel. 239660). General siesta-time is 12.30 p.m.–3.30 p.m. They'll help out on accommodation as well as providing the usual services.

POST OFFICE: Piazza Minghetti, Mon.–Fri.: 8.15 a.m.–6.40 p.m., Sat.: 8.15 a.m.–12.20 p.m.

STUDENT TRAVEL OFFICE: CTS, Via delle Belle Arti 20 (Tel. 264862).

24-HOUR CHEMIST: Tel. 192.

PHONE CODE: 051.

SEEING

The main street is VIA UGO BASSI with at one end the pedestrianized PIAZZA MAGGIORE where three Gothic structures tower up and supply shade to sit under. The PALAZZO COMUNALE is a complex of palaces which contains the municipal art gallery. Seven churches joined into another conglomeration is what you find at the BASILICA SANTO STEFANO; the octagonal church of the Holy Sepulchre, the eleventh-century church of the Crucifix and the church of St Peter and St Paul all merit a look. The courtyard behind the Holy Sepulchre has the BASIN OF PILATE where Pontius Pilate is said to have washed his hands when symbolically absolving himself of responsibility.

SLEEPING, EATING AND NIGHTLIFE

The scope isn't huge in Bologna for budget beds, especially since the youth hostel is about 3 miles from the city. The cheapest place in town is the Dormitorio Comunale. It has replaced the old hostel, but we can't vouch for it. Try Locanda Neva behind the station on Via Serra 7, Pensione Fiorita, Via San Felice 6 (Tel. 229560), or Locanda Testoni, Via Testoni 3 (Tel. 23968).

Eating's a totally different proposition: the only headache here is deciding where to go, as there are simply so many likely places. The cooking is terrific, and it's almost unheard of to have a bad meal. Though there is a university refectory, this is one place it'd be a shame to use as there are so many family-run trattorie. Try Osteria d'Orso on Via Montana, or the Trattoria at Via Broccaindosso 21A. If you're there in term-time, ask students in the university refectory for an idea of what's on; and pick up the rest of the events from tourist information. In the evening the young crowd hang out around Piazza Maggiore.

The Italian Riviera – Liguria

From the French Côte d'Azur to Tuscany lies the Italian Riviera. It's not quite as flash as its French counterpart, but it's cheaper, which results in some of the bigger resorts being packed out in summer. Genoa is the main town of this region, though it's hardly a resort. There's a very comprehensive line serving the Riviera which starts at Marseille in France, passes through the border at Ventimiglia and serves places like Bordighera, San Remo, Alassio, Albenga and Genoa. Rather than staying on the Cote d'Azur, you may wish to stop off on the border here. Worth checking out for accommodation are the Auberglia Cavour, via Cavour 3, or the Auberglia

Stella Marina on the same street. There are at least twenty-four trains a day, so hopping from one place to the next till you find the one you like best is easy. Each town has a tourist information office (Azienda di Turismo) and they'll help out on accommodation.

BORDIGHERA was a favourite among European royals and the English aristocracy in the nineteenth century. The oldest part of the town is on the hill, and along the shore is the new town. Bordighera is an attractive garden-filled resort which prides itself on its abundant palm trees (they supply the Vatican with palms on Palm Sunday). Prices tend to be high here, so try sleeping on the beach (in an unobtrusive place as the police aren't at all keen on this practice) and avoid the restaurants without fixed menus.

SAN REMO is the Riviera's largest resort, but unless you've money to waste in the Casino, stick tight to the beach. There are plenty of pizzerias and cafés, but this resort is one of the most commercialized and we're not recommending it too highly.

ALASSIO has a good mile-and-a-half beach. The new town's pretty grim, but the old town down by the beach is lovely. This used to be another haunt of the wealthy British, and there's tennis, golf and skiing on offer.

ALBENGA was a strategic Roman port and you can visit the ROMAN NAVAL MUSEUM here and see the remains of a Roman ship sunk in the first century BC. Today it is a market town and is more down-to-earth, and Italian, than many of the surrounding resorts.

Genoa (Genova)

The largest port of northern Italy with a medieval harbour-quarter, Renaissance upper town of merchants' palaces and, above all this, modern Genoa. Crowning this is the CIRCONVALLAZIONE A MONTE, a boulevard which winds its way in and out of the hills, giving a superb panorama over the city. Genoa became an important artistic centre in the sixteenth and seventeenth centuries when Flemish masters, including Rubens and Van Dyck, came over to paint the wealthy merchants' portraits. This is also the birthplace of Christopher Columbus.

STATION FACILITIES

Genoa has two stations: the Porta Principe (main station) and Brignole. Trains bound for the north use Principe, trains heading south use Brignole. Through-trains stop at both, except for those going north-west (Milano–Nice). They use only Principe. There are inter-station connecting trains regularly (at intervals of less than 30 minutes).

	PRINCIPE	BRIGNOLE
Train information	7 a.m.–11 p.m. (Tel. 284 081)	7 a.m.–11 p.m. (Tel. 284 081)
Reservations	7 a.m.–10 p.m.	7 a.m.–10 p.m.
Tourist information	Mon.–Sat.: 9 a.m.–12 noon 3 p.m.–7 p.m.	Mon.–Sat.: 8 a.m.–12 noon 4 p.m.–7 p.m.
Foreign exchange	Mon.–Fri.: 8.20 a.m.–1.20 p.m.	See train information
Left-luggage store	All hours	All hours
Cafeteria	11.30 a.m.–3.30 p.m. 7 p.m.–11 p.m.	6 a.m.–9.30 p.m.
Restaurant		11 a.m.–5 p.m.
Bar, Buffet	7 a.m.–11.30 p.m. (summer) 7 a.m.–11 p.m. (winter)	6 a.m.–9.30 p.m.
Post office	Mon.–Sat.: 8 a.m.–10 p.m. Sun.: 8 a.m.–12 noon	Mon.–Fri.: 8.15 a.m.–10 p.m. Sat.: 8.15 a.m.–2 p.m.

Daily trains to: Luxembourg, Frankfurt, Milan (1½ hours), Venice (4½ hours), Bologna (3 hours), Florence (4½ hours), Rome (5½ hours), Naples, Nice (3 hours).

TOURIST INFORMATION AND ADDRESSES

At the railway stations and the main office at Via Roma 11 (Tel. 581 407). Open Mon.–Thurs. 8 a.m.–2 p.m., and 2.30 p.m.–5 p.m. Fri.–Sat. 8 a.m.–1 p.m.

POST OFFICE: Palazzo Poste, Via G. Boccardo 2.

UK CONSULATE: Via XII Ottobre 2, 13th floor (Tel. 564 833).

24-HOUR CHEMIST: Piazza Acquaverde (Principe Station).

PHONE CODE: 010.

SEEING

Get hold of a map as it's a confusing city. Walk down VIA GARIBALDI and see the elegant sixteenth-century palaces. The PALAZZO BIANCO is now an art gallery with a Flemish collection. See the gallery and fine frescoes of PALAZZO CATALDI and the antiquities in PALAZZO DORIA TURSI. VIA BALBI and VIA CAIROLI are fine examples of old Genoa, as is PIAZZA DE FERRARI. SAN LORENZO CATHEDRAL was started in the twelfth century and finished in the sixteenth.

SLEEPING, EATING AND NIGHTLIFE

Tourist information will come up with plenty of pension suggestions and you shouldn't find any problems. The Hotel Astoria on Piazza Brignole (Tel. 893991), near Brignole Station, does some reasonable rooms (go for ones without baths). There's also Pension Principe at Piazza Acquaverde 2/12 and Riviera Liguria, 2 Via Colanza. Though the Youth Hostel is closed, women can use the Casa della Giovane, Via Fontane (12,000L).

There are scores of pizzerias and restaurants, and the prices all seem very much on a level in all quarters of the town, so go for one that's handy and displays its menu with prices quoted. Try the regional specialities of cima Genovese (stuffed cold veal) and pandolce (orange-flavoured cake).

Veneto

Veneto encompasses the north-eastern section of the Po Valley to the Dolomites and coastal resorts. This is the region around what many consider to be the most beautiful city in the world, Venice. Apart from this, there are the art towns of Padua and Verona close by.

Venice (Venezia)

Venice is absolutely unmatched by anything else in Europe; there really is nowhere else like it. It's a 'must' on any European tour, and it's worth all the crowds and higher-than-normal prices, because you'll never forget it. The town consists of 117 islets connected by 400 bridges with 150 canals winding their way through the maze. There are no cars, only boats.

The history of Venice is long and colourful. Her buildings reflect her glorious past when she, as an independent city-state, ruled over most of the Mediterranean. During the Renaissance, Venice was *the* trading port with the Middle East, and she became the centre of European commerce. The doges (the city dukes or rulers) had enough money not only to build sumptuous palaces and churches, but also to commission large-scale works of art from the Venetian school (Titian, Tintoretto, etc.) and patronize science and the arts. Their 1,000-year independence came to an end in 1797 when Napoleon gave Venice to the Austrians. When Italy was united, Venice joined on, and its popularity as a tourist trap of the twentieth century has brought it new wealth, much of which is used to prevent the entire city sinking and being lost for ever.

STATION FACILITIES

The station is situated at the west end of the town right on the Grand Canal. It's easily possible to walk everywhere by foot, but it's more fun to take the vaporetti (waterbuses) from outside the station. Nos. 1, 4 and 5 take you down the Grand Canal to San Marco Square. So does No. 2, which is the faster, limited-stop service.

SANTA LUCIA, VENEZIA	
Train information	7 a.m.–9 p.m.
	(Tel. 715555)
Reservations	7 a.m.–10 p.m.
Tourist information	8 a.m.–8 p.m.
Foreign exchange	Mon.–Sat.: 8 a.m.–7 p.m.
	Sun.: 8 a.m.–1 p.m.
Left-luggage store	Times vary according to season
Bar, Buffet	6 a.m.–9 p.m.
Waiting room	All hours
Post office	Mon.–Sat.: 8.30 a.m.–1.30 p.m.

Some trains stop only at Venezia–Mestre on the mainland, so check. To reach Venezia–Santa Lucia from Mestre, there are both trains and buses. Bus 2 from outside the station takes you into Venice proper.

TOURIST INFORMATION

The tourist office in the station (Tel. 715016) handles accommodation and little else except handing out maps. In summer, an office
at the bus station in Pizzale Roma does the same. (Tel. 27402). For
information your best bet is to head for the office near San Marco
Square at Ascensione 71F (Tel. 5226356), but this office will not
help you with accommodation. The student tourist office (CTGS) is
at Dorsoduro 3252 (Tel. 705660); they'll help you out with
accommodation and student travel. Tourist offices are always busy,
so try and fix up accommodation beforehand.

● **Addresses:**
POST OFFICE: Fondaco dei Tedeschi, near the eastern side of the
Rialto Bridge. Telephone office here also.
AMEX: San Marco, 1471 San Marco. Mon.–Sat.: 8 a.m.–8 p.m.
UK CONSULATE: Dorsoduro 1051 (Tel. 5227207).
FIRST AID: (Tel. 3000).
PHONE CODE: 041.

● **Getting about:** The waterbuses (vaporetti) cover all Venice. A trip
on Line 34 is good, as it takes in quite a few sights. They run every 10
minutes from 5 a.m. to 12 midnight. Fares are around the 2,000 L
mark. A 24-hour pass costs 10,000 L. A 3-day pass is also available.
There are also a few buses, but their routes are restricted. The
gondolas look beautiful, but at 60,000 L an hour it's not surprising
we haven't seen too many eurorailers on them.

SEEING

Venice is a place to wander in. There are so many little winding
back-streets and alleys, unexpected quiet squares and little hump-
back bridges that this is the easiest place in Europe to get lost in (no
wonder Venice's famous son Marco Polo was so good at exploring).
The sights that you can't miss are as follows:

1. ST MARK'S SQUARE: The city revolves round this incredible
   piazza. ST MARK'S BASILICA and the DOGES' PALACE are here, as
   are the LAW COURTS, the beautiful CLOCK TOWER and the OLD
   LIBRARY – now an archaeological museum. The PIAZZETTA leads
   off from the square to the GRAND CANAL.

2. ST MARK'S BASILICA: This amazing Byzantine church, built in the eleventh century, is a riot of gold, marble and mosaic. It was originally the chapel for the Doges, and became the city cathedral in 1807. The four massive bronze horses over the doorway were brought over from Constantinople after it was raided in 1207. (Girls: bring a shawl to cover your shoulders and arms; men: wear long trousers to be let in.) Climb up the Basilica for 2,000 L and a grand view.

3. DOGES' PALACE (Palazzo Ducale): This pink-and-white fairytale palace was the home of the Venetian government and the rulers of the republic. (Note the Tintoretto in the Grand Council Chamber.) The connecting bridge between the palace and the prison is known as the BRIDGE OF SIGHS. 4,000 L on ISIC.

4. THE ACADEMY OF FINE ART (Galleria dell'Accademia) has the best of the Venetian school's work: Canaletto, Tintoretto, Bellini, Veronese, etc. Closed Mondays. Entrance costs 4,000 L and there are no ISIC reductions. Check opening times before you go with the tourist office near San Marco Square.

5. CHIESA DEI FRARI: After St Mark's, this is Venice's most prized church. It houses two Titians and a Bellini. Next to it is the SCUOLA DI SAN ROCCO with a collection of fifty-six Tintorettos on biblical themes.

6. SCHOOL OF ST GEORGE: Beyond St Mark's Square at Calle dei Furlani. A frieze of paintings by Carpaccio – beautiful, and usually much quieter than the other museums.

A few streets away from the 'sights' is the quieter, less touristy western side of Venice; a great place to go to escape the hordes.

• **Excursions:** Just east of Venice lies the LIDO, the beach resort of the rich and famous. Wander past the villas, casino and hotels, and imagine it as it was when Thomas Mann used it to inspire his novel, *Death in Venice*. Also worth a trip is the island of MURANO where Venetian glass is blown (but buy it in Venice itself as prices in Murano are inflated); BURANO, a colourful little fishing village; and TORCELLO with its Byzantine cathedral.

SLEEPING

Here the problems start, especially in August. It's a seller's market and don't they know it. Having said that, in recent times prices have levelled out, and it's no more expensive here now than in Rome or Paris. The area near the station is as good as anywhere to look; just keep going from one pension to another. If all else fails, take the train (free on rail passes) to Mestre, 8 minutes away, and base yourself there where beds and food are cheaper. It is now illegal to sleep in railway stations in Italy and if you risk it you are likely to have a hose trained on you and end up with a soaking. You should also seriously consider travelling to Padua for accommodation in high summer. It's only 30 minutes by train from Santa Lucia station and there is a regular service. Accommodation is much cheaper, even in the incredibly busy summer season.

● **Hostels:** The youth hostel is on the island of Giudecca at Fondamenta delle Zitelle 86C (Tel. 52 38211), bus 5 from the station or waterbuses 5 and 8 from the landing stage along from the Piazza San Marco. Reception opens at 4 p.m. (11 p.m. curfew). Also out here are a few pensions and a religious hostel (women only), Istituto Canossiane, Ponte Piccolo 428 (Tel. 52 21157). Reception opens at 4 p.m., and it's 14,000 L each. Istituto Ciliota at San Marco 2976 (Tel. 5204888) caters for women and married couples only. Finally there's Domus Covanis, Dorsoduro 899, on Rio Foscarini (Tel. 52 87374). It's clean and convenient.

For camping, head to the beach on Litorale del Cavallino. Take the ferry from near San Marco to Punto Sabbioni, where there is also a good site. There is also a site at Fusina, which you can get to by waterbus or road bus no. 13 from the railway bridge near Mestre station, though reports differ as to cleanliness. It costs 6,000 L per person and mosquito repellent is an essential addition to your camping gear. There are a number of sites on the mainland. Best bet is to take buses 5 or 19 from the bus station and get off at whichever one takes your fancy. Expect to pay about 4,000 L per night. Further out, on the island of Lido, the clean and friendly campsite San Nicolo (Tel. 767415), charges 4,000 L and you have to join at a cost of 2,000 L so it's only worth it if you are staying for at least two nights. Bus A from Lido ferry.

● **Hotels and pensions:** Don't attempt to stay in a single room – it'll cripple you financially. If you are travelling alone, find a partner quick, or head for a hostel. I suggest the Lista di Spagna near the station as there are many cheap pensions in this area. Locanda Stefania, Fondamenta Tolentini 181A (Tel. 5203757), is across the bridge at the station. Doubles cost around 42,000 L. The Hotel Villa Rosa at Calle della Misericordia 389 (off the Lista di Spagna) (Tel. 5216569), costs 45,000 L for a double with shower and balcony. Only two minutes' walk from St Mark's square is the Pensione Apollo at the corner of Campo S. Angelo and Calle della Madonna (Tel. 5204909). It has only 15 rooms and charges about 30,000 L per person in a double or triple room. Breakfast is 7,200 L. Archie's House, Cannaregio 1814, San Leonardo (Tel. 5220884) is only 10 minutes from the station. Locanda Ca' Foscari, Dorsoduro 3888 (Tel. 5225817) is clean and reasonably priced. Near the Mestre station, at Via Parini 4, you should be able to get a double for under 36,000 L.

EATING AND NIGHTLIFE

There are quite a few fixed-price menus floating about and the food markets provide all you need for picnics. The main market is at the foot of the Rialto Bridge. There is also a cheap self-service restaurant here (expect to pay about 10,000 L). For trattorie the best area is Dorsoduro; there's a particularly good one at Dorsoduro 3922. If you're hard up and can't afford to eat at a trattoria, try the railworkers' café to the right of the station (Mensa Dopolavoro Ferroviario), or the students' Mensa at the end of Calle della Frescada.

Verona

It's not surprising Shakespeare chose Verona as his setting for *Romeo and Juliet* as it is a romantic city of palaces, churches, gardens and vineyards. It's about midway on the line from Milan to Venice and a popular destination with eurorailers. From the station it's a 15-minute walk to the centre of Verona, so take the bus No. 2 to the PIAZZA BRA where the incredibly preserved ROMAN ARENA is. Tourist information is at Dietro Anfiteatro 6 (Tel. 592828). At the PIAZZA DELL' ERBE are the Veronese merchants' palaces, and just close by at PIAZZA DEI SIGNORI are the tombs of the Scaligeri,

Verona's medieval enemies. Their house was the CASTELVECCHIO, now a museum. The Romanesque church of SAN ZENO MAGGIORE is worth seeing for its bronze door-panels and the altar-piece by Mantegna.

For a bed, try the Casa della Giovane (for women), Via Pigna 7 (Tel. 596880). Advance bookings taken. Open 8 a.m.–10.30 p.m. Pensione Marina, Via Ponte Nuovo 5 (Tel. 25968) do doubles for about 42,000 L, and there's camping at Via Castel San Pietro (Tel. 590360). Bus No. 3. There is also the hostel at Salita Fontana della Ferro 15 (Tel. 590360), just across the Ponte Pietra, and with bed and breakfast at 12,000 L a night it's good value. You can camp in the hostel grounds for 7,000 L.

Try Trattoria alla Canna at Via Scrimiari 5, Cucina Cristo at Piazzetta Pescheria or Trattoria da Mario, at Standone Porta Palio for cheap set menus. Wash it down with the local Soave or Valpolicella wine. During the summer there are performances of opera and Shakespearean dramas in the 22,000-capacity Roman Arena. Seats start at about 12,000 L, but it's an experience you won't easily forget (check with tourist information).

Padua (Padova)

About 30 minutes from Venice lies Padua, the famous thirteenth-century university town. Today, it's not as attractive as it once was, due to heavy industry, so one day should suffice. Tourist information is at the station. Pick up maps here, and make use of the accommodation service, which is free (open 9 a.m.–12.30 p.m., 3.30 p.m.–8 p.m., closed Saturday p.m. and Sunday). There is normally only one person working here, so don't be surprised if it suddenly shuts at odd times, while they nip off for a break. There also is a downtown office at Riviera Mugnai 22, which shuts at 6 p.m. The CAPPELLA SCROVEGNI is *the* sight of Padua: Giotto's masterpiece of medieval art that shook the artistic theories of the time. Next door is the CHIESA DEGLI EREMITANI where Mantegna's frescoes hang. Further up Corso Garibaldi is the university with its famous anatomical theatre. IL SANTO is the church dedicated to St Anthony, built in a mix of about six architectural styles. The

SCUOLA DI SANT'ANTONIO contains four Titians also dedicated to this saint, the patron of Padua.

Accommodation shouldn't be a problem. The youth hostel here is a renovated medieval castle. It's at Porta Legnano in Montagnana (Tel. 0429/81076), an hour's bus ride from the bus station at Via Trieste, just in front of the station. You can also take a local train to Monselice, and change there for Montagnana. Buy your tickets from the booth here instead of on the bus. You can also buy tickets at tobacconists. In town, try the Ostello Città di Padova at Via Aleardi 30 (Tel. 049–875 2219). Also worth checking out is the Albergo Pavia, Via Papafava 11 (Tel. 049–875 1566). Expect to pay about 30,000 L for a double, 20,000 L for a single. The Casa Famiglia at Via Bixio 4 (Tel. 049–875 1554) is also worth trying. It is across from the station and to the left. It's run by nuns and costs 15,000 L per night. For food, go to the excellent food market, the Salone, near the university, or try one of the three Mensas: at Via San Francesco 122 (closed August), Via Padovanino, or Via Leopardi.

Tuscany

Italy's wealthiest region in every way. This was the birthplace of the Renaissance and, apart from the mountains and coastal beaches, it offers some of the finest old art cities in the world: Siena, Pisa and the Renaissance town itself, Florence. The countryside is beautiful – without the south's poverty or the north's heavy industry, and the trains serve even the smallest towns.

Florence (Firenze)

The Medici family made Florence the central point of the Renaissance, and her citizens included names like da Vinci, Botticelli, Michelangelo, Galileo and Machiavelli. The legacy lives on in today's Florence, and even the pot-smoking, guitar-strumming crowd that camp outside the Uffizi in summer can't take away from the centuries of elegance and careful detail that make this a pilgrimage centre for artists the world over. There are enough churches, galleries, palaces and museums to interest everyone, but there aren't enough beds, so come early to Florence, and avoid joining the throngs of August station-sleepers who wake up to find they've lost more than a good night's sleep, if they haven't been arrested first, as it is illegal to sleep on public ground such as stations.

STATION FACILITIES

	FIRENZE SANTA MARIA NOVELLA
Train information	8 a.m.–9 p.m. (Tel. 278785)
Reservations	7 a.m.–9 p.m.
Tourist information	9 a.m.–9 p.m.
Foreign exchange	8 a.m.–12 noon, 1 p.m.–7 p.m. in train information (poor rates)
Left-luggage store	All hours
Bar, Buffet; Restaurant	5.30 a.m.–11.20 p.m.; 11.30 a.m.–9 p.m.
Shops	8 a.m.–12 noon, 5 p.m.–7.30 p.m. exc. Wed. and Sun.

Daily trains to: Bologna, Venice, Munich, Vienna, Frankfurt, Pisa, Rome, Naples, Sicily, Paris, Milan.

TOURIST INFORMATION

The tourist office at the station branch also deals with accommodation (commission 1,800 L). Expect long queues. The city tourist office is at Via Tornabuoni 15 (Tel. 216544).They give out good maps of the city. Open Mon.–Sat.: 9 a.m.–1 p.m. They do not book rooms.

● **Addresses:**
POST OFFICE: Via Pellicceria. Also poste restante and telephones. Open Mon.–Fri.: 8.15 a.m.–7 p.m.; Sat.: 8.15 a.m.–12 p.m.
AMEX: 49, Via Guicciardini (Tel. 278751), Mon.–Fri.: 9 a.m.–5.30 p.m., Sat.: 9 a.m.–12.30 p.m.
UK CONSULATE: Palazzo Castelbarco, Lungarno Corsini 2 (Tel. 284133).
US CONSULATE: Lungarno Vespucci 38 (Tel. 298276).

STUDENT TRAVEL: Via dei Ginori 11 (Tel. 263570).
24-HOUR CHEMIST: At the station by track 16.
PHONE CODE: 055.

SEEING

The DUOMO is the amazing multicolour cathedral with the huge dome which takes up a good chunk of the centre. It was started in 1296 and finished in 1434 – the dome was hailed as the wonder of the fifteenth century, but the façade of the cathedral today is only nineteenth-century. Climb the 464 steps (3,000 L) for an unrivalled view over Florence. The CAMPANILE was Giotto's idea and the BAPTISTRY is Romanesque and noted for its bronze doors by Ghiberti. The next sight of Florence has got to be the UFFIZI (5,000 L entrance), one of the world's greatest art galleries housed in a Renaissance palace. There's such a glut of sheer genius here, you really can't cope; visit it more than once and try to avoid the crowds. It isn't quite the same trying to study the finer points of a Leonardo with school parties whizzing past and real art enthusiasts elbowing you out of the way to get a closer look. It's open Tues.–Sat.: 9 a.m.–7 p.m., Sun.: 9 a.m.–1 p.m. Closed Monday, as are most of Florence's sights. Still, we must be grateful we still have the Uffizi to visit, as Hitler ordered the collections to be destroyed in 1945, and the terrible flood of 1966 badly damaged many of its treasures.

Across from the Uffizi is the PALAZZO PITTI, a fifteenth-century palace which the Medicis used during the sixteenth century. You can wander round it today and see the Raphaels, Rubens, Titians, and on its ground floor the ROYAL APARTMENTS and MUSEUM OF GEMS. The medieval BARGELLO PALACE holds the NATIONAL MUSEUM, an important sculpture collection (closed Mondays), and if you, like thousands of others, came to Florence to see Michelangelo's 'David' you'll find him in the GALLERIA DELL'ACCADEMIA on Via Ricasoli (also closed Mondays). The massive PALAZZO VECCHIO was the Medici residence from the fourteenth to the sixteenth century. Inside it's sumptuous – not surprisingly, they got the cream of Renaissance artists to decorate it. It's at Piazza della Signoria (closed Saturdays). The other palace you ought to see is the MEDICI on Via Cavour. They lived here from 1460 to 1540.

There's a tiny chapel on the first floor, and a Medici Museum downstairs which is free on Sundays.

As far as churches go, take in the Medicis' Renaissance parish church, ST LAURENCE'S. Most of them are buried here in the MEDICI CHAPELS (closed Mondays), and there's a LIBRARY considered to be Michelangelo's architectural masterpiece. SAN MARCO is worth seeing for the monks' cells which Fra Angelico painted his unique shade of blue, and the BRANCACCI CHAPEL of Santa Maria della Carmine has some beautiful Masaccio frescoes. Giotto has some work in SANTA CROCE and next to this is the interesting PAZZI CHAPEL.

The PONTE VECCHIO was the only bridge to survive the war intact, when the Germans blew-up all the others but were rushed by New Zealanders of the 8th Army before they could destroy it. It dates back to 1345 and is famous for the gold- and silversmith shops that line it. The STRAW MARKET (Mercato Nuovo) makes a good shopping trip, and the BOBOLI GARDENS, behind the Pitti Palace, are good for a picnic and sunbathe; they close at night, however, so a free sleep is impossible.

SLEEPING

Use the station tourist office and stress your price range. Florence is more expensive than average (now higher than Venetian levels), so be prepared to spend about 15,000 L in a hostel, 25,000 L in a pension and about 35,000 in a hotel for a single. Showers are invariably an extra 3,000 L and breakfast is rarely included.

• **Hostels:** The youth hostel is at Viale Augusto Righi (Tel. 601451) with around 400 beds, but it's for IYHF members only and costs 15,000 L a night. Reception opens at 2 p.m.; take bus 17B from the station. Pio X-Artigianelli is another hostel at Via dei Serragli 106 (Tel. 225044). It's near the Pitti Palace, but it's small so try to get there early. Ostello S. Monaca, Via Santa Monaca 6 (Tel. 268338), 13,000 L, is a private hostel near the centre, bus 11 or a fifteen-minute walk from the station. It is shut between 1 p.m. and 3 p.m., but you can reserve a place and leave your luggage at other times and register properly between 4 p.m. and 8 p.m.

• **Pensions:** There is a glut of suitable places within five minutes of the station. The only problem is that this is common knowledge, so get there early. If you come up with nothing in this area, drop off your pack if it's heavy as the other pensions are a good walk away. From the station, turn left then try places along Via Nazionale, Via Fiume, Via Fuenza, Via 28 Aprile, Via Guelfa and Via Cavour. We've tried the following and found them OK: Locanda Ester, Via Nazionale (Tel. 212741); Locanda Mia Cara at Via Fuenza 58 (Tel. 216053); Pensione Sofia, Via Cavour (Tel. 283930); Pension Fiume (Tel. 211045). Also try Locanda Sampaoli at Via S. Gallo 39 (Tel. 480316) and Locanda Giovanni, Via Firenze 69 (Tel. 261353).

Outside this section try Locanda Aldini, Via Calzaioli 13 (Tel. 214752), near the Duomo, or Pensione Davanzati at Via Porta Rossa 15 (Tel. 283414).

• **Camping:** Viale Michelangelo 80 (Tel. 6811977) is a site open April–Oct. but often full. It has good views of Florence. Take bus 13 from the station. For all-year camping try Camping Camerata next to the youth hostel (Tel. 610300). Neither will take bookings by phone although you can check how full they are first, before travelling. There is a municipal site at Villa Farvard which provides **free shelter and showers**. Take buses 14a, b or c from the station. Open from 7 p.m. to 10 a.m. Seven nights' stay allowed.

EATING AND NIGHTLIFE

The Santo Spirito–San Frediano quarter has more economy restaurants than elsewhere, but really Florence isn't geared up for subsistence-level living. Cheapest of all is the station buffet – spaghetti for 3100 L.

The self-service restaurant at Piazza della Stazione 25 does a really cheap meal; a favourite of mine (for a splurge) is Trattoria ZaZa at P. Mercato Centrale 26. A busy but good and cheap place is Trattoria il Constadino, Via Palazzuolo 69. If you've really reached rock bottom, Casa San Francesco on Piazza Sant' Annunziata (diagonally opposite Chiesa di Sant Annunziata), run by Franciscans, will do you a full lunch for about 9,000 L. They're only open for lunch, so you'll have to eat other meals elsewhere, and only use this if you are really broke. The university Mensas are on Via San Gallo 25 and Via dei Servi 66–68. For picnic food, the Mercato Centrale, near San Lorenzo, is your best bet. There are also a number of fast-food chains and, of course, ice-cream parlours.

Florence is reputed to have the best *gelati* in Italy. Vivoli, on Via dell' Isola delle Stinche, is still held by many to produce the world's best. It is closed in August, however. Use the take-away pizza places for economy shopping.

During July and August there are bi-weekly classical concerts held in the Pitti Palace courtyard, and there's a music festival in May. On 24 June there are fireworks on Piazzale Michelangelo after the parade in sixteenth-century costume, and the soccer match of the afternoon. On most summer nights, groups of students and travellers congregate on the Ponte Vecchio, and at the Duomo and Piazzale Michelangelo.

Siena

Siena is Tuscany's second art city, but while Florence is Renaissance, Siena is medieval. It's 1½ hours from Florence, and there are trains daily passing through Empoli and Poggibonsi. (Trains from Rome go via Chiusi, and you have to change at these stops unless you're taking a direct train.) The heart of the city is the PIAZZA DEL CAMPO, where the Palio (an inter-district horse-race) is held as part of the 2 July and 16 August celebrations, with fifteenth-century costume parades and all-night dances following on. The closest you'll get to the centre by bus from the station is Piazza Matteoti; walk the rest. The Gothic TOWN HALL (Palazzo Communale) and the bell tower in the piazza are well worth a visit. Entrance is only 2,500 L on ISIC. In the PIAZZA DEL DUOMO (bus 1: tickets at station) is ST CATHERINE'S CATHEDRAL with its museum of art and sculpture opposite. The CHIGI SARACINI PALACE is today a music academy, but on request they'll show you round the Renaissance apartments and gallery of Tuscan paintings. Further along you'll come to PIAZZA SALIMBENI with its four palaces dating from the thirteenth to the sixteenth centuries.

Cheap rooms are a bit of a problem here, but you can try Locanda Garibaldi, Via G. Dupré 18 (Tel. 0577–284204). It's central and one of the cheapest in Siena. Or ask tourist information: they're at Piazza del Campo 5 (Tel. 0577–280551). There's no shortage of good trattorie, and the Mensa Universitaria is on Via Sant' Agata. The IYHF hostel is at Via Fiorentina (Tel. 0577–52212) about 1 mile from the centre. Beds from about 12,000 L.

Pisa

Head straight for the PIAZZA DEL DUOMO with its famous Leaning
Tower (4,000 L entrance) which Galileo used in his experiments
(bus 1 from the station). Also here is the tourist office, though the
main one's at Lungarno Mediceo 42 (Tel. 050–203512). Beside the
tower is the CATHEDRAL AND BAPTISTRY, and the nearby CAMPO
SANTO is a twelfth-century cemetery built by the Crusaders.

Lodgings are difficult if you arrive late. Try Locanda Galileo, Via
Santa Maria 12 (Tel. 050–40621), down Via San Lorenzo, or the
campsite at Viale delle Cascine 86 (Tel. 050–560665). It's about
700 m from Rossore station and has free showers. On the way there
is a huge supermarket where you can stock up on food and drink at
reasonable prices. The Mensa's on Via Martiri and there are several
other cheap places round the university. If you're stuck, ask at
tourist information.

Florence–Rome

It's a bit more than three hours from Florence to Rome by the direct
line, via Arezzo, Orvieto and Orte, but why not take a detour to
visit the attractive towns of Perugia and Assisi? If you choose the
latter route and decide to stop off for a few hours at each place, here
is some basic information on these two places:

PERUGIA: This beautiful medieval hill town is about 2½ hours
from Florence. Although the centre and university are quite
modern, a walk up the side streets will take you back to the days of
Perugino – Raphael's teacher. The tourist office is at Via Mazzimi
21 (Tel. 075–25341), the main street. It's open 8.30 a.m.–1.30 p.m.,
4 p.m.–7 p.m. See the PALAZZO DEI PRIORI, CATHEDRAL, NATIONAL
GALLERY OF UNITORIA, NATIONAL ARCHAEOLOGICAL MUSEUM and
the ARCH OF AUGUSTUS.

ASSISI: The BASILICA OF ST FRANCIS is a noteworthy building
housing medieval and early Renaissance art. Opposite the Roman
columns of the TEMPLE OF MINERVA (now a church) is the tourist
office (Piazza del Comune, Tel. 075–812534), which is open 9
a.m.–1 p.m., 3.30 p.m.–6.30 p.m. Climb up the ROCCA MAGGIORE
(costs 2,000 L) for a stupendous view over the town and the valley.

Naturally the place is full of St Francis – visit the Church of SANTA
MARIA DEGLI ANGELI, which contains the Portiuncula, where it all
began for St Francis.

Rome (Roma)

Rome, the 'eternal city', is so called because it is a place of great
beauty, contrast and life. There are really three Romes: the
religious world centre of the Catholic Church, the incredible ruins
of the centre of the Roman Empire, and modern, dirty, bustling
Rome. All three seem incongruous, yet they live inside and beside
each other with great ease. You'll soon realize Rome was built to
rule and dominate the world. Everything is on a massive scale, solid
and 'eternal'. You'll find the Romans proud, arrogant and con-
ceited, but you'll look back on the overwhelming beauty and
dimensions of St Peter's, the atmosphere in the Colosseum at dusk,
and the Trevi Fountain when it's floodlit at night and buzzing with
young people, and remember it affectionately.

STATION FACILITIES

	ROMA TERMINI
Train information	7 a.m.–11 p.m. (Tel. 4775)
Reservations	7 a.m.–10 p.m.
Tourist information	9 a.m.–1 p.m.; 3 p.m.–8 p.m.
Foreign exchange (near platform 12)	Mon.–Fri.: 8.30 a.m.–1.30 p.m. in bank. Other times, window 28
Left-luggage store	All hours (Pay double for tents attached to outside of rucksack)
Bar, Buffet	6 a.m.–11.25 p.m. and 7.20 a.m.–8.40 p.m.
Cafeteria	10.30 a.m.–11 p.m.
Bath, Shower	7.20 a.m.–8.40 p.m.
Waiting room	Closed 4 a.m.–6 a.m.
Shops	7 a.m.–9 p.m.
Post office	Mon.–Fri.: 8.15 a.m.–8 p.m., Sat.: 8 a.m.–12 noon
Station shuts	1.30 a.m.–4.30 a.m.

It also has a morgue for 'departed' passengers.
Daily trains to: Pisa, Genoa, Nice, Milan, Innsbruck, Venice, Florence, Bologna,
Ancona, Naples, Brindisi, Sicily.

Trains running from the north of Italy to the south and vice versa stop at Tirbutina
station so you don't have to come into the centre.

TOURIST INFORMATION

Before leaving the station, go along to the EPT tourist office and pick up a map of the city, plus two booklets, 'Qui Roma' ('Here's Rome', current events, etc.) and 'Roma Giovane' ('Young Rome') as these are a great help in getting to know your way around.

Apart from the office at the station (Tel. 465461), there's one at Via Parigi 5 (Tel. 463748) (open Mon.–Sat.: 8.15 a.m.–7.15 p.m.). Pick up 'Qui Roma' here and, rather than leave yourself open to their accommodation suggestions (all over 18,000 L), hand them some of our telephone numbers and ask them to phone for a reservation for you.

Generally, shops and churches are open 9 a.m.–1 p.m., 4 p.m.–8 p.m. Museums generally close about 1 p.m. or 2 p.m. and all day Monday, though the Campidoglio museums open late on Tuesdays and Saturdays. In August, Romans take their holidays and you'll find many restaurants shut.

● **Addresses:**
POST OFFICE: Piazza San Silvestro 19, open Mon.–Fri.: 8.30 a.m.–9.40 p.m. for poste restante, Sat.: 8.30 a.m.–11.30 a.m., telephones 8 a.m.–12 midnight.
AMEX: Piazza di Spagna 38, open Mon.–Fri.: 9 a.m.–5.30 p.m., Sat.: 9 a.m.–12.30 p.m. (Tel. 67641).
UK EMBASSY: Via XX Settembre 80A (Tel. 475 5441).
US EMBASSY: Via Vittorio Veneto 119a (Tel. 46741).
CANADIAN EMBASSY: Via Zara 30 (Tel. 440 3028).
CTS (YOUTH TRAVEL SERVICE): Via Nazionale 66 (Tel. 479 931). They help out on accommodation, issue ISICs, etc. Also a Eurotrain office (Tel. 46791).
LATE CHEMIST: In station.
PHONE CODE: 06.

● **Getting about:** The buses are cheap, costing 700 L (6,000 L for 10) and the underground continues to expand yearly (costs the same), but it's difficult as they keep finding new archaeological sites where they want to lay tracks. Buy tickets from Tabac shops or the stations. Buses run from 5.45 a.m.–12 midnight. You can buy a cheap route map from the bus kiosk at the station. (Few people buy metro tickets!)

SEEING

Though the three sides of Rome (ancient, religious and modern) are virtually inseparable, we've tried to separate the sights into the three categories. If you give yourself a day for each you'll make it, but by the end you'll need to head for a beach to soothe your blisters in the sea. Ideally, give yourself 4–5 days here, and unless you're really flattened, use the afternoon siestas to get round the sights which are otherwise mobbed. A final word: be on your guard constantly for pickpockets, including young children begging to distract your attention and particularly the motorized ones who cruise about on mopeds and whip handbags off shoulders and wallets from pockets, then make off at great speed.

• **Ancient Rome:** The sites of ancient Rome are clustered round the Piazza Venezia, the modern city centre, and lie on the PALATINE, CAPITOLINE and AVENTINE hills.

The COLOSSEUM is the biggest site of ancient Rome (free for lower levels, 5,000 L for upper). This huge arena sat 55,000 Romans who passed many an afternoon watching the local Christians being eaten for dinner by lions, etc., or gladiators fighting it out to the bitter end. The Palatine Hill is where Nero, Mark Antony, Cicero and co. were based. The VILLA FARNESE incorporated many ancient structures into it when it was built in the sixteenth century, and the BOTANICAL GARDENS here were the world's first. See the frescoes on the HOUSE OF AUGUSTUS and the remains of the PALACE OF THE FLAVIANS and the PALACE OF SEPTIMIUS SEVERUS.

The ROMAN FORUM, adjoining the Palatine Hill, was the commercial, religious and civic centre of ancient Rome. Look out for the three TRIUMPHAL ARCHES, HOUSE OF THE VESTAL VIRGINS and the half-dozen temples. Enter by Via dei Fori Imperiali (closed Tuesdays, costs 5,000 L). Opposite is the IMPERIAL FORUM; Caesar started this annexe of the Roman Forum when the expanding empire's paperwork was getting too much for the one place. See TRAJAN'S FORUM with its famous column, and the BASILICA OF ST MAXENTIUS, the ancient law court and exchange (closed Mondays). the MAMERTINE PRISON, just off Via dei Fori Imperiali, is where Nero kept St Peter, and many others were tortured here.

The PANTHEON is the best preserved of all the sites of ancient Rome. It was started in 27 BC, rebuilt in AD 125 and, having been a temple to the gods for over 700 years, became a Christian church in the seventh century. The kings of Italy and the artist Raphael are buried here. It's at Piazza della Rotonda, near the Tiber.

On the APPIAN WAY, the 2,300-year-old Roman road stretching as far south as Brindisi, you'll find the third-century BATHS OF CARACALLA (near Piazzale Numa Pompilio), and the CATACOMBS OF ST CALIXTUS. There are five tiers of burial chambers, and many Christian saints and martyrs here, at 110 Via Appia Antica (closed Wednesdays). The NATIONAL MUSEUM OF ROME has the world's best collection of artefacts from the Roman Empire (Via delle Terme di Diocleziano, closed Mondays). CASTEL SANT' ANGELO, built by Hadrian in AD 139, was the Pope's fortress to flee to in times of danger. Now it's a museum of weapons, art and relics (Lungotevere Castello, closed Mondays). That leaves only the THEATRE OF MARCELLUS (13 BC), the PYRAMID OF CAIUS CESTIUS on Piazza San Paolo, and the remains of four ancient ROMAN TEMPLES in Largo Argentina. All the Roman remains that don't close on Mondays tend to close on Tuesdays.

• **Papal Rome:** The independent state of the VATICAN CITY is the spiritual centre for 627 million Roman Catholics. The Vatican has its own post office with stamps, printing press, currency, radio station, newspaper and railway, all within one square mile. The Pope's in charge here and the Swiss Guards keep order. ST PETER'S SQUARE is a seventeenth-century baroque masterpiece, designed by Bernini, which leads up to ST PETER'S BASILICA, the church whose incredible dome can be seen all over Rome. Inside the huge interior are works by Raphael, Michelangelo (his famous Pietà), Bernini and Bramante. (Don't wear shorts if you want to get in.) For the full emotion of this church to hit you – even if you're an atheist – come when it's just opened at 7 a.m. and climb the stairs to the top of the dome for a breathtaking view. The VATICAN MUSEUMS which include such treasures as Michelangelo's SISTINE CHAPEL, the RAPHAEL ROOMS, the GRAECO-ROMAN MUSEUMS, and the VATICAN LIBRARY are located north of St Peter's on Viale Vaticano. It costs about 5,000 L on ISIC, 8,000 L without, but it's well worth it. There are four alternative routes to follow through the museums; we suggest you take C or D, and skip through the bits you're not interested in. They are open Mon.–Sat. and the last Sunday of every month, when admission is free for everyone. Museums close at 5 p.m. in summer, and last entry is at 4 p.m. The two churches that must be included here, though they're not located in or near the Vatican, are ST JOHN LATERAN with the HOLY STAIRS and SANTA MARIA MAGGIORE. The former is the church of the popes, founded in the fourth century. The stairs are believed to be those from the palace of Pontius Pilate which Christ ascended during his Passion. You can only climb them, however, if you're officially worshipping, and then you have to do it on your knees. The church is south-east of the Colosseum at Piazza San Giovanni in Laterno. The latter is another fourth-century church, though rebuilt in the thirteenth and with an eighteenth-century façade. The campanile is the tallest in Rome and there are some interesting fifth-century mosaics (Via Liberiana 27). Mass is at 10 a.m. on Sundays, but come earlier to allow for queueing.

• **Modern Rome:** The squares of Rome are worth seeing as sights in themselves. The PIAZZA DEL CAMPIDOGLIO, designed by Michelangelo, is flanked by palaces and is considered to be the political city centre. Of the three palaces one is the senatorial office, one is the CAPITOLINE MUSEUM of antique sculptures, and the other is the CONSERVATORIO which has large chunks of hands, toes and heads from Roman statues.

The PIAZZA NAVONA is another Bernini work, as is PIAZZA BARBERINI. The SPANISH STEPS (Piazza di Spagna) are eighteenth-century and the Barcaccia fountain at the bottom attracts a young crowd of manwatchers, but *the* fountain of Rome has got to be the TREVI. This baroque work was finished in 1762. If you're looking for your Latin lover, come here after dark. The fountain's floodlit and the atmosphere typically Roman. It's at Piazza di Trevi.

The MONUMENT TO VICTOR EMMANUEL II, in the Piazza Venezia, is the huge white marble 'wedding cake' at the end of Via del Corso. It was built in 1911 to celebrate Italy's unification. The VILLA BORGHESE, in the north of Rome, is the most splendid of Rome's parks. The zoo and two art galleries are out here, and though this seems like the best place to sleep out in Rome, it is very dangerous.

SLEEPING

Though Rome gets packed in July and August, beds are never really a problem as there are literally hundreds of pensions, locande and alloggi. There are plenty of cheap places beside the station and, though this isn't right in the centre, it's not so far out you can't walk to the sights, and the prices are the cheapest in town. To help you find a place, use either CTS (see addresses), the Student Help Office or the tourist offices; but remember to get them to phone only your own suggested places, as theirs are all over the top.

There are three university halls of residence, which are open from the end of July to the end of September. They are at Via Cesare de Lollis, 24/B (take bus 492 from the station), Viale del Ministero degli Affari Esteri 6 (near the Youth Hostel, take Subway A to Ottaviano, then bus 32) and at Via D. De Dominicus (Subway A to Colli Albani, then bus 409). All charge around 20,000 L for bed and breakfast. Bookings for these hostels are handled by the one office (Tel. 385943 or 3599295).

• **Student hostels:** The youth hostel is at Viale delle Olimpiadi 61 (Tel. 3964709), quite far out and reports on it vary dramatically (costs 15,000 L per night). A better bet is the YMCA at Piazza Indipendenza 23c (Tel. 462520). It's near to the station and takes men and women, but is expensive with prices around 35,000 L. Locanda del Conservatorio, Via del Conservatorio 62 (Tel. 659612) has clean central rooms for around 15,000 L single, 27,000 L double, but reserve ahead. Near the station there's the Centro dei Giovane at Via degli Apuli 40 (Tel. 4953151); it's cheap and convenient but tends to fill up quickly, so get there early.

• **Pensions near the station:** As you leave the station you can turn either right or left to begin your search. On the right is Via Palestro. At No. 9 of this street is Pensione Lella which charges around 45,000 L per double and at No. 35 is Pensione Michele (Tel. 4743383), with Pensione Katty (Tel. 4751385) on the third floor at the same address. At No. 15 is Pensione Bolognese, which has clean rooms and showers and costs about 50,000 L for a double, 65,000 L if you want a shower room (Tel. 490045). Pensione Cina, Via Montebello 114, top floor (Tel. 4041379) asks about 20,000 L each for doubles and triples. The Pensione at Piemonte at Via Vicenza 34 (Tel. 4952240 or 495775) costs about 45,000 L for a double with showers.

On the left of the station you'll find another spate of pensions, and also several cheap eating-places. This is a very Roman working-class neighbourhood, full of colour and life. Via Principe Amedeo has a collection of very good bed bargains; all ask about 36,000 L a person. The pensions include Cotorillo, Contilla, Govoni and di Rienzo, which are all very acceptable. Next door at No. 79 is Pensione Pezzotti (Tel. 446875) with free showers and doubles for 38,000 L; and at 79d on the sixth floor is Pensione Tony (Tel. 736994). His rooms are clean and have their own shower. Another recommended place is the Pensione Papà Germano, 14a Via Calatafimi (Tel. 486919), which is clean, friendly and inexpensive.

If you want to be nearer the centre, try: Locanda Sud America, Via Cavour 116 (Tel. 464507), or Locanda Chic at No. 266 (Tel. 4758614). Both are near ancient Rome and in the 24,000–36,000 L per double range.

If things are desperate and you're sleeping out, no matter how desperate you are avoid flaking out in the park outside the station. Each summer the muggings seem to get more numerous and vicious, and the gypsies that hang out there should be watched like hawks. The park at Calle Oppio, near the Colosseum, is your best bet, but even that is to be avoided. One final piece of advice. Roman pensione owners are notorious for attempting the great tourist rip-off. Always check the prices with those posted in the room, and argue for the difference.

• **Camping:** There are several sites around Rome, but none are near the centre. One of the nearest, five miles out, is Falminio, at Via Flaminio (Tel. 3279006). It is quite good and open all year but relatively expensive. To get there take Metropolitan line A to Flaminio, then buses 202, 203, 204 or 205. Try also Camping Roma on Via Aurelio. Take bus 38 from the train station to Piazza Fiume, then bus 490 to the terminus where you change to bus 246. For Camping Nomentano, Via Nomentana, take bus 36 from outside Termini Station to Piazza Sempione, then bus 336 to Via Nomentana. Salaria Camping, Via Salaria 2141, offers a 20 per cent discount to *Europe by Train* readers.

EATING AND NIGHTLIFE

For about 15,000 L you can eat a good, filling meal in Rome. Almost every neighbourhood has its own collection of cheap trattorie and rosticcerie, as the Romans eat out a lot themselves. Go for the menu turistico and spoil yourself on the delicious pasta and pizza dishes which fill you up for very little money. There's little point buying food for picnics (though if you do, bar owners will let you eat it inside if you buy a drink from them) as good supermarkets are few and far between. Don't trail across town to follow our few suggestions; just eat at the nearest likely spot wherever you happen to find yourself. The Mensa Universitaria on Via Cesare de Lollis 20 is closed all August. Palmerie, Via Cimarra 415, is where some of the trendy Roman crowd hang out. The fixed-price menus are reasonable. The area on the right-hand side of the station as you leave is good for tourist menus. Especially good value is Osteria de Salvatore at Via Castelfidardo 39c. Expect to pay around 12,000 L, including drinks. For a good self-service restaurant, try the one at Piazza Cinquecento 47 near the station.

The Romans are big manwatchers, so when in Rome . . . Sit out and scrutinize the passers-by in Piazza Navona or Piazza del Popolo, or go and revisit some of the sights when they're floodlit: the Trevi, the Colosseum, St Peter's, etc. You're likely to encounter young Romans in a trattoria, disco or bar. If opera is your cup of tea, try and make it along to the outdoor performances in the Roman Baths of Caracalla. Buy tickets from the Teatro dell'Opera. Giolitti's are reputed to have the best ice-cream in Rome. They're near the Pantheon at Via Ufficio del Vicario 40.

• **Excursions:** Nineteen miles east of Rome is the sixteenth-century Renaissance cardinals' palace, VILLA D'ESTE at Tivoli. The gardens with their 500 fountains are the main attraction here, and your ISIC will get you in free in daytime, though the floodlit fountains do make a colourful nocturnal visit. Take a train from Rome station, or bus RT from Via Gaeta if you don't have a rail pass. If you bus it, you could also take in HADRIAN'S VILLA (closed Mondays).

Mussolini's 1940s quarter of Rome – the EUR – has an amusement park (LUNA PARK) and the MUSEUM OF ROMAN CIVILIZATION which reconstructs ancient Rome as it was under

Constantine in the early fourth century. Should you have hit a heatwave, the nearest beach is OSTIA-LIDO. It's not one of Italy's best but it's only eighteen miles away (metro Line B to Magliana then train to Ostia).

Southern Italy

Using the old geographical 'boot' analogy of Italy, CAMPANIA is the ankle, BASILICATA the arch, PUGLIA the heel (the departure point for the Brindisi ferry to Greece), and CALABRIA the toe.

There's a lot to take in in Campania. Apart from the colourful chaos of Naples, there's the smouldering volcano of Vesuvius, the archaeological remains of Pompeii, Herculaneum and Paestum, the romantic towns of Sorrento, Amalfi and Positano and the islands off the coast of Naples: Capri, Ischia and Procida. The Italians head for Agropoli, Catellabate and Santa Marco, all south of Naples, for their holidays so these are places to avoid in August when all the natives are there but worth the trip at other times of the year.

If you are planning on visiting Pompeii, get off at Pompeii Scavi station, which is a two-minute walk from the gates. Ignore the taxi drivers offering to take you there and also their directions when you refuse as they'll only send you the wrong way.

You have to be well clued-up to tackle Vesuvius. First of all make sure it is a clear day, then go early. There are only four buses a day (three in winter) and the last one leaves at 1 p.m. from Ercolano station. The journey takes between an hour and 90 minutes but the bus only waits for five minutes when you get there whereas you need at least an hour to go up and down with the compulsory guide, plus time at the top. The buses run to the chairlift station. The chairlift, which does not run in inclement weather, costs around 2,400 L, the guide around 1,000 L. Alternatively, if there is a group of around five of you, it might be just as cheap and certainly more flexible if you take advantage of the enterprising taxi drivers who hang around the bus stop at Ercolano station.

Naples (Napoli)

Naples is overcrowded, chaotic and often dirty, crime-ridden and chaotic. It's also a real experience. If you've come down from Florence or Venice, you'll feel you're in a different country: the people, the climate, and the colours and smells round the busy port all strengthen your belief that now you're really in southern Europe. More than anywhere else in Italy, watch your belongings here – over a third of Neapolitans are unemployed and the police officially put the number of smugglers at 40,000. Don't expect northern standards of hygiene either: until 1973 (when a cholera epidemic broke out), Naples had no sewers; but things are much better now. Despite all this it's a vibrant and exciting city.

STATION FACILITIES

Trains from Rome, and those going on to Sicily, invariably use the central station. The Rome–Bari trains stop at both stations, Piazza Garibaldi or Centrale. There's a connecting elevator between the two. Trains to Sorrento on the Circumvesuviana railway leave from Napoli PG. Space permits details of Napoli Centrale only as the most used by eurorailers.

	NAPOLI CENTRALE
Train information	7 a.m.–11 p.m.
Reservations	7 a.m.–10 p.m.
Tourist information	Mon.–Sat.: 8 a.m.–8 p.m.
	Sun.: 8 a.m.–1 p.m.
Foreign exchange	7 a.m.–9 p.m.
Left-luggage store	All hours
Bar, Buffet and Restaurant	6 a.m.–midnight
	(meals 11 a.m.–4 p.m.)
Bath, Shower	Tue.–Sat.: 8 a.m.–8 p.m.
	Sun.–Mon.: 8 a.m.–2 p.m.
Waiting room	All hours
Shops	6 a.m.–12 midnight
Post office	Mon.–Fri.: 8.15 a.m.–7.30 p.m.
	Sat.: 8.15 a.m.–1 p.m.

Daily trains to: Rome, Florence, Bologna, Genoa, Milan, Sicily, Venice, Brindisi.

TOURIST INFORMATION AND ADDRESSES

Apart from the one at the station, there's an office at Piazza Gesù
Nuovo (Tel. 5523328).
POST OFFICE: Via Matteotti, open Mon.–Fri.: 8.30 a.m.–7.30 p.m.,
Sat.: 8.30 a.m.–12 p.m.
AMEX: c/o Ashiba Travel, Piazza Municipio 1 (Tel. 5515303).
UK CONSULATE: Via Francesco Crispi 122 (Tel. 663 511).
US CONSULATE: Piazza della Repubblica (Tel. 660 966).
24-HOUR CHEMIST: Mattera, Via Carbonara 43.
PHONE CODE: 081.

SEEING

If you visited Pompeii or Herculaneum and were disappointed to
find none of the artefacts – or bodies – there, then visit the
NATIONAL ARCHAEOLOGICAL MUSEUM on Piazza del Museo. In this
sixteenth-century palace you'll find one of the best Graeco-Roman
collections in the world, as well as the Borgia collection of Etruscan
art. It's open mornings, except Wednesdays. The CAPODIMONTE
MUSEUM overlooks the city from its highest hill and has collections
of fine art from the fourteenth century on. The Royal Apartments
on the first floor of this former royal estate include a parlour
completely built from Capodimonte ceramics. Bus 24 takes you
there and it's closed on Mondays. Near Corso Vittorio Emanuele
III is the Vomero Hill where you find the CARTHUSIAN MONASTERY.
The NATIONAL MUSEUM is housed here, and it was the view from the
belvedere of Room 25 that inspired the saying 'See Naples and die'.
The CASTEL NUOVO was built in the late thirteenth century for
Charles I of Anjou, then rebuilt for the fifteenth-century Aragons.
Open daily at Piazza Municipio. The Neapolitans overdo everything and their over-ornate churches are a perfect example of
overkill. Look in SAN GENNARO CATHEDRAL (tours of its catacombs
at 9.30 a.m. and 12 noon), where every year St Gennaro's blood
apparently turns to liquid, SAN DOMENICO MAGGIORE and SAN
GREGORIO ARMENO.

SLEEPING

The only place near the station we suggest is at Corso Umberto 31.
Alberto Trentino costs 12,000 L per night with a 2,000 L charge for

showers. Try also Hotel Casanova, Corso Garibaldi 333 (Tel. 268 287).

The youth hostel's excellent and is at Salita della Grotta 23, Mergellina (Tel. 7612346). Go to the Margellirra stop on the underground. You can camp on the edge of the volcano crater at Camping Solfatara (Tel. 8673413). You can either take bus 152 direct, or a local train from Piazza Garibaldi (directly underneath the central station) to Pozzuoli (the end of the line) and then a walk of 850 m, mostly uphill. The train is free on Inter Rail.

EATING AND NIGHTLIFE

Pizza was born in Naples, so this is the place to find out just how far from the original the Pizzaland restaurant-chain really is. There are hundreds of cheap pizza places, and none charge more than 7,000 L for a plateful big enough for two. If you're flush, try one of the seafood restaurants down by the port in the Santa Lucia district. Renzo e Lucia on Via Tito Angelini 31/33 do good baked fish, and Caffe Osteria at Via Miroballo 14 gives good value for money. The university Mensa is on Via Mezzocanone.

There are plenty of shady bars and rip-off joints down by the port. You'll find your evening strolls being interrupted by people trying to sell you anything from cabbage-leaf Marlboros (which pass off as the real thing till you light them) to watches made from bottle lids – some of these are worth buying for the craftsmanship involved. Also the 'genuine Scotch' is sometimes only cold tea. Be warned!

• **Excursions:** The PHLEGREAN FIELDS, in the peninsula north of Naples, still has some active volcanoes you can visit. MOUNT VESUVIUS hasn't erupted since 1944, but they reckon it's due for another blow-out soon, so take the chairlift up to the crater at your peril. The Circumvesuviana line, from Stazione Vesuviana near Central Station, serves this area. It'll also take you to HERCULANEUM and POMPEII, which is not free on Inter Rail. There is a good campsite by the Villa dei Misteri station, and Camping Zeus is very convenient, cheap and friendly (no tent necessary). You can also get to Pompeii on the main Naples–Salerno line from Napoli PG (free on Inter Rail). These two towns fell foul of a Vesuvian outburst in AD 79. The latter was covered in ashes, the former with mud. Both offer unique insight into first-century Roman imperial life. From Naples it's possible to ferry over to the islands. CAPRI is the most touristy, while the Italians favour ISCHIA.

The beautiful AMALFI COAST south from Naples is a wonderful natural area of mountains and beaches; a great place to unwind after the chaos of Naples. AMALFI is a pleasant seaside town with a magnificent cathedral. The Tourist Office is at Corso delle Repubbliche Marinare 19/21. The best place to stay is the quiet fishing village of ATRANI (about a ten-minute walk). Stay at A Scalinatella, Piazza Umberto 1 (Tel. 089–871 492) for 10–15,000 L per night right near the beach. Also make sure to visit the EMERALD GROTTO about 2½ miles from Amalfi and the spectacular cliffside town of RAVELLO.

If you're heading south for Sicily, you can stop off at Salerno and head for PAESTUM where you'll find three Greek temples better than many in Greece. The bus takes an hour from Salerno.

Bari
Sailing to Greece from Brindisi? Then use the amazing free facilities at Bari. For one day you can enjoy free campsite, free buses throughout the town, free information centres, free museums, cheap meals, free luggage storage, free bikes, skateboards . . . all here for the under-thirties. Close to Brindisi for the ferry – just turn up.

Sicily

From Naples to Sicily takes about ten hours. Sicily is an interesting place to visit, and comes as a complete contrast to Italy, which is not surprising really as parts of it are nearer North Africa than mainland Italy. It's the largest island in the Mediterranean and because of its strategic position has been in the hands of just about every empire there ever was.

• **Getting there:** The standard ferry crossing is from VILLA SAN GIOVANNI to MESSINA on the train-ferry. In summer, the Rome–Sicily run gets crowded, so reserve ahead if you can. Once you're there you'll have to use the railway as your main sightseeing

medium. The services are slow and typical of the rest of the Italian
rail network. They are not, however, overwhelmingly crowded.
The buses are reasonably punctual and ususally air-conditioned.
Ignore the ferries from Naples to Catania, Syracuse and Palermo.
They're expensive and if you're on Inter Rail you'd have to pay to
get over.

Sicily: the east coast

The port town of MESSINA, founded by the Greeks in the eighth
century BC, has been rebuilt twice this century: once after the 1908
earthquake, and again after the bombing of the Second World War;
consequently, there's not *that* much to see, but if you've time to kill
waiting on a ferry, take in the following sights: the largest
ASTRONOMICAL MECHANICAL CLOCK in the world in the thirteenth-
century Norman cathedral, the church of ANNUNZIATA DEI CATA-
LANI, and the NATIONAL MUSEUM. The tourist office is on Via
Calabria Isolato 301, and there's another at the station. Half an
hour from Messina is TAORMINA, a historical resort popular with
middle-aged Italians. The GREEK THEATRE is overlooked by the
smoking live volcano of MOUNT ETNA which makes this setting for
Greek drama suitably dramatic. The PALAZZO CORVAIA, the
Sicilian parliament house dating from the fourteenth century, is in
Piazza Vittorio Emanuele, and the beach of MAZZARO can be
reached by funicular.

CATANIA hasn't been swamped by Mount Etna since 1693, so the
old town dates from the seventeenth century. At Piazza del Duomo
is the CHIERICI PALACE. From Catania you can visit Mount Etna, but
look out for a rip-off. The bus to Nicolosi seems reasonable at
around 3,800 L, but when you get there it costs 28,000 L in the
four-wheel drive buses (the only vehicles allowed) to get any further
up the mountain. Then you have to hire boots and a coat and even
then you only get to within 400 metres of the crater. SIRACUSA is a
strange mixture of ancient Greece and Rome. This was once as
important a centre as Rome or Athens and there are plenty of
archaeological sites to back this up. The ARCHAEOLOGICAL MUSEUM
is at Piazza del Duomo and the remains are behind the present city.

The GREEK THEATRE here is considered the best of its kind in the world. Opposite the theatre is the altar used for public sacrifices; a short walk takes you to the ROMAN AMPHITHEATRE from the fourth century BC. Tourist information is at Via San Sebastiano 43, and the youth hostel's at 45 Via Epipoli (Tel. 0931–711118). For pensions, try Centrale (Tel. 0931–60258) at the station, or Gran Bretagna, Via Savoia 21 (Tel. 0931–68765).

. Agrigento has frequent train services to other parts of Sicily. The main town is 8 km from the sea, where there is a resort called San Leone if you want to do the tourist bit. This hillside town is the site of the VALLEY OF TEMPLES, a collection of columns and temples dating from the sixth and fifth centuries BC. The tourist office is at Viale della Vittoria 255 (Tel. 0922–26926). There are two good campsites on the coast and the Nettuno has good showers and facilities and charges 3,500 L per night without tent. Take bus 10 from the station.

Palermo

The capital of Sicily has a modern north side and historic south side. The mixture of Arabic and Western is noticeable here, as can be seen in the PALACE OF THE NORMANS (see especially the PALATINE CHAPEL mosaics in the palace). Five miles away in MONREALE is the Norman CATHEDRAL with its unique biblical mosaics, and just next door the BENEDICTINE CLOISTER has a garden with medieval columns. Tourist information at Piazza Castelnuovo 35 (Tel. 091–586 122) is generally helpful. Try round the harbour for cheap rooms, or near the station on Via Roma and Via Maqueda. Albergo Pretoria, Via Maqueda 124 (Tel. 091–331 068), or Albergo Rosalia Conca d'Oro on Via Santa Rosalia 7 (Tel. 091–616 4543) are good places. Single rooms from about 18,000 L; doubles from about 28,000 L Also try Albergo Sicilia, Via Divisi 99 (Tel. 616 8460). Singles for 23,500 L.

Sardinia (Sardegna)

The mountainous and untamed island of Sardinia is about halfway between Italy and Africa's northern coast. The 1.6 million Sardinians have a strong independent streak; the region has been granted its own autonomous status. The west of the island is hilly but mainly cultivated; the east is wild and almost completely untouched. There are about half a dozen towns in all, and only a few real roads, so be prepared to rough it a bit if you're camping – but camp all the same, as this is by far the best means of accommodation on the island, and the scenery and climate are beautiful.

• **Getting there:** From Italy there are ferries to Cagliari (the capital), Olbia (on the east coast), Porto Torres (the northern tip) and Golfo Aranci (on the Costa Smeralda). The best overnight crossing is with the Tirrenia Line from Civitavecchia (one hour north of Rome) to Olbia. It costs about 21,000 L for deck class and reservations in summer are advisable. The Tirrenia office in Rome is at Via Bissolati 41.

For a daytime crossing, the state railways one from Civitavecchia to Golfo Aranci is the cheapest. A second-class reclining seat will cost 15,000 L plus. The crossing takes about nine hours, and there are five crossings a day. At the other end, there's a train waiting to take you on to Olbia or Sassari.

• **General information:** Once you're there, the rail network connects up the northern and western coasts, but that's about it. Services are slow and a bit unpredictable, but it's a lot better than hitching it round.

As far as accommodation goes, the tourist office will help you out. Good cheap pensions are thin on the ground and hotels, where they exist, expensive. In the north, youth hostels are your best bet. They're cheap (around 9,000 L) and usually on the beach. Generally, though, you can't beat camping. There are several official sites, but the true joy comes only with setting up on your own.

Avoid the restaurants – they're aimed at the wealthy tourists. Go for pizzerie, tavole calde or rosticcerie. Fish and seafood are cheap on the coast (cook them yourself), and the markets provide ample picnic food. The local wine is Vernaccia.

Sardinia: the east coast

South from Olbia is the most unspoiled region of Sardinia. There are miles of beautiful quiet beaches, and in these parts the women still wear the national costume. NUORO and ARBATAX are particularly beautiful and are the sites of archaeological remains. To get to this area, you'll need to take the train from Macomer or Cagliari. The coast around SANTA MARIA NAVARRESE is good for beaches.

Going north from Olbia you enter COSTA SMERALDA, the 'millionaires' playground'. This is the most commercialized part, though it's not yet spoilt. If you have enough time, take a trip to Porto Cervo and see some of the most expensive real estate in Italy. Don't attempt to stay the night, however, unless you don't mind paying Aga Khan prices. Golfo Aranci is in this region, and from here you really have to bus it. ARZACHENA is worth heading for, and has some very good beaches. Again not on the rail line but worth seeing is SANTA TERESA DI GALLURA on the northernmost tip of Sardinia with a view of Corsica. This little fishing village is currently becoming 'touristy', so get there before it finally succumbs.

Sardinia: the west coast

SASSARI, Sardinia's second city, has an interesting old medieval town which centres on the CATHEDRAL. There are a couple of churches and the SARDINIAN NATIONAL MUSEUM to see here, and tourist information is at Via Caprera 36. This is your best base for exploring north-west Sardinia and you'll find cheap rooms and meals along Corso Vittorio Emanuele. An hour from here is one of the prettiest towns on the island, ALGHERO. It's more Spanish than Italian as for many years this was a Catalan colony. The churches are the main sites of the town, and from here you can take a boat out to CAPO CACCIA and the Neptune Grotto: a series of underground caves, some of which are still unexplored.

Cagliari

The capital city of Sardinia. Ignore the new town and concentrate on the medieval centre, the CASTELLO, behind the harbour. The thirteenth-century CATHEDRAL is here and not far away is the ROMAN AMPHITHEATRE. The NATIONAL ARCHAEOLOGICAL MUSEUM (closed Mondays, open 9 a.m.–2 p.m. and 3.30 p.m.–6.30 p.m. Fri. and Sat., Sun.: 9 a.m.–1 p.m.) is famous for its collection of 'Nuraghic bronzes', and its Punic-Roman section. Tourist information is at Piazza Deffenu 9 (Tel. 663 207), and for cheap beds and meals try the streets between Corso Vittorio Emanuele and Via Roma.

Malta

If you're near to Naples, Calabria or Catania and fancy an island break which will steep you in history, a wonderful climate and won't break the bank, take a ferry over to the small country of Malta. Ferries are operated by the Tirrenia Navigation Co. and the Gozo Channel Co. and operate from Syracuse to Malta three times a week at a cost of around 17 Maltese pounds one way. There is also a daily catamaran service from Syracuse, Catania and Taormina/Naxos.

The island's main centres are Valletta, Sliema, Mdina and Rabat, while the little neighbouring island of Gozo also begs a visit as a day's excursion. The Youth Hostel Association on Malta ensures accommodation is no problem with cheap beds in all the main centres (average LM 1–2, which is around half-price; but you *must* show your 'Europe by Train' to qualify). Food too is good and cheap, and though the nightlife is tame by northern European standards the island has more than enough charm and colour to compensate for this.

The capital, VALLETTA, has as its not-to-be-missed-sights: the GRAND HARBOUR, which dates back to the days when Malta was the HQ for the Knights of St John in the sixteenth century; the GRAND

MASTERS' PALACE; ST JOHN'S CO-CATHEDRAL; the PALAZZO PARISIO, home to Napoleon in 1798; the UPPER BARRACCA, from where the view over the Grand Harbour and the FORTRESS OF ST ANGELO is breathtaking, and the eight Hostels of the Knights of St John – the AUBERGES. Tourist info is at 1 City Gate Arcade, Valletta (Tel. 227747). Open Mon.–Fri.: 9.30 a.m.–1 p.m., 3 p.m.–6 p.m., Sat.: 9.30 a.m.–12 p.m.

Seven miles from Valletta is the beautiful ancient capital of MDINA. See the MDINA GATE, the VILHENA PALACE, CASA INGUANEZ, the incredible baroque CATHEDRAL, the NORMAN HOUSE and the CHURCH OF THE ANNUNCIATION. Youth hostels to base yourself at are in PACEVILLE at 30b Wilga Street (bus 67); in PAWLA: 17 Tal-Borg Street (buses 1, 2, 3, 4, 5) (Tel. 29361); in GHAJNSIELEM: 21a Cordina Street on Gozo (book through the Pawla hostel). The hostels are clean, comfortable and undoubtedly the best places to stay in Malta. There are no opening and closing times (you are given a key) but there is a night-time curfew. This applies to all hostels. Family rooms are available and though preference is given to the under-30s, others can still get in.

Valletta abounds in cheap eating places. In SLIEMA, try the Magic Kiosk, St Anne's Square. To sample some freshly caught fish take the bus to the south-east coast village of MARSAXLOKK and eat in Hunter's Tower Restaurant. On Gozo there's a treat in store at Auberge Napoleon.

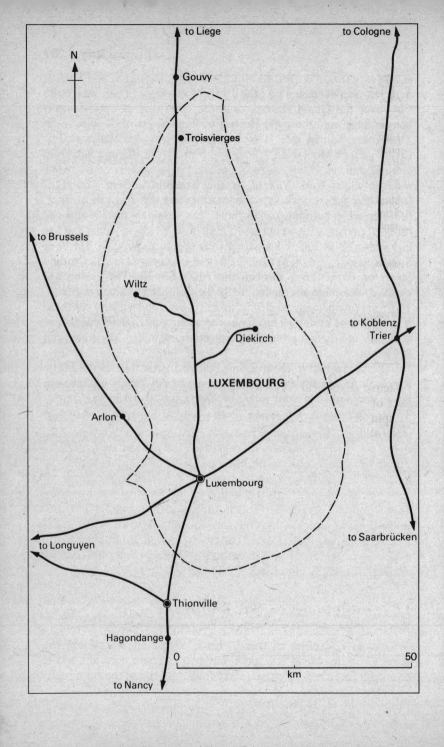

LUXEMBOURG

Entry requirements	Passport
Population	374,000
Capital	Luxembourg City (pop.: 100,000)
Currency	Luxembourg Franc (interchangeable with the Belgian but not vice versa)
	£1 = approx. 60.45 fr.
Political system	Constitutional Monarchy
Religion	Roman Catholic
Languages	Officially French although German and Letzeburgesch (the people's language) is spoken by everyone. English is widely spoken.
Public holidays	1 Jan.; 14 Feb.; Easter Sunday and Monday; 1 May; Ascension Day; Whit Monday; 23 June; Assumption Day; All Saints Day; 25, 26 Dec.
International dialling codes	From UK: 010 + 352 + number
	From USA: 011 + 352 + number
	To UK: 00 + 44 + number
	To USA: 00 + 1 + number

Luxembourg provides a welcome break from any train. The greater part of its 999 square miles is heavily wooded and makes ideal camping and hiking country. During the medieval period it was four times the size, and its royal house was so important that four of its members were elected as emperors of the Holy Roman Empire. All this changed in 1443 when Philip the Good of Burgundy seized the city and added it to his other investment, the Netherlands. It subsequently passed into the hands of the Spanish and Austrian Habsburgs, and finally the French. Independence came in 1815, and despite being overrun by Germany in both World Wars, it has managed to survive intact. Today its low unemployment and declining birthrate make Luxembourg a very prosperous country with a remarkably high GNP for its size.

LUXEMBOURG NATIONAL RAILWAYS
(Société Nationale des Chemins de Fer Luxembourgeois, CFL)

With only 210 miles of track, this is the smallest national rail network in the world – it takes only two hours to cross the whole country. There are, however, sixty-four stations, so the train really can take you to even the most obscure corners, and there are no supplements to worry about. CFL also run many bus services on which Inter Rail passes are valid. Network tickets are available for 1 day, 5 days or 1 month for 2nd class travel on all lines of the Luxembourg railway and bus system. Prices are 239 fr., 724 fr., and 1,923 fr. respectively.

TRAIN INFORMATION

For information on international trains, go to the Rail Tour Office where English is spoken. If there's a queue, or it's a simple question, look for the information officers wearing yellow capbands.

• **Reservations:** It's not possible to reserve on internal trains, and on internationals it's optional, but must be done twenty-four hours in advance. Luxembourg is connected to the German and French railways' computer, so it's possible to reserve sleepers and couchettes in these countries.

TOURIST INFORMATION

Apart from the National Tourist Office to the right of the main station in Luxembourg there are local offices (Syndicats d'Initiative) scattered throughout the country. Most open at 8 a.m. and shut at 6 p.m. with a two-hour lunch break.

• **ISIC bonuses:** Some museums and galleries half price.

• **Money matters:** 1 Luxembourg franc (fr.) = 100 centimes. Banking hours are Mon.–Fri.: 9 a.m.–12 noon and 1.30 p.m.–4.30 p.m., though some banks are open earlier, longer or do not close for lunch. The Luxembourg franc is interchangeable with the Belgian franc, but you're best to change them before leaving the country.

• **Post offices:** Open Mon.–Fri.: 9 a.m.–5 p.m. Station branch open 6 a.m.–8 p.m.

• **Shops and museums:** Vary in their times of opening. Tue.–Fri.: 9 a.m.–12 noon and 2 p.m.–6 p.m. seems to be the general rule. Some museums and shops shut on Mondays.

SLEEPING

Pick up the tourist board's excellent free guide on accommodation at the main office next to the station. This lists prices and facilities for all Luxembourg's hotels and pensions. If you're thinking about camping, ask for the free folder giving all the campsites and prices. There are twelve youth hostels for which you need IYHF membership, charging 210 fr. (170 fr. for under 26s) per night and 80 fr. more for breakfast. The Luxembourg City youth hostel costs an additional 40 fr. per night. In addition, there are a large number of campsites throughout the country, a free list of which is available from the national tourist office. Expect to pay from 100 fr. per tent plus a further 80/90 fr. per person.

EATING AND NIGHTLIFE

Dishes have a strong French flavour and specialities include Ardennes ham which you can pick up at supermarkets. Check up with the tourist offices for what's happening in the week ahead.

Luxembourg City

The old part of this 1,000-year-old city is on a high plateau overlooking cliffs, and the valleys of the Alzette River. Around the edge of the plateau is the PROMENADE DE LA CORNICHE which offers spectacular views over the city. Just below the promenade are the CASEMATES, thirteen miles of connecting underground passages from the times when this area was a fortress. You can explore these tunnels: enter from Place de la Constitution or from 'Bock' – fortress reconstruction. Also in the old town is the Renaissance GRAND DUCAL PALACE, the seventeenth-century CATHEDRAL OF NOTRE DAME and the NATIONAL MUSEUM on Fish Market Place (closed Mondays). If you've ever wondered what Radio Luxembourg looks like, the station is situated in a public park, five minutes' walk from Place d'Armes. See also the EUROPEAN CENTRE, located in the western suburbs and the home of a number of European agencies including the Supreme Court of the EEC, the

General Secretariat of the European Parliament and others. After Brussels, Luxembourg can be regarded as the most 'European' of European cities.

STATION FACILITIES

	GARE DE LUXEMBOURG
Train information	7 a.m.–8 p.m.
	(Tel. 492424)
Reservations	7 a.m.–7.30 p.m. (Tel. 4990573)
Tourist information	Mon.–Fri.: 9 a.m.–7.30 p.m. summer,
	9 a.m.–12 noon, 2 p.m.–6.30 p.m. winter
	Sat.: 9 a.m.–12 noon
	(in Luxair building)
Foreign exchange	Mon.–Sat.: 8.30 a.m.–9 p.m.
	Sun.: 9 a.m.–9 p.m.
Left-luggage lockers	No access 1.30 a.m.–4 a.m. (60 fr.)
Left-luggage store	No access 1.30 a.m.–4 a.m.
Bar, Buffet	8 a.m.–7 p.m.
Restaurant	Mon.–Fri.: 12 noon–3 p.m.
	5 a.m.–12 midnight
Shops	6.30 a.m.–8 p.m.
Bath, Shower	6 a.m.–9.30 p.m.
Waiting room	All hours (ticket required)
Post office	Across from station
Station shuts	1.30 a.m.–4 a.m.

Daily trains to: Brussels, Strasbourg, Basel, Zürich, Milan, Koblenz, Paris.

TOURIST INFORMATION AND ADDRESSES

Next to the station is the Luxair Terminal building. In summer it opens 9 a.m.–7.30 p.m., 9 a.m.–12 p.m. and 2 p.m.–6.30 p.m. the rest of the year, and hands out free information on all Luxembourg, as well as handling accommodation enquiries. The Tourist Information Centre is at Place d'Armes (Tel. 22809), open 9 a.m.–7 p.m. summer, 9 a.m.–1 p.m. and 2 p.m.–6 p.m. winter.
POST OFFICE: 38 Place de la Gare. Mon.–Sat.: 6 a.m.–10 p.m. Post restante till 8 p.m.

LUXEMBOURG STUDENT TRAVEL (TEJ): Voyage SOTOUR, 17 Place du Théâtre (Tel. 22673 or 46514), open Mon.–Fri.: 8 a.m.–6 p.m., Sat.: 10 a.m.–4 p.m.
24-HOUR CHEMIST: Tel. 012.
UK EMBASSY: 14 Boulevard Roosevelt (Tel. 29864).
US EMBASSY: 22 Bd E. Servais (Tel. 460123).
AMEX: 6–8 rue Origer (Tel. 496041).

SLEEPING

Stay close to the station for cheap hotels. Rue Joseph Junck is a safe bet, as is rue de la Liberté. Doubles average about 1,800 fr., but Axe, 34 rue J. Junck (Tel. 490953), has rooms for less. Hotel Delta, 74–78 rue A. Fischer (Tel. 493096), Hotel Windsor, 7 rue du Strasbourg and Bangkok Oriental, 19 Rue de Strasbourg (Tel. 60776) have cheapish doubles and triples. The youth hostel is good but is a bit out of town, although the scenery on the bus ride is worth the 10-minute trip. It can sometimes be full of adolescent groups and there is a 9 a.m. eviction, but apart from that it is comfortable and beautifully located. Take bus 9 from the station. The fare is about 30 fr. and it will cost you the same for your rucksack. If you don't fancy paying the extra you can walk through the town to it in half an hour and check out the places you want to come back to at night. The address is 2 rue du Fort Olisy (Tel. 26889).

Kockelscheuer Camping, 22 route de Bettembourg (Tel. 471815) is a 25–30-minute walk from the station. Prices from 100 fr. per tent and 90 fr. per person.

EATING AND NIGHTLIFE

Food isn't terribly cheap, so use the supermarkets and bakeries near the station. You'll find the usual McDonald's-type fast food places in this area as well. Try the tourist menu at Le Papillon, 9 rue Origer. Place d'Armes is where to head to in the evenings. People generally congregate here and often there are free concerts in the square. There are also fast food restaurants in this part of town and McDonald's opened a new branch recently right beside the bandstand. 'La Semaine à Luxembourg' is the 'what's on' and is available from tourist information.

The Countryside/Provincial Luxembourg

On the banks of the River Sauer lies the medieval village of ECHTERNACH. Though badly damaged in the Second World War (that's Germany just across the river) it has been well restored now, and the 1328 TOWN HALL is as good as ever. Echternach has a big International Music Festival each June. The BENEDICTINE ABBEY has some impressive frescoes and stained-glass windows. There's a youth hostel at 9 rue André Duchscher (Tel. 72158) or try Hotel Le Petit Poète, 13 Place du Marché (Tel. 72072). Doubles from about 1,200 fr. It's right in the centre of town. Just a few minutes north of Echternach is a small wedge of a hiker's paradise: LITTLE SWITZER-LAND. This is the Moellerdall section of the Ardennes, and a walk through the steep gorges and forest makes an exhilarating hour or so. In the northernmost part of the Ardennes is TROISVIERGES, the heart of hiking country. The Clerve Valley leads to CLERVAUX, about an hour on the line from Luxembourg City. The castles of BOURSCHEID and CLERVAUX, both eleventh-century and in good repair, are here in fairytale settings. There are permanent exhibitions in Clervaux Castle, including Steichen's 'Family of Man' collection. Admission 40 fr. The tourist office at Clervaux is next to the Castle (Tel. 92072). They'll help you find a bed. Not on the railway, but definitely worth a visit, is VIANDEN, with its cobbled streets and its magnificent castle (the biggest west of the Rhine). This was the cradle of the Grand-Ducal dynasty and dates back to the ninth century. Try the chairlift, and also the open-air swimming pool with impressive views over the castle. The newly restored youth hostel is at 3 Montée du Château (Tel. 84177), and the tourist office is in the Victor Hugo House, close by the bridge (Tel. 84257, closed 12 noon–2 p.m.).

MOROCCO

Entry requirements	Passport
Population	22,100,000
Capital	Rabat-Salé (pop.: 925,000)
Currency	Dirham
	£1 = approx. 15.4 dh.
Political system	Constitutional Monarchy
Religion	Muslim
Languages	Arabic (French and Spanish also official languages) (English spoken in tourist towns)
Public holidays	1, 11 Jan.; 1st of Moharram (moveable); 3 March; Moulid El Nabi (moveable); 1 May; Aid Es Seghir; 6 Nov.; 18 Nov.; Aid El Kebir (moveable).
International dialling codes	From UK: 010 + 212 + number
	From USA: 011 + 212 + number
	To UK: 00 + 44 + number
	To USA: 00 + 1 + number
Eurotrain office	112 avenue d'Espagne, Tangier (Tel. 09–35540)

After Europe, Morocco comes as a bit of a culture shock: everything appears alien, exotic and exciting, and if it's a 'far away from home' feeling you're after, this is your best destination. The further south you travel, the more 'foreign' things will appear – get down to Marrakesh if you possibly can to sample the vibrant colours, new smells and tastes, and baking hot sun of this Arab land. Recently the rail network has been vastly improved and travelling around the country is relatively trouble-free. Remember that Morocco is a Muslim country, therefore women should dress and act accordingly when travelling in more remote areas. For many Eurorailers Morocco is the highlight of their trip. It is certainly a country which makes a tremendous impression on you, and is a place which everyone 'doing Europe' should make an effort to get to in order to glimpse a non-European lifestyle. Most of Morocco was a French protectorate between 1912 and 1956, except for the north which was Spanish. The lowland areas, where the trains run, are the richest and most populous parts of Morocco.

• **Getting there:** There are various ferries from Spain to Tangier and Ceuta in Morocco, with the Algeciras–Ceuta being the shortest and cheapest crossing, but as it's not on the railway you'll do best to use the Algeciras–Tangier crossing. It costs about 2,100 pesetas and unless you've an Inter Rail or Eurail there are no reductions. Don't rely on the information posted in Algeciras Ferry Terminal; ask. Avoid any dealings in drugs *completely*. The border guards do not look kindly on anyone caught in possession.

MOROCCAN RAILWAYS
(Office National des Chemins de Fer, ONCF)

Recently there has been a big improvement in Moroccan trains, although they still do not run as frequently as you might wish. The Inter Rail card is valid here and the railway runs to the main tourist towns and regions. There are three classes on the trains: first, second and 'Economique'. Your Inter Rail or BIJ ticket entitles you to use the second-class facilities. It is well worth paying the supplement of around £2 to travel in an air-conditioned carriage. The rail network runs east from Marrakesh to Casablanca and Rabat, then splits at Sidi Kacem, one line going north to Tangier, the other to Oujda and over the border to Algeria. You can even charter a train!

• **Inter Rail bonuses:** The Algeciras–Tangier crossing has 30 per cent discount for Inter Rail, 20 per cent discount for Eurail.

• **Rover tickets:** The Carte d'Abonnement is valid for unlimited travel for one month on all trains but the fast TNR services. It costs 1,146 dh. for first-class and 767 dh. for second.

TRAIN INFORMATION

You'll find the odd official who speaks pidgin English, but in smaller places you'll have to resort to French.

• **Reservations:** Not compulsory, but not a bad idea if you're on a long haul in peak season.

• **Night travel:** Sleeping cars are first class only and come in singles or doubles. They're fairly expensive so unless you're feeling particularly delicate, try and schedule your travelling for daytime. Second class cars are often very full at night.

TOURIST INFORMATION

Most towns have both a tourist office and a Syndicat d'Initiative. The tourist office should be your first port of call as they have information on all of Morocco, and will also help find a bed if necessary. When you're organized, make your way back to the Syndicat d'Initiative which has leaflets on local sights, etc. Most offices have leaflets on all the places you are likely to visit in Morocco, so stock up at the first one you come to.

A word of warning: unofficial guides (mostly young boys) will pester you with their dubious services. A good impersonation of Finnish usually puts them off your track. Hustlers are another problem: they'll approach you in the medina and kasbah (old fortress), be incredibly friendly, and be conversant in a dozen languages. Ignore and avoid them. Finally, when you're at the sights don't feel obliged to accept the custodian's offer of a guided tour or feel it necessary to give him a tip, as he is already paid by the government and does very well from other tourists. If you wear contact lenses, bear in mind that it can be very dusty, and you may be more comfortable wearing glasses if you have them.

• **Money matters:** 1 dirham (dh.) = 100 francs.
Banking hours are Mon.–Fri.: 8.30 a.m.–11.30 a.m., 3 p.m.–5.30 p.m. Banks charge no commission and have the same rate of exchange everywhere. Buy dirhams in advance if arriving outside banking hours. Keep your receipts as you will probably be asked to produce them when changing dirhams back, and remember to use banks – the rate on the boat back to Spain is a rip-off.

• **Post offices:** Open Mon.–Sat.: 8.30 a.m.–12 noon, 2.30 p.m.–6 p.m. (Closed Sat. p.m.)

• **Shops:** Open Mon.–Sat.: 8.30 a.m.–12 noon, 2 p.m.–6.30 p.m. Bargain like mad wherever you go in the markets (souks), even when you see the 'prix fixe' sign. Haggling is a way of life here and, unless you manage to get the price down by at least 50 per cent, consider yourself a failure. Remember: you can never start low enough. Check with the Syndicats for opening times of museums and other sights.

SLEEPING

Morocco is a country where it pays dividends to be tough. You can live off next to nothing if you don't mind roughing it a bit. Camping and youth hostelling are very cheap, as little as 15 dh. a night under canvas or 20 dh. in a hostel dormitory, but you're not guaranteed central locations or Swiss conditions. The medina hotels/pensions offer the most central and colourful locations and are usually cheaper than the places in the new areas of town. Hotels are graded from one to five stars and there are fixed maximum prices for each category. You usually pay by the room, so doubling up with friends can bring the unit cost of a room down. If you find the water is hot at any time of day, seize the chance for a shower while you can (these usually cost 5–8 dh.) as the plumbing here is decidedly erratic. As far as public toilets go, always carry your own loo paper.

EATING AND NIGHTLIFE

If you've an iron stomach, take full advantage of it in Morocco by eating in the kasbahs and from shishkebab stands. Most decent restaurants offer a good selection of Moroccan dishes. Try harira, a rich soup of chicken and spices, followed by touojen (lamb or chicken stew) or couscous, Morocco's most famous dish (made from semolina, with lamb, fish or chicken). If you like something sweet to finish the meal, ask for kab el ghzal (almond pastries) and some mint tea. Don't take chances with tap water; drink only mineral water, which you have to ask for by brand name. You can usually trust Sidi Ali or Sidi Harazem brands. Often it is difficult in the more remote places to find meals during the day, so eat well at night; and don't expect alcohol to be widely available. The local Syndicat will let you know where the nearest belly-dancer performs and what's happening on the disco scene.

Tangier

This isn't the best Morocco has to offer, but if you're on a day trip from Spain, it'll show you some of the exotic and colourful differences between Europe and North Africa. As Tangier receives more than its fair share of tourists, be particularly on your guard for hustlers. Many readers feel the best advice on Tangier is to head straight for the rail station and take the first train out. This is primarily because of the excessive amount of hassle one experiences here, so be warned.

The GRAND SOCCO connects the medina and the new town. Tourist information (Tel. 09–32996) is at Boulevard Pasteur (open Mon.–Fri.: 9 a.m.–3 p.m. in summer, otherwise 8.30 a.m.–12 p.m. and 2.30 p.m.–6.30 p.m.), as is the post office. In the medina, the rue Mokhtar Ahardan is where to look for cheap hotels and restaurants. The Pensione Palace (Tel. 09–39248) is at No. 2 and costs about 30 dh. per person. If you really want to spoil yourself, head for the Grand Hotel Villa de France, which overlooks the town. In addition to the four-star view (Noel Coward used to stay here), you can expect an equally superb double room and service for about 180 dh. The beaches and nightlife are both good, though single girls on the beach are in for a hard time.

If you are leaving the country from here, remember to turn up early for the boat as you will end up having to queue for several things like passport control, forms for passport control, customs and – finally – the boat itself. To buy a discounted ferry ticket back to Algeciras you must produce a photocopy of your Inter Rail/Eurail Pass (the Cafe Terminal across from the main station will do one cheaply). The Eurotrain office is at 112 avenue d'Espagne (Tel. 09–35540).

Rabat

From Tangier to the capital of Morocco – Rabat – is about five hours on the main line. This is a clean, organized and structured city. It has numerous parks and gardens, and most of the town is new and affluent by Moroccan standards. There is a kasbah in the old town but the medina lacks atmosphere, and you feel you're back in Europe a lot of the time.

TOURIST INFORMATION AND ADDRESSES

TOURIST INFORMATION: 22 rue el Jazair (Tel. 21252) or Syndicat d'Initiative at rue Patrice Lumumba (Tel. 23272), which is nearer the station and is open from 8.30 a.m.–6.30 p.m. every day in season.

POST OFFICE: Avenue Mohammed V. Open Mon.–Fri.: 8 a.m.–noon; 2 p.m.–6.45 p.m., Sat.: 8.30 a.m.–12 noon.

AMEX: In Rabat Hilton (Tel. 72151). Take bus for Agdal.

UK EMBASSY: 17 Boulevard Tour Hassan (Tel. 20905).

US EMBASSY: 2 Avenue de Marrakesh (Tel. 66265).

CANADIAN EMBASSY: 13 Zankat Joafar Essodik, Agdal (Tel. 71376).

PHONE CODE: 07.

SEEING

The TOUR HASSAN minaret in the twelfth-century mosque and the MAUSOLEUM OF MOHAMMED V are close to each other, and about a mile's walk away is the CHELLAH, an Arab necropolis built in the old Roman section of Rabat called SALA COLONIA. There are gardens here that are ideal for a picnic. The OUDAIAS KASBAH fortress has another beautiful garden, a Moorish café, and the MUSEUM OF MOROCCAN HANDICRAFTS: carpets, musical instruments, furniture, etc. (open 8 a.m.–12 noon, 2 p.m.–6 p.m., closed Tuesday and Saturday p.m.). The ROYAL PALACE is also located here in the capital, though it dates only from the 1950s.

SLEEPING, EATING AND NIGHTLIFE

The youth hostel on 43 Rue Marassa (Tel. 25769) is cheap but not great. For camping, take bus 6 or 24 to Salé terminal and follow the signs for Camping Municipal. For cheap hotels, try the Hotel France which is on the edge of the Medina and costs around 50 dh. for a clean double with washing facilities (cold water, as in most cheap Moroccan hotels!). Alternatively, in the medina, try Hotel Marrakesh, rue Sebbahi (Tel. 27703). Enter the medina on Avenue Mohammed V and turn right three blocks later: singles around 30 dh. – good value. The medina is also the place for cheap eats. There are plenty of stalls and restaurants, with the Restaurant El Bahia on Avenue Hassan II offering good food at budget prices. It's located to your right as you approach the medina from Avenue

Mohammed V. For an evening stroll, walk round the Oudaias Kasbah as the sun is sinking.

Casablanca

This is the largest, and in many ways the least attractive, of Morocco's towns. With over two million inhabitants and a busy port, Casablanca is a crowded, modern and somewhat squalid city, and the only thing romantic about it is its name and Play-it-again-Sam image. Take the train to the Port Station for the medina, beaches etc, but be careful taking photographs as some of this is a sensitive military area. Casablanca has got some character and among its sights are the GREAT MOSQUE, neo-Moorish public buildings round the PLACE DES NATIONS UNIES and the MAHAKMA (regional courts). The journey south to Casablanca from Tangier is no problem as it involves the best trains in Morocco; however, if you're going further south make sure you have supplies with you as the buffets are awful. Also, if you can afford it, pay the supplement from second to first class (if you're travelling in peak season). Still, you shouldn't judge Morocco by Casablanca. Travel through to Fez or Marrakesh for a more representative image.

Marrakesh

This red-ochre city on the edge of the Sahara desert is what you expect Morocco to be like: vibrant markets with snake-charmers, fortune-tellers and acrobats; palm trees; remains from ancient dynasties, and incredible midday temperatures of around 105°F (August maximum).

On arrival get hold of a 'petit taxi' (not a regular one – they cost double) and haggle to fix a price for a ride to the Djemma el Fna. Or you can save 10 dh. and take a 3 or 6 bus from outside the station. You'll be dropped off in the city's main square, and from there it's no problem finding a cheap hotel bed.

TOURIST INFORMATION AND ADDRESSES

TOURIST OFFICE: Place Abdel Moumen ben Ali on Avenue Mohammed V (Tel. 30258). English spoken. Ask for a map and a list of
accommodation (though it doesn't list the real cheapies). Open
Mon.–Fri.: 8.30 a.m.–12 noon, 2.30 p.m.–6.30 p.m. Sat.: 8.30
a.m.–12.30 p.m. If you have already picked up leaflets on the city
elsewhere, don't bother making the one-mile trek here unless
you're desperate for them to book an hotel for you.
POST OFFICE: Place du 16 Novembre, off Avenue Mohammed V.
Open Mon.–Fri.: 8.30 a.m.–12.15 p.m. and 2.30 p.m.–6.45 p.m.
AMEX: c/o Voyages Schwartz, rue Mauritania, 2nd floor (Tel.
32831). Open Mon.–Fri.: 8.30 a.m.–12.30 p.m., 3 p.m.–6.30 p.m.
CHEMIST: Near Hotel Marrakesh, Place de la Liberté. Open till 10
p.m.
PHONE CODE: 04.

SEEING

The DJEMMA EL FNA (Assembly of the Dead) is the showpiece of
Marrakesh. This square is the hub of life of the city. In daytime it's a
busy colourful market, and at night the street artists arrive. (Be
particularly careful of your valuables here.) The medina is particularly lively and there are various photogenic markets like the ones
for musical instruments or wool dyers. The old theological school,
BEN YOUSSEF MEDERSA, has some fine marbles, mosaics and
wood-carvings, and the pale green twelfth-century minaret of the
KOUTOUBIA MOSQUE is Morocco's best example. the BAHIA PALACE
is nineteenth-century and the PALACE EL BEDI is eighteenth-century.
The SAADI MAUSOLEUM contains the remains of various sultans and
is free, though the guide expects a tip. The bus station is at Bab
Doukkala. Buses to the beach leave from here, but they travel at a
relaxed pace.

SLEEPING, EATING AND NIGHTLIFE

Head for the Djemma el Fna area for cheap hotels and restaurants.
Hôtel de France, Hôtel Cecil or Hôtel des Amis have doubles for
about 45 dh. The youth hostel's good by Moroccan standards. It's
near the station on Route Al Jahidh, Quartier Industriel (Tel.
44713); it closes 9 a.m.–2 p.m. and after 10 p.m. Further along the

same street is the campsite – Camping Caravanning – not too good. Café-Restaurant Oriental at 33 rue Bab Abnaou (off the Djemma el Fna) do good menus at reasonable prices.

Meknes

On the eastern line to Fez and the Algerian border, and 4½ hours from Tangier, lies the imperial city of Meknes. From the station, turn left for the medina, hotels and the old town. Tourist information is at Place Administrative (Tel. 05–21286) and is open Mon.–Fri.: 8 a.m.–2 p.m.; Sat.: 8.30 a.m.–12 noon, 3 p.m.–6 p.m. English is spoken, and some literature is available. MANSOUR, the pavilion where the seventeenth-century Sultan Moulay Ismail received ambassadors, is up here. There are UNDERGROUND CAVES where the Sultan's slaves were kept which can be viewed if you ask the guards nicely. The elaborate TOMB of Moulay Ismail is further up on the right. The mosque in which the tomb is located is the only one in the country to admit non-Muslims. Dress appropriately so as not to cause offence. The DAR JAMAI PALACE is now a museum. The theological school BOU INANIA is the elaborate fourteenth-century building in the medina.

SLEEPING, EATING AND NIGHTLIFE

Around Place el Hédime there are quite a few cheap hotels, but if you don't fancy these the best alternative is camping. The best site is Camping Esplanade near the Heri, on the other side of the medina from the tomb of Moulay Ismail. The youth hostel's a dead loss, but if you're desperate it's at Boulevard Okba Ben Nafii (Tel. 05–24698) (near Hôtel Transatlantique). For food, rue Dar Smen and Avenue de Rouamzine are the best ideas. Moroccan-style nightlife is not hard to find in Meknes.

Fez (Fes)

The oldest imperial city in Morocco is today considered her cultural and intellectual centre. The huge medina here is unmatched elsewhere in North Africa. You could easily spend days in it; the colours, smells, filth and constant arguments are as endless as the memories you will keep of Fez.

TOURIST INFORMATION AND ADDRESSES

TOURIST OFFICE: Avenue Hassan II (Tel. 23460). Open Mon.–Sat.: 9 a.m.–3 p.m. Take rue Chenguit, turn left at Place Kennedy, and left on to Hassan II.
POST OFFICE: On Avenue Hassan II there are three. Open Mon.–Fri.: 7 a.m.–2.30 p.m. in summer, otherwise 8.30 a.m.–6.45 p.m.
BUS STATION: CTM, Boulevard Mohammed V (Tel. 22041) with buses to Rabat, Casablanca, Marrakesh, Meknes, and Tangier. Private buses from Gare Routière in Bab Boujeloud.
PHONE CODE: 06.

SEEING

Expect to get lost in Fez. The MEDINA is so sprawling and unstructured it's inevitable, and there's no map to help you out. Refuse the offer of a guide unless you can get him down to 15 dh. or so. There are countless souks in the medina to look at, but only ferret out the tannery one if you've an iron stomach. The medina is the location of the tenth-century minaret of the KAROUIYNE MOSQUE, whose university claims to be the oldest in the world, and the theological schools of ATTARINE and BOU INANIA.

SLEEPING, EATING AND NIGHTLIFE

Round Bab Boujeloud you'll find a few cheap (and fairly nasty) hotels with doubles for 50–60 dh. The youth hostel on 18 rue Abdeslam Serghini (Tel. 24085) is good value and, by Fez standards, very clean and comfortable. Reach it by walking six blocks down from the tourist office along Boulevard Chefchaouni, turn left to street below and look for sign. Follow the arrows from

Place Mohammed V, it is about 5 km from the station. For a hotel try the Excelsior at 107 Rue Larbi el Kaghat (Tel. 25602).

Bab Boujeloud and the medina are the cheap eating districts. The youth hostel has a kitchen, so you could buy food there and cook it yourself (watch the meat). Avoid the local delicacy, bisteela (which is pigeon, vegetables and nuts, covered in sweet pastry!). An evening stroll in the old Jewish quarter is more rewarding than the formal entertainments you'll find.

Off-the-track places

Many of Morocco's best places are not on the railway, so buses are the only answer. TETUAN, 1½ hours away from Tangier (cost about 30 dh.), is a relatively unspoilt town with a fascinating medina – eat there and try round Place Hassan II for rooms. ASNI is thirty miles from Marrakesh and buses leave hourly from the station. It's more fun to share a taxi with several others and a full load should mean your share of the fare comes to between 10–15 dh. This is in the HIGH ATLAS mountain region in the Sahara. IMLIL, accessible by 'taxi' (communal truck), is even more spectacular. This is surrounded by the mountains and you can start a climb of MOUNT TOUBKAL (13,671 feet) from here. The town's refuge is your best bet for a bed, and it has cooking facilities. Don't attempt the mountain unless you're experienced and well equipped.

ESSAOUIRA is a Berber town on the south coast. If you're tired out with travelling and need a break before the long haul back home, sleep here free on the beaches and take advantage of this opportunity to share in a very un-European culture and lifestyle. Take a leisurely walk up to the eighteenth-century Moorish fortress (the SKALA) at sunset. The tourist office is on Porte Portugaise.

NETHERLANDS

Entry requirements	Passport
Population	14,700,000 +
Capital	Amsterdam (pop.: 1,000,000), though The Hague (pop.: 500,000) is the political capital
Currency	Guilder (Florin)
	£1 = approx. f. 3.18
Political system	Constitutional Monarchy
Religions	Protestant and Roman Catholic
Language	Dutch (English widely spoken in cities)
Public holidays	1 Jan.; Good Friday; Easter Monday; 30 Apr.; Ascension Day; Whit Monday; 25, 26 Dec.
International dialling codes	From UK: 010 + 31 + number
	From USA: 011 + 31 + number
	To UK: 10 + 44 + number
	To USA: 10 + 1 + number
Eurotrain office	Schipholweg 101, NL–2316XC Leiden (Tel. 071–253 333)

Most of Holland's major cities are concentrated in the flat Protestant west where one has visions of windmills, tulips and clogs. However, not all of Holland is like this; the south is very different: the land is not all flat, and many of the people are Catholic and much more like the French in many respects.

Under the Burgundians and the Habsburgs, Holland was politically linked to Belgium to form the Netherlands (lowlands). Then the Spanish King Philip II started to levy heavy taxes to pay for his army, fighting for the Catholic cause in Europe. As the northern Netherlands had mostly become Protestant by this time, you can imagine this didn't go down too well. Philip tried to smooth things over by sending in Spanish governors. This was the last straw for the Dutch who, under William of Orange, fought the Eighty Years War against the Spanish, emerging as an independent country in 1648.

After this, the Dutch really got it together for the remainder of the seventeenth century and showed the rest of Europe a thing or two about seafaring and commerce. At the same time, Rembrandt *et al.* were hard at work creating the Dutch golden age of arts and science. Symbolically, Holland's eclipse by Britain in the eighteenth century was begun by William III moving across to England to share the throne with Mary. After the Napoleonic Wars and French domination, life for the Dutch gradually developed into parliamentary democracy.

NETHERLANDS RAILWAYS
(Nederlandse Spoorwegen, NS)

Dutch Railways are as trouble-free and efficient as you're likely to find anywhere in Europe. There are frequent intercity services between all parts of Holland, at least once an hour. The short distances involved mean you can see most of Holland while based at one city. Be careful not to end up on the 'stop-trains' which do just that, before connecting up to the main intercity network. Supplements are only necessary on Eurocity trains. Electric trains often consist of portions for two different destinations.

• **Eurail bonuses:** Free passage on ships of BV Rederji NACO between Enkhuisen and Staveren or vice versa between 15 May and the first week in September.

TRAIN INFORMATION

There should be no problem with language as nearly everyone speaks English. Ask at the information desk for the booklet called 'Travelling By Rail in Holland' which has a useful map with frequency times.

• **Reservations:** It's not possible to reserve seats on inland trains. Also it's not necessary to reserve seats on the international trains, despite what they might tell you at Amsterdam Train Information Office. Trains are often very full, so if the queues are small, go ahead and reserve one. If they are not, you could literally be waiting for hours in the summer to make your reservation.

• **Night travel:** There are couchettes and sleepers on international routes only. There is an all-night service between Utrecht, Amsterdam, The Hague and Rotterdam running every hour.

• **Eating on trains:** All intercities have the usual mini-bars while only international trains have diners.

• **Scenic tips:** If you're fortunate enough to be travelling at any time from March to May through the bulb fields (Bollenvelden) region (on any runs between Amsterdam, Haarlem and Leiden) you will be amply rewarded.

• **Bikes:** Holland is ideal for cycling – it's flat and there are cycle tracks everywhere. Most stations hire out bikes and give reduced rates if you show your ticket. It usually costs only about £2 per day, but often you must leave a large deposit.

• **Rover tickets:** The Rail Rover ticket is available for 1 or 7 days. The prices are £15.50 and £33.50 for second class. In addition you can buy a Public Transport Link Rover which extends the Rail Rover ticket for use on all public transport, including Amsterdam and Rotterdam Metros, but excluding KLM Airport buses. The prices are an additional £1.70 and £6.50. The new Holland Rail Pass is valid for unlimited travel for any 3 days in a 15 day period and costs £24. Supplements still need to be paid for Eurocity trains but it is valid on ordinary Netherlands Railways intercity services. The frequency of service in Holland is such that you should never need to use an international express train for a domestic journey. You can buy it before you go from Netherlands Railways, 25/28 Buckingham Gate, London SW1E 6LD (Tel. 071–630 1735). If you buy it in Holland you need to show your passport and provide a passport-size photograph.

If you are travelling as a group, consider the Multi Rover Ticket which gives 2 to 6 passengers unlimited rail travel for one day (off peak only). It costs £23 for 2 passengers to £38 for 6. The Family Rover allows travel for a family for any four days in a ten-day period; the Teenage Rover is a similar ticket for those aged 10–18. Both of these are only available in June, July and August. Finally, there is the Benelux Tourrail which gives free rail travel in Belgium, Holland and Luxembourg (including Luxembourg country buses) on 5 out of 17 days. It cannot be used with the Public Transport Link Rover and is only valid when accompanied by a passport. The card costs £43.50 for adults, £31 for ages 4–25 and 50 per cent extra for first class use.

TOURIST INFORMATION (VVV)

The local offices are run by individual towns and can be found in every town and village in Holland. They find you accommodation if required and supply you with all the information about the area. If you plan to cycle, ask for a cycle map. Unfortunately it's not always free, so inquire first.

• **ISIC bonuses:** Up to 50 per cent reduction on museums. You can get into all state museums free once you've bought your museum card (f. 15 for those under 26, f. 30 for those over) from any state museum. For further information, contact NBBS, Dom 17, Amsterdam. In the States you can buy a Culture Card from the Netherlands National Tourist Office which for around $8 gives you free museum entrances and many other bonuses.

• **Money matters:** 1 guilder (florin) (f.) = 100 cents (c.).
Banking hours are Mon.–Fri.: 9 a.m.–4 or 5 p.m.; there are also exchange offices in twenty-seven railway stations, some of which are open in the evenings and at weekends. Some VVV tourist offices also exchange money. 'Store front' style exchange shops can charge as much as 9 per cent commission, so steer clear!

• **Post offices:** Open Mon.–Fri.: 9 a.m.–5 p.m. and, in major towns, 9 a.m.–4 p.m. on Sat.

• **Shops:** In general, Mon.–Fri.: 8.30/9 a.m.–5.30/6 p.m. and on Sat.: 8.30/9 a.m.–4 p.m.

• **Museums:** Most state museums are free on Wednesday afternoon. Anyone can buy a museum card which is essential for anyone taking sightseeing at all seriously. Most museums charge about f. 5 for admission.

SLEEPING

If you're spending a lot of time in Holland, it's a good idea to ask for the tourist board's publications on camping and hotels. If you're in luck, they will also have a photocopy of all the youth hostels in Holland. No special documents are necessary on any of Holland's 2,000 or so campsites. Expect to pay about f. 15 per night. For the fifty-two youth hostels, you have to be an IYHF member; charges vary from f. 20 to f. 30, depending on whether breakfast and an evening meal are included. Student hostels are open in summer and are fairly lax as long as you look like a student. Hotels are graded on a star basis with breakfast usually included in the price. Expect to pay f. 50 minimum for a one-star single room. Fortunately, Holland has plenty of boarding houses and private houses, most of which are very relaxed; these are your best bet. The local tourist offices keep a list and will find you a place for a small commission. Things get busy in July and August in Amsterdam and other tourist centres, so try and get along early.

EATING AND NIGHTLIFE

Most of the Dutch go in for a koffietafel (sandwich lunch and coffee) which is just as well, as evening meals have a tendency to be very high in carbohydrates. The best advice is: follow their example at lunchtime. There are over twenty-six types of cheese, so there's no excuse for sticking to just Edam and Gouda. There are numerous regional specialities to sample; one of the best is groene haring (new herring) – this is salted herring roe and is surprisingly tender and savoury. Follow the example of the Dutch and eat it from the street stalls. It's at its best during the first few weeks in May and makes a welcome change from hamburgers. For your main meal in the evening, keep your eyes skinned for one of the 600 restaurants which serve the tourist menu. This is filling and cheap and is the same price everywhere, so if you like what's on it, don't waste your time looking elsewhere. If you prefer something a little more exotic, try 'rijsttafel' from one of the numerous Indonesian restaurants in most cities. The VVV offices will keep you informed as to what's going on locally. In the larger cities there are plenty of nightclubs and discos, but expect to pay out quite a bit. Cinemas always show films in the original language with Dutch subtitles. Prices usually start at about f. 15 and performances begin at about 7 p.m.

The Northern Netherlands

Much of this area has been reclaimed from the sea and so is characteristically flat. FRIESLAND is a wildlife and bird sanctuary, and this area is more like a separate country (with its own language and separate history) than a part of Holland. The best places to make for are ZAANDAM, the 'living museum': a reconstructed village of mills and old houses; ALKMAAR (fifty minutes from Amsterdam) with its cheese market on Fridays at 10 a.m. from mid-April to mid-September; HOORN, which puts on a crafts and folklore market; and the capital of Friesland, LEEUWARDEN. Apart from being the birthplace of Mata Hari (her house is now the Museum of Frisian Literature), the town is also a birdwatchers' paradise; you can wade out to the islands on organized treks. See the FRIES MUSEUM, OLDEHOVE TOWER and PRINCESSEHOF MUSEUM of unique ceramics.

Amsterdam

There are two distinct faces to Amsterdam: one, the quiet graceful old town of endless canals, narrow houses and tiny winding streets; the other, the harsh reality of twentieth-century capitalist consumerism: fast food, fast sex, loud music and drug pushing. The two sides live incongruously together and have made Amsterdammers famed for their tolerance of different standards and others' opinions. There are so many things to experience in this city that it is pretty well essential to see it during any comprehensive European tour. The best time to visit Amsterdam is early June, for the Festival of Fools; you can also buy bulbs and herrings.

STATION FACILITIES

AMSTERDAM CENTRAAL STATION	
Train information	Mon.–Fri.: 8 a.m.–10 p.m., Sat. and Sun.: 9 a.m.–6 p.m. (Tel. 202 266)
Reservations	Mon.–Fri.: 8 a.m.–8 p.m., Sat. and Sun.: 9 a.m.–5 p.m.
Tourist information	April–Sept.: daily, 9 a.m.–11 p.m. Oct.–Mar.: Mon.–Fri.: 1 p.m.–9 p.m. (in VVV office outside station)
Foreign exchange	Mon.–Sat.: 7 a.m.–10.50 p.m., Sun.: 9 a.m.–10.45 p.m.
Left-luggage lockers	No access Mon.–Fri.: 1.25 a.m.–4.25 a.m. Sat.: 1.25 a.m.–5.15 a.m., Sun.: 1.25 a.m.–5.55 a.m.

Left-luggage store	Mon.–Sat.: 5 a.m.–1 a.m., Sun.: 6 a.m.–1 a.m.
Bar, Buffet	7 a.m.–7 p.m.
	6 a.m.–11 p.m. on platform 10a
Waiting room	All hours on platforms 7a, 10a, 13a
Shopping	6 a.m.–11 p.m. in central tunnel
Station shuts	Open 24 hours

Daily trains to: Hamburg (6 hours), Düsseldorf (2½ hours), The Hague (¾ hour), Brussels (2¾ hours), Paris (6 hours), Internal trains run approximately every 15 minutes.

TOURIST INFORMATION

The VVV office is just opposite the station at Stationsplein 10. From Easter–June and September Mon.–Sat.: 9 a.m.–9 p.m., July and August Mon.–Sun.: 9 a.m.–11 p.m., October–Easter Mon.–Fri.: 9 a.m.–6 p.m., Sat.: 9 a.m.–5 p.m., Sun.: 10 a.m.–1 p.m. and 2–5 p.m. (Tel. 266444). Another is at Leidsestraat 106, open daily: 9 a.m.–10 p.m. Change money elsewhere if you can; the rate here is poor. Ask for the publication 'Use It', a student-orientated magazine on what's where and how much. 'Amsterdam This Week' lists current events.

• Addresses:

POST OFFICE: Nieuwezijds Voorburgwal 182, Mon.–Fri.: 8.30 a.m.–6 p.m., Thurs. till 8.30 p.m., Sat.: 9 a.m.–12 noon. Good currency exchange here.

AMEX: Damrak 66 (Tel. 262042), Mon.–Fri.: 9 a.m.–5 p.m., Sat.: 9 a.m.–12 noon, Sun.: 10 a.m.–2 p.m.

UK CONSULATE: Koningslaan 44 (Tel. 764343).

US CONSULATE: Museumplein 19 (Tel. 790321), open 9 a.m.–12 noon, 2 p.m.–4 p.m.

MEDICAL HELP: Tel. 64 21 11 for doctor or dentist.

CRISIS CENTRE: JAC, Amstel 30 (Tel. 242949).

NBBS: Dam 17, Dam Square. Sells Eurotrain tickets.

PHONE CODE: 020.

• **Getting about:** Information and a map of the city's buses, trams and underground can be had from the GVB pavilion in front of the station. If you're going to make more than three journeys, invest in a twenty-four-hour pass. If you're there for a while, consider the two- or three-day pass or the multi-ride ticket. The fifteen-strip ticket (sold in post offices) is good value (ten-strip ticket sold on buses), and can be used throughout Holland. Bikes can be hired for about £2 per day, but shop around for the best bargain and watch out for thieves!

• **Drugs scene:** There are nearly as many pushers as eurorailers in Amsterdam station. It's up to you whether you get involved with them, but the best advice is not to. Contrary to what you might believe, possession of *any* amount of drugs is a criminal offence, although you are likely to be fined only for possession of less than 30 grams of hashish. Any more, and you are in serious trouble, with legal consequences to match.

SEEING

The four main canals (the Singel, Herengracht, Keizergracht and Prinsengracht) wind their way past the main sights, so in many ways the canal boats give you the best introduction to the city. They may really make you feel like a tourist but they're cheap during the day. Watch out at night – they can cost up to four times as much for the same trip. HERENGRACHT passes the rich seventeenth-century merchants' houses; at MUNT on the SINGEL is a colourful flower market.

DAM SQUARE is the heart of the city. It lies at the end of the main shopping thoroughfare, the DAMRAK, but its attraction is often clouded by the litter and the numbers of undesirables who hang around there. Still, it's always lively, and you can often find buskers and street artists performing. To the east of the Dam lies the old city centre, beautifully preserved in its seventeenth-century splendour. This area is known as WALLETJES, and you'll do best exploring it in daytime as parts of it (Oudezijds, Achterburgwal, Oude Zijds Voorburgwal and their surroundings) have a totally different character at night when they turn into the sex streets of Europe. JORDAAN is another district worth a wander. This is the Bohemian and working-class quarter bordered by Prinsengracht, Brouwersgracht, Marnixstraat and Elandsgracht. There's a good Saturday market on Lindemarkt.

Just west of the Dam is the WESTERKERK which has a good view from its tower (free). Round the back is ANNE FRANK'S HOUSE where she wrote her famous diary while in hiding with her family from the Nazis for two years. See the Anti-Semitic Exhibition downstairs. It's at Prinsengracht 263, open Monday to Saturday: 9 a.m.–5 p.m. and Sunday: 10 a.m.–5 p.m. Entrance f. 5.

The RIJKSMUSEUM at Stadhouderskade 42 is one of the world's great art museums and comes top of the list of Amsterdam's forty museums. It's really big on Rembrandts (his 'Night Watch' is there) and the Dutch masters. Open Tues.–Sat.: 10 a.m.–5 p.m., Sun.: 1 p.m.–5 p.m. Entrance f. 7 for adults. The ROYAL PALACE on Dam Square is held up by 13,659 bits of wood; this led it to be known as the 'Eighth Wonder of the World'. Also there is the NIEUWE KERK, though there's nothing new about this late Gothic church which dates from around 1500. Just behind it is a 'tasting house', THE THREE BOTTLES (De Drie Fleschjes), which dates from 1650. Try the Bols and Hoppe liqueurs.

As far as museums are concerned, the favourites are the AMSTELKRING (Our Lord in the Attic) at Oude Zijds Voorburgwal 40, a preserved seventeenth-century house where repressed Catholics used to hide. REMBRANDT'S HOUSE is at Jodenbreestraat 2–6; the STEDELIJK MUSEUM, modern art, Paulus Potterstraat 13; and the VAN GOGH MUSEUM, just along the street at No. 7 (closed Mon.).

The Fleamarket at Valkerburgersstraat is also worth a visit. Haggle and barter to get the best deal. Amsterdam is also the diamond centre of the world. Information about tours of cutting rooms is available from VVV.

Being so flat, the Dutch go in for cycling in a big way. It's a cheap and fun way to get about and in fact can also be the quickest. You can rent a bike at several places in the city, although the most convenient is next to the station at Stationsplein 6. You can extend this to the canals as well, by hiring a canal bike from four moorings in the city centre. The cost is f. 16.50 for two and f. 24.50 for four, per hour, with a returnable deposit of f. 50 when you 'park' the bike at any of the mooring points. Open from 9.00 a.m. to 11 p.m. in summer and 7.00 p.m. in autumn. You can pick up bikes at the Leidseplein (between the Marriot and American Hotels); between the Rijksmuseum and the Heineken Brewery; Prinsengracht at the

Westerkerk, near the Anne Frank House and on the Keizersgracht, near the Leidsestraat.

SLEEPING

As Amsterdam is the fourth most popular European city (after London, Paris and Rome), it's busy in summer, and often all the hotels are full. Still, you'll always find a bed in one of the hostels or the Sleep-In: check 'Use It' for current location. The VVV will find you a room for a small fee. Be prepared for hassles from hoteliers, as well as drug pushers at Amsterdam Centraal, trying to fill up their rooms out of season. Check out the prices from VVV to see you are getting the best deal.

• **Hotels:** One hotel which is good value is the Hotel Schröder, at 48b Haarlemmerdijk (Tel. 26 62 72), ten minutes west of the Central Station. Singles are around f. 35, doubles f. 60. This includes breakfast. Showers are f. 2. There is a minimum two-night stay in the busy season.

Also recommended is the Frisco Inn at Beursstraat 5 (Tel. 201610). Five minutes' stroll from Central Station. Centrally located with good security. Singles, doubles and dormitory accommodation, dorms from around f. 25, many with private showers. Very helpful and friendly staff with a lively bar. Even if you're not staying there it's worth checking out for its daily happy hour, weekly half price night, regular live music and for Rover, possibly Amsterdam's largest cat.

Other recommendations are:
Van Onna, Bloemgracht 102 (Tel. 26 58 01).
Pax, Raadhuisstraat 37 (Tel. 24 97 35).
Hotel De Beurs, Beursstraat 7 (Tel. 22 23 08/22 07 41).
Hotel Fantasia, 16 Nieuwe Keizergracht (Tel. 24 88 58).
Hotel Acro, Jan Luykenstraat 42–44 (Tel. 62 05 26). Clean, comfortable and quiet.
A walk down Raadhuisstraat, Beursstraat, Bloemgracht or Stadhouderskade will produce something, unless the city's bursting at the seams.

• **Private accommodation:** The average is f. 45 per person; VVV will fix you up for a f. 3.50 fee.

• **Hostels:** Vondelpark IYHF hostel, Zandpad 5 (Tel. 83 17 44). You'll need membership. Around f. 23 in dorms. Tram 1 or 2 from station to Leidseplein, then a five-minute walk. They don't take telephone reservations – go early.

Stadsdoelen IYHF hostel, Kloveniersburgwal 97 (Tel. 24 68 32). f. 21. This is more central. Take tram 4, 9 or 16 to Muntplein.

Hotel Kabul (Student Hostel), Warmoesstraat 42 (Tel. 23 71 58). Dormitory, single or double accommodation. Near station (and red-light district). Very noisy – the bar closes at 4 a.m. Dorm accommodation for f. 19.

The Sleep-In is open late June–early September and at Easter. Tends to be a bit sleazy and promiscuous. Check address as it changes location annually, currently at 'S Gravesandestraat 51 (Tel. 94 74 44). The two Christian hostels in Amsterdam are highly recommended at f. 13.50 for bed and breakfast. The Shelter is the more central at Barndesteeg 21 (Tel. 253230). It is near the Metro Nieuwmarkt. The Ebenhaezer is at Bloemstraat 179 (Tel. 244717) and is reached by taking tram 13 or 17 to Marnixstraat. Give the 'Boatels', behind the station, a miss, as they are illegal, dirty, smelly and dodgy for leaving luggage in. Hans Brinker Statel, Kirkstraat (Tel. 220687) is excellent and cheap.

For camping, try Vliegenbos at Meeuwenlaan 138 (Tel. 36 88 55). Bus 172 from Leidsplein.

To sleep out, try Julianapark, Beatrixpark or Vondelpark.

EATING AND NIGHTLIFE

There's a glut of cafés and restaurants near Dam Square, round the red-light district and Leidseplein: Dutch, Chinese, Italian and Indonesian. Go for the dag's menu and fill the gap with deep-fried poffertjes (mini-doughnuts) from street stalls. For Indonesian rijsttafel avoid the more expensive restaurants around Damrak and head for Binnen Bantammerstraat to the south-east of Central Station. Ask a local for precise directions. The many restaurants are authentic and great value. Although we have no particular preference, try the Azie or the Ling Nam.

For free beer, hit the Heineken Brewery at Van der Helstraat 30. The tours start at 10 a.m. and 2 p.m. Mon.–Fri., but get there 45 minutes beforehand to ensure a place. Sometimes they take a small collection at the beginning which goes to UNICEF. There are several good street markets to buy picnic supplies from, and if you want to go out for a drink, head for the Leidseplein, Rembrandtsplein or Thorbeckeplein.

If you want to see 'sin city' and wander through the notorious red-light district of Zeedijk, go east of the Damrak to the area bordered by Warmoesstraat, Zeedijk and Damstraat. Go carefully here as the crime rate is high. In particular, don't take photographs as some of the locals don't like it and your camera may end up in a canal.

Recommendations for restaurants are: H88 at Herengracht 88 (also a student hostel); Buddha's Belly at Rozenstraat 145; and Egg Cream at Sint Jacobsstraat 19, open 11 a.m.–7.30 p.m. Also worth checking out is the Great Rijstaffel at Mandarin Rokin 26, as are the Prins van Oranje behind Centraal Station and the Sonja in front of the station. For dancing, etc., try Melkweg at Lijnbaansgracht 243a or Bistrothèque at Korte, Leidsewarsstraat 26. The nicest old cafés are off Jordaan. Good for a gas (and it can literally be a 'gas' if you're on the wrong end of it) is the café Chris at Bloemstraat 42, whose toilet can be flushed only from the bar!

Carillon concerts are organized at the Old Church – check the noticeboard on the door for details. For free pop concerts head for the Vondelpark (Tuesdays).

Paradiso at Weteringschans 6 and Roxy at Singel 465 are two of the trendiest clubs.

Outside Amsterdam

LEIDEN is half an hour south-west of Amsterdam and makes a pleasant day trip. This is where Descartes first published his *Discourse on Method*, and the University is still considered Holland's finest. Tourist information is at Stationsplein 210. See the OLD TOWN, BOTANICAL MUSEUM, the RIJKSMUSEUM VAN OUDHEDEN (National Antiquities). Both these are on Rapenburg. To clamber in a windmill and nose about, go to the MOLEN MUSEUM DE VALK, Tweede Binnenvestgracht 1. Try sleeping at Witte, Wittesingel 80, and eating at Repelsteetje on Breestraat 19 (closed Mon. and weekends). The Eurotrain office is at Schipholweg 101 (Tel. 071–253 333).

The Hague (Den Haag)

As a major world political centre, The Hague has more than its fair share of smart elegant buildings and beautiful people. There

are three royal palaces, over twenty excellent museums and two
government bodies based in Den Haag: Holland's government
located in the attractive BINNENHOF, and the International Court
of Justice housed in the PEACE PALACE.

STATION FACILITIES

There are two stations in The Hague: Holland Spoor handles all
international trains and Amsterdam trains, while Centraal Station
handles trains to the east (Utrecht), south (Rotterdam) and short
intercity and suburban lines.

	HOLLAND SPOOR	CENTRAAL STATION
Train information	8 a.m.–10 p.m. (Tel. 471 681)	8 a.m.–10 p.m. (Tel. 471 681)
Reservations	Mon.–Fri.: 8 a.m.–8 p.m. Sat.: 9 a.m.–5 p.m.	Mon.–Fri.: 8 a.m.–8 p.m. Sat.: 9 a.m.–5 p.m. Sun.: 10 a.m.–5 p.m.
Tourist information	–	Summer: Mon.–Sat.: 8.30 a.m.–9 p.m. Sun.: 10 a.m.–7 p.m. Winter: Mon.–Sat.: 8.30 a.m.–8 p.m. Across street: Sun.: 10 a.m.–5 p.m.
Foreign exchange	Mon.–Sat.: 8 a.m.–9 p.m. Sun.: 10 a.m.–6 p.m.	Mon.–Sat.: 8 a.m.–9 p.m. Sun.: 10 a.m.–6 p.m.
Left-luggage lockers	No access 1.30 a.m.–4.30 a.m.	No access 1.30 a.m.–4 a.m.
Left-luggage store	6 a.m.–10 p.m.	Mon.–Sat.: 6 a.m.–10 p.m. Sun.: 6.30 a.m.–10.30 p.m.
Cafeteria	6.30 a.m.–10.30 p.m.	6.30 a.m.–11.30 p.m.
Restaurant	Mon.–Sat.: 7 a.m.–9 p.m. Sun.: 8 a.m.–9 p.m.	Mon.–Fri.: 11 a.m.–8 p.m. (upstairs) Mon.–Fri.: 10 a.m.–8 p.m. ('Pub')
Post office	–	Mon.–Fri.: 8 a.m.–6 p.m.
Waiting room	All hours	In self-service
Station shuts	1.30 a.m.–4.30 a.m.	1.30 a.m.–4 a.m.

Tram 12 connects the two stations, or take a through-going train (free).

Daily trains to: Amsterdam (¾ hour), Rotterdam (20 minutes), Antwerp (1½ hours),
Brussels (2 hours), Paris (5½ hours) and Cologne (4 hours).

TOURIST INFORMATION

Is outside Centraal Station at Koningin Julianaplein 30. Open Mon.–Sat.: 9 a.m.–9 p.m., Sun.: 9 a.m.–4 p.m.; there are also offices at Groenmarkt 7, Mon.: 12.30 p.m.–5 p.m., Tue.–Fri.: 10 a.m.–5 p.m., Sat.: 11 a.m.–4 p.m., and Swolsestraat, in Scheveningen, next to the Europe Hotel – open Mon.–Sat.: 9 a.m.–9 p.m., Sun.: 9 a.m.–6 p.m. (April–September). They'll all hand you free maps and an accommodation list or find a room for you.

● **Addresses:**
POST OFFICE: Nobelstraat, open Mon.–Fri.: 8.30 a.m.–7 p.m., Thur.: till 8.30 p.m., Sat.: 9 a.m.–12 p.m.
AMEX: Venestraat 20, open Mon.–Fri.: 9 a.m.–5 p.m., Sat.: 9.30 a.m.–12.30 p.m.
UK EMBASSY: Lange Voorhout 10 (Tel. 645800).
US EMBASSY: Lange Voorhout 102 (Tel. 624911).
CANADIAN EMBASSY: Sophialaan 7 (Tel. 614111).
AUSTRALIAN EMBASSY: Koninginnegracht 23–24 (Tel. 630983).
MEDICAL HELP: Tel. 455300.
NBBS (EUROTRAIN): Schoolstraat 24, Den Haag (Tel. 465819).
PHONE CODE: 070.

SEEING

The BINNENHOF – Holland's Westminster – is a complex of buildings with the thirteenth-century KNIGHT'S HALL at its centre. This is open to the public and is worth a look. There are carillon concerts at noon on Mondays, Wednesdays and Fridays in summer at the CHURCH OF ST JACOB, and on Thursday afternoons the imposing Lange Voorhout (where the Embassy is) turns into an open-air antique market. The museums not to miss are: the MAURITSHUIS MUSEUM, Plein 29, with its superb collection of Dutch art; the GEMEENTE MUSEUM, Stadhouderslaan 41, the city museum with a collection of musical instruments and Mondrian's major works; and the GEVANGENPOORT (Prison Gate) MUSEUM, Buitenhof 33, a morbid torture-chamber stuffed with medieval instruments to set your nerves on edge.

The main attraction of The Hague, however, is its miniature city, MADURODAM, open April–September till late at night. Tram 9 or bus 22 will take you out to Holland's Disneyland, admission f. 9.50. This city, built to a 1/25th scale, has everything from trains to houses and street lamps – and everything works.

As Holland's 'greenest city', there are plenty of picnic and unofficial camping places to be had. Try the Haagse Bos, Westbroekpark or Clingendael Park. If you fancy beach-bumming it, SCHEVENINGEN is your nearest place (it's also good to sleep out on). Ten minutes from The Hague is the town of DELFT, famous for its pottery. You can see it being made at the Porceleyne Fles, Rotterdamseweg 196.

SLEEPING

Hotels aren't cheap, so try the alternatives. The VVV have a nasty habit of not using private accommodation (f. 30) till they've filled all the hotels. Beds come cheaper in Scheveningen. Try Pension Centrale, Haagestraat 61 (Tel. 541653). There are campsites at Wijndaelerweg 16 (Tel. 252364) near the beach (bus 53 from the station) and Duinrell, Wassenaar (Tel. 01751/19314). The youth hostel at Monsterseweg 4 (Tel. 97 00 11) is very good. Take buses 122, 123 or 124 for the 5-mile journey from the station.

EATING AND NIGHTLIFE

Scheveningen is lively at night and your best bet for cheap eats and bars, though some can be fairly rough, so shop around. For groceries, try the market at Markthof, near Binnenhof, or on Grote Markt Straat. De Moglie Haan on Strandweg 137 do good meals for about f.13. The Padang restaurant, at Bagijinestraat is very good and is near the youth hostel.

Rotterdam

The largest port in Europe and second largest in the world, Rotterdam is Holland's second city after Amsterdam and, were it not for a Nazi air raid in 1940, would still be her rival in architectural terms. The rebuilt Rotterdam is an attractive, very modern city, best seen from the 600-foot-high Euromast.

ROTTERDAM CENTRAAL STATION	
Train information	Mon.–Fri.: 8 a.m.–10 p.m., Sat.: 9 a.m.–6 p.m., Sun.: 10 a.m.–9.30 p.m. (Tel. 4 117 100)
Reservations	Mon.–Fri.: 8 a.m.–10 p.m., Sat.: 9 a.m.–6 p.m., Sun.: 10 a.m.–5 p.m.
Tourist information	9 a.m.–10 p.m.
Foreign exchange	8 a.m.–9 p.m.
Left-luggage lockers	No access 1 a.m.–5 a.m.
Left-luggage store	6 a.m.–10 p.m.
Restaurant	6 a.m.–11 p.m.
Waiting room	All hours
Station shuts	1 a.m.–5 a.m.

TOURIST INFORMATION

MAIN OFFICE: VVV Stadhuisplein 19 (Tel. 4136006).
DOCTOR AND 24-HOUR CHEMIST: Tel. 4362244.
NBBS: Reiswinhel–Meent 126 (Tel. 4149485) sell Eurotrain tickets.
PHONE CODE: 010.

SEEING

You can tour round the massive port by boat if you've spare cash, or else wander round some of its thirty miles yourself. The BOYMANS-VAN-BEUNINGEN MUSEUM on Mathenesserlaan is a superb modern-art museum. Close to the station is the GROOTHANDELSGEBOUW (the nearest post office to the station is in here), a huge complex of offices, restaurants, entertainments, etc. One part of Rotterdam which wasn't wiped out was DELFSHAVEN from where the Pilgrim Fathers left in 1620 en route to discover America. In Delfshaven they are restoring the 110 buildings left and turning the area into a craft centre.

Not far from Rotterdam is the only remaining area with lots of windmills: Kinderdijk. Go on Saturday afternoons in summer and see all nineteen at work. The cheese town of GOUDA is 25 minutes by train from Rotterdam. See its colourful cheese market in the central market on Thursday mornings (9 a.m.–10 a.m.) in summer.

Rotterdam's youth hostel is at Rochussenstraat 107 (Tel. 4365763), and the Sleep-Inn (Tel. 121420) is open summers at Mauritsweg 29. There are plenty of cheap eating places all over town.

The Southern and Eastern Netherlands

The southern part of Holland, bordered by Belgium, has as its main stopping-off places the beautifully situated, historic town of BREDA, and the reconstructed medieval town of MIDDELBURG, with its miniature town on a 1/20th scale, 'Walcheren'.

When in LIMBURG, the south-eastern province between Germany and Holland, look in on MAASTRICHT with its nine castles and 120-mile network of man-made tunnels. UTRECHT is the main town of the east. It has a medieval city centre and a thirteenth-century cathedral. For real train buffs, there's a railway museum in the old station here, housing old steam locomotives. See also the CENTRAAL MUSEUM with its Viking ship, the MUSIC BOX MUSEUM and the RELIGIOUS HISTORY MUSEUM in Het Catherine Convent.

ARNHEM suffered great damage in 1944 (as seen in 'A Bridge Too Far'), but the twelfth-century DOORWERTH CASTLE outside the town has survived. The main reason to stay in Arnhem is for its proximity to the fascinating OPEN-AIR MUSEUM just north of the city. There are working farms, mills and houses here to give you a fully rounded picture of traditional Dutch rural life. There's also a zoo and safari park with a mini-train running through it, and a costume museum.

Haarlem

Fifteen minutes from Amsterdam is Haarlem, one of Holland's most historic and well-preserved towns. Tourist information is at Stationsplein 1, and after your call in here go to the GROTE MARKT where ST BAVO'S CHURCH, the RENAISSANCE MEAT MARKET and the fourteenth-century TOWN HALL are located. Also see the FRANZ HALS MUSEUM, especially when they're holding candlelight concerts in it.

Try the youth hostel at Jan Gijzenpad 3 (Tel. 023–373793). Take bus 6 from the station. Alternatively ask VVV to put you up in a private home, or camp out at Liewegje (Tel. 023–332360).

NORWAY

Entry requirements	Passport
Population	4,200,000
Capital	Oslo (pop.: 465,000)
Currency	Kroner
	£1 = approx. 11.36 kr.
Political system	Constitutional Monarchy
Religion	Lutheran
Language	Norwegian (English widely spoken)
Public holidays	1 Jan.; Maundy Thursday; Good Friday; Easter Monday; 1, 17 May; Ascension Day; Whit Monday; Whit Tuesday; 25, 26 Dec.
International dialling codes	From UK: 010 + 47 + number
	From USA: 011 + 47 + number
	To UK: 095 + 44 + number
	To USA: 095 + 1 + number

Norway has the lowest population density in Europe – even her cities are small by Western standards (Bergen 213,000, Stavanger 87,500) – a fact which is not surprising when one realizes that about a quarter of Norway's land is above the Arctic Circle. If you're lucky and it's not raining, one of Europe's most spectacular countries awaits you; 80 per cent of her land is taken up by forests and mountains. The Sognefjord, one of Norway's best-known fjords, runs for over 100 miles inland with 4,000-foot walls in places. It was from fjords like this that Harald Fairhair's longboats sailed westward, after his unification of Norway in 885, a process which continued until the death of Harald Hardrada, at Stamford Bridge in 1066, while trying to conquer England. During the medieval period, the plague knocked off most of the Norwegian population and left the German Hansa merchants in control of the country's trade. This was followed by 400 years of Danish rule, to be succeeded by rule by Sweden after the Napoleonic Wars. Independence came in 1905 when Haakon VII was elected king, and was succeeded by his son Olav in 1957. Today, Norway has one of the highest standards of living in Europe, thanks to cheap hydro-electric power and the discovery of oil. Norway's well worth the inconvenience of getting there – even if you can only afford a quick train through.

For ferries from the UK to Norway, use the excellent Norwegian Line from Newcastle to Bergen/Stavanger (Tel. 091–296 1313) and ask for student discount details.

NORWEGIAN STATE RAILWAYS
(Norges Statsbaner, NSB)

The Norwegians have one of the cleanest and most efficient railways in Europe and it passes through some of the most spectacular scenery. There are no supplements in Norway so Inter Rails are valid on all trains. The fastest and most comfortable trains are the Ekspresstog (Et, expresses). They run between all the major cities and stop only at main stations. The regular day-trains are the Hurtigtog (Ht, fast) but they're only slightly better than the locals (Persontog, Pt), which stop at every station. NSR have an office in London at 21–24 Cockspur Street (Tel. 071–930 6666). They are also agents for Danish and Swedish railways.

● **Inter Rail bonuses:**

Hirtshals–Kristiansand	50%
Larvik–Frederikshavn	50%
Flåm–Bergen and other services by Express Steamers and Fjord Steamers run by 'Fylkesbaatane i Sogn og Fjordane'	50%
Bodø/Fauske–Narvik (bus)	50%

● **Eurail bonuses:**

Hirtshals–Kristiansand	30%
Flåm–Bergen and other services by Express Steamers and Fjord Steamers run by 'Fylkesbaatane i Sogn og Fjordane'	50%

● **ScanRail bonuses:**

Flåm–Bergen and other services by Express Steamers and Fjord Steamers run by 'Fylkesbaatane i Sogn og Fjordane'	50%
Larvik–Frederikshavn	50%

● **Nordturist bonuses:**

Flåm–Bergen and other services by Express Steamers and Fjord Steamers run by 'Fylkesbaatane i Sogn og Fjordane'	50%
Larvik–Frederikshavn	50%
Fauske–Narvik–Kirkenes (bus)	50%

TRAIN INFORMATION

No problems here as everyone speaks good English. NSB also publish an excellent free series of leaflets giving maps and descriptions of their main tourist routes.

● **Reservations:** Domestic reservations are compulsory on all major routes, so check first. They should be made in advance, but if you don't have the time you can still do this on the train, though this won't guarantee you a seat, and you'll still have to pay. If you're travelling to Copenhagen you're advised to reserve thirty-six hours in advance and forty-eight hours at weekends. International seat reservations cost 1.3 kr. Reserved seats are not always marked, so don't be surprised if you get moved on, just when you thought it was safe to get comfortable. On the other hand, don't be too surprised to find someone already sitting in a seat you have reserved in advance.

• **Night travel:** Second-class sleepers with three berths cost about 90 kr; with two berths 190 kr. Standards are high – video and snacks are available. 50 kr. buys you an excellent hearty breakfast.

• **Eating on trains:** Expresses have dining cars, and if you have a bit of money to blow the food is excellent, as is the scenery. All other trains have buffets which serve hot meals as well as snacks.

• **Scenic tips:** There are more scenic routes in Norway than anywhere else in Scandinavia, and possibly even Europe. The jewel of them all is the Bergen–Oslo run. Be sure to get hold of the free NSB leaflets which give good descriptions of the various lines.

• **Rover tickets:** *Nordturist* (Nordic Tourist Ticket): available in the Nordic countries and in most European countries. Valid for unlimited railtravel in Norway, Sweden, Denmark and Finland for 21 days. Also valid for some ferries.

Class:	1st	1st	2nd	2nd
Prices in Kroner (1991):	adults	youth 12–25	adults	youth 12–25
	2.240	1.680	1.660	1.250

ScanRailpass: ScanRail is quite similar to Nordturist, but is only valid for certain days within a period of time. Available in North America (French Rail Inc.), Australia (Bentours) and Singapore. Valid for travel by train (and a few ferries) in Norway, Sweden, Denmark and Finland.

Class:	1st	2nd
4 days out of 15 days	USD 179	USD 139
9 days out of 21 days	USD 299	USD 229
14 days in 1 month	USD 459	USD 319

Midtukebillett and mini-group do not exist any more. *Minipris* has been introduced instead. Valid for direct travel on 'low-trafic' departures (most trains Monday–Thursday and Saturday). Price one way, unlimited distance (1990): 395 kr. With *'Customers Card'* you can obtain 30–50 per cent reduction on normal fare 2.cl. Price 1990: 295 kr., valid one year.

TOURIST INFORMATION

There's a tourist office at every major town in Norway. They help to find accommodation if necessary and have a good supply of local information leaflets. Norway's one of the most health-conscious of all European countries, and at weekends you'll find, depending on the season, the ski slopes, forest tracks and waterways well used by the 'great outdoors' fanatics. For detailed information on hiking and mountaineering, contact DNT, Stortingsgata 28, Oslo.

● **ISIC bonuses:** 50 per cent discounts on museums, theatres and some coastal steamers. Also 30 per cent reductions on some bus services. For further information, contact UR Universiterssentret, Blindern, Oslo (Tel. 02–466880).

● **Money matters:** 1 Norwegian kroner (kr.) = 100 øre.
Banking hours are Mon.–Fri.: 8.15 a.m.–3 p.m. (4 p.m. in winter). Some stay open till 5 p.m. on Thursdays.

● **Post offices and shops:** Mon.–Fri.: 8.30/9 a.m.–5 p.m., late-night opening Thursdays till 7 p.m.; closed Saturday p.m.

● **Museums:** Vary throughout Norway, but the general pattern is 10 a.m. opening and early closing at 3 p.m. or 4 p.m.

EATING AND NIGHTLIFE

Norway is one country you're bound to lose weight in; it's not that the food is bad, or that you'll be press-ganged into spending all day out hiking in the fjords – it's just that food is so expensive here that you'll rarely be able to afford the luxury of a full stomach. This is *the* problem in Norway: it's quite easy to spend 100 kr. a day just feeding yourself with average-quality meals. Avoid expensive meat dishes and turn instead to fish, and try and copy the locals: eat a full breakfast of smørbrødbord, have a snack at lunch (bought from a market/shop) and aim for a koldtbord (cold table) meal in the evening where you can eat as much as you like, or a fixed-price menu. If you're planning on self-catering a lot in Norway (and you should), bring some basic supplies with you from home.

The Norwegians have a reputation for being quite a serious lot, and to an extent that's fair comment – though catch them after a few drinks at night and you'd never believe it. They're very culture-conscious, and much effort is made to preserve the folk songs and dances of their forebears – the displays of these you may encounter are not put on purely as commercial stunts for the tourists.

The Southern Coast

If you've arrived in Norway at Stavanger, it'll take you about eight hours to get to Oslo. There's not that much to keep you here but if you've time to spare, the OLD TOWN gives you an idea what Norway was once like. The medieval CATHEDRAL is a good example, and is located in the colourful MARKETPLACE. If you've three or four hours to kill, the Stavanger–Sand ferry takes you through some fjords which will whet your appetite for what's to come. The 'Stavanger Guide' from the tourist pavilion has a map and all the information you'll need if you decide to stay longer.

Between Stavanger and Oslo is Kristiansand, which has ferry connections to Hirsthals in Denmark (50 per cent reduction with Inter Rail and Eurail). There is some good scenery here and some good beaches on the nearby islands.

Oslo

On Norway's south-eastern coast at the head of a 60-mile fjord lies Oslo, the oldest of the Scandinavian capitals. Outside the city limits are acres of forests, hills and unspoilt countryside which the Oslo-ites use at every opportunity to pursue their many outdoor activities. The town itself has no distinctive style, and you have to look below the surface for its real attractions: the museums and parks.

STATION FACILITIES

Smoking is banned in the Central Station as in all public buildings in Norway. There is an Inter Rail Centre, open 7 a.m.–11 p.m. end June–mid September, offering showers (10 kr.), phones, food and information. All Eurorailers welcome.

OSLO (CENTRAL)	
Train information	6.30 a.m.–11 p.m.
	(Tel. 171400)
Reservations	8 a.m.–9 p.m. (Tel. 171401)
Tourist information	8 a.m.–11 p.m. daily (Closed winter 3 p.m.–4.30 p.m.)
Foreign exchange + post office	7.00 a.m.–11 p.m., summer, 7 a.m.–8 p.m. winter
Left-luggage lockers	No access at night
Bar/Café	7 a.m.–11 p.m.
Restaurant	7 a.m.–11 p.m.
Waiting room	All hours

Daily trains to: Gothenburg, Stockholm, Stavanger, Trondheim, Bergen, Copenhagen, Hamburg.

TOURIST INFORMATION

Pick up maps and booklets from train information in Central Station, and use the Innkvartering (room-finding service) who ask a 5 kr. commission, but it's worth it. The Oslo Tourist Information Centre is at the Town Hall. They are extremely helpful and will give you maps, the 'Oslo Guide', 'Oslo This Week' and ferry and bus timetables. Mon.–Fri. (May–Sept.): 8.30 a.m.–7 p.m., Sat.–Sun.: 9 a.m.–5 p.m.

• **Addresses:**

POST OFFICE: Dronningensgate 15, open Mon.–Fri.: 8 a.m.–8 p.m., Sat.: 8 a.m.–3 p.m. Kongensgate 21 for twenty-four-hour telephones.

AMEX: c/o Winge Travel, Karl Johansgate 33 (Tel. 429150), open Mon.–Fri.: 8.30 a.m.–5 p.m., Sat.: 8.30 a.m.–1 p.m. No traveller's cheques exchange.

STUDENT TRAVEL: Terra Nova Travel, Dronningensgate 26 (Tel. 421410), open Mon.–Fri.: 8.15 a.m.–3.15 p.m.

NUH (Norwegian Youth Hostel headquarters): Dronningensgate 26. Pick up list of hostels here.

DEN NORSKE TURISTFORENING (Norwegian Mountain Touring Association): Roald Amundsengate 28 (Tel. 418020). If you've come to Norway to climb or camp, call in for leaflets on mountain huts, etc. Open weekdays: 8.20 a.m.–4 p.m., Thursday till 6 p.m.

UK EMBASSY: Thomas Heftyesgate 8 (Tel. 552400).

US EMBASSY: Drammensveien 18 (Tel. 448550).

CANADIAN EMBASSY: Oscargate 20 (Tel. 466955).

AUSTRALIAN EMBASSY: Jernbanstorget 2 (Tel. 414433).

24-HOUR CHEMIST: Jernbanstorget Apotek. In front of Central Station.

PHONE CODE: 02.

• **Getting about:** City transport is good and you can use your ticket to transfer to any form of transport within an hour. These include buses, trams, undergrounds, ferries and local trains (free on Inter Rail). Pick up the transit map at the station or tourist information. The Oslo Card (80 kr. for one day, 120 kr. for two and 150 kr. for three) is good value and gives free transport and entry to most of the sights.

SEEING

The Rådhus (Town Hall) is down by the harbour. This avant-garde 1950s structure was decorated by contemporary Norwegian artists and can be visited free. From the Rådhus Gate you can enter AKERSHUS CASTLE, built by King Haakon V around 1300, then rebuilt in Renaissance style by Christian IV. It's open weekdays 10 a.m.–4 p.m. (May to September); and in the grounds of the castle is the NORWEGIAN RESISTANCE MUSEUM describing the Nazi occupation of Norway. The ferry from the Rådhus over to the peninsula of BYGDØY takes you to five very interesting places:

1. The incredible NORSK FOLKEMUSEUM with 150 wooden buildings filled with material artefacts recreating Norway's past. These include Ibsen's study, houses from Lapland and museums of domestic furniture, clothes and implements.
2. THE VIKING SHIP HOUSE: Three preserved Viking longboats from AD 800–900.
3. KON-TIKI MUSEUM: The rafts used by the explorer Thor Heyerdahl on his voyages.
4. The NORWEGIAN MARITIME MUSEUM.
5. The FRAM MUSEUM: The ship used in the Polar expeditions of the nineteenth and early twentieth centuries.

All these museums are within walking distance of one another and are open 10 a.m.–6 p.m.

The VIGELAND SCULPTURE PARK and VIGELAND MUSEUM show the work and the background of the Norwegian artist Gustav Vigeland. This park is one of Norway's finest and 1,750 sculptures dotted round it have been termed everything from 'obscene' to 'serene'. The other famous Norwegian artist, EDVARD MUNCH, has his

MUSEUM in the east of the city. It's a particularly fine gallery, housing literally thousands of his Expressionist works. Both these museums tend to close on Mondays, except in high season. Check first with tourist information. The NATIONAL GALLERY is at Universitetsgata 13, and has Norway's principal art collection.

SLEEPING

Oslo's not easy on eurorailers. Forget hotels completely and concentrate on the few hostels and campsites, or settle for private accommodation. You can get a room in a private house for 145 kr. single, 240 kr. double, and you must stay at least two nights. Both youth hostels are very good, clean, efficient, and with plenty of facilities, but they could hardly be called central.

Haraldsheim is at Haraldsheimveien 4 (Tel. 222965). It charges average prices. Reservations cost 13 kr. and are recommended. It's open all year and is at the bottom of the hill from Sinsen tram terminus. The other Oslo Youth Hostel is at Sognsvn 218 (Tel. 237640) and costs 132 kr. including breakfast. It is open from the beginning of June to late August. Take tram 13 to Kringsja Station. The Seamen's Hostel, Oslo Sjømannshjemmet, Fred Olsengate 2 (Tel. 412005), have fair rooms and serve reasonably priced meals. Reception is open twenty-four hours.

If you don't mind an institutional atmosphere, Holtekilen Summer Hotel at Micheletsvei 55 (Tel. 533853) is good value. You can choose between the ten-bed classroom accommodation (it's a school except in summer) or if you're keen to escape the classroom, the hotel side does doubles for a bit more.

The campsites are Bogstad Camping at Ankerveien 117 (Tel. 247619) (bus 41) and the Ekeberg site at Ekebergveien 65 (Tel. 198568) which is more central but only open late June to late August (bus 24 from in front of Central Station. Showers are hot and free, but shared with the adjacent football pitches). The cheapest camping you will find in Oslo is around 40 kr. although you are allowed to camp free in any of the wooded areas north of the city provided it is away from public areas.

EATING AND NIGHTLIFE

Here more than anywhere else in Europe, you'll find prices sky-high. Don't attempt restaurants or stopping off for a coffee and cake (25 kr.). Eat like the Norwegians: a hearty breakfast and big dinner and expect to average 60 kr. for a full meal. There are fast-food chains – Wimpy and Kaffistovas – which can help eke out the finances, and Kveldsmat on Universitetgata, off Karl Johansgate, is cheap. Friskporten on Grensen 18 do superb vegetarian meals for about 45 kr. Or try Torgstova, Karl Johans gate 13.

● **Excursions:** Skiers should find the world's oldest SKI MUSEUM interesting. It's located inside the take-off point of the huge Holmenkollen ski jump. Exhibits here trace the history of the sport and produce evidence that it dates as far back as about 500 BC. Take the Holmenkollen railway from its underground station and walk about ten minutes from the station. EKEBERG PARK gives a great view over Oslo from its hills where Stone Age carvings from 1,000 BC have been found. If you're a group of four and have cash to spare, why not take a torch-lit sleigh ride through the woods here? (Contact Ekeberg Rideskole through tourist information.)

Oslo–Bergen: the Sognefjord

The rail run from Oslo to Bergen is one you should go out of your way to take. The scenery is incredible and during the course of this six-hour journey, you'll pass through fjords, glaciers, tundra, mountains, lakes, plateaux and gorges. Should you choose to break this journey and savour its delights slowly, stop off at MYRDAL and take the other line for the twelve-mile and 3,000-foot journey down to FLÅM. Should you decide to stay at Flåm, the Solhammer Pension, across the river from the station, is reasonable, and there's camping next door (though if you don't camp freelance here you never will). The campsite has good facilities, but showers are extra. Expect to pay around 40 kr. per tent. From Flåm you can tackle the fjords. A favourite trip of mine (and it won't take you out of your way from Bergen) is to take the ferry to GUDVANGEN from Flåm. This two-hour trip takes you past the spectacular scenery of the Nerøfjord, and calls at some isolated settlements en route whose sole means of communication is the ferry. From Gudvangen take the bus to Voss where you're back on the Bergen line again.

Another trip worth taking is from Flåm to Voss. It costs around 76 kr. with Inter Rail and includes bus and ferry connections. There is a commentary in English on both the train section (from Flåm to Myrdal) and the ferry. The bus ride is particularly spectacular as you cross the roof of Norway via the steep road and many hairpin bends. If you stop off in Voss there is a very good folk museum including a restored farm which dates back to the seventeenth century.

Bergen

The colourful harbour, red-roofed houses and spruce trees nestling under imposing Mount Fløyen give Bergen the reputation of being Norway's most attractive city. This was the northernmost city in the Hanseatic League and the HANSEATIC MUSEUM – a reconstruction of a sixteenth-century merchant's house – makes an interesting visit. This is in the quarter called BRYGGEN, and in the old timber houses today weavers and craftsmen carry on their trade. ROSENKRANTZ TOWER and KING HAAKON'S HALL aren't terribly interesting, so don't bother unless you're really bored. Do, however, take the funicular up Mount Fløyen and see the view. The RASMUS MEYER collection is an art gallery on the edge of the LILLE LUNGENGARDSVATNET park, and the GAMLE BERGEN (old town) with its traditional timbered buildings makes a pleasant walk. The Romanesque church of ST MARY'S is considered Norway's most beautiful church. Tourist information have details on the May–June INTERNATIONAL FESTIVAL held here, and also about the trips to the fjords that start from Bergen.

TOURIST INFORMATION AND ADDRESSES

Tourist information pavilion at Torgalmenning (Tel. 321480): walk for ten minutes up Kaigaten from the station. Open Mon.–Sat.: 8.30 a.m.–9 p.m. in summer. They change money, book you into private houses and supply maps and 'The Bergen Guide'.
POST OFFICE: Smästrandgate. Open 8 a.m.–5 p.m., Thur.: till 7 p.m., Sat.: 9 a.m.–1 p.m.
24-HOUR CHEMIST: Accident Clinic, Lars Millesgate (Tel. 210185).
STUDENT TRAVEL: Parkveien 1 (Tel. 321160). 25 per cent reductions on steamer fare to Newcastle.
PHONE CODE: 05.

SLEEPING, EATING AND NIGHTLIFE

If you are dumping rucksacks, note that left luggage is much cheaper than the lockers. Use the tourist pavilion who charge 10 kr. commission. Private homes ask about 130 kr. single, 200 kr. double.

The youth hostel is nearly always full (Bergen is very touristy), so call first. It's in a good position, halfway up Mount Ulriken. It costs 89 kr. Open May–Oct. On bus route 4 at Ravneberget (Tel. 292900), but apply at IYHA office at Strandgaten 4.

Lone is Bergen's main campsite (Tel. 240820), but it's quite far out and not that cheap. If you are feeling energetic, it is a good hour's walk up to the top of Flyen. The path is good and the views from the top quite spectacular. If you're not feeling like the climb, take the funicular.

The food and nightlife news is not too good. All you'll be able to afford are picnics and some of the fairly boring café-type places. Try Peppe's Pizza in Bryggen's – all-you-can-eat pizza and salad for 65 kr. on Mondays (no wine though!). The restaurant in the Fantoft Sommerhotel is decent and offers a 20 per cent students' discount (bus 14 or 15) and Hulen is a club run by the town's university students in an old air-raid shelter beneath Nygaardsparken. If you're over 20 (and can prove it) you can go to the disco and drink there.

Trondheim to the North Cape

The rail line runs to Bodø, capital of the Nordland province and land of the midnight sun. This is the northernmost region of Europe and its beauty is beyond the scope of any guidebook's description, so we won't start coming out with the standard string of superlatives, as you'd probably find it corny. Just take it from us you won't regret your trip up there. From Bodø you can take a ferry through the LOFOTEN ISLANDS up to Narvik (330 kr.) or a bus from Fanske (228 kr., 114 kr. with an Inter Rail card), then on to FINNMARK and LAPLAND (unfortunately there's no train). If you decide to head for Sweden at Narvik instead of going further north, you will travel on the Ofoten Line the 27 miles to the Swedish border. It is a particularly scenic journey and for many years it was the world's most northerly railway. Today it is still the most northerly electrified line and carries about half the total goods transported by Norwegian Railways, mainly about 20 million tons of Swedish iron ore. Tourist information is at Kongensgate 66 (Tel. 082–43309) and the youth hostel is beside the harbour at Havnegate 3 (Tel. 082–42598). The campsite is crowded and uneven and doesn't have showers, but you can get cheap showers and sauna in town at the Seaman's Mission, near the harbour. It is open from 4 p.m. to 10 p.m. and has a pool table, as well as cheap coffee and snacks. The Norwegian Mountain Touring Association (Den Norske Tukistforening) provide a series of well equipped mountain huts costing 50 kr. per night, if you are a member (60 kr. if not). Contact them at Roald Amundsengate 28, Oslo. To see the fjord and where the historic battles of Narvik took place during the last war you can take a two-hour boat trip from the harbour for approximately 70 kr. From June to August you can take a 15-minute cable car ride in the 'Gondolbaner' for magnificent views of the area and, at night, the midnight sun. The service runs from 10 a.m. to midnight or later depending on weather conditions and costs 50 kr. If you are intending to take the early morning train out of Narvik bear in mind that the station closes from 10.30 p.m. to 5 a.m. As things go the station buffet is reasonably priced, with coffee at around 8 kr.

Trondheim

Trondheim is a university town whose main purpose is to produce and export timber, fish, farm products and ships. Pick up a map and the 'Trondheim Guide' at the station. The tourist office is over the bridge along Søndregate, then turn right into Kongensgate and walk along to the market place. The office is on the corner (open Mon.–Fri.: 8.30 a.m.–8 p.m.; Sat.–Sun.: till 6 p.m. before Aug.). The sights of the city are the medieval NIDAROS CATHEDRAL, the twelfth-century ARCHBISHOP'S PALACE and the interesting RINGVE MUSEUM OF MUSIC HISTORY, the KRISTIANSEN FORTRESS and BRYGGEREKKEN – the wharf row – from where the view of the town bridge is excellent. The recently opened TYHOLT TOWER is worth visiting. From this rotating 80-metre tower you can view all Trondheim and the Trondheimsfjord. The youth hostel is at Weidemannsvei 41 (Tel. 530490).

There is an Inter Rail Centre at Trondheim which offers cooking facilities, seat reservations and all the usual Inter Rail facilities.
POST OFFICE: Dronningersgate 10. Open Mon.–Fri.: 10 a.m.–5 p.m., Sat.: 9 a.m.–1 p.m.
UK CONSULATE: Sluppenveien 10 (Tel. 968211).
CHEMIST: Søndregate 9 (Tel. 523122). Open 8.30 a.m.–12 p.m. all week.
PHONE CODE: 07.

Bodø

It's 11½ hours from Trondheim to Bodø, but the scenery and the comfortable trains make it feel a lot less. The bus ride from Bodø to Narvik joins up the northern part of the Norwegian railway system and is a fabulous experience. 50 per cent discount on fare with Inter Rail. From 1 June–12 July, the sun never sets here. 3½ hours before Bodø is MO-I-RANA, located on a magnificent fjord. The Youth Hostel (Tel. 087–50963) is open from May to September and costs 70 kr. If you hit a particularly good spell of weather, walk up Mount Ronvik, taking your camera with you. The 1956 CATHEDRAL is about the only noteworthy building in the town, but you don't come here for the towns. Head instead for SALSTRAUMEN where every six hours millions of gallons of water squeeze through a tiny passage between two fjords, making a spectacular sight. Buses sometimes run to coincide with the tides – ask for the timetable at tourist information, 32 kr. with Inter Rail.

TOURIST INFORMATION AND ADDRESSES

Tourist office is at Sjøgata 21, open Mon.–Fri.: 9 a.m.–5 p.m.; Sat.: 10 a.m. to 2 p.m. in season. Books private accommodation for you. Flatvold Youth Hostel is at Nordstrandvn 1 (Tel. 081–25666). A new, very good hostel with all facilities, ¾ mile from station. Open 20 June–16 Aug. The station buffet is OK for good and filling food. If you stay at the campsite you may get the occasional free fish from fishermen nearby. The site, 3 km from town at Bodøsjøen, has free cooking facilities and superb views of the fjord. It is on bus route 12 (Tel. 081–22902).

POLAND

Entry requirements	Passport and visa
Population	37,000,000
Capital	Warsaw (pop.: 1,700,000)
Currency	Zloty
	£1 = approx. 15,440 zl.
Political system	Republic
	(some Communists still in government)
Religion	Roman Catholic
Language	Polish (a little German and English spoken)
Public holidays	1 Jan.; Good Friday; Easter Monday; 1 May;
	Corpus Christi; 22 July; 1 Nov.; 25, 26 Dec.
International dialling codes	From UK: 010 + 48 + number
	From USA: 011 + 48 + number
	To UK: 00 + 44 + number
	To USA: 00 + 1 + number

The seemingly impossible has happened in Poland with the election of a Solidarity prime minister, but the harsh economic measures that have been adopted to pay for the failures of Communism have made life difficult. Solidarity's long struggle reflects the independent spirit of the Poles who resent outside pressure from the Soviet Union or wherever. This fact becomes understandable when one looks at the history of Poland, a country which has had more than its fair share of invasion and occupation. This process began in the tenth century with the eastward expansion of Germanic tribes, and continued long after the area came under the protection of the Holy Roman Empire. As an independent kingdom, Poland came into being in 1025; since then the country has been conquered and boundaries changed many times. In 1795 and 1939 Poland disappeared off the map altogether as it looked like doing again for a time in 1982. Eastern Europe's quiet revolution affected this country too in late 1989–90. It is today in a state of flux: food shortages are common, but it's more worth visiting than ever. Since 1991 it is in the Inter Rail scheme.

POLISH STATE RAILWAYS
(Polskie Koleje Państwowe, PKP)

Polish trains are among the slowest and busiest in Europe. Tickets are sold according to the type of train you want to travel on. Avoid the Osobowe and Pośpieszne categories and go for the Exspresowe expresses whenever possible. All the large cities have their own commuter trains called Pociągi Elektryczne which are even more crowded than normal. Don't be talked into buying a Polrailpass from any Orbis office unless you plan on spending a lot of time going around in circles as fares as so cheap. The pass costs from £33 for 8 days to £50 for one month second class. Poland is in Inter Rail and is now covered by the new 15-day East Rail Pass available from Danish State Railways (see Introduction).

If you are one of those steam train buffs, you will see plenty to interest you in Poland, as steam trains are still used regularly in certain areas (especially the north-east and south-east). They are being phased out but are still used in winter for their steam heating.

TRAIN INFORMATION

Few officials speak English, so if you want to make a reservation write down the name of your destination and the time your train leaves. Speaking German is best in the south, French in the north. If you get stuck, try: 'Z którego peronu odjezdza pociąg do . . . ?' (From which platform does the train to . . . leave?)

• **Reservations:** If you want a seat, you'll have to make a reservation as trains are always crowded to capacity. Go to the station at least one day in advance (several days for the Warsaw–Kraków–Zakopane run). For international trains you'll have to use Orbis and face the even longer queues. Look out for windows marked 'Polres': they deal with seat reservations (miejscówka) which are compulsory on express and international trains.

• **Night travel:** Don't expect high standards unless you're willing to travel first class. Reserve well ahead of time at Orbis, particularly for couchettes, which are always cheaper than paying for a night's accommodation. You may have no alternative but to reserve a couchette if you are going to Czechoslovakia, as you will probably be told they are the only seats available. International journeys are still cheaper to countries of the former Eastern Bloc.

• **Eating on trains:** There's either a WARS restaurant or buffet car on all long hauls in Poland, but some international trains have few facilities.

TOURIST INFORMATION

There are local Informacja Turystyczna (IT) offices in every major town as well as at many stations. If you plan to stay for a while, it's worth buying 'A Guide for Young Tourists' from any Ruch kiosks in Poland.

● **ISIC bonuses:** For an IUS card you have to go to Almatur in Warsaw; this gives you 25 per cent reductions on international trains within the former Eastern Bloc. New ISIC cards are combined with the IUS card.

● **Money matters:** 1 zloty (zl.) = 100 groszy (g.) (never used). Banking hours are Mon.–Fri.: 8 a.m.–1 p.m. Some banks Sat.: 8 a.m.–10.45 a.m. It's also possible to exchange money at Orbis and at travel agents.

Currency exchange has been opened to the free market, thus eliminating the need for a black market at a stroke. You now get the same rate everywhere and so living here for foreigners can be very, very cheap. You should still keep your exchange receipts as they may be checked when you leave. You aren't allowed to take zlotys out of the country, and as it is worthless anywhere else anyway you might as well spend it all.

● **Post offices:** Open Mon.–Fri.: 8 a.m.–8 p.m. Getting mail sent on is more trouble than it's worth (allow at least three weeks). Most embassies will keep your letters for at least two weeks.

● **Shops:** For food, 8 a.m.–7 p.m., others 11 a.m.–6 p.m. For opening times of museums, etc., check with the local IT office.

SLEEPING

It can be difficult to find a room in Poland without having fixed it up beforehand. To do this contact Polorbis (see p. 56 for address). They will issue you with student accommodation vouchers ($7 for students). These vouchers allow you to stay at any of the ISHs (international student hostels) (open July, Aug. and Sept.) in Poland if you're a student or under 25. If you haven't already done this, then your best plan is to arrive as early as possible in the day –

and even this does not ensure you a bed at an ISH. Vouchers are a prerequisite in Warsaw, so don't waste time going along unless you have them. If you've no luck with the ISHs, try the Polish Youth Hostel Federation (PTSM). Most require an IYHF card, but it's not always essential. The good news is that they're very cheap, the bad news is that they're like overcrowded prisons. There are a huge number of hostels ('schroniska mlodziezowe') in Poland all of which are spartan even by Western YH standards.

The more money you have, the less your problems are likely to be. PTTK is an organization which runs cheap hotels called 'Domy Turysty'; you can find out about these from the local IT office, but don't build your hopes up as they are nearly always full. Another organization called 'Biuro Zakwaterowania' arranges for you to stay with private families. Be careful about accepting offers of private rooms on the street as the room in question might well be a long way out of town. Finally, if you're really desperate, try the long queue at the Orbis office; they might have a spare bed in one of their hotels, if you're prepared to pay the high prices asked.

EATING AND NIGHTLIFE

The austere economic measures have affected tourists as well as the Poles. Things are not as bad as the media make out, however, for it's still possible to eat very well if you know where to look. It's best to stick to fish or poultry with which the Poles have had plenty of experience. You can get a good meal – but not a gastronomical delight – at the top hotels. Expect to pay around 20,000 zlotys for a three-course meal. Avoid station restaurants completely, except Warsaw, and only go there if you are stuck.

Nightlife is slowly resurfacing with the freeing up of society. It revolves around kawiarnie (cafés) and winiarnie (wine bars), and in some places student clubs.

Warsaw (Warszawa)

The beautiful city of Warsaw could have looked very different today had the patriotic Poles decided to replace the bombed buildings of 1944 with concrete blocks, instead of rebuilding replicas of the original nineteenth-century structures. Ignore the few Stalinesque buildings that have crept in, and judge the city instead on her elegant palaces and parks. Her past is bloody and tragic, and you only have to look back to 1943 when Hitler ordered that no stone of Warsaw should be left standing, for evidence of this. The HIS-TORICAL MUSEUM OF THE CITY, on the Old Town Market Square, has film captured from the Nazis which shows the systematic destruction of this city, and there are reminders of the holocaust dotted all round the centre.

TOURIST INFORMATION

The Warsaw information office is located at pl Zamkowy 1/13 (Tel. 270000). The main Orbis office is at ul Bracka 16 (Tel. 260271), open Mon.–Fri.: 8 a.m.–7 p.m., Sat.: 8 a.m.–5 p.m. The Orbis branch at Marszalkowska 142 sells international train tickets.

● **Addresses:**
POST OFFICE: Świętokrzyska.
AMEX: Orbis, Marszalkowska 142.
ALMATUR (Polish Student Travel): At the university on ul Koper-nika 15 (Tel. 262356). Open Mon.–Fri.: 8.30 a.m.–8 p.m. (4.30 p.m. Sept.–June).
UK EMBASSY: Aleja Róz 1 (Tel. 281001).
US EMBASSY: Al Ujazdowskie 29/31 (Tel. 283041).
CANADIAN EMBASSY: ul Matejki 1/5 (Tel. 298051).
FIRST AID: Hoza 56 (Tel. 999).
STATIONS: There are three stations in Warsaw, but the only one you're likely to use consistently is the new Centralna. Train information: Tel. 200361.
PHONE CODE: 022.

● **Getting about:** Buy your tram and bus tickets at the kiosks marked Ruch (bilety tramwajowe and bilety autobusowe). Buy as many as you think you'll use in one go (at the station) to avoid queues. Buses marked with letters are expresses and cost twice as much as normal buses. After 11 p.m. all fares are doubled.

SEEING

Between the STARE MIASTO (old town) and the LAZIENKI PARK lie the main sights of Warsaw. The centre of the old town is the beautiful RYNEK (market square). Rebuilt baroque houses line the square and a block to the south lies ST JOHN'S CATHEDRAL, the main church for Warsaw's deeply religious Catholics. In Zamkowy Square stands Warsaw's oldest monument, the Sigismund III column (1644), and this adjoins the ROYAL CASTLE which dates back to the fourteenth century and is still being worked on to repair its 1940s damage. The tin-roofed baroque PALACE is close by.

The Jewish population of Warsaw was wiped out under Nazism and the PAWIAK PRISON where 35,000 were executed and 65,000 detained is now a museum. The JEWISH HISTORICAL INSTITUTE at Al Świerczewskiego 79 looks at what happened in the famous Warsaw Ghetto, and the MAUSOLEUM TO STRUGGLE AND MARTYRDOM, across the river in Praga, is housed in the former Gestapo HQ and prison.

LAZIENKI PALACE AND PARK were built for the last Polish king in the eighteenth century. The palace has been restored and there are many other buildings and monuments in this graceful park. On the southern edge of the park is the monument to Chopin, and on Sunday afternoons there are often Chopin recitals. The WILANÓW PALACE AND PARK was one of the seventeenth-century kings' summer houses. The restored palace can be visited, and while you're out here you can visit the MUSEUM OF THE POLISH POSTER in the palace grounds. The palace is closed Tuesdays, the museum shuts Mondays and you reach them by bus B from ul Marszalkowska.

SLEEPING

Finding a bed in Warsaw can be a depressing and soul-destroying experience. Your best course of action is to go to the Almatur office (see above) and ask them for the addresses of their current ISHs (they change locations annually). These are open July–August and are cheaper if you are a student. Almatur also have lists of the campsites. If you're an IYHF member, go along to PTSM at ul Chocimska 28 for a list of Polish hostels. The two in Warsaw are cheap, rule-ridden and fairly depressing. They're at Karolkowa 53a (Tel. 328829) and Smolna 30 (Tel. 278952), but you must arrive before 9 a.m. to be in with a chance. PTTK at ul Marszalkowska 124 will give you a list of their Domy Turysty. The best campsite is Gromada on ul Zwirki i Wigury (Tel. 254391). There are bungalows here as well as tent sites, and they offer one of the best deals going: about 10,000 zl. per person in a four-person bungalow (bus 128, 136 or 175 from Centralna, direction airport). The two-tier price structure (one price for Eastern European residents, one for Western tourists) puts hotels right out of the picture, so don't even contemplate them.

EATING AND NIGHTLIFE

Make up for all the hardships you've had to endure by eating out in style. Food here is cheap enough to let you eat in all the best restaurants and still think you got a bargain. If you're cutting back on food too, eat in the milk bars (bar mleczny) or at the university cafeteria on campus at ul Krakowskie Przedmieście. Cristal-Budapest, ul Marszalkowska 21–25, does good Hungarian dishes, or try the Krokodyl, Starego Miasta 21, on the old town market square.

The kawiarnie and winiarnie are the hub of social life in Warsaw, as elsewhere in Poland. It's not difficult to find good ones, but Fukier, Rynek Starego Miasta, is Poland's best and dates back to the seventeenth century. For dancing, Hybrydy, ul Kniewskiego 7/9, is a lively student disco. The cinema is cheap, and Baja, ul Marszalkowska 136/138, shows Polish films with English or French subtitles. For opera, concert or theatre tickets, go to the Orbis office. If you need to get rid of some zlotys try the Centrum shopping centre on ul Marszalkowska near Central Station.

Cracow (Kraków)

A visit to Cracow in the south is a must as it is the ancient city of Polish kings and culture. Gothic, Renaissance and Baroque architecture reflect this long history. It is the only city in Poland to survive the war and has retained its medieval air.

TOURIST INFORMATION

Wawel Tourist is near Główny station at ul Pawia 6/8 (Tel. 229730). Pick up 'What, Where, When in Cracow', open Mon.–Fri.: 8 a.m.–7 p.m. Orbis is in the main square at Rynek Główny 41 (Tel. 224035).

Addresses:
POST OFFICE: corner of Westerplatte and Wielopole.
AMEX: at Orbis in the Hotel Cracovia, ul Puszkina 1 (Tel. 222885).
ALMATUR: Rynek Główny 7/8 (Tel. 226123).
US CONSULATE: ul Stolarska 9 (Tel. 221400).
PHARMACY: Komorowskiego 11 (Tel. 223027). Open 24 hours.
TRAINS: Make sure you get off at Kraków Główny, a 10-minute walk from the centre, and not one of the suburban stations. Train information: Tel. 222248.
PHONE CODE: 012.

SEEING

To see the sights, wander around the old town (STARE MIASTO) which is surrounded by a park where the old walls once stood. At the centre is the huge central market square, RYNEK GŁÓWNY, with its Renaissance mercantile CLOTH HALL (museum upstairs). WAWEL CASTLE dominates the River Vistula and encloses a CATHEDRAL, overseen for many years by Karol Wojtyla (now Pope John Paul II). The fifteenth-century COLLEGIUM MAIUS on sw Anny is the oldest building of the famous JAGIELLONIAN UNIVERSITY and is well worth a visit. The old Jewish quarter of KAZIMIERZ has Poland's oldest synagogue, the STARA SYNAGOGA at Szeroka 40.

SLEEPING

The Biuro Zakwaterowan, ul Pawia 8 (Tel. 221921) will arrange accommodation. There are three hostels – ul Oleandry 4 (Tel. 338822), tram 17, ul Kosciuszki 88 (Tel. 221951) and ul Zlotejkielni 1 (Tel. 372441). You could also try the Dom Turysty at Westerplatte 15–16 (Tel. 229566) which is on the edge of the old town. For camping try Camping Krak on ul Radzikowskiego 99 (Tel. 372122), bus 208, open mid-May to mid-September.

EATING AND NIGHTLIFE

Street stalls are often the best place to eat, but few restaurants will stretch your budget either. Try Staropolska, ul Sienna 4.

Cracow has better nightlife than much of Poland because of the university. Try the student club Pod Jaczczurami at Rynek Główny 8 or the disco Rotunda, ul Oleandry 1.

• **Excursions:** Less than two hours away is the town of OSWIECIM, better known as AUSCHWITZ, site of the largest concentration camp in Hitler's 'Final Solution'. There are actually two camps, Auschwitz itself and the huge BIRKENAU about a mile and a half away. The Auschwitz camp, now a museum providing a harrowing impression of life and death in the camps, is within walking distance of the station and is well signposted. You may prefer to take a bus or taxi; neither will stretch your budget. Watch the spine-chilling film showing the camp just after liberation.

The salt mine at WIELICZKA is an amazing complex of underground chambers, including the CHAPEL OF THE BLESSED KINGS, intricately carved from salt. The guided tour lasts 3–4 hours. Try and go early to be finished by lunchtime.

Czestochowa

Czestochowa is the most important religious site in deeply Catholic Poland. Pilgrims come from around the world to the JASNA GORA MONASTERY to see the BLACK MADONNA, an icon which is said to have cried during a seventeenth-century Swedish siege. The tourist office is at Aleje NMP 40. The youth hostel, at ul Waclawy Marek 12 (Tel. 0331–31296), is on the other side of town.

Tatra Mountains

Sixty miles south of Cracow is the beautiful TATRA NATIONAL PARK with lofty 6,000-foot mountains of granite and limestone. ZAKO-PANE is the largest town in the area and is a good place to base yourself to explore the surrounding area. A funicular railway runs to the top of MT GUBALOWKA (3,720 feet) and a cable car up MT KASPROWY WIERCH (6,510 feet). There is a great hike to the top of MT GIEWONT (6,260 feet) which takes about 6 hours. You will have a magnificent view from each peak. The tourist office is at ul Kosciuszki 7 and the PTTK at ul Krupówki 37 will give you information on mountain shelters. The youth hostel is at ul Nowotarska 45 (Tel. 0165–4203).

Gdańsk

The port of Gdańsk in north-eastern Poland is famous as the birthplace of Solidarity and has a lot to offer the eurorailer with its historic old town dating from the time of the medieval Hanseatic League, when the city was known as Danzig.

TOURIST INFORMATION AND ADDRESSES

TOURIST OFFICE: ul Heweliusza 8 (Tel. 310338), open Mon.–Fri.: 9 a.m.–3 p.m., Sat.: 8 a.m.–4 p.m., Sun.: 8 a.m.–3 p.m.
ORBIS: in Hotel Hevelius, ul Heweliusza 22 (Tel. 314777), open Mon.–Fri.: 10 a.m.–5 p.m.
POST OFFICE: ul Pocztowa and ul Dluga.
AMEX: at Orbis in Monopol Orbis, pl Gorkiego (Tel. 311466).
ALMATUR: Dlugi Targ 11 (Tel. 317801), open Mon.–Tues. and Thurs.–Fri.: 9 a.m.–3 p.m.
TRAINS: Gdańsk Główny is 10 minutes from the centre. Train information: Tel. 310051.
PHONE CODE: 058.

SEEING

Around the market square, DLUGI TARG, is the headquarters of the old Hanseatic League and the imposing TOWN HALL which contains a very interesting HISTORICAL MUSEUM (closed Mondays). There is a great view from the tower. Walk along ul Mariacka to see the grand façades of seventeenth-century burghers' houses. North of the old town is the home of Solidarity, the LENIN SHIPYARDS, and a monument to workers killed during the rising of 1970. During the summer Gdańsk is packed with beachgoers, try STOGI BEACH (tram 9).

SLEEPING

There are many hostels in the area, but the most central is at ul Walowa 21 (Tel. 312313), five minutes from the station, closed 10 a.m.–5 p.m. Use the Biuro Zakwaterowan at ul Elzbietanska 10–11 (Tel. 312634) to help you find a room. For camping try Gdańsk-Jelitkowo, ul Jelitkowska (Tel. 532731).

EATING AND NIGHTLIFE

Milk bars are probably your best bet. If you want to splash out try Pod Lososiem, ul Szeroka 54, which serves excellent fresh fish. Flisak, ul Chlebnicka and Kameralna, ul Dluga 57 are popular student clubs.

PORTUGAL

Entry requirements	Passport
Population	10,100,000
Capital	Lisbon (pop.: 1,500,000 +)
Currency	Escudo
	£1 = approx. 248 $
Political system	Republic
Religion	Roman Catholic
Language	Portuguese (some English spoken in cities)
Public holidays	1 Jan.; Shrove Tuesday; Good Friday;
	25 Apr.; 1 May; Corpus Christi; 10 June;
	15 Aug.; 5 Oct.; 1 Nov.; 1, 8, 25 Dec.
International dialling codes	From UK: 010 + 351 + number
	From USA: 011 + 351 + number
	To UK: 07 + 44 + number
	To USA: 07 + 1 + number
Eurotrain office	Rua C.C. Branco 20, P–1100 Lisboa
	(Tel. 01–525709)

There's a lot of rubbish talked about Portugal, not least about the beautiful unspoilt Algarve where, according to most guidebooks, inviting a girl out can still be misinterpreted as a proposal. Today, certainly in the main tourist areas, attitudes of the young people are likely to be the same as their contemporaries in any other European country.

Portugal's early history is shared with the rest of the Iberian peninsula, with the Phoenicians, Greeks and Romans all leaving their mark. Portugal was recognized as a separate nation in 1143 with the Moors being pushed out in 1249. Throughout the fifteenth century, explorers such as Vasco da Gama helped Portugal's overseas empire to grow quickly through the discovery and exploration of the African coast, India, China and finally Brazil. Before long, Portugal had the world's largest empire, but her glory was to be short-lived, as conflict with Spain and rivalry with other European powers gradually brought about her decline. Britain and Portugal share a 'special relationship' with an alliance going back more than 600 years. Eventually, even the royal family packed their bags and set off to Brazil during the Napoleonic Wars. Recently, the 1974 revolution has brought about a more liberal constitution. Portugal remains one of Europe's most affordable countries, where it's possible to cultivate a good tan and eat well while doing it.

PORTUGUESE RAILWAYS
(Caminhos de Ferro Portugueses, CP)

The British originally built the Portuguese network with a wide gauge for extra comfort. Much of the 3,600-km network is electrified, but you will also find some of the more remote inland lines are narrow-gauge and steam-hauled. The fastest of the non-supplement trains are the expresses (directo). Next down the list are the semi directos, which stop nearly as often as the slow regionals. Away from the Lisbon area, services can be very slow, so you might feel justified in paying the extra supplements for the intercity rápidos; this works out at about 25 per cent above the normal tariff. The standard has improved in recent years, though.

TRAIN INFORMATION

English is spoken by most information staff.

• **Reservations:** Are optional on inland trains and are quite cheap. For international and express trains, reservations are free of charge providing they are made the day before departure. In general, trains are crowded so it's best to reserve seats in advance.

• **Supplements:** Inter Rail and Eurail pass holders need to pay a supplement to travel on express trains. Some Rápido trains carry a saloon observation car which requires a supplement to travel in it. Don't buy tickets on the train as you face a whopping surcharge. It's far better to queue at the station, unless unavoidable. Ask first about the train you are taking. It is worth paying the small supplement on the Lisbon–Porto line.

• **Night travel:** There are no couchettes, but the sleepers are cheap.

• **Eating on trains:** All trains except the regionals have mini-bars, but only the rápidos can be relied upon to have dining cars.

• **Scenic tips:** As with Spain, there are enough problems getting where you want to go without worrying about scenic routes; however, the run from Valença in the north down to Lisbon is one of the best Portugal has to offer. Also try the line from Porto along the Douro valley and its branch lines, such as the one to Braganza.

Always check the timetabling of trains with the posters on station walls, as printed timetables cannot always be relied upon to be accurate.

● **Rover tickets:** Available for 7, 14 or 21 days in first and second class. The 'Tourist Ticket' is valid for all trains on the network and costs 11,500 $, 16,700 $ and 24,000 $ respectively for second-class travel.

TOURIST INFORMATION

Is provided by the government-run Postos do Turismo. They have offices all over the country and stalls at major stations.

● **ISIC bonuses:** The main perk here is admission to the cheap student restaurants on your ISIC. In addition about 1,200 places – discos, theatres and so on – also offer discounts. For further information contact Turismo Social e Juvenil, Turicoop (1st floor), Rua Pascual do Melo, Lisbon.

● **Money matters:** 1 escudo ($) = 100 centavos.
Banking hours are Mon.–Fri.: 8.30 a.m.–11.45 a.m., 1 p.m.–2.45 p.m. There are late-night exchange facilities at major tourist resorts.

● **Post offices and shops:** Open Mon.–Sat.: 9 a.m.–1 p.m., 3 p.m.–7 p.m. (closed Saturday p.m.).

● **Museums:** Open 10 a.m.–5 p.m.

SLEEPING

The government-run tourist board controls all the accommodation within Portugal and will book you a room if required. Hotels are graded from one star to five, boarding houses (estalagern, albergaria, pensão), one to four. By law, prices should be shown at reception and behind the door of each room. A double room in a three-star hotel costs about 4,000 $ a night. A student hostel tends to be more expensive than a cheap pensão. There are nineteen youth hostels (Pousadas de Juventude) in Portugal, all requiring IYHF cards, and most with an 11 p.m. curfew. Camping is another possibility, but don't expect too many facilities except in the

Algarve, where you have to have a Camping Carnet. I recommend cheap hotels and boarding houses. They're normally near the stations, and as prices are unaffected by location it's not really worth shopping around.

EATING AND NIGHTLIFE

Food is cheap in Portugal and eating out is a relatively inexpensive affair (900 $ to 1,400 $), except in the Algarve where prices are marked up for the tourists.

Go for fish dishes, especially chowders if you get the chance: they're invariably cheaper and tastier than meat dishes. National specialities include 'linguado delícia' (sole cooked with banana). If you don't like fish, pork represents the best value among the meat dishes. A bottle of wine is often thrown in for the price of the meal; if not ask for the local plonk (vinho da casa). The port is excellent but, rather surprisingly, it's not drunk a lot in Portugal.

If you're living on the beaches and need a meat 'booster', keep your eyes skinned for the mobile shops which serve cheap steak sandwiches (pregos).

Taverns tend to be very basic, but go down well with the local lads.

Bullfighting in Portugal is not as gory as it is in Spain – they're not allowed to kill the bull – but it's still a national obsession. Of the two types of Portuguese bullfights, the 'tourada à antiga' is perhaps the more spectacular. Here the bullfighter is dressed in thirteenth-century costume and fights from a horse.

Discos and bars are at their best in Lisbon, though by northern European standards many of the discos are pretty tame, and you'll do better heading for a bar which has 'fados' (melancholy Portuguese ballads) on the bill. There are no licensing hours in Portugal, so things can often drag right through the night till dawn.

Lisbon (Lisboa)

This westernmost capital of Europe escaped many of the influences that shaped the rest of the continent: among them the Reformation, the Industrial Revolution and the Second World War. It has developed out on a limb at a different pace and in a different way, and if any one force can be said to have affected its development, it was – and is – the sea. Lisbon was rebuilt after the 1755 earthquake; only the old Moorish quarter of Alfama escaped destruction. Essentially, it's a pleasant city to visit: beds and meals are cheap and plentiful, the nightlife's lively and there are several places of great interest to visit.

STATION FACILITIES

International trains and northern and eastern trains use Santa Apolónia Station. Trains to the south and south-east leave from Barreiro Station (linked to Santa Apolónia by a ferry across the Tagus – free on Inter Rail); trains to Sintra and the west use Rossio (on bus routes 9, 39–59 from Santa Apolónia), and trains for Estoril and Cascais use Cais do Sodré Station (bus 35).

	SANTA APOLÓNIA
Train information	8 a.m.–10 p.m. (Tel. 326226)
Reservations	9 a.m.–8 p.m. Window 11
Tourist information	9 a.m.–2 p.m., 4 p.m.–7 p.m.
Foreign exchange	9 a.m.–8 p.m.
Left-luggage lockers	No access 2 a.m.–5 a.m.
Left-luggage store	7 a.m.–1 a.m.
Bar, Buffet	7 a.m.–11 p.m.
Shops	Mon.–Sat.: 7 a.m.–12 midnight
Waiting room	All hours
Post office	Mon.–Fri.: 9 a.m.–7 p.m.
Station shuts	2 a.m.–5 a.m.

Daily trains to: Porto, Madrid, Irún, Paris.

TOURIST INFORMATION

The Portuguese National Tourist Office (Tel. 363624) is in Palácio Foz on Praça dos Restauradores, open Mon.–Sat.: 9 a.m.–8 p.m., Sun.: 10 a.m.–6 p.m. The Municipal Tourist Office is at Rua Jardim do Regedor; and the national tourist office headquarters is at Avenida Augusto de Aguiar 86 (Tel. 575015), open Mon.–Fri.: 9.30 a.m.–5.30 p.m. (by Rossio Station).

● **Addresses:**

POST OFFICE ('Correio'): Praça do Comércio, open Mon.–Fri.: 9 a.m.–7 p.m.

AMEX: Star Travel Service, Avenida Sidónio Pais 4A, open Mon.–Fri.: 9.15 a.m.–12.30 p.m., 2 p.m.–6 p.m. (Tel. 539871).

UK EMBASSY: Rua S. Domingos à Lapa 35–39 (Tel. 661191).

US EMBASSY: Avenida Dos Forças Armadas (Tel. 725600).

CANADIAN EMBASSY: Rua Rosa Aranjo 2, 6th floor (Tel. 562547).

AUSTRALIAN EMBASSY: Avenida da Liberdade 244 (Tel. 539108).

EUROTRAIN: Rua C.C. Branco 20 (Tel. 525709).

24-HOUR CHEMIST: British Hospital, Rua Saraiva de Carvalho 49 (Tel. 602020).

PHONE CODE: 01.

● **Getting about:** It's best to get your tram or bus ticket from a Carris kiosk rather than on the vehicle, where it costs about 110 $. A 4-day pass costs 1,000 $ and is valid on buses, trolleys and subways. Buy it from Carris booths in the main stations. The metro system is limited, but a fast way of getting around and only costs around 50 $. If you're travelling in a group taxis work out cheap at 75 $ per kilometre.

SEEING

It's pointless us suggesting a route round the ALFAMA district as it's so sprawling you're bound to get lost, so just wander through at your own pace, and if you happen to pass the church of SÃO MIGUEL or LARGO DO SALVADOR 22 (sixteenth-century mansion house), look in. This is one of Europe's most colourful districts, especially in the morning when the fish market's on, or on Fridays (washday) when the narrow streets are hung with locals' shirts and undies. The area is enclosed roughly by the banks of the Tagus, the castle, the church of St Vincent-outside-the-walls, and the cathedral. ST GEORGE'S CASTLE, the fortress on the hill, has dominated Lisbon in one form or another for 1,500 years. Its gardens of peacocks and flamingos make a good vantage point to look over the city. Near the centre is the SÉ (cathedral), worth a look for its ambulatory and burial chapel.

On the outskirts of the city are quite a few sights worth visiting. Go to the BELÉM quarter (tram 15, 16 or 17 from Praça do

Comércio), get off at the Museu Nacional dos Coches, and head for the HIERONYMITE MONASTERY (Mosteiro dos Jerónimos, closed Mondays). Here Vasco da Gama is buried, as are various Portuguese kings. The affluent merchants in the spice trade put up most of the money for this beautiful place which was built in the early sixteenth century. Opposite is the MONUMENT TO THE DISCOVERIES (180 $, free with ISIC). Take the lift (free) for a view of the city. Also in this district is the TOWER OF BELÉM (400 $, free with ISIC), one of Lisbon's landmarks.

As far as museums go, the GULBENKIAN arts and culture centre, Av. de Berna 45 (closed Mondays), the MUSEU NACIONAL DE ARTE ANTIGA, Rua das Janelas Verdes 95, and the FOLK ART MUSEUM, Av. Marginal, Belém, are the best.

• **Excursions:** SINTRA, twenty miles north-west of Lisbon, is one of Portugal's oldest towns. The summer residence of the royal family was here and PENA PALACE AND PARK are well worth the day trip (closed Wednesdays and public holidays). The MOORISH CASTLE, with a fantastic view, is a must. The park has more than 400 kinds of trees and many rare plants. Also out here is the sixteenth-century Capuchinhos monastery and Monserrate Park (closed Tuesdays). If you want a day on the beach, head for ESTORIL, a jet-set resort sixteen miles west of the city, or CASCAIS, two miles further on. If you want to stop off here but can't afford the hotel prices, head a few miles back towards Lisbon and get off the train at Oeiras. Here you can enjoy a fine beach and an excellent modern, cheap and friendly hostel just a stone's throw away. It is at Catalazete, Santa Amaro de Oeiras (Tel. 2430638). It's quite small and fills up quickly so don't waste time in booking your place. From Cascais you can catch a bus to CABO DA ROCA, the most westerly point in Europe, with a memorable view from the lighthouse. No. 45 departs from Cascais at 11 a.m., 3 p.m. and 6.45 p.m. and returns at 11.50 a.m., 4 p.m. and 7.30 p.m. A more frequent bus (no. 403) runs from Sintra. Get off at the Azoia turn-off and walk the last couple of miles. Another idea is to visit QUELUZ, the town eight miles north-west of Lisbon, where the rococo palace used to entertain VIPs of the Portuguese government. It's stuffed full of antiques and can be reached by train from Rossio Station (closed Tuesdays).

SLEEPING

An average double in a pension is about 2–3,000 $, a single 3–4,000 $. There are plenty of cheap places in Lisbon – not everywhere is clean and quiet, but the ones listed are about as close as you'll get. If these don't come up lucky, try yourself round Rua da Alegria, Rua dos Correiros, Rua Augusta and Praça da Figueira. The youth hostel, at Rua Andrade Corvo 46, is cheap and a 20-minute walk from the centre, but next to Picoas Metro (Tel. 532696). As far as camping goes, there are plenty of sites – and free beach camping close by – but the best site is the Parque Nacional de Turismo e Campismo (Tel. 704413) (bus to Parque Florestal, Monsanto). Residencial Mansarde, Avenida da Liberdade 141, 5th floor (Tel. 372963), charges about 3,000 $ for doubles, and there are two other places on this stair. Also at No. 53 of this street, Pensão do Sul (Tel. 365647) has cheap rooms. Pensão Ninho de Águias, Costa do Castelo 74 (Tel. 860391), is of very high quality. Doubles start at 3,200 $ including breakfast. Pensão São João da Praça on São João da Praça 97 (Tel. 862591) is near the Alfama district and asks from 2,500 $ per double.

EATING AND NIGHTLIFE

Between the port and the Praça da Figueira is the best district. Lisbon is no longer as cheap as in the eighties, so choose your district carefully. Try Rua dos Correeiros (near Terreiro do Paco). There are cheap places in most areas. Use the Mercado da Ribeira outside the Cais do Sodré for picnic food, and watch out you don't get stuck on Sundays, especially in July, when many places close. Fish is generally good value, but don't eat the bread and savouries put out on the tables unless you're prepared to pay the extortionate prices that are often asked for them. Restaurante Trevo da Madalena and Restaurante Central on Rua da Madalena both do meals around 900 $, or try Gloria on Rua da Gloria 39A. The area near the youth hostel is quite good for eating places.

Nightlife starts late and can get pretty lively. The authentic Portuguese folk music, the fado, is performed in several restaurants and cafés. Don't go till around midnight, unless you're happy to share your evenings with coach parties from package tours. Sr Vinho, Rua Praças 18, and the Patio das Cantigas, Rua São Caetano 27, offer authentic fados, but not for under 1,000 $. Port, the national drink, can be sampled at the Port Wine Institute, Rua S. Pedro de Alcantara 45, from 10 a.m.–12 midnight. From May–Sept. the Lisbon Amusement Park gives you somewhere to spend time before heading for the bars or cafés later on. The fair goes on till 1 a.m. and can be reached by the underground (station Entre-Campos). The best club in town is Trump's on Rua da Imprensa Nacional.

Northern Portugal

If you're approaching Portugal from the north, the places worth stopping for are Viana do Castelo, Óbidos on the Costa de Prata, and Coimbra. PORTO is an industrial town, very much a mixture of old and new. Climb the Igrejados Clerijos church tower, then visit one of the 20 or so Porthouses for a free tour and tasting, though avoid buying any in the Porthouses' own shops as you will probably find it cheaper in town. Much of this region is unspoilt, as most eurorailers head for either Lisbon or the overrated Algarve. A day trip to REGNA in the Douro Valley is possible from Porto. This is one of Europe's most scenic routes.

VIANA DO CASTELO: this pretty little fishing resort, 1½ hours from Porto, has a vantage point for views over the whole region: the BASÍLICA OF SANTA LUZIA. You can take the funicular up or, better still, walk up the twisting road past the pine and eucalyptus trees till you reach the top. Back down in the town, look out for the reminders of the Renaissance in the buildings of the PRAÇA DA REPÚBLICA and the church of SÃO DOMINGOS. If you're here in the third week of August, you'll catch the festival: bullfights, processions, fireworks, dancing, etc. The MUNICIPAL MUSEUM has a collection of the ceramics Portugal is famous for. Rooms aren't a problem: try the streets off Avenida dos Combatentes, or camp at CABEDELO BEACH.

ÓBIDOS is a little medieval village, seven miles from the sea, and is worth seeing for its preserved CASTLE, old TOWN WALLS and the two churches of SANTA MARIA and the MISERICÓRDIA. Tourist information is on Rua Direita.

COIMBRA: this university town is second only to Lisbon in terms of historical and cultural importance. It is set among the beautiful forests and woods of the Beira Litoral region, and is about 2½ hours from the capital. Get off at Coimbra 'A' station, walk two blocks east for the turismo in Largo da Portagem. It's open Mon.–Sat.: 9 a.m.–8 p.m., Sun.: 10 a.m.–5 p.m., and operates a currency exchange desk.

The UNIVERSITY is the best sight of the town. The OLD LIBRARY (Biblioteca), the CHAPEL and the MUSEUM are all impressive (knock on the door to be let in) and the CEREMONIAL HALL is decorated with some fine 'azulejos' (ceramic tiles). The MACHADO MUSEUM nearby was a former episcopal palace, and today houses many of Portugal's artistic treasures. The town's CATHEDRAL is twelfth-century, as is the Cistercian convent, MOSTEIRO DE CELAS. Not far out is a reconstructed village of all the famous buildings in Portugal, miniature-size: PORTUGAL DOS PEQUENINOS.

For cheap beds, look out for 'dormidas' round the station: Rua da Sota and the streets around should produce something. For eats, try 'Zé Manel', Beco do Forno 12, just off Rua da Sota. Apart from good cheap food, this place has character. Open 12 noon–3 p.m., 5 p.m.–10 p.m. and closed Mondays. Much cheaper food than in Lisbon.

An unspoilt resort where traditional Portugal survives alongside tourism is Nazare, 5 km (bus) from Valado on the Lisbon–Coimbra line. There is a nice beach and a funicular (20 $) to the old town.

The Alentejo

This huge region is the hinterland of Portugal between Spain and the Tagus. It is off the beaten track – a good place for avoiding your fellow tourists. The main town is EVORA, three hours from Lisbon. See the fourth-century ROMAN TEMPLE OF DIANA, the chapel (CAPELA DE OSSOS) containing the bones of 5,000 monks, the SÉ (cathedral) and the MUSEU D'EVORA (free on ISIC).

The youth hostel is at Largo Cândido dos Reis 70 (Tel. 044–31868). Camping is on the Alcáçovas Road (282 $ per person).

The Algarve

Portugal's famous southern region used to be one of the best-kept secrets in continental Europe; mile after mile of white sand interspersed with picturesque fishing villages. Sadly that is no longer the case as the package holiday industry has really taken off in a big way in the Algarve since the early 1970s. Many of the small villages have been turned into overgrown building sites, crowded with British package holidaymakers and overpriced accordingly.

The Algarve has practically no evidence left of its historical past. Most of the small villages were flattened by a major earthquake in 1755, and only FARO, LAGOS and SAGRES (home of Prince Henry the Navigator) have any traces worth visiting. The region as a whole retains some appeal, if you can manage to avoid all the busy package resorts, including QUARTEIRA, VILAMOURA, MONTE GORDO and (especially) ALBUFEIRA. These over-commercialized villages really have nothing to offer other than superb beaches. If you're lucky, you might find a few empty feet of sand all to yourself among the package tourists. One good place to base yourself is the small town of Lagoa, between Albufeira and Lagos. There is a complex specially designed for young travellers, and has the main advantage of sending transport to meet all local trains in the small towns. It is open from the end of May to the beginning of October. It is a self-contained unit with a choice of three restaurants/snack bars, and a disco with parties most nights. Accommodation is in dormitories or tents. Also there is a shuttle bus all day to its own beach which gives access to other, more secluded beaches. It is very popular among eurorailers because of the cosmopolitan atmosphere. For further information contact Astor Hostels, Thurloe St, London SW7.

One advantage of the huge package trade is that English is practically the second language of the region. The local cuisine is worth investigating – plenty of fish and seafood delicacies – and regional wines are really cheap. House wines are normally less than a pound (about 240 $) even in some of the better cafés and restaurants. The region is a sportsman's paradise, assuming he's not short of a few quid, and there are many exclusive golf and sports clubs tagged on to the bigger hotels.

Finding an inexpensive base in the Algarve is next to impossible during the peak summer months from June to August. Look out for 'casas particulares' (private accommodation) or else consider sleeping on the beach. If you've really set your heart on spending a few days in the Algarve then you ought to consider arriving out of season. March and April are good months, when the weather is mild with temperatures occasionally straying into the low 70sF. Cheap accommodation is also relatively plentiful in towns like Faro and Lagos. The weather can become quite windy after September so bear this in mind before packing too much suntan lotion later on in the year.

The Algarve is well connected by rail from Lisbon and the north, and the region's main line runs across from Lagos, through Faro, to Vila Real de Santo António in the east.

LAGOS is the region's westernmost town of any size and has a colourful past dating back to the time of the Celts. There's still quite a bit to see, including the scattered remains of the MEDIEVAL WALLS and the magnificent church of SANTO ANTONIO, on Rua Silva Lopes, which contains some of Portugal's finest gilt carvings. The REGIONAL MUSEUM next door has an interesting, if rather disjointed, collection of artifacts telling the town's history. The TOURIST OFFICE. is on Largo Marquês de Pombal.

FARO, the Algarve's capital, is well worth at least a day trip. Its jumbled streets spread out from a small MARINA just along from the railway station. Faro has an empty old CATHEDRAL just opposite the BISHOP'S PALACE. Nearby is an ARCHAEOLOGICAL MUSEUM, the better of a couple of modest museums in town. Try and get to the CARMELITE CHURCH at Largo do Carmo, near the main POST OFFICE as the church has a spectacular gilt interior, and a bizarre CHAPEL OF BONES behind it. The chapel was built by an over-zealous bishop in the last century using the skulls and bones of over 1,200 monks. Faro is your best bet for accommodation in the Algarve if you insist on arriving mid-summer. Room prices are over-inflated but you may find something away from the smart shopping centre part of town – aimed very much at the British tourist with lots of cash. Try PENSÃO RESIDENCIAL MARIM on Rua Gonçalo Barreto (Tel. 089–240–63). The TOURIST OFFICE, open daily 9 a.m.–8 p.m. in the summer, is on Rua da Misericórdia but don't expect much help in finding cheap accommodation.

If you are coming from Spain, remember there is a one-hour time difference when planning your onward journey after coming off the ferry at Vila Real, where you get the train to Faro and Lisbon.

For a total contrast, head inland for a day. The contrast with the heaving coastal resorts in many of the isolated rural villages is amazing, although you'll need to take the bus or cycle since the railway sticks rigidly to the coast! If you're heading east into Spain, VILA REAL DE SANTO ANTÓNIO sits right on the border and is a pleasant little town for a few hours' stop. Even if you're not heading onward through Spain, day trips from Vila Real across to AYAMONTE take 15 minutes by ferry (every half-hour, costs 70 $) and customs formalities are minimal.

ROMANIA

Entry requirements	Passport and visa (available at border)
Population	22,800,000
Capital	Bucharest (pop.: 2,090,000)
Currency	Leu
	£1 = approx. 34.22 lei
Political system	Republic
Religion	Romanian Orthodox
Language	Romanian (some French and German spoken)
Public holidays	1, 2 Jan.; 1, 2 May; 23, 24 Aug.
International dialling codes	From UK: 010 + 40 + number
	From USA: 011 + 40 + number
	To UK: 00 + 44 + number
	To USA: 00 + 1 + number

Romania is keen on encouraging tourism, especially after Romania's bloody Christmas revolution of 1989. Although the new government is still in the process of establishing its democratic credentials, things have become more lax for the eurorailer.

Once a Roman province, the area was overrun by Asian, Slavonic and Turkish tribes giving a real mixture of peoples. Moldavia in the north and Wallachia in the south were united to form Romania in 1859. Transylvania, the area in between, is full of forests and fortified towns and was once a good place for blood donors, but the demand has fallen away with the death of Count Dracula. Following German occupation in the two World Wars, Romania became part of the Soviet Bloc. Although Romania broke away from Moscow's foreign policy line, it remained firmly Stalinist with Ceauşescu as a total dictator. Economic mismanagement has made Romania the poorest country in Europe. The new government has taken steps to combat this but it will be very difficult, and energy shortages and food queues may continue. It's fascinating travelling through, and the fiery Romanians are interesting hosts.

ROMANIAN RAILWAYS
(Căile Ferate Române, CFR)

In recent years Romania has improved its services considerably in response to increased demand. Most trains are still dirty and overcrowded by Western standards, so imagine what they were like before. To travel at reasonable speed and comfort on any of the Rapide (fast) and Accelerate (semi-fast) trains you will have to pay a supplement. To avoid this, you have to travel on the local tren de persoane trains – a fate worse than death. In other words, pay the supplement.

• **Inter Rail bonuses:** Free entry to the railway museum at Gara de Nord, Bucharest.

TRAIN INFORMATION

English is not widely spoken, so be prepared with a French back-up. (French is Romania's second language.) If all else fails, try: 'De la ce peron pleacă trenul spre . . . ?' (From which platform does the train to . . . leave?)

• **Reservations:** Compulsory on all trains except the tren de persoane. The best strategy is to reserve your place out as soon as you arrive, especially on crowded routes, such as Bucharest–Constanta. Reserve your exit seat before entering the country – queues are horrendous.

• **Night travel:** Couchettes and sleepers hardly come up to Western standards and need to be booked well in advance, particularly on the Bucharest–Budapest run. Rates vary according to distance.

• **Eating on trains:** There are restaurants on many long-distance fast trains, and buffets on shorter-distance fast trains.

TOURIST INFORMATION

ONT is the national tourist organization. They have offices in all large towns which give out information and help in finding a room.

• **ISIC bonuses:** Reductions for all international rail travel in the Eastern Bloc. Also museum entrances reduced with an IUS card. For further information, contact BTT, Str. Oneşti 4–6, Bucharest 1.

• **Money matters:** 1 leu (plural, lei) = 100 bani (b).
Banking hours are Mon.–Sat.: 9 a.m.–12 noon, 1 p.m.–3 p.m. (closed Saturday p.m.).
    The leu has undergone high inflation recently and there is a lucrative black market paying seven to ten times the official rate.

However, the risks are also greater, as there are many informers. There is also a good black market for coffee. Kent cigarettes are useful for tipping.

• **Post offices, shops and museums:** All vary their times of opening, depending on the district. Most keep to the 9–5 routine six days a week. In Bucharest, some shops open on Sunday mornings.

SLEEPING

One's choices are limited in Romania by the absence of cheap class-three hotels but rooms in private homes may now fill this gap. Hostels (caminul de studenti) are run by the student travel service, BTT, and give preference to large groups when they open during July and August. If you're lucky and make the effort to get to the hostel direct, you will find it inexpensive. Most eurorailers camp and accept the poor facilities, or pay for a class-two hotel which can be anything up to 800 lei for a double room.

EATING AND NIGHTLIFE

Unlike elsewhere in Eastern Europe, eating is expensive and the food is generally of very low quality, as is the beer. Don't expect to be able to put a picnic lunch together from a supermarket unless you happen to like jam, which is colossally oversupplied. Romania's nightlife is not up to Hungary's standards, but after a few glasses of tzuica, the local plum spirit, you'll never know the difference.

Bucharest (Bucureşti)

The journey here on the dismal trains is not one of Europe's best and you'll probably wish you hadn't bothered halfway through the night, but take heart: Bucharest is known as the 'Paris of Eastern Europe', though considering the lack of nightlife and scarcity of actual 'sights', this is a bit over the top. The atmosphere post 1989–90 is exciting, though.

STATION FACILITIES

There are four train stations, Gara de Nord, Băneasa, Obor and Basarab. Gara de Nord is the biggest station and is used most by eurorailers.

	GARA DE NORD
Train information	24 hours (Tel. 052)
Reservations	24 hours
Tourist information	See below
Foreign exchange	8 a.m.–6 p.m.
Left-luggage lockers/store	24 hours
Café, Restaurant	6 a.m.–12 midnight
Waiting room	24 hours
Post office	24 hours

Daily trains to: Athens, Cluj, Belgrade, Berlin, Basel, Budapest, Munich, Paris, London, Prague, Sofia, Warsaw, Vienna, Zürich.

TOURIST INFORMATION

The station office is open 7 a.m.–9 p.m. weekdays, 7 a.m.–3 p.m. weekends. The main tourist office is at Blvd Magheru 7, open Mon.–Sat.: 7.30 a.m.–9.30 p.m., Sun.: 8.30 a.m.–1 p.m. However, the staff vary these hours at their own convenience. Don't expect the office to be open even if the door is. Also, don't be surprised if there are no street maps available – if this is so, the main tourist office has one on its wall which you can consult. Take tram 87 from the station to Piata Romana. You can change money at all offices. BTT, the youth tourist service that deals with groups (the whole of Romanian tourism centres on groups), is at Strada Oneşti 4–6, and opens 25 May–15 Sept., 8 a.m.–5 p.m., Sat.: 8 a.m.–1.30 p.m. Left-luggage is only for Romanians – foreigners have to use the 'Hand Luggage' office near Platform 13. The CFR offices are at Brezoianu Street 10, in the Tarom Building, and on Calea Griviţei.

● **Addresses:**
POST OFFICE: Str. Matei Millo 10, off Calea Victoriei, open 7 a.m.–midnight daily.
UK EMBASSY: Str. Jules Michelet 24 (Tel. 111635).
US EMBASSY: Tudor Arghezi 7–9 (Tel. 124040).
CANADIAN EMBASSY: Nicolae Iorga 36 (Tel. 506140).

24-HOUR CHEMIST: Blvd Magheru 18. Also at Gara de Nord.
PHONE CODE: 0.

• **Getting about:** Buses, trolley buses and trams are cheap, and tickets can be bought from all kiosks. Taxis too are a bargain. You will see many buses with huge grey cylinders on top, running the length of the bus. These have been converted to gas due to the petrol shortage. A metro system is still being built in Bucharest, with two lines having been completed. This merely adds to the chaos as some roads have been closed and many tram routes have been cancelled. Beware of pickpockets.

SEEING

Modern Bucharest is hard on the eye, so ignore the new and concentrate on the old. The name Bucharest was given to this town in 1459 by none other than Dracula, a local lad, known here as Vlad the Impaler. By far the most pleasant day's sightseeing is spent out on the HERĂSTRĂU PARK where the VILLAGE MUSEUM is. This collection of peasant houses gathered from all over the country is open 9 a.m.–6 p.m. (5 p.m. Monday). Parks and museums are Bucharest's main assets. LIBERTY PARK, the STUDENT PARK on Lacul Tei, or the central CISMIGIU PARK are great meeting places and the places to head for to meet young Romanians. Go to Piaţa Unirii for the bustling market where Romania's gypsies sell their wares. As far as museums go, out of the forty or so to choose from, I'd recommend the HISTORY MUSEUM; the former royal palace, today the NATIONAL ART MUSEUM; and the GEORGES ENESCO MUSEUM.

SLEEPING

For a bed in a student hostel, go to ONT or BTT (see above) and ask them for addresses as these change yearly. Camping is out at Camping Băneasa (Tel. 794525). It is cheap and has free hot showers. It is reached by taking bus 105 from Gara de Nord to its terminus at Plata Scinteli, then bus 148. The site is hidden in the trees. Grade-two hotels are your best bet here. Get a list from ONT and if you're told they're all full, ignore it and go along to the hotels regardless and ask at reception. There are quite a few near the Gara de Nord, charging about 440–510 lei single, and 700–880 lei for a double. Try Hotel Dunarea, Calea Grivitei 140 (Tel. 173220); Hotel Bucegi, Strada Witing 2 (Tel. 495100); Hotel Cismigiu, Blvd Gheorghiu-Dej 18 (Tel. 147410).

EATING AND NIGHTLIFE

The twenty-four-hour stand-up Buffet Expres are the cheapest form of eats, but a lot of the food is fairly revolting and high in stodge content. La Doi Cocqsi, Soseaua, Străulești is well worth finding for good food and authentic gypsy music, and next to the History Museum at Stavropoleos 5 is Carcul cu Bere, which does some particularly fine snacks.

As far as nightlife goes, don't build your hopes up as it's a bit of a non-event. ONT will tell you what's on in town, but usually the choice is between the Circus at Aleea Circului, the cinema, or the theatre. The University Student Club is an alternative where you can meet young Romanians, a surprising number of whom speak English. It's on Calea Plevnei 61, and you need your ISIC/IUS.

• **Excursions:** SNAGOV, 25 miles to the north, is well worth a day trip. The lake here is a great place for swimming and boating during the summer. Take a boat to the island in the middle of the lake, to visit the sixteenth-century MONASTERY where the infamous Vlad the Impaler (Dracula to some) has his final resting place.

Transylvania

This picturesque region, home of the notorious Count Dracula, is Romania's most scenic. The Transylvanian Alps and the small peasant villages with their rich, active folklore make travelling here interesting and rewarding. The best towns to base yourself in are Brașov or Sighisoara.

BRAȘOV, about 2½ hours from Bucharest, is on the edge of the Carpathian Mountains and set among the Transylvanian Alps. In its old town are the BLACK CHURCH and the TOWN HALL – both fourteenth-century, but the main attractions are outside the town. The CASTLE OF BRAN, Dracula's summer house, is reached by bus 12 to the bus station, then bus 23 (runs Mon–Sat. only) to the castle, and is open from 9 a.m.–6 p.m. (closed Monday). ONT, in Hotel Carpati, 9 Ch. Gheorghiu-Dej Blvd (open 7.30 a.m.–10 p.m. daily), will give you details of the best excursions. BTT in Strasma Armata Roşie will hand you this year's list of student hostels (bus 4 from station).

SIGHISOARA, 2¼ hours away from Braşov, is a beautiful medieval town, as yet unspoilt by tourism. This is an ideal spot to break the long haul from Bucharest to Budapest (nearly 14 hours), and it offers more in the way of sights than Braşov. The OLD WALLED TOWN is well preserved and among its sights are the CLOCK TOWER, the TOWN MUSEUM (closed Monday), the GUILD TOWERS, and the BERGKIRCHE, a church with good views over the town. The CHURCH OF THE MONASTERY off Clock Tower Square is the town's oldest building and not far from here is Dracula's father's house. ONT is across from the main thoroughfare of Str. Ch. Gheorghiu-Dej. It's open Mon.–Sat.: 8 a.m.–1 p.m., 2 p.m.–8 p.m., Sun.: 8 a.m.–11 a.m. Get your map here. You've a choice of camping at Campground Hula Danes (bus direction 'Mhedias') or paying up for Hotel Steaua (Tel. 950–71930). To meet the locals and have a drink, try the beer hall at 34 Piata Lenin.

The FAGARAS MOUNTAINS of the Carpathian Range make a great place to go hiking amongst the 6,000-foot peaks and 70 lakes. GARA SEBES OLT on the main line from Braşov is a good place to start. There are mountain huts (Cabanas) spread throughout the region high up on the slopes. Get a map ahead of time in Braşov and reserve Cabana beds through the tourist office there. Make sure to bring a lot of food and a good pair of shoes.

Moldavia

This region of Europe is known for beautiful painted mountain monasteries of southern Bucovina, small rural villages and its completely unspoilt lifestyle, where locals still wear national costume and not a word of English seems to be spoken. The trains are pitifully slow and you can't afford to be in a rush. Ask at Bucharest for times and routes – mostly you have to change to the smaller lines at Cluj.

SUCEAVA is the capital of Moldavia and the best starting point for a tour of the monasteries. The FOLK ART MUSEUM is a worthwhile visit. It's in the sixteenth-century 'Princely Inn' at Strada Ciprian Porumbescu 5 and in only an hour or two fills you in on the culture of the people that surround you. The ONT office is at Nicolae Balcescu 2 (open Mon.–Sat.: 8 a.m.–8 p.m., Sun.: 9 a.m.–12 noon), and they'll supply you with bus schedules and details on the monasteries.

THE MONASTERIES: VORONET is the most famous and ancient of the monasteries, dating back to 1488. It's known as the 'Sistine Chapel of the East', owing to its amazing frescoes and unique shade of blue. 'The Last Judgement' is the most amazing fresco in Moldavia, showing a whole panoply of figures and scenes from the Bible. HUMOR, a nearby village, has a monastery obviously built by misogynists (the devil is portrayed as a woman in the frescoes), and from here you can set off for SUCEVITA MONASTERY. This one is absolutely covered in fascinating frescoes inside and out, from portraits of Plato to the 'Arabian Nights'. There is also a small museum here. The actual village of Sucevita has got to be the most charming in Romania. There is a wonderful view over the monastery from the hill opposite and you can camp at the bottom of the hill.

To experience religious life visit the PUTNA MONASTERY where you will rub shoulders with chanting monks. There is no shortage of accommodation here with a large hotel, campsite and bungalows.

The Black Sea Coast

Romania's coastline starts at the Danube delta on the Russian frontier and stretches south for about 150 miles to the Bulgarian border. The resorts are dominated by huge hotels, and the main town on the coast is the ancient port of CONSTANŢA. The city is a curious mixture of Roman, Greek and Eastern Byzantine (there's even a mosque and minaret here). See the remains of the ROMAN DOCKS with its huge piece of preserved mosaic, the ARCHAEOLOGICAL MUSEUM and the ROMANIAN NAVAL MUSEUM. Outside the Archaeological Museum is a statue of the city's most famous resident, the poet OVID. Part of the beach is sheltered by a tree-and-hedge wind-break; however, you may find that Constanta gets busier than the other resorts in summer, so use your rail ticket to the full and head off for somewhere smaller down the line. Camping at Constanta is at Mamaia. Take trolley bus 150 from the station, and it is a two-minute walk to the site, situated by the sea and usually very crowded in summer.

TULCEA is the gateway to the Danube delta. Nature lovers should take a boat trip to see the wildlife. They are organized by ONT in the Hotel Delta, ten minutes' walk down the quay from the station at Strada Isaccea 2. Hotel Egreta is the cheaper hotel. The nearest camping site is at Maliuc (two hours by ferry) and infested with mosquitoes.

Western Romania

All trains east to Romania from Hungary and Yugoslavia pass through this area, once known as THE BANAT when it formed part of the great Hapsburg Empire. The land is mostly flat and is dominated by the three cities of Timişoara, Oradea and Arad.

Timişoara

TIMIŞOARA, which played such an important role in the revolution of 1989, is an interesting city whose architecture reflects its population of Hungarians and Serbs (now deported). The Hungarian people of western Romania led the fight against Ceauşescu and so it is no surprise that the December 1989 revolution started here and made the city world famous. The impressive DICASTERIAL PALACE on str. Ceahlău is an indication of the great opulence of the old Hapsburg rulers. Around the picturesque square PIATA UNIRII is a baroque CATHOLIC CATHEDRAL and a SERBIAN CATHEDRAL, as well as the MUSEUM OF FINE ARTS. The ETHNOGRAPHIC MUSEUM at str. Popa Şapcă is in the remains of the old Magyar fort around which the city grew. Take a walk along the BEGA CANAL through a whole series of parks and visit the THERMAL

BATHS on Bulevard Vasile Parvan. For a bit of fun go to the PUPPET THEATRE at Piata Furtuna. The tourist office and CFR international booking office are both at 6 B-dul Republicii. The cheapest place to stay is the campground in the Pădurea Forest (tram 1) where there are also bungalows. You could also try to get a place in the dormitories from BTT, 26 B-dul 23 August, but these are often full with groups.

Arad

ARAD is dominated by a huge star-shaped eighteenth-century CITADEL, around which the River Mureş flows through a park. The HISTORY MUSEUM (closed Mondays) is housed in the PALACE OF CULTURE on Piata George Tonescu and has displays on the complex history of the whole area. The Philharmonic Orchestra is also located here. Bulevard Republicii is the main street and here you will find the tourist office at number 72 just across from the neoclassical TOWN HALL. There is also a tourist office geared towards foreigners next door in the Hotel Astoria. For accommodation the youth hostel organization BTT is at 16 Piata Avram Iancu. To get to the Subcetate campsite follow the river south of the Citadel, about a mile or so from the bridge near the Park Hotel.

There are a whole series of fairs and gatherings in the villages around Arad well worth day visits, especially the 'Kiss Fair' in HALMAGIU in March, as well as festivals in PINCOTA (February), BÎRSA (April), SÎNTANA (May) and AVRAM IANCU (June). Ask at the tourist office for exact dates.

Oradea

ORADEA is a common stopping-off point on journeys from Budapest to Bucharest although probably does not warrant any more than a day's visit. Oradea has its own CITADEL and the largest baroque CATHOLIC CATHEDRAL in Romania. Nearby is the grand BISHOP'S

PALACE which was based on the Belvedere Palace in Vienna and is now a large MUSEUM (open Tues.–Sun.: 10 a.m.–6 p.m.) which has displays on the history and people of the Crişana region. Tourist information is on the main shopping street at 4 Piata Republicii and the CFR Railway office is at number 2. Cheap places to stay are hard to come by so you should try the campground five miles south east of Oradea at Baile Felix (tram 4 or 5), near the famous thermal baths, or else contact BTT at 9 str. Vulcan. There are many fascinating caves in the area, try to visit the VADU CRIŞULUI CAVE (take a slow train east from Oradea) which has tours 9 a.m.–6 p.m. each day.

SPAIN (España)

Entry requirements	Passport
Population	39,000,000
Capital	Madrid (pop.: 3,250,000)
Currency	Peseta
	£1 = approx. 175 ptas.
Political system	Constitutional Monarchy
Religion	Roman Catholic
Language	Spanish (some English spoken)
Public holidays	1, 6 Jan.; 19 Mar.;
	Maundy Thursday; Good Friday;
	Easter Monday; 1 May; 23 May; Corpus Christi;
	29 July; 15 Aug.; 12 Oct.;
	1 Nov.; 8, 25 Dec.
International dialling codes	From UK: 010 + 34 + number
	From USA: 011 + 34 + number
	To UK: 07 + 44 + number
	To USA: 07 + 1 + number
Eurotrain office	Jose Ortega y Gasset 71, E–28006 Madrid
	(Tel. 91–4011300)

Spain is the third largest country in Europe and culturally one of the most diverse. The Phoenicians, Greeks, Celts, Carthaginians, Romans, Visigoths and Moors were all here. Throughout the Christian reconquest, Spain consisted of several independent kingdoms united in 1479 by the marriage of Isabella of Castile to Ferdinand of Aragon. Shortly after this unification, the new king, Charles I, landed well and truly on his feet by inheriting the Netherlands and becoming Holy Roman Emperor in 1519. At the same time his 'conquistadores' were bringing enough gold and silver back from South America to make Spain a major world power. The defeat of the Spanish Armada in 1588 began a slow period of decline which ended in the loss of her colonies after the Napoleonic Wars. More recently, the abdication of the king was followed by a left-wing republic which gave rise to the Civil War of 1936–9. Since the death of the dictator Franco in 1975, King Juan Carlos has steered Spain towards democracy.

SPANISH NATIONAL RAILWAYS
(Red Nacional de los Ferrocarriles Españoles, RENFE)

The last year or two has seen significant improvements on RENFE. Supplements required on all fast trains: Talgos, TERs and ELTs, or the less steep Rápido supplement. RENFE are spending a lot of money ordering 155 m.p.h. trains to develop the Madrid–Seville line and cut the travel time from 6 hours to 3 by 1992. You'll have to change trains at the Spanish border, so don't go for a sleeper from France unless you're travelling on a Talgo which adjusts its wheels to the broader gauge. This is one time when a few pounds' worth of supplement is money well spent. The 'Automotor' trains which cover the medium-haul routes at semi-fast speeds are both comfortable and air-conditioned, and are a better bet than non-air-conditioned expresses. It's safe to say that all non-supplement trains are pretty slow and crowded, but they'll get you there in the end. The Tranvias and Correos (locals) crawl along and are only for the stalwart. Some routes are now impossible without supplements being paid, Algeciras–Madrid being an example. The RENFE computer is linked to BR, so you can book ahead before you leave, either at Victoria Station or through appointed BR travel agents.

● **Inter Rail bonuses:**

	FROM	TO	REDUCTION (%)
Cie de Navegación			
Transmediterránea	Algeciras	Tangier	30
	Barcelona	Palma/Ibiza/Mahon	30
	Valencia	Palma/Ibiza	30
	Melilla	Almeria/Málaga	30
	Cádiz	Las Palmas/Tenerife/	
		Lanzarote	30

RENFE – Free entrance to Railway Museum, San Cosme y San Damián, 2 Madrid.

● **Non-RENFE lines:** A few lines in Spain are not run by RENFE and do not accept rail passes. They are the narrow-gauge lines Hendaye to Gijon, Gijon to Ferrol, Palma to Inca, Valencia to Gandia and Barcelona to Montserrat.

TRAIN INFORMATION

English is not always spoken, so always have a Spanish back-up prepared. Expect long queues. At present, due to the ETA terrorist attacks, left-luggage facilities at Spanish stations are sometimes withdrawn, or subject to security checks such as X-ray examination. There are usually alternative non-official facilities though; usually in the form of some little fellow posted by the station door or in the nearest café who'll guard your luggage for the same hours at the same fee. If in doubt ask at the station.

• **Reservations:** If you can face the queues it's always advisable to reserve a seat in Spain. Unfortunately, if you decide not to reserve there's often no way of telling if someone else has, as reserved seats are not always indicated. On many occasions you settle down in an apparently empty compartment, only to be thrown out just when you thought you were safe. *Reservations are obligatory on all expresses.*

• **Night travel:** Spanish couchettes sleep six and are sometimes very old and dirty – more often than not you are better off on the floor. Sleepers are cheap, however, so all's not lost. For a journey under 550 km, a berth in a tourist-class sleeper will cost about 1,800 ptas.

• **Scenic tips:** In Spain, it's normally effort enough to get from A to B without thinking about scenic routes. Entering from France, the most scenic route is from Toulouse over the Pyrenees, arriving at Barcelona. The main line from here on to Madrid takes in much that is typically Spanish without you having to go out of your way. If it's mountains you're after, then it's best to head towards the northwest (León–Túy) or the south (Córdoba–Málaga, Granada–Almería).

• **Rover tickets:** In 1987, RENFE introduced their first rover ticket, the Tarjeta Turistica, which allows unrestricted travel within the country and covers all supplements except sleepers and seat reservations. Prices range from £60 for a second-class ticket valid for 8 days to £150 for first class valid for 22 days. Children between 4 and 12 pay half the appropriate adult fare. The ticket can be bought by anyone living outside Spain and can be used at any time of the year. A Flexi Card has just been introduced allowing 4 days travel in 15 days and costs about £45 second class. Also, the

Chequetren is available for individuals or families and gives a discount of 15 per cent when tickets or services to the value of either 25,000 ptas. or 35,000 ptas. are bought in advance for 21,000 and 30,000 ptas. respectively. There is a 50 per cent discount for families of at least three people travelling on journeys of more than 100 km. The first person pays the full fare while the rest pay only half fare. Children aged between 4 and 12 pay only 25 per cent of the full fare. This discount also applies to supplements. RENFE operates a discount for all standard fares on about 300 days per year called Blue Days (*dias azules*) when you can expect a further 25 per cent or so reduction (50 per cent with a RENFE Youth Pass). The number of Blue Days varies according to the time of year with all of February included but only 16 days in June. There is also a straight 20 per cent reduction for individuals taking return journeys of more than 100 km, which is applicable to all types of train and all classes. At the top end of the market there is the Al Andalus Express (a sort of Spanish Orient Express), which runs from Seville to Málaga. Prices are expensive, so it's beyond the means of most eurorailers. For further information contact Marsans Travel Ltd, 7A Henrietta Place, London W1M 9AG, Tel. 071–493 4934.

TOURIST INFORMATION

The government-run tourist office has branches in all major towns and at many stations. They have an excellent collection of free handouts on all the regions of Spain. In addition, there are local city tourist offices which supply maps and more detailed information.

• **ISIC bonuses:** Reduced entrance to the Prado and Bellas Artes museums. For further information, contact Viajes TIVE, Fernando el Católico 88, Madrid.

• **Money matters:** 1 peseta (pta.) = 100 centimos (c).
Banking hours are Mon.–Fri.: 8.30 a.m.–1.30/2 p.m., Sat.: 8.30 a.m.–1 p.m. Shop about, as there's no set rate of exchange, and exchange rates are high. The 'La Caixa' bank rate is very poor.

• **Post offices:** Open Mon.–Sat.: 9 a.m.–2 p.m. and often later in larger cities. 'Lista de Correos' = poste restante.

• **Shops:** Open Mon.–Sat.: 9 a.m.–1.30 p.m., 5 p.m.–7.30/8 p.m. (closed Saturday p.m.).

• **Museums:** Vary considerably; most open 10 a.m. and shut again for lunch 12.30/1 p.m., opening again at 4 p.m. till 7 p.m.

• Spain's entry into the EEC in 1986 means that Britons (and other EEC residents) get free medical assistance. As with Britain, entry into the EEC meant the introduction of VAT and higher prices all round. Although this should not be the case, some tourist-minded Spanish shopkeepers have been adding 30 per cent to everything (only supposed to be for luxury goods) and blaming it on VAT while pocketing the difference. Two ways to avoid this are to ensure that the advertised price includes all taxes, and the old favourite – haggling.

SLEEPING

Every large town in Spain has a Brujula office to help find rooms for a small fee. In addition the tourist information office issues lists to help freelancers. You shouldn't have any problems as there's always plenty of cheap accommodation around the stations, all of which is inspected and graded by the government. By law, prices should be shown behind the door of each room. During the summer it's legal for prices to be increased by about 15 per cent, so don't get too excited until you've worked it out. Hotels start at about 1,200 ptas. for a single and prices are nearly always charged by the room, not per person. Pensiones and Hostales are officially graded (Hs = hostal, HsR = hostal residencia, P = pensión, CH = casa de huéspedes and, cheapest of all, F = fonda). For the bare necessities, expect to pay about 900 ptas. per person. Always check to see if breakfast is included in the price; don't assume the management will tell you. Hot showers are another extra which can cost up to 150 ptas. If you think you're being done, the mere mention of 'libro de reclamaciones' (complaints book) should sort out your problems. To use any of Spain's seventy youth hostels, you'll need an IYHF card. At 500–650 ptas. a night, they are easily the cheapest accommodation you're likely to find. If you are thinking about camping, go to ANCE, Principe De Vergara 85, 2° Ocha, 28006 Madrid; they will give you a map and a rundown on official campsites. Prices start at about 275 ptas. per person per night. Sleeping on the beaches is another alternative, but don't make it too obvious or you'll attract trouble from the police or worse.

EATING AND NIGHTLIFE

Spain offers some of the most affordable restaurants in Europe. Give your stomach a chance to adapt to the excess of olive oil, and don't have too much seafood to start with. Once you've adapted to local conditions, there's an endless variety of regional specialities to sample, all at reasonable prices. Go for the tourist or house menu where possible, as it's usually a safe bet and works out a lot cheaper than ordering individual dishes. Expect to pay anything from 600 to 1,300 ptas. for your evening meal and remember that the Spaniards don't eat until at least 9 p.m.–10 p.m. If there's no fixed tourist menu, ask if they do combinados – an all-in feast on one plate which often includes something to drink as well. For those low in funds, try tapas – delicious and varied titbits that are sometimes free – available at most bars. Local wine is cheap at about 180 ptas. a bottle, and is a much better buy than beer, though it's often rough and tastes like weak sherry. Wine cellars and bars are cheaper and have more local colour than the discos which make their living by fleecing tourists at the resorts.

The bullfighting season runs from March to October and is recommended only for the bloodthirsty. Anyone who wants to see one, but is put off by the violence, should head for Portugal.

Madrid

Madrid is not one of Europe's most attractive capitals. The old town has charm, the nightlife is amongst the hottest in Europe and the Prado is definitely one of the world's great art galleries, but the sprawling concrete districts and lack of major sights entice one to leave Madrid in favour of Toledo or Seville. Still, sleeping and eating aren't a problem and many argue that Madrid is worth the trip for the tapas and fandangos alone.

STATION FACILITIES

Madrid has three stations: Chamartín, serving the north-east, France and eastern Spain; Atocha, serving Portugal and the south of Spain; and Norte (also called Principe Pio) handling what's left. Some trains, e.g. the Paris–Algeciras Express, pass through more than one of them. There are interconnecting trains every 20 minutes, and also an underground service. Due to bomb scares, the left-luggage lockers can only be used after your kit has been X-rayed. This is tough luck at Chamartín, but at Atocha head for some of the bars behind the station (round Calle de Rafael de Riego), and deposit your rucksack for 150 ptas. There is tourist information at Chamartín. (We give no information on the Norte Station as it is little used by eurorailers.) Trains may be diverted from Atocha to Chamartín due to building work – check locally and in Thomas Cook's timetable.

	CHAMARTÍN	ATOCHA
Train information	7 a.m.–10 p.m. (Tel. 247 7400)	7 a.m.–10 p.m.
Reservations	8 a.m.–9 p.m.	9 a.m.–9 p.m.
Hotel reservations	9 a.m.–11 p.m.	–
Foreign exchange	7 a.m.–10 p.m.	8.30 a.m.–9.30 p.m.
Restaurant, Cafeteria	12 noon–4 p.m. 7 p.m.–12 midnight	7 a.m.–12 midnight
Shops	7 a.m.–11 p.m.	–
Waiting room	All hours	All hours
Tourist information	Mon.–Fri.: 8 a.m.–8 p.m. Sat.: 9 a.m.–1 p.m.	–
Post office	Mon.–Fri.: 9 a.m.– 2 p.m., 5 p.m.–10 p.m. Sat.: 9 a.m.–2 p.m.	Mon.–Sat.: 9 a.m.–2 p.m. 7 p.m.–10.30 p.m.
Station shuts	12 midnight–5 a.m.	12 midnight–5 a.m.

Daily trains to: Bilbao, Paris, Zaragoza, Barcelona, Valencia, Alicante, Granada, Córdoba, Seville, Lisbon.

TOURIST INFORMATION

The main national office is at
Maria de Molina 50, and there's
another one at Plaza de España.
Both are open 9 a.m.–7 p.m.,
Mon.–Fri., Sat. 9.30 a.m.–1.30
p.m. The municipal office is at
Plaza Mayor 3, open 10 a.m.–1.30
p.m., 4 p.m.–7 p.m., Saturday 10
a.m.–2 p.m. and 4 p.m.–7 p.m.,
closed Sunday; and the provincial
office is at Duque de Medinaceli
2. Pick up a free map and
information leaflets here including a very good list of pensions.

- **Addresses:**
POST OFFICE: Palácio de Comunicaciones, Plaza de Cibeles. Open 9
a.m.–10 p.m. Poste restante and telegraphs here.
AMEX: Plaza de las Cortes 2 (Tel. 4295775). Open Mon.–Fri.: 9
a.m.–5.30 p.m., Sat.: 9 a.m.–12 noon.
UK EMBASSY: Fernando el Católico 16 (Tel. 4191528).
US EMBASSY: Serrano 75 (Tel. 2763400).
CANADIAN EMBASSY: Núñez de Balboa 35 (Tel. 4314300).
AUSTRALIAN EMBASSY: Paseo de la Castellana 143 (Tel. 2798501).
BRITISH-AMERICAN HOSPITAL: Paseo de Juan XXIII (Tel. 234 6700).
EUROTRAIN: José Ortega y Gasset 71 (Tel. 4011300).
PHONE CODE: 91.

- **Getting about:** For price and speed, the metro is the best means of
getting about. It runs till 1.30 a.m. and has nine lines. Buy tickets
from machines (65 ptas. per trip, 410 ptas. for ten) or kiosks and
hang on to your ticket till you've finished the journey. Buses are
pretty efficient, microbuses are the more luxurious versions of the
same theme and both cost the same as the metro.

SEEING

The PRADO MUSEUM is the reason why thousands of art-lovers
descend on this city each summer. There are over 3,000

masterpieces here, mainly collected by the Spanish royal family in the seventeenth and eighteenth centuries. The old Spanish masters (El Greco, Goya, etc.) are well represented, and there's a fair number of Flemish works collected by the Habsburg kings of the sixteenth century. There's such a glut of genius here, you'll need to pay two or three visits at least. The entrance is reasonable at 400 ptas., but ISIC holders are free. Near the exit is a shop selling very reasonably priced reproductions, postcards and books. The Prado is open daily, except Mondays, May–October, Tues.–Sat.: 9 a.m.–7 p.m., Sun.: 9 a.m.–2 p.m., November–April, Tues.–Sat.: 10 a.m.–5 p.m., Sun.: 10 a.m.–2 p.m. The ROYAL PALACE is the only other 'must' in Madrid. A 45-minute guided tour will take you through the various apartments and the Royal Armoury, which is considered one of the world's best collections of medieval weapons. The palace gardens, especially the CAMPO DEL MORO, are particularly fine and make good venues for regal picnic lunches. Entrance costs 500 ptas., 300 ptas. on ISIC. The BOTANIC GARDENS, near the Prado, is also a nice place to have a quiet picnic. Entrance costs 50 ptas.

Parks are, in fact, Madrid's speciality. The RETIRO PARK in the city centre is huge and, apart from its rowing lake, theatre, fountains and statues, the CRYSTAL PALACE of the Bourbon kings is here. North-west of the palace is another park on ten times the scale of the Retiro, which the young Spaniards tend to patronize at weekends: the CASA DE CAMPO has among its attractions a zoo, amusement park, swimming pool and outdoor theatre.

OLD MADRID lies between PUERTA DEL SOL (known as the centre of Spain) and the Crystal Palace; notice the descriptive pictures above the street signs to help the illiterate seventeenth-century locals. These narrow winding streets are the most colourful in Madrid, and the taverns in the alleys off the PLAZA MAYOR are good starting places for your evening's pub crawl, Madrid-style. On Sunday mornings there's a flea market (the Rastro) off the southern corner of the square where gypsies often congregate and put on street shows.

SLEEPING

Cheap beds aren't a problem here, even in summer. The tourist offices will advise you on accommodation, but won't arrange it for you; Brujula, a private placing agency, will do this for a small fee.

They have kiosks at the stations, but you shouldn't even need them as there are hundreds of suitable places, many near the centrally located Atocha Station, in streets like Calle Toledo. Try the Hotel Residencia Finister᷿ at No. 113, where you can expect to pay around 4,000 ptas. for a double with a shower. If you're really cutting corners and don't mind other people's nocturnal 'goings-on', or the odd bed-bug, the area south of Puerta del Sol will produce some very cheap (750–1,500 ptas.) casas de huéspedes. The university let out rooms to those wanting to stay five or more days, and there are two youth hostels which aren't too far away from the centre. One's at Calle Santa Cruz de Marcenado 28 (Tel. 247 4532) and the other's at Casa de Campo (Tel. 463 5699) in the park there. You need IYHF membership, and a bed will cost about 500 ptas. Ask at Turismo for the camping leaflet, and don't risk the parks unless you're desperate.

The street with more cheap beds than anywhere else is Gran Vía in central Madrid. Hostal Alcázar-Regis, on the 5th floor of No. 61 (Tel. 247 3549), is good value for what you get; La Costa Verde (9th floor) is cheaper, and Buenos Aires (Tel. 247 8800) on the 2nd floor have singles for around 900 ptas. and doubles for 1,500 ptas. Hostal Amayo (Tel. 222 2151) on the 1st floor of No. 12 and at No. 38, Hostal California (Tel. 222 4703) and Don José (Tel. 232 1385) have good rooms, and Hostal Margarita at No. 50 (Tel. 247 3549) is reasonable and cheap.

EATING AND NIGHTLIFE

Tapas (the tasty snacks served in infinite varieties to accompany your drink) are at their best in Madrid. Most Madrileños spend between 6 p.m. and 10 p.m. on the tapas circuit in either Pasage de Matheu or the area round Plaza Mayor. Mussels, mushrooms, omelettes and filled rolls are some of the savouries with which to bridge the gap till dinner, washed down with sangría or wine. The main meal of the day is eaten at lunchtime (2 p.m.–4 p.m.) and dinner, around 10 p.m., is quite a light affair. Argüelles, on the metro, is the city's main student quarter. Make for this area to eat cheaply and meet the university students. The bars along Calle de la Princesa are a safe bet to make friends, and back in the centre Calle Echegaray and Ventura de la Vega, off Calle San Jerónimo, also have cheap restaurants. Restaurant Copatisan, Calle del Barco

16–18, is very cheap and very good. Closed Aug. For a good paella try Restaurant El Parque, Fernando el Católico 78.

The nightlife starts with the pub crawl and continues in the salas de fiesta (nightclubs), winding up around 3 a.m.–4 a.m. At weekends, things are twice as lively and the discotecas (which are on the expensive side) hold afternoon as well as evening sessions to cope with the insatiable demand ('afternoon' in Spain seems to mean 7 p.m.–10 p.m.), try Archy's at Marquis de Riscal 11. The salas de fiesta shows range from awful cabarets to sex shows.

This list of current events in the 'Guía del Ocio' is all you need. Avoid the heavily advertised flamenco shows, as they're incredibly commercial and plastic, and ask about for the best discos, etc., in the bars along the Aurrera in the Argüelles quarter.

• **Excursions:** Thirty miles from the Norte Station is the huge granite palace of EL ESCORIAL. This was King Philip II's country house and though it took over twenty years to complete, it still looks more like a high-security prison than a palace. The guided tours take you round the museums, library, church, art gallery and royal apartments and costs 500 ptas. (open 10 a.m.–1 p.m., 3 p.m.–7 p.m.). A few miles further on is the VALLE DE LOS CAÍDOS – a memorial to those who died in the Civil War, and where Franco is buried. Or if you just want to cool off, stay in the train to Cercedilla and take the branch line up into the Sierra de Guadarrama Mountains.

ARANJUEZ, en route south to Córdoba or Seville, is worth a stop-off to see the ROYAL PALACE, the SAILOR'S HOUSE, the PRINCE'S GARDEN and the FARMER'S HOUSE. The campsite here, Soto del Castillo, will entice you to stay a night or two as it's about the best one in Spain.

Northern Spain and the Basque Country

This region runs from the foot of the Pyrenees to close to Portugal. It is one of Spain's least touristy areas, and the lush forests, good beaches and historic towns make it worth exploration. The Basques – possibly the oldest ethnic group in Europe – have their own very separate history, culture and language. Since Franco's death, the

ETA (Basque Liberation Front) have been increasingly active in their terrorist acts of bombings and murder, and the issue is still anything but settled.

San Sebastián

This was, until recent terrorist attacks, one of Spain's major holiday resorts for the rich and famous. Now its position as one of the main Basque cities makes it a slightly less safe bet for a family holiday, but the choice is yours; the odds of anything nasty happening are weighted heavily in your favour. It's an interesting and attractive place; the beaches are good and it will break up a run from Paris to Madrid nicely.

TOURIST INFORMATION AND ADDRESSES

TOURIST OFFICES: C. Andia 13, and Reina Regente (ground floor, Victoria Eugenia Theatre), open Mon.–Fri.: 9 a.m.–1.30 p.m., 4 p.m.–7 p.m., Sat.: 9 a.m.–1 p.m.
POST OFFICE: Calle Urdaneta 9.
FIRST AID: Cruz Roja, Calle Matia 7 (Tel. 214600).
PHONE CODE: 943.

SEEING

The SAN TELMO MUSEUM, in a sixteenth-century Renaissance monastery on Calle Coro, will fill you in on the differences between the Basques and the Spanish or French; or visit the AQUARIUM down on the port to see the collection of sea creatures. From the beach you can rent out a boat and go over to the island of SANTA CLARA, or else just laze about on the beaches of LA CONCHA and ONDARRETA.

SLEEPING

During the summer, cheap beds are hard to find. Try the excellent campsite on the Carretera de Monte Igueldo (about 5 miles from the station) or the two youth hostels at Ciudad Deportiva Anoeta

(Tel. 452970) and Parque Ulia (Tel. 293751). The best pension deals are at Pensión La Perla, Loyola 10 (Tel. 428123), and Hostal Gran Bahía, Embeltran (Tel. 423838), with doubles for 3,000 ptas. It's also possible to sleep on the beach.

EATING AND NIGHTLIFE

It's not easy to cut corners in San Sebastián for two reasons: first, there are hardly any places with tourist menus in the eurorailer's budget range; and secondly, the food is so good you won't feel like living off bread, cheese and fruit. This is one Spanish town where the food is consistently good and, of course, the fish dishes are excellent. The city actually has a Gastronomic Academy, and the exclusive and chauvinistic male-only dining clubs frequently sponsor eating contests. There are several bars and restaurants in the central square, Plaza del 18 de Julio, but watch the prices here.

For pre-dinner 'tapas', try the bars along Calle Fermin Calberton and, for dancing, Zorongo, San Martín 66, is meant to be pretty hot. There are festivals all summer, the most interesting being the Basque folklore one. Ask tourist information for details. If you're there 6–14 July and enjoy the blood and gore of bullfighting, take a bus a few miles to PAMPLONA where you can join in the 'Running of the Bulls' festival. There are twenty-four-hour celebrations and, from all the stories, the bulls aren't the only wild animals in town.

Santander

The port town of Santander is wedged between the Basque and Galician regions in the province of Cantabria. This part of northern Spain is mountainous with a rugged coastline, and contains some of the world's best prehistoric cave art in the ALTAMIRA CAVES.

The beaches at Santander are the main reason to stop off, particularly the ones at EL SARDINERO, COMILLAS and LIENCRES. The area by the harbour is the 'new town' and this is where the restaurants and bars are located. Tourist information is at Jardina de Pereda, open Mon.–Fri.: 9 a.m.–1.30 p.m., 4.30 p.m.–7.30 p.m.; Sat.: 9 a.m.–12 noon. There are plenty of cheap hostales, or campsites outside the town.

Santiago de Compostela

This is the main town in the beautiful province of Galicia, though if you really wanted to explore the dramatic Atlantic coastline you'd be better staying at La Coruña, on the main line to Madrid. Santiago was a popular place of pilgrimage in the Middle Ages for up to two million Christians a year who made the journey here to see where the Apostle St James is buried. The CATHEDRAL dominates the town, but it's difficult to isolate other main sights as the whole inner town is a national monument, and deserving of it. The cathedral was started in the eleventh century but encompasses many architectural styles. The student quarter lies between the cathedral and the university and this is the best area to head for at night. The tourist office is at Rúa del Villar 43 (closed Saturday p.m., all day Sunday and 2 p.m.–4.30 p.m. daily), and they have a list of the pensions with their prices posted up, but once you're at Turismo you're already in Santiago's main hostel street. Try Hospedaje Santa Cruz at No. 42, or Pensión Lens at No. 73. You may have trouble during the annual festival (25 July) or around religious feast days when pilgrims still flock into the town.

Barcelona

Situated across the Pyrenees from France and on the Mediterranean south of the Costa Brava, Barcelona seems to have as many links with France as with Spain. It's proud of its position as capital of Cataluña, and the language you'll hear in the streets, Catalan, is derived not from Spanish but from the French langue d'oc.

The old quarter of BARRIO GÓTICO with its medieval streets is particularly lively, though the whole city is bustling and vivacious. Regarded as the literary capital of Spain, and with an important university, Barcelona has the added attraction of its proximity to the Mediterranean and good beaches.

STATION FACILITIES

Barcelona has three main stations: Término, Sants and Paseo de Gracia. By and large, international trains use Término; rápidos to Valencia stop at Paseo de Gracia, some inland trains to the west and south originate at Término and most make stops at both Paseo de Gracia and Sants. Trains for the north-west leave from Sants. There are interconnecting trains between the stations every twenty minutes. Space permits information on only Término and Sants as the two stations most used by eurorailers.

	SANTS	TÉRMINO
Train information	6.30 a.m.–10.30 p.m. (Tel. 310 7200)	6.30 a.m.–10.30 p.m.
Reservations	7 a.m.–8 p.m.	7 a.m.–7 p.m.
Tourist information	7.30 a.m.–10.30 p.m. daily	Mon.–Fri.: 8 a.m.–8 p.m. Sat.: 8 a.m.–1 p.m.
Foreign exchange	Open weekends	8 a.m.–10 p.m.
Bar, Buffet	7 a.m.–11 p.m.	7 a.m.–11 p.m.
Restaurant	12 noon–3 p.m.	12 noon–3 p.m.
Shops	7 a.m.–10.30 p.m.	–
Post office	–	Mon.–Fri.: 9.30 a.m.–2 p.m.
Station shuts	12 midnight–4 a.m.	12 midnight–4 a.m.

Daily trains to: Paris, Geneva, Valencia, Zaragoza, Madrid, Irún.

TOURIST INFORMATION AND ADDRESSES

TOURIST OFFICE: Gran Vía de Les Corts Catalanes 658, open Mon.–Fri.: 9 a.m.–7 p.m., closed Saturday p.m. and Sundays. Ask them for their list of budget accommodation, along with your map and leaflets. Also in Término Station.
POST OFFICE: Plaza d'Antoni López, open Mon.–Sat.: 8.30 a.m.–9.55 p.m., Sun.: 10 a.m.–noon.
AMEX: Paseo de Gracia 101, open Mon.–Fri.: 9.30 a.m.–6 p.m., Sat.: 10 a.m.–12 noon (Tel. 217 0070).
UK CONSULATE: Avenida Diagonal 477 (Tel. 322 2151).
US CONSULATE: Vía Laietana 33 (Tel. 319 9550).
PHONE CODE: 93.

SEEING

Head for the BARRIO GÓTICO and look out for the GREAT ROYAL PALACE in Plaza del Rey, the CATEDRAL DE SANTA EULALIA and the DIPUTACIÓN PROVINCIAL (council buildings). The hub of the city, however, is LAS RAMBLAS. This collection of streets starts at the port and runs to the city centre at Plaza de Catuluña. For sheer entertainment value you can't beat Las Ramblas. It's the Piccadilly Circus of Barcelona, so popular that you pay for a folding chair to spectate, come nightfall. The incredible and unmissable cathedral of TEMPLO EXPIATORIO DE LA SAGRADA FAMILIA is the work of the Catalan architect Gaudí; however, his death before construction was completed put a spanner in the works as he didn't leave any plans. Work is now proceeding, however. South of Barrio Gótico is MONTJUICH PARK. The buildings erected here for the 1929 International Exhibition are of varying interest, but the model town in PUEBLO ESPAÑOL is well worth seeing as it shows all the different regional styles of architecture in Spain. Take the funicular up, and admire the view over the port and city or for even more dramatic views, take the tram and the funicular up to TIBIDABO. There are also good views from Palan Nacional and Mirador de L'Alcade (near Parc d'Attractions).

The PICASSO MUSEUM is at Calle de Montcada 15 (entrance 400 ptas.) and has lots of his works from the early sketches to his final masterpieces.

SLEEPING

The youth hostel on Passeig Pujadas 29 (Tel. 300 3104) charges 500 ptas., breakfast extra. Reception closed 10 a.m.–5 p.m. but you can leave luggage and reserve a bed after 3 p.m. It has only 68 beds, so get there as soon after 8 a.m. as possible. There are also youth hostels at Passeig de Nostra Senyora del Coll. 41–51 (Tel. 321 0004), Numancia 149–151 (Tel. 410 2309) and Duquesa d'Orleans 58 (Tel. 205 0961). For camping, there are quite a few sites; the nearest one is four miles out on the Espluges bus route: Camping Barcino. The university at Calle Mestre Nicolau 14 (Tel. 250 1419) offers both sexes bed and breakfast for 800 ptas. Your best bet for cheap casas and hostels is in Las Ramblas. Pensión Fernando, Calle Ferran 31 (Tel. 301 7993), is cheap and friendly; Hostal Alicante, Ronda

Universidad 4 (Tel. 318 3470), is a good splurge. Hostal Noya, Ramblas 133 (Tel. 301 4831), and Hostal Canaletas on the 3rd floor (Tel. 301 5660) start around 800 ptas. for singles and are situated right in the city centre. Although it can be quite rowdy, the Kabul Young Budget Hotel is cheap and central at Pl. Reial 17 (Tel. 318 5190). Mixed dormitories and free (but cold) showers. There is no curfew or lock-out and it costs only 800 ptas. or so. Although you get breakfast and can buy sandwiches at the bar, you are better eating around the Plaça de Sant Jaume. Some distance out is the Youth Hostel Ocata at El Masnou. To get there, take a suburban train from Barceloneta metro station to Ocata station (20 minutes). Turn right out of the station, left at the Banco de Bilbao and head up the hill. If all else fails, there's a Brujula (accommodation-finding kiosk) at Término Station, and if you arrive exhausted in mid-August this is your best move.

EATING AND NIGHTLIFE

The Catalans eat late. Dinner time averages 9 p.m.–11 p.m. There are plenty of places offering menu del día in Barrio Gótico, and if you get a chance to sample the regional speciality, Catalan stew, escudella i carne d'olla, do so. Casa José, Pl. San José Oriol 10, is the cheapest, though not friendliest, feed in Barcelona and Cosmos, at Ramblas 34, does a good meal with coffee for about 600 ptas. For a splurge, go to Barceloneta, the area of colourful winding streets down by the port, and savour the fresh seafood concoctions in Casa Costa on Juicio.

If you've money to blow, go to the nightclubs and discos like Georgia, Pelayo 58, or El Cordobés on Ramblas Capuchinos, but for our money strolling through the Ramblas, stopping at a few cafés en route, is better value. It gets quite lively at the top of the Montjuich on summer evenings, but if that's too sedate for you, head down to El Barrio Chino (near the docks). By Spanish standards some of the shows down there are pretty hot stuff.

● **Excursions:** The town of MONTSERRAT is 38 miles from Barcelona, reached by Catalan Railways (from Plaza de España – about £5 with Inter Rail discount). Set among the mountain peaks, there is a Benedictine monastery and a Gothic basilica. It's a nice day trip if you're sick of crowds.

If the oppressive heat of the city is getting you down, you've not far to go to get to the good but crowded beaches of the COSTA BRAVA and the COSTA DORADA. LLORET DE MAR is infested with package tourists but pretty, while S' AGARÓ is the St Trop of the Costa Brava. Stay at SAN FELÍU DE GUIXOLS and travel in the two miles to S' Agaró to save yourself a fortune. Buses run to these and other, closer resorts from Vergara 5, Barcelona.

About 60 miles south of Barcelona, on the Costa Dorada, lies TARRAGONA. Although touristy and surrounded by oil refineries, the culture vultures may wish to stop off here and visit the ruins of the provincial Roman capital of Hispania. If you are coming from Barcelona, sit on the right-hand side of the train for a visual extravaganza! Tourist information is at 4 Fortuny (Mon.–Fri.: 8.45 a.m.–2.35 p.m., Sat.: 9 a.m.–2 p.m.) where you can pick up leaflets with lots of useful information. Rambla Nova is the main street in Tarragona, and along this long, tree-lined avenue you will find an information kiosk and the post office, as well as countless places offering cheap food. The ARCHAEOLOGICAL MUSEUM has a fascinating collection of mosaics and is one of the most important in Spain. It is part of the CYCLOPEAN WALLS, which run for about 1 km along the highest part of town, starting at the end of Rambla Vella which runs parallel to Rambla Nova. The wall, which varies in height from 12–40 feet, was built around 600 BC. Also visit the ROMAN AMPHITHEATRE and the thirteenth-century CATHEDRAL in the old town. The youth hostel is at Avenida President Companys s/n (Tel. 977–210195). It normally has 90 beds, but in July and August the number jumps to 190. There are also a number of cheap hotels south of the Rambla Nova and the campsite is a couple of miles east of the town. Take a bus 3 or 3A from the Rambla Nova.

Just over the border from France is PORT BOU. Situated in a natural amphitheatre and nestling beside the Mediterranean, Port Bou is a delightful spot for the travel-weary eurorailer to relax and toast for a day or two. The vast railway station is out of all proportion to its surroundings but it is only a short walk to hotels and the rather pebbly beach. Tourist information at the harbour is open throughout the day Mon.–Sat., but only on Sunday mornings. Although there is no youth hostel and the locals don't like you sleeping on the beach, the Hotel Juventas is highly recommended at around 1,300 ptas. for a double with washbasin and shower next door. It is at Avenue de Barcelona 3. There isn't really much to do in Port Bou but lie on the beach and watch the skinny-dippers. There are plenty of good cafés, but although the seafood is good value the prices are not all that cheap.

An unusual excursion is to the tiny independent state of ANDORRA high in the Pyrenees. To get there take a train from Barcelona to Puigcerdà (3½ hours, or only 2 hours and 40 minutes on the Barcelona–Paris train via La Tour-de-Carol but you'll pay a supplement) and then a bus through Seu d'Urgell to the tiny capital Andorra la Vella. It is a beautiful but unexciting place, the best thing to do is shop as there is no tax, or ski at one of the five resorts. The tourist office is at Carrer Dr Vilanova in Andorra la Vella.

Valencia

If you're taking a detour off the railway to visit the Balearic islands of Majorca, Menorca or Ibiza, Valencia is logically en route, so you may feel like stopping off here. There's nothing very exciting here, but it is the point of departure for steamers to the islands, as are Alicante and Barcelona.

STATION FACILITIES

	VALENCIA TÉRMINO
Train information	7.30 a.m.–10 p.m. (Tel. 3214561)
Reservations	8 a.m.–8 p.m.
Tourist information	At town hall
Foreign exchange	8 a.m.–9 p.m.
Left-luggage store	All hours
Bar, Buffet	6 a.m.–1.30 a.m.
Cafeteria	7.30 a.m.–11.30 p.m.
Waiting room	All hours
Station shuts	3 a.m.–5 a.m.

Daily trains to: Barcelona, Alicante, Córdoba, Madrid.

TOURIST INFORMATION AND ADDRESSES

TOURIST OFFICE: Calle de la Paz, open Mon.–Fri.: 9 a.m.–2 p.m., 5 p.m.–7 p.m., closed Saturday p.m. and all day Sunday.

POST OFFICE: Plaza del Pais, Valenciano 24.

AMEX: c/o Viajes Melia, Calle de la Paz 41, open Mon.–Fri.: 9.30 a.m.–1.30 p.m., 4.30 p.m.–8 p.m., Sat.: 9.30 a.m.–1 p.m.

US CONSULATE: Calle de Ribera 3 (Tel. 3216973). Mon.–Fri.: 10 a.m.–1.30 p.m.

FERRIES TO THE ISLANDS: Transmediterránea, Avenida Manuel Soto Ingeniero 15.

PHONE CODE: 96.

SEEING

The PALACE OF THE MARQUÉS DE DOS AGUAS is about the most interesting building around. It's eighteenth-century rococo and contains about the best collection of Spanish pottery in Spain (2 p.m.–4 p.m., siesta, closed Sunday p.m. and all day Monday). The GOTHIC CATHEDRAL is also worth a look: climb its tower for a view over the city. Apart from these, the MUSEO PROVINCIAL DE BELLAS ARTES is the only other place really worth visiting. The best beaches are further south at BENIDORM and ALICANTE, but there are closer ones on the Costa del Azahar accessible by bus.

SLEEPING, EATING AND NIGHTLIFE

The youth hostel is at Avenida del Puerto 69 (Tel. 3690152) on bus route 19. Round the Plaza del Mercado are plenty of grotty casas and fondas with beds around 800 ptas. The Barrio del Carmen is the area both for cheap eating and for nightlife. Rice dishes are the Valencian speciality, but you often have to watch the prices. There are lots of spit'n'sawdust bars in this area which vary from colourful and 'ethnic' to grimy and revolting.

Castile: Central Spain

About two hours from Madrid lie two towns which should ideally be included on any Spanish itinerary: ÁVILA and SEGOVIA. Ávila

(famous because of Saint Teresa) has some of Europe's best-preserved medieval battlements, dating from the eleventh century, and
there are other buildings in the town from this same period. Tourist
information is at Pl. de la Catedral (Tel. 918–21 13 87) and there's
no problem finding cheap rooms. Segovia has a ROMAN AQUEDUCT
antedating Christ, a fourteenth-century ALCÁZAR (palace) (rebuilt
in the nineteenth century), and dozens of churches in different
architectural styles. The tourist office is at Plaza Mayor 10 and
there's plenty of cheap rooms nearby. Try Fonda Cubo, third floor
at 4 Pl. de Franco. Whilst both these towns are interesting enough to
make the effort to get to them, you'd be absolutely crazy not to
make it to the town of Toledo.

Toledo

This is the town which can show you the past four centuries of
Spanish history and culture in one or two days. From the Moorish
and Visigothic mosques and synagogues to the Renaissance buildings of the Spanish Inquisition, every architectural style is represented and wonderfully preserved. It's interesting to note that
Toledo was one of the world's few centres of Arab, Jewish and
Christian co-existence. It's possible to make Toledo a day trip from
Madrid (it takes 1½ hours) but you'll kill yourself trying to see all the
sights in just one afternoon. Perched up on the high town are
buildings such as the MOSQUE OF THE CHRIST OF LIGHT (tenth
century), the SYNAGOGUE OF SANTA MARÍA LA BLANCA, the
incredible medieval CATHEDRAL; and dominating the violet-
coloured sky is the ALCÁZAR which once housed El Cid. EL GRECO
lived in Toledo, and his HOUSE AND MUSEUM can be seen (closed
Saturday p.m. and Mondays, admission 200 ptas.). There are many
more things to see: go along to Turismo, just outside the Puerta de
Bisagra (closed Saturday p.m. and Sundays), and pick up your
glossy leaflets and map. This office, like many of the sights, takes a
long siesta and doesn't reopen till 4 p.m. From the station (at the
foot of the hill) take the bus marked Santa Barbara to the centre.
  For accommodation, there are two campsites: Camping El Greco
(Tel. 925–213537) and Circo Ronano (Tel. 925–220442). Tourist

information will suggest pensions. Fonda Lumbreras, Calle Juan Labrador 7 (Tel. 925–221571), or Fonda Escobar, Cuesta de Santa Leocadia 4 (Tel. 925–229465), are good bets. Shop around for your meals and eat at the fixed-price menu places near the central Plaza de Zocodover if possible. This is where it all happens in Toledo, especially at night. There is a RENFE office here too, where you can get info. or book tickets.

The youth hostel is in a castle ten minutes' walk from the station and town centre. It's at Castillo de San Servando (Tel. 925–224554) and is beautiful inside with a super pool.

Salamanca

Further down the line from Ávila is Spain's oldest university town, Salamanca. The main reason for going there is to see Spain's most beautiful square, the PLAZA MAYOR, built by Philip V in the eighteenth century. From the station take bus 1 to the centre of the town where tourist information is at Gran Vía 41 (Tel. 923–268571), closed Saturday afternoon and all day Sunday. An afternoon should be long enough to take in the main sights: the square, university, OLD AND NEW CATHEDRALS, and HOUSE OF SHELLS, but if you come in term-time you might want to stay a night for the active student nightlife. Look for a room round the Plaza Mayor and call in at Calle Meléndez for a cheap meal.

Burgos

Most Madrid–Paris runs go through this old tenth-century capital of Castile. Franco was declared military commander here in 1936 and none other than El Cid is buried in the CATHEDRAL that you should head for, as the rest of the town has nothing spectacular in it. Tourist information is at 7 Pl. de Alonso Martínez (Tel. 947–20 31 25). Open Mon.–Fri.: 9 a.m.–2 p.m., 4.30 p.m.–6 p.m., Sat.: 9 a.m.–2 p.m. The youth hostel is at C. General Vigón (Tel. 947–22 03 62) or try Hostal Victoria, C. San Juan 3 (Tel. 947–20 15 42), near the tourist office.

Valladolid

Just over an hour from Burgos is the university city of Valladolid. If you take a break here, visit the sixteenth-century house of MIGUEL DE CERVANTES, who wrote *Don Quixote*, off the Calle Miguel Iscar, the CATHEDRAL, the cloisters of the sixteenth-century S. GREGORIO COLLEGE, and the UNIVERSITY. Tourist information is at 3 Pl. de Zorrilla.

Cuenca

If you're heading for Valencia and the Costa del Azahar, and fancy a short break in the 5-hour journey from Madrid, take an hour or two off at Cuenca, about halfway up the line. Walk round the old town, starting at the PLAZA MAYOR, and take in the CITY HALL, the CATHEDRAL and the incredible fourteenth-century HANGING HOUSES on the banks of the Huécar River. Turismo is at Dalmacio Garcia Izcara 8 (Tel. 966–22 22 31). Open Mon.–Fri.: 9 a.m.–2 p.m., 4.30 p.m.–6.30 p.m., Sat.: 9.30 a.m.–1 p.m.

Costa del Sol

This exploited cement-heap of coastline, best reached via Málaga, is all that you'd expect. It's difficult to know you're in Spain, the food and nightlife are plastic and often vulgar, and you'll begin to understand the background to the jokes about package deals to Torremolinos. Don't come here to look for quiet fishing villages, deserted beaches or friendly locals. However, if you're low on cash, keen to rough it on the beach, meet Europeans and pick up a tan, then you'd be hard pressed to find a better deal in Europe. If you avoid July and August and the main package-holiday resorts, you'd be amazed how different a picture can emerge.

Málaga

Don't stay in Málaga too long: not just because you run a higher risk of getting mugged here than anywhere else in Spain, but because the resorts are often crowded, and it's advisable to make for one and get established first, then head back for a day trip to see this city's sights.

Tourist information in Málaga is at Calle de Larios 5, open 9 a.m.–2 p.m. (1 p.m. on Sat., closed Sun.). If you feel you're being followed from the station, turn round and take a good look, then stick to major streets. The instances of eurorailers being followed from station to tourist information and being mugged en route are amazing. Whatever happens, don't even think about sleeping out at Málaga Station. We realize you'll probably know plenty of people who have and have come out unscathed, but we also know scores who've had their rucksacks actually cut off their backs and been threatened at knife-point to hand over their valuables. Honestly, it's not worth the risk. The British Consulate is at Edificio Duquesa, Duquesa de Parcent 8 (Tel. 952–217571), in case anything nasty happens. The US one is at Avenida Fuengirola (Tel. 952–461865). Tourist information will give you a leaflet on Málaga's sights. Take in the ALCAZABA Moorish palace and GIBRALFARO CASTLE if you can. 'El Corte Inglés', the big department store, is useful to stock up in. Usually its toiletries, etc., are cheaper than at the resorts, and its cafeterias are worth a visit too.

The Resorts

The resorts to the east of Málaga are less exploited, but the beaches aren't so good. In places like CASTELL DE FERRO and TORRENUEVA you'll avoid the package tourists, but will find the facilities basic. It's easier coming down from Granada to get to the eastern resorts and using the bus for the last lap.

West of Málaga, the electric train runs as far as FUENGIROLA, stopping at Torremolinos, Benalmadena, and Los Boliches en route. This train is free on Inter Rail, but to get on to Marbella or further west, you have to resort to buses.

TORREMOLINOS is the most commercialized centre. Look for rooms in hostels leading down to the beach and, as far as eating and nightlife goes, you'd have a job actually to miss the tourist menus, bars and discos, so there's no problem there. Tourist information is on Bajos de la Nogalera (1 p.m.–4.30 p.m. siesta). If this doesn't appeal, move on to other resorts till you find a suitable one. MARBELLA is slightly more 'up market', so prices can be higher here. There's a good youth hostel here on Trapiche (Tel. 952–771491) but it may be closed temporarily, and for pensions, try round Aduar or Germán Porras. FUENGIROLA'S a good compromise between the two and, with its four miles of beaches and many cheap beds and restaurants, an attractive proposition to the footsore eurorailer.

Andalusia (Andalucía)

This is stereotyped Spain: flamencos, bullfights, Moorish palaces and hilltop villages. This province is bordered by the Mediterranean, the Straits of Gibraltar and the Gulf of Cádiz, and the principal centres are Seville, Granada and Córdoba.

Seville (Sevilla)

If Madrid disappointed you, head for Seville. It's a great city to visit: typically Spanish and colourful, and as alive at night as in the day. There are plenty of sights and cheap beds and it seems impossible to hit a day in summer when the heat doesn't drive you into the nearest shady park for a siesta, no matter how dedicated a sun-worshipper you might be.

STATION FACILITIES

There are two stations in Seville: San Bernardo (known as Cádiz Railway Station) and Plaza de Armas, which the locals call Córdoba Railway Station.

TOURIST INFORMATION AND ADDRESSES

TOURIST OFFICE: Avenida de la Constitución 21B, open 9.30 a.m.–7 p.m., Mon.–Fri. and 9.30 a.m.–2 p.m. Saturday.

POST OFFICE: Avenida de la Constitución 32, open Mon.–Fri.: 9 a.m.–8 p.m., Sat.: 9 a.m.–1 p.m.

AMEX: c/o Viajes Alhambra, Teniente Coronel Segui 3, open Mon.–Fri.: 9.30 a.m.–1.30 p.m. and 4.30 p.m.–8 p.m., Sat.: 9.30 a.m.–1.30 p.m.

UK CONSULATE: Plaza Neuva 8 (Tel. 228875).

US CONSULATE: PEU Paseo de las Delicias 7 (Tel. 231885), open 9 a.m.–1 p.m., 2 p.m.–4.30 p.m., closed Wednesday p.m., Saturdays and Sundays.

FIRST AID: Jesús del Gran Poder 34 (Tel. 224760).

PHONE CODE: 954.

SEEING

The CATHEDRAL and ALCÁZAR complex should be your first stops. The cathedral, the third largest in the world, is built on the site of a former mosque (entrance 200 ptas.), and the Moorish tower, LA GIRALDA, is a leftover from this period. Leave the cathedral at Puerta de los Naranjos, cross the plaza to Puerta Oriente and you'll come to the fourteenth-century Alcázar palace with its combination of Moorish and Gothic architecture (250 ptas., free with ISIC).

PLAZA DE ESPAÑA and the nearby parks offer romantic settings for the evening stroll, and you can hire out boats at reasonable rates and row round the Spanish Square taking it all in.

Behind the cathedral is the picturesque old Jewish quarter of SANTA CRUZ. There are guided tours, but you're better off wandering round yourself.

SLEEPING

Concentrate your efforts on finding a cheap pension (there's no convenient campsite or central youth hostel). Down from the Plaza de Armas Station or in the Santa Cruz area are your best bets. Rooms start about 1,000 ptas. single. Try to get fixed up early as Seville's popular with eurorailers and Spaniards alike. The hostels on Archeros are among the best in town. Try Pérez Montilla at No. 14 (Tel. 361740) or Casa de Huéspedes Orellana (Tel. 362259) at No. 19. Another good street to try is Calle San Eloy with the Hostal La Gloria at No. 58 (Tel. 222673) among the best. Sleeping rough in the parks is a dicey proposition as you have not only the police to contend with, but also the local rats. The youth hostel is at Calle Issac Peral 2 (Tel. 613150). Take buses C1 or C2 to the Resolana stop, or C3 or C4 to the Alameda stop. Also bus 34 to the last but one stop, from opposite the tourist office on Plaza Nueva.

EATING AND NIGHTLIFE

Prices in Seville tend to be over the top, but there are plenty of central places with fixed tourist menus, and there are even a few fast-food places creeping in now. Again, the area round the Plaza de Armas Station isn't bad, and you can eat for about 900 ptas., but some of these places aren't too fussy about hygiene.

The Barrio Triana is a good place to make for to try the local tapas, though some bars seem a bit hostile to women coming in on their own. Casa Manola at San Jorge 16 in the Barrio Triana is cheap and lively. But best value is El Diamante, Constitución 10, where an all-you-can-eat buffet costs under 900 ptas.

Going to a flamenco is *the* thing to do in Seville. There is no shortage of venues, and by and large they're good value. Avoid the heavily advertised ones and try and make your drinks last as long as possible, as they're (surprise, surprise) overpriced. Los Gallos at Plaza Santa Cruz 11 charge about 2,000 ptas. for entrance, including your first drink. This is about average, but the entertainment here is above average.

• **Excursions from Seville:** The sherry capital of JEREZ DE LA FRON-TERA is about 2 hours from Seville. If you're in this region in the second week of September go down for the fiesta. There are free guided tours and liberal samplings at the bodegas of Sandeman, Gonzalez Byass, etc. CÁDIZ, another 50 minutes away, hasn't much to commend it unless you're after a heavy nightlife scene.

If you are going on to Portugal, take the train to Huelva, then a 15-minute walk to the bus station for the bus to the ferry at Ayamonte (about 500 ptas.).

Granada

Bus 4, 5, 9 or 11 will take you from the station to the centre of Granada, and once you've found your bed and left off your things, you should walk up to the incredible ALHAMBRA, *the* sight of the city.

TOURIST INFORMATION AND ADDRESSES

TOURIST OFFICE: Calle Libreros 2 (behind the cathedral) (Tel. 221022). Mon.–Fri.: 10 a.m.–1 p.m., 4 p.m.–7 p.m. Sat.: 10 a.m.–1 p.m.

TRAIN INFORMATION: Tel. 223497.

POST OFFICE: Puerta Real, open 9 a.m.–2 p.m., 4 p.m.–6 p.m., closed Saturday p.m. and Sunday (Tel. 224835).

AMEX: c/o Viajes Bonal, Avenida Calvo Sotelo 19, open Mon.–Fri.: 9.30 a.m.–1.30 p.m., 4.30 p.m.–7 p.m., Sat.: 9.30 a.m.–1 p.m.

PHONE CODE: 958.

SEEING

The huge Arabic fortress on the hill dominating the city – the ALHAMBRA – is one of the world's best-preserved Moorish palaces. The ALCAZABA and WATCH TOWER go back to the ninth century, and you should visit GENERALIFE, the summer house of the sultans, the fourteenth-century palace, and see the incredible mosaics and examples of Muslim art. Go early in the day to get its full atmosphere. If you want to see the whole lot – castle, Generalife, royal palace, as well as the remaining grounds – the cost is 440 ptas.

Opposite the Alhambra is ALBAICÍN, the hilltop Arab quarter with its crowded, winding streets; and on the other hilltop is the gypsy quarter of SACROMONTE. Down in the town take in the Renaissance CATHEDRAL (100 ptas.) and ROYAL CHAPEL.

SLEEPING

The youth hostel is the best deal in Granada. It's in the Colegio Emperador Carlos at Camino de Ronda (Tel. 272638). It's not too

far from the station and a 20-minute walk from the town centre.
Other hostels near the station abound in Calle San Juan de Dios.
For pensions, try round the station on Avenida Andaluces, or the
road up to the Alhambra, Cuesta de Gomérez. Hostal Residencia
San Joaquin, Mano de Mierra 14 (Tel. 282879), is excellent, and the
Sierra Nevada campsite at Carretera Madrid (Tel. 232504) is OK,
but charges almost as much as a pension.

EATING AND NIGHTLIFE

Round Cetti Meriem is the place for cheap meals. La Riviera at No.
5 starts meals around 600 ptas. Avoid the 'gypsy flamenco' at
Sacromonte come what may, and instead head for the bars in the
centre. As far as nightlife's concerned, save your pesetas and go for
a nocturnal stroll up by the Alhambra instead.

Córdoba

The Roman and Moorish remains are the reasons to include
Córdoba in an itinerary. This was the eighth-century capital of
Moorish Spain, though in many ways today's Córdoba looks as if
it's had its heyday.

TOURIST INFORMATION AND ADDRESSES

TOURIST OFFICE: C. Torrijos 10, open Mon.–Fri.: 9.30 a.m.–2.30
p.m. and 5 p.m.–7 p.m., Sat.: 9.30 a.m.–1.30 p.m. (Tel. 471235).
The Municipal Tourist Office is at Plaza de Juda Levi 3 (off
Manriques), open Mon.–Fri.: 8.30 a.m.–1.30 p.m. (Tel. 290740).
POST OFFICE: Cruz Conde 21, open 9 a.m.–2 p.m., 4 p.m.–6 p.m.,
closed Saturday p.m. and Sunday.
PHONE CODE: 957.

SEEING

LA MEZQUITA was a mosque before the Christians made it into a
cathedral in the eighth century. The structure has an incredible

array of decorated arches and pillars, and if you climb the tower you'll see how big the mosque must have been, as the cathedral fits into its original centre. During the summer it is open from 10.30 a.m.–1.30 p.m. and 4 p.m.–7 p.m. and at other times from 10.30 a.m.–1.30 p.m. and 3.30 p.m.–5.30 p.m. Entry is 300 ptas. The fourteenth-century SYNAGOGUE isn't exactly riveting, and the MUSEO MUNICIPAL could be missed out too. The ALCÁZAR is at its best floodlit at night. It's on the banks of the Río Guadalquivir and the Moorish gardens, towers and fountains make it an interesting place to take in.

SLEEPING, EATING AND NIGHTLIFE

Cheap pensions are on Calle Rey Heredia, at La Milagrosa, No. 12 (Tel. 473317); 1,100 ptas. per person. Check out the Hostel Mari, Calle Pimentero 6 for only 800 ptas. per person. There's camping about a mile out at Carretera Córdoba–Villaviciosa (Tel. 275048). Tourist menus are found most easily in the old quarter and, for tapas and bar crawls, try the Jewish quarter (round the Mezquita).

Ronda

The main line from Córdoba to Algeciras passes through this delightful town impressively perched on a gorge. See the CASA DEL REY MORO and the RENAISSANCE PALACE. Also take a look at the eighteenth-century bridge spanning the deep gorge beneath the town, as well as the former Moorish fortress and baths, and the cathedral. For a room try around the tourist information office at Pl. de España. Open Mon.–Fri.: 9.30 a.m.–2 p.m., 5 p.m.–7 p.m., closed Saturday afternoon and Sunday.

Algeciras

TOURIST OFFICE: Acera de la Marina, open Mon.–Fri.: 9.30 a.m.–1.30 p.m. and 4.30 p.m.–7.30 p.m. Sat.: 9 a.m.–2 p.m. There is also a tourist office at the station which is often unmanned but displays a town map and location of hostels. These are cheap and plentiful, so accommodation shouldn't be too much of a problem here.

If you are using Algeciras as the departure point for a trip to Morocco, buy your ticket from the first office selling ferry tickets to Tangier. Although there are a number of operators on this route they all charge roughly the same and are quite expensive at around 2,700 ptas. single and 5,400 ptas. return. It's no cheaper to buy at the ferry terminal than at any of the offices in town. If you are going on this trip remember to get your passport stamped during the voyage. The town itself is rather unremarkable and down at heel.

Avoid the overnight Paris–Irún–Algeciras train (particularly on Thursday and Friday nights) as it is very overcrowded and full of Arab immigrant workers returning to North Africa. The guard has a permanent escort of two armed security guards – which says it all!

Gibraltar

First settled by the Moors, the Spanish took over, followed by the British in 1704. Despite strong Mediterranean influences, Gibraltar is distinctively British, with British police, troops, beer and currency. The reopening of the frontier with Spain in 1985 means that Eurorailers can get here easily. The most convenient way is by bus from Algeciras to La Linea (140 ptas.), then walking across the border.

See the MOORISH CASTLE (entrance 40p) and the Galleries in the Rock (£1). Another 'hole' in the Rock is the natural ST MICHAEL'S CAVE (£1.50). Concerts and *son et lumières* are often held here. The GIBRALTAR MUSEUM (70p) chronicles the Rock's history from Neanderthal times. All these sights are open 10 a.m.–7 p.m. in the summer. Also, take the cable car to the top of the Rock. The famous apes are up here, cared for by the British Army. Feeding times are 8 a.m. and 4 p.m.

Tourist Information is in Cathedral Square (Tel. 76400); the London office is at 179 The Strand, WC2R 1EH (Tel. 071–836 0777). Accommodation in Gibraltar is difficult as there are no youth hostels or campsites. The cheapest hotel is Queen's on Boyd Street (Tel. 74000). Singles cost £22 and doubles £32.

Ferries run from Gibraltar to Tangier, but, at about £26 return, it is cheaper to go from Algeciras. In general, though, Gibraltar represents good value as there is no VAT.

SWEDEN (Sverige)

Entry requirements	Passport
Population	8,400,000
Capital	Stockholm (pop.: 1,600,000)
Currency	Krona
	£1 = approx. 10.25 kr.
Political system	Constitutional Monarchy
Religion	Lutheran
Languages	Swedish, English
Public holidays	1, 6 Jan.; Good Friday; Easter Monday; 1 May; Ascension Day; Whit Monday; Midsummer's Day; All Saints' Day; 24, 25, 26 Dec.
International dialling codes	From UK: 010 + 46 + number
	From USA: 011 + 46 + number
	To UK: 009 + 44 + number
	To USA: 009 + 1 + number

Over half of Sweden's land surface is covered by forests and lakes, an area larger than the whole of the British Isles.

Geographically isolated in the ninth and tenth centuries, the Swedish Vikings pushed eastwards down the Russian rivers to trade their furs. This trade eventually caught the attention of the Hanseatic League who were always keen to capitalize on others' labour. By the fourteenth century, all Scandinavia had had enough of these German merchants who controlled so much. The Swedes hoped that the Union of Kalmar between Sweden, Norway and Denmark (1397) would change all this; instead, all that happened was that Denmark came out on top.

In 1523 Gustavus Vasa was elected king for successfully defeating the Danes, and from then on the Swedes never looked back.

Sweden reached her zenith in the seventeenth century under Gustavus Adolphus who procured a Baltic empire for her. Defending this new position meant constant warfare until the early nineteenth century; it was therefore widely welcomed when Sweden declared herself neutral at the end of the century.

Today Sweden enjoys one of the highest standards of living in the world and a quality of life to go with it (though why it then has the highest suicide rate is anyone's guess!), thanks to the highly developed social welfare system.

• **Getting there:** The alternative routes are London–Dover–Ostend and up through Germany, or from Harwich to the Hook of Holland, then up. This takes about 22–25 hours to reach Stockholm. By sea there are four sailings a week from Harwich to Gothenburg (50 per cent discount for ISIC card holders) and twice a week from Newcastle to Gothenburg in high season. Also there's another ferry to Esbjerg in Denmark which connects up to a through-train to Copenhagen, and a line operates from Newcastle to Esbjerg.

SWEDISH STATE RAILWAYS
(Statens Järnvägar, SJ)

Swedish trains are efficient, clean and comfortable. They are very rarely late and run frequent services (every hour or so) to most of the major cities. The journey from Stockholm to Malmö takes only six hours, and to Narvik in the far north of Norway twenty hours. New fast trains have started running between Stockholm and Gothenburg travelling at 130 m.p.h. They have audio channels in seats and outlets for computers! The long-distance Inter City and Rapid trains are the fastest, followed by the expresses which are used on regular routes. The local trains are not as slow as in some countries, but still stop at every station. There are supplements only on City Express trains, but see Reservations. Ask at stations for a free copy of SJ Tågtider timetables.

• **Inter Rail bonuses:**

	FROM	TO	REDUCTION %
Stena Sessan Line	Gothenburg	Frederikshavn	50
Silja Line	Stockholm (1)	Helsinki (1)	50
	Stockholm (1)	Turku (1)	50
T.T. Line	Trelleborg	Lübeck–Travemünde	50

(1) A ticket bought for Stockholm–Turku is not valid for Stockholm–Helsinki.

• **Eurail bonsues:** Free:
—Steamer service of the Silja Line between Stockholm and Helsinki and between Stockholm and Aland Islands–Turku. (Full fare is charged for cabin space.)

—Ferry crossings operated by the Swedish and Danish State Railways between Helsingborg and Helsingør (Denmark).

—Ferry crossings operated by Stena Sessan Line between Gothen-burg and Frederikshavn (Denmark).

Reduced fares:

—50 per cent reduction on the Danish Navigation Company, Øresund, on the hydrofoil between Malmö and Copenhagen.

—50 per cent reduction to Eurail Pass and Eurail Youthpass holders on the normal fares of the ferry crossings operated by TT Line between Malmö and Lübeck–Travemünde (Federal Republic of Germany).

TRAIN INFORMATION

No problems here, as everyone speaks perfect English and queues are never too long.

• **Reservations:** (20 kr.) Are compulsory on all Rapid and Inter City trains. Failure to reserve means paying heavily. Reservations can be made at the ticket desk.

• **Night travel:** Is relatively cheap in Sweden at about 80 kr. for a couchette and about 120 kr. for a tourist-class sleeper.

• **Eating on trains:** All long-distance expresses have a buffet or dining car, other trains have only snack bars.

• **Scenic tips:** Any line north of Stockholm is of interest, particularly from Östersund onwards, either to Trondheim in Norway or to Kiruna in the far north.

• **Bikes:** Bikes go as luggage as Swedish trains have no guard's vans. This means that your bike may not travel on the same train, so to be sure it arrives with you, send it two days in advance. Cost per bike is 50–100 kr.

• **Rover tickets:** The Nordic Railpass ('Nordturist Medtåg') is valid for 21 days in Sweden, Denmark, Norway and Finland for unlimited rail travel. It costs around £135 for second class and around £181 for first class for those over 25 and £101 and £136 respectively for those under, with children aged from 4 to 12 paying half price for the card but full price for seat reservations and couchettes/sleeping car berths. If you want to extend your holiday, you can buy several tickets in succession. The ticket is also valid on the SJ and DSB ferries between Helsingborg and Helsingør, on all the domestic DSB ferries in Denmark and the routes Rødby Færge–Puttgarten Mitte See, Gedser–Warnemunde Mitte See and Trelleborg–Sassnitz Mitte See, on the boat-lines Stockholm–Turku (Siljia Line), Göteborg–Frederikshavn (Stena Line) and Kristiansand–Hirtshals (Fred Olsen Lines/KDS), on the NSB bus service from Storlien to Trondheim, and on the combined boat and bus route between Halden/Sarpsborg and Strømstad (by Halden Turisttrafikk A/S SSV Bilselskap A/S, SJ Busstrafik and AB Koster-Trafic).

A 50 per cent reduction on the normal fare is available on the following boat-lines: Stockholm–Tallin (N and T Estline), Stockholm–Helsinki (Silja Line), Copenhagen Havnegade–Malmö Skeppsbron (DSÖ hydrofoil), Copenhagen–Oslo (DFDS, reclining seats), Copenhagen–Rønne (Bomholmstrafiken), Ystad–Rønne (Bomholmstrafiken), Hjørring–Hirtshals (Hjørring Privat-baner), Umeå–Vasa (Vasabåtama AB), Travemünde–Trelleborg (TT-Line), Bodö–Fauske–Narvik (Nord–Norway–Coach), Narvik–Kirkenaes (Nord–Norway–Coach), Växjö–Hultsfred–Västerviks railway company (12 May–26 August, Saturday and Sunday 1–23 September).

A 25 per cent reduction is available on Bicka Cruises Cruises Stockholm–Mariehamn. Don't forget your 'Nordturist' railway ticket allows you free entry to the railway museums in Gävle, Hamar, Hyvinkää and Odense. A popular card is the 'Inlandsba-nan' which is valid for the Inland Railway travelling 800 miles down the backbone of Sweden from Gallivare in the north to Kristine-hamn in the south, with one stretch involving travel by bus. The card, which gives unlimited travel on the line, is valid for either 14 or 21 days and gives discounts on overnight accommodation, restaur-ant meals and sightseeing tours. It costs around 490 kr. for 14 days and 545 kr. for 21 days. The ticket also gives a further 50 per cent reduction off the mini-fare on domestic flights to airports which link up with the line. The new structure has put a price ceiling on long-distance journeys with a flat rate fare for all trips over 560 miles (900 km). Children under 16 travel at half the full or reduced fare, depending on the day of travel.

TOURIST INFORMATION

Every Swedish county has a tourist board in addition to the local tourist information offices called 'Turistbyrå'. They are very helpful and always have a good selection of maps and brochures.

• **ISIC bonuses:** Few reductions here; the main one is 20 per cent off tours and day trips to historic places. For further information, contact SFS Resebyra, Kungsgatan 4, Box 7144, 10387, Stockholm (Tel. 08–234515).

• **Money matters:** 1 krona (kr.) = 100 öre.
Banking hours are Mon.–Fri.: 9.30 a.m.–3 p.m. Bank charges are high for traveller's cheques (approximately 30 kr.) so it makes sense to cash large denominations. Credit cards are widely accepted.

• **Post offices and shops:** Post offices open Mon.–Fri.: 9 a.m.–6 p.m., and 9 a.m.–2 p.m. on Saturdays. Most shops are open 9.30 a.m.–6 p.m., most shops close Sat. afternoons. The poste restante service is free in Sweden, and stamps are sold at newsagents as well as post offices.

• **Museums:** Normally open from about 10 a.m.–5 p.m.

SLEEPING

All regional and local tourist offices have free lists of hotels and campsites; many also have a room-finding service called Rumsför-medling. They charge a commission of about 20 kr., and can find you a room in a private house or in a hotel. In smaller towns and villages look for the sign Rum (the Swedish equivalent of B&B, except there's no breakfast). At about 200 kr. for a single, this represents as good value as you're likely to get. Youth hostels are great and cost about 50–83 kr. per night; add another 28 kr. to this if you're not a member. Camping's no problem thanks to the Allmansrätt law which allows anyone to camp on unfenced land for one night only – and please be careful about fire. Tourist information will direct you to suitable places. If you prefer your comforts, most towns have campsites with excellent facilities costing about

40–100 kr. per tent, but these require a camping pass (25 kr.) obtainable at the site.

EATING AND NIGHTLIFE

Eating out is incredibly expensive in Sweden even at fast-food joints (£4 for a hamburger; £1 for a coke). Always check to see if there's a tourist menu or a cheap set meal (dagens rätt). More often than not, you'll be forced to eat from supermarkets, which is no bad thing as the quality and choice are excellent. Most of the regional specialities, such as smoked reindeer meat from Lapland, are expensive and confined to the best restaurants. Smörgåsbord is cheaper here than in Norway, so if you feel like a Scandinavian splash-out do it here.

Nightlife is what you make it in Sweden, and there's no shortage of options in the larger towns. Alcohol and tobacco are expensive and controlled by the government, but there's not much the government can do during the midsummer festival when everyone lets rip with non-stop dancing and drinking, particularly in the north.

Stockholm

All the qualities one associates with the Swedes are reflected in their capital. It's tidy and well laid-out, socially minded and efficiently run, and the high level of money floating around has permitted them to improve their environment with schemes like making the city's waterway safe for swimming and erecting new buildings with more of an eye towards appearance than to economy. Stockholm has a reputation as the 'porn capital of Europe' but is in many ways more discreet about it than Amsterdam or Copenhagen. It's very much an 'it's there if you want it' attitude; by the way, men will be in for a disappointment if they go there believing all the stories they've heard about Swedish girls.

It's difficult to make out on a tight budget here, as even supermarket food is expensive, but you'll get by if you follow our suggestions and use your common sense.

STATION FACILITIES

	STOCKHOLM CENTRAL
Train information	24 hours (Tel. 225060)
Reservations	Domestic: 24 hours (Tel. 225060)
	International: 7 a.m.–10 p.m. (Tel. 248040)
Tourist information	Summer: 8 a.m.–9 p.m.
	Winter: 8.30 a.m.–5 p.m.
Foreign exchange	8 a.m.–9 p.m.
Left-luggage lockers	No access 1 a.m.–4.30 a.m.
Left-luggage store	6 a.m.–10.30 p.m.
Café, Bar	6.30 a.m.–10.30 p.m.
Restaurant	6.30 a.m.–12 midnight
Provisions	7 a.m.–11 p.m.
Post office	Mon.–Fri.: 7 a.m.–9 p.m., Sat.: 8 a.m.–4 p.m.
Station shuts	Mon.–Sat.: 1 a.m.–4.30 a.m., Sun.: 1 a.m.–5 a.m.

Frequent trains to: Malmö, Copenhagen, Gothenburg, Oslo, and all Sweden.

TOURIST INFORMATION

Apart from the station, there's an office in the centre at Sweden House (Sverigehuset), Kungstradgården, opposite the department store NK. Pick up maps and 'Stockholm This Week' and take a look at 'Stockholm on a Shoestring'. The Swedish Institute on the first floor gives out free fact-sheets on Sweden, and everyone involved seems incredibly helpful.

• **Addresses:**
POST OFFICE: Vasagatan 28–34, open 8 a.m.–8 p.m., Sat.: 9 a.m.–3 p.m., Sun.: 9 a.m.–11 a.m. Also Central Station.
AMEX: Birger Jarlsgatan 1 (Tel. 143981). Open Mon.–Fri.: 9 a.m.–5 p.m., Sat.: 9 a.m.–1 p.m.
UK EMBASSY: Skarpögatan 6 (Tel. 670140).
US EMBASSY: Strandvägen 101 (Tel. 630520).
CANADIAN EMBASSY: Tegelbacken 4, 7th floor (Tel. 237920).
AUSTRALIAN EMBASSY: Sergelstorg 12 (Tel. 244660).
24-HOUR CHEMIST: Apoteke Scheele, Klarabergsgatan 64 (Tel. 248280).
SVENSKA TURISTFÖRENINGEN: Vasagatan 48. Call in for information if you're camping or hostelling in Sweden.

INTERNATIONAL YOUTH CENTRE: Valhallavägen 142. A helpful lot who offer cheap bus excursions, free cooking facilities, games rooms, etc. Great place to meet students.
PHONE CODE: 08.

• **Getting about:** The underground and buses are good and charge by the zone. Three-day transit passes cost about 95 kr. (including free entry to some museums and ferries); twenty-four-hour passes cost about 25/50 kr., depending on the areas covered. Buy these at tourist information or stalls in the underground. The 'Stockholm Card' (Stockholmskortet), also known as the 'Key to Stockholm', is available for two or three days (190 kr. or 285 kr.) and gives you free travel on buses and underground trains as well as suburban trains (also free on Inter Rail), museum entrances and sightseeing trips by bus or boat. It also gives you a free excursion by boat to Drottningholm Palace. If you are only staying one day, you will need to cram in a lot to make it worthwhile, as many museums shut at 3 or 4 p.m. The banks also hand out free city maps, and if nature calls the best toilets are in the department stores such as NK.

SEEING

Close to the centre lie the islands of GAMLA STAN, SKEPPSHOLMEN and DJURGÅRDEN where the vast majority of sights are located. Gamla Stan, or the Old Town, dates back to the mid-thirteenth century. The narrow medieval streets are full of trendy shops and restaurants, nightclubs and studios. The eighteenth-century ROYAL PALACE is in Gamla Stan, and parts of it are open to the public till about 3 p.m. daily, except Mondays. The NATIONAL MUSEUM and MODERN ART GALLERY are located east of the Old Town at Skeppsholmen, and east of this again is the Djurgården, an island almost entirely devoted to recreation. Take the ferry over from Slussen or Nybroplan, or walk from Strandvägen. This is where the seventeenth-century warship *Wasa* is on view. This flagship of the Swedish navy only lasted ten minutes on her maiden voyage before sinking into oblivion, till she was rediscovered in 1956 and brought up. She's in a remarkable state of preservation and is well worth the 25 kr. fee (students 15 kr.).

If you're heavily into ships and naval history, the MUSEUM SHIPS at Sjöhistoriska museet (Tel. 6664890) will be of interest. Here you can see an ice-breaker, lightship and medieval ship. Open daily 10 a.m. to 5 p.m. during the summer.

Sweden's open-air museum, SKANSEN, is definitely one of Europe's best. It's called 'Sweden in Miniature' with good reason, as an afternoon spent there will fill you in more on Swedish folklore, architecture and history than will a week touring the country. There are over 150 buildings of authentic Swedish design, demonstrations of folk dancing, craftsmen at work, a zoo and lots more. Open Apr.–Sept.: 8 a.m.–11.30 p.m.; Oct.–Mar.: 8 a.m.–9 p.m. (the buildings 11 a.m.–5 p.m.).

GRÖNA LUND, or Tivoli, is the amusement park on Djurgården. It's better than Copenhagen's and averages 12 kr. on most rides.

The Swedish 'House of Culture' (KULTURHUSET) at Sergelstorg is a good example of the country's social-mindedness. Exhibitions of crafts and art are always on and there are free 'creative activities' for anyone who wants to participate so, if you're feeling inspired, jog along and model or paint your masterpiece. There's also a library and access to foreign newspapers and records. It's open in summer, Mon.–Thur.: 9 a.m.–8.30 p.m., Fri.: 9 a.m.–6 p.m. and Sat.–Sun.: noon–4 p.m.

SLEEPING

Hotellcentralen at Central Station will give you a map and list of hostels and hotels or find you a hostel space for a fee of 10 kr. or a hotel bed for a fee of 20 kr. The International Youth Centre will also help out if you're really stuck. You'd do well to make use of these services, especially in peak season, as beds (especially cheap ones) are thin on the ground. Theoretically they can arrange private accommodation at the station if you're staying more than a few days, but in general in summer there are never enough to go around. If it's at all feasible to call ahead and reserve, do so; and this goes for hostels, campsites or hotels. (English is widely spoken.)

The most memorable place to stay in Stockholm is definitely on board the AF *Chapman*. This youth hostel is a nineteenth-century sailing ship, fully rigged and decked out, and harboured opposite the Gamla Stan; it costs 72 kr. for a 'berth' in a 4–8-bed cabin. You need to pre-book or turn up early – 9 a.m. at the latest – to stand a chance; to reserve, call 103715. The other central youth hostel, open only in summer, is also popular and good: Frescati Hostel at

Professorsslingan (Tel. 157996) is part of Hotel Frescati and offers great doubles for around 200 kr. There's also a youth hostel on Skeppsholmen beside AF *Chapman* (Tel. 202506). Large and good value.

For hotels try one of the following: Hotel Domus, Körsbärsvägen 1 (Tel. 160195), Pensionat Oden, Odengatan 38 (Tel. 306349), or Gustavsvikshemmet at Västmannagatan (Tel. 214450). All are within the 350–450 kr. per double range.

Out of the four city campsites, the nearest ones are Ängby Camping on Lake Mälaren (Tel. 370420) on underground 17 or 18, and Bredäng Camping (Tel. 977071) on subway 13 or 15 to Bredäng Station. For a list of Swedish youth hostels contact STF at Vasagatan 48, and for student hostels contact SFS at Kungsgatan 4, Box 7144, Stockholm (Tel. 234515).

EATING AND NIGHTLIFE

Face the fact, you're going to have to spend twice as much as you would in southern Europe to eat out here. Picnics are the answer, in conjunction with bar meals ('Bars' are basic self-service restaurants here). Buy in supplies at Östermalms Saluhall or Hötorgshallen, the two big indoor markets. The central supermarkets also do a good line in groceries. There are some old cellar restaurants offering dagens rätt (today's special) in the Gamla Stan. While smörgåsbord are filling and tasty, they also tend to be pricey; however, if you arrive in Stockholm Central after a long train journey, treat yourself to the excellent stora frukost (eat-as-much-as-you-like breakfast 6.30 a.m.–10 a.m., closed Sunday). It's about 49 kr. and will keep you going all day. Annorlunda, a vegetarian place, at Malmskillnadsgatan 50 does good healthy meals for around 60 kr. If you're cutting all corners and don't mind plastic atmospheres and fast food, there are several outlets to choose from. There's a Wimpy beside the Kulturhuset. In the evening Gamla Stan tends to be the best area to head for. There are plenty of pubs and clubs with bands for around 50 kr. For cheaper entertainment, go over to Skansen or Gröna Lund where there's usually dancing, etc. Check with 'Stockholm This Week' for current events and, unless you're rolling in cash or desperate, steer clear of the notorious sex clubs – not that they'll short-change you in what they offer, but the admission fee's about half the price of your train ticket.

• **Excursions:** The old university town of UPPSALA is 45 minutes away by train. On a day trip here you can see the medieval CATHEDRAL, sixteenth-century CASTLE, the oldest UNIVERSITY in Sweden, pre-VIKING BURIAL MOUNDS, and the UPPLANDS MUSEUM which details the city's history and customs. Turn right on leaving the station for tourist information at Kungsgatan 44 (closed Saturday and Sunday). An alternative excursion is to DROTTNING-HOLM PALACE, built in the seventeenth century, five miles west of the capital on the island of Lovön. It's all very pretty: Chinese pavilion, rococo summerhouse, etc. To get there, either head for Klara Mälarstrand (near City Hall) and take the steamer, or take the underground to Brommaplan and then change to Mälarö-buses. To see at least some of Stockholm's 24,000 islands in the archipelago take a bus out to the TV tower at KAKNÄSTORNET. This 508-foot tower is reputed to have the fastest lift in Europe, but the view is worth it once your stomach has settled down. There is also a cafeteria and restaurant with prices which are not as extortionate as you will find in similar towers in other countries. Open from 9 a.m. to midnight during the summer, 9 a.m.–6 p.m. in winter.

Gotland

Sweden's largest island of Gotland is known for its medieval remains and its connections with the Hanseatic League. You'll find few tourists here, since to get here you need a ferry from Oskarshamn or Nynäshamn over to VISBY, the major town on Gotland. Ask tourist information for connection times and details. In Visby, tourist information is at Strandgatan 9 at the harbour. Before heading off to the unspoilt countryside of Gotland (prefer-ably on a bike), wander through Visby and take a look at the OLD CITY WALLS, the Viking remains in the GOTLANDS FORNSAL MUSEUM and the ST MARIA CATHEDRAL.

Gothenburg (Göteborg)

Sweden's second city is about four hours from Stockholm, and the detour to the west coast provides an interesting alternative route to get down to Copenhagen, as the direct line running straight down to Malmö is not that interesting. But if you go down that way it is worthwhile stopping off at the pleasant university town of LUND, four hours from Gothenburg, which has a magnificent cathedral with moving clock and an interesting outdoor museum (Kulturen) with demonstration crafts and old houses. Gothenburg's big on parks, museums and canals – in fact there's a distinct British feel to it, and it is known as Little London. Its harbour is the largest in Scandinavia.

STATION FACILITIES

	GÖTEBORG CENTRAL
Train information and *reservations by phone*	Sun.–Fri.: 8 a.m.–8 p.m. Sat.: 8 a.m.–7 p.m. (Tel. 031–805000)
Tourist information	At 'Östra Nordstan' (2 minutes away) in Nordstan Shopping Centre Mon.–Fri.: 9 a.m.–6 p.m., Sat.: 9.30 a.m.–3 p.m.
Foreign exchange	Mon.–Fri.: 8 a.m.–9 p.m.
Left-luggage lockers	24 hours
Left-luggage store	Sun.–Fri.: 7 a.m.–9 p.m. Sat.: 7 a.m.–8 p.m.
Cafeteria	Mon.:–Sat.: 6.30 a.m.–8.30 p.m. Sun.: 6.30 a.m.–9 p.m.
Restaurant and bar	Mon.–Thurs.: 11 a.m.–1 a.m. Fri.: 11 a.m.–2 a.m., Sat.: 1 p.m.–2 a.m. Sun.: 1 p.m.–12 midnight
Shops	Supermarket at station Mon.–Fri.: 6 a.m.–11 p.m. Sat.–Sun.: 7 a.m.–11 p.m. Other shops at 'Östra Nordstan' (2 minutes away)
Post office	At 'Östra Nordstan' (2 minutes away) Mon.–Fri.: 8 a.m.–7 p.m., Sat.: 9 a.m.–3 p.m.
Station shuts	12 midnight–5 a.m. Access to waiting room with ticket

Daily trains to: Oslo, Stockholm, Malmö, Copenhagen, northern Sweden. From Göteborg harbour, ferry services to: Denmark (daily), West Germany (daily), England (3 times/week) and Holland (2 times/week).

TOURIST INFORMATION AND SLEEPING

Apart from Östra Nordstan, the main tourist office is at Kungsport-splatsen 2, open daily 10 a.m.–8 p.m. Both offer an accommodation service including private accommodation lodgings for 150 kr. each. Their hotels start from about 350 kr. single, 450 kr. double, and they take 25 kr. commission. The youth hostel is good and not too far out. Ostkupan (Tel. 031–401050) at Kallebäck is about two miles from the centre on tram 5 to St Sigfridsplan, then bus 62 or 64 to Gräddgatan, open summer only. There is a new private hostel (Tel. 031–136467) on board a boat, the M/S *Seaside*, about 300 m from the station.

Kärralund (Tel. 031–252761) is the most central campsite and is reached by tram 5 to Welandergatan.

You can either buy a 24-hour pass for the excellent bus and tram system for around 25 kr., or invest in the 'Key to Gothenburg' (Goteborgskortet) which gives you free public transport, museum entrance, a sightseeing tour of the city centre, free on the famous 'Paddan' sightseeing boats, and many other things such as a free day trip to Denmark, free entrance to the Liseberg amusement park and much more. It costs around 75 kr. for 24 hours, 140 kr. for 48 hours and 195 kr. for 72 hours. Children pay approximately 50 per cent of the adult price. Always check prices and discounts on offer first.

If you are going on from Kiruna to Narvik the north side of the train is the one to sit on to see the most spectacular scenery.

SEEING

The centre of Gothenburg is very modern but if you head off to HAGA, the old district of wooden houses and coffee shops, you'll see a different side of the city. Of the many parks worth visiting try to take in the BOTANICAL GARDENS, SLOTTSKOGEN with its zoo, lakes and birds, and LISEBERG LEISURE PARK which has everything from discos to fun fairs. The INDUSTRIAL MUSEUM and ART CENTRE on Götaplatsen are interesting places, and for the nautically minded the MARITIME MUSEUM (Sjöfartsmuseet) has ships from Viking times to the present day. The KRONHUSET is the oldest building in the city and its museum, telling Gothenburg's history, includes such exhibits as reconstructed shops of the last century. The neo-classical

CATHEDRAL is also worth visiting. In the harbour is the FESKE-KÖRKA, a nineteenth-century church filled with fish stalls and vendors. The 7 a.m. auction is worth getting up for.

EATING AND NIGHTLIFE

Along Kungsportsavenyn (the main boulevard) are restaurants of all kinds and descriptions (from Chinese to Scottish), and alongside them are the increasingly popular fast-food chains. Fish and seafood are naturally in abundance in Gothenburg and often the dagens rätt will include a local fish dish. La Gondola at Kungsportsavenyn 4 does good large meals at moderate prices, and they have outside table service. For picnic food, the markets on Kungstorget are best.

At night, a lot of the young locals seem to gather round Kungsportsavenyn to cast an eye over the visiting talent; otherwise, you're most likely to meet the resident students in the bar at the Students' Union, Kårhuskällaren, which is near Götaplatsen. Behind the market on Kungstorget is Ölhallen, an authentic Swedish pub, and there are quite a few disco and jazz clubs, though their entrance fees put most of them safely out of the average eurorailer's reach.

Lapland

If you were put off going up to Lapland in Norway, let yourself be persuaded now you're in Sweden. It's easier here: the trains run right up to RIKSGRÄNSEN, just before the border and NARVIK in Norway. From Stockholm to the border is a straight 24 hours, though the conditions on the trains don't make this seem as much of an ordeal as it sounds, and the scenery once you're around GÄLLIVARE or KIRUNA is breathtaking. Once you're up there, there's an inland line from Gällivare down through JOKKMOKK and ARVIDSJAUR to ÖSTERSUND. It's legal to camp on unfenced land for one night so you can go it alone in a big way, especially out of season. Make sure you leave the place tidy afterwards though, and treat the plants with respect! Unless you've skin like leather, take with you mosquito repellent of some sort as they're out in force up there. The Svenska Turistföreningen, Box 7615, Stockholm, are the people to write to for information on mountain tourist stations and huts, and suggested hiking routes. To get the most out of a trip to Lapland, plan and book ahead as much as possible. Don't just wander aimlessly on to the train in Stockholm with no food or proper walking boots and expect to pick up relevant supplies once you're there, and don't go with fantasies in your head of great wilderness adventures with Lapps, reindeer and huskies. It's a bit like that, but in reality the towns are a bit grey and morose, and the Lapps (they call themselves Sami) are pretty sick of wide-eyed tourists pointing and gawping at them from June to September. If you do go make sure you have the right equipment with you.

Gällivare

This strategic mining town is at the junction of the main line to Narvik and inland line to Jokkmokk. If you've time to kill here waiting for connections, go to the nearby iron mines at MALMBER-GET and take the tour round (check times with tourist information), or go to the museum at VASARA where there are skis dating back before the time of Christ. Apart from the ETTORE CHURCH and the largest log cabin in the world, that's about it here. The tourist office is near the station at Storgatan 16, and is open Mon.–Sun.: 9 a.m.–11 p.m. in summer. They'll give you details on how to get up to the Stora Sjöfallet National Park and the surrounding mountains. If you're staying, ask about the private accommodation here. The youth hostel is at Andra Sidan (Tel. 0970–14380).

If you're travelling up to Kiruna and beyond, consider returning via Narvik and Fauske in Norway. (A bus connects the two and Fauske is on the Bodø line.) If, on the other hand, you are heading down to LULEA, take some time out to visit the excellent Museum of Lapp Culture. In addition to being free of charge, you can also get cassettes to wander around with, explaining the exhibits as you go along. The youth hostel (Tel. 0920–52325) is open all year round, take bus 6 from Lulea.

Kiruna

As the city's fairly unattractive, use Kiruna as a base for the surrounding countryside. Tourist information is at Hjalmar Lund-bohmsvägen 42, open 9 a.m.–8 p.m. weekdays, 1 p.m.–8 p.m. Sun. in season. There's a youth hostel called Strandstigen, which is 500 metres from the station and is only open from June to September. It's OK but avoid getting there towards the end of the season because it charges for heating! (Tel. 0980–17195). Or tourist information will get you into private houses. There are mine tours at Kiruna for 45 kr.

Jokkmokk

The SWEDISH MOUNTAIN AND LAPP MUSEUM has special displays on Lapp history and culture and is well worth the 10 kr. entrance fee. You'll find tourist information at Stortorget 4, open Mon.–Fri.: 8 a.m.–9 p.m.; Sat. and Sun.: 9 a.m.–9 p.m., during the summer. The tourist office give out 'Polar Certificates' to prove you've made it to, and crossed, the Arctic Circle (well, your Mum'll like it). The GAMLA KYRKA (Old Church) is the other main sight. There's a youth hostel at Stockgatan 22 (Tel. 0971–11977), open summer only, and an official campsite, Notuddens, a couple of miles from the centre.

Arvidsjaur

The LAPP VILLAGE in the town of Arvidsjaur is still used today by Lapps visiting the town for festivals and gatherings. Tourist information is at Östra Skolgatan 18, open 9 a.m.–8 p.m. daily in the summer, and they'll arrange private accommodation for you. The campsite at Järnvägsgatan 111 (Tel. 0960–13420) does huts as well as tent sites, and opposite the station is the Central Hotel at Järnvägsgatan with rooms at 200 kr. single, 300 kr. double. The youth hostel is at Östra Skolgatan 9 (Tel. 0960–12413), 300 m from the station.

SWITZERLAND

Entry requirements	Passport
Population	6,600,000
Capital	Bern (pop.: 145,000)
Currency	Swiss franc
	£1 = approx. SFr. 2.38
Political system	Federal Republic
Religions	Roman Catholic and Protestant
Languages	German, French, Italian, Romansch
	(English widely spoken)
Public holidays	1, 2 Jan.; Good Friday; Easter Monday;
	Whit Monday; Ascension Day; Corpus Christi;
	1, 15 Aug.; 1 Nov.; 25, 26 Dec.
International dialling codes	From UK: 010 + 41 + number
	From USA: 011 + 41 + number
	To UK: 00 + 44 + number
	To USA: 00 + 1 + number
Eurotrain office	Backerstrasse 52, CH–8026 Zürich
	(Tel. 01–2423000)

Cross the border from France or Italy to Switzerland and almost immediately you'll notice even the wood-piles are neater. Where the Swiss obsession for punctuality and cleanliness comes from is open to debate, but we suspect it's an ongoing process started when the Romans cleaned up after the Celts. Then along came the Germanic tribes who brought with them the work ethic we still see in their Swiss descendants, only now it's in the form of high finance and flashy watches. By the end of the thirteenth century, William Tell and his friends were demanding independence from the Habsburgs. This sparked off a proud tradition of self-government among the cantons which continues to this day. One of the reasons why the Swiss are so prosperous is the country's neutrality since Napoleon's invasion of 1815. Physically, Switzerland is one of the most beautiful countries in Europe and yet despite this apparent good fortune, many Swiss seem a bit tight-lipped and lacking in the vitality of their Italian neighbours.

SWISS FEDERAL RAILWAYS
(Schweizerische Bundesbahnen, SBB)
(Chemins de fer fédéraux suisses, CFF)
(Ferrovie federali svizzere, FFS)

Swiss federal railways and various private railway companies combine to give one of the most extensive and efficient services in Europe. There are even plans (called Rail 2000) to improve services with new lines and half-hourly service with fast new trains to rise to the challenge of 1992. The private outfits tend to serve the resort areas, except for the two largest. Most notable is the Bern–Lötschberg–Simplon line (BLS), Europe's largest private operation, which runs in friendly rivalry with the federal railway. International and intercity trains are federal-run, and intercity or express trains run hourly between all the main centres, while inland expresses run at least every other hour. There is a supplement on only two inland routes: the Bernina Express and the Glacier Express. From Chur to Tirano or v.v. it is about 20 F each way and from Zermatt to St Montz or v.v. it is about 8 F each way including seat reservation. A useful spin-off are the free maps and leaflets given out to lure custom.

● **Inter Rail bonuses:** Free entrance to Swiss Transport and Communications Museum, Lidostrasse, Lucerne.
   On most private railways of Switzerland, Inter Rail will bring you a 50 per cent reduction, so always ask first (see Appendix I). One that doesn't is Furka Oberalp.

● **Eurail bonuses:** Free:
—Regular steamer services on the lakes of Geneva, Lucerne, Thun, Brienz, Zürich, Neuchâtel, Biel, Murten, on the Rhine from Schaffhausen to Kreuzlingen and on the Aare from Biel/Bienne to Solothurn. Seasonal services – please consult timetables.

Reduced fares:
—50 per cent reduction on steamer services on Lake Constance between Romanshorn and Friedrichshafen and between Rorschach and Lindau.

● **Europabus:**
A 10 per cent reduction is granted by Europabus on transportation costs only and by local offices in Europe on:
200 St Moritz–Munich.

TRAIN INFORMATION

English is widely spoken throughout Switzerland and most Swiss timetables have an English section. If you have no luck finding anywhere to stay, look out for the travel-aid men with red, white and yellow armbands.

• **Reservations:** Must be made for the Glacier Express and the Bernina Express. It's probably only worthwhile reserving if you are going to Italy, where overcrowding can be a problem. Otherwise, don't bother unless you hit a particularly busy weekend. It's not possible to reserve on internal Swiss trains anyway. EuroCity trains have supplements, so ask first.

• **Night travel:** Wagons-Lits run sleepers on all international routes at their standard rates and couchettes are also available. SBB have no services on any inland runs.

• **Eating on trains:** Most stations are fairly well provided for, which is just as well as even the mini-bars are very expensive. If you've money to burn, the self-service buffet is much better value than the dining cars.

• **Scenic tips:** To get to grips with Switzerland's many scenic rail routes would take at least a month and involve paying out vast amounts for private lines. Swiss Pass or Swiss Card holders get round this problem, but most eurorailers have to be content with mainline runs. The possibilities are endless, without even leaving the main lines. All the main centres make excellent bases for touring the Alps. From Zürich take the main line to Chur, then the narrow-gauge Rhaetian Railway to Tirano – Europe's highest line at 7,400 feet as well as one of the most spectacular. At Chur an alternative is to head towards Zermatt. This line passes over the Oberalp (6,700 feet) and through the Furka tunnel but it gives no reduction to Inter-Railers.

Lucerne offers the greatest possibilities; foremost among them is the main line to Milan through the nine-mile-long Gotthard tunnel which took 2,500 men over seven years to construct in the 1880s. If this isn't spectacular enough, take the branch line to Locarno where you change trains for Domodossola in Italy. This line is a real favourite, passing through some incredible gorges. For the best view sit on the left-hand side. Also from Lucerne, the line to

Interlaken is equally awe-inspiring. If you haven't already seen enough and don't mind paying out, take the private line up to Kleine Scheidegg where, after you change trains, the line goes under the Eiger and on to the Jungfraujoch, Europe's highest station at 11,300 feet. Private lines also take you up to Mounts Rigi, Pilatus and Titlis from Lucerne, so good luck if you've got the money. Bern makes an alternative base for any of these trips, but if, like most eurorailers, you're in a hurry the main line to Milan via Brig will not be a disappointment. At Brig, if you've spare cash why not head for Zermatt, and take the cogwheel train up to Gornergrat and see the Matterhorn from close to. Approaching from the west, the train follows Lake Geneva as far as Lausanne where the line splits to enter Bern or Brig – either route is beautiful. The Martigny to Le Châtelard (and on to Chamonix) route is another classic. Sit on the left-hand side for the best view.

● **Rover tickets:** There are a number of tickets available in Switzerland, but a lot of these are designed to get people from airports and border crossings to ski resorts. The most useful is the Swiss Pass. It is available for eight days, fifteen days or one month (prices: £78, £94, £130 in second class) and gives free travel on state railways, steamers, post buses, town buses and trams plus reductions on private lines. The new Flexipass is valid for 3 days within 15 and costs £64 in second class. A number of Regional tickets are also available. They are valid for fifteen days. The holder gets five days of free travel plus ten days of half-price travel. Prices range from £24 to £59 depending on the region and class.

If you intend to stay mainly in one place and/or use many private lines, consider the Swiss Card which gives free travel from the border to a destination and back plus reductions on other journeys. £40 for one month. In general, though, the Swiss Pass is the best bargain. The Swiss Half-Fare Card costs £26 for one month or £44 for a year.

● **Bikes:** Can be hired at most SBB stations and some private ones; cost approximately 14 F a day for a basic six-gear model. Racing and mountain bikes are also available.

TOURIST INFORMATION

Every town has its own well-organized tourist office usually situated near the station. They keep a good selection of maps and leaflets, as well as running a room-finding service. Ask for the Swiss Holiday Card map: this shows the rail network of the country.

• **ISIC bonuses:** There's a variety of reductions on internal fares and in some museums. For further information, contact SSR Leonhardstrasse 10, Zürich, or SSTE, 3 rue Vignier, Geneva.

• **Money matters:** 1 franc (F) = 100 centimes (c.).
Banking hours are Mon.–Fri.: 8.30 a.m.–4.30 p.m. (often closed 12 noon–2 p.m.). Many stations have exchanges which stay open seven days a week. Post offices open Mon.–Fri.: 7.30 a.m.–6 p.m. (often closed 12 noon–1.45 p.m.), Sat.: 7.30 a.m.–11 a.m. Shops open Tues.–Fri.: 8.30 a.m.–6.30 p.m., and Saturdays until mid-afternoon. Many shops shut for lunch 12 noon–2 p.m., particularly in small towns.

SLEEPING

Availability and price are the two main problems you're likely to face in Switzerland. During the summer, the tourist resorts are packed and then there's always that unexpected conference in town. To avoid paying through the nose for somewhere to stay, arrive as early in the day as possible and start looking right away. Tourist offices keep lists of hotels and hostels in the area, and some will find you a room if required for a small charge. Hotels tend to be expensive with singles costing around 40 F, so think twice before committing yourself. Even a dormitory bed in a student hostel will set you back 28 F or more. Youth hostels often provide the only answer; there are over 100 of them in Switzerland, most of which are very clean and have excellent facilities. IYHF cards are required and you can expect to pay 9–18 F for a bed. Swiss campsites are among the best in Europe, and at only 7 or 8 F per person you can't go wrong. If you're forced to the hills to sleep out, remember it can get bitterly cold in Switzerland at night even during the summer.

EATING AND NIGHTLIFE

Although Switzerland used to be *very* expensive, prices have not risen so fast here, although budget travellers will still find it a bit of a struggle to eat out, and not sometimes particularly spectacular for what you get. Fortunately, a lot of the regional specialities can be bought from supermarkets (try Co-op or Migros). Alpine areas have a good selection of cheeses and cold meats ideal for picnics. The cheapest restaurants (Gemeindestube) don't serve alcohol, so if you want a glass of wine with your meal you'll have to check out the fixed-price menus. Look out for Rösti (a filling potato dish from the German area) or Berner Platte (a mixture of ham, bacon, and sausage with potatoes and green beans or pickled cabbage). If you can get a group together it's worth going for a fondue. The Swiss don't exactly specialize in budget entertainment; as a result, most young people take to the bars which serve excellent beer. During the summer, but also in spring and autumn there are plenty of local folk festivals going on in the mountains, and on 1 August the sky is set alight by fireworks commemorating the founding of the Swiss Confederation.

Zürich

The largest city of Switzerland and home of the 'gnomes' (as Harold Wilson so aptly put it) of the international money market. Walking on the average Zürich pavement, you're literally on top of gold: vaults containing much of the world's gold reserves lie buried beneath them. Zürich is one of Europe's most expensive cities, and in our estimation doesn't merit more than a couple of days of a tight timetable, though there's no denying the Old Town is picturesque. Situated in northern Switzerland, not far from the West German border, Zürich handles trains to an impressive number of destinations in Switzerland, France, Germany, Belgium, Holland, Hungary, Austria, Yugoslavia and Italy.

STATION FACILITIES

	ZÜRICH HAUPTBAHNHOF
Train information	Mon.–Fri.: 6.30 a.m.–8.45 p.m., weekends: 6.30 a.m.–8.45 p.m. (Tel. 2115010)
Reservations	7 a.m.–7.30 p.m.
Tourist information	8 a.m.–10 p.m.
Foreign exchange	6.30 a.m.–11.30 p.m.
Left-luggage lockers	No access 12 midnight–4 a.m.
Left-luggage store	Closed late evening to early morning
Self-service buffet	6 a.m.–1 a.m.
Restaurant	6 a.m.–11.40 p.m.
Bath, Shower and Shops	In complex under Bahnhofplatz
Post office	Mon.–Fri.: 7.30 a.m.–6.30 p.m. Sat.: 7.30 a.m.–11 a.m.
Station shuts	12 midnight–4 a.m.

TOURIST INFORMATION

The main office is on Bahnhofplatz 15, just outside the station. It's open Mon.–Fri.: 8 a.m.–10 p.m. (8 p.m. in winter), weekends: 8 a.m.–8.30 p.m. There are leaflets on everything here and an accommodation service for 3–5 F (Tel. 2114000).

Though the Swiss Student Reception Service is mainly a travel agent, it does also have information on Switzerland. It's at Leonhardstrasse 10 (Tel. 472955) and sells Eurotrain tickets.

● **Addresses:**
AMEX: Bahnhofstrasse 20, open Mon.–Fri.: 8.30 a.m.–5.30 p.m., Sat.: 8.30 a.m.–noon (Tel. 2118370).
UK CONSULATE: Dufourstrasse 56 (Tel. 471520).
US CONSULATE: Zollikerstrasse 141 (Tel. 552566).
PHONE CODE: 01.

SEEING

To the right of the Limmat River is OLD ZÜRICH with its sixteenth- and seventeenth-century guild houses, now restaurants and trendy shops, and close by the town's two medieval churches: FRAUMÜN-STER on the left bank and GROSSMÜNSTER, the austere Protestant cathedral, on the right. For a view over the old town, climb to LINDENHOF just up from the Fraumünster. BAHNHOFSTRASSE is said to be 'the most beautiful shopping street in the world' – it may well be, but it's certainly one of the most expensive; it runs down from the station to the lake where you can indulge in a boat trip if the weather's up to it. The ZOO in the Zürichberg woods and BOTANICS at Zollikerstrasse are wonderful picnic spots on good days, and on bad the SWISS NATIONAL MUSEUM behind the station and the RIETBERG MUSEUM in the Wessendonck villa at Gablerstrasse are excellent. The latter has one of the best collections of non-European art in Europe. There are all sorts of boat trips on Lake Zürich lasting 1½–4 hours which Inter-Railers get concessions on, or there's the trip down the River Limmat which takes you through old Zürich. Enquire at Selnau Station about the private mountain trains (Inter-Railers: always check in case you don't get half price on the line you've chosen) and strongly consider the chance to get up to an Alpine village, away from the bourgeois bustle of Zürich. From the Hauptbahnhof, take the train for about an hour to SCHAFFHAUSEN, then a further 20 minutes to STEIN AM RHEIN. This beautiful little place with its half-timbered houses and wonderful location can also be reached by boat from Schaffhausen quay. Inter-Railers get concessions and you can take the boat as far as Konstanz.

SLEEPING

It's probably best to forget hotels and keep it as basic as you can. The campsite on the Zürichsee is very good (train to Wollishofen, then 10-minute walk) and works out as your cheapest option. It's at Seestrasse 559 (Tel. 4821612).

The youth hostel's big and not strictly run. It's at Mutschellen-strasse 114 (Tel. 4823544) and is reached by tram 7 to Morgental (1 a.m. curfew; reception closes 9 a.m.–2 p.m.). For cheap pensions, try the following: Foyer Hottingen, Hottingerstrasse 31 (Tel. 479315); Josephsheim, Hirschengraben 64 (Tel. 2512757); Justi-nusheim, Freudenberg Strasse 146 (Tel. 3613806); or Schaefli, Badergasse 6 (Tel. 2514144). These range from 25–35 F singles, 55–65 F doubles.

EATING AND NIGHTLIFE

Round the station's as good as anywhere for cheap places, or use one of the many central Migros cafeterias. Jelmoli, the department store on Bahnhofstrasse, do good meals, but their best value is the all-you-can-eat breakfast for 13 F. There's enough there to keep you sustained till dinner. The Mensa at Rämistrasse 71 does cheap meals for students (shut during the summer), and there are a few beer halls where you can pick up Würst snacks for not a lot. The bars, discos and clubs are all around Niederdorfstrasse, but don't get too excited if you're a night owl, as most places close at midnight. There are also a substantial number of gay bars in the city.

Lucerne (Luzern)

If you can only stop once in Switzerland, make it at Lucerne. It's Switzerland's prettiest, and most touristy, town, and in this country that's saying something on both scores. Set on Lake Lucerne with the Alps in the background, it's beautifully preserved and has everything you always associated with Switzerland. It's 1½ hours from Bern and only ¾ hour from Zürich.

TOURIST INFORMATION AND ADDRESSES

The tourist office is a few blocks from the station at Frankenstrasse 1, open Mon.–Fri.: 8 a.m.–noon and 2 p.m.–6 p.m., Sat.: 9 a.m.–noon. Closed Sun. (Tel. 517171). When closed use room-finding service at the station. If you're staying a while, consider the Lucerne season ticket, which admits you to monuments, the beach and trips on cable railways and steamers.

POST OFFICE: Frohburgstrasse, open Mon.–Fri.: 7.30 a.m.–6.30 p.m., Sat.: 7.30 a.m.–11 a.m.

AMEX: Schweizerhofquai 4, open Mon.–Fri.: 8 a.m.–12 noon, 2 p.m.–6 p.m. Sat.: 8 a.m.–noon. Exchange till 5 p.m.

PHONE CODE: 041.

SEEING

The fourteenth-century covered wooden bridge, KAPELLBRÜCKE, spanning the River Reuss, is the symbol of the town. Walk over it to see the 120 paintings dating from the sixteenth to the eighteenth century which tell the town's history. The adjoining WATER TOWER served as a lookout tower, prison, and archive store. On Kornmarkt is the beautiful old TOWN HALL, and on WEINMARKT are old painted houses. The SPREUERBRÜCKE is another covered bridge, this time with paintings on the 'Dance of Death'. For a superb view of the town and its environs, climb the westernmost tower on the old city wall.

The SWISS TRANSPORT MUSEUM sounds boring as hell, but is actually quite interesting, and free to Inter-Railers. It's at the end of the park en route to the campsite. The WAGNER MUSEUM in the suburb of TRIBSCHEN shows the house where he worked and lived, and some of his possessions. You can get here by bus 6/7 or by the boat from in front of the station (Inter Rail concession). The GLACIER GARDEN is a beautiful rocky area formed during the Ice Age. Entrance to it and the PANORAMA (a huge 360° painting) is 10 F (5 F with ISIC).

SLEEPING

If you're intent on a pension or hotel (you must be mad), use the station's accommodation service (open 2.30 p.m.–10 p.m.) and clearly state your price range. The campsite is excellent: its situation couldn't be improved – near the beach and the lake – and to get to it you can walk through the park. It's at Lidostrasse (Tel. 312146) on bus route 2 and costs 4.80 F per person and 1.50 F per tent. The youth hostel Am Rotsee on Sedelstrasse 12 (Tel. 368800) has over 200 beds and is very reasonable at about 18 F. It's not central and closes 9.30 a.m.–6 p.m. Bus 18 to Friedental, then a two-minute walk or the more frequent bus 1 to Schlossberg, then a 10-minute walk will get you there. Try to arrive early, as we've had reports of 1½ hours queueing, even at 5 p.m.; the wise arrive early, leave their form and YHA card in the box provided and return before 10 p.m. Hotel Weisses Kreuz at Furrengasse 19 (Tel. 514040) is an old city hotel within the 35–40 F bracket, and is as good as you can expect. Hotel Jlge, Pfistergasse 17 (Tel. 220918), is in the Old Town and one of the best buys in Lucerne. Dormitory beds are cheap, and include use of the pool and breakfast. You can also try the Touristenhotel, St. Karliquai 12 (Tel. 512474).

EATING AND NIGHTLIFE

In general both tend to cater for monied European tourists, but if you walk the length of Hertensteinstrasse, you should come up with some suitable pub or restaurant, even if it's just Migros at No. 46, or a fast-food place.

Apart from the International Music Festival (mid-August–early September), Lucerne is exceptionally sedate. A pub with a collection of eurorailers determined to make merry will probably be your high spot, unless your budget is elastic.

• **Excursions:** The steamer cruises down the VIERWALDSTÄTTERSEE are well worth it. Inter-Railers go half price, and you leave from the quay near the station (ask tourist information for details of the alternatives).

The huge towering mountain dominating Lucerne is MOUNT PILA-TUS (7,000 feet). To get up there, you'd do best to take the boat from Lucerne to ALPNACHSTAD (half price Inter Rail) and then travel up on the steepest cogwheel railway in the world. Return by cable car to KRIENS then bus 1 back to Lucerne. It's well worth the effort, and really is an experience you won't forget, assuming you manage to avoid the mid-afternoon crowds and can afford the fare of around 45 F.

Bern

There's nothing to keep you in Bern for much more than a day if you're a restless type, even though it is the capital of Switzerland. It's pretty but not spectacular, and once you've seen the CLOCK TOWER, BEAR PIT (complete with bears), GOTHIC CATHEDRAL and BERNESE HISTORICAL MUSEUM you've more or less done the rounds unless you collect Swiss stamps and want to visit the POSTAL MUSEUM.

STATION FACILITIES

	BERN BAHNHOF
Train information	7.30 a.m.–8.30 p.m. (Tel. 211111)
Reservations	7.30 a.m.–8.30 p.m.
Tourist information	Mon.–Sat.: 8 a.m.–6.30 p.m. Sun.: 10 a.m.–5 p.m.
Foreign exchange	6.10 a.m.–10 p.m.
Left-luggage lockers	No access 12 midnight–4 a.m.
Left-luggage store	6 a.m.–11 p.m.
Bar, Buffet	4 a.m.–11.30 p.m.
Shops	Tue.–Fri.: 6.30 a.m.–6.30 p.m. Sat.: 6.30 a.m.–5 p.m. Mon.: 2 p.m.–6.30 p.m.
Bath, Shower	6.30 a.m.–8 p.m.
Station shuts	12 midnight–4 a.m.

Daily trains to: Brussels, Basel, Milan, Zürich, Lausanne, Geneva.

TOURIST INFORMATION AND ADDRESSES

The main tourist office is the one at the station. When they close, they leave information on accommodation posted up outside, and there's a free phone to make reservations. Open Mon.–Sat.: 8 a.m.–6.30 p.m., Sun.: 10 a.m.–5 p.m. (Tel. 227676).

POST OFFICE: Schanzenpost 1, open Mon.–Fri.: 7.30 a.m.–6.30 p.m., Sat.: 7.30 a.m.–11 a.m.

AMEX: Bubenbergplatz 11, open Mon.–Fri.: 8.15 a.m.–12.30 p.m., 1.30 p.m.–6 p.m., Sat.: 8.15 a.m.–12 noon (Tel. 229401).

UK EMBASSY: Thunstrasse 50 (Tel. 445021).

US EMBASSY: Jubiläumstrasse 93 (Tel. 437011).

CANADIAN EMBASSY: Kirchenfeldstrasse 88 (Tel. 446381).

AUSTRALIAN EMBASSY: Alpenstrasse 29 (Tel. 430143).

PHONE CODE: 031.

SLEEPING

Definitely avoid hotels here and stick to the youth hostel or campsite. The hostel is at Weihergasse 4 (Tel. 226316) near the Houses of Parliament. It closes 10 a.m.–5 p.m. and is run quite strictly and costs 13 F including breakfast. Camping Eichholz is down by the river (Tel. 542602), a bit out of the city. Tram 9 to Eichholz. For a central pension, try Hotel Bahnhof-Süd, Bumpliz-strasse 189 (Tel. 565111), or Hotel National, Hirschengraben 24 (Tel. 251988) next to the station.

EATING AND NIGHTLIFE

For picnic food there are shops in Marktgasse and Zeughausgasse near the station, or there are always Migros for cheap meals. About the only place you can afford, or would find remotely lively, is the Kornhauskeller on Kornhausplatz. It may bust your budget to eat there, but go for the local beer.

• **Excursions:** The best day trip you can take from Bern is to the ancient town of FRIBOURG, only 20 minutes away. The river that runs through it, the Sarine, is commonly regarded as the boundary line between the French- and German-speaking sections of Switzerland. Visit the ÉGLISE DES CORDELIERS with its original St Anthony altar-piece, and take in the view from the bridges that span the river. Most of the sights are on rue de Morat: the church mentioned above, the CATHEDRAL, the sixteenth-century TOWN HALL and the MUSEUM OF ART AND HISTORY.

The Bernese Oberland

The region round INTERLAKEN is stunning in its beauty, but from a eurorailer's point of view, unless you're stopping off to ski or climb, there's not that much to see apart from the scenery. The youth hostel 'Balmers' is good value: for 15 F in dormitory, 25 F in doubles, it provides space under shelters outside. Only an hour from Bern, Interlaken is a good base for heading off into the Bernese Oberland. Inter-Railers get a 50 per cent reduction on the private railways that take you there. If you've decided that, now you're this far, you want to spend a bit of time here, consider buying the rail pass from this area's private railways board. It costs 110 F for five days' unlimited travel out of 15 days on most trains, cable cars and 'gondolas' which hoist you up the thousands of feet in next to no time. It also gives you the remaining ten days' travel at half price; still it is a lot of money, and remember you can still travel half price on your Inter Rail. Tourist information is at Höheweg 37, as well as at Westbahnhof; and for rooms, look at the bulletin board at Westbahnhof listing the Zimmer frei alternatives.

GRINDELWALD is *the* destination for serious climbers (though LAUTERBRÜNNEN is equally beautiful if you're not a climber). What with the NORTH FACE OF THE EIGER, the JUNGFRAU and the MÖNCH, you won't know where to begin. There are hourly trains here from Interlaken, and Inter Rail's only valid on the route to Jungfraujoch. If you get this far, don't leave till you've taken the cable car to MÄNNLICHEN, WENGEN and from Grindelwald up to PFINGSTEGG. From Pfingstegg, walk to STIEREGG. More than likely, this will be the high spot of your travels in this spectacular country. KLEINE SCHEIDEGG and JUNGFRAUJOCH are also in this area and accessible with the help of an extortionately priced mountain railway. If you're staying, try for the youth hostel Die Weid at Terrassenweg (Tel. 036–531009), or camp. If this has whetted your appetite, you might as well carry on to the MATTERHORN. Your best base for excursions here is ZERMATT which you reach by private railway from BRIG or VISP (Inter-Railers half price). Tourist information is to the right of the station. They'll fix you up with maps, hiking suggestions and a bed. Hotel Bahnhof opposite the station is reasonable and has dormitories as well as rooms. The youth hostel costs about £6 per night (including breakfast). Curfew is at 10 p.m.

Lausanne

The French Alps are visible from Lausanne, home of the most spectacular Gothic building in Switzerland: its cathedral; the old medieval quarter is the most interesting (as the rest of the town is very modern) and here you'll find the HÔTEL DE VILLE, the EARLY GOTHIC CATHEDRAL and the CHÂTEAU SAINTE MAIRE, the Bishop's Palace. The funicular to OUCHY will take you down to the busy port which looks over to Lake Geneva and the Alps. Of the museums try to take in COLLECTION DE L'ART BRUT in the Château de Beaulieu where there are interesting exhibits by psychologically disturbed people, criminals and recluses.

TOURIST INFORMATION AND ADDRESSES

TOURIST OFFICE: 2 Avenue de Rhodanie, open Mon.–Fri.: 7 a.m.–6 p.m., Sat. and Sun.: 8 a.m.–12 noon, 1 p.m.–6 p.m., and at the station. They'll kit you out with maps, etc., and arrange accommodation.
POST OFFICE: Avenue de la Gare, open Mon.–Fri.: 7.30 a.m.–12 noon, 1.45 p.m.–6.30 p.m. (closed Saturday p.m.).
AMEX: 14 Avenue Mon Repos, open Mon.–Thurs.: 8 a.m.–12.15 p.m., 1.45 p.m.–5.30 p.m., Fri.: 8 a.m.–5.30 p.m.
PHONE CODE: 021.

SLEEPING

The youth hostel's down by the lake at Chemin du Muguet 1 (Tel. 265782), 14.75 F includes breakfast. Bus 1 to Batelière (direction La Maladière), then follow the signs. There is another hostel a little further out on the same bus route at Prés de Vidy, Chemin du Bois de Vaux (Tel. 242479). From 14 F (showers free). The very good campsite is also by the lake: Camping de Vidy-Lausanne (Tel. 242031). For rooms or dormitories, try Foyer la Croisée, 15 Avenue Marc Dufour (Tel. 204231).

EATING AND NIGHTLIFE

Food shouldn't be a problem. There are plenty of grocers' and bakers' shops to buy from, and no shortage of affordable restaurants, but watch out down in Ouchy – many restaurants are overpriced. There's no unique nightlife here, except in the Festival and Fête in late June, when the town offers plenty to do at night.

If you're staying at the youth hostel consider taking a wander into the park opposite and eating at the café bar next to the tennis courts. Although the menu is somewhat restricted, they do an excellent range of pizzas at reasonable prices and both the staff and the customers are young and friendly. If you've just come off a train after a long journey and can't wait for food, McDonald's is facing the main entrance to the station. But watch the traffic as the trolley-bus terminal is here and these vehicles are noise-free as well as pollution-free.

Basel (Basle)

Situated on the crossroads of France, Germany and Switzerland, Basel is the country's second city and is considered the cultural capital of Switzerland. From Basel you can take the train just about anywhere in Europe, from Warsaw to Stockholm.

STATION FACILITIES

As Basel is the border, the French effectively share the station with the Swiss. You'll find information for both SNCF and SBB at the station. French trains stop at the west end of the station.

	BASLE BAHNHOF
Train information	SBB 6 a.m–9.45 p.m.
	(Tel. 212321)
	SNCF 7.30 a.m.–7 p.m.
	(Tel. 225033)
Reservations	8 a.m.–7.30 p.m.
Tourist information	Mon.–Fri.: 8.30 a.m.–7 p.m.
	Sat.: 8.30 a.m.–12.30 p.m., 1.30 p.m.–6 p.m.
Foreign exchange	Mon.–Sat.: 6 a.m.–11.15 p.m.
	Sun.: 6 a.m.–10.30 p.m.
Left-luggage lockers	No access 0.30 a.m.–4 a.m.
Left-luggage store	5.30 a.m.–12 midnight
Bar, Buffet	6 a.m.–11 p.m.
Shops	Mon.–Fri.: 7 a.m.–6.30 p.m.
	Sat.: 7.30 a.m.–4 p.m.
Bath, Shower	Mon.–Sat.: 7.30 a.m.–4 p.m.
Post office	Mon.–Fri.: 7.30 a.m.–12 noon,
	1.45 p.m.–6.30 p.m.
	Sat.: 7.30 a.m.–11 a.m.
Station shuts	0.30 a.m.–4 a.m.

TOURIST INFORMATION AND ADDRESSES

As well as the one at the station, there's a tourist office at Blumenrain 2. Closed noon–1.30 p.m. weekdays, Sat. p.m. and Sun. (Tel. 255050).

POST OFFICE: Nauenstrasse, next to station. Open Mon.–Fri.: till 6.30 p.m., Sat.: till 11 a.m.

AMEX: c/o Reisebüro Kundig, Aeschengraben 10, open Mon.–Fri.: 8.15 a.m.–6 p.m.

PHONE CODE: 061.

SEEING

It's the museums in Basel that hog the limelight. If you're tired of trudging round museums and galleries, just take in the two bare essentials: the FINE ARTS MUSEUM and the KIKSCHGARTEN MUSEUM, housed in an old patrician mansion at Elisabethenstrasse 27. As for the town itself, the twelfth-century MÜNSTER (cathedral) is surrounded by medieval houses and stands in an attractive square. The TOWN HALL is on Market Square, and there are still markets held here today; THREE COUNTRIES' CORNER is the spot where the Swiss, French and German borders all meet. Just east of the tourist office lies the Münsterplatz where walking tours start.

SLEEPING

The large youth hostel is at 10 St Alban-Kirchrain (Tel. 230572). It's clean, friendly and has double rooms and dorms. A 3-course supper costs 7 F. 1 a.m. curfew. Take tram 1 one stop, then tram 3 to second stop. As far as hotels go, try the following, but insist on their cheapest rooms: Hotel Rheinblick, Oberer Rheinweg 75 (Tel. 336926); Hotel Stackhof, Gerbergasse 84 (Tel. 258711); Hotel Klingental Garm, Klingental 20 (Tel. 336248). These one-star hotels have single rooms (without bath) starting at about 40 F.

Cheaper hotels are a short journey over the French border in Mulhouse.

EATING AND NIGHTLIFE

You shouldn't have many problems finding shops and cafés to feed yourself from, there are plenty of alternatives. Zum Goldenen

Sternen, the oldest pub in Switzerland, at St Albanrheinweg 70, is good for a drink, but watch the food prices. 'This Week in Basel' will fill you in on events, and if you're there around Ash Wednesday, you should catch some local festivities.

Geneva (Genève)

This is perhaps the most international of all European cities, home to dozens of multinational organizations and peace-negotiating bodies such as the Red Cross and United Nations. The town has a rich and well-cared-for air, and is a good place to break up a long haul like Paris–Rome.

STATION FACILITIES

	GENÈVE CORNAVIN
Train information	7.00 a.m.–8 p.m.; Sat.: 7 a.m.–7 p.m.; Sun.: 10 a.m.–7 p.m. (Tel. 7316450)
Reservations	7 a.m.–8 p.m.
Tourist information	*Summer*: 8 a.m.–10 p.m.
Foreign exchange	Mon.–Sun.: 6 a.m.–10.45 p.m.
Left-luggage lockers	No access 1 a.m.–4 a.m.
Left-luggage store	Early morning to late evening
Snack bar	5 a.m.–12 midnight
Bath, Shower	Mon.–Sat.: 7 a.m.–7 p.m. Sun.: 7 a.m.–12 noon
Post office	6 a.m.–10.45 p.m. (next building)
Station shuts	1 a.m.–4 a.m.

Daily trains to: Lausanne, Basel, Bern, Zürich, Milan, Rome, Nice, Barcelona, Lyon, Paris.

TOURIST INFORMATION

The station office operates July to September. The main office is at 2 Tour de l'Ile, open Mon.–Fri.: 8 a.m.–10 p.m., Sat.: 9 a.m.–10 p.m. (Tel. 455200).

● **Addresses:**
POST OFFICE: Poste Gare Cornavin (next to the station).
AMEX: 7 rue du Mont Blanc, open Mon.–Fri.: 8.30 a.m.–5.30 p.m.,
Sat.: 9 a.m.–12 noon (Tel. 7317600).
UK CONSULATE: 37–39 rue Vermont (Tel. 7343800).
US CONSULATE: 11 route Pregny (Tel. 7335537).
MEDICAL HELP: PMC 'Permanence', rue Chantepoulet 21.
PHONE CODE: 022.

SEEING

Most of the things to see in Geneva can be taken in on the one main
walk. Starting from the station, walk down RUE DU MONT BLANC till
you're at the lake, then turn right on QUAI DES BERGUES, cross the
river on the PONT DE L'ILE to the PLACE BEL-AIR, then head on to the
PLACE NEUVE down RUE DE LA CORRATERIE. Once here, enter the
park which contains the university and the famous statue to the
Reformation. The VIEILLE VILLE is the old cobblestoned quarter
round the CATHÉDRALE ST PIERRE, where Calvin preached. On RUE
HÔTEL-DE-VILLE is the TOWN HALL where the Geneva Convention
was signed, and some seventeenth-century houses built by Italian
religious refugees. The best museums are the PETIT PALAIS (Impressionist paintings), INSTITUT ET MUSÉE VOLTAIRE, 25 rue des Délices
(Voltaire's house), and the PALAIS DES NATIONS on Avenue de la
Paix. Geneva is the world's top watchmaking centre, so hide your
Japanese digital and wander round the superb CLOCK MUSEUM, 1 rue
de Malagnou (closed Mondays). Boat trips on Lake Geneva (Lac
Léman) are pleasant, but compare prices first. The cheapest way to
get around is on a 'pink' bicycle. If you see one, ride it to where you
are going, and leave it for someone else to use. Sunbathers should
head for Nyon, on the way to Lausanne, which has a good lakeside
beach.

SLEEPING

Summer in Geneva makes affordable beds scarce, so arrive early
and immediately aim at getting fixed up. Ask tourist information for
their list of foyers, dormitories, etc., and phone around. The youth
hostel is at 30 rue Rothschild (Tel. 7326260, 10 minutes from
Cornavin station via rue de Lausanne). Reception closes 10 a.m.–

5 p.m. and costs 16 F including breakfast. The nearest campsite is Sylvabelle, 10 Chemin de Conches (Tel. 470603); take bus 3 to Rond Point de Rive, then bus 8 or 88. Maison des Jeunes, 5 rue du Temple (Tel. 7322060), is a hostel for anyone. It's central but basic. Home St Pierre, at Cour St Pierre by the cathedral, is a great place. It takes only women and is deservedly popular (Tel. 283707). Probably the safest accommodation you will find anywhere in Europe is at 37 rue du Nant – it's a nuclear shelter! Clean and efficient – but quite claustrophobic – it costs about 12 F. Take bus 5 to Rive then a five-minute walk. The Coopérative du Logement, rue H. Senger 2 (Tel. 292033), is the handling office to fill the four university dormitories. They charge around 30 F each. Alternatively, you could stay just over the border in France, at Bellegande, which is much cheaper.

EATING AND NIGHTLIFE

Geneva definitely aims its tourism at the well-heeled, but there are some Migros and budget restaurants dotted around. A picnic down by the lake is your cheapest and most memorable option, but if it's wet, try the restaurant opposite the station on 17 Place Montbrillant, or Le Zofage, the university's place at rue des Voisins, with cheap filling plats du jour.

Tourist information will tell you what's on. Geneva actually has the most swinging nightlife in Switzerland, but then that's not hard. Before you get excited, I'm afraid there's probably nothing much you can afford, so content yourself manwatching in Place Molard or head for a lively bar like Mr Pickwick's Pub, 80 rue Lausanne.

The Grisons (Graubünden)

From the source of the Rhine east to the River Inn and on to Austria is the canton of Grisons. Here you'll still hear Romansch spoken along with Swiss-German. CHUR is the cultural and administrative centre, and such flashy resorts as St Moritz are in this region. The trains are narrow-gauge, but Inter Rails are valid. Take the CHUR–ST MORITZ line (2 hours), even if you don't get off at the other end, as the scenery is quite beautiful.

Chur

Walk through the old-town streets with their medieval houses and pass through the old gate to the CATHEDRAL, with its pre-Christian sacrificial stone. The HOF (Bishop's Palace) next door is still in use, so don't nose about too much. The pub in there (the Hofkellerei) is a good watering-hole, but a bit touristy in summer. Tourist information is at Alexanderstrasse 24, Bahnhofplatz, and there's a good youth hostel at Berggasse 28 (Tel. 081–226563). Ask at the station for a map to get you there.

St Moritz

The actual town's nothing special, and apart from the ENGADINE MUSEUM en route to the famed healing waters of the MAURITIUS SPRINGS which reconstructs life of days long ago, there's not much else to see. But people don't come here to sightsee, they come to ski or climb. The general information centre is Kur-und-Verkehrsverein on Via Marstra 12, open Mon.–Fri.: 9 a.m.–12 noon, 2 p.m.–6 p.m., Sat.: 9 a.m.–noon.

If your time's short, do just two things: take the cable car up the 8,000-foot MUOTTAS MURAGL and walk the path along the SILS LAKE. If you're staying, try your best to get into the youth hostel at Via Surpunt 60 (Tel. 082–33969). It's beautiful, and cheap by Swiss standards. There's camping at Olympiaschanze (Tel. 082–34090) about 30 minutes from the station. Forget hotels; you're outclassed here, I'm afraid.

If you're heading for Italy, take the train in the direction of TIRANO on the Italian border (1½ hours) as the scenery around here and on the Passo del Bernina is incredible. Get off at every station and make a day of it, if you've time, as this is the highest line in Europe without cogs or cables.

Ticino

This region, next to Italy and known as the 'Swiss Riviera', has the best· of both countries: the scenery, tidiness and efficiency of Switzerland, and the sun, language and ambience of Italy. Lugano and Locarno are the main centres and the area round the lakes of Lugano and Maggiore makes wonderful camping, swimming and walking, away from the crowds.

Lugano

This is a particularly pretty town of sunny piazzas, palm trees and the dominating Monte San Salvatore. It's on LAKE LUGANO, and lies on the Zürich–Milan main line. Stroll through the little winding streets on the hill at SAN LORENZO for a view over the town, stopping off at SANTA MARIA DEGLI ANGIOLI to admire the sixteenth-century frescoes. Walk down to the lake and Riva Albertolli 5 where the tourist office is. They're open daily 8 a.m.–6 p.m., Sat.: 9 a.m.–5 p.m. and they'll give you maps, lists of the local mountain huts, and arrange accommodation.

The VILLA FAVORITA CASTAGNOLA houses one of Europe's finest private art collections: Rembrandts, Dürers, Rubens, etc. It's open Fri. and Sat.: 10 a.m.–12 noon, 2 p.m.–5 p.m., Sun.: 2 p.m.–5 p.m., 7 F. From the Paradiso quarter, it's a 10-minute ride on the funicular up MONTE SAN SALVATORE, with a great view over the Alps and lakes. The funicular from Via Cassarate up to MONTE BRÉ on the other side of the town is another scenic excursion.

There's a youth hostel in Lugano-Crocifisso at 6942 Savosa (at the terminus of bus 5) of an exceptionally high standard (Tel. 091–562728). Aris Pensioni, Via Geretta 8 (Tel. 091–541478), in nearby Paradiso is a good place to stay or eat, with rooms averaging 30 F per person and meals 15 F. For hotels, try the Montarina which has rooms from 30–40 F and dormitory accommodation at 15 F. It's at Via Basilta 28 (Tel. 091–561112). There are plenty of markets and food shops offering Swiss-quality Italian food. Commercios on Via

Lodovico Ariosto do great pizzas. In the evening there are often concerts down by the lake, but nightlife here is fairly sedate in general.

Locarno

From Lugano it's about half an hour to Ticino's capital BELLIN-ZONA, and from there another half-hour will take you into Locarno, the best place to base yourself for trips round LAKE MAGGIORE. To explore this region you'll need to resort to buses. One of the buses from Locarno station goes through Ascona, Brissago and crosses the Italian border at Madonna di Ponte. Get off at Brissago and make for the island where there's a beautiful botanical garden.

Back in Locarno itself there's a MUSEUM OF MODERN ART in Castello Visconti, and funiculars to take you up to see the town's landmark, the MADONNA OF THE ROCK. Try the Gottardo (Tel. 334454) above the station for a bed. The private Centrovalli railway from Locarno to Domodossola on the Milan–Brig line is well worth re-routing for. The left-hand side offers the best views of the fantastic scenery.

Liechtenstein

This small Alpine principality of only 26,500 people nestles between Switzerland and Austria. It has enjoyed sovereign status as an independent country since the early 1800s, although the Swiss currency is used. There is a separate identity to this little country making it worth a quick stop. You will see their royal family all over the country – on their famous postage stamps, postcards or quite possibly in person as the Prince of Liechtenstein and his family live near VADUZ, the capital 'city'. The tourist information office is in the centre of Vaduz at Städtle 37–38 (Tel. 075–21443) across the road from the post office and you can pick up information and maps on the whole principality here as well as getting fixed up with accommodation. The youth hostel here is one of the friendliest we have come across. It's at Rüttigasse 6 (Tel. 075–25022) and is modern and clean. Showers, sheets and breakfast are included in the price (16 F for seniors, 11 F for juniors).

Apart from good hiking, Liechtenstein also has a couple of museums worth checking out if the weather isn't. The POSTAGE STAMP MUSEUM in the centre of Vaduz has many rare stamps produced by Liechtenstein and other countries, and the ART COLLECTION at Städtle 37 has a fine collection of Viennese works collected by the Princes of Liechtenstein.

Although Liechtenstein does have some railway stations, the best way to get into the principality is by Postbus from either Sargans or Buchs in Switzerland. Services are frequent and the journey times to Vaduz are thirty minutes and fifteen minutes respectively.

Since 1988, all buses in Liechtenstein have been free of charge.

TURKEY

Entry requirements	Passport and visa (£5 at border)
Population	53,000,000
Capital	Ankara (pop.: 3,460,000)
Currency	Lira
	£1 = approx. 4,650 TL
Political system	Republic
Religion	Muslim
Language	Turkish (some English, French and German spoken in cities)
Public holidays	1 Jan.; 23 April; 19 May; 3-day Muslim lunar holiday in spring; 30 Aug.; 4-day Muslim lunar holiday in summer; 28, 29 Oct.
International dialling codes	From UK: 010 + 90 + number
	From USA: 011 + 90 + number
	To UK: 99 + 44 + number
	To USA: 99 + 1 + number

Only 3 per cent of Turkey is in Europe, the rest lies firmly in Asia. The Islamic and European blend of culture makes Turkey a fascinating experience and quite different from a jaunt through Europe. Of its previous civilizations, the best-preserved remains are to be found on the west and south coasts, the Aegean and Mediterranean. Until 1453 the European area of Turkey was under the umbrella of the Christian Byzantine Empire, but the Ottoman conquest put a stop to this. From then on there was no looking back, and under Süleiman the Magnificent (1520–63) the Ottoman Empire reached its zenith; it was largely thanks to him that the Christianity-versus-Islam wars of the sixteenth century were staged. It wasn't till the eighteenth and nineteenth centuries that this powerful empire went into decline; however, once it did the gradual process of westernization began. After the First World War Turkey was divided into British, French and Italian spheres of influence. The result was the War of Independence 1919–23. No one did more for the modernization of Turkey in the twentieth century than their national hero Atatürk, and tremendous progress has been made. Travelling in Turkey for women alone is no worse than anywhere else in southern Europe, so don't get the idea the Turks are a hostile and unfriendly lot as portrayed by the film *Midnight Express*. If you're befriended over there by a local, the hospitality they'll show you will leave any European pleasantries standing. Don't be surprised if Turks come up to you in the street and ask if they can talk to you to practise their English.

Nevertheless, steer very well clear of anything likely to be remotely connected with drugs. In particular, don't carry any loose tablets, even aspirin, and if you do have medicines with you carry a copy of the prescription if possible, or the original container. Since November 1989 British citizens (although not Americans, Canadians or Australians) require a £5 visa which you can get when you arrive. It must be paid for in hard currency – no coins are accepted.

TURKISH STATE RAILWAYS
(Turkiye Cumhuriyeti Devlet Demiryollari Isletmesi, TCDD)

In 1990 all of Turkey joined the Inter Rail scheme ('European Turkey' joined in 1985). To coincide with this there has been a general improvement in services, although you can still expect the journey from northern Greece to Istanbul to take more than a day and the trip from Athens to take up to 40 hours. If you are coming direct from central Europe remember that you *must* have a transit visa for Bulgaria unless you travel through Yugoslavia and change at Thessaloniki in northern Greece. If you decide to travel through Bulgaria (not available on Inter Rail), get your transit visa before you leave home.

Railway services in Turkey are slow. Students can get a 10 per cent discount on train fares (20 per cent on return tickets). Apart from the lines in European Turkey and the Haydarpaşa–Ankara run, you are well advised to use the buses. These are fast, cheap and often modern Mercedes-Benz vehicles. Free drinks en route are often included. For a rough guide to the main services, consult Thomas Cook's Overseas Timetable.

For short journeys, use a Dolmuş – these are communal taxis which run on set routes. Stop them by waving. Outside the cities they are usually beat-up Ford Transit or VW vans. Very cheap.

TRAIN INFORMATION

English is spoken by the information staff in big cities, while German and French are more useful elsewhere.

• **Reservations:** It's always advisable to reserve between Istanbul and Ankara, particularly if you want a couchette or to travel first class.

• **Night travel:** Generally, this is the best way of travelling in Turkey. There are first- and second-class couchettes to choose from.

• **Eating on trains:** Always be prepared with your own drinks. All expresses have a mini-bar or buffet.

TOURIST INFORMATION

There are tourist offices in all the major cities and tourist centres.

• **ISIC bonuses:** 50 per cent off museums, cinemas, concerts, and 10–20 per cent off rail tickets within Turkey. For further information, contact the nearest Turkish tourism and information office. Some places will not accept student cards as there are so many Turkish fakes.

• **Money matters:** 1 Turkish lira (TL).
Banking hours are Mon.–Fri.: 8.30 a.m.–12 noon, 1.30 p.m.–5 p.m. Twenty-four hour exchange facilities are thin on the ground and there are none at the stations, although there is a small exchange office at Istanbul station, if you can find it at the opposite end of the platform from the station entrance. It is open at weekends and has an average exchange rate; also inflation is a way of life in Turkey. In 1980 the rate was 120 per cent, and although it dropped a couple of years later to only 30 per cent, it has been creeping up again. The rate last year was around 63 per cent, so bear this in mind when looking at prices. Remember to spend all of your lira before leaving the country as you will find it difficult, if not downright impossible, to exchange – particularly in Greece, although relations between these two countries have been improving in recent years.

• **Post offices:** Open Mon.–Fri.: 8.30 a.m.–12 noon, 1 p.m.–5.30 p.m. Major post offices stay open till 12 midnight, Mon.–Sat. and 9 a.m.–7 p.m., Sun. Many post offices have exchange facilities; compare the rate to the banks'.

• **Shops:** Open Mon.–Sat.: 9 a.m.–1 p.m., 2 p.m.–7 p.m., Sun.: closed.

• **Museums:** All museums shut on Mondays, except for the Topkapi Palace which shuts on Tuesdays. Most offer half price at weekends.

SLEEPING

There's no problem finding cheap accommodation in Turkey, but we can't guarantee you'll be happy with the standards of cleanliness. Tourist information help out here and will find you a room in your price bracket. Basically, the hotels registered with the tourist board are called 'touristic' and are graded de luxe, or 1–5 stars. Also there are plenty with no grades at all, many of which are dirty but safe enough. In general, though, discretion is the better part of valour when it comes to a shady set-up. Expect to pay from $10 upwards for a half-decent double (more in Istanbul). Always check the room first and be prepared to bargain if the price seems too high. This tends to be the norm along the Bosphorus, but you can get a reduction with an ISIC card in some places off season. There are a few 'pansiyons' in Turkey and they can be the best places to stay but there still aren't too many of them. Student dormitories are another option during July and August, as are youth hostels of which there are about 45 in Turkey; most of them allow you to stay if you have a student card, but it's best to have an IYHC to be on the safe side. Campsites are growing in number but are still a bit primitive in their facilities.

EATING AND NIGHTLIFE

Turkish cuisine is among the best in Europe for sheer good value. The variety of dishes is staggering and, as often as not, you're invited into the kitchen to choose your own. (If you don't like the look of things while you're in, now's your chance to skip out with a suitable excuse.) Turkish specialities include dolmas (just about anything stuffed with rice) and anything called 'sis' (like siskebabh) is done on a spit. Kadin budu is a concoction of fried rice and meatballs and, literally translated, means 'woman's thigh' (we don't quite see the analogy). Then how about kadin gobegi ('woman's navel') for dessert? The wine's not bad and the grape brandy, raki, is hot stuff. Expect to pay around 20–25,000 TL for a full meal including wine, though you *can* eat for a lot less. For a snack, try lahmacun, a type of pizza. Water, especially in western Turkey, is heavily chlorinated and safe to drink. As part of its Islamic heritage, drinking fountains are very common.

The Turks are big folk-dancers and you should be able to catch each region's favourite without too many problems. The Turkish coffee houses (Kahve) are great meeting places and, of course, there's always the Turkish bath. Go and see a belly dancer if there's one advertised, even though they're terribly commercialized these days, but avoid the poor Western imitations of discos and clubs.

Istanbul

Incredible mosques share the spotlight with bazaars and the largest Roman building in the world in this fascinating city, and the blend of Asia and Europe makes it quite unique. If you're thinking of a trip to Turkey, make this your destination. It's often dirty and is pretty rough in some parts (women alone should take extra care), and the intensive train travel will give you ulcers, but there's so much here to catch the eye and imagination that it's all worthwhile.

STATION FACILITIES

Sirkeci (Tel. 5270050) is the main station of Istanbul; from here leave the trains bound for Sofia, Belgrade, Athens and the West. Haydarpaşa (Tel. 3362063) is the city's other station, on the opposite shore of the Bosphorus; services to Asia, Ankara, Anatolia, Iran, Syria and Baghdad leave from here.

Facilities at both stations tend to close down at night and there is no bath/shower at either station. Sirkeci Station has tourist information, exchange facilities and left-luggage. Although this is only a trolley on the platform it is fairly safe as there are many attendants about.

TOURIST INFORMATION AND ADDRESSES

TOURIST OFFICES: 57 Meşrutiyet Caddesi, Galatasaray; Divan Yolu Caddesi, Sultanahmet; entrance of Hilton Hotel; Karaköy Harbour Terminal; Yeşilköy Airport; Sirkeci Station; Yalova

Harbour Terminal. Open Mon.–Fri.: 8.30 a.m.–6.30 p.m., Sat.–
Sun.: 9 a.m.–5 p.m.

POST OFFICE: 25 Yeni Postane Sokak (two blocks from Sirkeci
Station).

AMEX: Hilton Hotel. Open daily 8.30 a.m.–8 p.m. (Tel. 1410431).

TOURIST POLICE: Across from St Sophia at beginning of Yerebetan
Caddesi, open 9 a.m.–8 p.m. (Tel. 5274503).

UK CONSULATE: 34 North Meşrutiyet Caddesi, Tepebasi (Tel.
1447540).

US CONSULATE: 104 Meşrutiyet Caddesi, Tepebasi (Tel. 1436200).

STUDENT TRAVEL: YEDITUR, Inönü Caddesi 37/2, Gümüssuyu
(Tel. 1499619/1525921). Student cards and travel.

MEDICAL HELP: For an ambulance call 100 Siracevizler Caddesi
(Tel. 1444998).

PHONE CODE: 1 (Taksim, etc.), 3 (Asian side), 5 (Sultanahmet,
etc.).

● **Getting about:** There are cheap buses which leave from Taksim
Square. The communal taxis are also a good buy. They have routes
between the main quarters, though if you specify you should get
dropped off where you ask. Most taxis now have meters, but check,
and if there isn't one then agree a price before you start your
journey. Frequent suburban trains run along the main line from
Sirkeci. Inter Rail is valid.

SEEING

Basically, Istanbul divides into two main areas which are further
subdivided into several small districts. The European part of the
city is divided by the GOLDEN HORN, and the European and Asian
parts are separated by the BOSPHORUS STRAIT. The vast majority of
sights are on the southern bank of the Golden Horn.

OLD STAMBOUL is the old walled city across the Golden Horn and
it looks like something out of the 'Fry's Turkish Delight' advert.
The mosques and palaces are wonderful examples, as good as you'll
find anywhere, especially ST SOPHIA, built in AD 347 by Constantine,
then rebuilt in the sixth century after a fire, and turned into a
mosque after the Turks captured the city in 1453. Today it's a
museum, though some of the original mosaics can still be seen. The
BLUE MOSQUE dating from the seventeenth century is an amazing
feat of engineering, built, as it was, to bend with the force in times of

earthquakes – a performance it has done twenty times already. You can go into any mosque in Istanbul as long as you take off your shoes and keep quiet. Not far from the Blue Mosque is the ornate FOUNTAIN OF SULTAN AHMED. The Roman HIPPODROME was the venue for chariot racing, and today there's a MOSAIC MUSEUM.

The GRAND BAZAAR (or Kapaliçarşi) is colourful and entertaining, but barter like mad before buying anything. The palace of the Ottoman Sultans, TOPKAPI SARAY, is today a complex of museums: have a look in the HAREM and TREASURY. There's enough here to interest you for hours (open 9 a.m.–5 p.m., closed Tuesdays and half price at weekends). The other notable museums are: the ARCHAEOLOGICAL MUSEUM, the MUSEUM OF THE ANCIENT ORIENT, and the MUSEUM OF TURKISH AND ISLAMIC ARTS, all of which are self-explanatory. Another couple of mosques worth taking in on your itinerary are the BEYAZIT, near the university, and the sixteenth-century SULEYMANIYE. As a break from the hot dirty city, take a cruise down the Bosphorus. Boats leave Galata Bridge on three-hour round cruises between Europe and Asia. They are dirt cheap, great fun and highly recommended. You can also get five-hour trips which stop off in Asia for four hours' sightseeing (fare about $8.50).

The 'modern' city is on the north side of the Galata Bridge and includes Istanbul's underground – the Tünel – with only two stations. Tickets are 400 TL. The Genoese Galata tower is now a nightclub. Also on this side of the Golden Horn is the nineteenth-century Dolhambaçe Palace.

SLEEPING

As long as you're not expecting Scandinavian-style cleanliness, you'll cope fine in Istanbul. Beds are cheap and plentiful, and as prices vary little between districts aim for the most central or convenient. Round the station is OK, but a bit on the noisy side. The central Sultanahmet quarter is near the sights and about the best place to head for. Although we concentrate on the Sultanahmet quarter, you may also find cheap places on the Haydarpaşa side of the Bosphorus.

Istanbul Youth Hostel, 63 Cerrahpaşa Cad, Aksaray (Tel. 212455), is OK, but hardly central, open only in summer. The only IYHF hostel in Turkey, the Yücelt Hostel, is in the Sultanahmet district at 6 Caferiye Sok (Tel. 5136150/1) and is clean, if crowded. Beds from $5. There are several campsites, but Yeşilyurt (Tel. 5738408) or Ataköy (Tel. 5720802) are two of the nicest. The Sultan Tourist Hotel on Yerebatan Cad (Tel. 5207676) is good, with doubles around $12, or try the Gögür on Divan Yolu Cad (Tel. 5262319), or the Yöruk at 35 Inçiliçavuş Sok (Tel. 5276476).

Also worth checking out is 'Family Pansion' at Piyerloti Cad, Kadirga Harman, Sokah No. 4, Çemberlitas (Tel. 5283746). A safe bet is the Hotel Buyuk Sanid, at Hudavendigar Cad 35a (Tel. 5267229). You'll find the rooms as clean and secure as any you'll find in Turkey. Camping Florya is good. Take local train to Florya. Next to the beach.

Don't try sleeping rough in Istanbul, it's not worth the risk; there are too many stories of muggings and rape. Don't bother with the black market here either, as police informers are out in abundance, especially in summer, and manage to make a good living out of turning in mugs who accept their offers. The same goes for drugs.

EATING AND NIGHTLIFE

You'll be pleasantly surprised on both scores here. It's possible to eat exceptionally well for next to nothing, whether you eat from the street stalls or at top restaurants. Fish and seafood are particularly good: go down to the Galata Bridge where there are dozens of seafood restaurants, or eat from the pavement fish-grilling stalls. If you've saved sufficient by getting into cheap accommodation, treat yourself to a proper Bosphorus meal (about 40,000 TL) of meze (mixed starters) and fresh fish. You'll have no trouble finding plenty of suitable places to patronize. The area behind the station (Eminonu) is a good area. Our only particular recommendation is the Murat Restaurant on Ordu Cad, Aksaray. Reasonable menus at good prices, next to the Hacibozan Ógullari Baklavaci.

Don't bother with the fabricated westernized nightlife of discos and nightclubs. To get a taste of real Istanbul, eat late and wander along Meşrutiyet Cad and sample the music in the little cafés. Sultanahmet Square will also be lively but can get pretty seedy late-on. There are a few pubs in the area, however, where you'll meet up with other eurorailers and hitchers. One in particular worth a visit is the Pudding Shop, on Divan Yolu Cad (off the Sultanahmet), which is one of Europe's classic meeting places, like Harry's

Bar in Venice. Although the draught beer is OK, we cannot emphasize too strongly that you must instantly forget any notion of eating here, no matter how hungry you are. The cases of salmonella are legion. The Istanbul Festival is on from mid-June to mid-July but it's fairly classically minded (opera, concerts, etc.). Ask at tourist information for details. If you're after belly dancing, head for the Galatasaray district and Istiklâl St; or if you've promised yourself an authentic Turkish bath, ask at tourist information for their recommendations. Cağaloglu Hamami at Yerebatan Cad in Cağaloglu is excellent – the full works for 30,000 TL.

North-west Turkey

BURSA was, for a short while, the capital of the Ottoman Empire. It is a popular resort area because it is only 20 minutes from the sea and is also close to the best-known Turkish ski resort ULUDAG. You can get to Bursa by taking a ferry from Istanbul to Yalova and then a bus. While in Bursa see the GREAT MOSQUE, GREEN MOSQUE and GREEN TOMB. Nearby are two interesting museums, the ETHNO-GRAPHIC MUSEUM and the TURKISH AND ISLAMIC ART MUSEUM (entrance $1, closed Mondays). Tourist information is in the centre of town near the covered market. For accommodation try the Yeni Ankara at 48 Inebey Caddesi or camp on top of Uludag at Millipark Camping (take the cable car).

Çanakkale is a good case to visit the area of the First World War Dardenelles Campaign and the scene of a much earlier campaign, Troy. The bus from Bursa takes about five and a half hours (costs $5). In Çanakkale itself there is a museum with archaeological artifacts from Troy and a CASTLE with its World War One artillery and damage. A minesweeper in the park around the castle is now a monument to Atatürk, who was the Turkish commander during the Dardenelles Campaign. The helpful tourist office is next to the harbour. The best place to look for hotels is around the town centre. Çanakkale comes to life every August with the Troy festival. Across the water from Çanakkale lie the DARDANELLES, scene of the bloody campaign. You can take a ferry across to ECEABAT and then hire a taxi to look around the battlefield. Twenty miles south is TRUVA (TROY). There are many buses from the bus station to Troy.

The ruins of nine separate cities are not that interesting themselves, but with a bit of background knowledge and some imagination they can be evocative (entrance $2.50), especially with the wooden horse replica.

Aegean Coast

KUŞADASI has not benefited from the growth of tourism, but it is a good base to explore the fascinating Greek and Roman site of Ephesus. To get to Kuşadasi either take a train to Izmir and then a two-hour bus ride or take the ferry straight from Istanbul. The small fortified PIGEON ISLAND is about the only thing worth a visit in Kuşadasi. The tourist office is in the port and is very helpful. There are many cheap sea-front hotels and pensions here. The real reason for coming here is EPHESUS (EFES), a huge 2,000-acre site chock full of classical ruins. To reach the site take a dolmuş to Selçuk and ask to get off at Ephesus. It is best to look around yourself as tours can be very pricey. See the GRAND THEATRE, the TEMPLE OF HADRIAN and the FOUNTAIN OF TRAJAN just to name a few. The site is open each day 8 a.m.–6.30 p.m. and admission is about $5.

Three and a half hours east by bus are the amazing white cliffs and thermal pools of PAMUKKALE. There are also ruins of the ancient city of HIERAPOLIS at the top of the cliffs. Other classical ruins along the Aegean coast are BODRUM (HALICARNASSUS) and BERGAMA (PERGAMON) and are well worth a visit.

Ferries link a number of ports to the nearby Greek islands. Although fares are quite steep, this is a way of avoiding the sometimes nightmarish Athens–Istanbul run. Ferry services include Cesme–Chios (single $20), Kuşadasi–Samos ($25), Bodrum–Kos ($15), Marmaris–Rhodes ($20), Ayvalik–Lesbos ($30).

Mediterranean Coast

This coastline has many beautiful beaches and resorts and is a good place to unwind and relax, but beware: there are often thousands of other people there with the same objective. The train runs down to MERSIN, in the eastern part of the coast, which is a bustling place and is best passed through. The tourist office is at the harbour, near where Turkish Maritime Lines run a service to the Turkish-controlled NORTHERN CYPRUS (ferry $16, students get a 10 per cent discount). If you go to Northern Cyprus, get the immigration authorities to stamp a separate sheet of paper rather than your passport because you may not be allowed entry back into Greece if they see you have been to the Turkish-controlled area of Cyprus.

Small beach towns run along the coast west of Mersin. KOCAHA-SANLI can be reached by bus and is a large campground right on the beach, a beautiful place. Also try the town of KORYKOS, with its two scenic castles, one on an island offshore, and beaches. There is no shortage of pensions or campsites here.

Central Anatolia

Central Anatolia is a desolate plateau region of extreme temperatures. It is also home to the capital of modern Turkey, Ankara, and the old capital of the Seljuk Turks, Konya.

Ankara

Ankara was once a small, unimportant town, but in the 1920s Atatürk made it the capital of the new Turkish Republic and it has boomed ever since to become a sprawling metropolis.

TOURIST INFORMATION

The main tourist office is at 33 Gazi Kemal, Demirtepe. There is also an information office at 4 Istanbul Caddesi. Ask for a map and the useful 'Ankara Guide'. Both are open Mon.–Fri.: 8.30 a.m.–5.30 p.m., and in season Sat.: 8.30 a.m.–5 p.m. and Sun.: 8.30 a.m.–2 p.m.

● **Addresses:**
POST OFFICE: Atatürk Bulvari, open 24 hours.
AMEX: 7 Cinnah Caddesi (Tel. 1677334), open Mon.–Fri.: 9 a.m.–6
p.m., Sat.: 9 a.m.–1 p.m.
STUDENT TRAVEL: Emek Işhani, Kat. 11 No. 1109, Kizilay (Tel.
1181326).
UK EMBASSY: 46A Sehit Ersan Caddesi (Tel. 1274310).
US EMBASSY: Atatürk Bulvari 110 (Tel. 1265470).
CANADIAN EMBASSY: 75 Nenehatun Caddesi (Tel. 1361290).
AUSTRALIAN EMBASSY: 83 Nenehatun Caddesi (Tel. 1361240).
MEDICAL HELP: Hacettepe University Hospital, Hasircilar Caddesi
(Tel. 3103545).
TRAINS: Railway station on Hippodron Caddesi. Overnight services
from Istanbul, also connections east.
PHONE CODE: 4.

SEEING

The ULUS is the old section of town where many of the sights are,
including the Citadel and the Museum of Anatolian Civilizations.
The CITADEL is itself a small walled city with winding lanes, a great
place to wander. The BAZAAR and a MOSQUE are also within the
Citadel's walls. The MUSEUM OF ANATOLIAN CIVILIZATIONS is a
world class museum with exhibits from the huge number of cultures
which grew up in this cradle of civilization (open Tues.–Sun.: 9
a.m.–5.20 p.m., admission $2.50).

The other main sight of Ankara is the huge MAUSOLEUM OF
ATATÜRK, the national hero, in a large park. It is a monument to
the man whose adopted name means literally 'Father of the Turks'.
There is also a museum of his life and personal effects, open
Tues.–Sun.: 9 a.m.–noon and 1 p.m.–5 p.m. Also check out the
ETHNOGRAPHIC MUSEUM and the TEMPLE OF AUGUSTUS.

SLEEPING

Most of the cheap places to stay are in the Ulus. You could try the
Cumhuriyet Student Hostel in Cebici (Tel. 193634), open summers.
Ask the tourist office for a list of hotels. Also try the Beyrut Palas

Oteli at 11 Denzciler Caddesi (Tel. 3108407) or the Otel Bulduk, Sanyi Caddesi 26 (Tel. 3104915).

EATING AND NIGHTLIFE

The Ulus does not have that great a selection of restaurants, try along the Çankiri Caddesi and near the main tourist office. The bazaar is always a good place to explore. To meet some Turkish students try the Café Melodi on Atatürk Bulvari.

Konya

KONYA is an important centre of Islam in Turkey and was once capital of the Seljuks. It is still a big pilgrimage centre. It was here that the famous Order of the Whirling Dervishes started. See the MONASTERY and TOMB OF MEVLANA, the founder of the Dervishes, the ARCHAEOLOGICAL MUSEUM and the MARKET. The tourist office is on Mevlana Caddesi. For accommodation try the Çatal Pansiyon (Tel. 33–114981) near the tourist office or Otel Konfor, 51 Eski Garaj Caddesi (Tel. 33–113103).

Eastern Turkey

The east of Turkey becomes wilder and harsher, that is until you get to LAKE VAN, where the land is green and the mountains beautiful. The city of VAN is three miles from the lake, the largest in Turkey. Outside the city is the imposing CITADEL and ANCIENT CITY on the ROCK OF VAN, once the capital of the Urartian Empire. There is also a small archaeological museum. The tourist office is at 127 Cumhuriyet Caddesi. Other places to visit around the lake are the ARMENIAN CHURCH on the island of AKDAMAR or the scenic mountains around the town of HAKKARI. The ferry across Lake Van takes about four hours.

KARS in the north-east is not too thrilling itself, but from here you can visit the incredible remains of the ancient Armenian city of ANI, 28 miles away. For accommodation try Hayat Oteli, 155 Faikbey Caddesi. The tourist office on Lise Caddesi will get you the permit you will need to visit Ani as it is very close to the border with the Soviet Union. To get to the ancient city either rent a minibus, get a taxi or catch the early bus (6 a.m.). The ruins are very impressive but unexcavated and well worth a visit to this spooky abandoned city.

UNITED KINGDOM

Entry requirements	Passport
Population	57,100,000
Capital	London (pop.: 7,550,000)
Currency	Sterling
	$1 = approx. 59p
Political system	Constitutional Monarchy
Religion	Protestant
Language	English, also some Welsh and Gaelic in some areas
Public holidays	1, (2, 3 Scotland) Jan.; (17 March Northern Ireland); Good Friday; Easter Monday; 1st Monday in May; Spring Bank Holiday; (Early August Bank Holiday, Scotland), Late August Bank Holiday; 25, 26 Dec.
International dialling codes	To USA: 010 + 1 + number
	From USA: 011 + 44 + number
Eurotrain office	52 Grosvenor Gardens, London SW1 (Tel. 071–730 3402)

Even the British get confused about their nationhood, so it's not uncommon to hear 'England', 'Great Britain' and the 'United Kingdom' used incorrectly in conversation. The island of Great Britain isn't just England; it comprises Wales and Scotland too. Add to this Northern Ireland, and you have the United Kingdom of Great Britain and Northern Ireland, more commonly known as the UK.

England, the largest of the four countries, has always attracted the majority of immigrants from pre-Celtic times to the present day. With the Normans in 1066 came feudalism and a power struggle among the nobles. Pretty soon the barons were in a position to lay down the law and force King John to recognize their rights in 1215. By the end of the Tudor era, Henry VIII had been through six wives, and England was a prosperous nation. The seventeenth century saw a Civil War between the Parliamentarians and Cromwell, and the royalist supporters of Charles I. The eighteenth century began with the union of Scotland and England and continued with the development of the British Empire in North America and India. Britain was the world's leader in the Industrial Revolution, and became known as the 'workshop of the world'.

The economic strain of being heavily involved in two World

576   Europe by Train

Wars, and increased rivalry in the marketplace, has led to her decline as a world power. From a eurorailer's point of view, the United Kingdom offers a diversity of not just geography but of history and culture too – all you'd expect from a country made up of four separate nations.

BRITISH RAIL (BR)

In recent years, British Rail have streamlined their services and improved their corporate image, gearing up for their privatization. In terms of speed and comfort the InterCity 225 and other InterCity services rank almost on a par with France and are certainly as good as in Germany although, as in most other countries, the commuter services could be improved. There are three main categories of trains: (1) The new electric InterCity 225s which run from London to Leeds and will run to Edinburgh soon. (2) InterCity 125s, named for the speed they travel at. These excellent trains, the fastest diesels in the world, are still used on most long hauls. (3) The other InterCity services are either diesel or electric and reach 110 m.p.h. on long runs. (4) The cross-country and local trains run on the more out-of-the-way routes or in the suburbs of the large towns. There are no supplements to worry about on any of these services. New fast trains are planned for the Channel Tunnel when it opens in 1993, but the route from London to the Channel is still the cause of heated debate.

• **Inter Rail bonuses:** Up to half price to point of departure from the UK, plus reduction as follows:

Company	Route	Reduction
Sealink UK Ltd/SNCF	Dover–Calais	30%
	Folkestone–Boulogne	30%
	Weymouth–Cherbourg	30%
Sealink UK Ltd	Portsmouth–Ryde	30%
	Lymington–Yarmouth	30%
	Fishguard–Rosslare	30%
	Holyhead–Dun Laoghaire	50%
	Stranraer–Larne	33%
Sealink Dieppe Ferries	Newhaven–Dieppe	30%
Sealink UK Ltd/Stena Line	Harwich–Hoek van Holland	30%

Company	Route	Reduction
Hoverspeed (Hovercraft)	Dover Hoverport–Calais/Boulogne	50%
P&O (European Ferries)	Dover–Calais/Boulogne	30%
	Dover–Oostende	30%
	Portsmouth–Le Havre	30%
Scandinavian Seaways (DFDS)	Harwich–Esbjerg	50%
	Newcastle–Esbjerg	50%
B&I Line	Holyhead–Dublin	50%

TRAIN INFORMATION

All main stations have their own information counters and there are free timetables for the main-line routes.

• **Reservations:** Only compulsory on certain services, as indicated by [R] in the BR timetable, otherwise advisable on main lines in summer, particularly around holiday weekends. Cost £1 for standard class, £2 for first class.

• **Night travel:** No couchettes, only sleepers at £18. Standard-class ticket holders share a two-berth compartment. A bonus is free tea and biscuits in the morning. All sleepers are air-conditioned and manufactured within the last five years.

• **Eating on trains:** Expensive restaurant cars run on all main lines, Mon.–Sat. Buffets with average-priced snacks run daily on the major routes.

• **Scenic tips:** There's nothing in Britain to compare with Switzerland or Norway, but the Lake District and parts of North Wales are interesting enough. The really scenic routes are up in the Scottish Highlands, particularly the Fort William–Mallaig and Glasgow–Oban runs. Ask for the 'Scenic Rail Journeys' leaflet at the British Tourist Authority.

• **Rover tickets:** There are several, depending on how much of the country you want to see. The All-Line Ticket is valid for either 7 or 14 days and costs around £265 and £400 respectively for first class. Standard-class tickets for the same periods are £160 and £225 respectively, with children aged between 5 and 15 paying two-thirds of the appropriate adult fare. This ticket is valid for all stations and Sealink services to the Isle of Wight. In addition, free travel on the

Vale of Rheidol Narrow Gauge Steam Railway in Wales and a 20 per cent reduction on the Windermere Iron Steamboat Company's steamers in the Lake District. The BritRail Pass and Flexipass are available only outside the UK and are valid for 8, 15, 22 days or 1 month (or 4 days from 8, 8 from 15 and 15 from 1 month). For prices see the Introduction, pp. 29–30). If you just want to visit a certain part of England and Wales there are a total of 19 regional rover tickets available for seven consecutive days between Easter and October. They cost from £27.50 to £48. All prices are standard class and some tickets are restricted to outside of weekday morning rush hours. If you are visiting or staying in Scotland, the Freedom of Scotland Ticket is a good buy and costs £56 for 7 days and £92 for 15 days. It is available only in standard class and also gives you free use of Caledonian MacBrayne sailings on the Firth of Clyde. If you are particularly attracted to the Highlands and Islands, an all-encompassing pass valid for all forms of land and sea transport called the 'Travelpass' is available for £35 for 7 days in March, April, May and October and £55 between June and September. For 13 days the price is £50 and £70 respectively. Note: British Rail calls itself ScotRail in Scotland and has recently embarked on an ambitious programme to modernize and improve stations and rolling stock. The Freedom of Wales pass is good for 7 days and costs £40 and the Northern Ireland Rail Runabout costs £27.50 and is valid for 7 days from April to October.

● **Bikes:** There are no facilities for hiring out bikes at British Rail stations, so ask at the tourist office for local suggestions.

● **Coach travel:** If you have bought your Inter Rail card in the UK or are travelling with a Eurailpass, you can save money travelling to London and on to Dover with National Express (Caledonian Express in Scotland). They travel to 1,500 locations. A single from Edinburgh to London can be as low as £10. Those under 23 can get a 33 per cent Discount Card for £5.

TOURIST INFORMATION

Every major city or town has its own tourist information office, and they will fix you up with accommodation for around £1 and supply you with maps and leaflets. There are also regional and national tourist boards who supply information.

• **ISIC bonuses:** Up to 50 per cent reduction at some monuments where you have to pay, but (in the main) museums and galleries are free. For further information, contact ISIC, London Student Travel, 52 Grosvenor Gardens, London SW1W 0AG (Tel. 071–730 3402), or NUS Travel, 12 Dublin Street, Edinburgh (Tel. 031–556 6598).

• **Money matters:** 1 pound (£) = 100 pence (p).
Banking hours are generally Mon.–Fri.: 9.30 a.m.–3.30 p.m. but over the last year or so have started to vary, particularly in Scotland where the much greater use of cash dispensers and computers means many banks, particularly in cities, now open to 4.45 p.m. All Scottish banks used to close between 12.30 p.m.–1.30 p.m. but many are now open all day. You may still find some banks in Scotland opening late on a Thursday and in England some banks even open on a Saturday morning. Beware of unfamiliar Bureaux de Change which charge high commissions and have poor exchange rates. Scottish banks issue their own notes and you may get some funny looks if you use them in England. When leaving the UK take English notes as Scottish ones might as well be from Paraguay.

• **Post offices:** Open 9 a.m.–5.30 p.m., with sub-post offices generally closing for lunch; Sat.: 9 a.m.–1 p.m.

• **Shops:** 9 a.m.–5.30 p.m. is average. Large stores take no lunch breaks, and in London and major cities shops are open late on several days of the week. Many cities have shops that stay open very late and open all day Sunday – these are convenient, but watch the prices.

• **Museums:** 10 a.m.–5 p.m. is the norm, and in many cases entrance is free.

SLEEPING

The wonderful institution of Bed-and-Breakfast (B&B) is the cornerstone of accommodation in Britain, and between B&Bs and youth or student hostels you should easily get by. B&Bs average £10 (£15 in London) and this includes an English breakfast (bacon, eggs, etc.) which should keep you going all day. Always go for small B&Bs where you'll feel like one of the family and will get good value for money. Hotels in Britain are very expensive and are best avoided. Many universities let out their student flats and hostels in summer, and these average about £10 a night. Youth hostels charge according to your age and the facilities on offer. The borderline for reduced rates is age 21, and hostels are either 'simple, standard or superior' grade: expect to pay between £2 and £9. If you're thinking of doing much hostelling, pick up the 'YHA Guide to England and Wales' or 'Scotland YHA Guide' which will show you the locations, etc., of the hostels. It's possible to join the IYHA at most of the large hostels for around £8 (£4 for under 21s). As far as camping goes, the vagaries of British weather may make this a dicey proposition, but if you're keen count on £2–4 a night, and bring mosquito repellent and warm clothes.

The English, Scottish and Welsh Tourist Boards have guides called 'Where to Stay' costing £5.95, £3.25, and £2.25 respectively. These aren't bad, though they're a bit sparse on cheap suggestions. You'll do better getting the lists of local campsites and accommodation from tourist information, or using their bed-booking service for about £1.

EATING AND NIGHTLIFE

British food has a bit of a bad reputation, but during the past decade or so much has been done to overcome this, and eating out in Britain today is no longer an expensive and tasteless affair. If you've got the cash, go for the traditional dishes like roast beef and Yorkshire pudding, or Scotch salmon and beefsteak. Often you'll find these on the set-lunch menus offered by hotels, and this is your chance to cash in and sample them at a reasonable price (£5 upwards). Always check if VAT (a 15 per cent tax) is included in the price, before deciding. For your picnics, look out for the impressive variety of British cheeses, Cheddar, Cheshire, Wensleydale, Double Gloucester, Stilton, etc., and shop at stores like Marks & Spencer, British Home Stores, Safeway and Sainsbury's, where you can be sure the produce is fresh and reasonably priced. While in the UK, at least once try to partake in the age-old custom of afternoon tea. This filling snack of scones, jam, cream and tea is often served in even the most luxurious hotels for only a pound or two, and it really gives an insight into the civilized Britain of yesteryear.

It's possible to make out in Britain on very little indeed if you know where to look. All the major centres have fast-food chains of some description, and even the smallest village has its own local fish'n'chip shop where you can fill up for just about £2. Chinese and Indian meals are also good value, as (in general) are pub lunches.

The pub is the mainstay of British social life and this is where you should make for to meet the locals. Many pubs, however, are soulless places and don't merit five minutes of your time, so be selective and choose either one with a historical connection or those that go to the effort of putting on live music. Pubs open 11 a.m.– 10.30 p.m. (11 p.m. in London), though many close between 2 or 3 p.m. and 5.30 p.m. All pubs close for about three hours in the afternoon on Sundays. You must be over 18 to drink alcohol. The English and Welsh pride themselves on their 'real ale', the Scots on their whisky and the Irish on their Guinness.

London is the home of British theatre and cinema – but this doesn't mean other cities are dead ducks; Edinburgh's International Festival and Fringe in August–September puts London in the shade for the three or four weeks it's on. In general, the live music and dancing scene is better in Britain than in most other European countries. Pick up the tourist board's list of current happenings from whichever town you're in, and remember to try for student discounts on theatre tickets, etc.

London

London is a must in any European wanderings. There are three Londons to take into account: the CITY of London (the financial and administrative centre of Great Britain), WESTMINSTER (the political, royal and religious centre), and the WEST END (home of the British theatre and cinema, smart shops and clubs). Each area has a different feel to it, and the combination of all three with over a thousand years of history and traditions, plenty of open green spaces and the buzz of Europe's largest city, makes a visit here unforgettable.

STATION FACILITIES

There are eight major stations in London, all interconnected by the fast and efficient tube (underground railway). To ensure you're at the right station, here's a quick checklist of which station serves where:

• **Charing Cross:** Handles suburban lines and the London–Folkestone and London–Hastings trains.

• **Euston:** Central England and the north-west, Birmingham, Coventry, Liverpool, Manchester, Glasgow and on to Dublin.

• **King's Cross:** The north-east, Leeds, York, Hull, Newcastle and on to Edinburgh and Aberdeen. From Newcastle you sail to Norway, Denmark and Sweden.

• **Liverpool Street:** The area north-east of London, Cambridge, Harwich, Norwich. From Harwich you can sail to Holland, Germany, Sweden, Norway and Denmark.

• **Paddington:** The south-west of England, Exeter, Plymouth, Penzance, Bristol, Swansea, Oxford, Gloucester.

• **St Pancras:** Trains bound due north, Nottingham, Derby, Leicester, Sheffield.

• **Victoria:** South-east England, Newhaven, Brighton, Eastbourne, Hastings and Dover, the main gateway to France, Belgium, Spain, Italy, etc. The 30-minute train journey to Gatwick Airport leaves from here too. If you're travelling by hovercraft to France, this is also where you depart for Dover Priory. The Continental travel office is here.

• **Waterloo:** Trains to the south of England, Bournemouth, Portsmouth, Southampton and Weymouth.

We are reliably informed by British Rail that the stations detailed on page 583 are the ones you are most likely to use.

	KING'S CROSS	VICTORIA
Train information	24 hours (Tel. 071–278 2477)	7.30 a.m.–9.30 p.m. (Tel. 071–928 5100)
Reservations	Mon.–Sat.: 7.15 a.m.–10.30 p.m. Sun.: 8 a.m.–10.30 p.m.	8 a.m.–9.30 p.m.
Tourist information	–	9 a.m.–9 p.m.
Foreign exchange	Sun.–Thur.: 8 a.m.–8 p.m. Fri. and Sat.: 8 a.m.–9.30 p.m.	T. Cook office 8.15 a.m.–9 p.m.
Left-luggage lockers	–	Always access
Left-luggage store	24 hours except Sat.: 11 p.m.– Sun. 7 a.m.	7 a.m.–10.30 p.m.
Bar, Buffet	Mon.–Sat.: 11 a.m.–3 p.m. 4.30 p.m.–11 p.m., Sun.: 12 noon– 2 p.m., 7 p.m.–10.35 p.m.	7 a.m.–10.40 p.m.
Restaurant	Mon.–Sat.: 7 a.m.–10 a.m. 11 a.m.–7 p.m.	7 a.m.–10 p.m.
Self-service	7 a.m.–9 p.m. daily	–
Showers	Open 24 hours	None
Post office	In road opposite station	None
Station shuts	Only Christmas Day	Always open

	EUSTON	LIVERPOOL STREET
Train information	Mon.–Sat.: 7.15 a.m.–10.30 p.m. Sun.: 8 a.m.–10.30 p.m. 24-hour telephone service (Tel. 071–387 7070)	7.15 a.m.–10.30 p.m. daily (Tel. 071–283 7171)
Reservations	7 a.m.–11 p.m.	Mon.–Sat.: 8 a.m.–6.45 p.m.
Tourist information	Mon.–Fri.: 8 a.m.–8 p.m. Sat.: 8 a.m.–6 p.m.	8 a.m.–6 p.m.
Foreign exchange	6.30 a.m.–11 p.m.	7.30 a.m.–8.30 p.m.
Left-luggage lockers	None	None
Left-luggage store	Open 24 hours	7 a.m.–10.30 p.m.
Bar, Buffet	7 a.m.–10 p.m.	7.30 a.m.–10.30 p.m.
Restaurant	7.30 a.m.–10 p.m.	Mon.–Fri.: 8 a.m.–9 p.m.
Bath, Shower	Mon.–Fri.: 7.30 a.m.–10 p.m. Sat: 11 a.m.–10 p.m. Closed Sunday	None
Shops	8 a.m.–6 p.m.	Various times, Mon.–Sat.
Post office	None	None
Station shuts	Open 24 hours	Open 24 hours

CROSS-CHANNEL FERRIES

The ferries to Calais, Dieppe, Boulogne and Ostend are usually packed out in high season, so before embarking on the crossing take a look at the alternatives open to you. Sealink, Hoverspeed, P&O and Scandinavian Seaways ferries offer discounts to Inter Rail holders. By far the most civilized form of Channel crossing is to use the Jetfoil from Dover to Ostend, or the hovercraft from Dover to Boulogne. For the £8 jetfoil supplement you get a guaranteed seat, far shorter crossing, and a speedier city-to-city connection. Another good alternative is to route your journey via Holland. The Harwich–Hook of Holland ferries are very good and there's not much in it financially, although these cruise-liner ships offer either an overnight or full-day sailing.

TOURIST INFORMATION

England, Wales and Scotland have separate Tourist Boards, all of which have offices in London. The Tourist Information Centre at Victoria Station forecourt carries information on London. Leaflets, maps, guidebooks, tourist tickets for buses and the underground, and sightseeing tour and theatre tickets are available. Same-day hotel accommodation can be booked. The Centre is open seven days a week, 9 a.m.–8.30 p.m. with longer hours in July and August.

The British Travel Centre provides information on all of the United Kingdom and is located at 12 Regent Street, Piccadilly Circus, London SW1, open Mon.–Fri.: 9 a.m.–6.30 p.m., Sat. and Sun.: 10 a.m.–4 p.m. (open later on Saturday May–September). Information on Northern Ireland is available from the Ireland desk of the British Travel Centre. The Scottish Tourist Board is at 19 Cockspur Street, London SW1, and is open Mon.–Fri.: 9 a.m.–5 p.m., and the Wales Tourist Board is at 34 Piccadilly, London W1, open Mon.–Thur.: 9.15 a.m.–5.15 p.m. and Fri.: 9.15 a.m.–5 p.m.

The City of London Information Centre, with detailed information on the City as well as more general information, is directly across the road from St Paul's Cathedral. It is open Mon.–Fri.: 9.30 a.m.–5 p.m., Sat.: 10 a.m.–4 p.m. during April–September and 9.30 a.m.–12 noon October–March.

• **Addresses:**
POST OFFICE: King Edward Building, King Edward Street (tube, St

Paul's), open Mon.–Fri.: 8 a.m.–7 p.m., Sat.: 9 a.m.–12.30 p.m. This is where all poste restante mail will end up. The twenty-four-hour post office is at St Martin's Place, Trafalgar Square.

AMEX: 6 Haymarket (tube, Piccadilly). Exchange open Mon.–Fri.: 9 a.m.–5 p.m., Sat.: 9 a.m.–6 p.m. (8 p.m. in season), Sun.: 10 a.m.–6 p.m. (Tel. 930 4411).

US EMBASSY: 24 Grosvenor Square, W1 (Tel. 499 9000) (tube, Bond St).

EUROTRAIN: Tel. 730 3402, or kiosk at Victoria Station (Tel. 630 8132).

PHONE CODE: 071 (inner London), 081 (outer).

• **Getting about:** The tube is efficient and fast, but expensive and crowded. Pick up an underground map, free at any station, and hang on to your ticket till the journey's through. Tubes run 5 a.m.–12 midnight. Like the tube, the red double-decker buses operate on a zone system, and you pay the driver or conductor on the bus, while the single-decker Red Arrows are express buses with ticket machines on board. There is an excellent network of night buses which run 12 midnight–5 a.m. on certain routes, all leave from Trafalgar Square.

If you're in London for a while, pick up the leaflets on the London Explorer tickets and Travelcards, but these are expensive by other European standards. Travelcards are valid on tubes, buses and local BR services. A one-day card (all zones) costs £2.60 (not valid on night buses) and also covers BR services in and around London. Cards for longer periods require a photograph. The prices vary according to the number of zones. Most sights are in zone one. The newly introduced Visitor Travelcard is only available from travel agents outside south-east England – get it or a voucher for it before you leave home. It is available for one, three, four or seven days (costs about £2.60, £8.80, £12.40, £20.50) and comes with a wallet of discount vouchers. If you're taking a tube after 10 a.m. and returning to the same place the same day, buy a cheap day return which will save you up to a third. Unless you're in a desperate rush, don't bother with the expensive taxis and, though it's impossible to get round all the sights on foot, try to see as much as you can of London through walks. The 'London A–Z' (about £1.95) is the best long-term map investment you can make.

SEEING

London has swallowed many villages into its bulk in the course of its development, but even today each village (now district) has its own character and traditions. Soho, Hampstead and Chelsea are as different from each other as individual towns. It's easy to divide London into its three sections but this would neglect the areas that fall between, like trendy COVENT GARDEN, or the intellectual centre of BLOOMSBURY where the BRITISH MUSEUM and London University are located. Don't forget either the wonderful days out you can have at the maritime centre of GREENWICH, or at the Royal Botanical Gardens at KEW, or HAMPTON COURT PALACE, and many more. This rundown is just a small sample of what you can see, but once you've made your visit to tourist information, you should be in a position to work out your own best itinerary.

The City of London

The London of the eleventh century is that area known as 'the City'. In this 'square mile', the wheelings and dealings of the Stock Exchange and big business take place, and the Bank of England and Royal Exchange have their headquarters here. The sights include: the beautiful Renaissance cathedral of ST PAUL'S (the one Charles and Di chose for their wedding in 1981), where Nelson and Wellington are buried; FLEET STREET, the former home of the British press; the INNS OF COURT and the OLD BAILEY – the heart of the British legal system; and the TOWER OF LONDON which dates back to William the Conqueror and has served as prison, palace and mint. The Crown Jewels, the White Tower and Tower Green where Henry VIII had Anne Boleyn and Katherine Howard executed, are among some of the sights to see here. Near the Tower is the famous TOWER BRIDGE. The BARBICAN is also in the City (tube Barbican or Moorgate). This arts centre has concerts, plays and exhibitions as well as the superb MUSEUM OF LONDON (free).

Westminster and the West End

Roughly, this stretches from HYDE PARK (the famous expanse with Speakers' Corner – a national venue for impromptu free speech on Sundays) to WESTMINSTER ABBEY, the incredible Gothic church so central to the country's history. WHITEHALL and the HOUSES OF PARLIAMENT, the centres of British government and administration, are along here, and so is the timekeeping landmark of London, BIG BEN. To go in and listen to Parliament (a fascinating experience), line up at St Stephen's entrance opposite the Abbey. THE MALL is the boulevard leading from TRAFALGAR SQUARE, home of the NATIONAL GALLERY, to BUCKINGHAM PALACE, the home of the monarchy, which is not open to the public. The hub of the capital is PICCADILLY CIRCUS with its statue of Eros. Leicester Square, London's movie centre, is near here. Just to the north is SOHO; the recent cleaning up of this area means that it no longer lives up to its seamy reputation. London's CHINATOWN is here, centred on Gerard Street. To the east is Covent Garden, once a vegetable market, now a shopping arcade. Look out for street performances and the London Transport Museum.

The BRITISH MUSEUM (tube Tottenham Court Road or Russell Square) is worth at least a day of anyone's time (everything, from the Elgin Marbles to Magna Carta is here). The other main museums are at South Kensington: the VICTORIA AND ALBERT, the NATURAL HISTORY, the GEOLOGICAL and SCIENCE MUSEUMS are next door to each other. Some of these have started to charge for entrance – check with tourist information. The ROYAL ALBERT HALL is close by. See the posters outside for what's on.

The famous department store HARRODS where you can buy 'absolutely anything', is in KNIGHTSBRIDGE. Wander round the food hall there – they sell every type and variety of eats you'd ever imagined. Other shops worth taking in for their sheer entertainment value are LIBERTY'S (the neo-Tudor building on Regent Street) and FORTNUM AND MASON, Piccadilly.

MADAME TUSSAUD'S wax museum, where the famous are immortalized, is on the Marylebone Road (tube Baker Street). If you are tired of the city's rush, head into one of the parks – tour LONDON ZOO (Regent's Park), try rowing on the Serpentine (Hyde Park) and look out for the Buddhist Pagoda (Battersea Park).

SLEEPING

The possibilities are endless, but in the lower price-bracket
(£10–15) you can't expect much in the way of comfort. London is
busy all year, but in summer it's absolutely packed. Student and
youth hostels average £7, halls of residence about £15, and B&B
£18. Ask for leaflets on hostels, etc., at the London Tourist Board
office in Victoria Station. There are five youth hostels: 36 Carter
Lane (Tel. 071–236 4965) (tube, St Paul's), the largest in Britain;
Holland House, Holland Walk, Kensington (Tel. 071–937 0748)
(tube, Holland Park); 4 Wellgarth Rd, Hampstead (Tel. 071–458
9054) (tube, Golders Green, followed by bus 210 or 260); 38 Bolton
Gdns (Tel. 071–373 7083) (tube, Earls Court); 84 Highgate West
Hill (Tel. 071–340 1831) (tube, Archway, then bus 148, 210 or 271).

Other hostels: These range from a tent city to charity set-ups. Try
some of the following: Tent City, Old Oak Common Lane (Tel.
081–743 5708) (tube, East Acton); Fieldcourt House, 32 Courtfield
Gdns (Tel. 071–373 0152) (tube, Gloucester Rd); Astor Museum
Hostel, 27 Montague St (Tel. 071–580 5360) (tube, Tottenham
Court Rd); International Students House, 229 Gt Portland St (Tel.
071–631 3223) (tube, Great Portland St). If you're staying a while,
two good ideas are to contact either the London University
Students' Union (Tel. 071–636 2818) or Universal Aunts (Tel.
071–351 5767). Some of the cheaper B&Bs are really depressing,
and you're invariably better in hostels, but anyway the areas to head
for are Earls Court, Paddington and Bayswater. Simone House
Hotel, 49 Belgrave Rd (Tel. 071–828 2474) (tube, Victoria);
Leinster Hotel, 7–11 Leinster Square (Tel. 071–229 9641) (tube,
Bayswater); Vicarage Hotel, 10 Vicarage Gate (Tel. 071–229 4030)
(tube, Kensington High St). As far as camping goes, there are
plenty of sites. Ask at tourist information. The best one is Pickett's
Lock Centre, Pickett's Lock Lane (Tel. 081–803 4756) (tube, Seven
Sisters, then bus 149, 259 or 279 or, alternatively, by BR to Angel
Road Station then a W8 bus). It's a bit out of the way but very well
equipped. The Tent City (see above) is probably the most central
and your best bet.

With violence on the increase, it's stupid to sleep rough in
London, but if you're determined to spend nothing, the
embankment at Westminster Bridge, or Hyde Park are your best
bets, though the police are becoming increasingly active in stamping
this out.

EATING AND NIGHTLIFE

Eating for under £4 is no great problem with the spate of fast-food chains, Indian and Chinese restaurants and very good supermarkets increasing every year. Many pubs serve lunches and, of course, there's always the great British invention, fish'n'chips. Always check if VAT is included on a menu as this tax can fairly bump up the bill. You can't go too far wrong for fast food in McDonalds and Pizzaland, but branches of Wimpy vary dramatically. For the best non-European meals, head for Soho. Marks & Spencer, Safeway, Sainsbury's and British Home Stores are all reliable for high-quality groceries, and if it's a good day you can do no better than get a picnic together and head for one of the parks.

Cranks Health Foods, Covent Garden, and 196 Tottenham Court Road, are excellent but a bit pricey. For something a bit cheaper, try the Country Life vegetarian restaurant at 123 Regent Street, W1. Open Mon. 1.30 a.m.–6 p.m., Fri. 10.30 a.m.–3 p.m. In Soho, Poons, Leicester St, Lee Ho Fook, Macclesfield St, and Chan May Mai, Lisle St, are all good value. For Indian food try around Bayswater, or for unbeatable value the Oval Tandoori Restaurant at 64A Brixton Road, SW9, which, although out of the centre, is worth the effort to get there. For good value Chinese food, try the Man Lee Hong restaurant on Lisle Street near Leicester Square. For excellent crêpes try Le Shop (formerly the Asterix Créperie) at 329 King's Road, Chelsea SW3.

Nightlife and London are inseparable from each other. London's no longer swinging the way it was in the 1960s, but there's still a lot happening. Your best source of information is the weekly magazine *Time Out*. The theatre is firmly entrenched in London's nightlife, and you really ought to try and make it along to a show. Pick up the fortnightly London Theatre Guide at any theatre or information office. Take along your ISIC to any theatre displaying (S) in its write-up, and you will be able to get cheap standby tickets before the curtain rises. In summer there's open-air Shakespeare in Regent's Park. Expect an average theatre ticket to cost £9. There's a half-price theatre ticket booth in Leicester Square. There's music to suit all tastes on offer, from the 'Proms' classics in the Albert Hall to punk in The Marquee, 105 Charing Cross Road. Also try the Wag Club at 35 Wardour Street.

There are endless lists of pubs, and these are as good a place as any to watch the locals in their habitat. Try the Sherlock Holmes, 10 Northumberland St, The Sun in Lamb's Conduit St, WC1, or Ye Olde Cheshire Cheese, just off Fleet St. The Firkin chain of pubs are well worth visiting. There are three in the city centre and several more spread round the periphery. The Goose & Firkin in Borough Road (Tube: Elephant & Castle) has a piano player on Friday and Saturday nights which livens up the friendly atmosphere. The Flounder & Firkin is in Holloway Road in the north, the Ferret & Firkin is in Lots Road, Chelsea, the Phoenix & Firkin at Denmark Hill Station (nine minutes from Victoria) and the Fox & Firkin is in Tavistock Crescent in Notting Hill. With over 4,000 pubs in London, you're bound to find one to your liking. If you're after some 'heavy nightlife', a wander through Soho should take good care of that, or if you want to be entertained while having a drink, try the Allsop Arms, 137 Gloucester Place. The Centre at 12 Adelaide St, WC2 is a good meeting place for the under 25s.

South-east England

If you're arriving in Britain from France or Belgium, chances are your first impressions will be of DOVER or FOLKESTONE. Dover, with its famous chalky white cliffs, dates back to the Romans and there are still remains to be seen from their time. If you've a bit of time to spend before making the direct two-hour journey to London, take in the CASTLE, with its Roman PHAROS, the PAINTED HOUSE (a Roman townhouse off New St, closed Monday). Tourist information is near Dover Priory Station and at Townwall St. They'll give you help with accommodation if you're staying overnight.

Half an hour up one of the lines to London lies the ancient pilgrimage centre of CANTERBURY. The CATHEDRAL, where St Thomas à Becket was murdered in 1170, is well worth breaking your journey for, and not far from here you can see the remnants of the old city walls at DANE JOHN GARDENS. ST MARTIN'S CHURCH has evolved from fourth-century Roman villas and is one of the oldest churches in England. There are various remains of long-defunct religious orders: ST AUGUSTINE'S ABBEY outside the city's East Wall, and EASTBRIDGE HOSPITAL on St Peter's St, open Mon.–Sat.: 9.30 a.m.–5.30 p.m. Food and beds shouldn't cause you any problems, but Canterbury can easily be seen as a day trip from London. The tourist office is at 34 St Margaret's Street.

Other noteworthy places in this area, though not on the Dover–London line, are Chichester, Winchester and Brighton. Lying 1½ hours from the capital on the London–Portsmouth line, CHICHESTER holds a summer theatre festival worth investigation, and has a ROMAN PALACE and CATHEDRAL of note. Tourist information is at St Peter's Market, West St, open Mon.–Sat.: 9.15 a.m.–5.30 p.m. WINCHESTER is a wonderful place, an archetypal English town. The CATHEDRAL is its pride, and rightly so. Walking down Cathedral Close, you'll come to WINCHESTER SCHOOL, England's first 'public' (private) school, which has nurtured the sons of the élite for six centuries. Not far from here (on bus route 214) is CHAWTON, home of the English novelist Jane Austen of *Pride and Prejudice* fame. Her house is open 11 a.m.–4.30 p.m. Winchester is on the London–Weymouth line, about 1½ hours down the line from London. Another ideal day trip from the capital is to BRIGHTON. Since the mid-eighteenth century, this has been a popular holiday resort, especially with the Victorians. In 1783 the ROYAL PAVILION was constructed when the Prince Regent came to settle here, and it's here and to the PALACE PIER you should head. Wander round the narrow streets from the Old Steine to West St. Tourist information is in the Guildhall on the Broadway, open Mon.–Sat.: 9.30 a.m.–6 p.m., Sun.: 2 p.m.–5 p.m. in season.

PORTSMOUTH is less than two hours from London Waterloo. It is a centre of Britain's maritime heritage. The naval dockyard contains a museum and two historic ships: HMS *Victory* (Nelson's flagship at Trafalgar) and HMS *Warrior* (Britain's first ironclad). The Tudor warship MARY ROSE is preserved in Portsmouth after being salvaged from the seabed. See SOUTHSEA CASTLE where Henry VIII stood as he watched *Mary Rose* sink. Take the ferry across the harbour to Gosport to see the submarine museum. Take the local train to Portchester and see the Roman and Norman castle with its huge keep and a church inside the walls.

South-west England

From the rail network point of view, we've divided the country so that we start the south-west at Salisbury and Bath, and extend down to Devon and Cornwall. This region is one of England's most picturesque and has some of the country's best weather.

Salisbury

Salisbury is dominated by its thirteenth-century CATHEDRAL, with the tallest spire in England. Take the tour round the cathedral and visit the cloisters and Chapter House. CATHEDRAL CLOSE was a religious city and you can still see some of its buildings, especially MOMPESSON HOUSE, now cared for by the National Trust.

Salisbury is on the London–Exeter and Bristol–Portsmouth lines, 1½ hours from London. This is the best place to stay if you want to visit the ancient religious site of STONEHENGE, ten miles north of Salisbury. If you know nothing of its history or aren't really interested don't bother making the trip as you won't understand what all the fuss is over. All that's there is a circle of stones they make you pay £1.30 (£1 for students) to see, but they date back at least to 1500 BC, so that makes them rather special. It's thought they were an astronomical calendar, and later on, in 250 BC, the Druids used them for their sun-worshipping festivals. Another stone circle is at AVEBURY – the village is actually inside the circle, so it is free. Ask at tourist information about getting there. The CITY MUSEUM in Cathedral Street has a fascinating exhibition which tells you everything but 'why', about the site. The Salisbury tourist office is at Fish Row, open Mon.–Sat.: 9 a.m.–7 p.m. in season, and they'll help with accommodation. There's a youth hostel at Milford Hill (Tel. 0722–27572) and several reasonable B&Bs.

Bath

Just 15 minutes from the city of BRISTOL, and in the south-west corner of the Cotswolds, lies the elegant Georgian spa town of Bath. This town was second only to London for style in the eighteenth century; successive generations of the aristocracy came to 'take the waters' and left behind an architectural legacy as rich as you'll find in England. Trains run hourly from London and the journey takes only 1¼ hours; if you're travelling on to Oxford you change at Didcot and Bath's proximity to Bristol means you could also use it as a jumping-off point for Devon and Cornwall.

SEEING

The heart of Georgian Bath is the CIRCUS, the circle of townhouses where the artist Gainsborough lived at No. 17, and William Pitt, the Prime Minister, at Nos. 7 and 8. Leaving the Circus at Brock St, you come to ROYAL CRESCENT, considered England's most attractive street. Visit No. 1 for an idea of elegant Georgian living. The MUSEUM OF COSTUME is particularly interesting, housed in the ASSEMBLY ROOMS on the Circus. From the Abbey Churchyard you enter the ROMAN BATHS AND MUSEUM. Take the tour, and visit the PUMP ROOM where the hot spring water is pumped. This complex is open 9 a.m.–7 p.m. daily. If you're there in the mornings and fancy treating yourself to a taste of elegant British life, sit down in the Pump Room for a coffee and enjoy the sounds of The Pump Room Trio (Mon.–Sat.: 10 a.m.–noon).

SLEEPING

Tourist information at The Collonades will find you a room for a commission, or pick up a list of places from them. There's a youth hostel at Bathwick Hill (Tel. 0225–465674), about a mile from the city (take minibus 18 from Orange Grove, by the Abbey), and a YMCA House at Broad Street Place (Tel. 0225–60471) accepts both sexes. For B&Bs, look around the Wells Road or, for one nearer the station, try Prior House, 3 Marlborough Lane (Tel. 0225–313587), around £10 each.

EATING AND NIGHTLIFE

There are plenty of bakers, pubs and supermarkets, so meals shouldn't pose any problems. The City Market is good for fruit and vegetables, and Molehill Café, 14 George St, is about the best place in town. After 8 p.m., it becomes a club with live music. Take out a weekly membership for about a pound, if you're staying for a while. The Bath Festival is on in late May, and ask at tourist information for the monthly 'What's On'.

Devon and Cornwall

The main centres to base yourself to explore these regions are Exeter, Plymouth or Penzance.

EXETER is the county town of Devon and is dominated by its impressive medieval CATHEDRAL. From the station of St David's, take the bus into the centre. Tourist information in the Civic Centre on Paris St will give you all you need on the region, including the national parks of Dartmoor and Exmoor. While in Exeter, take in the fourteenth-century GUILDHALL and go for a drink in the SHIP INN where Sir Francis Drake went for a jar. The youth hostel at 47 Countess Wear Rd, Topsham (Tel. 039287–3329), is a short distance out, but good (bus 187 or 356 from Paris St bus station). Alternatively, try the Exeter Student Guest House, 16 New North Rd (Tel. 0392–52493).

PLYMOUTH has been a major port since the fourteenth century. It was here Drake spotted the Spanish Armada and the *Mayflower* set sail to discover the New World. Spend an afternoon wandering round the Elizabethan BARBICAN QUAY, NEW ST with its timber merchant houses and the ruins of the fourteenth-century castle.

PENZANCE, 2½ hours further down the line, has a history of pirates and invaders, and makes an interesting day trip. Take in the MARKET HOUSE and MORRAB GARDENS where subtropical plants flourish, thanks to the exceptionally mild climate. From Penzance you can sail out to the Scilly Isles, or visit ST MICHAEL'S MOUNT, three miles east of the town – a castle and mountain where St Michael is said to have appeared.

The Midlands and East Anglia

The university towns of OXFORD and CAMBRIDGE, with their beautiful cloisters and unique building formations, are a must on a serious tour of Great Britain, and Shakespeare's home town STRATFORD-UPON-AVON, however commercialized it is becoming, is still well worth a visit. Most of the Midlands is industrial and not worth stopping off at, while East Anglia is the flat land, taking in places like Cambridge, NORWICH, KING'S LYNN and the NORFOLK BROADS.

Oxford

Home of Britain's oldest and most prestigious university, which has dominated the town for over 700 years, Oxford lies 45 minutes from London's Paddington Station, and can easily be taken in on a day trip from the capital.

STATION FACILITIES

Train information	Mon.–Sat.: 8.30 a.m.–7.30 p.m.,
	Sun.: 9.30 a.m.–7.30 p.m.
Reservations	Mon.–Fri.: 9 a.m.–5 p.m., Sat.: 9 a.m.–12 noon
Tourist information	8 a.m.–7 p.m.
Foreign exchange	8 a.m.–7 p.m.
Left-luggage lockers	All hours

Daily trains to: London, Reading, Birmingham, Manchester, Liverpool, Worcester.

TOURIST INFORMATION AND ADDRESSES

Tourist information is at St Aldate's, open Mon.–Sat.: 9 a.m.–5.30 p.m., Sun.: 10 a.m.–4 p.m. Pick up their 40p leaflet and their accommodation list.

STUDENT TRAVEL: 13 High Street. Open Mon.–Fri.: 9.30 a.m.–5.30 p.m., Sat.: 10 a.m.–3 p.m.

LATE MONEY EXCHANGE: Lewis's Bank, in Selfridge's department store, Westgate. Open till 5 p.m. Mon.–Fri., Sat. till noon.

PHONE CODE: 0865.

SEEING

Carfax Tower is at the centre, and from here most of the university colleges are only a few minutes away. CHRIST CHURCH, the sixteenth-century college with its beautiful library, housing the spoils of Henry VIII's monastic plunderings, is down St Aldate's. North of this is MERTON COLLEGE, dating from the thirteenth century and with a notably attractive chapel; and next door is ORIEL. Take Bear Lane now, then cross the High Street to reach BRASENOSE COLLEGE and ALL SOULS (probably the most prestigious collection of academics around – all specially appointed to the college). At the north end of the square is the BODLEIAN LIBRARY, built in 1602 and containing over three million books. The atmosphere in here must be sampled at first hand. MAGDALEN COLLEGE (pronounced 'maudlin') on the High Street makes a lovely walk through its fifteenth-century cloisters, and the ASHMOLEAN MUSEUM on Beaumont Street (Italian and English art) is worth seeing. Turn up Cornmarket Street at Carfax and, after the new shopping centre, you'll reach BALLIOL and ST JOHN'S colleges. Opposite Balliol, Latimer and Ridley were burned by Bloody Mary in 1555, with Bishop Cranmer following a year later.

If you want to be terribly traditional and you've managed to hit a sunny afternoon, hire out a punt at the CHERWELL BOATHOUSE for about £4 an hour. Worth a quick mention here is BLENHEIM PALACE, birthplace of Winston Churchill and ancestral home of the Dukes of Marlborough. You can visit the mansion for £4.20 in season (bus 420 or 423 from Cornmarket Street).

SLEEPING

If you don't use the tourist office's services, try calling in at the many B&Bs in Abingdon Road. The youth hostel is a little too like school to be comfortable; it's on bus routes 72 and Nipper 73 at Jack Straw's Lane (Tel. 62997). There's camping at Cassington Mill Caravan Park, five miles out (Tel. 881490). Mrs R. Old at 58 St John Street (Tel. 55454) is worth a try for B&B. Oxford does get busy in summer, but owing to its proximity to London, it's possible to take it in as a day trip.

EATING AND NIGHTLIFE

There are plenty of places ideal for eurorailers for, though an Oxford student may be a cut above the average, all students still look for the same type of things when it comes to eating and what to do at night. Brown's Restaurant and Wine Bar seems pretty popular from all appearances. It's at 7 Woodstock Road, and the food and atmosphere are very acceptable. Another place worth a mention is the local for Christ Church college, The Bear in Bear Lane. There are plenty of pubs; and if you want to meet the students, simply go to the pubs closest to the colleges. Oxford's July–August Festival is fairly classical; to find out the latest events, pick up the 'What's On' at the tourist office.

Stratford-upon-Avon

About 1½ hours from Oxford and 2½ from London (Paddington Station) lies the Elizabethan town of Stratford, birthplace of William Shakespeare. The house where he was born in HANLEY STREET in 1564 is charming, or would be if it weren't for the hundreds of tourists trying to get around it. He's buried in Holy Trinity Church. Shakespeare's wife's house ANNE HATHAWAY'S COTTAGE can be visited at Shottery. Americans might also like to visit the Elizabethan HARVARD HOUSE, where the parents of John Harvard (of University fame) lived. The Royal Shakespeare Theatre and the new Swan Theatre put on productions of outstanding quality, though the cheapest tickets are about £3–£5 (Tel. 0789–292271 for information on what's playing). While you're in the area, you can pop into Shakespeare's mother's house and complete the family socializing. The HOME OF MARY ARDEN in the village of Wilmcote can be reached by local train in a matter of minutes.

TOURIST INFORMATION AND ADDRESSES

The tourist office is at 1 High St, open Mon.–Sat.: 9 a.m.–5.30 p.m., Sun.: 2 p.m.–5 p.m. in season. They'll give you a leaflet on accommodation, but the best bets are B&Bs on Evesham Place or Shipston Road.

- **Youth hostel:** Hemmingford House, Alveston (Tel. 0789–297093). Bus 518 from the bus station.

- **Camping:** The Elms, Tiddington (Tel. 0789–292312). Bus 518.

Cambridge

Oxford's great rival is the equally ancient market town and prestigious university of Cambridge which dates back to the thirteenth century and has names like Darwin, Newton, Byron and Milton in its old registers. Cambridge is 60 minutes from London (Liverpool Street Station), and once you arrive at the station, the bus to Market Square will take you to the centre of things.

STATION FACILITIES

Train information	Mon.–Sat.: 5.35 a.m.–10.35 p.m.
	Sun.: 7 a.m.–10.45 p.m.
	(Tel. 311999)
Reservations	Mon.–Sat.: 8 a.m.–8.30 p.m., British
	Mon.–Sat.: 9 a.m.–5.30 p.m., Continental
Left-luggage lockers	All hours
Left-luggage store	Mon.–Fri.: 7 a.m.–7 p.m., weekend: 9 a.m.–1 p.m.
Bar, Buffet	Mon.–Sat.: 7.30 a.m.–9.45 p.m., Sun.: 9.30 a.m.–9.30 p.m.
Station shuts	1.20 a.m.

Daily trains to: London, Birmingham, Peterborough, Norwich.

TOURIST INFORMATION AND ADDRESSES

The tourist office is at Wheeler St, open Mon.–Fri.: 9 a.m.–6 p.m., Sat.: 9 a.m.–5 p.m., Sun.: 10.30 a.m.–3.30 p.m. in season. Pick up the 35p 'Brief Guide' leaflet and ask about their walking tours.
CYCLE HIRE: Cambridge Cycle Hire, 118 Milton Road. £3 a day.
PUNT HIRE: Scudamore's Boatyards, Silver Street, or Magdalene Bridge. £4 an hour.
PHONE CODE: 0223.

SEEING

The area between Magdalene Bridge and Silver Street is the one to concentrate on. The town itself is quite substantial, and the university colleges are set apart, literally in a world of their own. THE BACKS are the meadows and fields on the other side of the Cam, and the best way to drink in this pastoral atmosphere is to hire a punt and picnic on the banks.

The main colleges to take in are: KING'S, QUEENS', CHRIST'S and TRINITY. At King's, look into the CHAPEL, and at Christ's visit the gardens which open weekdays, 2 p.m.–4 p.m.

SLEEPING

Tourist information will find you a bed for a £1 fee or hand you a list of local B&Bs. The best place to find a cheap B&B is near the station at Tenison Road or Jesus Lane in the town. Try any of the following in that lane: Mrs Spalding at No. 56 (Tel. 353858), Mrs Day at No. 72 (Tel. 356961), or Mrs Owen at No. 65 (Tel. 60648). The youth hostel is at 97 Tenison Road (Tel. 354601), and there's camping at Cambspeed Caravan Site, Wimpole Road, Barton. Not that good, 2½ miles west on bus routes 118, 120 or 175 from Drummer Street.

EATING AND NIGHTLIFE

There are hundreds of pubs and shops, and the outdoor market in Market Square is the best source for picnic food. Try the Purleigh Arms, Purleigh Street, for good meals, or the Man on the Moon, near the Grafton Centre, the King's Pantry at 9 King's Parade or the Fort St George on Jesus Green. The Maypole, in Portugal Place, does excellent cocktails. Try also the Cambridge Arms in King Street.

Ask tourist information for the 'What's On', as there's always a round of plays, films or debates. The best value is the Cambridge University Amateur Dramatic Club, Park Street. Their productions are good and their prices low, £1.50–£4 (Tel. 352000 to see what's playing).

During the last two weeks of July see the Cambridge Festival which is not all classical; some of their folk concerts are excellent.

Get tickets from Central Library, Lion Yard. For live music, try Old Orleans on Mill Lane.

Wales

Wales is a rugged land of 8,000 square miles and 2¾ million people, about a fifth of whom still speak Welsh. It is wilder than England and less dramatic than Scotland, and for a while you'd never know you were over the English border; but travel to the SNOWDONIA NATIONAL PARK in the north-west, taking the SNOWDON MOUNTAIN RAILWAY up Mount Snowdon, or listen to the soft-spoken Welsh in the north, and you'll be glad you took in this extra country.

South Wales

South Wales was once a centre of coal mining and heavy industry. This has now receded but elements of it remain. CARDIFF, the capital, is about 2 hours from London and an hour from Bristol. There's an increasing amount here to merit a stop, and the CASTLE and WELSH NATIONAL MUSEUM are worth seeing, and the WELSH OPEN-AIR FOLK MUSEUM, five miles out at St Fagans (bus 32), is fascinating.

From the eurorailer's point of view, southern Wales is not ideally planned, as most of the interesting places aren't on any line. The BRECON BEACONS NATIONAL PARK is best reached from ABERGAVENNY, which is on the Crewe–Cardiff line. There's tourist information about the park at Swan Meadow, Monmouth Road (open Easter–October) and you're OK to camp where you like in the park, provided you check with the local farmer first. There are six youth hostels in all, and many B&Bs, and the countryside is marvellous. The other big attraction of the south is the other National Park: the PEMBROKESHIRE COAST, a similar set-up on the west coast.

ABERYSTWYTH, seat of the University of Wales and popular resort with Welsh grannies, is worth a look. Early Welsh manuscripts are in the NATIONAL LIBRARY, and visit the ABERYSTWYTH ARTS CENTRE while you're here. Tourist information at 13 Eastgate Street is open 9 a.m.–6 p.m. in season. The Vale of Rheidol Steam Railway leaves for the waterfalls at DEVIL'S BRIDGE daily – a must for train buffs.

North Wales

The SNOWDONIA NATIONAL PARK covers half of North Wales and is one of Europe's best regions for getting away from it all. The terrain is ideal for climbing, hiking, camping or hostelling. Make your way to the town of CAERNARFON, the thirteenth-century town with its incredibly well-preserved medieval CASTLE where the investiture of Prince Charles took place. Take the train to BANGOR, on the Holyhead line, then bus it to Caernarfon, and from there bus to LLANBERIS, where the SNOWDON MOUNTAIN RAILWAY will hoist you to the mountain's summit (but it's expensive: about £10 return). Other great castles in this area are at Harlech, Conwy and Beaumaris on the island of Anglesey (Yns Mon).

If you are interested in ecology, conservation and the environment a visit to the Centre for Alternative Technology is a must. Set in a slate quarry overlooking the Snowdonia National Park, near Machynlleth, the centre is a maze of windmills, aerogenerators, solar heating panels and water turbines. It is situated three miles from Machynlleth Station, where you can get a bus to the adjacent village of Pantperthog. Open every day 10 a.m.–7 p.m. (Tel. 0654–2400). Entrance costs £2.50 (students £1.50).

Each July the small town of LLANGOLLEN hosts the EISTEDDFOD, an international music festival of Welsh culture. There's also a steam railway here. Buses run from Wrexham and Chirk railway stations to Llangollen.

Northern England

LIVERPOOL

Liverpool is similar to Glasgow in that it has received a lot of bad press internationally and has a bad public image. In fact the crime rate is no higher than in any other major city and the people are renowned for their wit and friendliness. Tourism is a growth industry in Merseyside, and many people who come solely because of the Beatles are surprised to find much more.

STATION FACILITIES

	LIME STREET STATION (INTER CITY)
Ticket office	Mon.–Sun.: 5 a.m.–1 a.m.
Travel centre	Mon.–Sun.: 8 a.m.–8 p.m.
Left-luggage	Mon.–Sat.: 6.30 a.m.–10 a.m., 10.30 a.m.–6 p.m., 6.30 p.m.–9.30 p.m. Opens 7 a.m. Sun.
Restaurant	Mon.–Sun.: 7 a.m.–10 p.m.
Telephone	051-709 9696

Daily trains to: London, Manchester, Birmingham, South-West, Wales, Scotland, Lake District, Newcastle.

● **Merseyrail Underground:** Lime Street, James Street, Central and Moorfields stations in the city centre. Underground and bus information (Tel. 051–236 7676). Frequent trains to Southport, Chester, Ormskirk, Wirral, North Wales, Manchester.

TOURIST INFORMATION

There are information offices on Lime Street and in Clayton Square shopping centre and the Albert Dock. Bus information from Merseytravel office, Williamson Square.
PHONE CODE: 051.

SEEING

ALBERT DOCK on the waterfront is the largest grade 1 listed building in the country. It has been restored and now hosts an array of small shops, cafés and exclusive apartments. It is rapidly becoming one of the most popular tourist attractions in the country. The Albert Dock also hosts the northern branch of London's famous TATE GALLERY. Admission is free although there is often a small charge for admission to special exhibitions. Also at the Albert Dock is the MERSEYSIDE MARITIME MUSEUM – a museum which traces

Liverpool's maritime history. Nearby is the PIER HEAD which holds the three buildings which dominate Liverpool's skyline. From here you can still get a Ferry 'Cross the Mersey. Other things to see in the city centre include the two modern cathedrals. LIVERPOOL CATHEDRAL is a huge gothic building completed in the 1980s. It is the second largest Anglican cathedral in the world after St Paul's and houses the largest pipe organ in Europe. There are often recitals on bank holidays. In complete contrast at the other end of Hope Street is the Catholic LIVERPOOL METROPOLITAN CATHEDRAL – a concrete and glass circular structure known locally as 'Paddy's Wigwam'. Inside the spray of light from the stained glass can be quite beautiful. If you've come to Liverpool in search of the Beatles, stop off at one of the information shops first. These will give you information about all the walking and coach tours available. The original Cavern club was demolished some years ago but a faithful replica has been constructed a little further down Matthew Street in the Cavern Walks Shopping Centre. If you want to see Penny Lane, Strawberry Fields etc., take a coach trip. Liverpool is famous for its footballing tradition. During the football season, matches can be seen on a Saturday at Liverpool or Everton FCs.

SLEEPING

The YMCA, YWCA and numerous small B&B hotels can be found on Mount Pleasant near the Catholic cathedral and 10 minutes' walk from the station.

EATING

There are numerous fast-food and fish and chip shops dotted throughout the city centre. Alternatively, make a picnic with food from one of the city centre shops.

The industrial north has a few saving graces from its heavy-industry towns in the form of the YORKSHIRE MOORS in the east, and the LAKE DISTRICT in the west. The moors are wild, untouched terrain, ideal for hiking and camping as long as you don't mind isolation. The NORTH YORK MOORS NATIONAL PARK has a tourist office at PICKERING STATION, which is as good a place as any to base yourself. The

LAKE DISTRICT NATIONAL PARK is considered to be the country's best. The main centres, and also the most touristy in summer, are KESWICK, WINDERMERE and GRASMERE. There's a station at Windermere, and for Keswick use PENRITH. For tourist information, contact the office in Victoria Street, Penrith, open 10 a.m.–8.30 p.m. in season. There are thirty youth hostels (the world's highest density) and the Park Service run a series of free guided walks and courses in summer.

York

York dates back to Roman times and is considered Britain's best-preserved medieval city with the finest Gothic cathedral. It lies about halfway between London and Edinburgh on the east-coast line, and with the fast 125 intercity service, it takes only 2½ hours from the capital. However, as this route is being electrified at present, delays – particularly at weekends – may be expected.

STATION FACILITIES

Train information	8 a.m.–9 p.m.
	(Tel. 25671)
Reservations	8 a.m.–9 p.m.
Left-luggage store	Open 24 hours
Bar, Buffet	24 hours (Platform 14)
Restaurant	6.30 a.m.–10 p.m.
Bookshop	6.15 a.m.–7 p.m.

Daily trains to: London, Edinburgh, Leeds, the Midlands, the West Country, South Wales, Liverpool, Manchester, Scarborough, Harrogate.

TOURIST INFORMATION AND ADDRESSES

The tourist information centre is in Exhibition Square and at the station, and is open Mon.–Sat.: 9 a.m.–8 p.m., Sun.: 2 p.m.–5 p.m. in season. They run a free two-hour walking tour from the Art Gallery at 10.15 a.m., 2.15 p.m. and 7.15 p.m.
PHONE CODE: 0904.

SEEING

There are four main entrances to the city: BOOTHAM GATE, MICKLE-GATE, MONKGATE and WALMGATE, and the city is surrounded by three miles of defensive walls. York MINSTER (the cathedral which had a tied school) is amazing: the Great East Window is as big as a tennis court, and all the stained glass is medieval. Once you've wandered around the cathedral, visit the CASTLE MUSEUM which is an exceptionally good folk museum with reconstructions of streets, people and implements of the last century. For evidence of the Romans, go to the MULTI-ANGULAR TOWER in the Yorkshire Museum Gardens. The JORVIK VIKING CENTRE in Coppergate is an essential stopping-off place if you are keen on history. York of 1,000 years ago comes to life in this fascinating museum. Real train enthusiasts will like the NATIONAL RAILWAY MUSEUM down by the station – plenty of steam locos, etc. There are many other historic and interesting places, like the TREASURER'S HOUSE, CLIFFORD'S TOWER, and the wonderful old shopping streets of medieval York like the SHAMBLES, and the site of the old whipping post, WHIP-MA-WHOP-MA-GATE. Pick up detailed leaflets from tourist information. While you're in the area, you might want to visit CASTLE HOWARD, the beautiful eighteenth-century setting of *Brideshead Revisited*. Ask tourist information for the best buses.

SLEEPING

Tourist information will give you lists of B&Bs and hostels, or find you a room for free (with a £1.75 deposit). York can get very busy in summer, so get fixed up as soon as you arrive. The area round Bootham is not bad for B&B, and there's a youth hostel at Water End, Clifton (Tel. 653147), though it's rule-ridden and usually full. Bishophill House is a private hostel at 11–13 Bishophill Senior Road (Tel. 625904) or there's the International House, 33 Bootham (Tel. 622874). For B&B try Bishopthorpe Road in Bootham, or the Mount area down Blossom Street. The campsite, open May–Sept., is three miles out of town at Bishopsthorpe (Tel. 704442).

EATING AND NIGHTLIFE

There are bakers' shops, markets and pubs a-plenty in York. York Wholefood, 98 Micklegate, do good meals upstairs, and Kooks at

108 Fishergate (closed Mon.) is also worth a try. With over 150 pubs, you shouldn't get stuck for a watering hole. The Black Swan in Peasholme Green is a suitably olde-worlde place, but there are many more dotted around.

York–Edinburgh

Fifty minutes further up the line from York is the cathedral town of DURHAM. You should take an hour or two of even the most hurried journey off, and catch the next 125, to see the magnificent CATHEDRAL and CASTLE there (not open to the public as it is part of the university). They face each other over Palace Green in a dramatic setting. The cathedral is eleventh-century and is considered one of Europe's finest Romanesque examples; and the castle dates from the same time with fourteenth-century additions. The fortified town of BERWICK-UPON-TWEED is the border between the ancient enemies, Scotland and England. Should you break your journey here, see the old city walls and elegant eighteenth-century TOWN HALL. From the border it's an hour to Edinburgh, Scotland's majestic capital.

Scotland

The scenery in the Scottish Highlands is outstanding: the glens and mountains, lochs and islands are unique in their unspoilt beauty. Were the weather only a bit better, Scotland would be the answer to everyone's holiday problems; however, let's be honest – you don't come here for a tan, you come to hike on the hills or wander through the historic streets of Edinburgh. The rail network is a bit restricted up north, but if you travel up the east coast to Inverness, then over to Kyle of Lochalsh, taking the boat from Mallaig, then back down the west coast via Oban to Glasgow, Scotland's largest industrial city, you'll get a good idea of the geography. Now, without going into a detailed account, until the eighteenth century, the English and the Scots shared nothing in common and, as far as many Scots are concerned, they still don't. Remember this when you're making small talk with them, and do try not to refer to the whole of Great Britain as just 'England' – it doesn't go down too well in these parts.

Edinburgh

The elegant city of Edinburgh can't fail to strike the visitor as dramatic: built on extinct volcanoes with a fairytale castle dominating the city, and hills and the sea all around. It's the artistic, commercial, academic and legal centre of Scotland and its history goes back to the seventh century. As soon as you walk up the hill from Waverley Station you're in the centre of things, with the castle and 'old town' behind and to your left, and the 'new town' from the Georgian era on your right.

STATION FACILITIES

	WAVERLEY STATION
Train information	Mon.–Sat.: 8 a.m.–11 p.m., Sun.: 9 a.m.–11 p.m. (Tel. 556 2451, 24 hours)
Reservations	Mon.–Sat.: 8 a.m.–8 p.m., Sun.: 9 a.m.–8 p.m.
Tourist information	100 yards from station
Foreign exchange	3 a.m.–12 midnight
Left-luggage store	Mon.–Sat.: 6 a.m.–10.50 p.m. Sun.: 7 a.m.–10.50 p.m.
Bar	Mon.–Sat.: 7 a.m.–1 a.m. Sun.: 12.30 a.m.–2.30 p.m., 6.30 p.m.–11 p.m.
Restaurant	6.30 a.m.–10.30 p.m.
Bath, Shower	3 a.m.–12 midnight
Station shuts	0.30 a.m.–2.30 a.m.

Daily trains to: Aberdeen, Birmingham, Bristol, Glasgow, Inverness, Liverpool, London, Manchester, Perth, Stirling.

TOURIST INFORMATION AND ADDRESSES

The Tourist Information and Accommodation Centre is in the Waverley Market, just up the ramp and to your right from the station, open weekdays 8.30 a.m.–9 p.m., Sun.: 11 a.m.–9 p.m. in season. Ask for 'What's On', and get details on the rest of the country from the Scottish Tourist Board desk in there. Good Bureau de Change (Tel. 557 2727). There's also the Scottish Tourist Board Travel Centre at 14 South St Andrew Street (Tel. 557 5522), open weekdays 9 a.m.–5.30 p.m., Sat. 9 a.m.–1 p.m. Pick up literature on the whole of Scotland here. Packed with useful information, such as where to eat and what to see, the pocket-sized EDINBURGH CITY GUIDE is one of the best all-round city guidebooks. Good value at around £2.50 in bookshops.

POST OFFICE: 2–4 Waterloo Place (at east end of Princes Street), open Mon.–Fri.: 9 a.m.–5.30 p.m., Sat.: 9 a.m.–12.30 p.m. Currency exchange.

AMEX: 139 Princes Street, open Mon.–Fri.: 9 a.m.–5 p.m., Sat.: 9 a.m.–12 noon (Tel. 225 7881).

US CONSULATE: 3 Regent Terrace (Tel. 556 8315).

AUSTRALIAN CONSULATE: 80 Hanover Street (Tel. 226 6271).

MEDICAL HELP: University Health Service, Bristo Square (Tel. 667 1011).

CAMPUS TRAVEL EUROTRAIN: 5 Nicolson Square (Tel. 668 3303).

PHONE CODE: 031.

SEEING

The medieval ROYAL MILE was so called because it stretches from the CASTLE to the royal palace of HOLYROOD. You can't possibly miss the castle which dates back to the seventh century. It stands on an extinct volcano and can be seen from virtually every corner of Edinburgh. Though entrance is £2.20 (there's no student discount), if you're keen on history it's worth it. The Scottish Crown Jewels are on display here and you can see QUEEN MARGARET'S CHAPEL, the smallest in Scotland and the oldest building in the city. Walking down the Royal Mile, you'll find GLADSTONE'S LAND, a beautifully preserved medieval townhouse in the Lawnmarket, well worth a visit, and behind this is LADY STAIR'S HOUSE with Burns, Stevenson and Scott mementoes. ST GILES' CATHEDRAL, the Gothic 1385 High Church of Scotland, is on the right, as are various buildings of the Scottish parliament. Halfway down in the Canongate is JOHN KNOX'S HOUSE and the MUSEUM OF CHILDHOOD, an interesting collection of toys and games from bygone days. After a tour of the sixteenth-century palace, clear your head with a good blast of Scottish air up another of Edinburgh's extinct volcanoes, ARTHUR'S SEAT, or walk to CALTON HILL at the east end of Princes Street to look at 'Edinburgh's Disgrace': the replica of the Athens Parthenon that ran out of money and remains unfinished.

On one side of Princes Street are the city's main shops, while opposite are gardens and the two neo-classical art galleries: the NATIONAL GALLERY OF SCOTLAND and the ROYAL ACADEMY, both particularly impressive. WALTER SCOTT'S MONUMENT, the huge Gothic tower in Princes Street Gardens, affords a good view from the top, and from here a walk up Hanover Street will take you down to Queen Street where, along on the right, you'll find Scotland's MUSEUM OF ANTIQUITIES. Bus 23 or 27 from Hanover Street will take you down to the BOTANICAL GARDENS which are a glorious picnic venue and you'll find the NATIONAL GALLERY OF MODERN ART near DEAN VILLAGE on Belford Road. If you've any time left, search out the GEORGIAN HOUSE, on CHARLOTTE SQUARE, THE ZOO, one of the finest in Britain, and take bus 41 out to CRAMOND, down by the sea. During the International Festival and its Fringe, literally hundreds of events are staged: plays, concerts, exhibitions; and every church hall in the city has some group performing in it. Thousands of students descend on the city, as tickets start as low as £2. Running at the same time are the film and jazz festivals, and the bonanza of the MILITARY TATTOO with enough kilts and bagpipes to satisfy even the most ardent American. Tattoo office: Tel. 225 1188, Fringe office: Tel. 226 5257.

Go to INCHCOLM ISLAND in the Firth of Forth for a great day out. The 'Iona of the East' has a beautiful medieval abbey and hundreds of seabirds nest here. It is also home to grey seals. To get there take a train to SOUTH QUEENSFERRY and then a ferry which leaves across from the Hawes Inn, where Robert Louis Stevenson is known to have downed a few (cost £4.50 return, £3.50 for students). Runs May to September.

SLEEPING

Aside from late August–September (Festival time), a bed's not too much of a hassle, and the tourist information centre will help you out. They're open till 9 p.m. and have a free list of suggestions. For

B&Bs, take a bus out to Newington and look along Newington and Minto Streets, or try the Bruntsfield area.

• **Hostels:** The youth hostels are at 18 Eglinton Crescent (Tel. 337 1120) and 7–8 Bruntsfield Crescent (Tel. 447 2994).

The University Halls of Residence, Pollock Halls, 18 Holyrood Park Road (Tel. 667 1971), are very good and offer 1,500 single rooms at around £9.70 for students, £16.25 otherwise. Take buses 21 or 33 to the Commonwealth Pool.

The High Street Hostel (Tel. 557 3984) at 8 Blackfriars Street is situated halfway between the castle and the Palace of Holyrood House and only a few minutes' walk up the hill from Waverley Station. It costs £5 and you don't need an IYHF card. It is open from 7 a.m. to 2 a.m. although 24-hour access can be arranged. There is a free left-luggage service and showers. Accommodation is in dormitories of about 12 beds. To camp, take bus 33 out to Little France, Old Dalkeith Road (Tel. 664 4742).

• **Hotels:** The Roxburghe Hotel, Charlotte Square (Tel. 225 3921) is a fine, central first-class hotel for the Adult Eurail market while Johnstonburn House Hotel at Humbie, half an hour south of Edinburgh, is a country house hotel of great character and quality, offering traditional comforts and excellent cuisine in an historic setting. The Adult Eurail market will also find the Greywalls Hotel in Gullane, near Edinburgh a delightful place to dine or spend a weekend. This luxury country house hotel is a fine example of a traditional British estate, and apart from its exceptional restaurant and good accommodation, it has the luck to be situated right next to one of Britain's finest golf courses – Muirfield, dramatically positioned right next to the sea. Take the train to Drem and a cab from there. Booking ahead in summer is advisable. (Tel. 0620–842144).

EATING AND NIGHTLIFE

Cheap eats are no problem in Edinburgh and it's possible to fill up for under £1.50 at either a fish'n'chip shop or a filled baked potato carry-out; Edinburgh specializes in these, and there are Spud-U-Like shops dotted around the centre. Pick up the free leaflet from tourist information on restaurants. Pubs often offer cheap lunches, and this capital has over 500 to choose from. The University

Students' Union at Teviot Row (up the Mound, and George IV Bridge) do meals for about £1.50, or try Henderson's Salad Table, 94 Hanover Street, for healthy meals around £5. Also good value is Bell's diner at 26 St Stephen Street in Stockbridge (Tel. 225 8116). It's a very popular eating place, selling home-made burgers, salads, delicious sweet courses and house wines. Book ahead. Edinburgh has restaurants representing a huge number of countries, try the French Ma Cuisine on St Stephen's Street and Viva Mexico just off Cockburn Street.

If you're here in Festival time, the nightlife position is unmatched anywhere else in Britain. Go along to the Fringe Club, in Teviot Row, off Bristo Square (Tel. 667 2091), where performers, the media and the public gather to socialize (£16 membership for the Festival's duration, bring a passport photo). Be sure to pick up the Fringe programme for the widest range of entertainment you're likely to find anywhere. If you're visiting at any other time, pick up 'What's On' from tourist information and combine some events with a visit to some of the city's pubs; a popular pub crawl is along the nineteen bars of Rose Street. Many students hang out in the George Square area pubs such as the Pear Tree, Maxie's, Bristo, and the up-market, continental wine bar, Negociants, opposite the Teviot Row Students' Union. Café Royal, just behind the large Wimpy at the east end of Princes Street, is an outstanding example of a fine Victorian pub. Check out the ceiling in their upstairs bar. They do good bar lunches too.

If you are splashing out, try Jackson's Restaurant in Jackson's Close, off the Royal Mile. They do an excellent menu including traditional Scottish food and wine.

Check out what's playing in the Film House, Calton Studios or Traverse Theatre.

Glasgow

Just 45 minutes on one of the half-hourly expresses from Edinburgh is Glasgow, Scotland's largest city and business centre. While it does not have the immediate visual presence of Edinburgh, Glasgow is still a beautiful Victorian city and well worth a visit.

Thanks to the 'Glasgow's Miles Better' campaign which started some years ago, it is gradually shaking off an unfair reputation for being violent and dirty. In recent years many buildings have been cleaned and the environment generally improved, although for many years it has had more parks per head of population (780,000) than any other city in Europe – a fact which has surprised many visitors. In Glasgow it's not so much the buildings you come to see (as with Edinburgh) but the people. They are regarded as the warmest, most outgoing lot in Britain, and a visit to a few pubs will confirm that. Last year it hosted a Garden Festival and it is the 1990 European City of Culture.

SEEING

When you get off the train at Queen Street Station go straight ahead into George Square and turn right into St Vincent Place. The tourist office is on the left-hand side (Tel. 041–227 4880), where you can pick up leaflets, get information about places to see and book accommodation. Without doubt the major attraction is the BURRELL COLLECTION, an 8,000-piece artistic treasure trove, gathered together over a lifetime of collecting on every continent by Glasgow shipping magnate Sir William Burrell. Entry is free to the collection, which was donated to the people of Glasgow in 1944 but opened only in 1983. The award-winning building housing the collection is situated in POLLOK COUNTRY PARK. Take a train from Glasgow Central to Pollokshaws West and then the free bus from the entrance next to the station. If you don't want to wait for the bus (every 20 minutes) walk through the 361 acres of parkland and gardens and see the herd of Highland cattle near to Pollok House. In Pollok House is one of the finest collections of Spanish paintings in Britain. Entry to both museums is free of charge and they have the same opening hours: Mon.–Sat.: 10 a.m.–5 p.m., Sun.: 2 p.m.–5 p.m. The ART GALLERY AND MUSEUM, at Kelvingrove, is also worth visiting as it houses Britain's finest civic collection of British and European paintings including Salvador Dali's 'Crucifixion'. Charles Rennie Macintosh came from Glasgow and many of the buildings he designed can be seen in the city. The Headquarters of the CHARLES RENNIE MACINTOSH SOCIETY (formerly Queen's Cross Church) are at 866 Garscube Road, open Tue., Thur., Fri.: 12 noon–5.30 p.m., Sun.: 2.30 p.m.–5.30 p.m. In the city centre you can visit and have tea at the WILLOW TEA ROOM, a famous Macintosh building recently restored, at 217 Sauchiehall Street (Tel. 041–332 0521) Mon.–Sat.: 9.30 a.m.–5 p.m.

It is only a short distance from Glasgow to the spectacular scenery of the TROSSACHS or LOCH LOMOND and bus tours to both places – and many others – run from Buchanan Bus Station in the city centre (Tel. 041–332 7133). Alternatively you can head over to the Island of ARRAN. Trains to Ardrossan Harbour leave from Central Station and take just over an hour. The ferry takes under an hour to Brodick and there are connecting buses there to take you to the two hostels on the island, one in the south at Whiting Bay (Tel. 077 07–339) and the other in the more mountainous north at Lochranza (Tel. 077 083–631).

SLEEPING

The youth hostel is near the Art Gallery. Take a train from Queen Street low level one stop to Charing Cross and head up the hill following the signs. It's at 11 Woodlands Terrace (Tel. 041–332 3004). Alternatively, try the University of Glasgow Halls of Residence, bookable through the tourist office. An unofficial hostel, run on foreign lines with a relaxed attitude to curfews and duties, it operates each summer. The Glasgow Central Tourist Hostel is situated in the Balmanno Building, 81 Rottenrow East (Tel. 041–552 2401/2). It is a few minutes' walk from George Square and Queen Street Station, close to the University of Strathclyde.

EATING AND NIGHTLIFE

In the same area are two restaurants worth seeking out. The Ubiquitous Chip, at 12 Ashton Lane, also specializes in traditional Scottish food but is better known for its wine cellar, reputed to be among the top ten in Britain. Imaginative top-grade food served at medium-grade prices makes this an essential meeting place for the young, arty crowd (Tel. 041–334 5007). Glasgow also has a fine selection of Indian restaurants. One definitely not to be missed is the Shish Mahal in Gibson Street, near Glasgow University. The popularity of this place makes booking more or less essential (Tel. 041–339 8256) and you'll find well-prepared Indian dishes at reasonable prices, as well as meeting a few Glaswegian students. In the city centre try Babbity Bowster, a café/bar/restaurant which is full of character. The food is excellent and reasonably priced. It is at 16/18 Blackfriars Street (Tel. 041–552 5055). Texas Fever at 46 West George Street is one of the grooviest nightclubs in town.

On to Inverness

From Edinburgh or Glasgow it's a 4-hour journey up to Inverness, capital of the Highlands. The route is via Perth and Aviemore and, once you're up at Pitlochry, the scenery is wonderful. Perthshire is one of Britain's most splendid regions. Majestic landscapes and pretty villages; neat, clean towns and wonderful old country houses, many of which now serve as de luxe hotels and restaurants, are some of the attractions of this area. Perth and Stirling are the two main stopping-off stations, and from there regular buses allow you to explore the hidden corners of this unspoilt part of the UK.

A quick rundown on Inverness is all that is needed, for while it's a pleasant enough place, you should really just use it as a base for the surrounding country. While there, wander round LOCH NESS where the elusive monster is said to live, and visit CAWDOR CASTLE (twelve miles east) where Shakespeare set *Macbeth*. There are plenty of B&Bs around Old Edinburgh Road, as is the youth hostel at No. 1 (Tel. 0463–231771), and camping down by the river on the Craig Dunain bus route (Tel. 0463–236920).

Culloden House Hotel, three miles from the town centre, where the station is located, is the recommended luxury hotel in this area of the Highlands. While it is strictly in the 'afternoon tea only' category to most Inter-Railers, those on the Adult Eurail Pass may well consider splurging on a night in sumptuous historic surroundings, enjoying traditionally prepared dishes, and relaxing in the sort of luxury you'd forgotten existed after a few weeks on the road. It's well worth the trip out, even if just to see the eighteenth-century buildings and enjoy the surrounding countryside (Tel. 0463–790461). Tourist information at 23 Church Street is open Mon.–Sat.: 9 a.m.–8 p.m., Sun.: 2 p.m.–6 p.m. in summer. To get into the corners not covered by rail, rent a bike from Ness Motors or the youth hostel and, armed with a map, head for the north side of Loch Ness and Urquhart Castle. If you're lucky you may even see the monster here.

The Highlands and Islands

From Inverness, take the train west to KYLE OF LOCHALSH, a 170-minute journey of beautiful unspoilt scenery through the Wester Ross mountains. From Kyle there's a frequent five-minute ferry over to Kyleakin on the ISLE OF SKYE, Britain's most dramatic island. The peace and beauty of the Black Cuillin Hills and the haunting cloud formations are quite unmatched elsewhere. POR-TREE, the island's capital, has a tourist office overlooking the harbour. Skye can also be approached from MALLAIG, and from Mallaig you're back on the main line to FORT WILLIAM and GLASGOW. If you were thinking of heading further north, there's a line from Inverness to WICK; but it's pretty desolate up there, so think twice. If it's isolation you're after, try the ORKNEY ISLANDS. These ex-Danish colonies are well worth visiting; the easiest approach is the ferry from John O'Groats. Visit the Stone Age settlement of SKARA BRAE and the Bronze Age STANDING STONES OF STENNESS and RING OF BRODGAR. The Oban–Glasgow run is another favourite for Highland scenery, 3½ hours of it. From OBAN you can visit the beautiful ISLE OF MULL, and from there go to the smaller, more isolated islands of Iona, Staffa, Coll and Tiree. Tourist information in Oban is at Argyll Square, turn right from the station; and there's a hostel on the Esplanade (Tel. 0631–62025).

Northern Ireland

Many more tourists are now visiting Northern Ireland despite the current 'troubles'. Bear in mind that the media tend to inflate it out of all proportion, and that most of the province is safe to visit, particularly if you're obviously a tourist. However, you may lay yourself open to security-checks from the armed forces in the affected areas. That said, the scenery is nice and varied for such a small area, with lots of mountains, lakes, caves, cliffs and some wonderful sandy beaches.

The Northern Ireland Railways Board offer a 50 per cent discount if you bought your Inter Rail from BR, NIR or IE. There are three main rail routes from Belfast Central Station (Tel. 0232–230310) – north to Londonderry via Ballymena and Coleraine, east to Bangor, and south to Dublin via Lisburn, Portadown and Newry. The Dublin–Belfast Express takes about 2 hours. The boat-train for Scotland leaves from York Street Station, Belfast (Tel. 0232–235282) to the ferry from Larne to Stranraer in south-west Scotland.

Taking the capital, Belfast, as the centre, you'll find COUNTY DOWN and the MOURNE MOUNTAINS to the south, ARMAGH to the west, FERMANAGH further west and TYRONE inland. COUNTY LONDONDERRY is in the north-west corner and COUNTY ANTRIM in the north-east. At TORR HEAD you're only thirteen miles from Scotland, and in the north-west of Antrim's coast is the GIANT'S CAUSEWAY, the famous rock formation. The Whitepark Bay Youth Hostel (Tel. 02657–31745) is nearby.

The main things to see in BELFAST are in the UNIVERSITY area and the city centre round DONEGALL SQUARE where the Renaissance City Hall is. Also worth a mention are the OPERA HOUSE and the ULSTER MUSEUM and ART GALLERY in the Botanic Gardens. The ULSTER FOLK AND TRANSPORT MUSEUM at Cultra Manor, Holywood, six miles from Belfast, is well worth the detour. There are reconstructions of nineteenth-century life from farms to craft centres. Tourist information is at 48–52 High Street and there's a youth hostel at 11 Saintfield Rd (Tel. 0232–647865) on bus routes 83, 84 or 38. The city bus tour is as good a way as any of seeing Belfast's sights.

LONDONDERRY, 2 hours from Belfast, is one of Northern Ireland's most attractive towns. The OLD CITY WALLS have withstood invaders for over 350 years, and while you can walk the one-mile circuit to see good views of the city, they are hardly laid out as a walk. The GUILDHALL in Shipquay Place is a modern Gothic building whose stained-glass windows tell the city's history. You'll find tourist information down here too, at Foyle Street, and the seventeenth-century Protestant cathedral.

YUGOSLAVIA (Jugoslavija)

Entry requirements	Passport
Population	23,600,000
Capital	Belgrade (pop.: 1,850,000)
Currency	New Dinar
	£1 = approx. 19.50 D
Political system	Socialist Federal Republic
Religions	Serbian Orthodox, Muslim, Catholic, Protestant
Languages	Serbo-Croat, Slovenian, Macedonian (some English, German, Italian and French understood)
Public holidays	1, 2 Jan.; 1, 2 May; 4 July; 29, 30 Nov.
International dialling codes	From UK: 010 + 38 + number
	From USA: 011 + 38 + number
	To UK: 99 + 44 + number
	To USA: 99 + 1 + number

Yugoslavia is one of the most complex and culturally diverse countries in Europe. There are no less than six republics (Bosnia–Hercegovina, Montenegro, Croatia, Macedonia, Slovenia and Serbia) inhabited by at least eight nationalities, speaking five different languages and using two alphabets (Cyrillic and Latin). To make matters even more complicated, they practise four separate religions. Understandably, the country is rich in folklore and the Yugoslavs are proud of their traditional differences, although they are leading to strong tensions as the other Socialist countries are being transformed. For several centuries Yugoslavia was dominated by the Austro-Hungarian Empire in the north and by the Turks in the south. Then, in the aftermath of the First World War, present-day Yugoslavia was created. During the Second World War about a fifth of the country's population was killed, many by fellow Yugoslavs in the civil war which developed. From this period emerged Marshal Tito who died in 1980. He managed to keep the country together and preserve a non-aligned status until his death. Today Yugoslavia is a centralized economy, where tourism is encouraged as an important source of revenue. The country is suffering the effects of over-borrowing from the West in the '70s and in 1988 inflation reached a frightening 140 per cent. The value of the dinar has sunk in recent years, having dropped from 175 to the £ in the summer of 1984 to 10,000 to the £ in 1989. The dinar was revalued in January 1990 to make transactions more manageable. While this means you get bargains everywhere, they are constantly being eroded by rapidly rising prices. The prices mentioned in this chapter are therefore only a rough guide.

YUGOSLAV STATE RAILWAYS
(Jugoslovenske Železnica, JZ)

Most Yugoslav trains have a well-deserved reputation for being slow and dirty, although recent investment has seen a vast improvement in some services. Most expresses are electric, but many local trains and railcars, particularly the newest ones, are diesel. The majority of JZ rolling stock consists of redundant German carriages pensioned off years ago, so if you have to travel through Yugoslavia stick to international expresses and head for carriages from other countries such as Austria, France and Switzerland. Despite that, JZ has recently bought some new stock and on these trains air-conditioning means something other than a permanently open door. The afternoon express from Zagreb to Ljubljana, for instance, uses the most modern railcars, with aircraft-style seating, air-conditioning, piped music, free newspapers, soft drinks and sandwiches. Coffee, however, is extra. But like the rest of Yugoslavia, the railway system is full of contrasts, and your next train is likely to be an ancient carriage with blocked loos, opaque windows and hard seats.

All the major towns are linked by rail, but only a few lines go as far as the coast. Don't be misled by the impressive variety of trains operating within Yugoslavia, as only the international expresses are worth travelling on. Listed here in descending order of comfort and speed are the options open to the eurorailer: international expresses, inland expresses (Ekspresni), rapides (Poslovni), fast (Brzi) and the unspeakably slow trains (Putnički). Unless you plan to visit Belgrade, go for a through express, as changing trains here nearly always means no seat for the second leg of your journey. To make things easier, here are the origins and destinations of the main international expresses:

Simplon: London–Paris–Milan–Belgrade
Venezia: Venice–Belgrade–(Sofia–Istanbul)–Athens

Acropolis: Munich–Ljubljana–Belgrade–Kosovo Polje–Skopje–Athens
Yugoslavia: Frankfurt–Munich–Ljubljana–Zagreb
Hellas: Dortmund–Munich–Belgrade–Skopje–Athens
Tauern: London–Ostend–Aachen–Cologne–Munich–Zagreb–Knin–Split
Istanbul: Munich–Belgrade–Sofia–Istanbul
Mostar: Stuttgart–Munich–Zagreb–Sarajevo–Kardeljevo   (in winter also Zagreb–Knin–Split)

It's strongly advisable to reserve a seat on any of these expresses, all of which are valid on Inter Rail. Reservations are obligatory from stations in Germany to stations in Yugoslavia and Greece. Beware guards trying to collect unofficial supplements.

TRAIN INFORMATION

English is spoken by most information staff; if not, try German. In the backwaters, rely on your ingenuity as there won't be any information staff, let alone English speakers.

• **Reservations:** Are obligatory on some internal routes. Trains from Belgrade south to Athens and north to Zagreb or Budapest are invariably packed – get a reservation if you can, otherwise you may end up in the corridor or (better) the baggage car, a practice that guards tend to tolerate. Note that reserved seats are not marked.

• **Night travel:** Yugoslavian couchettes are quite comfortable but difficult to get hold of (if possible, try for a couchette from Vienna). The price of sleepers will keep you awake worrying, so you may as well forget them.

• **Buses:** Yugoslavia has an extensive network of bus services linking major and minor towns. The bus station is usually next door to the railway station, and often has better facilities. The staff are generally helpful. The buses themselves, like the trains, range from the ultra-modern to the decrepit, but they serve many places where the railway doesn't run and are always faster than Putnički trains. Fares are very cheap. Inter-Railers can save money by buying green bus tokens at news stands.

• **Eating on trains:** Most expresses and fast trains have bars and diners. Other trains may have mini-bars but the food is expensive and drink even worse. It is far cheaper and better to buy bread, cheese and meat in shops near the station. Also, go for the excellent range of Fructal carton fruit drinks. Most stations have drinking water taps on the platforms.

• **Scenic tips:** Three-quarters of Yugoslavia is covered by mountains and one-third by forests, so there are plenty of options. The most spectacular route is the recently opened Belgrade–Bar line to the Montenegrin coast. A particularly breathtaking bus ride is Cetinje to Kotor.

TOURIST INFORMATION

All major cities have a tourist office (Turističko Društno); they're normally near the stations. They keep maps and leaflets on their region and help find a room if required.

• **ISIC bonuses:** Discounts are given on some museums and cultural tours. For further information contact Karavan Student Travel Agency, Takovska 2, Belgrade.

• **Money matters:** The currency is the new dinar (D). 1 dinar = 100 paras.
Banking hours fluctuate. The longest are 7 a.m.–7 or 8 p.m. Away from the tourist centres, some banks shut from 12 noon to 3 p.m. It's also possible to change money at many travel agencies, though expect to pay 2 per cent commission on all transactions. Banks do not charge commission. Remember to keep your exchange slips for reconversion. It's the same rate everywhere so don't bother to shop around. It's illegal to take in or out more than 1,200 D. Don't change much, particularly if you are not staying long, as exchange facilities – if they exist at all – will give you a poor rate at the border. The black market is thriving, though you won't get a much better rate than at a bank. Restaurant waiters are usually very willing to change money. Remember, Yugoslavs hate the dinar; take hard currency everywhere. Knock four noughts off old notes.

• **Post offices:** Open Mon.–Sat.: 7 a.m.–8 p.m. Stamps can also be bought from tobacconists and Trafik shops. Glavna Pošta = poste restante.

• **Shops:** Open Mon.–Sat.: 8 a.m.–8 p.m. with an optional 12 noon–3 p.m. siesta.

SLEEPING

Tourist offices help out a bit by supplying booklets and information on camping, private accommodation and hotels, as well as running a room-finding service. Hotels are pricey, with even the cheapest C grades charging upwards of $30 per person. Private accommodation (sobe) is a much better bet at about $10 per person. If you're approached at the station by locals offering a room in their house you could try and negotiate but it is illegal. Student hostels are another alternative in July and August, with doubles at about $20. Also, there are thirty-five youth hostels scattered throughout the country, most of which are very basic, though the ones in the major cities are better. For camping, pick up the tourist information booklet which gives facilities and distances from the nearest town. Prices range between $2–6 per person.

Finally, you can be sure to be moved on if you try to sleep at the stations, as the authorities don't look too kindly on this.

EATING AND NIGHTLIFE

The endless variety of regional specialities should make eating out in Yugoslavia a pleasure, but if you go for westernized restaurants you'll find prices high. Your best bets are the self-service places or take-away stalls. If you're really low on readies, try the workers' communal eating halls (large soup-kitchen-type places full of men putting away mundane meals at an incredible pace). These are very cheap but not for those of a delicate disposition, as you'll see a lot of spitting (and worse) which can lessen the appetite somewhat. As a general rule, meat dishes represent the best value, particularly from the take-aways. Try ćevapčići (grilled and spiced beef), or raznjići (grilled pork, veal or lamb, on a spit). If you're really hard up, go for a burek (a pastry with meat, cheese or vegetable filling) or just a plain pancake washed down with yoghourt, as the locals do. If you're eating out, it's best to stay with the local wines: Riesling and Smederevka are the most popular white, Zupsko and Prokupac the most popular red.

The korzo is a pre-dinner evening stroll where everyone eyes up their neighbours in the town to see who's with who and what they're wearing. It's as good a way as any to meet the locals.

Slovenia

The proximity and influence of Austria over this rural region of Yugoslavia have helped make it one of the more comfortable to travel in. Hygiene and standards are generally more westernized than further south; in fact, northern Slovenia is just like an extension of Austria, and it's not till the Julian Alps that the scenery begins to flatten out and change. In southern Slovenia, there are some smallish beaches at KOPER and PIRAN; and some winter sports centres.

Ljubljana

This is the capital of the region, but it's an industrial centre and not really worth special attention. However, if you are breaking a journey here, take in the OLD TOWN with its castle, cathedral and medieval streets, or the old NATIONAL MUSEUM (a good rainy-afternoon alternative). In summer, the cultural festival means there are plenty of concerts and plays going on. Sleeping and eating shouldn't put you out: get the tourist office to fix you up with private accommodation or camp at Titova 260a (Tel. 371382) on bus route 6.

TOURIST INFORMATION AND ADDRESSES

TOURIST OFFICE: Titova Cesta 11, open Mon.–Sat.: 7 a.m.–10 p.m., Sun.: 8 a.m.–12 noon, 5 p.m.–8 p.m.
POST OFFICE: Titova Cesta 8, open Mon.–Fri.: 8 a.m.–8 p.m., Sat.: 8 a.m.–2 p.m.
AMEX: c/o Atlas, Trg Mestni 8, open Mon.–Fri.: 7.30 a.m.–9.30 p.m.; Sat.: 7.30 a.m.–1 p.m.

STUDENT TRAVEL: Celovšuka 49. Pick up youth hostel lists here and let them help you out on accommodation, open Mon.–Fri.: 10 a.m.–2 p.m., 3 p.m.–5 p.m.
PHONE CODE: 061.

A great day trip from Ljubljana is to the famous POSTOJNA CAVES. Although the entrance fee is quite expensive by Yugoslavian standards (£7 – half with ISIC – there is a Bureau de Change next to the pay booth), it is worth every penny and the trip lasts for several hours. The caves are one of the natural wonders of Europe and the system of underground chambers, stalactites and stalagmites gets more and more breathtaking the further you go on your tour by electric train and on foot. Take some warm clothing as it can get cold. You can get to Postojna either by train or bus; although the bus service is more frequent and takes you nearer the cave entrance, there is still a 15–20 minute walk from the bus station and almost half an hour's walk from the train station.

Julian Alps

One of the most famous Yugoslavian tourist postcard views is of the church on an island in the middle of LAKE BLED at the foot of the Julian Alps. Bled has been a spa resort for many years and is as popular in summer as it is in winter as a ski resort. The town is situated near the Austrian border about 35 miles from Ljubljana, and there is an hourly bus service to it from the bus station in front of the train station. The fare is only around $1.50 and the journey takes about 90 minutes. You could take the less regular train service, but the station marked Bled is actually about three miles away and you'll only end up waiting for the next bus to take you there. It is well worth a day's outing and you can get some spectacular views of the island from the castle and museum overlooking the lake if you decide not to take a boat trip to the island itself. The youth hostel is a few minutes' walk along the road from the bus station at Grajska 17 (Tel. 064–78230), should you be so enchanted with the place you decide to stay overnight. Food tends to be slightly dearer here than in towns like Ljubljana, but there is a market town so stock up here if you intend staying any length of time or heading on to do some climbing in the Julian Alps. Bled is a popular starting-out point for those who wish to attempt an assault on MOUNT TRIGLAV, at 2,834 metres the highest mountain in the Julian Alps.

Zagreb

The regional capital of Croatia and cultural centre of Yugoslavia. This is a city which is only 250 miles (but can be more than seven hours in a train – I speak from bitter experience) from Belgrade but feels like it is in another world. For Yugoslavia, this city really ticks and is quite sophisticated and westernized. The people are very friendly and helpful and the contrast with Belgrade is quite marked.

The station has the full range of facilities, left luggage, restaurants, Bureau de Change (open 6 a.m.), Information and the city's main post office and phone office is next door, past the old steam train which is a feature of many Yugoslav stations. Although nicely painted and highly polished, many of these trains are kept in working order so they can be used if the electricity network is destroyed.

The city is divided into three main areas: the Upper Town, dating back to the thirteenth century; the Lower Town, which is nineteenth-century; and the modern, postwar New Zagreb. Concentrate your efforts on Upper Zagreb (north of the station) and see: ST STEPHEN'S CATHEDRAL, ST MARK'S, the CROATIAN NATIONAL THEATRE and some of the many galleries and museums. There are several festivals, and the nightlife here is the most cosmopolitan you'll get. Use the cheap and excellent accommodation at the Studentski Centar Turist Biro, Savska Cesta 25 (Tel. 041–278611); or the youth hostel, Petrinjska 77 (Tel. 041–434964). Near Zagreb (1 hr by bus, 1½ hrs by train) is Kumrovec, Tito's birthplace. This old home is now a museum.

Trieste–Dubrovnik

The Adriatic is fast becoming the goldmine of Yugoslavia as intensified tourism increases each year. Trains run as far south as Split. To get to Dubrovnik, you have to bus it from Kardeljevo (Ploče). The coast is Yugoslavia's main redeeming feature – in fact, it's the only part of the country where touring isn't hard work, and even here it's bad enough; but console yourself with the fact that there are over 1,000 little islands out there in the Adriatic, and that there are towns like Split and Dubrovnik, which are well worth visiting. You're bound to find somewhere to take off your shirt and relax for a day or two. If you're interested: Yugoslavia's Adriatic coast is *the* centre for 'naturism' in southern Europe. Though unofficial camping's illegal, you should get away with it in the less obvious places, though there are quite a few youth hostels on the coast.

Probably the easiest option, though, is to forget the train trip to Split and head for RIJEKA from Ljubljana or Trieste, depending on whether you enter the country from Austria or Italy respectively. There is a regular ferry service by the Jadrolinija Line down the coast stopping at many of the islands. The ticket will cost around $30 (less October–December) but you could spend several times that on a cabin on the overnight service. Don't bother, as the bench seats are very wide and comfortable, but get on early and book your space as the ship tends to get full at Rijeka, gradually emptying as it calls at the islands on the way down the coast. If you're peckish, check out the price of the restaurant meals. Depending on inflation, it should still cost less to have a blow-out on a silver service dinner in the restaurant than a hamburger and Coke in McDonald's in the West.

On the way down, stop off at HVAR. This lovely island has lots of private accommodation and the hotels are reasonably priced, even in summer. It is well worth spending a day or two discovering Hvar village, parts of it dating back to the thirteenth century, including the oldest theatre in the Adriatic. As for other islands, ask amongst eurorailers for their recommendations. Suggestions are KRK, RAB, CRES and BRAC.

Jadrolinija ferries go on down the coast and call at Split, Dubrovnik and Bar, continuing to Corfu and Igoumenitsa in Greece. From Hvar it is a 6-hour journey by boat to DUBROVNIK, but as with the trains, don't be surprised if it takes you twice as long as timetabled, particularly if the weather is rough.

Split

The regional capital of Dalmatia dates back to the fourth century AD and to the Romans. The magnificent PALACE built by Diocletian in the third century developed into a medieval town, and the former palatial apartments have over the years become houses, while the corridors became streets. The basement now houses several museums and galleries. Other things to look out for are the CATHEDRAL, the ARCHAEOLÓGICAL MUSEUM, with many of the palace's fittings, and the BAZAAR. The city outside the walls is the new commercial centre where the hotels and nightclubs are.

Sleeping's a problem in Split as prices are high and it's a seller's market. You could try camping at Put Trstenika (Tel. 058–521971) on bus route 7 or 17, but it's usually pretty unsavoury; or for a dormitory bed you could try the student hostel at Maslešina 66 (Tel. 058–551744), bus 18. The best of the cheap hotels is the Srebrena Vrata inside the east gate at Bulićeva Poljana (Tel. 058–46869).

There are 12 ferries per day to and from Supetar on the nearby island of Brac (approx. $3.50 each way) where there is a good natural beach.

TOURIST INFORMATION AND ADDRESSES

TOURIST OFFICE: Titova Obala 12, open Mon.–Sat.: 7 a.m.–10 p.m., Sun.: 8 a.m.–12.30 p.m., 4 p.m.–8 p.m. in season. They handle private accommodation, but it's not cheap.
AMEX: Atlas, Trg Preporoda 7 (just west of the palace), open Mon.–Sat.: 8 a.m.–10 a.m. and 2 p.m.–5 p.m. in season.

Dubrovnik

This is undoubtedly the most attractive city Yugoslavia has to offer. It was one of Europe's leading centres in the fifteenth century – so much so it rivalled Venice in looks and wealth, and the Renaissance palaces and churches can still be seen today.

• **Transport:** The railway line to Dubrovnik has disappeared. The nearest railhead is Kardeljevo on the line from Sarajevo. Buses from Kardeljevo are fairly frequent and cheap. Dubrovnik bus station is about twenty minutes' walk from the old town. Buses also run south to Bar (3–5 hours) which is on the end of a new line from Belgrade. If you are thinking of heading down to Greece you can get a ferry several times a week from Dubrovnik. Check the times at the ferry terminal or with tourist information because they are liable to sudden changes. You have to pay in hard currency for travel to destinations outside Yugoslavia.

TOURIST INFORMATION AND ADDRESSES

TOURIST OFFICE: Poljana Paška Milićěvića 20, open daily: 9 a.m.–9.30 p.m. Located by the west gate, they'll arrange accommodation and hand out maps and leaflets.
AMEX: c/o Atlas, Pile 1, open daily: 8 a.m.–8 p.m.
MEDICAL HELP: Maršala Tita 61 (Tel. 32677).
PHONE CODE: 050.

SEEING

A wonderful introduction to the city is to walk along on top of the old city walls – don't worry, they're thick enough to be safe. This'll give you an idea of the layout ($.75). Dubrovnik's actually tiny, so you can quite easily get round the sights on foot.

The most inspiring buildings are the DOGE'S PALACE, the baroque CHURCH OF ST VLAHO beside ONOFRIO'S FOUNTAIN, the FRANCISCAN MONASTERY and the DOMINICAN CLOISTER AND MUSEUM (closed Sundays). The beaches are always busy in summer and charge, so you're actually far better taking the ferry over to LOKRUM, the island offering a national park and bathing area. (The nudist beach here is known to get quite lively in peak season!)

SLEEPING

As with most commercial resorts, sleeping can be a problem: hotels are over the top and there aren't enough hostels to go round. Sleeping on the beaches seems the natural solution – only the police don't quite view it that way, and for the kind of fines they'll impose, you could have slept at the best hotel in town. The International Student Centre is very good, but unless you reserve, you don't stand a chance. It's at Ivanska 14 (Tel. 23841), bus 2 or 4 from the bus or ferry stations. There are two youth hostels, one at Oktobarske Revolucije 17 (Tel. 23241), open April–October and worth a try and the other at Vinka Sagrestena 3 (Tel. 415038). For hotels, try the Lapad (Tel. 23473) or Gruž, Gruška Obala 68 (Tel. 24777), but even they're in the $30 per double range. There is a campsite one and a half miles east of the station (Tel. 22666). Three buses an hour to the old city (numbers 4 or 6). If you are arriving late off the ferry, and haven't booked in advance, it may be worth your while considering accommodation offered to you on the quayside. Strictly speaking this is illegal, but in practice the police prefer this to fining people found sleeping rough on the beach. This doesn't mean to say you can't haggle with them to reduce the price.

EATING AND NIGHTLIFE

Neither is a problem. To cater for the tourists there are plenty of restaurants with reasonable menus although the price of food in the old town is about twice that of anywhere else in Yugoslavia, or you could live out of any of the self-service Expresses. The summer festival draws top names in 'high culture' to the town, but if that leaves you cold, there's always good manwatching potential, once everyone changes at night (or gets dressed for the first time, in many cases) and parades up and down the main streets, having an occasional drink or ice-cream. There are also nightclubs, strippers, etc., in some of the flashy hotels.

Bosnia–Hercegovina

The Turkish-influenced region of Bosnia–Hercegovina, set among the central mountains, is en route to Dubrovnik from Zagreb or

Belgrade. The stretch of line from Sarajevo to MOSTAR runs through this region, and a day's stop-off in either of these towns will be an interesting experience.

SARAJEVO, 8½ hours from Zagreb and 6½ hours from Belgrade, was under Turkish rule for over 500 years and there are still minarets, mosques, and culinary reminders of this all around. There are also reminders of the 1984 Winter Olympics in the shape of Sarajevo's above-average facilities. Tourist information is at Jugoslovenske Narodne Armije 50, open 7.30 a.m.–8 p.m., and to get fixed up with private accommodation, go to Unis Turist, Vase Miskina 16. There's a youth hostel at Zadrugina 17 (Tel. 071–36163). The campsite is at Ilidza, tram 3 to the end. Eat in the Turkish quarter and on your sightseeing tour look out for BEY'S MOSQUE, the bridge where Archduke Ferdinand was shot (think back to your First World War history), and the SERBIAN ORTHODOX CHURCH. Take a stroll around the restored BASCARSIJA MARKET area. It has a pleasant atmosphere, although it has obviously been reconstructed for tourists. You can get cheap snacks and cakes here.

An interesting side trip is to the new pilgrimage site of MEDUJORDE where four young people see visions of the Virgin Mary daily. Bus 48 from Mostar costs about $2.

Belgrade (Beograd)

The capital of Serbia (the eastern half of Yugoslavia), and of the country as a whole, is not one of Europe's best cities. This is probably because since its founding in the third century the city has been destroyed and rebuilt thirty-six times, and little but grey, high-rise, concrete blocks stand there today. Despite this, Belgrade is friendlier than many Eastern European cities. The station is old, but its facilities are usable, though those in the bus station next door are superior. The station does have a cafeteria, left-luggage office (obligatory passport check), tourist information office and late night bureau de change. Building work is likely to add to the noise and chaos. A new station is under construction to the south of Belgrade. Trains coming in from this direction often stop here for long periods.

Belgrade also has its Donau station which serves the daily Bucharest train. Bus number 34 connects.

TOURIST INFORMATION AND ADDRESSES

There's an information booth inside the station, open 7 a.m.–9 p.m., but the main office is in the subway at the Albanija Building on Terazije, and is open 8 a.m.–8 p.m. All the main hotels will hand you a free map if you ask at reception.

POST OFFICE: Takovska 2, open Mon.–Fri.: 7 a.m.–7 p.m., Sat.: 8 a.m.–2 p.m. Poste restante and telephones also here.

AMEX: Zmaj Jovina 10, open Mon.–Fri.: 8 a.m.–8 p.m., Sat.: 8 a.m.–3 p.m.

UK EMBASSY: Generala Ždanova 46 (Tel. 645055).

US EMBASSY: Kneza Miloša 50 (Tel. 645655).

CANADIAN EMBASSY: Kneza Miloša 75 (Tel. 644666).

KARAVAN STUDENT TRAVEL: Takovska 2, open Mon.–Fri.: 7 a.m.–6 p.m., Sat.: 8 a.m.–6 p.m.

PHONE CODE: 011.

SEEING

Belgrade has one main attraction: the KALEMEGDAN PARK. It is a remarkable place that contains the KALEMEGDAN FORTRESS, built by the Serbs, Austrians and Turks; it now contains an observatory and the Military Museum (closed Mondays). The fortress has a commanding view over the confluence of the rivers Sava and Danube. Come here for a picnic and to watch the locals' afternoon strolls. Apart from this, head for the NATIONAL MUSEUM at Trg Republike. The nineteenth-century Bohemian quarter, SKADARLIJA, is good for a stroll.

• **Excursion:** The massive fortress of SMEDEREVO on the banks of the Danube is well worth a visit. 1½ hours by bus or over 2 hours by train. A good half-day trip. The fortress, railway station and bus station are next to each other.

SLEEPING

Go to the tourist office and ask them to help you out, as there are very few affordable beds. The youth hostel at Bulevar Jug. Narodne Armije 56a (Tel. 463846) is on tram 9 or 10. University halls around

130 D a night. Studentski Grad, 11070 Novi Beograd. Bus 601 outside station. Get off at the fourth stop. You're usually deluged with offers if you hang round the station long enough, but haggle with them to reduce prices dramatically. Across from the station is the Pansion Centar, at Trg Bratsva i Jedinstva 17. The station closes from midnight till 5 a.m., and if you try hanging around the police give you a hard time, so take bus 53 from the station, walk up Nemanijina and turn left at Kneza Miloša out to its terminus, and camp out in the forest.

EATING AND NIGHTLIFE

For both activities the Skadarlija district is best. There are plenty of places to eat cheaply, but avoid stopping off for just a drink in cafés, as prices are high. There are enough stalls selling snacks dotted round Skadarlija to get a meal together as you walk, and there are street performances and music and dancing in most of the restaurants in this part.

Montenegro

South of Dubrovnik is the varied region of Montenegro. The train services are restricted, and to get to the interesting places you really have to resort to buses. However, if you want to try and see some of Montenegro, the main line to concentrate on is the one from Belgrade to Bar, which runs via TITOGRAD. Titograd is a rather pleasant, fairly modern town rebuilt after almost total destruction in 1944. There isn't much to see in the town itself, but an hour's bus ride to Cetinje is worth it for the former Royal Palace of Montenegro.

Macedonia

This is one of the most backward regions of Europe, and the pleasure of seeing a primitive land such as this is greatly diminished by the many inconveniences you'll have to put up with: hardly any trains, and expect great problems with eating and sleeping. If you're one of the brave ones on the Belgrade–Athens run, you'll pass through SKOPJE, the capital of the region. Unless you're feeling really grotty and don't think you could make it straight down to Athens, don't break your journey in Skopje. It is not very attractive and is unfriendly and uninteresting. If you're staying the night, try Studentski Dom, Kuzman Josifonski (Tel. 091–235360) or youth hostel at Prolet 25 (Tel. 091–233866). See the OLD TOWN at the foot of the ruined CASTLE.

The area to head for in Macedonia is LAKE OHRID, along the Albanian border. OHRID is a charming town containing medieval Serbian remains. It stands on a beautiful clear lake in which you can swim. The local fish is a speciality. Tourist information is at Partizanska 3 (open 7 a.m.–9 p.m.), and they'll help you out with accommodation.

To get to Ohrid, take a bus from Kicevo or Bitola. Both of these can be reached by train from Skopje. One train per day also runs from Florina in Greece to Bitola. There is no other reason for going to Bitola, although it does have a free campsite – a field behind a restaurant; take bus number 1 from the station.

APPENDICES

Appendix I

CIEE Offices

USA

California
2511 Channing Way
Berkeley, CA 94704
(415) 848–8604

UCSD Price Center
Q–076

La Jolla, CA 92093
(619) 452–0630

1818 Palo Verde Avenue
Suite E
Long Beach, CA 90815
(213) 598–3338
(714) 527–7950

1093 Broxton Avenue
Suite 220
Los Angeles, CA 90024
(213) 208–3551

4429 Cass Street
San Diego, CA 92109
(619) 270–6401

312 Sutter Street
Suite 407
San Francisco, CA 94108
(415) 421–3473

919 Irving Street
Suite 102
San Francisco, CA 94122
(415) 566–6222

14515 Ventura Blvd
Suite 250
Sherman Oaks, CA 914403
(818) 905–57777

Connecticut
Yale Co-op East
77 Broadway
New Haven, CT 06520
(203) 562–5335

District of Columbia
1210 Potomac Street, NW
Washington, DC 20007
(202) 337–6464

Georgia
12 Park Place South
Atlanta, GA 30303
(404) 577–1678

Illinois
29 East Delaware Place
Chicago, IL 60611
(312) 951–0585

831 Foster Street
Evanston, IL 60201
(708) 475–5070

Louisiana
8141 Maple Street
New Orleans, LA 70118
(504) 860–1767

Massachusetts
79 South Pleasant Street
(2nd floor, rear)
Amherst, MA 01002
(413) 256–1261

729 Boylston Street
Suite 201
Boston, MA 02116
(617) 266–1926

1384 Mass. Avenue
No. 206
Cambridge, MA 02138
(617) 497–1497

Stratton Student Center
MIT, W20–024
84 Mass. Avenue
Cambridge, MA 02139
(617) 225–2555

Minnesota
1501 University Avenue, SE
No. 300
Minneapolis, MN 55414
(612) 379–2323

New York
205 East 42nd Street
New York, NY 10017
(212) 661–1450

35 West 8th Street
New York, NY 10011
(212) 254–2525

356 West 34th Street
New York, NY 10001
(212) 564–0142

Oregon
715 S.W. Morrison
No. 600
Portland, OR 97205
(503) 228–1900

Rhode Island
171 Angell Street (corner
of Thayer), Suite 212
Providence, RI 02906
(401) 331–5810

Texas
1904 Guadalupe Street
Suite 6
Austin, TX 78705
(512) 472–1931

Exec. Tower Office Ctr.
3300 W Mockingbird Ln.
Suite 101
Dallas, TX 75235
(214) 350–6166

Washington
1314 Northeast 43rd Street
Suite 210
Seattle, WA 98105
(206) 632–2448

Wisconsin
2615 North Hackett Avenue
Milwaukee, WI 53211
(414) 332–4740

EUROPE

France
12, rue Leydet
13100 Aix-en-Provence
(42) 38.58.82

37 bis, rue d'Angletere
06000 Nice
(93) 82.32.83

31, rue St Augustin
75002 Paris
(1) 42.66.20.87

49, rue Pierre Charron
75008 Paris
(1) 43.59.23.69

51, rue Dauphine
75006 Paris
(1) 43.25.09.86

16, rue de Vaugirard
75006 Paris
(1) 46.34.02.90

Germany
18, Graf Adolph Strasse
4000 Düsseldorf 1
(211) 329.088

Appendix II

INTER-RAIL 1991
DISCOUNTS AVAILABLE TO INTER-RAILERS

SEA OPERATORS

Sealink UK Ltd/SNCF	Dover–Calais	30%
Sealink UK Ltd/SNCF	Folkestone–Boulogne	30%
Sealink UK Ltd/SNCF	Weymouth–Cherbourg	30%
Sealink UK Ltd/Stena Line	Harwich–Hoek van Holland	30%[1]
Hoverspeed (Hovercraft)	Dover Hoverport–Calais/Boulogne	50%
P&O (European Ferries)	Dover–Calais/Boulogne	30%
P&O (European Ferries)/RMT	Dover–Oostende	30%
P&O (European Ferries)	Portsmouth–Le Havre	30%
Sealink Dieppe Ferries	Newhaven–Dieppe	30%
Scandinavian Seaways (DFDS)	Harwich–Esbjerg	50%
Scandinavian Seaways (DFDS)	Newcastle–Esbjerg	50%
Sealink UK Ltd	Fishguard–Rosslare	30%
Sealink UK Ltd	Holyhead–Dun Laoghaire	50%
Sealink UK Ltd	Stranraer–Larne	33%
B&I Line	Holyhead–Dublin	50%
Irish Continental Line	Cork/Rosslare–Le Havre	50%
Sealink UK Ltd	Portsmouth–Ryde	30%
Sealink UK Ltd	Lymington–Yarmouth	30%

[1] Reductions only on night boats on condition you book a reclining seat. Day sailings are not subject to reservations.

AUSTRIA

Puchberg Schneeberg–Hochschneeberg	50%
St Wolfgang Schafbergbahnhof–Schafbergspitze	50%
OeBB Wolfgangseeschiffahrt	50%
Vereinigte Schiffahrtsverwaltungen fur den Bodensee und Rhein	50%
Erste Donau–Dampfschiffarhrts–Gesellschaft Passau–Wien	50%
Chemins de fer regionaux de la Styrie (Steiermark) Feldbach–Bad Gleichenberg	50%
Chemins de fer regionaux de la Styrie (Steiermark) Gleisdorf–Weiz	50%
Chemins de fer regionaux de la Styrie (Steiermark) Peggau Deutsch feistritz–Ubelbach	50%
Chemins de fer regionaux de la Styrie (Steiermark) Unzmarkt–Tamsweg	50%

DENMARK

Det Forenbde Dampskibsselskab (DFDS)	Kobenhavn–Oslo	50%
Hjorring Privatbaner (HP)	Hjorring–Hirtshals	50%
Flyvebadene (Hovercraft)	Kobenhavn–Malmo	50%

FINLAND

Oy Finnjet Lines	Helsinki–Lubeck Travemunde	50%
Oy Vaasanlaivat	Vassa–Umea	50%

FRANCE

Chemins de fer de la Corse		50%
Chemins de fer de la Provence	Nice–Digne	50%
Societe Nationale Maritime Corse–Mediterranee	Marseille–Ajaccio	30%
Societe Nationale Maritime Corse–Mediterranee	Toulon–Bastia	30%
Societe Nationale Maritime Corse–Mediterranee	Nice–Calvi	30%
Societe Nationale Maritime Corse–Mediterranee	Marseille–Propriano	30%

GERMAN FEDERAL REPUBLIC

Schauinslandbahn GmbH, Freiburg (Breisgau)	50%
Kahlgrund–Verkehrs–GmbH, Schollkrippen	50%
Oberrheinische Eisenbahn–Gesellschaft AG, Mannheim	50%
Regentalbahn AG, Viechtach	50%
Lokalbahn Lam-Kitzting, Lam	50%
Tegernsee–Bhan AG, Tegernsee	50%
Kreisbahn Aurich GmbH, Aurich	50%
Eisenbahn–Gesellschaft Altona–Kaltenkirchen–Neumunster, Hamburg–Kaltenkirchen–Neumunster	50%
Regionalverkehr Munsterland GmbH	50%
Regionalverkehr Ruhr–Lippe GmbH	50%
Vereinigte Schiffahrtsunternehman fur den Bodensee und Rhein, Frankfurt (M) Postal & Railway Coaches	50%
Verkehrsbetriebe Kreis Tecklenburg–Tecklenburger Nordbahn – AG	50%

ITALY

Societe de Navigation Adriatica and HML	Brindisi–Patras	30%
Societe de Navigation Adriatica and HML	Brindisi–Corfu	30%
Societe de Navigation Adriatica and HML	Brindisi–Igoumenitsa	30%

MOROCCO

Cie Limadet Ferry	Malaga–Tanger	30%
Cie Marocaine de navigation	Tanger–Sete	20%

NORWAY

Fred Olsen Lines/KDS	Hirtshals–Kristiansand	50%
Ofotens Bilruter–Autobus	Narvik–Bodo	50%
Larvik Line A/S	Larvik–Frederikshavn	50%

SPAIN

Cie de Navigation Trasmediterranea	Barcelona–Palma/Ibiza/Mahon	30%
Cie de Navigation Trasmediterranea	Valencia–Palma/Ibiza	30%
Cie de Navigation Trasmediterranea	Melilla–Almeria/Malaga	30%
Cie de Navigation Trasmediterranea	Cadiz–Las Palmas/Tenerife/Lanzarote	30%
Cie de Navigation Trasmediterranea	Algeciras–Tanger	30%

SWEDEN

Stena Sessan Line	Goteborg–Frederikshavn	50%
Silja Line	Stockholm–Helsinki	50%
Silja Line	Stockholm–Turku S	50%
TT–Line	Trelleborg–Lubeck Travemunde	50%
From 01-07-90		
Swedish State Railways	Haparanda–Boden	50%
	Storuman–Haellnaes	50%
	Jorn–Arvidsjaur	No Reduction
	Bastutraesk–Skellefteaa	No Reduction
	Mellansel–Oernskoeldsvik	No Reduction

SWITZERLAND

All these companies give a 50 per cent reduction:

AB	Appenzellerbahn
BAM	Biere–Apples–Morges
BGF	Grindelwald–First
BLM	Lauterbrunnen–Murren
BOB	Berner Oberland–Bahnen
BOW	Oberdorf–Weissenstein
BrS	Brienzersee
BTI	Blei–Tauffelen–Ins
BVD	Bex–Villars–Bretaye
BVZ	Brig–Visp–Zermatt
CEV	Chemins de fer du Veveysans
CJ	Chemins de fer du Jura
CMN	Chemins de fer des Montagnes Neuchateloises
EBT	Emmental–Burgdorf–Thun
FB	Forchbahn
GBS	Gurbetal–Bern–Schwarzenburg
GFM	Chemins de fer fribourgeois
GFM/VMCV	Vevey/Chatel/St Denis–Bossennens
GGB	Gornergratbahn
GN	Glion–Rochers-de-Naye
JB	Jungfraubahn
LAF	Adliswil–Felsenegg

SWITZERLAND

LAS	Les Avants–Sonloup
LEB	Lausanne–Echallens–Bercher
LLB	Leuk–Leukerbad
LLPR	Lenzerheide–Parpener Rothorn
LSE	Luzern–Stans–Engelberg
LSM	Stockalp–Melchsee–Frutt
LSMS	Stechelberg–Schilthorn
LWM	Wengen–Mannlichen
MC	Martigny–Chatelard
MGI	Montreux–Glion
MO	Martigny–Orsieres
NStCM	Nyon–Sant-Cergue–Morez
OeBB	Oesingen–Balsthal
OJB	Oberaargau–Jura
PBr	Pont–Brassus
RBS	Regional Verkehr Bern–Solothurn
RVT	Regional du Val-de-Travers
SBN	Beatenberg–Neiderhorn
SGA	St Gallen–Gais–Appenzell–Alstatten
SGV	Vierwaldstaltersee
SMB	Solothurn–Moutier
SMtS	Stimier–Mont-Soleil
SNB	Solothurn–Neiderbipp
STB	Sensetalbahn
STI	Steffisburg–Thun–Interlaken
SZU	Sihltal–Zurich–Uetliberg–Bahn
TB	Trogenerbahn
TBB	Thunersee–Beatenberg
Ths	Thunersee
URh	Untersee und Rhein
VBW	Bern–Worb
VCP	Vevey–Mont-Pelerin
VHB	Vereinigte Huttwil–Bahnen
WAB	Wengenalpbahn
WB	Waldenburgebahn
WSB	Whynental–und Suhrentalbahn
YSteC	Yverdon–Ste-Croix
ZSG	Zurichsee

Details of the discounts are compiled according to information provided to British Rail by the operators concerned. However, this information may be subject to change without notice.

TRANSPORT MUSEUMS

The following Transport Museums offer free or reduced admittance to holders of Inter-Rail Cards:

Austria	Railway Museum, 212, Mariahilfer Strasse – Wien 14e – reduction only
Belgium	Railway Museum, Gare de Bruxelles Nord – free
Denmark	Railway Museum, Jernbanemuseum, Odense – free
France	French Railway Museum, 2 Rue Alfred de Glehn – Mulhouse – free
Federal Republic of Germany	Transport Museum, Lessingstrasse 6, Nürnberg – free
Finland	Railway Museum, Hyvinkää – free
	Narrow Gauge Railway Museum, Jokioinen (Gare Minkio) – free
Hungary	Transport Museum, Varosligeti, Körut II, Budapest XIV – free
	Metro Museum, Metro Station Deák Ferenc tér, Budapest – free
	Horse Carriage Museum, Paradfürdo – free
Norway	Railway Museum, Hamar – free
Portugal	Railway Museum, Gare de Santarem – free
Romania	Railway Museum, Bucuresti (Nord) – free
Spain	Railway Museum, San Cosmey y San Damien, 2, Madrid – free
Switzerland	Swiss Transport and Communications Museum, Lidostrasse, Luzern – free

---

INTER-RAIL CENTRE, KOBENHAVN

A special Inter-Rail centre is open during the summer months, between 7 a.m. and midnight, at Kobenhavn Central Station (Hovebanegard) and provides information, refreshment and free showers. Overnight sleeping is not allowed!

IMPORTANT INFORMATION

1. Replacement cards cannot be issued under any circumstances. You are advised to take out insurance to cover you in the event of loss or theft of your Inter-Rail card.

2. Inter-Rail card holders must pay the usual reservation fees for seats, couchettes and sleeping berths.

3. When returning your completed card for rebate, please ensure that you take it to the office which issued it, with a complete record of the journeys you made.

4. **B&I Line sailing, Dublin Ferryport/Holyhead**
During peak periods in 1990, B&I will require Inter-Railers to have control tickets for sailings at 10.00 and 21.45 from Dublin and at 04.00 and 15.45 from Holyhead.

This applies during the whole of August, on most dates in June and July, during Bank Holiday periods and in March around St Patrick's Day. Control tickets are free and can be obtained in the UK from B&I at 150 New Bond Street, London W1 or at Reliance House, Water Street, Liverpool L2. Passengers without control tickets will be able to board if space is available after control ticket holders have boarded.

CHANGES IN 1991

Please note that Czechoslovak State Railways (CSD) are now included in the list of participating railways. All of Turkey is still included; Bulgaria, Poland and Germany are also participating members of Inter Rail. There are no flexi cards and no Inter Rail or boat tickets.

Appendix III

BASIC VOCABULARY

Although it is sometimes possible to get by in English, often it's not. We've kept it pretty simple as there's no point getting too involved in a language you don't know the basics of. German can often be used in Eastern Europe. Useful books are the Berlitz *European Phrase Book* (14 languages, £3.95) and the Pan *Traveller's Multilingual Phrase Book* (8 languages, £3.99).

ENGLISH	CZECH	DANISH	DUTCH
Yes	Ano	Ja	Ja
No	Ne	Nej	Nee
Please	Prosím	Vaer så venlig	Alstublieft
Thank you	Děkuji	Tak	Dank U
Good morning	Dobrý den	Godmorgen	Goedemorgen
Goodbye	Na shledanou	Farvel	Tot ziens
Where is/are...	Kde je/jsou...	Hvor er...	Waar is/zijn...
Excuse me	Promiňte	Undskyld	Neemt U me niet kwalijk
How much?	Kolik to stojí?	Hvor meget?	Hoeveel?
Can I have...	Chtěla bych...	Kan jeg få...	Mag ik...hebben
I don't understand	Nerozumím	Jeg forstår ikke	Ik begrijp het niet
Do you speak English?	Mluvíte anglicky?	Taler De engelsk?	Spreekt U Engels?
My name is...	Jmenuji se...	Mit navn er...	Mijn naam is...

ENGLISH	FINNISH	FRENCH	GERMAN
Yes	Kyllä	Oui	Ja
No	Ei	Non	Nein
Please	Olkaa hyvä	S'il vous plaît	Bitte
Thank you	Kiitos	Merci	Danke
Good morning	Hyvää houmenta	Bonjour	Guten morgen
Goodbye	Näkemiin	Au revoir	Auf Wiedersehen
Where is/are...	Missä on/ovat...	Où se trouve/trouvent...	Wo ist/sind...
Excuse me	Anteeksi	Excusez-moi	Verzeihung
How much?	Kuinka paljon?	Combien?	Wieviel?
Can I have...	Voinko saada...	Je voudrais...	Kann ich...haben
I don't understand	En ymmärrä	Je ne comprends pas	Ich verstehe nicht
Do you speak English?	Puhutteko englantia?	Parlez-vous anglais?	Sprechen Sie Englisch?
My name is...	Nimeni on...	Je m'appelle...	Ich heiße...

ENGLISH	HUNGARIAN	ITALIAN	NORWEGIAN
Yes	Igen	Sí	Ja
No	Nem	No	Nei
Please	Kérem	Per favore	Vennligst
Thank you	Köszönöm	Grazie	Takk
Good morning	Jó reggelt	Bongiorno	God morgen
Goodbye	Viszontlátásra	Arrivederci	Adjø
Where is/are...	Hol van/vannak...	Dov'è/Dove sono...	Hvor er...
Excuse me	Elnézést	Mi scusi	Unnskyld
How much?	Mennyi/Mennyit?	Quanto?	Hvor mye?
Can I have...	Kaphatok...	Posso avere...	Kan jeg få...
I don't understand	Nem értem	Non capisco	Jeg forstår ikke
Do you speak English?	Beszél angólul?	Parla inglese?	Snakker De engelsk?
My name is...	Nevem...vagyok	Mi chiamo...	Mitt navn er...

ENGLISH	PORTUGUESE	SPANISH	SWEDISH
Yes	Sim	Sí	Ja
No	Não	No	Nej
Please	Por favor	Por favor	Varsågod
Thank you	Obrigado	Gracias	Tack
Good morning	Bom dia	Buenos días	God morgon
Goodbye	Adeus	Adiós	Adjö
Where is/are...	Onde está/estão...	Dónde está/están...	Var är...
Excuse me	Descuple	Dispénseme	Förlåt
How much?	Quanto?	¿Cuánto?	Hur mycket?
Can I have...	Pode dar-me...	Puede darme...	Kan jag få...
I don't understand	Não compreendo	No comprendo	Jag förstår inte
Do you speak English?	Fala inlês?	¿Habla usted inglés?	Talar Ni engelska?
My name is...	O meu nome é...	Mi llamo...	Mitt namm är...

ENGLISH	TURKISH	YUGOSLAVIAN (SERBO-CROATIAN)
Yes	Evet	Da
No	Hayir	Ne
Please	Lütfen	Molim
Thank you	Teşekkür ederim	Hvala
Good morning	Günaydin	Dobro jutro
Goodbye	Güle güle/Allahaismarladik	Zbogom
Where is/are...	Nerede/Neredeler...	Gde je/su...
Excuse me	Affedersiniz	Izvinite
How much?	Ne kadar?	Koliko?
Can I have...	...rica edebilir miyim	Mogu li dobiti...
I don't understand	Anlamiyorum	Ne razumem
Do you speak English?	Ingilizce Biliyor musunuz?	Gavorite li engleski?
My name is...	Adim...'dir	Ja se Zovem...

ACKNOWLEDGEMENTS

We would like to thank the following people for their support and cooperation throughout this project: Gill Edwards, Philip Wilks and Rupert Brown of British Rail who have been invaluable with their up-to-date information and late-night checkings (and Czech spellings, Phil!), I Ole Egholm of Danish State Railways, Janet Ennor of Eurotrain. Last but not least, thanks to my family for their kindness and encouragement.

Each year I receive dozens and dozens of letters from you, the readers, telling me of your eurorailing experiences, and how you found the book. Without your help I would find it very difficult to keep abreast of all the changes in all 27 countries, so please keep up the good work. Please, however, keep these letters brief, concise and under two pages! I can't cope with any more 15-pagers! I try to acknowledge each letter individually, but sometimes it gets hard, and between trips, meeting publishing deadlines and organizing future research trips some people may wait longer than I'd ideally like for their personal 'thank you'. This year your response has been great, and to those of you who wrote especially detailed letters I'd like to take this opportunity to acknowledge your contributions: Stephen Kerish from Keele; E. Jones from Hastings; Dawn Morris from Watford; John Pindar from London; V. Hilton of Sheffield; Michael Connell of Rippenden; Dorothy and George Smith from Liverpool; Melanie Clark of Leeds; Allan and Liz Williams of Buxton; Radar Kuča of Ostrava, Czechoslovakia; Scott Ferguson of Phoenix Arizona USA; R. F. Phillips of Ashton Helston; Greta Harris of Cardiff and Dr Peter Hedges of Liverpool.

Also, Robert Palmer of Bedford; Glen Williams of Waterlooville; Saul Richmond of Liverpool; Antonia Reed of Preston; Rachel Collier of Tübingen; Richard Long of Leeds; Clare Sutton of Twickenham; P. Gibson of Huntingdon; Julie Haggen of Reading; Geraldine Friel of Co. Donegal; Suzanne Dickenson and Maeve Carrell of Dublin; Neil Gosling of Luton, Peter Ede of Waterlooville; Kirsty Parry of Cheshire; Louise Carr of Dublin; Crispin Waymouth of Appledore; Sharon Harris of Newport; Tracey Acres of Dorset; Jack Alexander of Stockport; Neil Sinclair of Perth; Ian

Waterfield of Cambridge; Carol Browne of Glasgow; Kate Smith and Juliet Richardson of Cambridge and Calvin Quinnell of Gillingham.

To you all, a sincere thank you.

Katie Wood, October 1990.

INDEX

Index